J. R. R. TOLKIEN
A Descriptive Bibliography

Wayne G. Hammond is Assistant Librarian in the Chapin Library of Rare Books at Williams College, Williamstown, Massachusetts. He is a regular contributor of bibliographic notes to the journal *Mythlore*, and was awarded a 1991 Clyde S. Kilby Research Grant from the Marion E. Wade Center, Wheaton College, for the completion of this book. His collection of Tolkieniana is one of the finest in private hands.

Douglas Anderson, a bookseller in Ithaca, New York, wrote the introduction to the authoritative American edition of *The Lord of the Rings* and the introduction and notes to *The Annotated Hobbit*: the latter won the 1989 Mythopoeic Society Award for scholarship.

J.R.R. TOLKIEN

A Descriptive Bibliography

WAYNE G. HAMMOND

with the assistance of

DOUGLAS A. ANDERSON

ST PAUL'S BIBLIOGRAPHIES · WINCHESTER

OAK KNOLL BOOKS · NEW CASTLE · DELAWARE

1993

In Memory
of Joy Hill

First published by St Paul's Bibliographies,
West End House, 1 Step Terrace, Winchester, UK in 1993
as part of the *Winchester Bibliographies of 20th Century Writers*

Published in North and South America by
Oak Knoll Books, 414 Delaware Street,
New Castle, DE 19720, USA

British Library Cataloguing in Publication Data
A catalogue record for this book is available
from the British Library.

Library of Congress Cataloging-in-Publication Data
Hammond, Wayne G.
    J.R.R. Tolkien : a descriptive bibliography / Wayne G. Hammond,
  with the assistance of Douglas A. Anderson.
        p.   cm. — (Winchester bibliographies of 20th century writers)
    Includes bibliographical references and index.
    ISBN 1-873040-11-3 (UK).—ISBN 0-938768-42-5 (USA)
    1. Tolkien, J. R. R. (John Ronald Reuel), 1892–1973—Bibliography.
  2. Fantastic literature, English—Bibliography. I. Anderson.
  Douglas A. (Douglas Allen), 1959– . II. Title III. Series.
  Z8883.45.H36   1992
  [PR6039.032]
  016.828′91209—dc20   92–35912

Excerpts from letters and other unpublished works by
J. R. R. Tolkien are printed with the permission of the
Tolkien Trust. Excerpts from the published works of
J. R. R. Tolkien are printed with the permission of
HarperCollins*Publishers*.

ISBN 1-873040-11-3 (UK).—ISBN 0-938768-42-5 (USA)

Printed in Great Britain by The Alden Press Ltd., Oxford

Contents

List of Plates

The Tolkien Society

The Tolkien Society, founded in 1969, is a focal point for the many people interested in the works of J. R. R. Tolkien (1892–1973). Its membership is international and varied. Professor Tolkien is Honorary President of the Society *in perpetuo*, and his daughter Priscilla is Honorary Vice President.

The members of The Tolkien Society are kept in touch by a bulletin, *Amon Hen*, which contains news of Society events, book reviews, and short articles on Tolkien and his works. The annual Society journal, *Mallorn*, contains longer articles and reviews, as well as poetry and fiction in the Tolkien tradition.

The Society holds three meetings each year: the Annual General Meeting and Dinner, with a notable guest speaker, in spring; a summer Seminar; and 'Oxonmoot', an autumn weekend in Oxford. In addition, informal gatherings, or 'moots', are held throughout the year by local Society groups, called 'smials'.

For details of membership, or for more information about the Society or about Tolkien and his works, write to: *The Tolkien Society (WH), 12 Mortimer Court, Abbey Road, London NW8 9AB, U.K.*

The Tolkien Society is a registered charity in the U.K., and is independent of Tolkien's publisher HarperCollins.

Foreword

A bibliographer, like a lexicographer, may easily be dismissed as a harmless drudge; but, as I found to my chagrin when I thumbed through the pages of Wayne Hammond's admirable and exhaustive bibliography of J. R. R. Tolkien's writings, it was as often as not the publisher who had caused the drudgery.

I have been associated with Tolkien's works for most of my life. Admittedly my first encounter as a ten-year-old publisher's reader may have initiated, but did nothing else to influence, the instant complexities of *The Hobbit*'s publishing history. But from the early nineteen-fifties for about forty years I have discovered in Wayne Hammond's pages a sort of database of all the decisions and indecisions; mistakes and belated correction of mistakes; marketing wheezes and failures; compromises and conciliations (at least possible expense) with author or printer, that have been the stock-in-trade of a working publisher's life.

In an ideal world few, if any, modifications should be called for once a book has been established in printed form; the few, inevitable misprints could swiftly be corrected in subsequent impressions, the verso of the title page would record and date these reprints accurately, and the need for a bibliography *raisonné* would be non-existent. The lamentable failure of the publisher over many years to live in an ideal world is reflected by the very size—even the existence—of this bibliography.

Assembling a detailed publishing history retrospectively is never an easy task. The ledgers and records of George Allen & Unwin were probably no worse than average, though they suffered from being moved and, latterly, weeded by inexperienced gardeners. But even the publisher could not guess the bibliographic entanglements that might be caused when, for instance, a straightforward reprint from standing type of *The Fellowship of the Ring* was ordered. The printer, without permission, had distributed the type and, having failed to persuade the publisher to offset, said nothing, but quietly reset the book with a new quota of inexplicable errors.

I remember as a child being told (possibly as an incentive to improve my religious knowledge) that the University Presses would pay five pounds to anyone who detected a printer's error in one of their authorized Bibles. I never heard of anyone who earned this small fortune, but I have often imagined an equivalent reward being offered three centuries after the first publication of *The Lord of the Rings*. It would take at least that long to achieve typographical perfection.

Most readers of Tolkien's books have been impressed by his command of detail and complexity. Why, they may reasonably ask, were his publishers such muddlers? It would be difficult, and inappropriate here, to mount a well-argued defence. I can only say, wincing from the stark record of so many, seemingly gratuitous, changes, that publishing Tolkien was never straightforward. The harder one tried, the more ensnared one became. Why, for example, when Houghton Mifflin had chosen four of the author's colour plates to embellish their first edition of *The Hobbit* did Allen & Unwin, emboldened by the need for a new printing themselves, choose to include four colour plates in their own second printing, three of which were the same and one of which was different on each side of the Atlantic? The reason for this decision—if decision it was—is inexplicable, but the bibliographer is left to pick up the bits. Likewise the inability of publishers to read runes led to such curious anomalies as the runic rubric 'Published by George Allen and Unwin' that for a long time embellished the Houghton Mifflin copies of *The Hobbit*.

Bibliographic simplicity also suffers as a result of the demand for newfangledness that invariably overtakes any book that is successful. Indeed, good marketing demands constant re-presentation of the product. Between ourselves Tolkien and I referred to this as 'The Philosophy of Restlessness', and we agreed that although we personally didn't need it, it brought tangible results by way of sales. If a top is spinning you have to keep whipping it and, without any consideration for a bibliographer's future labours, the publishers whipped away when Tolkien's books took off in the nineteen-sixties, and have kept whipping ever since.

It seems appropriate, therefore, that as Wayne Hammond has invited me to write a foreword to his useful and meticulous work, I as Tolkien's long-standing publisher should accept responsibility, and offer a modest *apologia*, after having added so inconsiderately to his task.

RAYNER UNWIN

Introduction

D. W. Krummel, in his *Bibliographies: Their Aims and Methods*, compares bibliographical research to burrowing, which can become 'seductive, even exciting, when unexpected things turn up, as they so often do'—leading to still more burrowing, for burrowing's sake. This seems a particularly hobbitish analogy, and is one I have thought of many times while writing this first descriptive bibliography of J. R. R. Tolkien (a 'burrower' himself, among the roots of words). Though I have not delved as deep as I could, I have dug much too long. Like *The Lord of the Rings*, this book was written over many years, was often interrupted, and 'grew in the telling'. It was begun when *The Silmarillion* seemed to conclude the Tolkien canon and a young bibliographer might optimistically (or naïvely) project completion of his book within two or three years. I did not foresee the astonishing number of additional works by Tolkien, new editions, and collections that would be published in the next decade and a half, which more than doubled the size of this book and my task. And I did not suspect the terrible complexity of the publishing and textual history of Tolkien's writings, which needed long hours to research and explain. Even the end of the Soviet Bloc contributed to delay, as linguists in the East celebrated their freedom by making new translations of Tolkien's works in a dozen tongues.

I have kept up, and could continue to do so; and I would gladly enlarge or improve what I have done already, especially my study of textual changes in *The Lord of the Rings*. But this bibliography has been promised time and again, and too often. Tolkien's centenary is a good occasion to put it between covers at last and in the hands of the many (I hope) who will find it useful.

The popularity of *The Hobbit* and *The Lord of the Rings* gave rise to a widespread fan movement and inevitably to amateur guides to Tolkien's works. The first of these now seem amusingly brief. Their authors only scratched the surface. Only later did the extent of Tolkien's writings become better known. The labours of Richard West and Bonniejean Christensen to this end in the nineteen-sixties and seventies are most notable. Humphrey Carpenter's bibliographical appendix in his 1977 biography of Tolkien (revised in 1982) was far more extensive than all previous lists and immediately became a standard reference. But there was not yet a descriptive bibliography of Tolkien, with details of title pages, contents, illustrations, format, bindings, and jackets. Librarians, booksellers, collectors, and especially students of Tolkien's works still were not adequately served.

Douglas Anderson and I independently recognized their need and began to fulfil it. It was also our own: we were both avid readers and collectors of Tolkien. We soon learned of each other and pooled our knowledge. By happy coincidence, in my early research I had focused on Tolkien's books, while Anderson had compiled an almost complete list of Tolkien's writings in periodicals; and while I had professional expertise in the mechanics of bibliography, he was an enthusiastic 'burrower' with a knack for *minutiae*. Together we devised a shape for this book and agreed that it should be not merely a guide for collectors, but a thorough history of the publication of Tolkien's writings and art, and as complete an account as possible of the many errors, corrections, and revisions in Tolkien's texts. However, we did not agree on a division of labour or a schedule for completion, and in time Anderson concentrated on other projects, notably the 1987 American edition of *The Lord of the Rings* and the valuable *Annotated Hobbit*. The bibliography as it is finally published remains a collaboration in its framework, in part of the textual notes for *The Hobbit*, in section C (Periodicals), in the list of interviews in section F, and in a few other respects. I gratefully acknowledge Douglas Anderson's contributions. But the actual writing and preparation for press are entirely my own, and I must accept responsibility for any errors this book contains.

Section A describes books written by Tolkien himself, including 'The History of Middle-earth' in which Christopher Tolkien's comments are extensive but his father's texts predominate. Books to which J. R. R. Tolkien was a contributing author or for which he acted as editor or translator are described in section B. All entries in sections A and B include quasi-facsimile transcriptions and are arranged so that all editions, impressions, issues, and states of a work (except later collections) are considered together, in order of publication (as far as the chronology can be determined). Classification is first by capital letter and number, then by lower case letter: for example, in 'A3g' *A3* denotes *The Hobbit*, the third work in section A, and *g* denotes the revised Ballantine Books edition, the seventh *Hobbit* described. New sub-entries are made for new or revised typesettings, and separate sub-entries for hardcover and paperback formats.

The focus in sections A and B is on British and American trade editions. Most subsidiary and reprint editions in English are noted only, except *reset* book club and collector's editions, which are fully described in separate entries. Proof copies are omitted. Special bindings for libraries are noted only when significant.

Section C is devoted to Tolkien's works (except letters) first published in periodicals; section D to collections of Tolkien's letters and to letters and parts of letters published in periodicals, catalogues, etc.; section E to Tolkien's art; section F to audio recordings by Tolkien and other miscellaneous works not included in other sections; and section G to translations of Tolkien's works. Further notes on the contents and arrangement of sections C through G are given in each section.

In transcriptions, qualifications in square brackets apply to the text that follows until the end of the description is reached or a superseding qualification is made. For example, text described as printed '[*in red:*]' continues in red until otherwise qualified, e.g. '[*in black:*]'. Italics are printed as such in transcriptions; all other type and lettering should be considered roman unless otherwise stated. Black letter and uncials are noted, but in general, 'fancy' lettering has not been described as such. No attempt has been made to distinguish serifed from sans serif type, or boldface from regular printing, or small caps from regular upper case fonts. The letter- and wordspacing of transcriptions may suggest, but is not meant to accurately depict, the spacing as it appears in the items described.

Pagination statements in A, B, Di, and Ei are for quick reference only and are meant to be used in conjunction with contents notes. Each pagination statement represents the extent of the book, including blanks, according to the pagination scheme used in the book (or inferred). Plates are noted when present. In the contents note, inferred pagination is given in square brackets, initial and final blanks are specified, and internal unnumbered pages and blanks are noted when at the beginning or end of a sequence. Collations are expressed according to Bowers' formulary, when sewn signatures can be distinguished. The collations of books (including most paperbacks) trimmed at the spine folds and glued are expressed in terms of leaves rather than gatherings. Statements of size refer to the dimensions of leaves, not bindings except wrappers trimmed flush, and are given to the nearest 0.1 centimeter. The size stated is, for each dimension, the largest measured among all copies examined.

Binding and dust-jacket illustrations and decorations are described in detail, so that a book may be more easily identified on a bookshop or library shelf. Internal illustrations and decorations are only indicated when present, unless they are especially significant or Tolkien's own art.

Text paper and endpapers are described as wove or laid, and are to be considered white or off-white unless otherwise stated. Watermarks are noted only when present.

For hardcover books, the presence or absence of headbands is noted (*headbands*, plural, indicates a band at both the top and bottom of the spine). Type and lettering are to be considered printed in black unless otherwise stated. Illustrations are to be considered printed in black and white unless stated to be in colour. Colours are described subjectively, but with as much accuracy and consistency as humanly possible, in order of prominence or in the descending order of priority *red, orange, yellow, green, blue, purple, black, white, grey*. Also used, usually for bindings, are *gold, silver*, and *copper*. These common terms, alone or combined with each other and/or with qualifiers such as *light, dark*, and *pale*, are used unless a more exotic but still commonly understood description (e.g. *wine red*) seemed more appropriate.

For each book fully described, the date of publication, original price, and number of copies in the first impression are given to the extent they can be learned. Some publishers unfortunately chose not to provide information, while others have lost all or part of their records, or kept none. Some of Tolkien's publishers no longer exist, and their records (if any survive) have not been located. When 'official' data was not available, I drew upon standard references such as *British Books in Print*, press releases, and announcements in trade journals such as *Publishers Weekly*. However— and here let the user of any bibliography beware—even publishers' own records are sometimes confused or incomplete, even incorrect, and the printing figures they contain are usually rounded off.

Textual citations do not include running heads in the count of lines. Titling is included in line counts unless otherwise stated. The symbols < and > indicate the direction of textual change.

The reader is generally assumed to be familiar with *The Hobbit, The Lord of the Rings*, and *The Silmarillion*. For convenience I have described Tolkien's own illustrations by title only; for further reference to his art, see *Pictures by J. R. R. Tolkien* (Ei2). After Tolkien's *Letters* (Di1), Humphrey Carpenter's biography of Tolkien and his *The Inklings* are the two best sources for further biographical information. When referring to Carpenter's books, I have cited pages in their first editions, A32a–b (and A32f) and A33a–b.

The surname *Tolkien* used by itself refers always to J. R. R. Tolkien. *Certar* and *tengwar* refer to writing systems invented by Tolkien; see Plate VI, in which the upper inscription is in certar and the lower inscription is in tengwar. The runic certar should not be confused with the Anglo-Saxon runes used in *The Hobbit*.

George Allen & Unwin's 'St. George' device, frequently noted in descriptions, depicts St. George and the dragon and exists in three versions: two, designed by Walter Crane in 1890, are square and elaborated with vines and lettering; the third, a less fussy design by Joan Hassall, is 'open' rather than squared.

Terminology follows Fredson Bowers' *Principles of Bibliographical Description* and John Carter's *ABC for Book Collectors*. The recommendations of G. Thomas Tanselle have also been instructive, especially with regard to *issue* and *state*.

Throughout this book I have tried to be consistent without allowing a false ideal of consistency to come before readers' understanding; to be complete, within reason and stated limits, though I am certain to have missed something; and to be accurate, while under no illusion that even the best copy-editing and proofreading (by man or word processor) will prevent all errors. I will gratefully receive corrections and additions.

WAYNE G. HAMMOND
Williamstown, Massachusetts
June 1992

Acknowledgements

Most of the descriptions in this book are based on my own collection, or on that of Christina Scull. Christina herself spent many hours examining copies and sifting through archives—and encouraging the author—in support of this book. She has my gratitude and my love. The collection of the Marion E. Wade Center, Wheaton College, Wheaton, Illinois, was also invaluable. My thanks go to the Center and its staff, especially Marjorie Lamp Mead, Associate Director, for their help on several occasions, and for their generous award to me of a 1991 Clyde S. Kilby Research Grant. I am also grateful to the Marquette University Library, Milwaukee, Wisconsin, Charles B. Elston, Archivist, for access to their important collection of Tolkien's manuscripts; to the University of Reading Library, Michael Bott, Keeper of Archives and Manuscripts, who allowed Christina Scull and me to browse freely in their George Allen & Unwin files; to the Bodleian Library, Oxford, especially Dr. Judith Priestman; and to my employer, the Chapin Library of Rare Books, Williams College, Williamstown, Massachusetts, and its Custodian, Robert L. Volz.

In the course of research Douglas Anderson and I received assistance from numerous libraries in addition to those already acknowledged. These include the British Library; the Libraries of the Claremont Colleges; the Cleveland (Ohio) Public Library; the Columbia University Library; the Cornell University Library; the libraries of the University of Illinois at Chicago and Urbana; the Lilly Library, Indiana University; the library of the University of Maryland; the libraries of the University of Michigan, Ann Arbor; the New York Public Library; the Central University Libraries of Southern Methodist University; the Lillian H. Smith Collection and the Spaced-Out Library, both of the Toronto Public Library; the Valparaiso University Library; Falvey Memorial Library, Villanova University; Margaret Clapp Library, Wellesley College; the Library of the University of Wisconsin at Madison; and the Williams College Library.

My thanks also to those publishers, manuscript dealers, booksellers, and friends who provided information, allowed me to examine their collections, or located items for me. I would especially like to acknowledge: Douglas Anderson; Pauline Baynes; Rhona Beare; Dainis Bisenieks; Richard Blackwelder; David Bratman; Mary Faith Boyle; Marjorie Burns; Raoul Chandrasakera; Jeffrey Drefke; Verlyn Flieger; Robert Fraker; Russell Freedman; Glen GoodKnight; Gary and Sylvia Hunnewell; Andy McQuiddy; Nancy Martsch; Charles Noad; John Rateliff and Janice Coulter; Patricia and Trevor Reynolds; Pamela Robinson; Anthony Rota; Julian Rota; the late Taum Santoski; Jonathan Simons; Lester Simons; Arden Smith; Anders Stenström; Donn Stephan; Eric Thompson; Richard West; and Jessica Yates. Special thanks to my fellow Tolkien bibliographer Åke Bertenstam, for his help with section G and many other references; to David Doughan, for his notes on translations published (and continuing to proliferate) in the former Soviet Union; to The Tolkien Society, for encouragement in the early stages of this book and for the use of their archives; to Peter Foden, Archivist of the Oxford University Press, and to Morton H. Baker and Susanna Tecce of the Houghton Mifflin Co., for publication data; to Doris Ayres of Unwin Hyman, for her help and courtesy; to HarperCollins, especially Mary Butler, for access to and permission to quote from their Tolkien files; to Rayner Unwin, for allowing me to read the invaluable Allen & Unwin/Unwin Hyman archive, for permission to quote his reader's reports, and for his flattering foreword; to Christopher Tolkien, for his notes on *The Lord of the Rings*, for 'The History of Middle-earth', and for his enthusiasm; to Christopher Tolkien and F. R. Williamson, executors of the Estate of J. R. R. Tolkien, for permission to quote from published works and unpublished letters; to B. C. Bloomfield and Colin Hutchens for their advice; to Robert Cross of St Paul's Bibliographies; and to the dedicatee of this book, my dear friend Joy Hill, whose memory I treasure.

W. G. H.

Abbreviations

ATB	*The Adventures of Tom Bombadil*
Biography	*J. R. R. Tolkien: A Biography* by Humphrey Carpenter
BLT1	*The Book of Lost Tales, Part One*
BLT2	*The Book of Lost Tales, Part Two*
Drawings	*Drawings by J. R. R. Tolkien*
EPCW	*Essays Presented to Charles Williams*
FCL	*The Father Christmas Letters*
FGH	*Farmer Giles of Ham*
FR	*The Fellowship of the Ring*
H	*The Hobbit*
HBBS	'The Homecoming of Beorhtnoth Beorhthelm's Son'
Lays	*The Lays of Beleriand*
LBN	'Leaf by Niggle'
Letters	*Letters of J. R. R. Tolkien*
LR	*The Lord of the Rings*
OFS	'On Fairy-Stories'
Pictures	*Pictures by J. R. R. Tolkien*
RGEO	*The Road Goes Ever On*
RK	*The Return of the King*
GPO	*Sir Gawain and the Green Knight, Pearl, and Sir Orfeo*
Shadow	*The Return of the Shadow*
Shaping	*The Shaping of Middle-earth*
Silm	*The Silmarillion*
SWM	*Smith of Wootton Major*
TL	*Tree and Leaf*
TR	*The Tolkien Reader*
Treason	*The Treason of Isengard*
TT	*The Two Towers*
UT	*Unfinished Tales*

Chronology

1892 John Ronald Reuel Tolkien born, 3 January, at Bloemfontein, South Africa.
1900 Begins to attend King Edward's School, Birmingham.
1908 Meets Edith Bratt.
1911 Formation of the 'T. C. B. S.' an informal club of Tolkien and his literary schoolmates; enters Exeter College, Oxford.
1913 Awarded Second Class in Honour Moderations; begins to read for the Honours School of English Language and Literature.
1915 Awarded First Class Honours; commissioned in the Lancashire Fusiliers.
1916 Marries Edith Bratt, 22 March; in June, embarks for France; Battle of the Somme; in November, returns to England suffering from trench fever; begins to write (in substantial form) his 'Silmarillion' mythology.
1917 Birth of eldest son, John.
1918 Joins the staff of the *Oxford English Dictionary*.
1920 Appointed Reader in English Language at Leeds University; birth of second son, Michael.
1922 *A Middle English Vocabulary* published.
1924 Becomes Professor of English Language at Leeds; birth of third son, Christopher.
1925 *Sir Gawain and the Green Knight* (edited with E. V. Gordon) published; elected Rawlinson and Bosworth Professor of Anglo-Saxon at Oxford.
1926 Meets C. S. Lewis.
1929 Birth of daughter, Priscilla.
1933 (*circa*) Tolkien, C. S. Lewis, and other friends begin to meet as 'The Inklings'.
1936 Delivers British Academy lecture, 'Beowulf: The Monsters and the Critics'.
1937 *The Hobbit* published; begins to write *The Lord of the Rings*.
1939 Delivers Andrew Lang Lecture, 'On Fairy-Stories'.
1945 Elected Merton Professor of English Language and Literature at Oxford; 'Leaf by Niggle' published.
1949 *Farmer Giles of Ham* published.
1953 'The Homecoming of Beorhtnoth Beorhthelm's Son' published.
1954 *The Fellowship of the Ring* and *The Two Towers* (vols. 1 and 2 of *The Lord of the Rings*) published; receives honorary degrees from the National University of Ireland and the University of Liège.
1955 *The Return of the King* (vol. 3 of *The Lord of the Rings*) published; delivers O'Donnell Lecture, 'English and Welsh'.
1959 Retires from his professorship.
1962 *The Adventures of Tom Bombadil* and *Ancrene Wisse* published.
1964 *Tree and Leaf* published.
1965 Ace Books and Ballantine Books publish paperback editions of *The Lord of the Rings*; 'Tolkien cult' begins in the United States.
1967 *The Road Goes Ever On* (with Donald Swann) and *Smith of Wootton Major* published.
1971 Edith Tolkien dies.
1972 Awarded C.B.E.; receives honorary degree from Oxford University.
1973 Dies, 2 September, in Bournemouth.
1975 *Sir Gawain and the Green Knight, Pearl, and Sir Orfeo* published.
1976 *The Father Christmas Letters* published.
1977 *The Silmarillion* published.
1979 *Pictures by J. R. R. Tolkien* published.
1980 *Unfinished Tales* published.
1981 *Letters of J. R. R. Tolkien* published.
1983– *The History of Middle-earth* published.

A

Books by J. R. R. Tolkien

[*within a single rule frame, within a frame of 184 ornaments (56 at left and right, 36 at top and bottom):*] A | MIDDLE ENGLISH | VOCABULARY | BY | *J. R. R. TOLKIEN* | [*rule*] | *Designed for use with* | SISAM'S Fourteenth Century Verse & Prose | [*rule*] | [*ornaments*] | [*rule*] | OXFORD | AT THE CLARENDON PRESS | M DCCCC XXII

168 pp. Collation: $\pi^4 1–9^8 10^{10}$. 18.8 × 12.2 cm.

[1] title; [2] list of abbreviations; [3] note; [4] list of principal variations of form or spelling; [5–162] text; [163–8] index of names; [168, following index] '[*corrigenda to Sisam's* Fourteenth Century Verse & Prose] | Printed in England at the Oxford University Press'.

Laid paper. Bound in light brown wove wrappers. All edges trimmed and unstained. Three binding variants, priority as follows:

(1) Upper cover printed as for the title page, except that 186 ornaments are in the outer frame (57 at left and right, 36 at top and bottom), and the type varies in spacing and leading from the title page setting. (See Plate I.) Printed on spine, running up: 'A MIDDLE ENGLISH VOCABULARY–TOLKIEN'. Printed on lower cover within frames as on upper cover: 'OXFORD ENGLISH | DICTIONARIES & GLOSSARIES | FOR STUDENTS | [*7 titles, beginning with Sweet,* The Student's Dictionary of Anglo-Saxon, *ending with H. W. and F. G. Fowler,* The Concise Oxford Dictionary of Current English]'. Wove front endpapers, unprinted; wove back endsheet is a folio of advertisements headed on p. [1] 'EARLY AND MIDDLE ENGLISH | Editions of Chaucer by Professor Skeat | *October 1921*', 3 pp. on 2 leaves (leaf 2 pasted down).

(2) As (1), but also with advertisements printed on recto and verso of front free endpaper, headed on recto 'Oxford Books of Reference', dated on verso January 1922.

(3) As (1), but the folio of advertisements at back is dated September 1922.

Copies, presumably later, have been noted (1) with 'PRINTED IN ENGLAND.' rubber-stamped on the title page below the outer frame, and with no inserted advertisements; and (2) with the line rubber-stamped within the frames, below the imprint date, and with advertisements following at back dated September 1922. A later impression has been noted with 'Printed in England' printed from type at the foot of the title page below the outer frame, with no corrigenda on p. [168], and with advertisements at back not dated. Melissa and Mark Hime (booksellers), *Precious Stones* (catalogue, Idyllwild, Calif., 1980, see Dii46), item 5, describes a copy with 184 ornaments on the title page and 184 ornaments on the upper cover (the latter illustrated in the catalogue), and with advertisements not dated.

Published 11 May 1922 at 4s. 6d.; 2,000 copies printed, of which some were bound separately and some with Kenneth Sisam, *Fourteenth Century Verse & Prose* (B3). It was the custom at the time to keep copies in sheets until there was demand for binding.

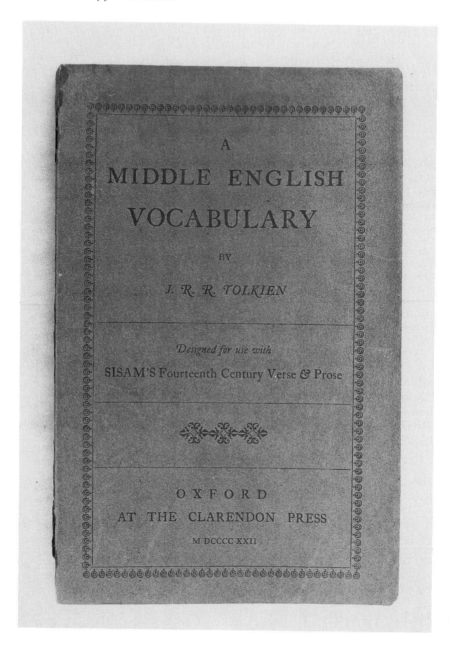

I. *A Middle English Vocabulary* (A1).

Tolkien remarked on 13 February 1923, in a letter to E. M. (Mrs. Joseph) Wright, that he had 'lavished an amount of time' on his Middle English glossary 'which is terrible to recall, and long delayed the Reader bringing curses on my head'. He was otherwise occupied with settling his wife and sons in Leeds and invigorating the linguistic curriculum at Leeds University.

A2   BEOWULF: THE MONSTERS AND THE CRITICS   1937

BEOWULF | THE MONSTERS AND | THE CRITICS | BY | J. R. R. TOLKIEN | SIR ISRAEL GOLLANCZ | MEMORIAL LECTURE | BRITISH ACADEMY | 1936 | FROM THE PROCEEDINGS OF THE | BRITISH ACADEMY. VOLUME XXII | LONDON: HUMPHREY MILFORD | AMEN HOUSE, E.C.

56 pp. Collation: [A]⁴B–G⁴. 25.4–25.6 × 15.8–16.2 cm. (height and width vary).

[1] title; [2] 'PRINTED IN GREAT BRITAIN'; [3]–36 text; 36–47 appendix; 47–53 notes; [54] 'PRINTED IN | GREAT BRITAIN | AT THE | UNIVERSITY PRESS | OXFORD | BY | JOHN JOHNSON | PRINTER | TO THE | UNIVERSITY'; [55–6] blank.

Laid paper, watermarked 'Cassiobury'. Bound in grey wove wrappers. Printed on upper cover: 'BEOWULF | THE MONSTERS AND | THE CRITICS | BY | J. R. R. TOLKIEN | SIR ISRAEL GOLLANCZ | MEMORIAL LECTURE | BRITISH ACADEMY | 1936 | *Price 3s. net* | FROM THE PROCEEDINGS OF THE | BRITISH ACADEMY. VOLUME XXII | LONDON: HUMPHREY MILFORD | AMEN HOUSE, E.C.' Printed on lower cover: 'SIR ISRAEL GOLLANCZ MEMORIAL | LECTURES | *Already Published* | THE ART OF GEOFFREY CHAUCER, by *John Livingstone Lowes.* | 1930. *2s. net.* | CYNEWULF AND HIS POETRY, by *Kenneth Sisam*. 1932. *2s. net.* | LAURENCE NOWELL AND THE DISCOVERY OF ENGLAND | IN TUDOR TIMES, by *Robin Flower*. 1935. *2s. net.* | *Published for the* BRITISH ACADEMY | *By* HUMPHREY MILFORD, OXFORD UNIVERSITY PRESS | AMEN HOUSE, E.C.' Top edge trimmed, fore- and bottom edges untrimmed. All edges unstained.

Published 1 July 1937 at 3s.; 500 copies printed.

Tolkien read his landmark Sir Israel Gollancz Memorial Lecture on 25 November 1936. It was published separately six months before its appearance in vol. 22 of the printed annual *Proceedings* of the Academy, published 30 December 1937, pp. [245]–95. It was reprinted in 1958 and later by Oxford University Press, and by Folcroft Press (Folcroft, Pa., 1969), Norwood Editions (Norwood, Pa., 1975), R. West (Philadelphia, 1977), and Arden Library (Darby, Pa., 1978). The essay was included in *An Anthology of Beowulf Criticism*, ed. Lewis E. Nicholson (Notre Dame, Ind.: University of Notre Dame Press, 1963); *The Beowulf Poet: A Collection of Critical Essays*, ed. Donald K. Fry (Englewood Cliffs, N.J.: Prentice-Hall, 1968); *Beowulf*, ed. Harold Bloom (New York: Chelsea House, 1987), lacking the appendix, and with Modern English translations by Bloom of Tolkien's Old English quotations; *Interpretations of Beowulf: A Critical Anthology*, ed. R. D. Fulk (Bloomington: Indiana University Press, 1991); and *The Monsters and the Critics and Other Essays* (A19).

   Pertinent manuscript and typescript materials, correspondence, and revised proofs, and other materials by Tolkien on *Beowulf* studies (cf. B17a), are in the Bodleian Library, Oxford.

a. First edition:

The Hobbit | or | There and Back | Again | by | J. R. R. Tolkien | London | George Allen & Unwin Ltd | Museum Street

312 pp. + 1 plate. Collation: [A]^{8}B–T^{8}U^4. 19.0 × 13.5 cm.

[1–2] blank; [3] 'The Hobbit'; [4] illustration; [5] title; [6] 'FIRST PUBLISHED IN 1937 | *All rights reserved* | PRINTED IN GREAT BRITAIN BY | UNWIN BROTHERS LTD., WOKING'; [7] table of contents; [8] blank; [9] list of illustrations; [10] blank; [11]–310 text and illustrations; [311] '*OVERLEAF* | *particulars of publications* | *of similar interest* | *issued by* | [*publisher's square "St. George" device with lettered border*] | GEORGE ALLEN & UNWIN LTD | [*7 addresses, London to Sydney*]'; [312] advertisement of Čapek, *Fairy Tales* and *Dashenka*, and Huxley, *At the Zoo.*

Illustrations, by Tolkien: *The Hill: Hobbiton across the Water*, p. [4]; *The Trolls*, p. 49; *The Mountain-path*, p. 68; *The Misty Mountains Looking West from the Eyrie towards Goblin Gate*, p. 117; *Beorn's Hall*, p. 126; *Mirkwood*, halftone plate facing p. 146; *The Elvenking's Gate*, p. 177; *Lake Town*, p. 196; *The Front Gate*, p. 209; *The Hall at Bag-End, Residence of B. Baggins Esquire*, p. 307. Maps, by Tolkien, in black and red: *Thror's Map*, front endsheet; *Wilderland*, back endsheet.

Wove paper. Bound in light green cloth over boards. Stamped on upper cover in dark blue: '[*decoration by Tolkien, mountains, moon, and sun, wraps around covers and spine*] | The | Hobbit | [*decoration by Tolkien, a dragon looking left*]'. Stamped on spine in dark blue: '[*wraparound decoration*] | The | Hobbit | *by* | J. R. R. | Tolkien | [TH *rune*] | [D *rune*] | [TH *rune*] | George Allen | *&* Unwin L^{td}'. Wraparound decoration stamped at top of lower cover, decoration by Tolkien (dragon looking right) at bottom, in dark blue. (See Plate II.) Wove endpapers (maps). No headbands. All edges trimmed. Top edge stained light green, fore- and bottom edges unstained. The publisher's cost book records 152 copies in 'paper cover binding', i.e. wrappers (not seen), presumably for review and samples.

Dust-jacket, wove paper. (See Plate III.) Wraparound illustration by Tolkien, in black, green, and blue, of the Lonely Mountain and neighboring mountains and forest, with a dragon flying near a crescent moon on the lower cover, eagles and the sun in the sky on the upper cover, the whole bordered by an inscription in runes read anticlockwise from lower left: 'THE HOBBIT OR THERE AND BACK AGAIN BEING THE RECORD OF A YEARS JOURNEY MADE BY BILBO BAGGINS OF HOBBITON COMPILED FROM HIS MEMOIRS BY J. R. R. TOLKIEN AND PUBLISHED BY GEORGE ALLEN AND UNWIN LTD'. Lettered on upper cover against the illustration: '[*in white:*] THE | HOBBIT | *by* | [*in black:*] J. R. R. Tolkien'. Lettered on spine against the illustration: '[*in black:*] THE | [*in white:*] HOBBIT | [*in black:*] TOLKIEN | [*against a white panel outlined and shadowed at bottom in black:*] GEORGE ALLEN | AND UNWIN'. Printed on front flap: '[*blurb*] | THIS COVER AND THE DRAWINGS | IN THE BOOK ARE BY THE AUTHOR | 7s. 6d.' Blurb printed on back flap, 'Dodgson' misspelled 'Dodgeson'.

Published 21 September 1937 at 7s. 6d.; 1,500 copies printed.

Includes the errors:

   p. 14, ll. 17–18, 'find morning' for 'fine morning'

II. *The Hobbit* (A3a). Binding design by J. R. R. Tolkien. Photograph from the first edition, second impression, 1937.

III. *The Hobbit* (A3). Dust-jacket design by J. R. R. Tolkien. Photograph from the third edition, 'fifth impression', 1970.

p. 17, ll. 29–30, ' "So you have got here at last!" what [*for* That] was what he was going to say'

p. 25, l. 11, 'more fierce then fire' for 'more fierce than fire'

p. 62, ll. 2–3, 'uncomfortable palpitating' for 'uncomfortable, palpitating'

p. 62, l. 31, 'their bruises their tempers and their hopes' for 'their bruises, their tempers and their hopes'

p. 64, l. 21, 'where the thrush knocks' for 'when the thrush knocks'

p. 85, l. 10, 'far under under the mountains' for 'far under the mountains'

p. 104, l. 17, 'back tops' for 'black tops'

p. 147, l. 16, 'nor what you call' for 'not what you call'

p. 183, l. 26, ' "Very' for ' "Very' (reversed double quotation mark)

p. 205, l. 32, 'dwarves good feeling' for 'dwarves' good feeling'

p. 210, l. 29, 'above stream' for 'above the stream'

p. 216, l. 4, 'leas' for 'least'

p. 215, l. 13, 'door step' for 'doorstep'

p. 229, ll. 16–17, 'you imagination' for 'your imagination'

p. 248, l. 32, 'nay breakfast' for 'any breakfast'

The history of the writing of *The Hobbit* is sketched by Humphrey Carpenter in *J. R. R. Tolkien: A Biography*, and will be fully told by John D. Rateliff in a forthcoming book; but a few words on the subject are appropriate here as preface to its publishing history. The origin of the book cannot be dated precisely. Tolkien's eldest sons, John and Michael, remembered having heard elements of the story in their father's study at 22 Northmoor Road, Oxford, where the family lived between early 1926 and the beginning of 1930. Michael wrote stories in imitation of *The Hobbit* which he dated '1929', and speculated that it was no later than that year when his father idly wrote the first sentence of his book. J. R. R. Tolkien recalled on 7 June 1955, in a letter to W. H. Auden: 'All I can remember about the start of *The Hobbit* is sitting correcting School Certificate papers in the everlasting weariness of that annual task forced on impecunious academics with children. On a blank leaf I scrawled: "In a hole in the ground there lived a hobbit." I did not and do not know why. I did nothing about it, for a long time, and for some years I got no further than the production of Thror's Map. But it became *The Hobbit* in the early 1930s. . . .' That is, it took shape as a written story. The earliest manuscript did not reach past the first chapter (two pages are reproduced in A3y, A3aa, and A3bb, and one in A3dd–ee). But the work was sufficiently complete and presentable by the winter of 1932–3 to be read by C. S. Lewis, who in a letter of 4 February 1933 remarked on the 'children's story which Tolkien has just written' (*They Stand Together: The Letters of C. S. Lewis to Arthur Greeves (1914–1963)*, ed. Walter Hooper [London: Collins, 1979], p. 449). In late 1937 Christopher Tolkien remarked (in a letter to Father Christmas) that his father had written *The Hobbit* 'ages ago' and had read it aloud to John, Michael, and Christopher in their 'Winter "Reads" after tea in the evening; but the ending chapters were rather roughly done, and not typed out at all'. Tolkien hesitated after writing about Smaug's death, and made only rough notes for the end of the story. The rest of the book was neatly typed, with the songs in italics.

Other friends besides Lewis knew of Tolkien's children's book. One was Elaine Griffiths, a former pupil and in 1936 a young graduate in Oxford. On Tolkien's recommendation she was engaged by Allen & Unwin to revise Clark Hall's translation of *Beowulf* (see B17a). In the late spring or early summer of 1936 she was visited by Susan Dagnall, a fellow Oxford graduate now employed by Allen & Unwin. Griffiths recommended *The Hobbit* to Dagnall, who called upon Tolkien and borrowed the typescript. Dagnall saw merit in the work and encouraged Tolkien to complete it for publication by Allen & Unwin. On 10 August 1936 Tolkien noted in a letter (quoted in *Biography*, p. 180) that '*The Hobbit* is now nearly finished, and the publishers [are] clamouring for it.' He sent the finished typescript to Allen & Unwin on 3 October 1936. Stanley Unwin, chairman of the firm, acknowledged its receipt on 5 October and soon accepted it for publication, guided by the favourable report given the work by his ten-year-old son, Rayner:

> Bilbo Baggins was a hobbit who lived in his hobbit-hole and *never* went for adventures, at last Gandalf the wizard and his dwarves perswaded him to go. He had a very exiting time fighting goblins and wargs. at last they got to the lonley mountain; Smaug, the dragon who gawreds it is killed and after a terrific battle with the goblins he returned home—rich!
> This book, with the help of maps, does not need any illustrations it is good and should appeal to all children between the ages of 5 and 9.

The report is date-stamped 30 October 1936. Specimen pages were first sent to Tolkien probably in November of that year. On 4 December Susan Dagnall sent a revised specimen page for approval. Tolkien objected to a star-shaped ornament at the chapter openings, and it was removed. Dagnall also asked on 4 December for 'a short paragraph describing the book, for use in our forthcoming Announcement List and for the basis of all preliminary notices of the book'. Tolkien wrote a paragraph, evidently by 10 December 1936, which was printed not only in the Allen & Unwin 1937 *Summer Announcements* but (with remarks by the publisher) on the flap of the *Hobbit* dust-jacket:

> If you care for journeys there and back, out of the comfortable Western world, over the edge of the Wild, and home again, and can take an interest in a humble hero (blessed with a little wisdom and a little courage and considerable good luck), here is the record of such a journey and such a traveller. The period is the ancient time between the age of Faerie and the dominion of men, when the famous forest of Mirkwood was still standing, and the mountains were full of danger. In following the path of this humble adventurer, you will learn by the way (as he did)—if you do not already know all about these things—much about trolls, goblins, dwarves, and elves, and get some glimpses into the history and politics of a neglected but important period. For Mr. Bilbo Baggins visited various notable persons; conversed with the dragon, Smaug the Magnificent; and was present, rather unwillingly, at the Battle of Five Armies. This is all the more remarkable, since he was a hobbit. Hobbits have hitherto been passed over in history and legend, perhaps because they as a rule preferred comfort to excitement. But this account, based on his personal memoirs, of the one exciting year in the otherwise quiet life of Mr. Baggins will give you a fair idea of this estimable people, now (it is said) becoming rather rare. They do not like noise.

On 10 December Dagnall reported to Tolkien that the Allen & Unwin production staff were having problems with the five maps then planned for the book: 'What is worrying our Production Department chiefly is (a) the number of colours, and (b) the chalk shading, as in the circumstances these could only be reproduced by the three-colour half-tone process, which means splitting the drawings up into minute dots, which will spoil the line, and also printing them on a different paper from the text, which makes them so formal.' She suggested that *Thror's Map* and *Wilderland* be printed as endpapers, in red and blue

> or any other two colours you prefer. This means in the Mirkwood map [i.e. *Wilderland*] showing the Misty Mountains and the Grey Mountains only by hatching in one colour, the higher ranges being indicated by closer hatching.

The rivers may then be shown by parallel lines. Possibly it will be best to indicate Mirkwood in the same colour as the Mountains, leaving the second colour for all the paths and all the lettering. All that is needed with the lettering is that you should do it a little more neatly. This is indeed the only alteration needed in Thror's map. But in the latter are the moon-runes very important? They can be reproduced, but it will be a little difficult.

The other three maps can then be printed in with the text in a single colour. The Esgaroth map . . . only needs rather more careful lettering. Would it be possible for you to redraw the other Esgaroth map, which you have in done in two colours, in one, indicating the water not by shading as at present, but by three or four parallel lines round the coast, as done by professional carto- graphers! The Lonely Mountain will then have to be redrawn in one colour with the shading indicated please by fine, but not too fine, lines. Would it be possible to make some sort of ripple effect in line for the river? This question of shading unfortunately also applies to Mirkwood, which will have to be indicated by hard lines.

By 4 January 1937 Tolkien redrew *Thror's Map*, which he intended to be tipped in at its first mention in the text ('a piece of parchment rather like a map', p. 30). He also redrew the general map, *Wilderland*, which was to appear at the end of the book. The other maps, he now decided, were not wanted. On 7 January C. A. Furth of Allen & Unwin's production department also suggested that the maps be printed as endpapers. But if this were done, he admitted, the 'magic runes' on *Thror's Map* would present a problem. As described in *The Hobbit*, these letters could be seen only when the moon shone on them. Tolkien hoped that the effect could be approximated by printing a mirror image of the 'moon-letters' on the back of the sheet, so that they would be seen, reading correctly, when the map was held up to a light. 'Rather a complication with an end-paper', Furth wrote. 'Moreover, will not people just turn over [the sheet] instead of looking at them through the page as they should? We are trying a rather more cunning method of letting the runes be both there and not there and shall submit the result to you.' Tolkien replied on 17 January: 'The maps could be used as end-papers as you suggest—though I would rather the *chart with runes* was inserted in the text, perhaps (rather than in I) in ch. III where the secret runes are first observed by Elrond.' On 23 January Susan Dagnall asked that Tolkien return to the publisher the original of *Thror's Map*, because the blockmaker had misunderstood his instructions and left out the 'magic' of the runes. Tolkien complied, also on 23 January, and again made his point that the 'magic runes' would be more effective on the back of the map. 'I have drawn a copy in reverse so that when printed they would read right way round held up to the light. But I leave this up to the Production Dept., hoping nonetheless that it will not be necessary to put the magic runes on the face of the chart, which rather spoils it (unless yr. reference to "magic" refers to something "magical").' The 'more cunning method' was perhaps to print the runes in a tone to distinguish them from the line art of the map; in the event, they were distinguished merely by being drawn with a noticeably thinner line.

The responsible member of the Allen & Unwin production department and the blockmaker's representative who had worked out the method went down with influenza simultaneously, and the blockmaker did not follow their written instruc- tions. Susan Dagnall assured Tolkien on 1 February that with a fresh block the runes would not appear 'so blatantly on the front'—but they *would* be printed on the front of the sheet, not on the back as Tolkien wished. The maps, Dagnall explained, would have to be printed as endpapers for economic reasons. As a children's book, *The*

Hobbit had to be sold at a modest price, Allen & Unwin had not allowed any cost margin for illustrations (but see below), and tipping in would have meant extra cost. On 5 February Tolkien finally conceded: 'Let the Production Dept. do as it will with the chart.'

Discussion of the endpapers in fact continued into April, and Tolkien's regrets into May (and beyond). Furth agreed with him on 23 March that black and red would be better colours for the endpapers than blue and red, an 'excess of patriotism' when printed on a white background. Tolkien passed proofs of the endpapers on 13 April, commenting that 'the change from *blue* to *red* on end-paper 2 [*Wilderland*] is detrimental. I wonder if it would not be better (since only 2 colours are possible) to substitute *blue* for *red* in end-paper 1 [*Thror's Map*]? This would entail a change in text from *red* to *blue* in 2 places on page 30. . . .' But the complications of this route seem to have become suddenly clear to him (or he could be bothered with the matter no more), and he footnoted his remarks: 'On second & last thought—I think not.' He made a 'more careful drawing' of the runes for *Thror's Map*, but it was not possible to substitute them for the earlier version, which Tolkien thought 'ill-done (and not quite upright)' (letter of 13 April). And he continued to prefer his own design for the book. If the British edition was now largely a *fait accompli*, perhaps there was hope for the American edition he learned of in early May? He wrote to Allen & Unwin on 28 May 1937 and pointedly wondered: 'Do you think they [the American publisher] would contemplate enlarging the Mirkwood drawing into an end-paper [see below], and inserting the maps in text (in original colours), with the runic map re-drawn? That *would* be an improvement, I think.' But in this too he was disappointed: see A3b note.

Rayner Unwin concluded in his reader's report that *The Hobbit*, 'with the help of maps, does not need any illustrations'. Nevertheless, Tolkien submitted drawings for the story. According to Carpenter, *Biography*, he did so at the publisher's suggestion, and Tolkien implies as much in his letter of 5 February 1937, noting that originally he had forsworn illustrations on the assumption that they could not be afforded. But the contrary is suggested by Susan Dagnall in her letter to Tolkien of 1 February 1937: Allen & Unwin had not allowed any cost margin for illustrations, she wrote, 'but when you sent us these drawings they were so charming that we could not but insert them, although economically it was quite wrong to do so. And when you sent us the second batch we felt just the same!' And Tolkien seems to be advancing his pictures tentatively in his letter to Dagnall of 4 January 1937. He had 'redrawn (as far as I am capable) one or two of the amateur illustrations of the "home manuscript" [master copy],' he wrote, 'conceiving that they might serve as endpapers, frontispiece or what not. I think on the whole such things, if they were better, might be an improvement [to the book]. But it may be impossible at this stage, and in any case they are not very good and may be technically unsuitable.'

These illustrations were *Mirkwood*, which Tolkien intended for the front endpaper; *The Elvenking's Gate*, for the end of ch. 8; *Lake Town*, in ch. 10; and *The Front Gate*, in ch. 11. Tolkien had made other drawings as well, but not to his satisfaction. As he feared, there were problems with some of those submitted. C. A. Furth remarked on 7 January 1937 that the *Hobbit* drawings were admirable and had been handed on to the blockmaker, but *Mirkwood*, shaded with ink wash, 'will present a little difficulty in reproduction—unless it were to be printed separately on glossy paper, which we think would be disturbing.' And except for *The Front Gate*, the drawings were horizontal rather than vertical, so that they had to be turned parallel with the spine of the book if they were not to be reduced so greatly that Tolkien's intricate detail was lost. On 17 January Tolkien replied to Furth, leaving the drawings in the publisher's hands to reproduce and use in the best way. He also specified where the drawings should be placed in the text, and in doing so found that the maps and pictures were concentrated toward the end. 'This is due to no plan,' he wrote, 'but occurs simply because I failed to reduce the other illustrations to even passable shape [i.e. draw them to his satisfaction]. I was also advised that those with a geographical or landscape content were the most suitable—even apart from my inability to draw anything else!' He now submitted, for balance, six additional drawings: *The Hill: Hobbiton across the Water*, for ch. 1; *The Trolls*, for the beginning of ch. 2; *The Mountain-path*, beginning of ch. 4; *The Misty Mountains Looking West*, beginning of ch. 6; *Beorn's Hall*, at any point in ch. 7; and *The Hall at Bag-End* in ch. 19, 'thus beginning and ending with the "quiet life"'. *Mirkwood* he now wanted at the beginning of ch. 8 and *The Elvenking's Gate* at the beginning of ch. 9. 'They all are obviously defective,' he remarked to Furth, 'and quite apart from this may, each or some, present difficulties of reproduction. Also you may be quite unwilling to consider thus belatedly any more complications, and a change of plan.'

By 23 January 1937 Allen & Unwin decided that four additional illustrations could be included without raising the price of the book—*The Hill*, *The Misty Mountains Looking West*, *Beorn's Hall*, and *The Hall at Bag-End*, with perhaps a fifth drawing reproduced on the dust-jacket. On 1 February Susan Dagnall remarked that the fifth and sixth drawings might be squeezed in at the ends of chapters, where space was available on the page. In the event, all of the drawings were included. On 5 February Tolkien approved rough proofs of the new illustrations, though he found defects in *The Trolls* and was sorry that he had 'misguidedly put' in *The Hall at Bag-End* 'a wash shadow reaching up to the side beam,' which had come out black, obscuring the key in the door. The toned drawing *Mirkwood* was printed on a coated stock after all, without its upper decorative border.

Allen & Unwin admired Tolkien's art despite his frequent self-criticism, and now asked him to design the dust-jacket for his book. C. A. Furth wrote to him on 23 March 1937: 'We are still hoping to persuade you of your ability to produce a jacket (provided you have the time) but the matter does not press since you have still to see revised proofs.' Tolkien replied on 30 March that he would do what he could about a jacket, and within two weeks submitted a preliminary design. He wrote to Allen & Unwin on 13 April:

> I discovered (as I anticipated) that it was rather beyond my craft and experience. But perhaps the general design would do?
>
> I foresee the main objections.
>
> There are too many colours: blue, green, red, black. (The 2 reds are an accident; the 2 greens inessential.) This could be met, with possible improvement, by substituting *white* for *red*; and omitting the sun, or drawing a line round it. The presence of the sun and moon in the sky together refers to the magic attaching to the door [in the Lonely Mountain, at the centre of the design].
>
> It is too complicated, and needs simplifying: e.g. by reducing the mountains to a single colour, and simplification of the jagged 'fir-trees'.
>
> The lettering is probably not clear enough. The cutting of the main title is an accident. In redrawing I should place the zig-zag below the HOBBIT and place author's name on the bottom of [the] line of trees (as per affixed label).
>
> The design *inside* the runic border is of the size of the model you gave me. Could you tell me if this was correct? It seems to be too small, unless the proof-page is reduced in margin-cutting by ⅞ of an inch (approx.) in height, and then that allows for no overhang of the boards. But the border (1 cm. all round)

could be cut off and a heavy black line substituted; or in redrawing the whole thing could be reduced—if you think the runes are attractive. Though magical in appearance they merely run: *The Hobbit or There and Back Again, being the record of a year's journey made by Bilbo Baggins; compiled from his memoirs by J. R. R. Tolkien and published by George Allen and Unwin.* The white edge is not intended to be included.

I should be glad to hear as soon as possible whether this design is of any use, or contains any hope—for term begins on April 24th, and once it arrives there will be no time for anything for some weeks. Redrawing even a simplified form on proper paper (I apologize for the two pieces of philological waste paper that have been used) would take a day or two.

C. A. Furth found the jacket design 'admirable' and made to the correct proportions. But in a letter to Tolkien of 15 April, he suggested that its red colour be removed

both because the title will show up better in white [Tolkien had lettered 'THE HOBBIT' in red] and because the only feature about which we are not entirely happy in the cover is the flush on the central mountain [the snowcap], which makes it look to our eyes just a trifle like a cake. If the red is omitted, would you put the marginal runes on a green background [originally, it seems, drawn on a red background]? Otherwise the lettering seems to us entirely satisfactory, since it will become neater when reduced and can also be slightly touched up by the blockmaker.

Actually we could probably work straight from this first drawing, but as you have suggested being good enough to re-draw it, we are returning it to you herewith. The only other point is that your name ought really to appear somewhere on the shelf-back, if necessary in substitution for ours.

Tolkien reported to Furth on 25 April that he had re-drawn the jacket

with some labour, but I fear no great improvement. I have not altered it in much save size, since you gave your general approval. It is now in intention of exact size for actual cover. I have omitted the offending pink icing on the mountain-ous cake. It is now arranged in blue, black, green. The sun and dragon still have some red, which can be left out, in which case the sun will vanish or can have a thin black outline.

The colours of the original draft were, I think, more attractive. I may say that my children (if they are anything to go by) much prefer the original, including the red flush on the central mountain—but possibly the cake-suggestion is attractive to them. Personally, being ignorant of costs and possibilities in reproduction, I should say that if effect alone is considered, *red* is very desirable, and should be used for dragon and sun; for HOBBIT on front cover; instead of blue in the ground of the forest immediately behind the first row of black trunks (as in first draft but one row forward); for the runic border; and possibly for author's name on shelf-back. The whole would, of course, also be much improved by the use of a *dark green* for the front row of large trees, and also for the green spaces (with wavy top edges) behind last row of pointed 'trees', on either side of white path. But such questions are, of course, for you to settle. The design is probably too complicated already.

I send back separately the dummy [given him by Furth to guide his jacket revisions], with your (now rather tattered) paper model of the jacket, and a brown-paper model of the same size as design now submitted; the original draft and the redrawing (unfolded as it is on stiff paper) came with this letter.

Tolkien's elaborate instructions to the printer written on the new design are transcribed in *Drawings* (Ei1), item 32.

Furth replied on 28 April that the red would have to be omitted from the jacket and the sun outlined. Production commenced, and a proof jacket was sent to Tolkien in late May. He approved it on 28 May with the comment: 'The sun in outline is my chief sorrow, but I realise that it cannot be helped. A slightly finer outline would have been better but it is a small point.' A colour photograph of Tolkien's final dust-jacket art is printed on the jacket of A3ee.

A dummy jacket by Tolkien, now in fragments mounted on rice paper, is in the Tolkien archive at Marquette University, Milwaukee, Wisconsin, and is reproduced (in black and white) in *J. R. R. Tolkien: The Hobbit Drawings, Watercolors, and Manuscripts* (Dii66), pp. 8–9. It is not, however, one of the designs discussed in Tolkien's correspondence with C. A. Furth, but appears to be an earlier draft, if not his first attempt *circa* 30 March 1937. It was drawn on white paper in black, dark grey, light and dark green, and light brown, with a red dragon (on the upper cover) and the title THE HOBBIT in red. The lowest jagged line modelling the large mountain at far right (upper cover) partly runs through the word HOBBIT in the lettered titling, a 'cutting of the main title' which Tolkien may have repeated in the design he first sent to Allen & Unwin. There are no 'jagged "fir-trees"' to need simplification. The lower third of the upper cover and the lower two-thirds of the spine are lost to wear or damage, and there are no flaps. The runic border is not present, and perhaps was never part of this draft, for there is no evidence of excision. Here the eagles fly near the crescent moon on the lower cover and the dragon with the sun on the upper cover, opposite to the final design.

The binding case of *The Hobbit* was originally designed by the Allen & Unwin production staff. Two wavy lines wrapped around the covers and spine at top and bottom, perhaps to suggest mountains. 'The | Hobbit' was stamped in italic type asymmetrically on the upper cover, and two more wavy lines were stamped below the title. Two copies of the suggested case, one in blue cloth and one in green, were submitted to Tolkien for approval. He commented to C. A. Furth on 28 May that he preferred the green cloth, that the title would be better centred, and that roman rather than italic letters should be used. He also wrote, urgently, that 'the *wavy line* at edges and (especially) *under title is bad*. None or straight? A small design would be an improvement. I suppose it must be in black blocked in or thick outline. I will try one at once.' Furth agreed on 1 June that the wavy lines might be removed from under the title, but the publisher wanted something at the edges. Roman letters would be substituted for the italics, 'although our choice of italic was made because upright sometimes looks rather jejune in a position like this.' On 3 July he sent Tolkien a new sample case with revised lettering and without the wavy lines below the title, 'which we agree is a great improvement, but unless you feel strongly we should like to leave the lines top and bottom, because without them we feel the binding will be bare and that if they are made straight lines it will look too much like a Macmillan textbook.'

Illness prevented Tolkien from attending to the binding design for five weeks. On 9? July 1937, though he imagined it now too late, he sent Allen & Unwin his attempt at a redesign

as far as it had got a month ago.... I thought the wavy line might be transformed into something significant; and tried to find an ornamental dragon-formula. The one intended for the bottom right hand corner might possibly have been of use in some way. The wavy mountains could have appeared at bottom or top, according to the dragon selected. But the whole thing is too elaborate. I never had a chance of reducing it. The revised cover, which I return, will do—though I still hanker after a dragon, or at least some sort of rune-formula such as I have put on the centre of back [spine]. I am sorry that disaster and procrastination have spoiled the project.

I have not seen the original of Tolkien's revised binding design, and find it difficult to picture from this letter. The 'wavy mountains' must be his wraparound decoration of mountains, moon, and sun; they may have been at both top and bottom to replace the Allen & Unwin version's wavy lines, without a dragon present, if Tolkien still 'hankered' for one. But it is clear that he submitted two dragons: one, drawn with a heavy line and printed on the upper and lower covers of the finished binding as mirror images (see Plate II); and another, drawn more delicately and elongated. The latter design is reproduced in *Catalogue of an Exhibition of Drawings by J. R. R. Tolkien* (Ei1), p. [11], where it is incorrectly stated that the dragon would have been 'a pendant to the dragon at the bottom'. Tolkien's letter of 9? July leaves no doubt that he intended his 'wavy mountains' to appear at the top if the first dragon were used at the bottom (as on the finished binding), or to appear at the bottom if his second dragon were stamped at the top.

    Tolkien received proofs of signatures A–H of *The Hobbit* on 20 February 1937. He corrected them but advised Allen & Unwin on 21 February that he would retain the proofs until he had the complete set. 'There are some minor discrepancies that come out in print and make it desirable to have the whole story together before passing for press. This will cause little delay, as there is little to do, and I can correct a batch of about 8 signatures within 24 hours of receipt. . . . The printing and interpretation of copy seem very good. Actual printer's errors are very rare; and very few corrections would be necessary, but for defects in the copy itself, and unfortunate discrepancies in the text (and between the text and the illustrations).' He was sent the remaining proofs on 24 February with the instruction to replace 'such alterations and deletions as are unavoidable' with 'words taking up as near as possible the same amount of space'. He returned the complete set of corrected proofs on 10? March, with the remarks: 'The type-setting throughout was guilty of very few divergences from copy, and in general proof-corrections are light. But I ought to have given the MS. a revision—in places there were considerable confusions of narrative and geography! About 16 pages have suffered severely. I have calculated the space line by line as carefully as possible and I hope made all corrections plain and intelligible.'

    In fact, as C. A. Furth wrote to Tolkien on 23 March, the author's corrections, apart from corrections of printer's errors, were 'pretty heavy'—heavy enough, in the event, that the printers revised the setting of the whole book rather than just the corrected passages. Tolkien received revised proofs in early April and returned them to Allen & Unwin on 13 April. This time, he wrote, he had 'altered 8 words, to rectify narrative errors that escaped my previous care; and have also corrected necessarily about 7 errors that descended from copy and also escaped.'

    On 10? March 1937 Tolkien asked C. A. Furth if Allen & Unwin had decided when they would publish. Furth replied on 23 March that the book should come out just when ready, 'without being held over to appear, somewhat unsuitably, amongst the Christmas "juveniles"'. On 14 May Furth explained that *The Hobbit* must appear during term-time. Since Allen & Unwin published on alternate Tuesdays, the nearest publication date considered was 8 June 1937; but this was made impossible by the need for revised proofs and by the Whitsun holidays, and in any case by the first week of June people in Oxford (where the publisher hoped the book would do well) would be preoccupied by examinations. Publication was possible at the end of

June, but Allen & Unwin, advised by the prominent Oxford bookseller Blackwell's, felt that it was best to hold the book over until after the middle of October, after the beginning of Michaelmas Term. Tolkien disagreed. 'I cannot help thinking,' he wrote on 28 May, 'that you are possibly mistaken in taking Oxford University and its terms into account; and alternatively, if you do, in considering early October better than June. Most of O. U. [Oxford University] will take no interest in such a story; that part of it that will is already clamouring, and indeed beginning to add *The Hobbit* to my long list of never-never procrastinations.' Late June, he felt, between last preparations for exams and 'the battle with scripts', is a time when lighter reading is sought. 'October with the inrush of a new academic year is most distracted.' By 1 June Allen & Unwin had decided to publish in September. 'The book itself is now printed, as you know,' Furth wrote, 'and if we rushed the binding we could publish before the end of this month [June]', but postponement would allow time for sending out advance copies, and would suit the American publisher best [see A3b].'

Tolkien received an advance copy of his book by 13 August. On 31 August he commented to C. A. Furth on inaccuracies in the publisher's remarks printed on the *Hobbit* jacket (see *Letters* no. 15). Furth assured Tolkien on 4 September that his corrections would be made in any reprint—though by then, he felt, most of the offending blurb would be crowded out by quotations from enthusiastic reviews.

The first impression was sold out by 15 December 1937 and a reprint hurried through press. Tolkien submitted a list of emendations to Allen & Unwin on 16 December 1937, too late to correct the new impression, already completed. The second impression consisted of 2,300 copies printed in December? 1937 and bound through November 1940. Though the book is marked 'SECOND IMPRESSION 1937' and was ready by 19 December 1937, official publication was on 25 January 1938. 423 copies in sheets in the warehouse of the binder Key & Whiting were destroyed in the bombing of London on 7 November 1940. The title page of the second impression reads: 'The Hobbit | or | There and Back | Again | by | J. R. R. Tolkien | Illustrated | by the Author | London | George Allen & Unwin Ltd | Museum Street'. Page 4 is blank, the line illustration *The Hill* replaced by a frontispiece plate. The list of illustrations, p. [9], was reset. Four plates of colour illustrations by Tolkien are present in addition to the black and white *Mirkwood* plate: *The Hill: Hobbiton across the Water*, facing p. [5]; *The Fair Valley of Rivendell* (i.e. *Rivendell*), facing p. 59; *The Dark River Opened Suddenly Wide* (i.e. *Bilbo Comes to the Huts of the Raft-Elves*), facing p. 192; '*O Smaug, the Chiefest and Greatest of All Calamities!*' (i.e. *Conversation with Smaug*), facing p. 228. These had been commissioned for the first American edition, and were in the American publisher's hands when Allen & Unwin decided to include them in the second impression. The original art was called back for reproduction in Britain, then returned across the Atlantic. Tolkien thought that the colour plates came out well, but was sorry that the 'Eagle picture' (*Bilbo Woke Up with the Early Sun in His Eyes*) was not included. On 19 December 1937 he wrote to C. A. Furth: 'I marvel that four can have been included without raising the price. Perhaps the Americans will use it? Odd folk.' See further, A3b.

Allen & Unwin planned the third impression of *The Hobbit* to be a 'cheaper edition' (at 5s.), and to this end began production *circa* January–February 1940 with the printing of 820 sets of endpapers and the moulding of the standing type. Publication was intended for 24 October 1940, but was delayed, probably by wartime conditions, and then was abandoned after the publisher's substantial loss (more than one million books) in the warehouse fire of 7 November 1940. Plates were cast, presumably from the early 1940 moulds, *circa* December 1941. In late

1942, Allen & Unwin printed 1,500 copies of *The Hobbit* with their own imprint, together with 3,000 copies for the Children's Book Club of the bookseller Foyles. The impression is dated 1942, but slow binding delayed publication by Allen & Unwin until 1943. Foyles' copies were supplied to the bookseller in sheets and bound independently, without plates or maps, in yellow, gilt-stamped cloth over boards, with a dust-jacket (which Tolkien thought hideous) in black, orange, and white, featuring a cartoon of a dandified hobbit. A black and white photograph of the upper cover of this jacket is printed in *The Annotated Hobbit* (A3dd–ee), p. 11. In the Allen & Unwin copies, bound between March? and December? 1943, all plates except the colour frontispiece (*The Hill*) were omitted, and at least three corrections were made to the text: ' "Very' > ' "Very' (reversing the double quotation mark), p. 183, l. 26; 'leas' > 'least', p. 216, l. 4; 'you imagination' > 'your imagination', p. 229, ll. 16–17.

Stanley Unwin remarked in a letter to Tolkien, 7 July 1944, that if Allen & Unwin had the paper, they would immediately reprint *The Hobbit* again, knowing that sales of the popular book were assured. But the severe wartime paper shortage delayed the next printing for another two years. The fourth impression consisted of 4,000 copies printed July? 1946 and dated 1946, but not bound until *circa* October 1947 and not officially published until 18 November 1947. At least two corrections were made in this impression: 'find morning' > 'fine morning', p. 14, ll. 17–18, and 'far under under the mountains' > 'far under the mountains', p. 85, l. 10.

For the 'fifth impression', see A3c.

The manuscript (lacking the first part of ch. 1), typescripts, and corrected proofs of A3a are in the Archives and Special Collections of the Marquette University Library, Milwaukee, who have published an inventory. Part of a page of the *Hobbit* typescript is reproduced in Karen Sodlink, 'J. R. R. Tolkien: Manuscripts of a Fairy Tale Writer', *Marquette Journal*, Milwaukee, September 1981, pp. 8–10. Most of the original art for *The Hobbit*, including the final dust-jacket art, is in the Bodleian Library, Oxford. The art for *Mirkwood* was given by Tolkien to a Chinese student, and has been lost. An unfinished sketch of a dragon, probably meant for the dust-jacket, is on the verso of the first leaf of Tolkien's letter of 9? July in the Tolkien/Allen & Unwin correspondence. See further, *Drawings* (Ei1), *Pictures* (Ei2), *Drawings for 'The Hobbit' by J. R. R. Tolkien* (Oxford: Bodleian Library, 1987), *J. R. R. Tolkien: The Hobbit Drawings, Watercolors, and Manuscripts* (Dii66), and the foreword by Christopher Tolkien to A3y, A3aa–bb. Also see further, Brian Alderson, *The Hobbit 50th Anniversary, 1937–1987* (Oxford: Blackwell Bookshops; London: Unwin Hyman, 1987), Dii65.

The first edition text of chapter 5 was reprinted in *Masterpieces of Terror and the Supernatural: A Treasury of Spellbinding Tales Old & New*, selected by Marvin Kaye with Saralee Kaye (Garden City, N.Y.: Doubleday, 1985). Portions of original chapter 5, with the revisions made in the second edition, were printed in *The Annotated Hobbit* (A3dd–ee). Poems and riddles from *The Hobbit* frequently appear in anthologies; for lists of reprints, see Åke Bertenstam, *En Tolkienbibliografi 1911–1980 = A Tolkien Bibliography 1911–1980* (Uppsala, 1986), and supplements in the journal *Arda*. For dramatizations of *The Hobbit*, see Bertenstam, and A3c note.

b. First American edition (1938):

Two impressions, or two states of the first impression, priority as follows:

1:

THE HOBBIT | or | There and Back | Again | BY | J. R. R. TOLKIEN |

ILLUSTRATIONS BY | THE AUTHOR | [*decoration, a bowing hobbit*] | BOSTON AND NEW YORK | HOUGHTON MIFFLIN COMPANY | 1938

146, [2], 147–312 pp. + 4 plates. Collation: $[1^8(-1_2)2–19^820^4(-20_{3,4}+20_3,20_{4,5})]$. 20.5 × 14.8 cm.

[1–2] blank; [3–4] excised, frontispiece plate attached to stub of $[1_2]$; [5] title; [6] 'COPYRIGHT, 1937 AND 1938, BY J. R. R. TOLKIEN | ALL RIGHTS RESERVED INCLUDING THE RIGHT TO REPRODUCE | THIS BOOK OR PARTS THEREOF IN ANY FORM | PRINTED IN THE U.S.A.'; [7] table of contents; [8] blank; [9] list of illustrations; [10] blank; [11]–146 text and illustrations; [146+1] illustration, *Mirkwood*; [146+2] blank; 147–310 text and illustrations; [311–12] blank.

Black and white illustrations, by Tolkien: *The Trolls*, p. 49; *The Mountain-path*, p. [68]; *The Misty Mountains Looking West from the Eyrie towards Goblin Gate*, p. 117; *Beorn's Hall*, p. [126]; *Mirkwood*, p. [146+1]; *The Elvenking's Gate*, p. 177; *Lake Town*, p. [196]; *The Front Gate*, p. 209; *The Hall at Bag-End, Residence of B. Baggins Esquire*, p. 307. *Mirkwood* is reproduced on an integral leaf, not included in the pagination, between pp. 146–7. Colour illustrations, by Tolkien, on 4 plates, each with title printed in blue below the illustration: *The Hill: Hobbiton across The Water*, facing p. [5]; *The Fair Valley of Rivendell* (i.e. *Rivendell*), facing p. 58; *Bilbo Woke Up with the Early Sun in His Eyes*, facing p. [118]; '*O Smaug, the Chiefest and Greatest of Calamities!*' (i.e. *Conversation with Smaug*), facing p. 228. Maps, by Tolkien, in red only: *Wilderland*, front endsheet; *Thror's Map*, back endsheet.

Wove paper. Bound in tan cloth over boards. Two binding cloths seen, no priority determined: (1) without ribbing; (2) with bands of horizontal ribbing. Only one copy of binding 2 has been seen. Stamped on upper cover: '[*in blue:*] THE | HOBBIT [*to right of title: decoration, a bowing hobbit in silhouette, in red*]'. Stamped on spine: '[*in blue:*] THE | HOBBIT | [*decoration, a dwarf's cap, in red*] | [*in blue:*] TOLKIEN | HOUGHTON | MIFFLIN CO.' Wove endpapers (maps). No headbands. All edges trimmed and unstained.

Dust-jacket, wove paper. Printed on upper cover against a blue background: '[*in white:*] The Hobbit | [*colour illustration by Tolkien*, The Hill: Hobbiton-across-the Water, *against a white panel outlined with a thick red rule*] | [*in white:*] By J. R. R. Tolkien'. Quotation from the (London) *Times* printed across upper cover in blue, against a white band. Printed on spine in blue, against a cream background, between two red rules running the length of the cover: '[*running down:*] The Hobbit · Tolkien | [*horizontal:*] H.M.Co.' Printed on lower cover against a blue background: '[*in white:*] The Hobbit | [*colour illustration by Tolkien*, Conversation with Smaug, *against a white panel outlined with a thick red rule*] | [*in white:*] By J. R. R. Tolkien'. Different quotation from the *Times* printed across lower cover in blue, against a white band. Printed on front flap in blue, against a cream background: '$2.50 | [*double rule*] | THE HOBBIT | *By J. R. R. Tolkien* | [*rule*] | [*blurb*] | *Illustrated* | [*double rule*]'. Printed on back flap in blue, against a cream background: '[*double rule*] | THE MAGIC | WALKING-STICK | *By John Buchan* | [*rule*] | [*blurb*] | [*double rule*]'. A black and white photograph of the covers and spine of the jacket is printed in *The Annotated Hobbit* (A3dd–ee), p. [3].

The Houghton Mifflin file copies, and the copies sent by the publisher to Tolkien, are as described above (binding 1).

2:

THE HOBBIT | or | There and Back | Again | BY | J. R. R. TOLKIEN | ILLUSTRATIONS BY | THE AUTHOR | [*publisher's 'flute-player' device*] | BOSTON AND NEW YORK | HOUGHTON MIFFLIN COMPANY | 1938

146, [2], 147–310 pp. + 4 plates. Collation: [1–19⁸20⁴]. 20.5 × 14.8 cm.

[1–2] blank; [3] 'The Hobbit'; [4] blank; [5] title; [6] 'COPYRIGHT, 1937 AND 1938, BY J. R. R. TOLKIEN | ALL RIGHTS RESERVED INCLUDING THE RIGHT TO REPRODUCE | THIS BOOK OR PARTS THEREOF IN ANY FORM | PRINTED IN THE U.S.A.'; [7] table of contents; [8] blank; [9] list of illustrations; [10] blank; [11]–146 text and illustrations; [146+1] illustration, *Mirkwood*; [146+2] blank; 147–310 text and illustrations.

Illustrations as for impression or state 1, except that the frontispiece is not inserted on a stub. [1₂] is a half-title and blank verso. The 'bowing hobbit' on the title page is replaced by a publisher's device (see Plate IV). The list of illustrations is corrected. Leaf [20₄] is integral.

Wove paper. Binding and endpapers as for impression or state 1, binding 1. Dust-jacket not seen, presumably as for impression or state 1.

Published 1 March 1938 at $2.50; 5,000 copies printed.

Typeset as for A3a, except pp. [5–6], [9]. Printed from plates, the type slightly enlarged. The endpaper maps are bound opposite to the order called for in the list of illustrations and by the instruction to the reader, p. 30, referring to *Thror's Map* as it was bound (and printed in two colours) in A3a: 'Look at the map at the beginning of this book, and you will see there the runes in red.'

On 11 May 1937 C. A. Furth reported to Tolkien that Allen & Unwin had interested 'one of the outstanding firms of American publishers' in *The Hobbit*, and that the book would be issued in the United States (unlike the British edition) 'more or less explicitly as a juvenile'. Paul Brooks, formerly of Houghton Mifflin, recalled in his memoir *Two Park Street* (Boston: Houghton Mifflin, 1986) that *The Hobbit* was published by his firm despite negative criticism by the editor in charge of children's books and by the children's librarian at the Boston Public Library, whose professional opinion was asked. Brooks himself 'fell for Mr. Bilbo Baggins and his crew'.

Houghton Mifflin wanted to include 'about four' colour illustrations, by American artists, in addition to Tolkien's line drawings. Allen & Unwin suggested to Tolkien that 'it would be better if all the illustrations were from your hand', and asked that he send, to be forwarded to Houghton Mifflin, five or six of the pictures (as C. A. Furth remembered) that he had tucked away in a drawer. Tolkien replied on 13 May that he was 'divided between knowledge of my own inability and fear of what American artists (doubtless of admirable skill) might produce', but he felt also that 'four professional pictures would make my own amateurish productions look rather silly'. The illustrations remembered by Furth were not, Tolkien pointed out, for *The Hobbit*, but scenes from his 'Silmarillion' mythology 'on the outskirts of which the Hobbit had his adventures'. He offered to make five or six new illustrations for the American edition, as time allowed in the middle of the Oxford term; but that if the matter did not allow of much delay, he wondered if it might be advisable, 'rather than lose the American interest', to let Houghton Mifflin 'do what seems good to them—as long [as] it was possible (I should like to add) to veto anything from or influenced by the Disney studios (for all whose work I have a heartfelt loathing)'.

THE HOBBIT

or

There and Back
Again

BY

J. R. R. TOLKIEN

ILLUSTRATIONS BY
THE AUTHOR

BOSTON AND NEW YORK
HOUGHTON MIFFLIN COMPANY
1938

THE HOBBIT

or

There and Back
Again

BY

J. R. R. TOLKIEN

ILLUSTRATIONS BY
THE AUTHOR

BOSTON AND NEW YORK
HOUGHTON MIFFLIN COMPANY
1938

IV. *The Hobbit* (A3b). Variant title pages of the first American edition.

Without Tolkien's permission, Allen & Unwin forwarded his letter of 13 May to Houghton Mifflin, which led Tolkien to feel, in a letter of 28 May, 'even greater hesitation in posing further as an illustrator'. But he resolved to try, and sent Allen & Unwin three 'coloured "pictures" ' as samples of his work. 'I cannot do much better', he complained,

> and if their standard is too low, the H.M.Co can say so at once and without offence. . . . These are casual and careless pastime-products, illustrating other stories. Having publication in view I could possibly improve the standard a little, make drawings rather bolder in colour & less messy and fussy in detail (and also larger). The Mirkwood picture [i.e. *Beleg Finds Gwindor in Taur-nu-Fuin*] is much the same as the plate in *The Hobbit*, but illustrates a different adventure. I think if the H.M.Co wish me to proceed I should leave that black and grey plate [*Mirkwood*] and do four other scenes.

In the event, he produced five paintings: *The Hill* (a new version of the A3a first impression frontispiece, there a line drawing), *Rivendell, Bilbo Woke Up with the Early Sun in His Eyes, Bilbo Comes to the Huts of the Raft-elves*, and *Conversation with Smaug*. The scenes were selected, Tolkien informed Allen & Unwin on 31 August 1937, 'so as to distribute illustrations fairly evenly throughout the book (especially when taken in conjunction with the black-and-white drawings)'. All except the frontispiece seem to have been made within a week or two in mid-July 1937, having been delayed by the artist's ill health and by uncertainty whether Houghton Mifflin (who had not replied to Furth) still wanted the colour illustrations. The colour version of *The Hill* was completed by 13 August. *Mirkwood* was re-drawn or traced for the American edition, apparently not by Tolkien (his monogram is not present in this version at lower right), and printed in line rather than as a halftone. Allen & Unwin added all of the new illustrations except *Bilbo Woke* to the second impression of their edition (see A3a note); Houghton Mifflin chose all except the *Raft-elves* painting. Two of the colour illustrations were also reproduced (partially obscured) on the American dust-jacket, which Houghton Mifflin preferred to Tolkien's design for A3a. That version, they felt, had a 'British look'.

Tolkien thought that the American edition was 'not so bad. I am glad they have included the eagle picture; but I cannot imagine why they have spoilt the Rivendell picture by slicing the top and cutting out the ornament at the bottom. All the numerous textual errors are of course included. I hope it will some day be possible to get rid of them.'

A curious feature of the American edition is the replacement of the 'bowing hobbit' on the title page with a (worn) publisher's device, within the first impression or (probably) with the second impression. The fine lines of the 'hobbit' block may have broken, or Tolkien's comments in a letter to his American publisher of March or April 1938 may have been taken to heart. Tolkien had remarked, in response to a query about illustrating hobbits and in regard to the figure of Bilbo in the *Smaug* plate, that 'there is in the text no mention of his acquiring of boots. There should be! It has dropped out somehow or other in the various revisions. . . . But since leathery soles, and well-brushed furry feet are a feature of essential hobbitness, he ought really to appear unbooted, except in special illustrations of episodes'. Perhaps Houghton Mifflin noticed that the 'bowing hobbit', from a line drawing (not by Tolkien) after the silhouette of Bilbo in *Conversation with Smaug*, was wearing boots, and decided to correct their 'error'. The 'bowing hobbit' silhouette on the binding is also after a detail of *Conversation with Smaug*.

The original colour illustrations for *The Hobbit* are in the Bodleian Library, Oxford.

c. Second edition ('fifth impression', 1951):

The Hobbit | or | There and Back | Again | by | J. R. R. Tolkien | Illustrated | by the Author | London | George Allen & Unwin Ltd | Museum Street

316 pp. + 1 plate. Collation: $[A]^8B–T^8U^6$, U2 signed '*'. 18.5 × 12.4 cm.

[1–4] blank; [5] 'The Hobbit'; [6] '*also by J. R. R. Tolkien* | FARMER GILES OF HAM'; [7] title; [8] 'FIRST PUBLISHED IN 1937 | SECOND IMPRESSION 1937 | REPRINTED 1942 | REPRINTED 1946 | SECOND EDITION (FIFTH IMPRESSION) 1951 | *This book is copyright under the Berne Convention* | *No portion may be produced by any process* | *without written permission. Inquiries* | *should be addressed to the publishers* | PRINTED IN GREAT BRITAIN BY | UNWIN BROTHERS LTD., WOKING & LONDON'; [9] table of contents; [10] author's note; [11]–315 text and illustrations; [316] '[*publisher's open "St. George" device*] | GEORGE ALLEN & UNWIN LTD | [*7 addresses, London to Wellington*]'.

Black and white illustrations, by Tolkien: *The Trolls*, p. 49; *The Mountain-path*, p. [68]; *The Misty Mountains Looking West from the Eyrie towards Goblin Gate*, p. 122; *Beorn's Hall*, p. [131]; *The Elvenking's Gate*, p. 182; *Lake Town*, p. [201]; *The Front Gate*, p. 214; *The Hall at Bag-End, Residence of B. Baggins Esquire*, p. 312. Colour illustration, by Tolkien: *The Hill: Hobbiton-across-the Water*, plate facing p. [7]. Maps, by Tolkien, in black and red: *Thror's Map*, front endsheet; *Wilderland*, back endsheet.

Wove paper. Bound in green cloth over boards. Stamped as for A3a, except stamped on spine, below wraparound decoration, in dark blue: 'The | Hobbit | *by* | J. R. R. | Tolkien | [TH *rune*] | [D *rune*] | [TH *rune*] | Allen | and | Unwin'. Wove endpapers (maps). No headbands. All edges trimmed. Top edge stained light green, fore- and bottom edges unstained.

Dust-jacket, wove paper. Covers and spine as for A3a. Printed on front flap: '[*blurb*] | FIFTH IMPRESSION | THIS COVER AND THE DRAWINGS | IN THE BOOK ARE BY THE AUTHOR | 8s. 6d. net'. Printed on back flap: '[*blurb, continued*] | SOME PRESS OPINIONS | [*4 quotations, from the* New Statesman and Nation, Observer, *London* Times, *and* Lady] | *Printed in Great Britain*'.

Published 19 July 1951 at 8s. 6d.; 3,500 copies printed. Bound November 1950 through March? 1953.

Partly reset, revised, based on the fourth impression of A3a, with corrections, but continuing the errors:

p. 17, ll. 29–30, ' "So you have got here at last!" what [*for* That] was what he was going to say'

p. 25, l. 11, 'more fierce then fire' for 'more fierce than fire'

p. 62, ll. 2–3, 'uncomfortable palpitating' for 'uncomfortable, palpitating'

p. 62, l. 31, 'their bruises their tempers and their hopes' for 'their bruises, their tempers and their hopes'

p. 152, l. 16, 'nor what you call' for 'not what you call'

p. 210, l. 32, 'dwarves good feeling' for 'dwarves' good feeling'

'In this reprint several minor inaccuracies, most of them noted by readers, have been corrected' (author's note, p. [10]). Among these were Gandalf's reading of the runes on Thror's Map, p. 30, made to accord with Elrond's reading on p. 64 (not, Tolkien remarked in a letter to G. E. Selby [Dii66], strictly an error in the original edition, but better in agreement); 'where the thrush knocks' > 'when the thrush knocks',

p. 64, 'misread' from the runes on Thror's Map, corrected after the error was pointed out to Tolkien by Selby; and references to 'men' when the text is not referring to Men (e.g. p. 27, Bilbo the hobbit as an 'excitable little man'), a feature noted by Arthur Ransome. (Tolkien retained 'little boys', p. 117, as an insult to goblins.) The following alterations (other than corrections to errors noted for A3a) and new errors were made in A3c:

p. [9], l. 16: Fore [*error, for* Fire] and Water

p. [10], author's note added

p. 27, l. 28: Excitable little fellow < A3a, p. 27, l. 28: Excitable little man

p. 30, ll. 26–7: Five feet high the door and three may walk abreast < A3a, p. 30, ll. 26–7: Five feet high is the door and three abreast may enter it

p. 35, l. 18: And your father went away on the twenty-first of April < A3a, p. 35, l. 18: And your father went away on the third of March

p. 84, l. 34–p. 85, l. 1: It like [*error, for* likes] riddles

p. 85, ll. 9–10: before he lost all his friends and was driven away, alone, and crept down, down, into the dark under the mountains < A3a, p. 85, ll. 9–10: before the goblins came, and he was cut off from his friends far under under [*sic*] the mountains

p. 85, ll. 25–7: If it asks us, and we doesn't answer, then we does what it wants, eh? We shows it the way out, yes! < A3a, p. 85, ll. 25–6: If it asks us, and we doesn't answer, we gives it a present, gollum!

p. 91, l. 15–p. 100, l. 13: He knew, of course, that the riddle-game was sacred and of immense antiquity. . . . They yelled twice as loud as before, but not so delightedly. < significantly revises and enlarges A3a, p. 91, l. 15–p. 95, l. 8: But funnily enough he need not have been alarmed. . . . Then they yelled twice as loud as before, but not so delightedly.

p. 105, ll. 13–20: So I said: 'what about your promise? Show me the way out!' But he came at me to kill me, and I ran, and fell over, and he missed me in the dark. Then I followed him, because I heard him talking to himself. He thought I really knew the way out, and so he was making for it. And then he sat down in the entrance, and I could not get by. So I jumped over him and escaped, and ran down to the gate. < A3a, p. 100, ll. 14–18: So I asked for my present, and he went to look for it, and couldn't find it. So I said 'very well, help me to get out of this nasty place!' and he showed me the passage to the door. 'Good-bye' I said, and I went on down.

p. 105, ll. 28–9: dodging guards, jumping over Gollum, and squeezing through < A3a, p. 100, l. 26: dodging guards, and squeezing through

p. 106, ll. 30–1: Gandalf knew all about the back-door, as the goblins called the lower gate, where Bilbo lost his buttons < A3a, p. 101, ll. 29–30: Gandalf knew all about the back-gate, as he called it, the lower door where Bilbo lost his buttons

p. 299, l. 11: If more of us < A3a, p. 294, l. 11: If more men

Probably in the 'seventh' impression (i.e. third impression of A3c, 1955), 'Fore and Water' in the table of contents, p. [9], was corrected to 'Fire and Water'; the reading 'what about your present?' was changed to 'what about your guess', p. 87, ll. 26–7; and the note beginning '*If you are interested in Hobbits*' was added at the end of the text, p. 315.

On 21 September 1947, while writing *The Lord of the Rings*, Tolkien sent Stanley Unwin a list of corrections to errors remaining in the 1946 fourth impression of *The Hobbit*, together with a 'specimen of re-writing', a new version of chapter 5 which brought the story better into accord with its sequel as it had developed. The 'specimen' was intended only as a proposal, but was seen by the publisher as another 'correction'. On 27 September Stanley Unwin notified Tolkien that he was passing the *Hobbit* corrections to the Allen & Unwin production department, and on 30

September Tolkien noted two additional errors in the text. Preparations for another printing of the book began in May 1950. Allen & Unwin took the opportunity to incorporate Tolkien's corrections as well as revised chapter 5, and on 26 July 1950 sent him rough proofs of the changes. Tolkien returned the proofs on 1 August, with the comment:

> They did not require much correction, but did need some consideration. The thing took me much by surprise. It is now a long while since I sent in the proposed alteration of Chapter V, and tentatively suggested the slight remodelling of the original *Hobbit*. I was then still engaged in trying to fit on the sequel [*LR*], which would have been a simpler task with the alteration, besides saving most of a chapter in that over-long work. However, I never heard any more about it at all; and I assumed that alteration of the original book was ruled out. The sequel now depends on the earlier version; and if the revision is really published, there must follow some considerable rewriting of the sequel. . . .
>
> I did not mean the suggested revision to be printed off; but it seems to have come out pretty well in the wash. As you will see I have made very few alterations (marked) that are not in the MS. If I had had warning I could possibly have shortened and tightened the revision; but if you are (as appears) content, and prepared to make the necessary changes in pagination etc. then I am quite content also.

In fact Tolkien's alterations to chapter 5, though very cleverly 'explained' in his author's note, p. [10] (and further in *The Lord of the Rings*), were not made seamlessly, and additional small corrections had to be made later—not, however, removing all inconsistencies. For further analysis of Tolkien's significant revision of chapter 5, see Bonniejean Christensen, 'Gollum's Character Transformation in *The Hobbit*', in *A Tolkien Compass* (B31), pp. 9–28; and *The Annotated Hobbit* (A3dd–ee).

The Hobbit was serialized in the British magazine *Princess*, with illustrations by Ferguson Dewar, in 1964–5? (not seen). Chapter 5 occasionally is reprinted, in whole or in part, e.g. in *The Fantastic Imagination: An Anthology of High Fantasy*, ed. Robert H. Boyer and Kenneth J. Zahorski (New York: Avon, 1977), with a brief introduction. Chapter 1 (as by 'John Tolkien') was reprinted in *Once upon a Time . . .: English Fairy Tale[s]* (Moscow: Progress Publishers, 1975), ed. S. Nikonova, with comments by D. Urnov, colour illustrations by F. Lemkul, and a biographical note and amusing glosses on *Midsummer Eve, the Blue,* and *pop-gun.*

An authorized condensation of *The Hobbit*, made by Harley Usill, read by Nicol Williamson, was issued in 1974 by the Decca Record Co., London on their Argo label, on four LP phonograph records, with printed notes by Usill and Lissa Demetriou. It was also issued in 1986 by the Clover Patch Collection, Providence, Rhode Island, on three audio cassettes, and in 1988 in England by Hamlyn Books on Tape in both two- and three-audio cassette versions. An unabridged recording of *The Hobbit*, read by Rob Inglis, was issued in 1991 by Recorded Books, Prince Frederick, Maryland, on eight audio cassettes. Tolkien's own recording of part of ch. 5, see section Fi.

The Hobbit has been adapted for the stage since at least March 1953, when Miss L. M. D. Patrick of St. Margaret's School, Edinburgh, with Tolkien's approval performed a version for the school and parents. Two published dramatizations are Patricia Gray, *J. R. R. Tolkien's The Hobbit* (Chicago: Dramatic Publishing Company, 1967); and *The Hobbit*, 'a musical play', music by Allan Jay Friedman, lyrics by David Rogers, book by Ruth Perry (Chicago: Dramatic Publishing Company, 1972 [libretto]), both 'authorized by Professor J. R. R. Tolkien'.

A musical adaptation by Paul Drayton in 1967 is described, with some of its music printed, in Paul Drayton and Humphrey Carpenter, 'A Preparatory School Approach', *Music Drama in Schools*, ed. Malcolm John (Cambridge [England]: University Press, 1971). Other adaptations include that of the Oxford University Experimental Theatre Club, 1971, adapted by Graham Devlin, music by Michael Hinton; Phoenix Arts, Leicester, 1984, adapted by Rony Robinson and Graham Watkins, music by Stephanie Nunn, later revised and abbreviated; an opera by Robert Hammersley, performed by the Iffley Community Opera at the Oxford (England) Town Hall in 1987; a one-man show by Rob Inglis, also recorded on an audio cassette (London: Chanticleer, 1987); and the Children's Theatre Company, Minneapolis production, adapted by Thomas W. Olson, music by Alan Shorter, 1990.

The Hobbit was serialized in the BBC *Children's Hour* radio programme, read by David Davis, thirteen weekly parts beginning 4 January 1961. The book was also broadcast, in a four-part weekly dramatization, in the BBC Schools Department *Adventures in English* programme, 5–26 October 1961, and also by the BBC in eight weekly parts adapted by Michael Kilgarriff, music by David Cain, broadcast 29 September–17 November 1968. The latter dramatization was issued by the BBC in 1988 on four audio cassettes. A dramatization by the Marleybone Players was issued in 1975 by The Drama Project on four audio cassettes. A 1979 dramatization by Bob Lewis was issued by Jabberwocky on two, four, or six audio cassettes, and was broadcast on American radio ('The Mind's Eye', 'Radio 2000') in ten parts.

Other adaptations of *The Hobbit* include the graphic novel by Charles Dixon, illustrated by David Wenzel, first published by Eclipse Books, Forestville, California, 1989–90, in 3 vols.

d. Second American edition (1951):

Sheets as for A3c. 18.4 × 12.6 cm.

Wove paper. Binding as for A3c, except imprint at foot of spine: 'HOUGHTON | MIFFLIN | COMPANY'.

Dust-jacket not seen, presumably as for A3c with spine imprint of Houghton Mifflin, and U.S. price on front flap.

Published in spring? 1951 at $2.50; 1,000 copies imported from Allen & Unwin, printed simultaneously with A3c.

In late 1964 or early 1965, a reader observed that the runes on the dust-jacket of the American edition of *The Hobbit* described the book as published by 'George Allen & Unwin', not 'Houghton Mifflin'. The runes were re-lettered for American copies by the twentieth U.S. impression.

e. First paperback edition (1961):

J. R. R. TOLKIEN | [*divided swelled rule*] | THE HOBBIT | OR | *There and Back* | *Again* | PENGUIN BOOKS

288 pp. Collation: 144 leaves. 17.9 × 11 cm.

[1] blurb; [2] blank; [3] title; [4] 'Penguin Books Ltd, Harmondsworth, Middlesex | AUSTRALIA: Penguin Books Pty Ltd, 762 Whitehorse Road, | Mitcham, Victoria | [*dash*] | First published by Allen & Unwin 1937 | Published in Puffin Books 1961 | [*dash*] | Made and printed in Great Britain | by Cox and Wyman Ltd, | London, Reading, and Fakenham | [*notice of restrictions under copyright*] | [*dash*] | A cloth-

bound edition of this book is published by Allen & Unwin | [*notice of restrictions of sale*]'; [5] table of contents; [6–7] *Thror's Map*; [8–9] *Wilderland* map; [10] author's note; 11–[284] text; [285] Allen & Unwin advertisement of *LR* and *H*; [286] publisher's advertisement of Streatfeild, *The Painted Garden*; [287] advertisement of Burnett, *A Little Princess*; [288] advertisement of Day Lewis, *The Otterbury Incident*.

Omits Tolkien's illustrations, except for the maps, in black only, pp. [6–9].

Wove paper. Bound in heavy wove wrappers. Wraparound colour illustration by Pauline Baynes, of Gandalf, the dwarves, and Bilbo ascending a mountain path, above a wraparound black panel. Printed on upper cover: '[*against the illustration:*] [*in yellow:*] The Hobbit | [*in pink:*] J. R. R. TOLKIEN | [*below the illustration:*] [*rule, in white*] | [*against the black panel:*] [*in yellow:*] A Puffin Book [*publisher's "puffin" device, in white and black*] [*in yellow:*] 3/6'. Printed on spine: '[*against the illustration:*] [*running down:*] [*in pink:*] J. R. R. Tolkien [*in white:*] THE HOBBIT | [*horizontal, in black:*] 161 | [*below the illustration:*] [*rule, in white*] | [*publisher's "puffin" device, in white and black, against the black panel*]'. Printed on lower cover: '[*in white, against the illustration:*] For copyright reasons this edition | is not for sale in the U.S.A. | [*below the illustration:*] [*rule, in white*] | [*in yellow, against the black panel:*] Published by Penguin Books'. All edges trimmed and unstained. A black and white photograph of the wrappers is printed in *The Annotated Hobbit* (A3dd–ee).

Published 26 October 1961 at 3s. 6d.; 35,000 copies printed.

Reset, based on the 'twelfth' impression of A3c (1961), with a few genuine corrections to minor errors, but with *dwarves, dwarves', dwarvish* 'corrected' to *dwarfs, dwarfs', dwarfish* (with one exception), and *elvish* to *elfish* seven out of ten times by Tolkien's count, and with other errors:

p. 24, l. 3, 'more fierce then fire' for 'more fierce than fire'

p. 32, l. 11, 'the dragon for them' for 'the dragon waiting for them'

p. 57, l. 13, 'their bruises their tempers and their hopes' for 'their bruises, their tempers and their hopes'

p. 76, ll. 23–4, 'It like riddles' for 'It likes riddles'

p. 87, l. 33, 'Gollum flip-flapping head' for 'Gollum flip-flapping ahead'

The author's note, p. [10], comprises only the second paragraph of the note as in A3c–d, with the first sentence and the beginning of the second sentence changed to: 'It has been suggested by several students of the lore of the period that there is an error in Thror's Map on pp. 6–7. On the Map is written *Here of old. . . .*' The reading of A3a–d, p. 17, ll. 29–30, ' "So you have got here at last!" what [*error, for* That] was what he was going to say', is here, p. 17, ll. 9–10, incorrectly abridged: ' "So you have got here at last!" was what he was going to say'. On p. 28, ll. 29–30, the instruction to the reader reads, in accord with *Thror's Map* printed, in this edition, in black only, on an integral leaf: 'Look at the map on page 6 of this book, and you will see there the runes in the left-hand panel.' The note about *LR* following the end of the text is omitted.

On p. 78, ll. 11–12, 'Bilbo was beginning to hope that he would not be able to answer' replaced 'Bilbo was beginning to wonder what Gollum's present would be like' (A3c–d, p. 86, ll. 25–6), as directed by Tolkien in a letter to Penguin Books in April 1961. This was an intermediate revision between the reading of A3c–d, which lost its meaning when chapter 5 was revised to omit Gollum's promise of a 'present', and the more expressive reading introduced in A3g–i (1966), 'Bilbo was beginning to hope that the wretch would not be able to answer'. An earlier intermediate revision, 'Bilbo was getting impatient', was tape-recorded by Tolkien; see *J. R. R. Tolkien Reads and Sings His* The Hobbit *and* The Fellowship of the Ring, section Fi.

On 30 November 1960 Margaret S. Clark of Penguin Books suggested that her firm publish a paperback edition of *The Hobbit* to coincide with the serialization of that work in the BBC *Children's Hour* radio programme scheduled for 1961. Tolkien was reluctant 'to cheapen the old Hobbit' and preferred to 'leave him to amble along' in hardcover, but he was 'no longer able to ignore cash-profit' (letter to Rayner Unwin, 10 December 1960). The paperback edition proceeded, under Penguin Books' 'Puffin' children's books imprint, though with restrictions: Tolkien and Allen & Unwin would authorize the paperback cover art (by Pauline Baynes), and the book could not be sold in any other binding; no more than 35,000 copies would be printed; and an advertisement of the Allen & Unwin hardcover *Hobbit*, and of their *Lord of the Rings*, would be included (p. [285]).

Tolkien received a copy of the new edition in late September 1961, but did not look at it until months later. When he did, he objected to Penguin Books' 'corrections'. 'I view this procedure with dudgeon', he wrote to Rayner Unwin on 30 December 1961.

> I deliberately used *dwarves* etc. for a special purpose and effect—that it has an effect can be gauged by comparing the passages with the substitutes *dwarfs*, especially in verse. The point is dealt with in L.R. [*LR*, A5a] iii, p. 415. Of course I do not expect compositors or proof-readers to know that, or to know anything about the history of the word 'dwarf'; but I should have thought it might have occurred, if not to a compositor, at least to a reader, that the author would not have used consistently getting on for 300 times a particular form, nor would your readers have passed it, if it was a mere casual mistake in 'grammar'.

Penguin Books' Kaye Webb apologized at length for the publisher's over-zealous production department, who had followed house style in the absence of special instructions, and promised to correct the setting with the next impression of the book, though a major part would have to be reset. Penguin were eager to reprint, having sold approximately 20,000 copies of their edition in just three months. But Allen & Unwin argued that the paperback edition had cut into their hardcover sales, and they held firm to the agreed limit of 35,000 copies. The stock of the Puffin *Hobbit* was exhausted by mid-August 1962.

Kaye Webb's offer to reset with Tolkien's preferred spellings was honoured, in part, by the printing of extracts from *The Hobbit* in two Puffin Books anthologies: part of ch. 5 in *I Like This Story: A Taste of Fifty Favorites*, ed. Kaye Webb, illus. Anthony Kerins (1986); and part of ch. 2 in *The Puffin Book of Twentieth-Century Children's Stories*, ed. Judith Elkin, illus. Michael Foreman (1991, also published in hardcover by Viking).

The original painting by Pauline Baynes for the cover illustration is in the Marion E. Wade Center, Wheaton College, Wheaton, Illinois, who have reproduced it on a postcard.

f. First American paperback edition (1965):

The Hobbit | or | There and Back | Again | [*strip of leaf ornaments*] | by | J. R. R. Tolkien | BALLANTINE BOOKS • NEW YORK

288 pp. Collation: 144 leaves. 17.8 × 10.7 cm.

[1] '*And what is a Hobbit?* | [*blurb*] | THIS IS THE AUTHORIZED PAPERBOUND EDITION | PUBLISHED BY BALLANTINE BOOKS'; [2] 'About the "Lord of the

Rings" Trilogy | by J. R. R. Tolkien: | PART I *The Fellowship of the Ring* | [2 *quotations, from the* New York Herald Tribune Book Week *and* New York Times Book Review] | PART II *The Two Towers* | [2 *quotations, from the* Chicago Tribune *and* Boston Herald Traveler]'; [3] 'PART III *The Return of the King* | [3 *quotations, from the* New York Herald Tribune Book Week, *Arthur C. Clarke, and the* New Republic]'; [4] 'THE AUTHORIZED EDITION | *of the works of J. R. R. Tolkien* | THE HOBBIT | *The Lord of the Rings Trilogy* | *Part I* | THE FELLOWSHIP OF THE RING | *Part II* | THE TWO TOWERS | *Part III* | THE RETURN OF THE KING | *Uniformly priced at 95¢ each* | [*note on Tolkien*]'; [5] title; [6] 'Copyright, 1937 and 1938, by J. R. R. Tolkien | All rights reserved including the right to reproduce | this book or parts thereof in any form. | This edition published by arrangement with | Houghton Mifflin Company. | First printing: August 1965. | *Printed in the United States of America.* | BALLANTINE BOOKS, INC. | 101 Fifth Avenue, New York, N.Y.'; [7] table of contents; [8] blank; [9] author's note; [10–11] *Thror's Map*; [12–13] *Wilderland* map; [14] blank; 15–287 text; [288] 'Available now *from Ballantine Books!* | [*advertisement of* H *and* LR]'.

Omits Tolkien's illustrations, except for the maps, in black only, pp. [10–13].

Wove paper. Bound in heavy wove wrappers. Printed on upper cover within a thick pink single rule frame: '[*at upper left, running up, in blue:*] BALLANTINE BOOKS U7039 [*to right of preceding, horizontal:*] [*publisher's "BB" device, in white and blue*] [*in black:*] 95¢ | THE AUTHORIZED EDITION | [*in green:*] THE | HOBBIT | [*in black:*] THE ENCHANTING PRELUDE TO | "THE LORD OF THE RINGS" | [*black letter:*] J. R. R. TOLKIEN | [*colour illustration by Barbara Remington, of a fantastic landscape with a lion*] | [*roman:*] [*in black, against a red-orange panel:*] HOUGHTON | MIFFLIN | COMPANY | [*in white:*] [*Houghton Mifflin "dolphin" device*] | *Dolphin* | *Edition* | [*in black:*] WITH | BALLANTINE BOOKS'. Printed on spine: '[*in blue:*] U7039 | [*running down:*] [*in green:*] THE HOBBIT [*black letter, in black:*] J. R. R. TOLKIEN | [*publisher's "BB" device, horizontal, in white and blue*]'. Printed on lower cover: '[*blurb*] | [*quotation from the* Times Literary Supplement] | BALLANTINE BOOKS IS THE PAPERBOUND PUB- | LISHER OF THE AUTHORIZED EDITIONS OF | "THE HOBBIT" AND "THE LORD OF THE RINGS" | [*against a green panel outlined in black:*] A STATEMENT FROM THE AUTHOR | *"This paperback edition, and no other,* | *has been published with my consent and* | *co-operation. Those who approve of* | *courtesy (at least) to living authors will* | *purchase it, and no other."* | [*facsimile signature, "J. R. R. Tolkien"*] | [*below the panel:*] Printed in U.S.A.' All edges trimmed and stained orange.

Published 16 August 1965 at $0.95; number of copies not known.

Reset, based on a (partly) corrected impression of A3c or A3d. Continues the errors:

p. 21, ll. 6–7, ' "So you have got here at last!" what [*for* That] was what he was going to say'

p. 27, l. 31, 'more fierce then fire' for 'more fierce than fire'

p. 60, ll. 19–20, 'uncomfortable palpitating' for 'uncomfortable, palpitating'

p. 61, l. 11, 'their bruises their tempers and their hopes' for 'their bruises, their tempers and their hopes'

p. 80, ll. 23–4, 'It like riddles' for 'It likes riddles'

p. 192, l. 3, 'dwarves good feeling' for 'dwarves' good feeling'

At least one additional error was introduced: 'they keep half an eye open' for 'they can keep half an eye open', p. 212, l. 8. The instruction to the reader, p. 32, ll. 21–2, regarding *Thror's Map* (in this edition printed only in black) incorrectly reads: 'Look at the map at the beginning of this book, and you will see there the runes in red.' The author's note, p. [9], was reset in the second impression with no change of text.

The Hobbit was first published in America when the United States had not yet joined the international copyright convention, and in 1965 there was some question whether the work was protected under U.S. copyright law. In May 1965 Ace Books published the first volume of a paperback edition of *The Lord of the Rings*, which they claimed had fallen into the public domain in the United States (see A5c note). Houghton Mifflin had already asked Tolkien for revisions to *The Lord of the Rings* and *The Hobbit* for new editions with which American copyright could be secured without question. Now they contracted with Ballantine Books to rush an authorized paperback edition of *The Hobbit* into print, in order to have a Ballantine-Tolkien presence in bookshops and forestall an unauthorized paperback *Hobbit* from Ace Books or any other American publisher. Tolkien's revised text could not be completed in time, and was not published by Ballantine until 1966. The original Ballantine edition had five impressions through December 1965, when it was replaced by A3g.

Production of A3f was so swift that the illustrator of the cover, Barbara Remington, had no time to read the book. Her illustration presumably depicts Hobbiton—at least, a cluster of 'hobbit-holes' on the side of a hill—but the landscape is fantastic, with strange flora and fauna. It puzzled Tolkien. 'What has it got to do with the story?' he asked Rayner Unwin in a letter of 12 September 1965. 'Where is this place? Why a lion and emus? And what is the thing in the foreground with pink bulbs?' He thought the cover ugly, with 'horrible colours and foul lettering'. Austin Olney of Houghton Mifflin responded that the art had been shown around the publisher's office with nothing but approval, and that they had received no negative comments from readers. But Tolkien was not satisfied. The 'grinning lion', if not the emus and pink bulbs, was removed from the cover after the fifth impression (see A3g). The illustration is an extended version of the extreme left side of the 'mural' painted by Remington for the covers of the Ballantine edition of *LR* (A5d). The artist later wrote to Tolkien that she had made the painting on very short notice, relying on the advice of others, and that after reading the books thoroughly she agreed that her art was inappropriate to the text.

g. Revised Ballantine Books edition (1966):

The Hobbit | or | There and Back | Again | *(Revised Edition)* | [*strip of leaf ornaments*] | by | J. R. R. Tolkien | BALLANTINE BOOKS • NEW YORK

288 pp. Collation: 144 leaves. 17.8 × 10.7 cm.

[1] '*And what is a Hobbit?* | [*blurb*] | THIS IS THE AUTHORIZED PAPERBOUND EDITION | PUBLISHED BY BALLANTINE BOOKS'; [3] 'About the "Lord of the Rings" Trilogy | by J. R. R. Tolkien: | PART I *The Fellowship of the Ring* | [2 quotations, from the New York Herald Tribune Book Week *and* New York Times Book Review] | PART II *The Two Towers* | [2 quotations, from the Chicago Tribune *and* Boston Herald Traveler]'; [3] 'PART III *The Return of the King* | [3 quotations, from the New York Herald Tribune Book Week, *Arthur C. Clarke, and the* New Republic]'; [4] 'THE AUTHORIZED EDITIONS | *of the works of J. R. R. Tolkien* | THE HOBBIT | *The Lord of the Rings Trilogy* | Part I | THE FELLOWSHIP OF THE RING | *Part II* | THE TWO TOWERS | *Part III* | THE RETURN OF THE KING | *Uniformly priced at 95¢ each* | [*note on Tolkien*]'; [5] title; [6] 'Copyright © 1937, 1938 and 1966 by J. R. R. Tolkien | All rights reserved including the right to reproduce | this book or parts thereof in any form. | This edition published by

arrangement with | Houghton Mifflin Company. | [*list of first-fifth impressions of original Ballantine edition*] | *Revised edition:* | First Printing: February, 1966. | *Printed in the United States of America.* | BALLANTINE BOOKS, INC. | 101 Fifth Avenue, New York, N.Y.'; [7] table of contents; [8] blank; [9] author's note; [10–11] *Thror's Map*; [12–13] *Wilderland* map; [14] blank; 15–287 text; [288] 'Available now from Ballantine Books! | [*advertisement of H and LR*]'.

Omits Tolkien's illustrations, except for the maps, in black only, pp. [10–13].

Wove paper. Bound in heavy wove wrappers. Printed on upper cover within a thick pink single rule frame: '[*at upper left, running up, in blue:*] BALLANTINE BOOKS U7039 [*to right of preceding, horizontal:*] [*publisher's "BB" device, in white and blue*] [*in black:*] 95¢ | THE AUTHORIZED EDITION | [*in blue:*] THE | HOBBIT | [*in black:*] THE ENCHANTING PRELUDE TO | "THE LORD OF THE RINGS" | [*black letter:*] J. R. R. TOLKIEN | [*colour illustration by Barbara Remington, of a fantastic landscape, as for A3f but with the lion omitted*] | [*roman, against a red-orange panel:*] [*in black:*] HOUGHTON | MIFFLIN | COMPANY | [*in white:*] [*Houghton Mifflin "dolphin" device*] | Dolphin | Edition | [*in black:*] WITH | BALLANTINE BOOKS'. Printed on spine: '[*in blue:*] U7039 | [*running down:*] [*in green:*] THE HOBBIT [*black letter, in black:*] J. R. R. TOLKIEN | [*publisher's "BB" device, horizontal, in white and blue*]'. Printed on lower cover: '[*blurb*] | [*quotation from the* Times Literary Supplement] | BALLANTINE BOOKS IS THE PAPERBOUND PUB- | LISHER OF THE AUTHORIZED EDITIONS OF | "THE HOBBIT" AND "THE LORD OF THE RINGS" | *REVISED EDITION* | [*against a green panel outlined in black:*] A STATEMENT FROM THE AUTHOR | "*This paperback edition, and no other,* | *has been published with my consent and* | *co-operation. Those who approve of* | *courtesy (at least) to living authors will* | *purchase it, and no other.*" | [*facsimile signature, "J. R. R. Tolkien"*] | [*below the panel:*] Printed in U.S.A.' All edges trimmed and stained orange.

Published February 1966 at $0.95; number of copies not known.

Partly reset, revised, based on A3f. All errors noted for A3f were corrected except for 'it like riddles' for 'it likes riddles', p. 80, ll. 23–4, and 'they keep half an eye open' for 'they can keep half an eye open', p. 212, l. 8. The following alterations (other than corrections to errors noted for A3f) and new errors were made in A3g:

p. [9], ll. 14–16: as it was set out in the chronicles of the Red Book of Westmarch, and is now told in *The Lord of the Rings* < A3f, p. [9], ll. 13–14: as it is set out in the chronicles of the Red Book of Westmarch, and it must await their publication

p. 16, ll. 9–11: They are (or were) a little people, about half our height, and smaller than the bearded Dwarves. Hobbits have no beards. < A3f, p. 16, ll. 9–11: They are (or were) small people, smaller than dwarves (and they have no beards) but very much larger than lilliputians.

p. 16, l. 24: the fabulous [*error, for* famous] Belladonna Took

p. 16, ll. 27–30: It was often said (in other families) that long ago one of the Took ancestors must have taken a fairy wife. That was, of course, absurd, but certainly there was < A3f, p. 16, ll. 27–30: It had always been said that long ago one or other of the Tooks had married into a fairy family (the less friendly said a goblin family); certainly there was

p. 17, ll. 31–2: an old man with a staff. He had a tall pointed blue hat, a long grey cloak, a silver scarf over which a white beard [*error, for* his long white beard] < A3f, p. 17, ll. 31–2: a little old man with a tall pointed blue hat, a long grey cloak, a silver scarf over which his long white beard

p. 19, ll. 19–21: mad adventures. [*error, for* adventures?] Anything from climbing trees to visiting Elves—or sailing in ships, sailing to other shores! < A3f, p. 19, ll. 19–21: mad adventures, anything from climbing trees to stowing away aboard the ships that sail to the Other Side?

p. 21, l. 8: odd-looking [*error, for* old-looking] dwarf

p. 24, l. 12: cold chicken and pickles < A3f, p. 24, l. 12: cold chicken and tomatoes

p. 26, ll. 5–8: Gandalf's smoke-ring would go green and come back to hover over the wizard's head. He had quite a cloud [*error, for* had a cloud] of them about him already, and in the dim light it made him look strange and sorcerous. < A3f, p. 26, ll. 5–8: Gandalf's smoke-ring would go green with the joke and come back to hover over the wizard's head. He had quite a cloud of them about him already, and it made him look positively sorcerous.

p. 32, l. 6: made by Thror, your grandfather, Thorin < A3f, p. 32, l. 6: made by your grandfather, Thorin

p. 32, ll. 30–1: devouring so many of the dwarves and men of Dale < A3f, p. 32, ll. 32–3: devouring so many of the maidens of the valley

p. 32, ll. 37–8, a footnote: Look at the map at the beginning of this book, and you will see the runes there. < A3f, p. 32, ll. 21–2: Look at the map at the beginning of this book, and you will see there the runes in red.

p. 34, ll. 25–30: Long ago in my grandfather Thror's time our family was driven out of the far North, and came back with all their wealth and their tools to this Mountain on the map. It had been discovered by my far ancestor, Thrain the Old, but now they mined and they tunnelled and they made huger halls and greater workshops < A3f, p. 34, ll. 26–30: Long ago in my grandfather's time some dwarves were driven out of the far North, and came with all their wealth and their tools to this Mountain on the map. There they mined and they tunnelled and they made hugh halls and great workshops

p. 34, ll. 33–4: King under the Mountain again and treated < A3f, p. 34, ll. 33–4: King under the Mountain, and treated

p. 35, ll. 9–11: full of armor [*sic*] and jewels and carvings and cups, and the toy-market of Dale was the wonder of the North < A3f, p. 35, ll. 9–11: full of wonderful jewels and carvings and cups, and the toyshops of Dale were a sight to behold

p. 37, ll. 1–2: Your grandfather Thror was killed, you remember, in the mines of Moria by Azog the Goblin— < A3f, p. 37, ll. 1–2: Your grandfather was killed, you remember, in the mines of Moria by a goblin—

p. 37, l. 18: said the wizard slowly and grimly < A3f, p. 37, l. 18: said the wizard slowly and crossly

p. 37, ll. 35–6: He is an enemy quite beyond the powers < A3f, p. 37, l. 35: That is a job quite beyond the powers

p. 38, l. 1: was for his son to read the map < A3f, p. 38, l. 1: was for you to read the map

p. 41, ll. 35–6: and then on for a whole mile or more < A3f, p. 41, ll. 35–6: and so for a whole mile or more

p. 42, l. 29: They had not been riding < A3f, p. 42, l. 29: They hadn't been riding

p. 42, l. 37–p. 43, l. 12: At first they had passed through hobbit-lands, a wild [*error, for* wide] respectable country inhabited by decent folk, with good roads, an inn or two, and now and then a dwarf or a farmer ambling by on business. Then they came to lands where people spoke strangely, and sang songs Bilbo had never heard before. Now they had gone on far into the Lone-lands, where there were no people left, no inns, and the roads grew steadily worse. Not far ahead were dreary hills, rising higher and higher, dark with trees. On some of them were old castles with an evil look, as if they had been built by wicked people. Everything seemed gloomy, for the weather that day had taken a nasty turn. Mostly it had been as good as May can be, even in merry tales, but now it was cold and wet. In the Lone-lands they had [*error, omits* been obliged] to camp when they could, but at least it had been dry. < A3f, p. 42, l. 37–p. 43, l. 12: Things went on like this for quite a long while. There was a good deal of wide respectable country to pass through, inhabited by decent respectable folk, men or hobbits or elves or what not, with good roads, an inn or two, and every now and then a dwarf, or a tinker, or a farmer ambling by on business. But after a time they came to places where people spoke strangely, and sang songs Bilbo had never heard before. Inns were rare and not good, the roads were worse, and there were hills in the distance rising higher and higher. There were castles on some of the hills, and many looked as if they had not been built for any good purpose. Also the weather which had often been as good as May can be, even in tales and legends, took a nasty turn.

p. 43, l. 13: 'To think it will soon be June,' grumbled Bilbo < A3f, p. 43, l. 13: 'To think it is June the first tomorrow,' grumbled Bilbo

p. 45, ll. 1–3: Travellers seldom come this way now. The old maps are no use: things have changed for the worse and the road is unguarded. < A3f, p. 45, ll. 1–2: Policemen never come so far, and the map-makers have not reached this country yet.

p. 48, ll. 18–20: said William. He had already had as much supper as he could hold; also he had had lots of beer. < A3f, p. 48, ll. 18–20: said William (I told you he had already had as much supper as he could hold; also he had had lots of beer)

p. 48, l. 31: when Bert dropped him < A3f, p. 48, l. 31: when they dropped him

p. 52, ll. 6–8: he stepped from behind a tree, and helped Bilbo to climb down out of a thorn-bush < A3f, p. 52, ll. 6–8: he stepped from behind the bushes, and helped Bilbo to climb down out of a thorn-tree

p. 52, l. 17: practising pinching < A3f, p. 52, l. 17: practising burglary

p. 55, l. 7 after titling: One morning they forded a river < A3f, p. 55, l. 7 after titling: One afternoon they forded the river

p. 56, ll. 12–14: That sounded nice and comforting, but they had not got there yet, and it was not so easy as it sounds to find the Last Homely House < A3f, p. 56, ll. 12–14: That sounded nice and comforting, and I daresay you think it ought to have been easy to make straight for the Last Homely House

p. 56, ll. 21–3: Morning passed, afternoon came; but in all the silent waste there was no sign of any dwelling. They were growing anxious, for they now saw that the house < A3f, p. 56, ll. 21–3: The afternoon sun shone down; but in all the silent waste there was no sign of any dwelling. They rode on for a while, and they soon saw that the house

p. 57, ll. 4–7: His head and beard wagged this way and that as he looked for the stones, and they followed his head [*error, for* lead], but they seemed no nearer to the end of the search when the day began to fail. < A3f, p. 57, ll. 4–7: They still seemed to have gone only a little way, carefully following the wizard, whose head and beard wagged this way and that as he searched for the path, when the day began to fail.

p. 61, ll. 20–1: swords of the High Elves of the West, my kin < A3f, p. 52, l. 17: swords of the elves that are now called Gnomes

p. 61, ll. 32–4: remnants of old robberies in some hold [*error? for* hole] in the mountains of the North [*error?, for* mountains of old]. I have heard that there are still forgotten treasures of old [*error?, for* forgotten treasures] to be found < A3f, p. 61, ll. 32–4: remnants of old robberies in some hold [*error? for* hole] in the mountains of the North [*error? for* mountains of old]. I have heard that there are still forgotten treasures to be found

p. 62, ll. 34–6: He was the father of the fathers of the eldest race of Dwarves, the Longbeards, and my first ancestor: I am his heir. < A3f, p. 62, ll. 34–6: He was the father of the fathers of one of the two races of dwarves, the Longbeards, and my grandfather's ancestor.

p. 63, l. 1: is as all should know the first day < A3f, p. 63, l. 1: is as everyone knows the first day

p. 65, ll. 10–11: in secret after the battle of the Mines of Moria < A3f, p. 65, ll. 10–11: in secret after the sack of the mines of Moria

p. 79, ll. 7–8: lived old Gollum, a small slimy creature. I don't know where < A3f, p. 79, ll. 7–8: lived old Gollum. I don't know where

p. 79, ll. 10–11: pale eyes in his thin face. He had a little boat < A3f, p. 79, l. 10: pale eyes. He had a boat

p. 82, ll. 13–14: Bilbo was beginning to hope that the wretch would not be able to answer, Gollum < A3f, p. 82, ll. 13–14: Bilbo was beginning to wonder what Gollum's present would be like, Gollum [Cf. intermediate revision, A3e note.]

p. 164, l. 11: take turns [*error, omits* at] watching

p. 164, l. 29: the Deep-elves and the Sea-elves < A3f, p. 164, l. 30: the Deep-elves (or Gnomes) and the Sea-elves

p. 164, l. 33: before some came back < A3f, p. 164, l. 33: before they came back

p. 164, ll. 34–7: lingered in the twilight of our Sun and Moon but loved best the stars; and they wandered in the great forests that grew tall in lands that are now lost. They dwelt most often by the edges of the woods < A3f, p. 164, ll. 34–7: lingered in the twilight before the raising of the Sun and Moon; and afterwards they wandered in the forests that grew beneath the sunrise. They loved best the edges of the woods

p. 228, ll. 24–5: It was of silver-steel, which the elves call *mithril*, and with it < A3f, p. 228, ll. 24–5: It was of silvered steel and ornamented with pearls, and with it

p. 232, ll. 10–12: Under the rocky wall to the right there was no path, so on they trudged among the stones on the left side of the river, and the emptiness and desolation < A3f, p. 232, ll. 10–12: So on they trudged among the stones on the left side of the river—to the right the rocky wall above the water was sheer and pathless—and the emptiness and desolation

p. 247, ll. 18–20: along a narrow ledge of the cliff, to the right as one looked outwards from the wall < A3f, p. 247, ll. 18–20: along a narrow path close to the cliff on the right (as you looked towards the gate from the outside)

p. 281, ll. 4–5: The North will be freed from that horror for many long years, I hope. < A3f, p. 281, ll. 4–5: The North is freed from that horror for many an age.

p. 285, l. 8: on friendly terms < A3f, p. 285, l. 8: on speaking terms p. 285, l. 25: was largely spent in presents < A3f, p. 285, l. 25: was mostly spent in presents

The new references to Thror and Thrain, pp. 32, 34, and 37, further explain the inscription on Thror's Map, 'Here of old was Thrain King under the Mountain' (cf. Tolkien's note, p. [10]). For further analysis of Tolkien's revisions, see Constance B. Hieatt, 'The Text of *The Hobbit*: Putting Tolkien's Notes in Order', *English Studies in Canada*, 7, no. 2 (Summer 1981), pp. [212]–24; David Cofield, 'Changes in Hobbits: Textual Differences in Editions of *The Hobbit*', *Beyond Bree* (newsletter of the American Mensa Tolkien Special Interest Group), April 1986, pp. 3–4; and Christopher Tolkien, 'Notes on the Differences in Editions of *The Hobbit* Cited by Mr. David Cofield', *Beyond Bree*, July 1986, pp. 1–3.

Tolkien's revisions to A3g were made in the first instance for the new edition planned by Houghton Mifflin (see A3f note), but were also intended for the first paperback edition by Allen & Unwin (A3h) and its hardcover version published by Longmans, Green (A3h note). In the event, they appeared first in the new Ballantine Books edition, later not only in the Allen & Unwin paperback and Longmans editions but also in a new hardcover edition by Allen & Unwin (A3i), and not until

1967 or 1968 in a new edition by Houghton Mifflin (A3j). These editions represent four new typesettings, each of which has different compositor's errors. Some of Tolkien's revisions were overlooked in partly resetting A3f for A3g, so that some readings from the second edition text were mistakenly continued. Tolkien seems to have been most directly concerned with A3h, which contains the fewest errors.

The later textual history of the Ballantine edition is murky. At least two 'twentieth' impressions were printed, dated 'June 1969' and 'September 1969'. The dates of other impressions vary in lists given on copyright pages in the edition. The text proper was partly reset at least twice. The error 'odd-looking' for 'old-looking', p. 21, l. 8, was corrected between the twenty-fourth (March 1970) and forty-third (September 1973) impressions. Between the fifty-sixth (October 1975) and fifty-ninth (June 1976) impressions, the errors 'We are met together' for 'We are not together', p. 29, ll. 6–7, and 'I like six eggs with my ham' for 'I like eggs with my ham', p. 38, l. 20, were introduced, and the break between pp. 286–7 was changed from 'I am | very fond' to 'I | am very fond'. An appreciation by Peter S. Beagle, dated 14 July 1973, was added between the forty-third (post-September 1973) and fiftieth (June 1974) impressions, and reset with the sixty-second impression (June 1977). Beginning with the seventy-seventh impression (April 1981), an unknown number of impressions (not reset) were published as a 'Special Silver Jubilee Edition'. Impression numbering was begun anew with the January 1982 impression, sometime after the seventy-seventh impression (April 1981). This book was completely reset in 1988 (see A3cc).

Tolkien hoped that Ballantine Books would soon replace the Remington cover illustration, but the design had established an 'identity' on paperback racks, and to change it too early would have risked lost sales. After the fortieth (March 1973) and no later than the forty-second (September 1973) impression, the cover was changed to feature *Bilbo Comes to the Huts of the Raft-elves* by Tolkien. Impressions with this cover were sold separately or with *LR* (A5d) in a slipcase, red (or blue, or gold) printed paper over boards, featuring Elvish heraldic devices by Tolkien. With the seventy-seventh impression (April 1981) the cover was changed to feature a colour illustration by Darrell K. Sweet, *The Lord of Eagles*, and after the new thirteenth (July 1985) and no later than the new seventeenth (July 1986) impression to again feature *Bilbo Comes to the Huts of the Raft-elves* by Tolkien. These later copies also were sold separately or in a slipcase with *LR* (A5d).

h. Unwin Books 'third edition' (1966):

J. R. R. TOLKIEN | THE HOBBIT | *or* | *There and Back Again* | [*facsimile signature, 'J. R. R. Tolkien'*] | LONDON · UNWIN BOOKS

viii, 280 pp. + 2 plates (maps). Collation: 144 leaves. 18.4 × 12.2 cm.

[i] '[*publisher's "U books" device, in white and black*] | THE HOBBIT | [*blurb*]'; [ii] '*by J. R. R. Tolkien* | [*3 titles, beginning with* ATB, *ending with* LR] | (*in three vols.*) | [*4 titles, beginning with* FR, *ending with* TL]'; [iii] title; [iv] '*First published in 1937* | *Second impression 1937* | *Reprinted 1942* | *Reprinted 1946* | *Second edition (fifth impression) 1951* | *Sixth impression (second edition) 1954* | [*list of seventh–fifteenth impressions, 1955–65*] | *Third edition (sixteenth impression) 1966* | [*notice of restrictions under copyright*] | *This edition* © *George Allen & Unwin Ltd., 1966* | UNWIN BOOKS | George Allen & Unwin Ltd. | Ruskin House, Museum Street | London W.C.1 | PRINTED IN GREAT BRITAIN | *in 10 on 11 point Baskerville* | BY NORTHUMBERLAND PRESS LIMITED | GATESHEAD'; [v] table of contents; [vi] blank; [vii] author's note; [viii] blank; 1–[279] text; [280] blank.

Omits Tolkien's illustrations, except for the maps, in black only, on 2 folded plates: *Thror's Map*, preceding p. [i]; *Wilderland*, following p. [280]. In later impressions, the maps are printed on integral leaves.

Wove paper. Bound in heavy wove wrappers. Printed on upper cover: '*J. R. R. Tolkien* | THE HOBBIT | [*colour illustration by Tolkien*, Death of Smaug, *wraps around upper cover, spine, and one-third of lower cover; at lower right, against the illustration:*] 8s 6d net | Unwin Books'. Printed on spine: '[*running up:*] [*against the illustration:*] THE HOBBIT [*above the illustration:*] Tolkien | [*horizontal, against the illustration:*] [*publisher's "U books" device, in white and black*] | 65'. Printed on lower cover: '[*at left, list of 64 titles published as Unwin Books, beginning with* Russell, On Education, *ending with* Hingley, Chekhov; *at upper right, above the illustration:*] UNWIN BOOKS [*publisher's "U books" device, in white and black*] | [*in black:*] An early sketch | by the author'.

Published 30 June 1966 at 8s. 6d.; 20,000 copies were planned as of 30 November 1964.

Reset, revised, based on the 'fourteenth' impression of A3c (i.e. the tenth impression of the second edition, 1963). Of the errors noted for A3c, only 'It like riddles' for 'It likes riddles', p. 67, ll. 29–30, was continued. The following alterations (other than corrections to errors noted for A3c) and new errors were made in A3h:

p. [vii], the author's note is new ('This is a story of long ago. . . .'); the reference to Thror's Map incorrectly reads '30 and 63' (as for A3c)

p. 2, ll. 10–12: They are (or were) a little people, about half our height, and smaller than the bearded Dwarves [*error, for* dwarves]. Hobbits have no beards. < A3c, p. 12, ll. 14–16: They are (or were) small people, smaller than dwarves (and they have no beards) but very much larger than lilliputians.

p. 2, ll. 29–32: It was often said (in other families) that long ago one of the Took ancestors must have taken a fairy wife. That was, of course, absurd, but certainly there was < A3c, p. 12, ll. 32–4: It had always been said that long ago one or other of the Tooks had married into a fairy family (the less friendly said a goblin family); certainly there was

p. 3, l. 36–p. 4, l. 1: an old man with a staff. He had a tall pointed blue hat, a long grey cloak, a silver scarf over which his long white beard < A3c, p. 14, ll. 6–7: a little old man with a tall pointed blue hat, a long grey cloak, a silver scarf over which his long white beard

p. 5, ll. 29–31: mad adventures? Anything from climbing trees to visiting Elves— or sailing in ships, sailing to other shores! < A3c, p. 16, ll. 2–3: mad adventures, anything from climbing trees to stowing away aboard the ships that sail to the Other Side?

p. 10, l. 33: cold chicken and pickles < A3c, p. 22, l. 12: cold chicken and tomatoes

p. 12, ll. 23–6: Gandalf's smoke-ring would go green and come back to hover over the wizard's head. He had a cloud of them about him already, and in the dim light it made him look strange and sorcerous. < A3c, p. 23, ll. 11–14: Gandalf's smoke-ring would go green with the joke and come back to hover over the wizard's head. He had quite a cloud of them about him already, and it made him look positively sorcerous.

p. 18, l. 37: made by Thror, your grandfather, Thorin < A3c, p. 30, l. 3: made by your grandfather, Thorin

p. 19, ll. 26–7: devouring so many of the dwarves and men of Dale < A3c, p. 30, ll. 29–30: devouring so many of the maidens of the valley

p. 21, ll. 23–9: Long ago in my grandfather Thror's time our family was driven out of the far North, and came back with all their wealth and their tools to this Mountain on the map. It had been discovered by my far ancestor, Thrain the Old, but now they mined and they tunnelled and they made huger halls and greater workshops < A3c, p. 32, ll. 30–4: Long ago in my grandfather's time some dwarves were driven out of the far North, and came with all their wealth and their tools to this Mountain on the map. There they mined and they tunnelled and they made hugh halls and great workshops

p. 21, l. 32: King under the Mountain again, and treated < A3c, p. 33, ll. 3–4: King under the Mountain, and treated

p. 22, ll. 9–11: full of armour and jewels and carvings and cups, and the toy-market of Dale was the wonder of the North < A3c, p. 33, ll. 17–19: full of wonderful jewels and carvings and cups, and the toyshops of Dale were a sight to behold

p. 24, ll. 4–5: Your grandfather Thror was killed, you remember, in the mines of Moria by Azog the Goblin. < A3c, p. 35, ll. 15–16: Your grandfather was killed, you remember, in the mines of Moria by a goblin—

p. 24, l. 21: said the wizard slowly and grimly < A3c, p. 35, l. 32: said the wizard slowly and crossly

p. 25, ll. 2–3: He is an enemy far beyond the powers < A3c, p. 36, l. 15: That is a job quite beyond the powers

p. 25, ll. 5–6: was for his son to read the map < A3c, p. 36, l. 18: was for you to read the map

p. 28, l. 14: and then on for a mile or more < A3c, p. 40, ll. 5–6: and so for a whole mile or more

p. 29, l. 6: They had not been riding < A3c, p. 41, l. 1: They hadn't been riding

p. 29, ll. 15–30: At first they had passed through hobbit-lands, a wide respectable country inhabited by decent folk, with good roads, an inn or two, and now and then a dwarf or a farmer ambling by on business. Then they came to lands where people spoke strangely, and sang songs Bilbo had never heard before. Now they had gone on far into the Lone-lands, where there were no people left, no inns, and the roads grew steadily worse. Not far ahead were dreary hills, rising higher and higher, dark with trees. On some of them were old castles with an evil look, as if they had been built by wicked people. Everything seemed gloomy, for the weather that day had taken a nasty turn. Mostly it had been as good as May can be, even in merry tales, but now it was cold and wet. In the Lone-lands they had been obliged to camp when they could, but at least it had been dry. < A3c, p. 41, ll. 9–22: Things went on like this for quite a long while. There was a good deal of wide respectable country to pass through, inhabited by decent respectable folk, men or hobbits or elves or what not, with good roads, an inn or two, and every now and then a dwarf, or a tinker, or a farmer ambling by on business. But after a time they came to places where people spoke strangely, and sang songs Bilbo had never heard before. Inns were rare and not good, the roads were worse, and there were hills in the distance rising higher and higher. There were castles on some of the hills, and many looked as if they had not been built for any good purpose. Also the weather which had often been as good as May can be, even in tales and legends, took a nasty turn.

p. 29, l. 31: 'To think it will soon be June!' [*error? for* June,'] grumbled Bilbo < A3c, p. 41, l. 23: 'To think it is June the first tomorrow,' grumbled Bilbo

p. 30, ll. 7–16: it began to get dark as they went down into a deep valley with a river at the bottom. Wind got up, and willows along its banks bent and sighed. Fortunately the road went over an ancient stone-bridge [*error, for* stone bridge], for the river, swollen with the rains, came rushing down from the hills and mountains in the north. ¶ It was nearly night when they had crossed over. The wind broke up the grey clouds, and a wandering moon appeared < A3c, p. 42, ll. 3–9: it began to get dark. Wind got up, and the willows along the river-bank bent and sighed. I don't know what river it was, a rushing red one, swollen with the rains of the last few days, that came down from the hills and mountains in front of them. ¶ Soon it was nearly dark. The winds broke up the grey clouds, and a waning moon appeared

p. 30, l. 29: where they were. They moved to a clump of trees < A3c, p. 42, ll. 22–7: where they were. So far they had not camped before on this journey, and though they knew that they soon would have to camp regularly, when they were among the Misty Mountains and far from the lands of respectable people, it seemed a bad wet evening to begin on. They moved to a clump of trees

p. 31, ll. 22–4: Travellers seldom come this way now. The old maps are no use: things have changed for the worse, and the road is unguarded. < A3c, p. 43, ll. 20–1: Policemen never come so far, and the map-makers have not reached this country yet.

p. 35, ll. 8–10: said William. He had already had as much supper as he could hold; also he had had lots of beer. < A3c, p. 47, ll. 13–15: said William (I told you he had already had as much supper as he could hold; also he had had lots of beer).

p. 35, l. 21: when Bert dropped him < A3c, p. 47, l. 26: when they dropped him

p. 39, ll. 8–10: he stepped from behind a tree, and helped Bilbo to climb down out of a thorn-bush < A3c, p. 52, ll. 17–18: he stepped from behind the bushes, and helped Bilbo to climb down out of a thorn-tree

p. 39, l. 20: practising pinching < A3c, p. 52, l. 28: practising burglary

p. 42, ll. 7–8 after titling: One morning they forded a river < A3c, p. 56, l. 7 after titling: One afternoon they forded the river

p. 43, ll. 12–14: That sounded nice and comforting, but they had not got there yet, and it was not so easy as it sounds to find the Last Homely House < A3c, p. 57, ll. 14–16: That sounded nice and comforting, and I daresay you think it ought to have been easy to make straight for the Last Homely House

p. 43, ll. 20–2: Morning passed, afternoon came; but in all the silent waste there was no sign of any dwelling. They were growing anxious, for they saw now that the house < A3c, p. 57, ll. 23–5: The afternoon sun shone down; but in all the silent waste there was no sign of any dwelling. They rode on for a while, and they soon saw that the house

p. 44, ll. 5–8: His head and beard wagged this way and that as he looked for the stones, and they followed his lead, but they seemed no nearer to the end of the search when the day began to fail. < A3c, p. 58, ll. 12–14: They still seemed to have gone only a little way, carefully following the wizard, whose head and beard wagged this way and that as he searched for the path, when the day began to fail.

p. 48, ll. 26–7: swords of the High Elves of the West, my kin < A3c, p. 63, ll. 6–7: swords of the elves that are now called Gnomes

p. 49, ll. 20–2: remnants of old robberies in some hold [*error? for* hole] in the mountains [*error? for* mountains of the North *or* mountains of old]. I have heard that there are still forgotten treasures of old [*error? for* forgotten treasures] to be found < A3c, p. 63, ll. 18–20: remnants of old robberies in some hold in the mountains of the North. I have heard that there are still forgotten treasures to be found

p. 50, ll. 7–9: He was the father of the fathers of the eldest race of Dwarves, the Longbeards, and my first ancestor: I am his heir. < A3c, p. 64, ll. 24–6: He was the father of the fathers of one of the two races of dwarves, the Longbeards, and my grandfather's ancestor.

p. 50, l. 12: is as all should know the first day < A3c, p. 64, l. 29: is as everyone knows the first day

p. 52, ll. 10–11: in secret after the battle of the Mines of Moria < A3c, p. 67, ll. 13–14: in secret after the sack of the mines of Moria

p. 64, ll. 11–12: nor fortunately had the goblins noticed it < A3c, p. 81, l. 13: nor do the goblins seem to have noticed it

p. 66, ll. 11–12: lived old Gollum, a small slimy creature < A3c, p. 83, ll. 16–17: lived old Gollum

p. 66, ll. 14–15: pale eyes in his thin face. He had a little boat < A3c, p. 83, l. 19: pale eyes. He had a boat

p. 66, l. 19: limp-like [*error, for* lamp-like] eyes

p. 69, ll. 20–1: Bilbo was beginning to hope that the wretch would not be able to answer < A3c, p. 86, ll. 25–6: Bilbo was beginning to wonder what Gollum's present would be like [Cf. intermediate revision, A3e note.]

p. 109, l. 33: Mr. Baggins, a hobbit [*error? for* Mr. Baggins a hobbit *as in all other editions*]

p. 155, ll. 21–2: the Deep-elves and the Sea-elves < A3c, p. 178, ll. 13–14: the Deep-elves (or Gnomes) and the Sea-elves

p. 155, l. 25: before some came back < A3c, p. 178, l. 17: before they came back

p. 155, ll. 26–30: twilight of our Sun and Moon, but loved best the stars; and they wandered in the great forests that grew tall in lands that are now lost. They dwelt most often by the edges of the woods < A3c, p. 178, ll. 18–21: twilight before the raising of the Sun and Moon; and afterwards they wandered in the forests that grew beneath the sunrise. They loved best the edges of the woods

p. 220, ll. 13–14: It was of silver-steel, which the elves call *mithril* < A3c, p. 251, ll. 7–8: It was of silvered steel and ornamented with pearls

p. 224, ll. 3–5: Under the rocky wall to the right there was no path, so on they trudged among the stones on the left side of the river, and the emptiness and desolation < A3c, p. 255, ll. 6–8: So on they trudged among the stones on the left side of the river—to the right the rocky wall above the water was sheer and pathless—and the emptiness and desolation

p. 238, ll. 28–9: in making a new path that led < A3c, p. 271, l. 4: in remaking the road that led

p. 239, l. 7: towards [*probably an error, for* toward] the mountain

p. 239, ll. 21–2: along a narrow ledge of the cliff, to the right as one looked outwards from the wall < A3c, p. 271, ll. 32–4: along a narrow path close to the cliff on the right (as you looked towards the gate from the outside)

p. 240, ll. 14–15: the camp was moved to the east of the river, right between < A3c, p. 272, ll. 25–6: the camp was moved and was brought right between

p. 266, l. 3: Beorn stopped [*error, for* stooped] and lifted Thorin

p. 272, l. 35–p. 273, ll. 1–2: the [*error? for* The] Forest will grow somewhat more wholesome. The North will be freed from that horror for many long years, I hope. < A3c, p. 308, ll. 3–5: The Forest will grow somewhat more wholesome. The North is freed from that horror for many an age.

p. 277, ll. 6–7: on friendly terms < A3c, p. 313, ll. 15–16: on speaking terms

p. 277, l. 24: was largely spent in presents < A3c, p. 313, ll. 32–3: was mostly spent in presents

The error on p. [vii] was later corrected. On p. 19, ll. 15–16, the reference to *Thror's Map* (printed in this edition in black only) reads: 'Look at the map at the beginning of this book, and you will see there the runes in red.' This sentence was later corrected to: 'Look at the map at the beginning of this book, and you will see there the runes.'

On 30 November 1964 Rayner Unwin informed Tolkien that the firm Longmans, Green were interested in publishing *The Hobbit* for schools. Allen & Unwin had their own small school book department, but it was cheaper to sub-contract to Longmans and run on, from the same printing, a large number of copies for publication in Allen & Unwin's paperback 'U Books' series. A deal was struck by 14 June 1965. Tolkien remarked on 23 June, in a letter to C. A. Furth:

> I feel that the matter is [in] the hands of those better able to judge what is good for the book and its sales than I am. All the same I feel some anxiety, particularly with regard to the *text*. I hope that I may be allowed some control over what is done. In the matter of 'Puffin Books' I had none, and the result was unhappy. . . .
>
> I have already and recently re-read *The Hobbit* in various forms down to a copy of the second edition, and have notes ready, but it is much simpler to indicate required corrections on a printed copy. The minor errors that still survive, or have later appeared, are very few. But since in effect a new edn. (for U. Books) is being re-set, I think the time has come to make a few alterations (in 6 places) which I have prepared: their object is to correct a small discrepancy; to make the note on *Thrain*, which was still necessary in the Puffin version, unnecessary; and to bring *The Hobbit* in line with *The Lord of the Rings* where needed. The changes are in each case very small in extent.

He also felt that since this was to be in the first instance a 'school' edition, a short note on *dwarves* was required, to explain his use of that plural form. His alterations, he told Furth, were all that he considered necessary,

> though much more could be introduced with advantage. Those that I here refer to are insufficient for the purposes of Houghton Mifflin and the copyright business. What view do you take of a divergence of text between the English and American editions? Should the 'revisions', which I shall be sending to Houghton Mifflin before the end of July, be made with any reference to the present proposals for re-setting as an 'Unwin Book'—in which case they must be cut to a minimum—or to any other future edition by Allen and Unwin?

Rayner Unwin decided that they would wait and incorporate Tolkien's changes to the American edition (see A3f, A3g notes) in the Unwin Books and Longmans editions. On 24 August Tolkien wrote to Unwin:

> I am doomed to be always late. However here at last is 'The Hobbit' revised.
>
> You will observe that the 'corrections etc.' are much the most heavy in Chapter I. After Ch. II there are few.
>
> I have (I hope) resisted the inclination to 'improve' *The Hobbit*—except for removing the 'author-to-reader' asides in some places: very irritating to intelligent children (as some have said). There are some correction[s] due to the actual errors and discrepancies in the tale itself; some that try to make things clearer. But since in order to spot these things—including printer's errors that still survive!—one has to read the whole with line-to-line care, it seemed to me a pity not to get rid of a few happy-go-lucky passages that are quite out of joint. *The Hobbit* is taken as a prologue to *The L.R.* [*Lord of the Rings*] and though no one expects consistency between the two to be exact, it is a pity that some passages in *The H.* should be completely impossible in *The L.R.* . . .

Tolkien was sent proofs of the new edition on 11 November and returned them corrected on 10 December. He read the text carefully one more time and made a few further alterations required by still more inconsistencies he discovered. His author's note with a runic heading, and chiefly about runes, was now introduced, for the benefit and pleasure of his young readers who found runes attractive.

On 19 June 1965 Tolkien sent Allen & Unwin 'a crude drawing (all I can find) of my attempt to catch a glimpse, beyond my skill, of the death of Smaug' as a help or inspiration to a cover artist. The publisher chose instead to use Tolkien's coloured sketch for the cover, though the artist considered it a scrawl, 'too much in the modern mode in which those who can draw try to conceal it. But perhaps there is a distinction between their productions and one by a man who obviously cannot draw what he sees' (letter to Rayner Unwin, 15 December 1965). He dated the drawing to *circa* 1936.

The Longmans, Green edition appeared in June 1966 (British Library copy received 6 June) in their 'Heritage of Literature' series, bound in black, grey, and white pictorial paper over boards, without dust-jacket. The edition was reprinted by Longmans in 1968, in their 'Pleasure in Reading' series, bound in colour pictorial paper over boards, without dust-jacket. It was reprinted also by Methuen, Toronto, in 1976. Their Magnum paperback, 1977, the second impression of the Methuen edition, is bound in heavy wove wrappers featuring *Conversation with Smaug* by Tolkien.

i. Allen & Unwin hardcover 'third edition' ('sixteenth impression', 1966):

The Hobbit | or | There and Back | Again | by | J. R. R. Tolkien | Illustrated | by the Author | London | George Allen & Unwin Ltd | Ruskin House Museum Street

320 pp. + 4 plates. Collation: $[A]^{16}B-K^{16}$. 18.4 × 12.4 cm.

[1] 'The Hobbit'; [2] '*also by J. R. R. Tolkien* | [*7 titles, beginning with* ATB, *ending with* TL]'; [3] title; [4] 'FIRST PUBLISHED IN 1937 | SECOND IMPRESSION 1937 | REPRINTED 1942 | REPRINTED 1946 | SECOND EDITION (FIFTH IMPRESSION) 1951 | SIXTH IMPRESSION (SECOND EDITION) 1954 | [*list of seventh–fourteenth impressions, 1955–63*] | THIRD EDITION (FIFTEENTH IMPRESSION) 1966 | SIXTEENTH IMPRESSION 1966 | [*notice of restrictions under copyright*] | *Third Edition* © *George Allen & Unwin,* 1966 | PRINTED IN GREAT BRITAIN BY | C. TINLING AND CO. LTD., | LIVERPOOL, LONDON AND PRESCOT'; [5] table of contents; [6] list of illustrations; [7] author's note; [8] blank; [9]–317 text and illustrations; [318] '[*publisher's square "St. George" device*] | GEORGE ALLEN & UNWIN LTD | [*19 addresses, London to Tokyo*]'; [319] advertisement of *LR*; [320] advertisement of *TL, FGH, ATB*.

Black and white illustrations, by Tolkien: *The Trolls*, p. 48; *The Mountain-path*, p. [67]; *The Misty Mountains Looking West from the Eyrie towards Goblin Gate*, p. 121; *Beorn's Hall*, p. [130]; *The Elvenking's Gate*, p. 184; *Lake Town*, p. [202]; *The Front Gate*, p. 215; *The Hall at Bag-End, Residence of B. Baggins Esquire*, p. 315. Colour illustrations, by Tolkien, on 4 plates: *The Hill: Hobbiton-across-the Water*, facing p. [3]; *Rivendell*, facing p. 64; *Bilbo Comes to the Huts of the Raft-elves*, facing p. 192; *Conversation with Smaug*, facing p. 228. Maps, by Tolkien, in black and red: *Thror's Map*, front endsheet; *Wilderland*, back endsheet.

Wove paper. Bound in green textured paper over boards. Stamping as for A3c. Wove endpapers (maps). No headbands. All edges trimmed and unstained.

Dust-jacket not seen, but probably: covers and spine as for A3a, spine imprint in type (not hand-lettered); front flap: '[*blurb*] | *Third Edition* | ALL THE ILLUS-TRATIONS IN THIS | BOOK ARE BY THE AUTHOR | [*price?*]'; back flap: list of books by Tolkien.

Published 30 June 1966 at 20s.; number of copies not known.

Reset, revised, based on the 'fourteenth' impression of A3c (i.e. the tenth impression of the second edition, 1963). Revision, see A3h note. Of the errors noted for A3c, only 'It like riddles' for 'It likes riddles', p. 67, ll. 29–30, was continued. The following alterations (other than corrections to errors noted for A3c) and new errors were made in A3h:

p. 6, l. 10: Ratelves [*error, for* Raft-elves]

p. 7, the author's note is new ('This is a story of long ago. . . .')

p. 10, l. 1: The Bagginses have lived [*error, for* had lived]

p. 10, ll. 15–17: They are (or were) a little people, about half our height, and smaller than the bearded dwarves. Hobbits have no beards. < A3c, p. 12, ll. 14–16: They are (or were) small people, smaller than dwarves (and they have no beards) but very much larger than lilliputians.

p. 10, l. 33–p. 11, l. 2: It was often said (in other families) that long ago one of the Took ancestors must have taken a fairy wife. That was, of course, absurd, but certainly there was < A3c, p. 12, ll. 32–4: It had always been said that long ago one or other of the Tooks had married into a fairy family (the less friendly said a goblin family); certainly there was

p. 12, ll. 7–9: an old man with a staff. He had a tall pointed blue hat, a long grey cloak, a silver scarf over which his long white beard < A3c, p. 14, ll. 6–7: a little old man with a tall pointed blue hat, a long grey cloak, a silver scarf over which his long white beard

p. 14, ll. 5–7: mad adventures? Anything from climbing trees to visiting Elves—or sailing in ships, sailing to other shores! < A3c, p. 16, ll. 2–3: mad adventures, anything from climbing trees to stowing away aboard the ships that sail to the Other Side?

p. 19, l. 19: cold chicken and pickles < A3c, p. 22, l. 12: cold chicken and tomatoes

p. 21, ll. 17–20: Gandalf's smoke-ring would go green and come back to hover over the wizard's head. He had a cloud of them about him already, and in the dim light it made him look strange and sorcerous. < A3c, p. 23, ll. 11–14: Gandalf's smoke-ring would go green with the joke and come back to hover over the wizard's head. He had quite a cloud of them about him already, and it made him look positively sorcerous.

p. 28, l. 14: made by Thror, your grandfather, Thorin < A3c, p. 30, l. 3: made by your grandfather, Thorin

p. 29, ll. 6–7: devouring so many of the dwarves and men of Dale < A3c, p. 30, ll. 29–30: devouring so many of the maidens of the valley

p. 31, ll. 9–15: Long ago in my grandfather Thror's time our family was driven out of the far North, and came back with all their wealth and their tools to this Mountain on the map. It had been discovered by my far ancestor, Thrain the Old, but now they mined and they tunnelled and they made huger halls and greater workshops < A3c, p. 32, ll. 30–4: Long ago in my grandfather's time some dwarves were driven out of the far North, and came with all their wealth and their tools to this Mountain on the map. There they mined and they tunnelled and they made hugh halls and great workshops

p. 31, l. 18: King under the Mountain again, and treated < A3c, p. 33, ll. 3–4: King under the Mountain, and treated

p. 31, ll. 31–2: full of armour and jewels and carvings and cups, and the toy market of Dale was the wonder of the North < A3c, p. 33, ll. 17–19: full of wonderful jewels and carvings and cups, and the toyshops of Dale were a sight to behold

p. 33, ll. 31–2: Your grandfather Thror was killed, you remember, in the mines of Moria by Azog the Goblin. < A3c, p. 35, ll. 15–16: Your grandfather was killed, you remember, in the mines of Moria by a goblin—

p. 34, l. 14: said the wizard slowly and grimly < A3c, p. 35, l. 32: said the wizard slowly and crossly

p. 34, ll. 31–2: He is an enemy far beyond the powers < A3c, p. 36, l. 15: That is a job quite beyond the powers

p. 34, l. 34–p. 35, l. 1: was for his son to read the map < A3c, p. 36, l. 18: was for you to read the map

p. 39, ll. 5–6: and then on for a mile or more < A3c, p. 40, ll. 5–6: and so for a whole mile or more

p. 40, l. 1: They had not been riding < A3c, p. 41, l. 1: They hadn't been riding

p. 40, ll. 10–25: At first they had passed through hobbit-lands, a wild [*error, for* wide] respectable country inhabited by decent folk, with good roads, an inn or two, and now and then a dwarf or a farmer ambling by on business. Then they came to lands where people spoke strangely, and sang songs Bilbo had never heard before. Now they had gone on far into the Lone-lands, where there were no people left, no inns, and the roads grew steadily worse. Not far ahead were dreary hills, rising higher and higher, dark with trees. On some of them were old castles with an evil look, as if they had been built by wicked people. Everything seemed gloomy, for the weather that day had taken a nasty turn. Mostly it had been as good as May can be, even in merry tales, but now it was cold and wet. In the Lone-lands they had been obliged to camp when they could, but at least it had been dry. < A3c, p. 41, ll. 9–22: Things went on like this for quite a long while. There was a good deal of wide respectable country to pass through, inhabited by decent respectable folk, men or hobbits or elves or what not, with good roads, an inn or two, and every now and then a dwarf, or a tinker, or a farmer ambling by on business. But after a time they came to places where people spoke strangely, and sang songs Bilbo had never heard before. Inns were rare and not good, the roads were worse, and there were hills in the distance rising higher and higher. There were castles on some of the hills, and many looked as if they had not been built for any good purpose. Also the weather which had often been as good as May can be, even in tales and legends, took a nasty turn.

p. 40, l. 26: 'To think it will soon be June,' grumbled Bilbo < A3c, p. 41, l. 23: 'To think it is June the first tomorrow,' grumbled Bilbo

p. 41, ll. 5–13: it began to get dark as they went down into a deep valley with a river at the bottom. Wind got up, and willows along its banks bent and sighed. Fortunately the road went over an ancient stone bridge [cf. A3h, 'ancient stone-bridge'], for the river, swollen with the rains, came rushing down from the hills and mountains in the north. ¶ It was nearly night when they had crossed over. The wind broke up the grey clouds, and a wandering moon appeared < A3c, p. 42, ll. 3–9: it began to get dark. Wind got up, and the willows along the river-bank bent and sighed. I don't know what river it was, a rushing red one, swollen with the rains of the last few days, that came down from the hills and mountains in front of them. ¶ Soon it was nearly dark. The winds broke up the grey clouds, and a waning moon appeared

p. 41, l. 25: where they were. They moved to a clump of trees < A3c, p. 42, ll. 22–7: where they were. So far they had not camped before on this journey, and though they knew that they soon would have to camp regularly, when they were among the Misty Mountains and far from the lands of respectable people, it seemed a bad wet evening to begin on. They moved to a clump of trees

p. 42, ll. 20–2: Travellers seldom come this way now. The old maps are no use:

things have changed for the worse and the road is unguarded. < A3c, p. 43, ll. 20–1: Policemen never come so far, and the map-makers have not reached this country yet.

p. 46, ll. 16–18: said William. He had already had as much supper as he could hold; also he had had lots of beer. < A3c, p. 47, ll. 13–15: said William (I told you he had already had as much supper as he could hold; also he had had lots of beer).

p. 46, l. 29: when Bert dropped him < A3c, p. 47, l. 26: when they dropped him

p. 51, ll. 24–5: he stepped from behind a tree, and helped Bilbo to climb down out of a thorn-bush < A3c, p. 52, ll. 17–18: he stepped from behind the bushes, and helped Bilbo to climb down out of a thorn-tree

p. 52, l. 1: practising pinching < A3c, p. 52, l. 28: practising burglary

p. [55], ll. 7–8 after titling: One morning they forded a river < A3c, p. 56, l. 7 after titling: One afternoon they forded the river

p. 56, ll. 15–17: That sounded nice and comforting, but they had not got there yet, and it was not so easy as it sounds to find the Last Homely House < A3c, p. 57, ll. 14–16: That sounded nice and comforting, and I daresay you think it ought to have been easy to make straight for the Last Homely House

p. 56, ll. 24–6: Morning passed, afternoon came; but in all the silent waste there was no sign of any dwelling. They were growing anxious, for they saw now that the house < A3c, p. 57, ll. 23–5: The afternoon sun shone down; but in all the silent waste there was no sign of any dwelling. They rode on for a while, and they soon saw that the house

p. 57, ll. 12–15: His head and beard wagged this way and that as he looked for the stones, and they followed his lead, but they seemed no nearer to the end of the search when the day began to fail. < A3c, p. 58, ll. 12–14: They still seemed to have gone only a little way, carefully following the wizard, whose head and beard wagged this way and that as he searched for the path, when the day began to fail.

p. 61, ll. 3–4: uncomfortable palpitating [*error, for* uncomfortable, palpitating]

p. 61, l. 32: their bruises their tempers and their hopes [*error, for* their bruises, their tempers and their hopes]

p. 62, ll. 7–8: swords of the High Elves of the West, my kin < A3c, p. 63, ll. 6–7: swords of the elves that are now called Gnomes

p. 62, ll. 20–2: remnants of old robberies in some hole [*error? for* hold] in the mountains of old [*error? for* of the North]. I have heard that there are still forgotten treasures [*error? omits* of old] to be found < A3c, p. 63, ll. 18–20: remnants of old robberies in some hold in the mountains of the North. I have heard that there are still forgotten treasures to be found

p. 63, ll. 27–9: He was the father of the fathers of the eldest race of Dwarves, the Longbeards, and my first ancestor: I am his heir. < A3c, p. 64, ll. 24–6: He was the father of the fathers of one of the two races of dwarves, the Longbeards, and my grandfather's ancestor.

p. 63, l. 32: is as all should know the first day < A3c, p. 64, l. 29: is as everyone knows the first day

p. 66, ll. 13–14: in secret after the battle of the Mines of Moria < A3c, p. 67, ll. 13–14: in secret after the sack of the mines of Moria

p. 80, ll. 13–14: nor fortunately had the goblins noticed it < A3c, p. 81, l. 13: nor do the goblins seem to have noticed it

p. 82, ll. 16–17: lived old Gollum, a small slimy creature < A3c, p. 83, l. 16: lived old Gollum

p. 82, ll. 19–20: pale eyes in his thin face. He had a little boat < A3c, p. 83, l. 19: pale eyes. He had a boat

p. 84, ll. 2–3: it like [*error, for* likes] riddles

p. 85, l. 13: *Toothless bits* [*error, for* bites]

p. 85, ll. 30–1: Bilbo was beginning to hope that the wretch would not be able to answer < A3c, p. 86, ll. 25–6: Bilbo was beginning to wonder what Gollum's present would be like [Cf. intermediate revision, A3e note.]

p. 120, l. 17: where men lives [*error, for* lived]

p. 134, l. 32: And so do it [*error, for* I]

p. 138, ll. 10–11: *on it went.* [*error, inserts full stop*] | *o'er shaken pool*

p. 152, l. 11: lives [*error, for* lived] at times

p. 165, l. 33: (as he thought; [*error, for right parenthesis*]

p. 168, l. 24: feeding none to [*error, for* too] well

p. 178, l. 29: the Deep-elves and the Sea-elves < A3c, p. 178, ll. 13–14: the Deep-elves (or Gnomes) and the Sea-elves

p. 178, ll. 32–3: before some came back < A3c, p. 178, l. 17: before they came back

p. 178, l. 34–p. 179, l. 3: twilight of our Sun and Moon, but loved best the stars; and they wandered in the great forests that grew tall in lands that are now lost. They dwelt most often by the edges of the woods < A3c, p. 178, ll. 19–21: twilight before the raising of the Sun and Moon; and afterwards they wandered in the forests that grew beneath the sunrise. They loved best the edges of the woods

p. 208, l. 22: travelled with [*error, omits* us] out of the West

p. 219, ll. 12–13: without a joint or crevice to be seen. ¶ [*paragraph break probably an error*] No sign was there < A3c, p. 218, l. 12: without a joint or crevice to be seen. No sign was there

p. 244, l. 14: Now [*error, for* No] trace of a keyhole

p. 252, ll. 10–11: It was of silver-steel, which the elves call *mithril* < A3c, p. 251, ll. 7–8: It was of silvered steel and ornamented with pearls

p. 224, ll. 3–5: Under the rocky wall to the right there was no path, so on they trudged among the stones on the left side of the river, and the emptiness and desolation < A3c, p. 255, ll. 6–8: So on they trudged among the stones on the left side of the river—to the right the rocky wall above the water was sheer and pathless—and the emptiness and desolation

p. 269, ll. 19–20: that old bird understand [*error, for* understands] us

p. 272, ll. 4–5: in making a new path that led < A3c, p. 271, l. 4: in remaking the road that led

p. 272, ll. 33–4: along a narrow ledge of the cliff, to the right as one looked outwards from the wall < A3c, p. 271, ll. 32–4: along a narrow path close to the cliff on the right (as you looked towards the gate from the outside)

p. 273, ll. 26–7: the camp was moved to the east of the river, right between < A3c, p. 272, ll. 25–6: the camp was moved and was brought right between

p. 291, l. 2: beseigers [*error, for* besiegers]

p. 310, ll. 6–8: The Forest will grow somewhat more wholesome. The North will be freed from that horror for many long years, I hope. < A3c, p. 308, ll. 3–5: The Forest will grow somewhat more wholesome. The North is freed from that horror for many an age.

p. 314, l. 24: on friendly terms < A3c, p. 313, ll. 15–16: on speaking terms

p. 316, l. 7: was largely spent in presents < A3c, p. 313, ll. 32–3: was mostly spent in presents

With the 'third' (1967) or 'fourth' (1968) impression, the impression numbering was revised, the count now beginning with the first impression of the third edition, formerly the 'fifteenth' (but see below). With the 'fifth' impression (1970) *The Hill* was moved to face p. 32, *Conversation with Smaug* was moved to face p. [224], and the list of illustrations was revised. With the 'seventh' (1972) or 'eighth' (1974) impression, but continuing the numbering of impressions, the type was completely reset; see A3m.

The numbering of A3i in and after the 'sixteenth' impression, 1966, suggests that the 'fifteenth' was the first impression of the new edition. The true 'fifteenth' impression of the Allen & Unwin hardcover *Hobbit*, however, published in 1965, was the final impression of the second edition (A3c). 'THIRD EDITION (FIFTEENTH IMPRESSION) 1966 | SIXTEENTH IMPRESSION 1966' on the copyright page is an error for 'THIRD EDITION (SIXTEENTH IMPRESSION) 1966'. The sequence is correctly listed in A3h.

Between the 'sixth' impression (1971) and the 'tenth' impression (= A3m, 1975) the dust-jacket (except the runic border) was re-lettered in a style similar to the earlier jacket but with heavier and straighter lines and smoother edges.

An abridged edition based on A3i, 'to introduce the Soviet reader to one of J. R. R. Tolkien's most famous books', was published in 1982 by Prosveshchenie, Moscow, in English with preliminaries and production notes in Russian, and commentary by Yu. L. Tret'yakova. The edition annotates *lo and behold, cash on delivery, gone cracked*, and *bunny*.

j. New Houghton Mifflin edition (1967 or 1968):

The Hobbit | or | There and Back | Again | by | J. R. R. Tolkien | Illustrated | by the Author | HOUGHTON MIFFLIN COMPANY | BOSTON

320 pp. Collation: [A]^{16}B–K^{16}. 20.2 × 13.6 cm.

[1] 'The Hobbit'; [2] blank; [3] title; [4] *'also by J. R. R. Tolkien* | [*3 titles, beginning with* ATB, *ending with* LR] 1. THE FELLOWSHIP OF THE RING | 2. THE TWO TOWERS | 3. THE RETURN OF THE KING | TREE AND LEAF | *Twenty-fifth Printing* C | COPYRIGHT © 1966 BY J. R. R. TOLKIEN | ALL RIGHTS RESERVED INCLUDING THE RIGHT | TO REPRODUCE THIS BOOK OR PARTS THEREOF IN ANY FORM | LIBRARY OF CONGRESS CATALOG CARD NUMBER: 67-29221 | PRINTED IN THE U.S.A.'; [5] table of contents; [6–7] *Thror's Map*; [8] author's note; [9]–317 text and illustrations; [318–19] *Wilderland* map; [320] blank.

Illustrations, by Tolkien: *The Trolls*, p. [48]; *The Mountain-path*, p. [67]; *The Misty Mountains Looking West from the Eyrie towards Goblin Gate*, p. 121; *Beorn's Hall*, p. [130]; *The Elvenking's Gate*, p. [184]; *Lake Town*, p. [202]; *The Front Gate*, p. [215]; *The Hall at Bag-End, Residence of B. Baggins Esquire*, p. [315]. Maps, by Tolkien, in black only, pp. [6–7], [318–19].

Wove paper. Bound in light blue-green cloth over boards. Stamped on upper cover in dark blue: 'THE | HOBBIT'. Stamped on spine in dark blue: 'THE | HOBBIT | [*decoration, a dwarf's cap*] | TOLKIEN | HOUGHTON | MIFFLIN CO.' Wove endpapers. No headbands. All edges trimmed and unstained.

Dust-jacket, wove paper. Covers as for A3a except with 'HOUGHTON MIFFLIN CO.' in place of 'GEORGE ALLEN AND UNWIN LTD' in the runic inscription, and '5–97090' at the foot of the lower cover. Spine as for A3a except with 'HMCo' against a white panel outlined, and shadowed at bottom, in black. Printed on front flap: '[*price? corner clipped from copy examined*] | THE HOBBIT | [*blurb*] | All ages'. Advertisement of *LR* printed on back flap.

Published in 1967 or 1968, price not known; number of copies, see below.

Reset, revised, based on A3i, page for page but not always line for line, with at least two corrections. Revision, see A3g note. The following errors were continued from A3i:

p. 40, ll. 10–11, 'wild respectable country' for 'wide respectable country'
p. 61, ll. 3–4, 'uncomfortable palpitating' for 'uncomfortable, palpitating'
p. 61, l. 32, 'their bruises their tempers and their hopes' for 'their bruises, their tempers and their hopes'
p. 84, ll. 2–3, 'it like riddles' for 'it likes riddles'
p. 85, l. 13, '*Toothless bits*' for '*Toothless bites*'
p. 134, l. 32, 'And so do it' for 'And so do I'
p. 138, l. 10, '*on it went.*' for '*on it went*'
p. 152, l. 11, 'lives at times' for 'lived at times'
p. 165, l. 33, '(as he thought;' for '(as he thought)'
p. 168, l. 24, 'feeding none to well' for 'feeding none too well'
p. 208, l. 22, 'travelled with out of the West' for 'travelled with us out of the West'
p. 219, ll. 12–13, 'without a joint or crevice to be seen. ¶ No sign was there' for the same without a paragraph break
p. 291, l. 2, 'beseigers' for 'besiegers'

Four new errors were introduced in A3j: 'the river swollen' for 'the river, swollen', p. 41, l. 9; 'where men live' for 'where men lived', p. 120, l. 17 (cf. A3i, 'where men lives' for 'where men lived'); 'I fear less there' for 'I fear lest there', p. [279], l. 21 after titling; and 'liften Thorin' for 'lifted Thorin', p. 302, l. 22.

On p. 28, ll. 29–30, the reference to *Thror's Map* reads: 'Look at the map at the beginning of this book, and you will see there the runes.' Elrond's statement, p. 62, l. 22, reads 'treasures of old to be found' (cf. A3i, 'treasures to be found').

In January 1963 Tolkien's American publisher, Houghton Mifflin, suggested that a more sumptuous *Hobbit* be published with illustrations by an artist other than Tolkien himself. Tolkien and Allen & Unwin agreed with Houghton Mifflin in principle; all parties found it hard to choose an artist. Rayner Unwin thought that the illustrator should be scrupulous in detail rather than impressionistic, and Austin Olney of Houghton Mifflin felt that the new art should maintain the 'mood' of the original illustrations. Pauline Baynes, illustrator of *Farmer Giles of Ham* (A4), came first to mind among possible artists, but her work was judged too 'delicate' for *The Hobbit*. A sample picture was obtained from noted science fiction illustrator Virgil Finlay, of which Tolkien remarked (letter to Joy Hill, 11 October 1963):

> ... though it gives prospects of a general treatment rather heavier and more violent and airless than I should like, I thought it was good, and actually I thought Bilbo's rather rotund and babyish (but anxious) face was in keeping with his character up to that point. After the horrors of the 'illustrations' to the translations [of *The Hobbit*] Mr Finlay is a welcome relief. As long (as seems likely) he will leave humour to the text and pay reasonable attention to what the text says, I shall I expect be quite happy.

An illustration by Finlay for *The Hobbit* was published in *The Book of Virgil Finlay*, ed. Gerry de la Ree (Saddle River, N.J.: De la Ree, 1975; New York: Avon Books, 1976).

Finlay seems to have abandoned the project, however, for on 20 February 1964 Austin Olney wrote to Tolkien that Houghton Mifflin had a new artist for *The Hobbit*: Maurice Sendak. Sendak had just won the Caldecott Award for *Where the Wild Things Are*, and commanded a high royalty. Houghton Mifflin changed their plans for an illustrated ordinary edition of *The Hobbit* and proposed a limited, deluxe edition which could be sold at a higher price. It would not appear soon, for

Sendak wanted approximately two years to make the illustrations. In the event, a sample sketch (of Bilbo and Gandalf at the door of Bag End) was not received from the artist until January 1967. Tolkien was unhappy about the proportions of Bilbo relative to Gandalf in the sketch (which in fact could be excused by the perspective), but he did not reject Sendak's work outright. In May 1967 Sendak suffered a heart attack during a visit to England, and though he recovered his health and continued to be a productive artist, he seems never to have returned to *The Hobbit*. When Houghton Mifflin published a 'collector's edition' of *The Hobbit* in 1973 (A3l), it was with Tolkien's own illustrations.

Houghton Mifflin's regular trade edition was reset with either the 'twenty-fourth' impression (15,500 copies, published 4 August 1967) or the 'twenty-fifth' impression (20,000 copies, published 13 February 1968). Douglas A. Anderson writes in *The Annotated Hobbit*, p. [321]: 'The American hardcover debut of the further revised text occurred in either the twenty-fourth printing (1967), of which I have yet to see a copy, or the twenty-fifth printing (1968). . . .' I too have not seen (or located) a copy of the 'twenty-fourth printing', and have found no evidence with which to choose conclusively between the two impressions. The 'twenty-fifth printing' is described here by default.

'A Comprehensive Index of Proper Names and Phrases in *The Hobbit*' by Paul Nolan Hyde, *Mythlore*, 17, no. 3, whole no. 65 (Spring 1991), pp. 39–42, applies primarily to A3j and its derivatives (A3l, aa, and dd–ee), and to a lesser extent to A3i and A3m.

An unauthorized reprint of this typesetting, in a smaller format, the text photographically reduced, was published by Bookcase Shop, Taiwan, their imprint shared with George Allen & Unwin, London, with erroneous date '1972'.

k. 'Fourth (school) edition' (1972):

J. R. R. TOLKIEN | THE HOBBIT | *or* | *There and Back Again* | [*facsimile signature, 'J. R. R. Tolkien'*] | Introduced for Schools by R. S. Fowler | *London* | GEORGE ALLEN & UNWIN LTD | Ruskin House Museum Street

xii, 308 pp. Collation: $[1]^8 2–9^8 10^4 11–19^8 [20]^4 [21]^8$. 17.9 × 12.3 cm.

[i] blank; [ii–iii] *Thror's Map*; [iv] blank; [v] 'THE HOBBIT | [*blurb*]'; [vi] '*by J. R. R. Tolkien* | [*7 titles, beginning with* ATB, *ending with* TL] | *By R. S. Fowler and A. J. B. Dick* | [*5 titles, beginning with* English 11/12, *ending with* English 15/ 16]'; [vii] title; [viii] 'First published 1937 | [*list of second–fourth impressions, 1937–46*] | Second edition 1951 | [*list of second–eleventh impressions, 1954–65*] | Third edition 1966 | [*list of second–fourteenth impressions, 1966–72*] | Fourth (school) edition 1972 | [*notice of restrictions under copyright*] | This edition © George Allen & Unwin Ltd, 1972 | ISBN 0 04 823105 3 | PRINTED IN GREAT BRITAIN | *in 10 on 11 point Baskerville* | by The Aldine Press, Letchworth'; [ix] table of contents; [x] blank; [xi] introduction, by R. S. Fowler; [xii] author's note; 1–[279] text; [280] blank; 281–303 ideas and suggestions for study; [304–5] blank; [306–7] *Wilderland* map; [308] blank.

Omits Tolkien's illustrations, except for the maps, in black only, pp. [ii–iii], [306–7].

Wove paper. Bound in limp cloth. Printed on upper cover against a black background: '[*uncials:*] [*in white:*] THE HOBBIT | [*in yellow:*] J. R. R. TOLKIEN | [*rule, in white*] | [*roman, in yellow:*] Introduced for Schools by R. S. Fowler | [*colour illustration by Tolkien*, Conversation with Smaug]'. Printed on spine, running down, against a black background: '[*uncials:*] [*in white:*] THE HOBBIT [*in yellow:*] J. R.

R. TOLKIEN [*roman:*] GEORGE ALLEN [*parallel to the preceding two words:*] & UNWIN'. Lower cover printed solid black. All edges trimmed and unstained.

Published in 1972 at £0.75; date of publication and number of copies not known.

Typeset as for A3h, except pp. [v–ix], [xi], 281–303. The incorrect reference, p. [xii], to Thror's Map ('30 and 63') was later corrected.

l. 'Collector's edition' (1973):

The HOBBIT | [*rule, in green*] | [*in black:*] or There and Back Again | [*decoration, in black, against a green panel*] | [*in black:*] by J. R. R. TOLKIEN | [*rule, in green*] | [*in black:*] Illustrated by the author | HOUGHTON MIFFLIN COMPANY BOSTON

320 pp. + 5 plates. Collation: $[1–10^{16}]$. 22.8 × 17.1 cm.

[1] 'The Hobbit'; [2] blank; [3] title; [4] '*First Printing Collector's Edition* H | COPYRIGHT © 1966 BY J. R. R. TOLKIEN | ALL RIGHTS RESERVED INCLUDING THE RIGHT | TO REPRODUCE THIS BOOK OR PARTS THEREOF IN ANY FORM | LIBRARY OF CONGRESS CARD NUMBER: 73-8769 | ISBN: 0-395-17711-1 | PRINTED IN THE U.S.A.'; [5] table of contents; [6–7] *Thror's Map*; [8] author's note, in black with runic title in green; [9]–317 text and illustrations; [318–19] *Wilderland* map; [320] blank. Rules at table of contents, at chapter titles, and below running heads, and runic titling on p. [8], in green.

Illustrations, by Tolkien, each in black against a green panel, except titles on pp. [48], [67] 121, [184], and [215] are outside the panel: *The Trolls*, p. [48]; *The Mountain-path*, p. [67]; *The Misty Mountains Looking West from the Eyrie towards Goblin Gate*, p. 121; *Beorn's Hall*, p. [130]; *The Elvenking's Gate*, p. [184]; *Lake Town*, [202]; *The Front Gate*, p. [215]; *The Hall at Bag-End, Residence of B. Baggins Esquire*, p. [315]. Colour illustrations, by Tolkien, on 5 plates: *The Hill: Hobbiton-across-the Water*, facing p. 32; *Rivendell*, facing p. 64; *Bilbo Woke up with the Early Sun in His Eyes*, without printed title, facing p. 128; *Bilbo Comes to the Huts of the Raft-elves*, facing p. 192; *Conversation with Smaug*, facing p. [224]. Maps, by Tolkien, each in black against a green panel, pp. [6–7], [318–19].

Wove paper. Bound in dark green imitation leather over boards. Decoration, mountains and trees, stamped on upper cover in gilt, within a gilt single rule frame, within a double frame of red rules, gilt runes within gilt single rule frames, and gilt corner ornaments, the whole within a gilt single rule frame. The runes read, clockwise from lower left: 'THE HOBBIT OR THERE AND BACK AGAIN BEING THE RECORD OF A YEARS JOURNEY BY BILBO BAGGINS CAMPILED [i.e. COMPILED] FROM HIS MEMOIRS'. The incorrect 'A' rune was corrected to 'O' in a later impression. Stamped on spine, running down, in gilt, within a double red rule frame, within a gilt single rule frame: '[*within a gilt single rule frame, in one compartment of the red frame:*] THE HOBBIT BY J. R. R. TOLKIEN HMCo [*parallel to the preceding, within a gilt single rule frame, within the second compartment of the red frame, the same words in runes*]'. Yellow-green laid endpapers. Yellow/green headbands. All edges trimmed and speckled green.

Slipcase, dark green imitation leather over boards. Gold label affixed to right side (open end of case toward viewer), printed in black: 'THE HOBBIT | [*decoration, mountains and trees, against a green panel*] | J. R. R. TOLKIEN'.

Published 24 October 1973 at $12.50; 20,000 copies printed. Houghton Mifflin announced a price of $12.50 until 31 December 1973, $15.00 thereafter, and that 'time permits only one printing before Christmas'. Publisher's records, however, indicate three impressions by 12 October (20,000; 5,000; 5,000).

Typeset as for A3j, except pp. [3–4]. Photographically enlarged.

Also published by the Book-of-the-Month Club.

In 1984 The Easton Press of Norwalk, Connecticut, reprinted this edition as an 'extra' for subscribers to Easton Press series, bound in dark green leather over boards stamped with a design of gilt rules and runes by George Herrick, with gold watered silk endsheets and a gold ribbon marker. Inserted is a specially commissioned colour frontispiece by Michael Hague, of Bilbo, Gandalf, and six dwarves with the Lonely Mountain in the background—a scene which does not occur in Tolkien's text, and which is not included among Hague's illustrations for A3v, w, z, ff.

m. Allen & Unwin hardcover 'third edition' (new 'eighth impression', 1974):

The Hobbit | or | There and Back | Again | by | J. R. R. Tolkien | Illustrated | by the Author | London | George Allen & Unwin Ltd | Ruskin House Museum Street

320 pp. + 5 plates. Collation: [A]^{16}B–K^{16}. 18.5 × 12.2 cm.

Contents as for A3i, except pp. [4] 'FIRST PUBLISHED IN 1937 | [*list of second–fourth impressions, 1937–46*] | SECOND EDITION 1951 | [*list of second–tenth impressions, 1954–63*] | THIRD EDITION 1966 | [*list of second–seventh impressions, 1966–72*] | EIGHTH IMPRESSION 1974 | [*notice of restrictions under copyright*] | *Third Edition* © *George Allen & Unwin*, 1966 | PRINTED IN GREAT BRITAIN BY | COX & WYMAN LTD, LONDON, FAKENHAM AND READING'; [318] advertisement of *LR*; [319] advertisement of *TL, FGH, ATB*; and [320] '[*publisher's square "St. George" device*] | GEORGE ALLEN & UNWIN LTD | *Head Office* | *40 Museum Street, London, W.C.1* | *Telephone: 01-405 8577* | *Sales, Distribution and Accounts Departments:* | *Park Lane, Hemel Hempstead, Hertfordshire* | *Telephone: 0442 3244* | [*20 addresses, Buenos Aires to Barbados*]'.

Illustrations and maps as for A3i, with one additional colour plate, *Bilbo Woke with the Early Sun in His Eyes* (printed title below illustration), facing p. [122].

Wove paper. Bound in dark green textured paper over boards. Stamping as for A3c, in black. Wove endpapers (maps). No headbands. All edges trimmed and unstained.

Dust-jacket not seen, but probably as for A3i as later re-lettered.

Published in 1974; date of publication, price, and number of copies not known.

Reset, based on A3i, page for page but not always line for line, with corrections, but continuing errors and with many new errors introduced. The following errors (or possible errors) were continued from A3i:

   p. 6, l. 10, 'Ratelves' for 'Raft-elves'
   p. 10, l. 1, 'The Bagginses have lived' for 'The Bagginses had lived'
   p. 40, ll. 10–11, 'wild respectable country' for 'wide respectable country'
   p. 61, ll. 3–4, 'uncomfortable palpitating' for 'uncomfortable, palpitating'
   p. 61, l. 32, 'their bruises their tempers and their hopes' for 'their bruises, their tempers and their hopes'
   p. 62, ll. 20–2, 'remnants of old robberies in some hole [*error? for* hold] in the mountains of old [*error? for* of the North]. I have heard that there are still forgotten treasures [*error? omits* of old] to be found'
   p. 84, ll. 2–3, 'It like riddles' for 'It likes riddles'
   p. 85, l. 13, '*Toothless bits*' for '*Toothless bites*'

p. 134, l. 32, 'And so do it' for 'And so do I'
p. 138, ll. 10–11: '*on it went.* | *o'er shaken pool*' for '*on it went* | *o'er shaken pool*'
p. 165, l. 33, '(as he thought;' for '(as he thought)'
p. 168, l. 24, 'feeding none to well' for 'feeding none too well'
p. 219, ll. 12–13, 'without a joint or crevice to be seen. ¶ [*error, paragraph break*] No sign was there'
p. 269, ll. 19–20, 'that old bird understand us' for 'that old bird understands us'
p. 291, l. 2, 'beseigers' for 'besiegers'

Many careless errors were made in the resetting, e.g. 'wizard's' for 'wizards', p. 14, l. 27, and 'my leg ache' for 'my legs ache', p. 109, l. 4. Following are the more significant (or amusing) new errors made in A3m:

p. 80, l. 7, 'what striking of matches' for 'what the striking of matches'
p. 82, l. 18, 'He was a Gollum' for 'He was Gollum'
p. 102, l. 25, 'He had been more trouble' for 'He has been more trouble'
p. 110, l. 2, 'You could have laughed' for 'You would have laughed'
p. 129, l. 16, 'We do not mean to' for 'We did not mean to'
p. 149, l. 32, 'he turned his horses' for 'he turned his horse'
p. 152, l. 11, 'live at times' for 'lived at times' (cf. A3i error, 'lives at times')
p. 165, l. 20, 'Bombur has described' for 'Bombur had described'
p. 167, ll. 2–3, 'stuck it with his sword' for 'struck it with his sword'
p. 183, l. 23, 'sat Elvenking' for 'sat the Elvenking'
p. [201], l. 25 after titling, 'that he had guessed' for 'than he had guessed'
p. 212, l. 3, 'more groan or grumbles' for 'more groans or grumbles'
p. [308], l. 24 after titling, '*Come! Tra-la-la-la-lally!*' for '*Come back to the valley!*'

At least one correction was made in the 'ninth' (1974) or 'tenth' (1975) impression, 'Bilbao's' > 'Bilbo's', p. 11, l. 9.

The 'sixth' impression (1971) of the Allen & Unwin hardcover third edition was printed from the typesetting of A3i; the 'eighth' impression (1974) was printed from new type. I have not seen the 'seventh' impression (1972), and it is possible that A3i was reset at that time. However, since the colour plate *Bilbo Woke* was added to the edition, and since that illustration was copyrighted in 1973, it seems reasonable to conclude that the resetting occurred no earlier than 1973, i.e. in 1974 and not 1972.

n. 'Reset (New Edition)' (1975):

The Hobbit | *or There and Back Again* | J. R. R. TOLKIEN | Illustrated by the Author | UNWIN BOOKS

256 pp. + 2 plates. Collation: 128 leaves. 19.7 × 12.9 cm.

[1] blank; [2–3] *Thror's Map*; [4] blank; [5] '[*publisher's "U" device, repeated, in black and white*] | UNWIN BOOKS | The Hobbit | [*blurb*]'; [6] '*by the same author* | [*3 titles, beginning with* ATB, *ending with* LR] | 1 THE FELLOWSHIP OF THE RING | 2 THE TWO TOWERS | 3 THE RETURN OF THE KING | [*3 titles, beginning with* TL, *ending with* SGPO] | *with Donald Swann* | THE ROAD GOES EVER ON'; [7] title; [8] 'First published in 1937 | Second edition 1951 | Third edition (Unwin Books) 1966 | [*list of second–nineteenth impressions, 1966–74*] | Reset (New Edition) 1975 | [*notice of restrictions under copyright*] | © This edition George Allen & Unwin Ltd, 1975 | ISBN 0 04 823126 6 | UNWIN BOOKS | George Allen & Unwin Ltd | Ruskin House, Museum Street | London W.C.1 | Printed in Great Britain | in 10 on 11 point Plantin | by Cox & Wyman Ltd, | London, Reading

and Fakenham'; [9] table of contents; [10] list of illustrations; [11] author's note; [12] blank; [13]–253 text and illustrations; [254–5] *Wilderland* map; [256] '[*publisher's "U" device, repeated, in black and white*] | UNWIN BOOKS | [*advertisement of* LR *and* Tree and Leaf, Smith of Wootton Major, The Homecoming of Beorhtnoth Beorhthelm's Son]'.

Black and white illustrations, by Tolkien: *The Trolls*, p. [43]; *The Mountain-path*, p. [58]; *The Misty Mountains Looking West from the Eyrie towards Goblin Gate*, p. 99; *Lake Town*, p. [161]; *The Front Gate*, p. [173]; *The Hall at Bag-End, Residence of B. Baggins Esquire*, p. [252]. Colour illustrations, by Tolkien, on 2 plates printed on both sides, inserted between pp. 192–3 and [224]–5 or pp. 32–3 and 64–5: *The Hill: Hobbiton-across-the Water*, facing p. 192 (or 32); *Rivendell*, facing p. 193 (or 33); *Bilbo Comes to the Huts of the Raft-elves*, facing p. [224] (or 64); *Conversation with Smaug*, facing p. 225 (or 65). Maps, by Tolkien, in black only, pp. [2–3], [254–5].

Wove paper. Bound in heavy wove wrappers. Wraparound colour illustration by Tolkien, from his original painting for the dust-jacket of the first edition of *The Hobbit* (cf. A3a, note), with pale green central snowcap and a red sun and red dragon, but re-lettered. Below the illustration, wrapping around covers and spine, is a blue strip, against which is printed the publisher's repeated 'U' device, alternating gold/blue, and at lower left on the upper and lower covers, 'UNWIN BOOKS' in gold. Printed on upper cover in red-orange outlined in black, against the illustration: 'THE | HOBBIT | J. R. R. Tolkien'. Printed on spine, running down, in red-orange, against the illustration and wraparound strip: 'THE HOBBIT J. R. R. Tolkien'. Printed on inside upper cover: 'PRICE NET | £1.50 | IN U.K. ONLY'. All edges trimmed and unstained.

Published 30 October 1975 at £1.50; number of copies not known.

Copies of the first impression of A3n were later sold in a slipcase with *Farmer Giles of Ham [and] The Adventures of Tom Bombadil* (A12) and *Tree and Leaf, Smith of Wootton Major, [and] The Homecoming of Beorhtnoth Beorhthelm's Son* (A13). Sides and spine of slipcase printed against a dark green background, top and bottom printed solid dark green. Printed on left side (open end of case toward viewer): '[*in white:*] TOLKIEN | [*illustration by Tolkien*, The Green Dragon, *in gold, white, and red*] | [*in white:*] The Hobbit | and | Other Stories'. Printed on spine: '[*in white:*] TOLKIEN | [*illustration*, The Green Dragon, *in gold, white, and red*] | [*in white:*] The | Hobbit | and | Other | Stories | [*in red:*] UNWIN | PAPERBACKS'. Printed on right side (open end of case toward viewer): '[*in white:*] TOLKIEN | [*illustration by Tolkien*, The Green Dragon, *in gold, white, and red*] | [*in white:*] The Hobbit | and | Other Stories | [*in dark green, against a white panel:*] ISBN 0 04 823134 7'. Round gold label affixed to bottom edge, printed in black: 'PRICE NET | £3.25 | IN U.K. ONLY'.

   Copies of the first impression were also sold in a six-volume set, *The Tolkien Collection*, in a slipcase with the two volumes noted above plus *LR* (A5j), at £6.95.

Reset, based on A3m, with many corrections but continuing a few errors (e.g. 'The Bagginses have lived' for 'The Bagginses had lived'; 'wild respectable country' for 'wide respectable country'; 'He was a Gollum' for 'He was Gollum') and with many new errors introduced (e.g. 'away from there' for 'away from here', p. 114, l. 21; 'Smaug's rolling eye' for 'Smaug's roving eye', p. 189, l. 29; 'eldest brother' for 'elder brother', p. 242, l. 34). On p. 114, l. 24, the reading 'easy enough, as you remember, to get' disagrees with all earlier editions ('easy enough, as you remember to get') but seems a valid correction. On p. 238, l. 8, the reading 'The Eagles! The Eagles!'

disagrees with most earlier editions (which have 'The Eagles! the Eagles!') but is consistent with the reading two paragraphs earlier (as for all earlier editions).

On *Thror's Map*, the first full word on the second line of 'moon-letters', previously 'hwen' (the Old English form, for 'when'), was altered to read 'when'.

Two different impressions marked 'second impression' (1976) have been seen. In both, the colour plates were omitted and the list of illustrations revised. In (1) the text was otherwise not altered; wrappers as for the first impression, except with red lettering, sun, and dragon, no green on snowcap, and price information (now £1.00) inset in black on the lower cover. In (2), probably the third impression marked 'second impression' in error, now in wrappers featuring *Conversation with Smaug* by Tolkien, many corrections were made (e.g. 'wild respectable country' > 'wide respectable country'). In (2) also the publisher regularized *goodbye* as *good-bye* (except p. 17, l. 10), *good morning* always with 'morning' not 'Morning', and *lookout* as *look-out*. Further corrections were made in the 'third' (1977) or 'fourth' (1977) impression (e.g. 'had not had a meal since the night before last', p. 88, l. 22 > 'had not had a meal since the night before the night before last', p. 88, ll. 22–3).

o. 'De Luxe edition' (1976):

[*in red:*] THE HOBBIT | OR | THERE AND BACK AGAIN | [*in black:*] J. R. R. Tolkien | *London* | GEORGE ALLEN & UNWIN LTD

288 pp. + 15 plates (including maps). Collation: [1–18^8]. 22.1 × 14.2 cm.

[1–2] blank; [3] 'THE HOBBIT'; [4] 'J. R. R. TOLKIEN | DE LUXE EDITIONS | *The Lord of the Rings* | *The Hobbit* | FORTHCOMING | *Poems and Stories*'; [5] title; [6] 'First published in 1937 | Fourth impression 1946 | Second edition 1951 | Tenth impression 1963 | Third edition (paperback) 1966 | Nineteenth impression 1974 | Reset (Fourth edition) 1975 | De Luxe edition 1976 | [*notice of restrictions under copyright*] | © George Allen & Unwin Ltd, 1966, 1975, 1976 | ISBN 0 04 823127 4 | Printed in Great Britain | in 11 point Garamond type | by W & J Mackay Limited, Chatham'; [7] table of contents; [8] blank; [9] list of illustrations; [10] blank; [11]–12 author's note; [13]–286 text; [287–8] blank.

Colour illustrations, by Tolkien (* with colour added by H. E. Riddett), on 13 plates: *The Hill: Hobbiton-across-the Water*, facing p. [5]; *The Trolls**, facing p. 48; *Rivendell*, facing p. 54; *The Mountain-path**, facing p. [62]; *The Misty Mountains Looking West from the Eyrie towards Goblin Gate**, facing p. 110; *Bilbo Woke with the Early Sun in His Eyes*, facing p. [114]; *Beorn's Hall**, facing p. 120; *The Elvenking's Gate**, facing p. 168; *Bilbo Comes to the Huts of the Raft-elves*, facing p. 182; *Lake Town**, facing p. 186; *The Front Gate**, facing p. [194]; *Conversation with Smaug*, facing p. 212; *The Hall at Bag-End, Residence of B. Baggins Esquire**, facing p. 284. Maps, by Tolkien, on 2 plates, each in black and red on a folded leaf: *Thror's Map*, inserted before [1$_1$]; *Wilderland*, inserted after [18$_8$].

Wove paper. Bound in black cloth over boards. Decoration, after *The Green Dragon* by Tolkien (see Ei2, no. 40), stamped on upper cover in gilt, silver, and red. Stamped on spine in gilt, within a gilt single rule frame: '[*2 rules*] | J. R. R. | Tolkien | [*dash*] | THE | HOBBIT | [*8 rules*] | George | Allen | & | Unwin'. Grey and black mottled wove endpapers. Green/white headbands. All edges trimmed and speckled green.

Black paper box. Label affixed to lid, printed: '[*double rule, in black*] | [*in red:*] THE HOBBIT | OR | THERE AND BACK AGAIN | [*in black:*] J. R. R. Tolkien | DE LUXE EDITION | [*double rule*]'.

Published 2 September 1976 at £15.00; number of copies not known.

Reset, based chiefly on the corrected 'second' (i.e. third) impression of A3n, with at least one further correction ('he had not had a meal since the night before last' > 'he had not had a meal since the night before the night before last'), but continuing some earlier errors (e.g. 'wild respectable country' for 'wide respectable country', 'uncomfortable palpitating' for 'uncomfortable, palpitating') as well as the remaining errors of A3n (e.g. 'The Bagginses have lived' for 'The Bagginses had lived', 'He was a Gollum' for 'He was Gollum', 'eldest brother' for 'elder brother'). The text was determined by Allen & Unwin by comparing A3n, A3m, and A3k—but not thoroughly, and some incorrect readings were chosen as 'correct'. In the list of illustrations, credit is not given to Riddett for colouring *The Elvenking's Gate* (corrected in the second impression, 1979).

The 'moon-letters' on *Thror's Map* are printed (altered) as for A3n.

In 1976 the Folio Society, London, used sheets from A3o, with the title page imprint 'GEORGE ALLEN & UNWIN LTD | *for* | THE FOLIO SOCIETY', for the first of two editions published for members of the Society (see also A3r). The 1976 edition was bound in light brown/black cloth over boards with a brown leather spine, stamped in gilt, with 'labyrinth' decorations by Jeff Clements, issued in a slipcase of tan and dark blue 'leather' papers over boards.

Later, impressions of A3o were issued in a slipcase, black cloth over boards.

p. Abrams edition (1977):

[*double-page title spread:*] TEXT BY | J. R. R. TOLKIEN | AND ILLUSTRATIONS FROM THE FILM BY | ARTHUR RANKIN, JR. | AND | JULES BASS | [*colour illustration*] [*two-word title proper extending across facing pages:*] THE HOBBIT [*colour illustration*] | OR THERE AND BACK AGAIN | HARRY N. ABRAMS, INC., PUBLISHERS, NEW YORK

220 pp. Collation: [1–15^{12}6^{4}7^{8}8–9^{12}10^{4}11^{6}12^4]. 26.8 × 28.8 cm.

[1] 'THE HOBBIT | [*colour illustration*]'; [2–3] colour illustration (enlarged detail of illustration on pp. [176]–7); [4–5] colour illustration (enlarged detail of illustration on pp. [60]–1); [6–7] colour illustration (enlarged detail of illustration on pp. [78]–9); [8–9] title; [10] 'Book design: Nai Y. Chung and John S. Lynch | Illustrators: Lester Abrams, Robert Jones, Tsuguyuki Kubo, John S. Lynch, | Gray Morrow, Minoru Nishida, Carol Ann Robson, Walter Simonson, Charles Vess | Library of Congress Catalogue [*sic*] Card Number: 77-78707 | Standard Book Number: 8109-1060-8 | Illustrations © copyright 1977 RANKIN/BASS PRODUCTIONS, INC., New York. All rights reserved | Published in 1977 by Harry N. Abrams, Incorporated, New York | Text © 1966 by J. R. R. Tolkien, published by arrangement with Houghton Mifflin Company | This edition is not authorized for distribution outside the United States of America, its territories and possessions, and Canada | Printed and bound in the United States of America'; [10–11] *Thror's Map*, after Tolkien, in colour; [12–13] *Wilderland* map, after Tolkien, in colour; [14–15] table of contents, with 3 colour illustrations; [16]–220 text and illustrations, most illustrations in colour.

Wove paper. Bound in paper over boards. Colour illustration, of dwarves ascending a mountain path, as on pp. 52–[3], printed on upper cover. Colour illustration, of Smaug's hoard, as on p. [173], printed on lower cover. Printed on spine: 'J. R. R. | TOLKIEN | [*running down:*] THE HOBBIT | [*horizontal:*] ABRAMS'. Wove endpapers. Pastedowns, recto, front free endpaper, and verso, back free endpaper printed solid black, except with colour illustration of Bilbo with smoke rings printed on recto, front free endpaper, and colour illustration of Bilbo seated at a table printed on verso, back free endpaper. Blue/white headbands. All edges trimmed and unstained.

Acetate dust-jacket. Printed on upper cover: '[*colour illustration, of the dragon Smaug in flight*] | [*in white:*] THE HOBBIT | AN ILLUSTRATED EDITION WITH TEXT BY | J. R. R. TOLKIEN'. Printed on lower cover: '[*colour illustration of Smaug, after the illustration on pp. [156]–7*] | [*at left, illustration of Bilbo 'invisible', in black and white; at right, in white:*] THE HOBBIT | AN ILLUSTRATED EDITION WITH TEXT BY | J. R. R. TOLKIEN'. Printed on front flap in white: '[*blurb*] | *Over 230 illustrations in full color* | This edition is not authorized for distribution outside the | United States of America, its territories and possessions and | Canada.' Printed on back flap in white: 'Some Other Abrams Artbooks | [*advertisement of 7 titles, beginning with Huygen and Poortvliet,* Gnomes, *ending with Descharnes,* Dali] | Prices subject to change without notice | Write for a complete catalogue of Abrams | Artbooks | Harry N. Abrams, Inc. | 110 East 59th Street, New York, N.Y. 10022 | Printed in the United States of America | 8109-1060-8'.

Published October 1977 at $29.95; 40,000 copies printed.

Reset, based on a later impression of A3g, continuing its errors (e.g. 'the fabulous [*for* famous] Belladonna Took', 'wild respectable country' for 'wide respectable country') but with 'odd-looking' corrected to 'old-looking' and without the later errors of A3g.

The first 3 leaves of gatherings [6] and [10] fold out as large illustrations. Each of these gatherings is inserted along the fold between its third and fourth leaves.

Illustrated with sketches and finished paintings from the Rankin/Bass animated television motion picture, *The Hobbit*, screenplay by Romeo Muller, first broadcast in the United States on 27 November 1977. The film was later issued on videocassette.

In 1989 Galahad Books, New York, reprinted A3p in a smaller format, without foldout illustrations, bound in red textured paper over boards, stamped in gilt, in a dust-jacket combining the binding and jacket illustrations of the Abrams edition except the 'invisible' Bilbo.

q. New Ballantine Books edition (1978):

[*double-page title spread:*] TEXT BY | J. R. R. TOLKIEN | AND ILLUSTRATIONS FROM THE FILM BY | ARTHUR RANKIN, JR. | AND | JULES BASS | [*colour illustration*] [*two-word title proper extends across facing pages:*] THE HOBBIT [*colour illustration*] | OR THERE AND BACK AGAIN | BALLANTINE BOOKS • NEW YORK

ii, 222 pp. Collation: 112 leaves. 22.6 × 24.0 cm.

[i] colour illustration, against a black background; [ii] blank; [1] 'THE HOBBIT | [*colour illustration*]'; [2–3] colour illustration (enlarged detail of illustration on pp. [176]–7); [4–5] colour illustration (enlarged detail of illustration on pp. [60]–1); [6–7] colour illustration (enlarged detail of illustration on pp. [78]–9); [8–9] title; [10] 'Book design: Nai Y. Chung and John S. Lynch | Illustrators: Lester Abrams, Robert Jones, Tsuguyuki Kubo, John S. Lynch, Gray Morrow, Minoru Nishida, | Carol Ann Robson, Walter Simonson, Charles Vess. | Illustrations © copyright 1977 RANKIN/BASS PRODUCTIONS, INC., New York. All rights reserved. | Published in 1977 by Harry N. Abrams, Incorporated, New York | Text © 1966 by J. R. R. Tolkien, published by arrangement with Houghton Mifflin Company | All

rights reserved under International and Pan-American Copyright Conventions. Published in the United | States by Ballantine Books, a division of Random House, Inc., New York. | Library of Congress Catalog Card Number: 77-78707 | ISBN 0-345-27711-2 | This edition published by arrangement with Harry N. Abrams, Inc., Publishers | Manufactured in the United States of America | First Ballantine Books Edition: September 1978'; [10–11] *Thror's Map*, after Tolkien, in colour; [12–13] *Wilderland* map, after Tolkien, in colour; [14–15] table of contents, with 3 colour illustrations; [16]–220 text and illustrations, most illustrations in colour; [221] blank; [222] colour illustration, against a black background.

Wove paper. Bound in heavy wove wrappers. Printed on upper cover: '[*at upper right:*] [*publisher's "BB" device, in white and black*] | Ballantine | 27711 | $8.95 [*at centre of cover:*] J. R. R. TOLKIEN'S | [*in yellow-orange outlined in dark brown, partly against the illustration:*] THE | HOBBIT | OR THERE AND BACK AGAIN | [*colour illustration, of dwarves ascending a mountain path with the dragon Smaug flying overhead (composite of upper cover and jacket of A3p), outlined in dark brown*] | [*below illustration, in black:*] THE DELUXE EDITION OF THE WORLD'S MOST BELOVED FANTASY | With over 230 full-color illustrations from the great animated film spectacle by Arthur Rankin, Jr., and Jules Bass'. Printed on spine: '[*publisher's "BB" device, in white and black*] | [*running down:*] [*in dark brown:*] THE HOBBIT J. R. R. TOLKIEN [*in black:*] ART BY RANKIN/ BASS 345-27711-2-895'. Printed on lower cover: '[*in dark brown:*] THE MAGIC, THE MYSTERY, THE MARVELS OF MIDDLE-EARTH | COME COLORFULLY ALIVE! | [*colour illustrations of the hobbit Bilbo and six dwarves, partly flanking the blurb*] | [*in black:*] [*blurb*] | [*at lower right, running down:*] Cover printed in USA'. All edges trimmed and unstained.

Published September 1978 at $8.95; number of copies not known.

Typeset as for A3p, except pp. [8–10]. Illustrations as for A3p.
  Published in Canada in 1978 by Methuen, Toronto.

r. 'Fourth edition' (1978):

[*2 lines in runes, each line between single rules*] | THE HOBBIT | OR | THERE AND BACK AGAIN | by | J. R. R. Tolkien | Illustrated | by the Author | London | GEORGE ALLEN & UNWIN | Boston Sydney | [*2 lines in runes, each line between single rules*]

256 pp. + 5 plates. Collation: [1–2⁸3–9¹⁶]. 22.1 × 14.1 cm.

[1–2] blank; [3] 'THE HOBBIT | [*decoration*]'; [4] '[*2 lines in runes, each line between single rules*] | *also by J. R. R. Tolkien* | [*11 titles, beginning with* ATB, *ending with* Silm] | *with Donald Swann* | THE ROAD GOES EVER ON | [*2 lines in runes, each line between single rules*]'; [5] title; [6] 'First published in 1937 | Fourth impression 1946 | Second edition 1951 | Tenth impression 1963 | Third edition 1966 | Tenth impression 1975 | Fourth edition 1978 | [*notice of restrictions under copyright*] | GEORGE ALLEN & UNWIN LTD | 40 Museum Street, London WC1A 1LU | Fourth edition © George Allen & Unwin (Publishers) Ltd, 1978 | [*British Library Cataloguing in Publication Data, within a single rule frame*] | Printed in Great Britain in 11 on 12 point Times type | by William Clowes & Sons Limited | London, Beccles and Colchester'; [7] table of contents; [8] list of illustrations; 9–10 author's note; 11–256 text and illustrations.

Black and white illustrations, by Tolkien: dragon looking left, p. [3], as for the binding of A3a; *The Trolls*, p. 43; *The Mountain-path*, p. 56; *The Misty Mountains*

Looking West from the Eyrie towards Goblin Gate, p. 98; *Beorn's Hall*, p. 108; *The Elvenking's Gate*, p. 149; *Lake Town*, p. 163; *The Front Gate*, p. 174; *The Hall at Bag-End, Residence of B. Baggins Esquire*, p. 256. Colour illustrations, by Tolkien, on 5 plates: *The Hill: Hobbiton-across-the Water*, facing p. 32; *Rivendell*, facing p. 64; *Bilbo Woke with the Early Sun in His Eyes* (title in type below illustration), facing p. 96; *Bilbo Comes to the Huts of the Raft-elves*, facing p. 160; *Conversation with Smaug*, facing p. 192. Maps, by Tolkien, in black only: *Thror's Map*, front endsheet; *Wilderland*, back endsheet.

Wove paper. Bound in dark green cloth over boards. Stamped on spine in gilt: '[TH *rune*] | [D *rune*] | [TH *rune*] | The | Hobbit | J. R. R. | TOLKIEN | GEORGE ALLEN | AND UNWIN'. Wove endpapers (maps). No headbands. All edges trimmed. Top edge stained dark green, fore- and bottom edges unstained.

Dust-jacket, wove paper. Covers and spine as for A3i as re-lettered. Printed on front flap: '[*blurb*] | *All the illustrations in this book are by* | *the author.* | PRICE NET | £3.95 | IN U.K. ONLY'. Printed on back flap: '*by J. R. R. Tolkien* | [*12 titles, beginning with* LR, *ending with* FCL] | also | J. R. R. Tolkien: A Biography | Humphrey Carpenter | ISBN 0 04 823147 9 | *Printed in Great Britain*'.

Published September 1978 at £3.95; number of copies not known.

Sold separately and in a set with *LR* (A5e) and *Silm* (A15a), *The Tolkien Library*, at £24.00. Slipcase, paper (sides and spine) and dark green cloth (top and bottom) over boards. Sides and spine printed against a dark green background. Printed on left side (open end of case toward viewer): '[*in white:*] THE | TOLKIEN | ["*JRRT*" *monogram, in gold and grey, within a grey single rule circle, within a gold single rule circle*] | [*in white:*] LIBRARY | ISBN 0 04 823158 4'. Right side printed as for left side, except without the ISBN. Printed on spine: '[*in white:*] THE | TOLKIEN | [*colour photograph of Tolkien, within a grey single rule circle, within a gold single rule circle*] | [*in white:*] LIBRARY | [*in gold:*] George Allen & Unwin'.

Reset. Text as for A3n as corrected in, and after, the 'second' (i.e. third) impression, with 'wide respectable country', 'uncomfortable, palpitating', 'had not had a meal since the night before the night before last', etc. correct, but continuing the remaining errors of A3n (e.g. 'The Bagginses have lived' for 'The Bagginses had lived', 'He was a Gollum' for 'He was Gollum', 'eldest brother' for 'elder brother'). The runic inscription on *Thror's Map* is printed in its earlier (unaltered) form.

 A book club edition was published in 1978 by Guild Publishing, London, without colour plates, bound in dark red imitation leather over boards, stamped in gilt, without dust-jacket.

 Reprinted, photographically enlarged, in 1982 by F. A. Thorpe, Leicester, in the Charnwood Library Series of large-print books, bound in paper over boards with colour illustration by Tolkien, *Conversation with Smaug*, without dust-jacket.

s. 'Reset third paperback edition' (1979):

The Hobbit | *or There and Back Again* | J. R. R. TOLKIEN | Illustrated by the Author | London | UNWIN PAPERBACKS | Boston Sydney

288 pp. Collation: 144 leaves. 17.8 × 11.2 cm.

[1] blurb; [2–3] *Thror's Map*; [4] '*also by J. R. R. Tolkien* | [*10 titles, beginning with* LR, *ending with* SGPO] | *with Donald Swann* | THE ROAD GOES EVER ON'; [5] title; [6] 'First published in Great Britain by George Allen & Unwin 1937 | Second edition 1951 | Reprinted eighteen times | First published in Unwin Paperbacks 1975 |

Reprinted five times | Reset third paperback edition 1979 | [*notice of restrictions under copyright*] | UNWIN® PAPERBACKS | 40 Museum Street, London WC1A 1LU | © George Allen & Unwin (Publishers) Ltd 1979 | [*British Library Cataloguing in Publication Data, within a single rule frame*] | Typeset in 10 on 11 point Times | and printed in Great Britain | by Cox & Wyman Ltd, London, Reading and Fakenham'; [7] table of contents; [8] blank; [9] list of illustrations; [10] blank; [11] author's note; [12] blank; [13]–285 text and illustrations; [286–7] *Wilderland* map; [288] '*Also by J. R. R. Tolkien* | [*advertisement of* LR, Silm, ATB, RGEO]'.

Illustrations, by Tolkien: *The Trolls*, p. [47]; *The Mountain-path*, p. [64]; *The Misty Mountains Looking West from the Eyrie towards Goblin Gate*, p. 111; *Beorn's Hall*, p. [119]; *The Elvenking's Gate*, p. [166]; *Lake Town*, p. [182]; *The Front Gate*, p. [195]; *The Hall at Bag-End, Residence of B. Baggins Esquire*, p. [283]. Maps, by Tolkien, in black only, pp. [2–3], [286–7].

Wove paper. Bound in heavy wove wrappers. Covers and spine printed against a brown background. Printed on upper cover: '[*in orange:*] TOLKIEN | [*in white:*] The Hobbit | [*colour illustration by Tolkien, detail from* Conversation with Smaug, *outlined in white, partly overlapping the outline at left and right*] | [*publisher's "unwin" device, in orange, white, and black*]'. Printed on spine, running down: '[*in orange:*] TOLKIEN [*in white:*] The Hobbit [*publisher's "unwin" device, in orange, white, and black*]'. Printed on lower cover against an orange panel outlined in white: '[*4 quotations, from the* Times Literary Supplement, *London* Times, Daily Mail, *and* Observer] | [*at left:*] UNITED KINGDOM £0.85 | AUSTRALIA $2.50 (Recommended) | CANADA $2.75 [*at right:*] CHILDREN/ | TOLKIEN/FANTASY | ISBN 0 04 823154 1'. All edges trimmed and unstained.

Published March 1979 at £0.85; number of copies not known.

Copies of the first impression of A3s were later sold in a box with *LR* (A5n), in the set *Stories from the Third Age*. All sides of box printed against a dark blue background. Printed on main flap: '[*in orange:*] Tolkien | [*in white:*] The Hobbit | [*rule, in orange*] | [*in white:*] The Lord of | the Rings | [*rule, in orange*] | [*publisher's "unwin" device, in orange, white, and black, outlined in white*]'. Printed on right side (main flap towards viewer): '[*in orange:*] Tolkien | [*in white:*] Stories from | the Third Age | [*colour photograph of Tolkien, overprinted in black:*] Picture: Billett Potter'. Left side printed as for right side, except without credit line. Printed on rear flap: '[*in orange:*] 4 | books | Tolkien | [*in white:*] The Hobbit | The Fellowship of the Ring | The Two Towers | The Return of the King | [*in orange:*] 4 | books | [*in white:*] UNWIN PAPERBACKS | 0 04 823169 X | *Printed in the United Kingdom*'. Printed on top in orange: 'Tolkien'. Bottom printed as for top, with round gold label affixed, printed in black: 'U.K. | £3.95 | INC. BOX'.

Copies of the first impression were also later sold in a box with *LR* (A5n) and *Silm* (A15f), in the set *The Middle-earth Collection*. All sides of box printed against a dark brown background. Printed on main flap: '[*in blue:*] Tolkien | [*in white:*] The Hobbit | [*rule, in blue*] | [*in white:*] The Lord of | the Rings | [*rule, in blue*] | [*in white:*] The | Silmarillion | [*rule, in blue*] | [*publisher's "unwin" device, in blue, white, and black, outlined in white*]'. Printed on right side (main flap towards viewer): '[*in blue:*] Tolkien | [*in white:*] The Middle-earth | Collection | [*colour photograph of Tolkien, overprinted in black:*] Picture by John Wyatt/Transworld Features'. Left side printed as for right side, except without credit line. Printed on rear flap: '[*in blue:*] 5 | books | Tolkien | [*in white:*] The Hobbit | The Fellowship of the Ring | The Two Towers | The Return of the King | The Silmarillion | [*in blue:*] 5 | books | [*in white:*] UNWIN PAPERBACKS | 0 04 823170 3 | *Printed in the United*

Kingdom'. Printed on top in blue: 'Tolkien'. Bottom printed as for top, with round gold label affixed, printed in black: 'U.K. | £5.20 | INC. BOX'.

Reset, based on a later impression of A3n, with 'wide respectable country', 'uncomfortable, palpitating', 'had not had a meal since the night before the night before last', etc. correct, but continuing the remaining errors of A3n (e.g. 'The Bagginses have lived' for 'The Bagginses had lived', 'He was a Gollum' for 'He was Gollum', 'eldest brother' for 'elder brother'). The runic inscription on *Thror's Map* is printed in its earlier (unaltered) form.

Published in Canada by Unwin Paperbacks in wrappers with different lettering and a black background.

A3s was reprinted, beginning in 1981, as the Unwin Paperbacks 'Fourth edition', bound in wrappers featuring *Conversation with Smaug* by Tolkien. With the twentieth impression (1987) the cover was changed to feature a colour illustration by Roger Garland, of Smaug, with a legend marking the fiftieth anniversary of *The Hobbit*. Subsequent impressions retained the Garland painting but not the anniversary legend. With the twenty-fifth impression (1989) the cover was changed to feature a colour illustration by Ted Nasmith, of Rivendell.

A 1987 impression of Unwin sheets was issued in new wrappers by ELT, Hamburg, as Bd. 33 in *Klassiker des Gebrauchs an Schule und Universität*.

Later published by HarperCollins under the Grafton Books imprint, with new preliminaries and impression numbering. In 1991 the cover was changed to feature a colour illustration by John Howe, of Smaug.

t. Houghton Mifflin trade paperback edition (1979):

The Hobbit | or | There and Back | Again | by | J. R. R. Tolkien | Illustrated | by the Author | BOSTON | HOUGHTON MIFFLIN COMPANY | 1979

320 pp. Collation: 160 leaves. 20.8 × 13.5 cm.

[1] 'The Hobbit'; [2] 'BOOKS BY | J. R. R. TOLKIEN | [*12 titles, beginning with* H, *ending with* Silm]'; [3] title; [4] 'COPYRIGHT © 1966 BY J. R. R. TOLKIEN | ALL RIGHTS RESERVED INCLUDING THE RIGHT TO | REPRODUCE THIS BOOK OR PARTS THEREOF IN ANY FORM | LIBRARY OF CONGRESS CATALOG CARD NUMBER: 67–29221 | ISBN 0-395-07122-4 | ISBN 0-395-28265-9 PBK | PRINTED IN THE UNITED STATES OF AMERICA | [*printing code, beginning* "M", *ending* "1"]'; [5] table of contents; [6–7] *Thror's Map*; [8] author's note; [9]–317 text and illustrations; [318–19] *Wilderland* map; [320] blank.

Illustrations, by Tolkien: *The Trolls*, p. [48]; *The Mountain-path*, p. [67]; *The Misty Mountains Looking West from the Eyrie towards Goblin Gate*, p. 121; *Beorn's Hall*, p. [130]; *The Elvenking's Gate*, p. [184]; *Lake Town*, p. [202]; *The Front Gate*, p. [215]; *The Hall at Bag-End, Residence of B. Baggins Esquire*, p. [315]. Maps, by Tolkien, in black only, pp. [6–7], [318–19].

Wove paper. Bound in heavy wove wrappers. Covers and spine printed against a gold background. Printed on upper cover: '[*facsimile signature, "J. R. R. Tolkien"*] | [*in red:*] THE | HOBBIT | [*decoration, the Lonely Mountain (after the jacket spine of A3a etc.), in black*]'. Printed on spine: '[*running down, in red:*] THE HOBBIT | [*decoration, as for cover, horizontal, in black*] | [*running down, in red:*] J. R. R. TOLKIEN [*parallel to the name:*] HOUGHTON MIFFLIN COMPANY | [*publisher's "dolphin" device, horizontal*]'. Printed on lower cover: '[*in red:*] "All those, young or old, who love a finely | imagined story, beautifully told, will take | The Hobbit to their hearts."—HORN BOOK | [*in black:*] [*blurb*] | ISBN 0-395-28265-9

| [*rule*] | 6-97090 | HOUGHTON MIFFLIN COMPANY © 1979'. All edges trimmed and unstained.

Issued with *LR* (A5m) in slipcase, printed paper over boards. Sides and spine printed against a green background, top and bottom printed solid green. Facsimile signature, 'J. R. R. Tolkien', in tan, above 'Ring and Eye' device, in black, red, tan, and white, printed on left side (open end of case toward viewer). Printed on spine: '[*in tan:*] THE | HOBBIT | [*"Ring and Eye" device, in black, red, tan, and white*] | [*in tan:*] THE | LORD | OF THE | RINGS | HOUGHTON MIFFLIN COMPANY © 1979 | [*publisher's "dolphin" device*] | ISBN: 0-395-28263-2 | [*rule*] | 6-97084'. Facsimile signature, 'J. R. R. Tolkien', in tan, above a detail of the Lonely Mountain from the *Hobbit* dust-jacket, in black, red, tan, and white outlined in black, printed on right side (open end of case toward viewer).

Published October 1979; number of copies not known. Announced in *Publishers Weekly* as issued in a set with *LR* (A5m) at $18.95.

Typeset as for A3j, except pp. [2–4]. Beginning no later than the fourth impression, the trade paperback became a reprint of the 1978 Allen & Unwin resetting (A3r), i.e. A3x.

u. Second Folio Society edition (1979):

J. R. R. TOLKIEN | [*uncials:*] THE HOBBIT | [*roman:*] or There and Back Again | Illustrations by | ERIC FRASER | LONDON | THE FOLIO SOCIETY | 1979

248 pp. Collation: [1–14⁸15⁴16⁸]. 22.1 × 14.3 cm.

[1] 'THE HOBBIT'; [2] illustration; [3] title; [4] '© *Text copyright George Allen & Unwin Ltd 1966* | © *Illustrations copyright The Folio Society Ltd 1979* | *The text of this edition is used by kind permission of* | *George Allen & Unwin Ltd* | PRINTED IN GREAT BRITAIN | *by W & J Mackay Limited, Chatham*'; [5] table of contents; [6] blank; [7]–8 author's note; [9] illustration; [10] blank; [11]–245 text and illustrations; [246] 'SET IN 11 POINT BARBOU LEADED 1 POINT | WITH LIBRA FOR DISPLAY | AND PRINTED BY W & J MACKAY LIMITED | ON WHITE CARTRIDGE PAPER | BOUND BY W & J MACKAY LIMITED | IN QUARTER ART LEATHER WITH SCHOLCO | ALMOLINE CLOTH SIDES | BLOCKED WITH A SPECIAL DESIGN | BY JEFF CLEMENTS'; [247–8] blank.

Wove paper. Bound in wine red cloth over boards, with dark wine red leather spine. 'Labyrinth' decoration stamped on upper cover in gilt. Stamped on spine in gilt: '[*"labyrinth" decoration*] | [*running up:*] J. R. R. Tolkien [*parallel to the author's name:*] The Hobbit'. Wove endpapers, in black and wine red: *Thror's Map*, by Tolkien, front endsheet; *Wilderland* map, by Tolkien, back endsheet. Wine red/white headband. All edges trimmed. Top edge stained wine red, fore- and bottom edges unstained.

Slipcase, light grey 'leather' paper over boards.

Published October? 1979 at £8.50; number of copies not known.

The second Folio Society edition, reset and with new illustrations. Text as for A3o, but with 'uncomfortable, palpitating' correct.

The binding repeats the earlier Folio Society design by Jeff Clements (see A3o note), with changes in colour.

v. Allen & Unwin illustrated edition (1984):

J. R. R. TOLKIEN | *The* | HOBBIT | [*thick-thin rule*] | *or, There and Back Again* | *Illustrated by Michael Hague* | London | GEORGE ALLEN & UNWIN | Boston Sydney

x, 294 pp. Collation: [1⁸2–13¹²]. 25.4 × 20.2 cm.

[i] '*The* | HOBBIT | [*thick-thin rule*]'; [ii] colour illustration; [iii] title; [iv] 'First published in Great Britain 1984 | This book is copyright under the Berne Convention. | No reproduction without permission. | All rights reserved. | Copyright © George Allen & Unwin (Publishers) Ltd 1937, 1951, 1966 | Illustrations copyright © 1984 by Oak, Ash & Thorn, Ltd | [*3 publisher's addresses, London to North Sydney*] | ISBN 0 04 823273 4'; [v] table of contents; [vi] blank; [vii] *Wilderland* map, by Tolkien; [viii] author's note; [ix] *Thror's Map*, by Tolkien; [x] colour illustration; 1–290 text and colour illustrations; [291–4] blank.

All illustrations are by Hague and in colour, except two maps by Tolkien, in black only, pp. [vii], [ix].

Wove paper. Bound in green imitation leather over boards. 'JRRT' monogram stamped on upper cover in gilt. Stamped on spine, running down, in gilt: '*The* HOBBIT J. R. R. TOLKIEN GEORGE ALLEN & UNWIN'. Wove endpapers. Green/yellow headbands. All edges trimmed and unstained.

Dust-jacket, wove paper. Printed on upper cover against a dark green background: '[*in light yellow:*] *The* | HOBBIT | J. R. R. TOLKIEN | [*colour illustration by Hague, of the dragon Smaug upon his hoard, detail from illustration on pp.* [208–9], *outlined in white*] | [*in light yellow:*] *Illustrated by Michael Hague*'. Printed on spine, running down, in light yellow, against a dark green background: '*The* HOBBIT J. R. R. TOLKIEN GEORGE ALLEN & UNWIN'. Lower cover printed solid dark green. Printed on front flap: '[*blurb*] | £11.95 | NET | IN U.K. ONLY'. Printed on back flap: '[*note on Tolkien*] | ISBN 0 04 823273 4'.

Published 27 September 1984 at £11.95; number of copies not known.

Reset, based on A3i, with a few corrections (e.g. '*Toothless bits*' > '*Toothless bites*'; 'And so do it' > 'And so do I'), but with new errors ('where men live [*for* lived]', p. 103, l. 9; 'live [*for* lived] at times', p. 130, l. 4).

w. Houghton Mifflin illustrated edition (1984):

J. R. R. TOLKIEN | *The* | HOBBIT | [*thick-thin rule*] | *or, There and Back Again* | *Illustrated by Michael Hague* | Houghton Mifflin Company Boston 1984

x, 294 pp. Collation: [1⁸2–13¹²]. 25.4 × 20.3 cm.

Contents as for A3v, except pp. [iii] title, as above; and [iv] 'Copyright © 1966 by J. R. R. Tolkien | Illustrations copyright © 1984 by Oak, Ash & Thorn, Ltd. | All rights reserved. | [*notice of restrictions under copyright*] | [*Library of Congress Cataloging in Publication Data*] | Printed in Italy | [*printing code, beginning "10", ending "1"*]'.

Wove paper. Binding as for A3v, except stamped on spine, running down, in gilt: '*The* HOBBIT J. R. R. TOLKIEN Houghton Mifflin Company'.

Dust-jacket, wove paper. Covers and spine printed against a dark green background. Upper cover as for A3v. Printed on spine, running down, in light yellow: '*The*

HOBBIT J. R. R. TOLKIEN Houghton Mifflin Company'. Printed on lower cover: '[*at left, in white:*] 5–97092 [*at right, in black, against a white panel:*] ISBN 0-395-36290-3'. Printed on front flap: 'FPT ISBN 0-395-36290-3 >>$19.95 | [*blurb*] | 10194584'. Printed on back flap: '*Critics have said of J. R. R. Tolkien's work:* | [4 *quotations, from the* New York Times Book Review *(Auden),* Nation, New York Times Book Review *(Barr), and* New York Herald Tribune Book World] | *And of Michael Hague's previous books:* | [4 *quotations, from* Booklist, Publishers Weekly, *the* Los Angeles Times, *and the* New York Times Book Review] | *Jacket* © 1984 *by Oak, Ash & Thorn, Ltd.*'

Published 29 October 1984 at $19.95; 81,000 copies printed.

Typeset as for A3v, except pp. [iii–iv]. Illustrations as for A3v.

x. New Houghton Mifflin edition ('fortieth printing', 1985):

[2 *lines in runes, each line between single rules*] | THE HOBBIT | OR | THERE AND BACK AGAIN | by | J. R. R. Tolkien | Illustrated | by the Author | Houghton Mifflin Company | Boston | [2 *lines in runes, each line between single rules*]

256 pp. Collation: [1–8^{16}]. 20.3 × 13.8 cm.

[1–2] blank; [3] 'THE HOBBIT | [*decoration*]'; [4] '[2 *lines in runes, each line between single rules*] | *by J. R. R. Tolkien* | [18 *titles, beginning with* The Hobbit De-luxe, *ending with* TL] | *also* | J. R. R. TOLKIEN: A BIOGRAPHY | HUMPHREY CARPENTER | [2 *lines in runes, each line between single rules*]'; [5] title; [6] 'The text of this edition of *The Hobbit* contains all revi- | sions and corrections that have been made since the | original publication and conforms in every respect to | that of the British Fourth Edition published by George | Allen & Unwin in 1978. | Copyright © 1966 by J. R. R. Tolkien | [*notice of restrictions under copyright*] | Library of Congress Card Catalog [*sic*] Number: 67-29221 | ISBN 0-395-07122-4 | Printed in the United States of America | A 40th printing'; [7] table of contents; [8] list of illustrations; 9–10 author's note; 11–256 text and illustrations.

Black and white illustrations by Tolkien as for A3r. Maps, by Tolkien, in black only: *Thror's Map*, front endsheet; *Wilderland*, back endsheet.

Wove paper. Bound in green cloth over boards. Stamped on upper cover in dark blue: 'THE | HOBBIT'. Stamped on spine in dark blue: '[*running down:*] THE HOBBIT | [*decoration, a dwarvish cap, horizontal*] | [*running down:*] TOLKIEN HOUGHTON MIFFLIN CO.' Wove endpapers (maps). Yellow/green headbands. All edges trimmed and unstained.

Dust-jacket, wove paper. Covers and spine as for A3j, with the addition of 'ISBN 0-395-07122-4' printed at the foot of the lower cover in black, against a white panel, against the illustration. Printed on front flap: 'FPT ISBN 0-395-07122-4 >$13.95 | THE HOBBIT | [*blurb*] | The text of this edition of THE | HOBBIT contains all revisions and | corrections that have been made | since the original publication and | conforms in every respect to that | of the British Fourth Edition pub- | lished by George Allen & Unwin | in 1978. | All ages | 04134585'. Printed on back flap: 'Also by J. R. R. Tolkien | [19 *titles, beginning with* LR, *ending with* The Monsters and the Critics and Other Essays]'.

Published in 1985 at $13.95; date of publication and number of copies not known.

Typeset as for A3r, except pp. [4–6].

y. Unwin Hyman fiftieth anniversary edition (1987):

[2 *lines in runes, each line between single rules*] | THE HOBBIT | OR | THERE AND BACK AGAIN | by | J. R. R. Tolkien | Illustrated | by the Author | UNWIN HYMAN | London Sydney | [2 *lines in runes, each line between single rules*]

8, xvi, 9–256 pp. + 6 plates. Collation: [1^{16}2^{8}3–9^{16}]. 22.1 × 14.1 cm.

[1–2] blank; [3] 'THE HOBBIT | [*decoration*]'; [4] '[2 *lines in runes, each line between single rules*] | *by J. R. R. Tolkien* | [18 *titles, beginning with* The Hobbit De-Luxe, *ending with* TL] | *also* | J. R. R. TOLKIEN: A BIOGRAPHY | HUMPHREY CARPENTER | [2 *lines in runes, each line between single rules*]'; [5] title; [6] 'First published by George Allen & Unwin 1937 | Fourth impression 1946 | Second edition 1951 | Tenth impression 1963 | Third edition 1966 | Tenth impression 1975 | Fourth edition 1978 | Fifth impression 1985 | This anniversary edition published by Unwin Hyman, an imprint of | Unwin Hyman Limited, 1987 | Fourth edition © George Allen & Unwin (Publishers) Ltd 1978 | Foreword © Christopher Tolkien 1987 | [*notice of restrictions*] | [4 *publisher's addresses, London (Denmark Street) to Wellington*] | [*rule*] | [*British Library Cataloguing in Publication Data*] | [*rule*] | Printed in Great Britain by Mackays of Chatham Ltd'; [7] table of contents; [8] list of illustrations; i–xvi foreword, by Christopher Tolkien; 9–10 author's note; 11–256 text and illustrations.

Black and white illustrations, by Tolkien: dragon looking left (cf. A3a), p. [3]; sheet from the first manuscript draft of *The Hobbit*, including 'the first sketch of Thror's Map,' pp. ii–iii; drawing, *Gate of the Elvenking's Halls*, p. viii; schematic drawing of the Lonely Mountain, p. xii; a sketch of 'The Back Door,' p. xiii; a sketch of the exterior of Bag-End, p. xiv; *Mirkwood*, plate facing p. ix; drawing, *The Lonely Mountain*, p. [xi]; *The Trolls*, p. 43; *The Mountain-path*, p. 56; *The Misty Mountains Looking West from the Eyrie towards Goblin Gate*, p. 98; *Beorn's Hall*, p. 108; *The Elvenking's Gate*, p. 149; *Lake Town*, p. 163; *The Front Gate*, p. 174; *The Hall at Bag-End, Residence of B. Baggins Esquire*, p. 256. Colour illustrations, by Tolkien, on 5 plates: *The Hill: Hobbiton-across-the Water*, facing p. 32; *Rivendell*, facing p. 64; *Bilbo Woke with the Early Sun in His Eyes* (title in type below illustration), facing p. 96; *Bilbo Comes to the Huts of the Raft-elves*, facing p. 160; *Conversation with Smaug*, facing p. 192. Maps, by Tolkien, in black and red: *Thror's Map*, front endsheet; *Wilderland*, back endsheet.

Wove paper. Bound in green textured paper over boards. Stamped on spine in gilt: '[TH *rune*] | [D *rune*] | [TH *rune*] | The | Hobbit | J. R. R. | TOLKIEN | UNWIN | HYMAN'. Wove endpapers (maps). No headbands. All edges trimmed and unstained.

Dust-jacket, wove paper. Covers as for A3i as re-lettered, except that the dragon and sun are coloured red; on the upper cover is a red band, on which is printed in white: '*The Hobbit* ["50" *large:*] *50th Anniversary*'; and on the lower cover is printed in black, against a white panel, within a black single rule frame: 'ISBN 0-04-823386-2 | [*bar code*]'. Spine as for A3i, except that the imprint reads, in type, 'UNWIN | HYMAN'. Printed on front flap: '[*blurb*] | *All the illustrations in this book are by the* | *author.* | Price net | £7.95 | U.K. only'. Printed on back flap: '*by J. R. R. Tolkien* | [18 *titles, beginning with* The Hobbit De-luxe, *ending with* TL] | *also* | J. R. R. Tolkien: A Biography | Humphrey Carpenter | ISBN 0 04 823386 2'.

Published March 1987 at £7.95; number of copies not known.

Typeset as for A3r, except pp. [4–6] and added pp. i–xvi. Includes a foreword by Christopher Tolkien on the history and illustration of *The Hobbit*.

A book club edition was published in 1987 by Guild Publishing, London, in similar binding and dust-jacket.

z. New Unwin Paperbacks edition (1987):

J. R. R. TOLKIEN | *The* | HOBBIT | [*thick-thin rule*] | *or, There and Back Again* | *Illustrated by Michael Hague* | UNWIN PAPERBACKS | London Sydney

x, 294 pp. Collation: [1⁸2–13¹²]. 25.5 × 20.3 cm.

Contents as for A3v, except pp. [iii] title, as above; and [iv] 'First published in Great Britain by George Allen & Unwin 1984 | First published by Unwin ® Paperbacks, | an imprint of Unwin Hyman Ltd, 1987 | Copyright © George Allen & Unwin (Publishers) Ltd, 1937, 1951, 1966 | Illustrations copyright © 1984 by Oak, Ash & Thorn, Ltd | [*notice of restrictions*] | Printed in Italy by International Publishing Enterprises | [*4 publisher's addresses, London to Wellington*] | [*rule*] | [*British Library Cataloguing in Publication Data*] | [*rule*]'.

Wove paper. Bound in heavy wove wrappers. Printed or stamped on upper cover against a colour illustration by Hague, of the dragon Smaug upon his hoard (detail of illustration on pp. [208–9]): '[*printed in green, against a cream panel outlined with a stamped gilt rule, the panel and rule partly overlapped by the illustration:*] [*rule*] The [*rule*] | HOBBIT | J. R. R. TOLKIEN | [*in white, at foot of cover:*] *Illustrated by* | *Michael Hague* | *The Hobbit* ["*50*" *large:*] *50th Anniversary*'. Printed on spine, running down, against a cream background: '[*in green:*] THE HOBBIT [*in black:*] J. R. R. TOLKIEN [*parallel to the author's name:*] *Illustrated by Michael Hague* [*followed by: publisher's* "*unwin*" *device, in green, white, and black*]'. Printed on lower cover against a cream background: '[*quotation from* The Hobbit] | [*blurb*] | [*3 quotations, from the* Daily Mail, Observer, *and* British Fantasy Newsletter, *in black and green*] | [*in black:*] [*at left:*] *cover illustration by Michael Hague* | UNWIN PAPERBACKS | TOLKIEN/FANTASY | £8.95 [*at right, against a white panel outlined in black:*] ISBN 0-04-823380-3 [*3 parallel rules*] | [*bar codes*]'. All edges trimmed and unstained.

Published 10 September 1987 at £8.95; 60,000 copies printed.

Typeset as for A3v, except pp. [iii–iv]. Illustrations as for A3v.

aa. Houghton Mifflin fiftieth anniversary edition (1987):

The HOBBIT | [*rule, in gold*] | [*in black:*] *or There and Back Again* | [*50th anniversary device, against a gold panel*] | *by* J. R. R. TOLKIEN | [*rule, in gold*] | [*in black:*] *Illustrated by the author* | HOUGHTON MIFFLIN COMPANY BOSTON

xvi, 320 pp. + 5 plates. Collation: [1¹⁶2⁸3–11¹⁶]. 22.7 × 17.1 cm.

[i] 'The Hobbit'; [ii] blank; [iii] title; [iv] 'Copyright © 1966 by J. R. R. Tolkien | [*notice of restrictions under copyright*] | Book-of-the-Month Records® offers recordings on | compact discs, cassettes and records. For information and | catalog write to BOMR, Department 901, Camp Hill, PA 17012. | Library of Congress Catalog Card Number: 73-8769 | ISBN: 0-395-17711-1 | Printed in the United States of America'; [v–xvi, 1–4] foreword, by Christopher Tolkien; [5] table of contents; [6–7] *Thror's Map*; [8] author's note, titling in gold; [9]–317 text and illustrations; [318–19] *Wilderland* map; [320] blank. Rules at table of contents, at chapter titles, and below running heads, and runic titling on p. [8], in gold.

Illustrations, by Tolkien, each in black against a gold panel, except titles on pp. [48], [67], 121, [184], and [215] are outside the panel: *The Trolls*, p. [48]; *The Mountain-path*, p. [67]; *The Misty Mountains Looking West from the Eyrie towards Goblin Gate*, p. 121; *Beorn's Hall*, p. [130]; *The Elvenking's Gate*, p. [184]; *Lake Town*, p. [202]; *The Front Gate*, p. [215]; *The Hall at Bag-End, Residence of B. Baggins Esquire*, p. [315]. Maps, by Tolkien, each in black against a gold panel, pp. [6–7], [318–19]. Additional black and white illustrations, by Tolkien, reproduced in the foreword: sheet from the first manuscript draft of *The Hobbit*, including 'the first sketch of Thror's Map,' pp. [vi–vii]; drawings, *Gate of the Elvenking's Halls* and *Mirkwood*, p. [xiii]; drawing, *The Lonely Mountain*, and a schematic drawing of the same, p. [1]; sketch of 'The Back Door,' p. [2]; sketch of the exterior of Bag-End, p. [4]. Colour illustrations, by Tolkien, on 5 plates: *The Hill: Hobbiton-across-the Water*, facing p. 32; *Rivendell*, facing p. 64; *Bilbo Woke Up with the Early Sun in His Eyes*, without printed title, facing p. 128; *Bilbo Comes to the Huts of the Raft-elves*, facing p. 192; *Conversation with Smaug*, facing p. [224].

Wove paper. Bound in gold imitation leather over boards. 50th anniversary device stamped on upper cover in green, within a green single rule frame, within a double frame of red rules, green runes within green single rule frames, and green corner ornaments, the whole within a green single rule frame. Cover runes as for A3l, later corrected version. Stamped on spine, running down, in green, within a double red rule frame, within a green single rule frame: '[*within a green single rule frame, in one compartment of the red frame:*] THE HOBBIT BY J. R. R. TOLKIEN HMCo [*parallel to the preceding, within a green single rule frame, within the second compartment of the red frame, the same words in runes*]'. Yellow-green wove endpapers. Yellow/green headbands. All edges trimmed and speckled green.

Slipcase, gold imitation leather over boards. Gold label affixed to right side of case (open end toward viewer), printed in black: 'THE HOBBIT | [*50th anniversary device, against a yellow-green panel*] | J. R. R. TOLKIEN'.

Published 26 October 1987 at $29.95; 15,000 copies printed. Sold as a regular trade book, despite the book club notice on p. [iv].

Typeset as for A3l, except pp. [iii–xvi, 1–4]. The foreword was reset from A3y.

Another, presumably later impression (but simultaneous publication?) has been seen, as above except with darker gold (slightly brown) ink; a cancel title leaf, with p. [iv]: 'Copyright © 1966 by J. R. R. Tolkien | Foreword copyright © Christopher Tolkien 1987 | [*notice of restrictions under copyright*] | Library of Congress Catalog Card Number: 73-8769 | ISBN: 0-395-17711-1 | Printed in the United States of America | H'; brighter stamping; and edges speckled a lighter green.

Copies for book club use have varying copyright pages and are in varying bindings, though all are bound in a brighter gold leatherette with a square stamped in red or blind on the lower cover.

A trade paperback version was published, possibly by the Quality Paperback Book Club, with the Houghton Mifflin imprint, bound in heavy wove wrappers printed with an asymmetrical design by Andrew Becker, featuring a colour illus-tration by Tolkien, *Bilbo Comes to the Huts of the Raft-elves*, against a beige 'marbled' background.

bb. '*Super de luxe edition*' *(1987):*

[*in red:*] THE HOBBIT | OR | THERE AND BACK AGAIN | [*in black:*] J. R. R. Tolkien | UNWIN HYMAN | London Sydney

1–10, xvi, 11–288 pp. + 16 plates (including maps). Collation: [1–20⁸]. 22.4 × 14.4 cm.

[1–2] blank; [3] 'THE HOBBIT'; [4] 'by J. R. R. TOLKIEN | [24 *titles, beginning with* H, *ending with* Pictures] | also | *J. R. R. Tolkien: A Biography by Humphrey Carpenter.*'; [5] title; [6] 'First published in 1937 | Fourth impression 1946 | Second edition 1951 | Tenth impression 1963 | Third edition (paperback) 1966 | Nineteenth impression 1974 | Reset (Fourth edition) 1975 | De luxe edition 1976 | Fourth impression 1986 | This anniversary super de luxe edition, | published by Unwin Hyman, an imprint of Unwin Hyman Ltd, 1987. | [*notice of restrictions*] | [4 *publisher's addresses, London (Denmark House) to Wellington*] | © George Allen & Unwin (Publishers) Ltd, 1937, 1966, 1975, 1976, 1987 | Foreword © Christopher Tolkien 1987 | ISBN 0-04-440091-8 | Printed in Great Britain by Mackays of Chatham | and bound by Cramp of Cornwall'; [7] table of contents; [8] blank; [9] list of illustrations; [10] blank; i–xvi foreword and illustrations; [11]–12 author's note; [13]–286 text; [287–8] blank.

Black and white illustrations, by Tolkien: sheet from the first manuscript draft of *The Hobbit*, including 'the first sketch of Thror's Map,' pp. ii–iii; drawing, *Gate of the Elvenking's Halls*, p. viii; *Mirkwood*, plate facing p. viii; schematic drawing of the Lonely Mountain, p. xii; sketch of 'The Back Door,' p. xiii; sketch of the exterior of Bag-End, p. xiv; drawing, *The Lonely Mountain*, p. [xi]. Colour illustrations, by Tolkien (* with colour added by H.E. Riddett), on 13 plates: *The Hill: Hobbiton-across-the Water*, facing p. [5]; *The Trolls*, facing p. 48; *Rivendell*, facing p. 54; *The Mountain-path*, facing p. [62]; *The Misty Mountains looking West from the Eyrie towards Goblin Gate*, facing p. 110; *Bilbo Woke with the Early Sun in His Eyes*, facing p. [114]; *Beorn's Hall*, facing p. 120; *The Elvenking's Gate*, facing p. 168; *Bilbo Comes to the Huts of the Raft-elves*, facing p. 182; *Lake Town*, facing p. 186; *The Front Gate*, facing p. [194]; *Conversation with Smaug*, facing p. 212; *The Hall at Bag-End, Residence of B. Baggins Esquire*, facing p. 284. Maps, by Tolkien, in black and red on 2 folded plates: *Thror's Map*, before p. [1]; *Wilderland*, after p. [288].

Wove paper. Bound in dark green leather over boards. 'JRRT' monogram stamped on upper cover in gilt within a gilt single rule frame. Stamped on spine in gilt, between blind-stamped bands: '[*band*] | THE | HOBBIT | [*band*] | J. R. R. | TOLKIEN | [*3 bands*] | UNWIN HYMAN'. Illustration by Tolkien, *The Green Dragon*, stamped on lower cover in blind. Tan wove endpapers. Limitation notice pasted onto recto, front free endpaper: '[*within a thick-thin rule frame:*] This is copy number [*numeral added in pen*] of a | limited collectors' edition of 500 copies | of The Hobbit by J. R. R. Tolkien | with a special foreword by Christopher Tolkien | commemorating the 50th anniversary | of first publication on 21st September 1937. | ['*JRRT*' *monogram*]'. Green/yellow headbands. Dark green ribbon marker. All edges trimmed. Top edge gilt, fore- and bottom edges plain.

Slipcase, green cloth over boards, open edges tipped with dark green leather.

Published 26 November 1987 at £100.00; 500 copies printed.

Typeset as for A3o, except pp. [4–6], new i–xvi.

cc. New Ballantine Books edition (1988):

The Hobbit | or | There and Back | Again | [*strip of leaf ornaments*] | by | J. R. R. Tolkien | BALLANTINE BOOKS • NEW YORK

xiv, 306 pp. Collation: 160 leaves. 17.4 × 10.5 cm.

[i] '*[blurb, within a single rule frame]* | And what is a Hobbit? | *[blurb]* | THIS IS THE AUTHORIZED PAPERBOUND EDITION | PUBLISHED BY BALLANTINE BOOKS'; [ii] 'About the "Lord of the Rings" Trilogy | by J. R. R. Tolkien: | PART I *The Fellowship of the Ring* | [2 quotations, from the New York Herald Tribune Book Week *and* New York Times Book Review] | PART II *The Two Towers* | [2 quotations, from the Chicago Tribune *and* Boston Herald Traveler] | PART III *The Return of the King* | [3 quotations, from the New York Herald Tribune Book Week, Arthur C. Clarke, and the New Republic]'; [iii] introduction, by Peter S. Beagle; [iv] 'THE AUTHORIZED EDITIONS | *of the works of J. R. R. Tolkien* | [10 titles, beginning with H, ending with Smith of Wootton Major and Farmer Giles of Ham] | [note on Tolkien]'; [v] title; [vi] 'Copyright © 1937, 1938 and 1966 by J. R. R. Tolkien | Introduction Copyright © 1973 by Peter Beagle | Maps of Middle-earth copyright © George Allen & Unwin Pub- | lishers Ltd. 1980 | *[notice of restrictions under copyright]* | ISBN 0-345-33968-1 | This edition published by arrangement with Houghton Mifflin | Company | Manufactured in the United States of America | First Ballantine Books Edition: August 1965 | *Revised Edition:* | First Printing: January 1982 | Twenty-third Printing: September 1988 | Cover Art by Michael Herring'; [vii] table of contents; [viii] blank; [ix] author's note; [x–xi] *Thror's Map*; [xii–xiii] *Wilderland* map; [xiv] blank; 1–304 text; [305] '[3 lines and blurb between thick-thin rules at left and right:] J. R. R. TOLKIEN'S | Epic Fantasy Classic | The Lord of the Rings | *[blurb]* | *[publisher's order form]*'; [306] blank.

Omits Tolkien's illustrations, except for the maps, in black only, pp. [x–xiii].

Wove paper. Bound in heavy wove wrappers. Two versions of upper cover, issued simultaneously:

(1) *on stock with gloss finish:* Printed or stamped on upper cover against a black background: '*[printed in white:]* THE AUTHORIZED EDITION OF THE FANTASY CLASSIC | *[rule]* | *[stamped in gilt:]* J. R. R. | TOLKIEN | *[printed in white:]* *[rule]* | THE ENCHANTING PRELUDE TO *The Lord of the Rings* | *[rule]* | *[in light blue:]* THE | HOBBIT | *[colour illustration by Michael Herring, of Bilbo Baggins and Gollum within an archway, on the base of which is "inscribed" in runes "THE HOBBIT"; within a gold ring at upper right of and partly overlapping the illustration, in white:]* 50TH | ANNIVERSARY | EDITION! | *[in lower left corner of cover:]* *[running up, in white:]* Ballantine/Fantasy/33968/U.S. $4.95 | *[below preceding line, publisher's "BB" device, horizontal, in black and white]*'. This version matches the covers of the Ballantine Books *LR* introduced in late 1988 (see A5d note).

(2) *on stock with matte finish:* Identical to version 1, except that 'J. R. R. | TOLKIEN' is printed in white; parallel to and to the right of 'Ballantine/Fantasy/ 33968/U.S. $4.95' in the lower left corner of the cover is a rule, in blue; and in white, parallel to and to the right of the blue rule, running up, is 'SPECIAL BOOK CLUB EDITION'. Despite the 'book club' legend, copies of version 2 were sold in the trade with version 1.

The spine and lower cover are identical on both versions, printed against a black background. Printed on spine: '*[publisher's "BB" device, in black and white]* | *[in white:]* Fantasy | *[running down, between single rules:]* J. R. R. TOLKIEN *[in gold:]* · | *[horizontal:]* *[colour illustration as on upper cover, reduced]* | *[running down, in light blue:]* THE *[parallel to preceding word:]* HOBBIT | *[horizontal, in white:]* U.S. 495 | *[rule]* | 345- | 33968-1'. Printed on lower cover: '*[at upper left, colour illustration as on upper cover, reduced; to right of illustration, in light blue:]* THE RELUCTANT | HOBBIT | *[rule]* | *[blurb, in white, to right of and extending below illustration*] | [*rule, in light blue*] | [*blurb, in white*] | [*in black, against a white panel:*] [*bar codes*] | ISBN 0-345-33968-1 [*to right of panel, running down, in white:*] Cover printed in USA'. All edges trimmed and stained yellow.

Published September 1988 at $4.95; number of copies not known.

Copies with binding 1 were also sold in a slipcase with *LR* (A5d), at $19.80. Sides and spine of slipcase printed against a black background, top and bottom printed solid black. Printed on left and right sides: '[*in white:*] [*rule*] J. R. R. [*rule*] | TOLKIEN | [*in light blue:*] THE HOBBIT | [*in white:*] and | [*in light blue:*] The Lord of the Rings | [*colour illustration by Michael Herring, of Aragorn, Gandalf, and three other figures within an archway, on the base of which is "inscribed" in runes* "THE LORD OF THE RINGS"; *within a white ring at upper right of and partly overlapping the illustration, in white:*] 50TH | ANNIVERSARY | EDITIONS!'. Printed on spine: '[*in white:*] [*rule*] J. R. R. [*rule*] | TOLKIEN | [*in light blue:*] THE HOBBIT | [*in white:*] and | [*in light blue:*] The Lord of the Rings | [*in white:*] PART ONE: | [*in red:*] THE FELLOWSHIP | OF THE RING | [*in white:*] PART TWO: | [*in light purple:*] THE TWO TOWERS | [*in white:*] PART THREE | [*in light green:*] THE RETURN | OF THE KING | [*publisher's "BB" device, in black and white*] | [*in white:*] Fantasy'.

Reset, based on a later impression of A3g with 'old-looking' correct, but continuing the errors noted for that edition, including 'We are not together' for 'We are met together', p. 16, ll. 9–10, and 'I like eggs with my ham' for 'I like six eggs with my ham', p. 26, ll. 20–1.

dd. First annotated edition (1988):

[*2 lines of runes, each line between single rules, in light yellow-brown*] | [*in yellow-brown:*] THE ANNOTATED | HOBBIT | [*in black:*] [*rule*] | INTRODUCTION AND NOTES BY | *Douglas A. Anderson* | [*against a tan panel outlined in yellow-brown:*] The Hobbit | or | There and Back | Again | J. R. R. Tolkien | Illustrated | by the Author | [*below the panel:*] [*publisher's 'dolphin' device*] | HOUGHTON MIFFLIN COMPANY · BOSTON | 1988 | [*2 lines of runes, each line between single rules, in light yellow-brown*]

xii, 340 pp. Collation: [1–11^{16}]. 27.7 × 21.6 cm.

[i] '[*decoration*] | [*in yellow-brown:*] THE ANNOTATED | HOBBIT | [*rule, in black*]'; [ii] '[*2 lines of runes, each line between single rules, in light yellow-brown*] | [*in black:*] [*photograph of Tolkien*] | J. R. R. Tolkien in the mid-1930s | [*2 lines of runes, each line between single rules, in light yellow-brown*]; [iii] title; [iv] 'The Hobbit copyright © 1966 by J. R. R. Tolkien | Annotations copyright © 1988 by Douglas A. Anderson | ALL RIGHTS RESERVED | For information about permission to reproduce selections from this book, write to | Permissions, Houghton Mifflin Company, 2 Park Street, | Boston, Massachusetts 02108. | [*Library of Congress Cataloging in Publication Data*] | [*extensive copyright notice*] | PRINTED IN THE UNITED STATES OF AMERICA | [*printing code, beginning "M", ending "1"*]'; [v] quotation, by André Maurois; [vi] blank; [vii] table of contents; [viii] blank; [ix]–x preface; [xi] '[*decoration*] | [*in yellow-brown:*] THE ANNOTATED | HOBBIT | [*rule, in black*]'; [xii] blank; [1]–[7] introduction and illustrations; [8] author's note and annotations; [9]–317 text; [318] blank; [319] '[*in yellow-brown:*] APPENDIX A: | [*in black:*] Textual and Revisional Notes | [*in yellow-brown:*] APPENDIX B: | [*in black:*] On Runes and Their Values | [*in yellow-brown:*] BIBLIOGRAPHY | MAP OF WILDERLAND'; [320] blank; [321]–8 Appendix A;

[329] Appendix B; [330] blank; [331]–5 bibliography; [336] *Wilderland* map, with caption running up right edge: '*J. R. R. Tolkien*'; [337] '[*in yellow-brown:*] THE END | [*decoration*]'; [338–40] blank. Some titling, all note numbers, and parts of some illustrations printed in light brown. Some illustrations printed against tan panels.

Decorations and illustrations, by Tolkien, in black and white except as noted: dragon, an unused decoration for the binding of A3a (see A3a note), pp. [i], [xi]; the dust-jacket and binding of the first edition of *H*, and the dust-jacket for the first American edition (A3b), the latter reproducing *The Hill: Hobbiton-across-the Water* and *Conversation with Smaug*, p. [3]; sketch of the exterior of Bag-End, p. 24; *Thror's Map* (with 'moon-letters' omitted), in black with yellow-brown runes, p. 28; a page from the original manuscript draft of *H*, with the first sketch of *Thror's Map*, p. 29; *The Hill: Hobbiton* (drawing), *The Hill: Hobbiton across the Water* (drawing, frontispiece for A3a), and *The Hill: Hobbiton-across-the Water* (painting), p. 39; sketch of dwarves marching (see *Drawings* [Ei1], p. [13]), p. 40; *Trolls' Hill*, p. 42; *The Trolls*, in black against a tan panel (except title printed below the panel), p. [48]; *The Three Trolls are Turned to Stone*, in black against a tan panel, p. 51; *Rivendell*, p. 57; *Thror's Map* with moon-runes visible, in black with runes at left in light yellow-brown, p. 63; *Rivendell Looking East*, p. 64; *The Mountain-path*, p. [67]; *The Misty Mountains Looking West from the Eyrie towards Goblin Gate*, p. 121; *Bilbo Woke with the Early Sun in His Eyes*, p. [122]; *Beorn's Hall*, p. [130]; *Mirkwood*, p. 153; *The Elvenking's Gate* and *Gate of the Elvenking's Halls*, p. [184]; *The Elvenking's Gate* (unfinished painting), p. 185; preliminary painting for *Bilbo Comes to the Huts of the Raft-elves* (i.e. *Sketch for The Forest River*), p. 198; *Bilbo Comes to the Huts of the Raft-elves* (finished painting), p. 199; *Lake Town*, in black with border in yellow-brown, p. [202]; *The Front Gate*, p. [215]; schematic drawing of the Lonely Mountain, p. 218; *The Lonely Mountain*, p. 230; *Conversation with Smaug*, p. 234; *Death of Smaug*, p. 261; *The Hall at Bag-End, Residence of B. Baggins, Esquire*, p. [315]; *Wilderland* map, p. [336]; dragon looking left, decoration for the upper cover of A3a, p. [337].

Wove paper. Bound in green textured paper over boards, blue cloth spine. Decoration by Tolkien, a dragon (as on pp. [i], [xi]), stamped on upper cover in gilt. Stamped on spine in gilt: '[*in runes, between single rules:*] THE · HOBBIT | [*roman:*] J. R. R. | TOLKIEN | INTRODUCTION | AND NOTES | BY | DOUGLAS A. | ANDERSON | [*running down:*] THE ANNOTATED [*parallel with the preceding words:*] HOBBIT | [*horizontal:*] [*publisher's "dolphin" device*] | HOUGHTON | MIFFLIN | COMPANY | [*in runes, between single rules:*] THE · HOBBIT'. Yellow-brown wove endpapers. Yellow/green headbands. All edges trimmed and unstained.

Dust-jacket, wove paper. Upper and lower illustrations adapted from the standard wraparound dust-jacket illustration by Tolkien for *The Hobbit* (see A3a), in black, dark blue, green, and white. Covers and spine printed against a green background. Printed on upper cover against a multi-sided decorative panel, in black, dark blue, and green against a cream background: '[*in dark blue:*] THE | [*in green:*] ANNOTATED | [*in dark blue:*] HOBBIT | J. R. R. TOLKIEN | [*in green:*] ANNOTATED BY | DOUGLAS A. ANDERSON'. Printed on spine: '[*running down:*] [*in white:*] THE [*in cream:*] ANNOTATED [*in white:*] HOBBIT [*in cream:*] J. R. R. TOLKIEN [*in dark blue:*] ANNOTATED BY [*parallel with the preceding two words:*] DOUGLAS A. ANDERSON | [*horizontal, publisher's "dolphin" device, in white*] | [*running down, in dark blue:*] HOUGHTON [*parallel with the preceding word:*] MIFFLIN'. Printed on lower cover below the illustration: '[*at left,*

in white:] 6-80604 [*at right, in black, against a white panel:*] ISBN 0-395-47690-9'.
Printed on front flap: '[*in black:*] FPT>$24.95 | [*2 lines of runes, each between
single rules, in dark blue*] | [*blurb, in black with green initial T*] | [*in black:*]
10244588 | ISBN 0-395-47690-9 | [*line of runes between single rules, in dark blue*]'.
Printed on back flap: '[*2 lines of runes, each between single rules, in dark blue*] | [*in
black:*] [*note on Tolkien*] | [*note on Anderson*] | Jacket art: J. R. R. Tolkien | Jacket
design: Michaela Sullivan | Houghton Mifflin Company | 2 Park Street, Boston,
Massachusetts 02108 | [*line of runes between single rules, in dark blue*]'.

Published 28 October 1988 at $24.95; 30,000 copies printed.

Text proper typeset as for A3j, with corrections. 'Each reset edition [of *The Hobbit*]
has its own peculiarities of misprints. . . . In preparing this annotated edition of *The
Hobbit*, I have attempted to correct these errors, and have a text which as perfectly
as is possible represents Tolkien's final intended form' (Anderson, p. [321]).
Continues, however, the following errors from A3j:

    p. 61, ll. 3–4, 'uncomfortable palpitating' for 'uncomfortable, palpitating'
    p. 120, l. 17, 'where men live' for 'where men lived'
    p. 134, l. 32, 'And so do it' for 'And so do I'
    p. 138, l. 10, '*on it went.*' for '*on it went*'
    p. 152, l. 11, 'lives at times' for 'lived at times'
    p. 165, l. 33, '(as he thought;' for '(as he thought)'
    p. 168, l. 24, 'feeding none to well' for 'feeding none too well'
    p. 208, l. 22, 'travelled with out of the West' for 'travelled with us out of the
West'
    p. 219, ll. 12–13, 'without a joint or crevice to be seen. ¶ No sign was there' for
the same without a paragraph break
    p. 291, l. 2, 'beseigers' for 'besiegers'

Anderson has concluded that Elrond's statement, p. 62, ll. 20–2, should correctly
read: '. . . remnants of old robberies in some hold in the mountains of old. I have
heard that there are still forgotten treasures to be found. . . .'
    The reference to *Thror's Map* reads, p. 28, ll. 29–30 (above the map on the same
page): 'Look at the map below, and you will see there the runes in gold.'
    Error in annotations, p. 262, l. 5, '*gleed*' for '*glede*'.
    The runes on the title spread read: 'THE HOBBIT OR THERE AND BACK
AGAIN BEING THE RECORD OF A YEARS JOURNEY MADE BY BILBO
BAGGINS OF HOBBITON COMPILED FROM HIS MEMOIRS BY J. R. R.
TOLKIEN AND ANNOTATED IN THIS EDITION BY DOUGLAS A. ANDER-
SON AND PUBLISHED BY THE HOUGHTON MIFFLIN COMPANY'. The runes
on the dust-jacket flaps form the same inscription through the word 'MEMOIRS'.
The shorter inscription is repeated, in light yellow-brown, as a decoration at the foot
of most spreads.
    Includes five related poems by Tolkien: 'The Root of the Boot', p. 45; 'Goblin
Feet', p. 77; 'Progress in Bimble Town', p. 212; 'The Dragon's Visit', pp. 262–3; and
'Iúmonna Gold Galdre Bewunden', pp. 288–9.
    Includes illustrations from twelve translations (see section G): Estonian 1, French
1, German 1, Hungarian 1, Japanese 1, Portuguese 1, Romanian 1, Russian 1,
Slovak 1, Slovenian 1, and Swedish 1, 4. Also includes two illustrations by Eric
Fraser for A3u.
    A book club edition was published in 1989, with changes to the copyright page,
printed on heavier paper, bound in dark blue paper over boards, dust-jacket with
'HOUGHTON MIFFLIN' on spine, '*Book Club Edition*' on front flap.

ee. First British annotated edition (1989):

[*2 lines of runes, each line between single rules, in light yellow-brown*] | [*in yellow-brown:*] THE ANNOTATED | HOBBIT | [*in black:*] [*rule*] | INTRODUCTION AND NOTES BY | *Douglas A. Anderson* | [*against a tan panel outlined in yellow-brown:*] The Hobbit | or | There and Back | Again | J. R. R. Tolkien | Illustrated | by the Author | [*below the panel:*] UNWIN | [*publisher's 'man drawing a circle' device*] | HYMAN | LONDON SYDNEY WELLINGTON | [*2 lines of runes, each line between single rules, in light yellow-brown*]

Pagination, collation, and size as for A3dd.

Contents as for A3dd, except pp. [iii] title, as above; and [iv] 'First published by George Allen & Unwin 1937 | Fourth impression 1946 | Second edition 1951 | Tenth impression 1963 | Third edition 1966 | Tenth impression 1975 | Fourth edition 1978 | Seventh impression 1987 | Fourth edition © George Allen & Unwin (Publishers) Ltd 1978 | Annotations © Douglas A. Anderson 1988 | [*notice of restrictions*] | [*3 publisher's addresses, London to Wellington*] | ISBN 0–04–440337–2 | [*extensive copyright notice*] | PRINTED IN THE UNITED STATES OF AMERICA | [*printing code, beginning "M", ending "1"*]'.

Illustrations as for A3dd.

Binding as for A3dd, including imprint.

Dust-jacket, wove paper. Covers and spine printed against a black background. Printed on upper cover against a black panel outlined in light orange and red-orange, against a white panel, against a purple panel: '[*in white:*] J. R. R. TOLKIEN | THE | ANNOTATED HOBBIT | [*colour reproduction of Tolkien's painting for the dust-jacket of the first edition of* H] | [*in white:*] ANNOTATED BY | DOUGLAS A. ANDERSON'. Printed on spine: '[*in white:*] J. R. R. | TOLKIEN | THE | ANNOTATED | HOBBIT | [*"JRRT" monogram*] | [*colour reproduction of centre portion of Tolkien's dust-jacket painting*] | [*in white:*] ANNOTATED BY | DOUGLAS | A. ANDERSON | UNWIN | [*publisher's "man drawing a circle" device*] | HYMAN'. Printed on lower cover against a purple panel: '[*"JRRT" monogram, in white*] | [*in black, against a white panel:*] ISBN 0-04-440337-2 | [*bar code*]'. Printed on front flap: '[*blurb*] | £14.95 | UK ONLY'. Printed on back flap: '*Jacket design by The Pinpoint Design Company*'.

Published 23 March 1989 at £14.95; 7,500 copies printed.

Typeset as for A3dd, except pp. [iii–iv].
   Sheets imported from Houghton Mifflin. An additional 1,500 copies were ordered for publication in Canada, as for A3dd but in a version of the American dust-jacket (with Unwin Hyman imprint on spine).
   A book club edition was published in 1989 by Guild Publishing, London, printed with the first U.K. impression (i.e. second impression) of the Unwin Hyman edition, bound in black paper over boards, publisher's 'GP' device on spine, dust-jacket similar to that for A3dd.

ff. New Houghton Mifflin trade paperback edition (1989):

J. R. R. TOLKIEN | *The* | HOBBIT | [*thick-thin rule*] | *or, There and Back Again* | *Illustrated by Michael Hague* | Houghton Mifflin Company Boston

x, 294 pp. Collation: 152 leaves. 25.2 × 19.7 cm.

Contents as for A3v, except pp. [iii] title, as above; and [iv] 'Copyright © 1966 by J. R. R. Tolkien | Illustrations copyright © 1984 by Oak, Ash & Thorn, Ltd. | All rights reserved. For information about permission | to reproduce selections from this book, write to | Permissions, Houghton Mifflin Company, 2 Park Street, | Boston, Massachusetts 02108. | Printed in the United States of America | [*Library of Congress Cataloging in Publication Data*] | RNF ISBN 0-395-36290-3 | PAP ISBN 0-395-52021-5 | [*printing code, beginning "Y", ending "3"*]'.

Wove paper. Bound in heavy wove wrappers. Covers and spine printed against an orange background. Printed on upper cover: '[*in green:*] The | HOBBIT | J. R. R. TOLKIEN | [*colour illustration by Hague, of the dragon Smaug upon his hoard (detail of illustration on pp. [208–9], against a white panel outlined in green*] | [*in green:*] Illustrated by Michael Hague'. Printed on spine, running down, in green: 'The HOBBIT J. R. R. TOLKIEN Houghton Mifflin Company'. Printed on lower cover: '[*in black:*] $12.95 | [*quotation from Booklist, in black with green initial T (actually T+J, derived from Tolkien's monogram)*] | [*in black:*] [*at left:*] 1089 | [*rule*] | 4-97177 [*at right, against a white panel:*] ISBN 0-395-52021-5 | [*bar code*]'. All edges trimmed and unstained.

Published 30 October 1989 at $12.95; 20,000 copies printed.

Typeset as for A3v, except pp. [iii–iv]. Illustrations as for A3v.

gg. Reset book club edition (1990):

[*within 3 concentric single rule frames, alternating thin-thick-thin:*] THE | HOBBIT | [*rule*] [*diamond*] [*rule*] | J. R. R. Tolkien | [*below the frames:*] GUILD PUBLISHING | LONDON · NEW YORK · SYDNEY · TORONTO

272 pp. Collation: [1–17⁸]. 19.8 × 12.5 cm.

[1] 'THE HOBBIT'; [2–3] *Thror's Map*; [4] blank; [5] title; [6] 'This edition published 1990 by | Guild Publishing by arrangement | with George Allen & Unwin Ltd. | First published 1937 | Fourth edition © George Allen & Unwin | (Publishers) Ltd 1978 | [*notice of restrictions under copyright*] | Typeset by Colset (Private) Ltd | Singapore | Printed and bound in Great Britain by | Mackays of Chatham PLC | Chatham, Kent'; 7 table of contents; 8 list of illustrations; 9–10 author's note; 11–264 text and illustrations; [265] blank; [266–7] *Wilderland* map; [268–72] blank.

Illustrations, by Tolkien: *The Trolls*, p. 45; *The Mountain-path*, p. 59; *The Misty Mountains Looking West from the Eyrie towards Goblin Gate*, p. 103; *Beorn's Hall*, p. 114; *The Elvenking's Gate*, p. 155; *Lake Town*, p. 169; *The Front Gate*, p. 181; *The Hall at Bag-End, Residence of B. Baggins Esquire*, p. 264. Maps, by Tolkien, in black only, pp. [2–3], [266–7].

Wove paper. Mottled blue-green-grey paper over boards, dark green imitation leather spine with raised bands. Thick vertical rule stamped in gilt on leatherette on upper and lower covers. Stamped on upper cover in gilt, within a thin gilt single rule frame, against a dark grey panel outlined by a thick gilt rule: 'THE | HOBBIT | [*rule*] [*diamond*] [*rule*] | J. R. R. Tolkien'. Stamped on spine in gilt: '[*thick rule*] | THE | HOBBIT | [*2 thick rules*] | [*thin rule*] | J. R. R. | TOLKIEN | [*thin rule*] | [*2 thick rules*] | [*thin rule*] | GUILD | CLASSICS | [*thin rule*] | [*2 thick rules*] | [*publisher's "gp" device within a decorative frame*] | [*thick rule*]'. Wove mottled blue-green-grey endpapers. Green/white headbands. Dark green ribbon marker. All edges trimmed and unstained.

Published December? 1990 at £7.95; number of copies not known.

Reset, based on A3r, continuing the errors of that edition. On p. 26, ll. 35–7, the reference to *Thror's Map* (printed in this edition in black only) reads: 'Look at the map at the beginning of this book, and you will see there the runes in red.'

hh. Large-print edition (1990):

The Hobbit | or | There and Back Again | BY | J. R. R. TOLKIEN | ILLUSTRATED BY | THE AUTHOR | [*Windrush 'rushes' device*] | Oxford

xii, 356 pp. Collation: [1⁸2–12¹⁶]. 23.3 × 15.5 cm.

[i] 'THE HOBBIT | [*decoration*]'; [ii] blank; [iii] title; [iv] 'Copyright © George Allen & Unwin (Publishers) Ltd | 1937, 1978 | First published in Great Britain 1937 | by George Allen & Unwin | Published in Large Print 1990 by Clio Press, | 55 St Thomas' Street, Oxford, OX1 1JG, | by arrangement with Unwin Hyman Ltd and | Houghton Mifflin Co. | All rights reserved | [*British Library Cataloguing in Publication Data*] | ISBN 1-85089-805-7 | Printed and bound by Hartnolls Ltd, | Bodmin, Cornwall | Cover designed by CGS Studios, Cheltenham'; [v] table of contents; [vi] blank; [vii] list of illustrations; [viii–ix] *Thror's Map*; [x] blank; [xi–xii] author's note; 1–351 text and illustrations; [352–3] *Wilderland* map; [354] 'ISIS | large print and audio books | [*advertisement*]'; [355] 'CHILDREN'S CLASSICS | [*publisher's advertisement of 26 authors and titles, beginning with Barrie, *Peter Pan*, ending with Wilder, *On the Banks of Plum Creek*]*'; [356] 'CHILDREN'S BOOKS IN | LARGE PRINT | [*publisher's advertisement of 21 authors and titles, beginning with J. and A. Ahlberg, *The Ha Ha Bonk Book*, ending with Danziger, *The Cat Ate My Gymsuit*]*'.

Decoration and illustrations, by Tolkien: decoration, dragon looking left, p. [i]; *The Trolls*, p. [45]; *The Mountain-path*, p. [66]; *The Misty Mountains Looking West from the Eyrie towards Goblin Gate*, p. 127; *Beorn's Hall*, p. [135]; *The Elvenking's Gate*, p. [197]; *Lake Town*, p. [218]; *The Front Gate*, p. [233]; *The Hall at Bag-End, Residence of B. Baggins Esquire*, p. [349]. Maps, by Tolkien, in black only, pp. [viii–ix], [352–3].

Wove paper. Bound in paper over boards. Covers as for the dust-jacket of A3r, except that the dragon and sun are coloured red, and printed against the lower cover, in black, against a white panel outlined in black: '[*blurb*] | ISBN 1 85089 805 7'. Printed on spine against a green background: '[*running down:*] [*in white:*] THE HOBBIT [*in black:*] J. R. R. TOLKIEN [*Windrush "rushes" device, horizontal*]'. Wove endpapers. No headbands. All edges trimmed and unstained.

Issued without dust-jacket.

Published October 1990 at £9.95; 1,250 copies printed.

Reset, based on A3r, continuing the errors of that edition.

A4   FARMER GILES OF HAM   1949

a. First edition:

FARMER GILES | OF HAM | [*black letter:*] Aegidii Ahenobarbi Julii Agricole de Hammo | Domini de Domito | Aule Draconarie Comitis | Regni Minimi Regis et Basilei | mira facinora et mirabilis | exortus | [*roman:*] or in the vulgar tongue | *The Rise and Wonderful Adventures of* | *Farmer Giles, Lord of Tame,* | *Count of Worminghall* | *and King of* | *the Little Kingdom* | by | J. R. R. TOLKIEN | embellished

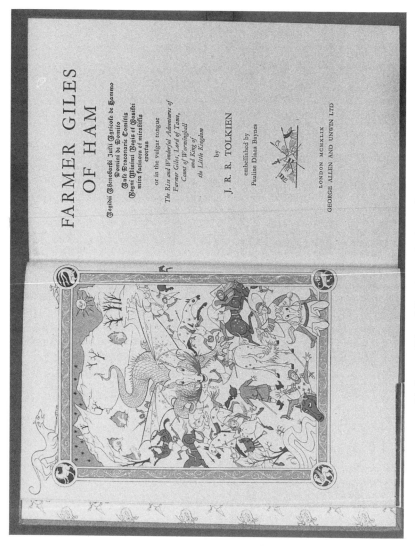

V. *Farmer Giles of Ham* (a4a). Art by Pauline Baynes.

by | Pauline Diana Baynes | [*decoration*] | LONDON MCMXLIX | GEORGE ALLEN AND UNWIN LTD

80 pp. + 2 plates. Collation: [A]⁸B–E⁸. 19.9 × 13.0 cm.

[1] 'FARMER GILES OF HAM | [*illustration*]'; [2] 'by J. R. R. Tolkien | THE HOBBIT | or *There and Back Again*'; [3] title; [4] '*First published in 1949 | This book is copyright | No portion of it may be reproduced without | written permission. Inquiries should be | addressed to the publishers | Printed in Great Britain | in 12 point Garamond type | by Unwin Brothers Limited | London and Woking*'; [5] '[*black letter:*] To C. H. Wilkinson | [*illustration*]'; [6] illustration; 7–8 foreword; 9–[79] text and illustrations; [80] '[*publisher's open "St. George" device*] | GEORGE ALLEN & UNWIN LTD | [*7 addresses, London to Wellington*]'. Additional illustrations by Pauline Baynes on 2 plates, in black, grey-blue, light brown, and white: [*the dragon Chrysophylax attacks*] ('Suddenly there came a rush of smoke that smothered them all, and right in the midst of it the dragon crashed into the head of the line', p. 59), facing p. [3]; [*Chrysophylax unhorses Farmer Giles*] ('The grey mare sat down plump, and Farmer Giles went off backwards into a ditch', p. 40), facing p. 40.

Wove paper. Bound in light orange textured paper over boards (later, for library sales, in orange-brown cloth over boards). Illustration by Baynes, of Chrysophylax (as on p. 42), stamped on upper cover in blue. Stamped on spine in blue: '[*black letter:*] Farmer | Giles | of | Ham | [*roman:*] J. R. R. | TOLKIEN | ALLEN | AND | UNWIN'. Wove endpapers, with repeated illustration by Baynes, of Chrysophylax (as on p. 25), in blue. No headbands. All edges trimmed. Top edge stained blue, fore- and bottom edges unstained.

Dust-jacket, wove paper. Decoration by Baynes, a tree, birds, a squirrel, the moon and sun, and ornaments within and partly overlapping a decorative frame, printed on upper cover in light brown. Printed within open area of decoration, in blue: '[*black letter:*] Farmer Giles | of Ham | [*roman:*] BY J. R. R. TOLKIEN | *embellished by* | *PAULINE DIANA BAYNES*'. Printed on spine: '[*in blue:*] [*black letter:*] Farmer | Giles | of | Ham | [*roman:*] J. R. R. | TOLKIEN | [*decoration by Baynes, a tree limb and birds, in light brown*] | [*in blue:*] ALLEN | AND | UNWIN'. Printed on lower cover in blue: '*also by J. R. R. Tolkien* | [*black letter:*] The Hobbit | [*roman:*] Cr. 8vo Fourth Impression 7s.6d. net | *Illustrated by the author* | [*blurb*] | GEORGE ALLEN AND UNWIN LTD'. Printed on front flap of trade dust-jacket in blue: '[*blurb*] | 6s. net'. Printed on back flap in light brown: 'NATIONAL | BOOK LEAGUE | *President: John Masefield O.M.* | [*advertisement*] | [*"NBL" device*] | *Printed in Great Britain*'. Dust-jacket for library binding as for the trade binding, except that the price is clipped from the lower corner of the front flap, and '7s. 6d. net' is separately printed at the foot of the flap, in blue.

4,500 copies in trade binding published 20 October 1949 at 6s.; 500 copies in library binding published 17 November 1949 at 7s. 6d.

John, the eldest son of J. R. R. Tolkien, recalled that 'Farmer Giles of Ham' was originally an impromptu story told to the Tolkien children when they took shelter under a bridge during a sudden rainstorm that interrupted a family picnic. It was first written down in the late nineteen-twenties or early nineteen-thirties. Its narrator then was 'Daddy', and most of its characters were nameless. The second draft expanded the tale and its chronology and substituted 'The Family Jester' for 'Daddy'. A third manuscript, written in the late nineteen-thirties, at about the time that Tolkien was completing *The Hobbit*, was more than doubled in length and greatly altered in tone, with scholarly references. This version, with all the characters now named and the scene and chronology altered, was read to the Lovelace Society of Worcester College, Oxford, in January 1938 and was submitted to Allen & Unwin (see below). It was later further revised and enlarged. See 'The Boundaries of the Little Kingdom' by Taum Santoski, *Selections from the Marquette J. R. R. Tolkien Collection* (Milwaukee: Marquette University Library, 1987), pp. [11–15], and 'Early Versions of *Farmer Giles of Ham*' by John D. Rateliff, pp. 45–8, *Leaves from the Tree: J. R. R. Tolkien's Shorter Fiction* (London: The Tolkien Society, 1991). Santoski believed that there was an intermediate stage of revision, now lost, between the second and third drafts described above (cf., perhaps, the d'Ardenne translation, section G, French 5).

Even before *The Hobbit* was proved a success, George Allen & Unwin were interested in publishing other children's stories by Tolkien. In early 1937 they saw 'Roverandum', Tolkien's (still unpublished) story of a dog, and 'Farmer Giles of Ham'. Young Rayner Unwin thought that these two stories together would make a good book. On 15 November 1937 Tolkien resubmitted 'Farmer Giles' to Allen & Unwin together with other manuscripts (see A15a note). Stanley Unwin returned 'Farmer Giles' on 16 November and suggested that an excellent book would be made if the story were put with material of a like character. Unwin wanted a sequel to *The Hobbit* for the 1938 Christmas season; and if not that, then a volume of stories like 'Farmer Giles'.

By 24 July 1938 Tolkien's *Hobbit* sequel, *The Lord of the Rings*, had come to a halt for want of inspiration, *The Silmarillion* was not finished, and another book was still wanted for publication. 'The only line I have,' he wrote to C. A. Furth of Allen & Unwin,

> quite outside [the 'Silmarillion' mythology], is 'Farmer Giles' and the Little Kingdom (with its capital at Thame). I rewrote that to about 50% longer [than the version submitted to Allen & Unwin], last January, and read it to the Lovelace Society in lieu of a paper 'on' fairy stories. I was very much surprised at the result. It took nearly twice as long as a proper 'paper' to read aloud, and the audience was apparently not bored—indeed they were generally convulsed with mirth. But I am afraid that means it has taken on a rather more adult and satiric flavour. Anyway I have not written the necessary two or three other stories of the Kingdom to go with it!

He sent the enlarged typescript to the publisher in September or October 1938, then waited months for a response while continuing work on *The Lord of the Rings*. He wrote to C. A. Furth on 2 February 1939: 'In spare time it would be easier and quicker to write up the plots already composed of the more lighthearted stories of the Little Kingdom to go into *Farmer Giles*. But I would rather finish the long tale [*LR*], and not let it go cold.' And to Furth again on 10 February: 'Did *Farmer Giles* in the enlarged form meet with any sort of approval? . . . Is it worth anything? Are two more stories, or any more stories of the Little Kingdom, worth contemplating? For instance the completion in the same form of the adventures of Prince George (the farmer's son) and the fat boy Suovetaurilius (vulgarly Suet), and the Battle of Otmoor. I just wonder whether this local family game played in the country just round us is more than silly.'

By 19 December 1939 Tolkien still was making slow progress with *The Lord of the Rings*. 'I wish you would publish poor "Farmer Giles" in the interim', he wrote to Stanley Unwin. 'He is at least finished, though very slender in bulk. But he amuses the same people, although Mr Furth seemed to think he had no obvious public. He has mouldered in a drawer since he amused [medievalist and literary historian] H. S. Bennett's children when I was in Cambridge last March. Admittedly they are bright children. . . .'

The burdens of world war now intervened in author's and publishers' lives, and it was not until 7 December 1942 (it seems from extant correspondence) that Tolkien again raised the subject of 'Farmer Giles'. He asked Stanley Unwin if Allen & Unwin would 'consider a volume containing three or four shorter "fairy" stories and some verses. "Farmer Giles", which I once submitted to you, has pleased a large number of children and grown-ups. If too short, I could add to it one or two similar tales, and include some verse on similar topics, including "[The Adventures of] Tom Bombadil".' Unwin replied with interest on 16 December, but the idea seems not to have been pursued immediately. Tolkien re-submitted 'Farmer Giles' in July 1946 to be read by Stanley Unwin's son David (the writer 'David Severn'), who in 1945 had read and liked Tolkien's 'Leaf by Niggle'. 'If I could have a little leisure,' Tolkien wrote to Stanley Unwin on 21 July 1946, 'I could add a few things of the same sort, still not finished. But *Niggle* has never bred any thing that consorts with himself at all.' David Unwin's report on 'Farmer Giles' was very favourable: it would make an excellent book if suitably illustrated, but better for young readers without the academic description of Farmer Giles' blunderbuss (a play on the *OED* definition, retained in the published text to the delight of adult readers).

On 30 September Tolkien wrote to Stanley Unwin:

> I should, of course, be delighted if you see your way to publish 'Farmer Giles of Ham'. In its present form it was revised from its primitive nursery form and read to the Lovelace Society at Worcester College, and Cyril Wilkinson (the old war-horse) has always been at me to publish it. He returned to the charge on September 3rd when we met at the Election of Nichol Smith's successor to the Merton Chair of Literature—a tiresome business which has gone far to destroy my chances of 'writing' this summer. All the same I feel, as you seem to do, that it is rather a short long and really needs some company.
>
> ... I think I once planned a volume of 'Farmer Giles' with (say) three other probably shorter stories interleaved with such verse as would consort with them from the *Oxford Magazine*: 'Errantry', 'Tom Bombadil', and possibly the 'Dragon's Visit' [cf. C24, 27, 29]. Of the stories one only is written—and might not seem so suitable though I have been urged to publish it. I send you a copy. The other, 'The King of the Green Dozen', would exactly consort, but is only half-written. The third an actual sequel to 'Farmer Giles' is a mere plot. My verse story, which I also enclose in the only copy I possess (as I seem to have mislaid the manuscript), might not be felt to go with it. As 'Leaf by Niggle' certainly would not?

The story which 'might not seem so suitable' was 'The Sellic Spell', still unpublished. The 'verse story' was 'The Lay of Aotrou and Itroun' from the *Welsh Review* (C33), which Tolkien felt (in a separate letter to Stanley Unwin of 30 September) would 'not consort' with 'Farmer Giles', 'at any rate not if a largely juvenile audience is aimed at. One or two other things, A troll song ["The Root of the Boot" from *Songs for the Philologists*, B15] and The true and full story of Hey diddle and the Cat and the fiddle ["The Cat and the Fiddle" from *Yorkshire Poetry*, C16] have got caught up into the Hobbit sequel: still on the stocks.' Enclosed with these were his poems 'The Hoard', 'Errantry', 'Tom Bombadil', 'The Dragon's Visit', 'The Bumpus' (later revised as 'Perry-the-Winkle'), and (if I correctly read and interpret Tolkien's manuscript note) 'The Man in the Moon Came Down Too Soon'.

David Unwin read these works, rejected 'The Sellic Spell' for its lack of humour compared with 'Farmer Giles of Ham', and advised against combining the latter with poetry, even poems which Severn thought admirable. 'Farmer Giles', he felt, would stand better alone, set wide and well illustrated (and, in the event, printed on thick paper). Stanley Unwin concurred, and informed Tolkien on 11 November 1946. On 5 July 1947 Tolkien sent Allen & Unwin a typescript of 'Farmer Giles' revised for press. 'I have as you will see gone through it carefully,' he wrote, 'making a good many alterations, for the better (I think and hope) in both style and narrative. The total will amount to about a page or less of increase in size. I have also inserted a Preface.' The latter was submitted as rough copy, with a short draft of a publicity paragraph. He added:

> You will note that, whoever may buy it, this story was *not* written *for* children; though as in the case of other books that will not necessarily prevent them from being amused by it. I think it might be well to emphasize the fact that this is a tale specially composed for reading aloud. It was, in fact, written to order, to be read to the Lovelace Society at Worcester College; and was read to them at a sitting.
>
> For that reason I should like to put an inscription to C. H. Wilkinson on a fly-leaf, since it was Col. Wilkinson of that College who egged me to it, and has since constantly egged me to publication.

Another typescript of 'Farmer Giles', with further corrections, was made in October 1948.

Tolkien was asked if he had made any illustrations for 'Farmer Giles', or if he had anyone specially in mind who could illustrate it. It was important, Stanley Unwin felt, to find an artist who would enter thoroughly into the spirit of the book. Tolkien had made no illustrations for 'Farmer Giles', but his daughter Priscilla was anxious that he should give a chance to a young artist she knew, Milein Cosman. Cosman visited Tolkien in late November 1946. As far as Tolkien could judge from her samples, she was an artist of merit; and on this basis Unwin commissioned her. But she made slow progress, and failed to please Tolkien despite having made specimen drawings in two different styles. At least some of her drawings were in the freely sketched style of Feliks Topolski and Edward Ardizzone, a manner which Allen & Unwin's art editor, Ronald Eames, termed 'fashionable', but which Tolkien thought 'unfinished' and unsuited to his book. At length, in August 1948, Cosman was released, and work by other artists was gathered for Tolkien's approval.

Among the new candidates was Pauline Diana Baynes, in whose portfolio were comical pen-and-watercolour cartoons drawn after medieval manuscript decorations. Tolkien was attracted to them at once. In mid-October 1948 Baynes was given a typescript of 'Farmer Giles' for consideration, and in mid-November made suggestions for one-colour illustrations and for the two planned colour plates, all of which were approved. Unaccustomed to roughs, she went ahead with finished drawings and produced a dozen more than were required, so that a selection could be made. The first were delivered in early December. Tolkien found them delightful and 'the perfect counterpart to the text (or an improvement on it) and to accord exactly in mood' (letter to Eames, 10 December 1948). On 16 March 1949, after the remaining illustrations were received from Pauline Baynes, Tolkien wrote to Eames that he was 'pleased with them beyond even the expectations aroused by the first examples. They are more than illustrations, they are a collateral theme. I showed them to my friends whose polite comment was that they reduced my text to a commentary on the drawings.' His remarks on Baynes' art continued to be favourable, except that he had hoped for more colour than the artist chose, and than could be afforded. By economizing on colour Allen & Unwin were able to include the majority of Baynes' line drawings, and thereby to increase the length of the book.

Tolkien received galley proofs in early April 1949 and returned them corrected on 4 May. He received page proofs at the end of June and returned them on 9 July. Stanley Unwin sent him an advance copy of *Farmer Giles of Ham* on 13 September.

A4a was reprinted in 1975 by Cedric Chivers, Bath, photographically enlarged for the vision-impaired, the two large illustrations in black and white, bound in dark blue textured paper over boards, in a dust-jacket similar to the jacket of A4a. Also published, reset, as *Selected English & American Children's Books* 27, ed. Shinichi Yoshida (Tokyo: Kenkyusha, [196–?]), with text in English, notes and introduction in Japanese, fewer illustrations by Pauline Baynes and with the large illustrations in black and white, bound in light blue wrappers and grey dust-jacket.

The manuscripts and typescripts of 'Farmer Giles of Ham', and corrected galley proofs, are in the Department of Special Collections and University Archives, Marquette University Library, Milwaukee, Wisconsin.

b. First American edition (1950):

FARMER GILES | OF HAM | [*black letter:*] Aegidii Ahenobarbi Julii Agricole de Hammo | Domini de Domito | Aule Draconarie Comitis | Regni Minimi Regis et Basilei | mira facinora et mirabilis | exortus | [*roman:*] or in the vulgar tongue | *The Rise and Wonderful Adventures of* | *Farmer Giles, Lord of Tame,* | *Count of Worminghall* | *and King of* | *the Little Kingdom* | by | J. R. R. TOLKIEN | embellished by | Pauline Diana Baynes | [*decoration*] | HOUGHTON MIFFLIN COMPANY— Boston | The Riverside Press, Cambridge | 1950

80 pp. + 2 plates. Collation: [A]⁸B–E⁸. 19.6 × 12.8 cm.

Contents as for A4a, except pp. [3] title, as above; [4] '*First published in the U.S.A. in 1950* | *Printed in Great Britain* | *in 12 point Garamond type* | *by Unwin Brothers Limited* | *Woking and London*'; and [80] blank.

Wove paper. Bound in blue cloth over boards. Stamped on upper cover in black: 'FARMER | GILES | OF | HAM | [*illustration, after Pauline Baynes, of the dog Garm and the dragon Chrysophylax*]'. Stamped on spine in black: '[*jagged thin-thick rule with points down*] | *Farmer* | *Giles* | *of* | *Ham* | [*jagged thick-thin rule with points up*] | *Tolkien* | [*jagged thick-thin rule with points up*] | H.M.Co. | [*jagged thin-thick rule with points down*]'. Wove endpapers. No headbands. All edges trimmed and unstained.

Dust-jacket, wove paper. Wraparound illustration by 'Franzen' after Baynes, of Farmer Giles with his sword and the dragon Chrysophylax laden with baggage, in black, orange, blue, and white above a black wraparound band. Printed on upper cover against the illustration: '[*in white:*] Farmer Giles | of Ham | [*against the band:*] By J. R. R. TOLKIEN | [*in orange:*] Illustrated by Pauline Diana Baynes'. Printed on spine against the illustration: '[*running down:*] [*in white:*] Farmer Giles of Ham [*in black:*] TOLKIEN | [*horizontal, in orange, against the band:*] H. | M. | Co.'. Lower cover identical with upper cover (the figure of Giles is centred on the spine, Chrysophylax appears on the upper and lower covers). Printed on front flap: '$2.00 | 10 up | FARMER GILES | OF HAM | By J. R. R. Tolkien | Illustrated by Pauline Diana Baynes | [*blurb*]'. Printed on back flap: '$2.50 | All ages | THE HOBBIT | By J. R. R. Tolkien | Illustrated by the Author | [*blurb*]'.

Published 2 October 1950 at $3.00; 5,000 copies printed. Sewn gatherings imported from Allen & Unwin, cased in the United States.

Typeset as for A4a, except pp. [3–4], [80]. Illustrations as for A4a.

On 16 August 1949 Stanley Unwin sent proofs of *Farmer Giles of Ham* to the Houghton Mifflin Co. for consideration. Houghton Mifflin responded favourably but suggested that Tolkien make a few changes in the first pages of his text, which seemed to the publisher too 'heavy' for American children. They also suggested that the book be reset, not so closely and without runarounds (because of the high wages of American typesetters), and that it have ten or fifteen additional illustrations by Pauline Baynes to further increase its bulk. In the event, Houghton Mifflin merely imported sheets of the British edition with new title and copyright pages and put them in a different binding and dust-jacket.

In September 1960 Houghton Mifflin allowed *FGH* to go out of print in the United States. The American publication rights reverted to Allen & Unwin, who in June 1961 offered them to Thomas Nelson & Sons, New York. Beginning in March 1962, Nelson's sold at least 3,000 copies of *FGH*, of which 2,000 were imported from Allen & Unwin with cancel titles, and at least 1,000 appear to have been sheets of the first impression (dated 1950) imported by Houghton Mifflin, which Nelson's obtained through a jobber. In October 1964 Nelson's reported their stock of *FGH* completely sold and did not reorder, citing poor recent sales. Within a month, the American rights were assigned again to Houghton Mifflin, who had continued as the American publisher of *The Hobbit* and by now had also published *The Lord of the Rings* and *The Adventures of Tom Bombadil*. Houghton Mifflin put another 2,000 copies of *FGH* in print in early 1965.

c. Second edition (1976):

J. R. R. TOLKIEN | FARMER GILES | OF HAM | [*black letter:*] Aegidii Ahenobarbi Julii Agricole de Hammo | Domini de Domito | Aule Draconarie Comitis | Regni Minimi Regis et Basilei | mira facinora et mirabilis exortus | [*roman:*] or in the vulgar tongue | *The Rise and Wonderful Adventures* | *of Farmer Giles, Lord of Tame* | *Count of Worminghall and* | *King of the Little Kingdom* | EMBELLISHED BY | PAULINE BAYNES | [*decoration*] | London | GEORGE ALLEN & UNWIN LTD | Ruskin House Museum Street

64 pp. + 2 plates. Collation: [1–4⁸]. 22.3 × 14.3 cm.

[1] 'FARMER GILES | OF HAM'; [2] 'BY J. R. R. TOLKIEN | [*10 titles, beginning with* LR, *ending with* FCL]'; [3] title; [4] 'First published in 1949 | [*list of second–eleventh impressions*] | Reset New Format 1976 | [*notice of restrictions under copyright*] | © George Allen & Unwin (Publishers) Ltd 1976 | ISBN 0 04 823131 2 | Printed in Great Britain | in 12 point Garamond type | by W & J Mackay Limited, Chatham | by photo-litho'; [5] '[*black letter:*] To C. H. Wilkinson | [*illustration*]'; [6] illustration; 7–8 foreword; 9–[64] text and illustrations. Illustrations by Pauline Baynes on 2 plates, in black, grey-blue, light brown, and white: [*Chrysophylax attacks*], facing p. [3]; [*Chrysophylax unhorses Farmer Giles*], facing p. 34. Cf. A4a.

Wove paper. Bound in paper over boards. Wraparound colour illustration by Pauline Baynes, of the dragon Chrysophylax breathing fire at Farmer Giles. Printed on upper cover within open area of the illustration: 'J. R. R. TOLKIEN | Farmer Giles | of Ham | EMBELLISHED BY | PAULINE BAYNES'. Printed on spine, running up, against the illustration: 'J. R. R. TOLKIEN Farmer Giles of Ham'. Printed on lower cover against the illustration: 'PRICE NET | £2.50 | IN UK ONLY'. Later, bound identically except no price printed on the board, with gold label affixed to the lower cover, printed
in black: 'PRICE NET | £2.75 | IN U.K. ONLY'. Wove endpapers. No headbands. All edges trimmed and unstained.

Issued without dust-jacket.

Published 2 September 1976 at £2.50; number of copies not known.

Reset. Illustrations as for A4a.

d. Second American edition (1978):

J. R. R. TOLKIEN | FARMER GILES | OF HAM | [*black letter:*] Aegidii Ahenobarbi Julii Agricole de Hammo | Domini de Domito | Aule Draconarie Comitis | Regni Minimi Regis et Basilei | mira facinora et mirabilis exortus | [*roman:*] or in the vulgar tongue | *The Rise and Wonderful Adventures* | *of Farmer Giles, Lord of Tame* | *Count of Worminghall and* | *King of the Little Kingdom* | EMBELLISHED BY | PAULINE BAYNES | [*decoration*] | HOUGHTON MIFFLIN COMPANY BOSTON | 1978

3–34, [2], 35–64 pp. Collation: [1–4⁸]. 22.1 × 13.9 cm.

[3] 'FARMER GILES | OF HAM'; [4] illustration (*Chrysophylax attacks*), in black, blue-grey, and light brown; [5] title; [6] 'BOOKS BY J. R. R. TOLKIEN | [*10 titles, beginning with* LR, *ending with* SGPO] | *The Father Christmas Letters* | *(edited by Baillie Tolkien)* | *The Silmarillion* | *(edited by Christopher Tolkien)* | WITH DONALD SWANN | The Road Goes Ever On | Copyright © 1976 by | George Allen & Unwin (Publishers) Ltd. | [notice of restrictions] | ISBN 0-395-26799-4 | Printed in the United States of America | [printing code, beginning "A", ending "1"]*'; 7–8 foreword; 9–34 text and illustrations; [34+1] illustration (*Chrysophylax unhorses Farmer Giles*), in black, blue-grey, and light brown; [34+2] blank; 35–[64] text and illustrations.

Wove paper. Bound in paper over boards. Wraparound colour illustration by Pauline Baynes, as for A4c. Printed on upper cover within open area of the illustration: 'J. R. R. TOLKIEN | Farmer Giles | of Ham EMBELLISHED BY | PAULINE BAYNES'. Printed on spine, running up, against the illustration: 'J. R. R. TOLKIEN Farmer Giles of Ham'. Printed on lower cover against a dark yellow panel, against the illustration: '[*blurb*] | [*at left:*] HOUGHTON MIFFLIN COMPANY © 1978 | $4.95 [*at right:*] ISBN 0-395-26799-4 | [*rule*] | 6–97061'. Wove endpapers. No headbands. All edges trimmed and unstained.

Issued without dust-jacket.

Published 3 October 1978 at $4.95; 10,000 copies printed. A second impression of 5,000 copies was printed before publication.

Typeset as for A4c. Illustrations as for A4c, except that the colour illustrations are printed on integral leaves.

e. New Unwin Paperbacks edition (1983):

J. R. R. TOLKIEN | FARMER GILES | OF HAM | [*black letter:*] Aegidii Ahenobarbi Julii Agricole de Hammo | Domini de Domito | Aule Draconarie Comitis | Regni Minimi Regis et Basilei | mira facinora et mirabilis exortus | [*roman:*] or in the vulgar tongue | *The Rise and Wonderful Adventures* | *of Farmer Giles, Lord of Tame* | *Count of Worminghall and* | *King of the Little Kingdom* | WITH ILLUSTRATIONS BY | PAULINE BAYNES | London | UNWIN PAPERBACKS | Boston Sydney

x, 86 pp. Collation: 48 leaves. 17.5 × 10.9 cm.

[i] blurb; [ii] '*also by J. R. R. Tolkien* | [*15 titles, beginning with* ATB, *ending with* UT] | *with Donald Swann* | The Road Goes Ever On'; [iii] title; [iv] '*Farmer Giles of Ham* first published in Great Britain | by George Allen & Unwin 1949 | Reprinted ten times | First published in Unwin Paperbacks 1975 | Reprinted 1977, 1979 (twice), 1981, 1982 | This edition first published 1983 | This book is copyright under the Berne Convention. No reproduction | without permission. All rights reserved. | [*3 publisher's addresses, London to North Sydney*] | © George Allen & Unwin

(Publishers) Ltd 1949, 1961, 1975, 1983 | ISBN 0-04-823233-5 | Set in 12 on 14 Bembo | by V & M Graphics Ltd, Aylesbury, Bucks | and printed in Great Britain | by Cox and Wyman Ltd, Reading'; [v] '[*black letter:*] To C. H. Wilkinson | [*illustration*]'; [vi] illustration; vii–viii foreword; [ix] illustration; [x] blank; 1–83 text and illustrations; [84] advertisement of 14 titles by or about Tolkien, beginning with *FR*, ending with Strachey, *Journeys of Frodo*; [85] advertisement of *H* and *LR*; [86] publisher's order form.

Wove paper. Bound in heavy wove wrappers. Colour illustration by Pauline Baynes, detail from the binding of A4c, printed on upper cover. Printed against the illustration: 'J. R. R. TOLKIEN | Farmer Giles | of Ham | Illustrated by | Pauline Baynes | [*publisher's "unwin" device in red, white, and black*]'. Printed on spine, running down, against an olive green background: 'Farmer Giles of Ham J. R. R. TOLKIEN [*publisher's "unwin" device, in red, white, and black*]'. Printed on lower cover against a light green background: '[*blurb*] | [*unidentified quotation (from* Sunday Times*), in white*] | [*at left, in black:*] UNWIN | PAPERBACKS | CHILDREN/ | FANTASY | £1.50 [*at right, against a white panel outlined in black:*] GB £ NET + 001.50 | ISBN 0-04-823233-5 | [*bar codes*]'. All edges trimmed and unstained. Copies of the first impression were later issued in a binding as above, except with 'Baines' misprinted for 'Baynes' on the upper cover; cf. A20.

Published 25 July 1983 at £1.50; number of copies not known.

Reset. Illustrations as for A4a, except that the large illustrations are in black and white and on integral leaves (pp. [vi], [39]).

f. New edition, hardcover copies (1990):

J. R. R. TOLKIEN | FARMER GILES | OF HAM | [*black letter:*] Aegidii Ahenobarbi Julii Agricole de Hammo | Domini de Domito | Aule Draconarie Comitis | Regni Minimi Regis et Basilei | mira facinora et mirabilis exortus | [*roman:*] or in the vulgar tongue | *The Rise and Wonderful Adventures* | *of Farmer Giles, Lord of Tame* | *Count of Worminghall and* | *King of the Little Kingdom* | With illustrations by Roger Garland | [*publisher's 'man drawing a circle' device*] | UNWIN | PAPERBACKS [*sic*] | LONDON SYDNEY WELLINGTON

xii, 84 pp. Collation: 48 leaves. 19.6 × 13.0 cm.

[i–ii] blank; [iii] 'FARMER GILES | OF HAM'; [iv] 'By J. R. R. Tolkien | [*13 titles, beginning with* H*, ending with* UT] | and, edited by Christopher Tolkien, | *The History of Middle-earth* | [*7 titles, beginning with* The Book of Lost Tales*, ending with* The War of the Ring]'; [v] blank; [vi] illustration; [vii] title; [viii] 'First published in 1949 | [*list of second–eleventh impressions, 1957–74*] | Reset New Format 1976 | Reset New Format 1990 | This new reset format first published in Great Britain by | Unwin Hyman, an imprint of Unwin Hyman Limited, 1990 | © Unwin Hyman Limited 1990 | [*notice of restrictions*] | [*3 publisher's addresses, London to Wellington*] | A CIP catalogue record for this book is available | from the British Library. | Paperback ISBN 0-04-440723-8 | Hardback ISBN 0-04-440724-6 | [*at left, publisher's "JRRT" device; at right, 2 lines:*] © Frank Richard Williamson and Christopher Reuel Tolkien, | executors of the Estate of the late John Ronald Reuel Tolkien | Set in 11½ on 13 point Bembo by | Nene Phototypesetters Ltd, Northampton | and printed in Great Britain by | Cox and Wyman Ltd, Reading'; [ix] '[*black letter:*] To C. H. Wilkinson'; [x] blank; [xi–xii] foreword; 1–79 text and illustrations; [80] blank; [81] advertisement of 'The Complete Tolkien Catalogue'; [82] '*Books by J. R. R. Tolkien in Unwin Paperbacks* | [*order form*]'; [83–4] blank.

Wove paper. Bound in black textured paper over boards. Stamped on spine in gilt: '[*running down:*] Farmer Giles of Ham J. R. R. TOLKIEN | [*horizontal:*] UNWIN | [*publisher's "man drawing a circle" device*] | HYMAN'. Wove pastedowns; no free endpapers. No headbands. All edges trimmed and unstained.

Dust-jacket, wove paper. Colour illustration by Roger Garland, of Farmer Giles, a dog, cow, horse, etc., above a dragon, all within and overlapping an architectural frame, printed on upper cover. Printed against the illustration, in white: 'J. R. R. TOLKIEN | Farmer Giles | Of Ham | Illustrated by Roger Garland | [*publisher's "JRRT" device*]'. Printed on spine: '[*running down:*] [*in red:*] Farmer Giles of Ham [*in black:*] J. R. R. TOLKIEN | [*horizontal:*] UNWIN | [*publisher's "man drawing a circle" device*] | HYMAN'. Printed on lower cover: '[*colour illustration, of a windmill, detail from upper cover illustration*] | [*in black within a black single rule frame:*] ISBN 0-04-440724-6 | [*bar code*]'. Printed on front flap: "*A fabulous tale of the days when* | *giants and dragons walked the* | *kingdom.*' | SUNDAY TIMES | [*blurb*] | [*illustration, of a windmill, from p. 76*] | [*at left, "JRRT" device; at right:*] £8.99 net U.K.' Printed on back flap: '[*note on Tolkien*] | [*note on Garland*] | Jacket illustration by Roger Garland'.

Published 23 August 1990 at £8.99; 1,000 copies printed, simultaneous with A4g.

Reset. Includes new illustrations, by Roger Garland.

g. New edition, paperback copies (1990):

Sheets, pagination, collation as for A4f. 19.6 × 12.8 cm.

Bound in heavy wove wrappers. Upper cover as for the upper jacket of A4f. Printed on spine: '[*running down:*] [*in red:*] Farmer Giles of Ham [*in black:*] J. R. R. TOLKIEN | [*horizontal, publisher's "man drawing a circle" device*]'. Printed on lower cover: '[*colour illustration, of a dragon, detail from upper cover illustration*] | [*in black:*] 'A fabulous tale of the days when giants and dragons | walked the kingdom.' | SUNDAY TIMES | [*blurb*] | [*at left:*] [*publisher's "JRRT" device*] | Cover illustration by Roger Garland | UNWIN PAPERBACKS | CHILDREN/FANTASY | £3.99 net U.K. [*at right, within a single rule frame:*] ISBN 0-04-440723-8 | [*bar code*]'. All edges trimmed and unstained.

Published 23 August 1990 at £3.99; 10,000 copies printed, simultaneous with A4f.

h. New American edition (1991):

J. R. R. TOLKIEN | FARMER GILES | OF HAM | [*black letter:*] Aegidii Ahenobarbi Julii Agricole de Hammo | Domini de Domito | Aule Draconarie Comitis | Regni Minimi Regis et Basilei | mira facinora et mirabilis exortus | [*roman:*] or in the vulgar tongue | *The Rise and Wonderful Adventures* | *of Farmer Giles, Lord of Tame* | *Count of Worminghall and* | *King of the Little Kingdom* | With illustrations by Roger Garland | [*publisher's 'dolphin' device*] | Houghton Mifflin Company | Boston 1991

xii, 84 pp. Collation: 96 leaves. 19.6 × 12.9 cm.

[i–ii] blank; [iii] 'FARMER GILES | OF HAM'; [iv] 'By J. R. R. Tolkien | [*15 titles, beginning with* H, *ending with* Bilbo's Last Song] | and, edited by Christopher Tolkien, | *The History of Middle-earth* | [*7 titles, beginning with* The Book of Lost Tales, *ending with* The War of the Ring]'; [v] blank; [vi] illustration; [vii] title; [viii] '[*on adhesive label:*] FARMER GILES OF HAM | Copyright © 1990 Unwin Hyman Ltd. | First American edition 1991 | Originally published in Great Britain in 1990 by Unwin Hyman Ltd. | All rights reserved. For information about permission to reproduce | selections from this book, write to Permissions, Houghton Mifflin | Company, 2 Park Street, Boston, Massachusetts 02108. | ISBN 0-395-57645-8 | Printed in Great Britian [*sic*] | [*printing code, beginning "10", ending "1"*] | [*below the label, printed directly on the page:*] [*at left, "JRRT" device; at right:*] is a trademark of Frank Richard Williamson and | Christopher Reuel Tolkien, executors of the Estate of | the late John Ronald Reuel Tolkien.'; [ix] '[*black letter:*] To C. H. Wilkinson'; [x] blank; [xi–xii] foreword; 1–79 text and illustrations; [80] blank; [81] advertisement of *H*; [82] advertisement of *LR*.

Wove paper. Bound in black textured paper over boards. Stamped on spine in gilt: '[*running down:*] Farmer Giles of Ham J. R. R. TOLKIEN | [*horizontal:*] [*publisher's "dolphin" device*] | HMCo'. Wove pastedowns; no free endpapers. No headbands. All edges trimmed and unstained.

Dust-jacket, wove paper. Upper cover as for A4f. Printed on spine: '[*running down:*] [*in red:*] Farmer Giles of Ham [*in black:*] J. R. R. TOLKIEN | [*horizontal:*] [*publisher's "dolphin" device*] | HMCo'. Printed on lower cover: '[*colour illustration, of a windmill, detail from upper cover illustration*] | [*in black:*] [*at left:*] 5-97095 [*at right:*] ISBN 0-395-57645-8 | [*bar codes*]'. Printed on front flap: '$13.95 | [*blurb*] | [*illustration, of a windmill, from p. 76*] | [*at left, "JRRT" device; at right:*] 0491.' Printed on back flap: '[*note on Tolkien*] | [*note on Garland*] | Jacket art © 1990 by Unwin Hyman Limited | Jacket illustration by Roger Garland'.

Published 29 April 1991 at $13.95; 5,000 copies printed.

Typeset as for A4f–g, except pp. [iv], [vii–viii], [81–2]. Illustrations as for A4f–g.

A5 THE LORD OF THE RINGS 1954–5

The textual history of *The Lord of the Rings* is much more complex than I have given it here. It needs a large book to itself (in fact, a variorum edition) and a team of scholars to compile it. Errors and inconsistencies, especially of spelling and punctuation, abound in the various editions. In part these are the fault of an author who had an enormous text to manage and often changed his mind, and in part are the result of careless typesetting. Some 'inconsistencies', though, are not errors but significant variation—e.g., *orcs* as well as *Orcs*—intended by the author. An editor forces 'consistency' on Tolkien's texts at his peril.

I have not listed all errors and corrections in *The Lord of the Rings*, a Herculean task; nor have I completely accounted for the many additions and alterations made to *The Lord of the Rings* over the years, first by J. R. R. Tolkien and later by Christopher Tolkien on his father's behalf. But I have at least suggested their extent and nature, which I hope will be a useful guide for students of these texts.

a. First edition:

i. THE FELLOWSHIP OF THE RING (1954):

[*1 line in certar, between double rules*] | The Fellowship | of the Ring | BEING THE FIRST PART OF | THE LORD OF THE RINGS | BY | J. R. R. TOLKIEN | George Allen & Unwin Ltd | RUSKIN HOUSE MUSEUM STREET LONDON | 1954 | [*2 lines in tengwar, between double rules*]

424 pp. + 1 plate (map). Collation: [1]⁸2–26⁸27⁴. 22.2 × 14.3 cm.

[1] 'THE FELLOWSHIP OF THE RING | [*publisher's open "St. George" device*]';

[2] '[*1 line in certar, between double rules*] | THE LORD OF THE RINGS | BY J. R. R. TOLKIEN | PART I | THE FELLOWSHIP OF THE RING | PART II | THE TWO TOWERS | PART III | THE RETURN OF THE KING | [*2 lines in tengwar, between double rules*]'; [3] title; [4] '*First published in 1954* | [*notice of restrictions under copyright*] | *Printed in Great Britain* | *in 11 on 12 point Imprint type* | *by Jarrold and Sons Limited* | *Norwich*'; [5] 'THE LORD OF THE RINGS | [*poem, "Three Rings for the Elven-kings" etc.*]'; [6] blank; [7]–8 foreword; [9] table of contents; [10] blank; 11–24 prologue; [25] map, *A Part of the Shire*, in black and red; [26] blank; [27] 'BOOK I | [*swelled rule*]'; [28] blank; 29–227 text and illustration; [228] blank; [229] 'BOOK II | [*swelled rule*]'; [230] blank; 231–423 text and illustrations; [424] '[*publisher's open "St. George" device*] | GEORGE ALLEN & UNWIN LTD | [*10 addresses, London to Sao Paulo*]'. Map of Middle-earth, in black and red on folded leaf, tipped onto recto, back free endpaper.

Illustrations, by Tolkien: Ring inscription, p. 59; Moria gate (redrawn by printer's artist), p. [319]; Balin's tomb inscription (redrawn by printer's artist), p. 333.

Wove paper. Bound in dark red cloth over boards. Stamped on spine in gilt: '[*within a decorative ring:*] The | Fellowship | of the | Ring | [*below the ring:*] J. R. R. | TOLKIEN | GEORGE ALLEN | AND UNWIN'. Wove endpapers. No headbands. All edges trimmed. Top edge stained red, fore- and bottom edges unstained.

Dust-jacket, grey wove paper. Printed on upper cover: 'THE | FELLOWSHIP | OF THE RING | [*"Ring and Eye" device, in black, red, and gold*] | [*in black:*] J. R. R. TOLKIEN'. Printed on spine: '[*in red:*] J. R. R. | TOLKIEN | [*in black:*] THE | FELLOWSHIP | OF THE | RING | [*in red:*] Being the | First Part | of | THE LORD | OF | THE RINGS | [*in black:*] GEORGE ALLEN | AND UNWIN'. Printed on lower cover in red: '*J. R. R. TOLKIEN* | [*swelled rule*] | [*advertisement of* H *and* FGH] | GEORGE ALLEN AND UNWIN LTD'. Printed on front flap: '[*blurb*] | 21s net'. Printed on back flap: '*THE LORD OF THE RINGS* | by J. R. R. TOLKIEN | * | PART ONE | THE FELLOWSHIP OF THE RING | PART TWO | THE TWO TOWERS | PART THREE | THE RETURN OF THE KING | Medium 8vo | [*at left:*] *The Fellowship of the Ring* | J. R. R. Tolkien | G. Allen & Unwin | 21s net [*at right:*] *Printed in Great Britain*'.

Published 29 July 1954 at 21s.; 3,000 copies printed. 2,500 copies bound before publication by Jarrold & Sons, 500 bound in September 1954 by Key & Whiting. The publisher's cost book records 20 copies bound in wrappers (not seen), presumably for review and samples.

ii. THE TWO TOWERS (1954):

[*1 line in certar, between double rules*] | The Two Towers | BEING THE SECOND PART OF | THE LORD OF THE RINGS | BY | J. R. R. TOLKIEN | George Allen & Unwin Ltd | RUSKIN HOUSE MUSEUM STREET LONDON | 1954 | [*2 lines in tengwar, between double rules*]

352 pp. + 1 plate (map). Collation: [1]⁸2–22⁸. 22.1 × 14.3 cm.

[1–2] blank; [3] 'THE TWO TOWERS | [*publisher's "St. George" device*]'; [4] '[*1 line in certar, between double rules*] | THE LORD OF THE RINGS | BY J. R. R. TOLKIEN | PART I | THE FELLOWSHIP OF THE RING | PART II | THE TWO TOWERS | PART III | THE RETURN OF THE KING | [*2 lines in tengwar, between double rules*]'; [5] title; [6] '*First published in 1954* | [*notice of restrictions under copyright*] | *Printed in Great Britain* | *in 11 on 12 point Imprint type* | *by Jarrold and Sons Limited* | *Norwich*'; [7] 'THE LORD OF THE RINGS | [*poem, "Three Rings for*

THE LORD OF THE RINGS
BY J. R. R. TOLKIEN
PART I
THE FELLOWSHIP OF THE RING
PART II
THE TWO TOWERS
PART III
THE RETURN OF THE KING

The Two Towers

BEING THE SECOND PART OF
THE LORD OF THE RINGS

BY

J. R. R. TOLKIEN

George Allen & Unwin Ltd
RUSKIN HOUSE MUSEUM STREET LONDON
1954

VI. *The Two Towers* (A5a). Photograph from the first edition, first impression, 1954.

the Elven-kings" etc.]'; [8] blank; 9–10 synopsis; 11 table of contents; [12] blank; [13] 'BOOK III | [*swelled rule*]'; [14] blank; 15–206 text; [207] 'BOOK IV | [*swelled rule*]'; [208] blank; 209–352 text. Map of Middle-earth, in black and red on folded leaf, tipped onto recto, back free endpaper.

Wove paper. Bound in dark red cloth over boards. Stamped on spine in gilt: '[*within a ring:*] The | Two | Towers | [*below the ring:*] J. R. R. | TOLKIEN | GEORGE ALLEN | AND UNWIN'. Wove endpapers. No headbands. All edges trimmed. Top edge stained dark red, fore- and bottom edges unstained.

Dust-jacket, grey wove paper. Printed on upper cover: '[*in red:*] THE | TWO | TOWERS | [*"Ring and Eye" device, in black, red, and gold*] | [*in red:*] J. R. R. TOLKIEN'. Printed on spine: 'J. R. R. | TOLKIEN | [*in red:*] THE | TWO | TOWERS | [*in black:*] Being the | Second Part | of | THE LORD | OF | THE RINGS | [*in red:*] GEORGE ALLEN | AND UNWIN'. Printed on lower cover in red: 'J. R. R. TOLKIEN | [*swelled rule*] | [*advertisement of* H *and* FGH] | GEORGE ALLEN AND UNWIN LTD'. Printed on front flap: '[*blurb*] | 21s net'. Printed on back flap: '*THE LORD OF THE RINGS* | by J. R. R. TOLKIEN | * | PART ONE | THE FELLOWSHIP OF THE RING | PART TWO | THE TWO TOWERS | PART THREE | THE RETURN OF THE KING | Medium 8vo 21s net each | [*at left:*] *The Two Towers* | J. R. R. Tolkien | G. Allen & Unwin | 21s net [*at right:*] *Printed in Great Britain*'.

Published 11 November 1954 at 21s.; 3,250 copies printed.

iii. THE RETURN OF THE KING (1955):

[*1 line in certar, between double rules*] | The Return of | the King | BEING THE THIRD PART OF | THE LORD OF THE RINGS | BY | J. R. R. TOLKIEN | George Allen & Unwin Ltd | RUSKIN HOUSE MUSEUM STREET LONDON | 1954 | [*2 lines in tengwar, between double rules*]

416 pp. + 1 plate (map). Collation: $[1–2]^8 3–26^8$. 22.0 × 14.1 cm.

[1–4] blank; [5] 'THE RETURN OF THE KING | [*publisher's "St. George" device*]'; [6] '[*1 line in certar, between double rules*] | THE LORD OF THE RINGS | BY J. R. R. TOLKIEN | PART I | THE FELLOWSHIP OF THE RING | PART II | THE TWO TOWERS | PART III | THE RETURN OF THE KING | [*2 lines in tengwar, between double rules*]'; [7] title; [8] '*First published in 1955* | [*notice of restrictions under copyright*] | *Printed in Great Britain* | *in 11 on 12 point Imprint type* | *by Jarrold and Sons Limited* | *Norwich*'; [9] 'THE LORD OF THE RINGS | [*poem, "Three Rings for the Elven-kings" etc.*]'; [10] blank; 11–13 synopsis; [14] blank; 15 table of contents; [16] blank; [17] 'BOOK V | [*swelled rule*]'; [18] blank; 19–169 text; [170] blank; [171] 'BOOK VI | [*swelled rule*]'; [172] blank; 173–311 text; [312] blank; 313–416 appendices; at foot of p. 416: 'PUBLISHER'S NOTE | We regret that it has not been possible to include as | an appendix to this edition the index of names an- | nounced in the Preface of *The Fellowship of the Ring*.' Map of Rohan, Gondor, and Mordor, in black and red on folded leaf, tipped onto recto, back free endpaper.

Wove paper. Bound in dark red cloth over boards. Stamped on spine in gilt: '[*within a ring:*] The | Return | of the | King | [*below the ring:*] J. R. R. | TOLKIEN | GEORGE ALLEN | AND UNWIN'. Wove endpapers. No headbands. All edges trimmed. Top edge stained dark red, fore- and bottom edges unstained.

Dust-jacket, grey wove paper. Printed on upper cover: 'THE | RETURN OF | THE KING | [*"Ring and Eye" device, in black, red, and gold*] | [*in black:*] J. R. R.

TOLKIEN'. Printed on spine: '[*in red:*] J. R. R. | TOLKIEN | [*in black:*] THE | RETURN | OF THE | KING | [*in red:*] *Being the* | *Third Part* | *of* | *THE LORD* | OF | *THE RINGS* | [*in black:*] GEORGE ALLEN | AND UNWIN'. Printed on lower cover in red: '*J. R. R. TOLKIEN* | [*swelled rule*] | [*advertisement of* H *and* FGH] | GEORGE ALLEN AND UNWIN LTD'. Printed on front flap: '[*blurb*] | 21s net'. Printed on back flap: '*THE LORD OF THE RINGS* | by J. R. R. TOLKIEN | * | PART ONE | THE FELLOWSHIP OF THE RING | 'An epic-romance . . . a most remarkable feat' | — *Manchester Guardian* | PART TWO | THE TWO TOWERS | 'Superb'—*The Observer* | PART THREE | THE RETURN OF THE KING | Medium 8vo 21s net each | [*at left:*] *The Return of the King* | J. R. R. Tolkien | G. Allen & Unwin | 21s. net [*at right:*] *Printed in Great Britain*'.

Published 20 October 1955 at 21s.; 7,000 copies printed.

Two states of the first impression, priority as follows: (1) on p. 49 (4_1 recto) the signature mark '4' is present, and all lines of type 'sag' in the middle; (2) on p. 49 no signature mark is present, and the lines of type are straight.

Maps drawn by Christopher Tolkien.
    The title page inscription in each volume reads (also printed on facing page): '[*in certar:*] THE LORD OF THE RINGS TRANSLATED FROM THE RED BOOK [*in tengwar:*] of Westmarch by John Ronald Reuel Tolkien herein is set forth the history of the War of the Ring and the return of the King as seen by the Hobbits'.

Tolkien began *The Lord of the Rings* between 16 and 19 December 1937. *The Hobbit*, published three months earlier, was a success, and George Allen & Unwin were encouraging Tolkien, against his inclination, to write a sequel. He could not think of anything more to say about hobbits, he had remarked to Stanley Unwin in a letter of 15 October 1937: 'Mr Baggins seems to have exhibited so fully both the Took and the Baggins sides of their nature. . . . But if it is true that *The Hobbit* has come to stay and more will be wanted, I will start the process of thought, and try to get some idea of a theme drawn from this material suitable for treatment in a similar style and for a similar audience—possibly including actual hobbits.' He would rather have returned to his 'Silmarillion' mythology, 'the world into which the hobbit intruded', and on 15 November 1937 submitted *The Silmarillion* and related manuscripts to Allen & Unwin for consideration (see A15a). But Stanley Unwin advised him that *The Silmarillion* was

> a mine to be explored in writing further books like *The Hobbit* rather than a book in itself. . . . What we badly need is another book with which to follow up our success with *The Hobbit* and alas! neither [*The Lay of Leithian* and the prose *Silmarillion*] . . . quite fills the bill. I still hope that you will feel inspired to write another book about THE HOBBIT; I am quite sure that it would be worth your while to make the effort because we should have a much easier time with the second book than we did with the first and it would help us to get additional sales for *The Hobbit* next Christmas season.

'I think it is plain', Tolkien wrote to Unwin on 16 December, 'that . . . a sequel or successor to *The Hobbit* is called for. But I am sure you will sympathize when I say that the construction of elaborate and consistent mythology (and two languages) rather occupies the mind, and the Silmarils are in my heart. So that goodness knows what will happen.' Three days later, he wrote to C. A. Furth at Allen & Unwin: 'I have written the first chapter of a new story about Hobbits—"A long expected party".'
    The history of the writing of *The Lord of the Rings* is told in detail by Christopher Tolkien in *The Return of the Shadow*, *The Treason of Isengard*, *The War of the Ring*,

and *Sauron Defeated* (A26–A29). Here it will suffice to say that the work was often delayed by Tolkien's duties at Oxford, by the Second World War, by ill health, by bouts of failed inspiration, and by the distraction of other writings (e.g. 'Leaf by Niggle'); and that at the same time, Tolkien tended to wrongly predict its date of completion and underestimate its final size.

As Tolkien remarked in the foreword to its second edition (A5d et al.), *The Lord of the Rings* 'grew in the telling' until it was not simply another story about hobbits, but part of the larger mythology that was in his heart. He came to feel that *The Lord of the Rings* was the 'continuation and completion' of *The Silmarillion*, and that the two works should be published 'in conjunction or in connexion' (letter to Stanley Unwin, 24 February 1950). Allen & Unwin, however, could not afford to publish both works as Tolkien wished, nor could the publisher Collins, with whom Tolkien dealt in 1949–52. The works together were enormous, and production costs were rising. (See further, A15a note.)

After Collins withdrew, Tolkien felt chastened. He now humbly replied to enquiries by Rayner Unwin, who had joined the family firm and had remained friendly with Tolkien. '*The Lord of the Rings* and *The Silmarillion* ... are where they were,' Tolkien wrote on 22 June 1952:

> The one finished (and the end revised), and the other still unfinished (or unrevised), and both gathering dust. I have been both off and on too unwell, and too burdened to do much about them, and too downhearted. Watching paper-shortages and costs mounting against me. But I have rather modified my views. Better something than nothing! Although to me all are one, and the 'L of the Rings' would be better far (and eased) as part of the whole, I would gladly consider the publication of any part of this stuff. . . .
>
> When I have a moment to turn round I will collect the *Silmarillion* fragments in process of completion. . . . But what about *The Lord of the Rings*? Can anything be done about that, to unlock gates I slammed myself?

Unwin seized the opportunity. If Tolkien could send Allen & Unwin a copy of *The Lord of the Rings*, he asked on 1 July,

> it would give us a chance to refresh our memories and get a definite idea of the best treatment for it. I expect it's been said many a time before, but the capital outlay will be terrific and if (as you now indicate you are willing to), you could let us split our expenses by keeping 'Silmarillion' and 'Lord of the Rings' a little apart, at any rate at the beginning, it would help us a lot. Arthur Waley did this with 'Tales of Genji', when we published that enormous book, and afterwards we were able to bring the separate parts together again in an omnibus edition.
>
> We do *want* to publish for you—it's only ways and means that have held us up. So please let us have the 'Ring' now, and when you are able the 'Silmarillion' too. . . .

Tolkien's academic duties prevented a reply until 29 August. 'I am anxious to publish *The Lord of the Rings* as soon as possible', he wrote to Unwin. 'I believe it to be a great (though not flawless) work. Let other things follow as they may.' Since Tolkien had only one copy of the book in typescript, Unwin visited Oxford on 19 September to collect it in person.

In October and November Allen & Unwin made casts and estimates, and determined that the most economical way to produce *The Lord of the Rings* would be in three volumes as 25s. each. But this was still an expensive project and a potential loss for the publisher. Philip Unwin recalled in his *The Publishing Unwins* (London: William Heinemann, 1972) how the firm wavered over the huge outlay involved. He put his vote in its favour, 'on the reckoning that at worst another and bigger book on Hobbits surely could not be a total flop.' Charles Knight, Secretary of the Company, suggested publishing in three volumes to give Allen & Unwin at least the possibility of withdrawing, after incurring one-third of the costs, if the first volume failed. Rayner Unwin wrote to his father, who was abroad, explaining that *The Lord of the Rings* was a work of genius, but if published could lose the firm £1,000. '*If* you believe it is a work of genius,' Stanley Unwin replied, '*then* you may lose a thousand pounds.' Even so, Allen & Unwin minimized their risk by publishing *The Lord of the Rings* under a profit-sharing agreement. Tolkien would not be paid royalties in the conventional way, but would receive no payment until sales of the book had covered its costs, and then would share all profits equally with the publisher. Allen & Unwin have been criticized for this agreement, which to some seems cold-hearted; but it was fair to the publisher and, in the event, very lucrative to the author.

Now began a long and difficult period of production, perhaps most clearly described in the form of a (staggered and abridged) chronology:

12 December 1952 Tolkien wants to insert a facsimile of the burnt pages of the 'Book of Mazarbul' (*LR*, bk. 2, ch. 5). Rayner Unwin suggests that it would be a mistake to insert a halftone plate in the middle of the narrative. A line block, he feels, would be better for this, as well as for the Moria gate illustration (bk. 2, ch. 4), which he now asks Tolkien to redraw with blacker ink and on smoother paper for a steadier line.

11 April 1953 Tolkien has completed his revision—'I hope to the last comma'—of the first volume (*LR* bks. 1 and 2) and will now send the manuscript to the publisher. He will also send his foreword, in which he promised as an appendix to the book 'some abridged family-trees', 'an index of names and strange words with some explanations,' and a 'brief account . . . of the languages, alphabets, and calendars that were used in the West-lands in the Third Age of Middle-earth' (A5a.i, p. 8). Of these Tolkien remarks to Unwin: 'It is no good promising things that are not going actually to appear; but I very much hope that precisely what is here promised, in however reduced a form, will in fact prove possible.' He has not yet had a chance to redraw the Moria gate, 'but I will attend to that as soon as it is needed. . . . That is, I will draw it as much better as my little skill allows, in black. But it should of course properly appear in white line on a black background, since it represents a silver line in the darkness.' He regrets the omission of the 'Book of Mazarbul' facsimiles and thinks line-blocks impracticable for that purpose. 'A page each is required, or the things will be too illegible to be interesting (or too unveracious to be worth inclusion). I earnestly hope it may be found possible to include them in the "appendix".' 'I shall not make such heavy weather with the remainder of the work', he promises. 'The first two books were written first a very long time ago, have been often altered, and needed a close consideration of the whole to bring them into line. As a result the later parts are nearly done; and two more books can follow as soon as you want them (that is, Vol. II).' Three maps are needed, at least one of them rather large. 'They exist, of course; though not in any form fit for reproduction—for of course in such a story one cannot make a map for the narrative, but must first make a map and make the narrative agree. . . . Shall I try and draw them in suitable form as soon as ever I can, and let you have them for the consideration of the Production Department?'

14 April 1953 White lines on black will present no technical difficulty, Unwin replies; but in the middle of the book such an illustration would be very noticeable. He suggests using a halftone tint rather than solid black. 'I am sorry about the burnt pages, you could certainly have a full page in line for each or alternatively they could go into the appendix.' He agrees that three maps are required, but warns Tolkien to avoid making them too large or with too many folds. 'If possible, for the small scale map of the whole field of action, I would suggest we use a double page leaving a gutter down the crack which would enable us to have quite a large area without any fold at all. Possibly the 2 small maps of the Shire & Gondor could be reproduced on a full page each.'

11 June–4 August 1953 The printers (Jarrold & Sons) are slower than Unwin anticipated. He offers to send galleys piecemeal; Tolkien asks to receive them collected. 'I am in a very hot spot with scripts,' he writes on 26 June, 'already lagging behind owing to many other calls, and from now on (i.e. till July 16) shall not have any time for anything else but marking. During *viva*, July 16–29, I may get some time in the evenings. After that I am more or less free for a few weeks.' The first galleys are sent to him on 20 July and 4 August. On the latter date Tolkien writes to his son Christopher:

> The galleys are proving rather a bore! There seem such an endless lot of them; and they have put me very much out of conceit with parts of the Great Work, which seems, I must confess, in print very long-winded in parts. But the printing is very good, as it ought to be from an almost faultless copy; except that the impertinent compositors have taken it upon themselves to correct, as they suppose, my spelling and grammar: altering throughout *dwarves* to *dwarfs*; *elvish* to *elfish*; *further* to *farther*; and worst of all, *elven-* to *elfin*. I let off my irritation in a snorter to A. & U. [not preserved in the Allen & Unwin archive] which produced a grovel.

Tolkien apparently referred in his last sentence to a letter of 4 August from W. N. Beard of Allen & Unwin's production staff: '. . . the printers have replied that they followed the Oxford Dictionary for style. It is quite true that this shows the variations in spelling which they have used, but as we have pointed out to them, the copy clearly indicated that the style of the author was to be followed. . . .' Beard had written earlier, on 24 July: 'We are really appalled that the printers have made such radical deviations from your copy in the course of the type setting. We have told them that the expense of correcting the book to the style which you have used through out must be their own expense.'

28 July–17 August 1953 Rayner Unwin suggests that the first volume be entitled *The Lord of the Rings*, and its two books 'The Ring Sets Out' and 'The Ring Goes South'; that the second volume be entitled *The Ring in the Shadow* or *The Shadow and the Ring*, with its two books 'The Treason of Isengard' and 'The Ring Goes East'; and that the third volume be entitled *The War of the Ring*, with the sixth book 'The End of the Third Age' and the title of fifth book to be determined later. Tolkien, however, prefers *The Lord of the Rings* as an overall title, with the three volumes entitled *The Return of the Shadow*, *The Shadow Lengthens*, and *The Return of the King*. He hopes to avoid sub-titles for the six books, 'for it is really impossible to devise ones that correspond to the contents; since the division into two "books" per volume is purely a matter of convenience with regard to length, and has no relation to the rhythm or ordering of the narrative.' On 17 August he writes to Unwin that he now prefers as volume titles *The Fellowship of the Ring*, *The Two Towers*, and *The War of the Ring*.

> *The Fellowship of the Ring* will do, I think, and fits well with the fact that the last chapter of the Volume is The Breaking of the Fellowship. *The Two Towers* gets as near as possible to finding a title to cover the widely divergent Books 3 and 4; and can be left ambiguous—it might refer to Isengard and Barad-dûr, or to Minas Tirith and B[arad-dûr]; or Isengard and Cirith Ungol. On reflection I prefer for Vol. III *The War of the Ring*, since it gets in the Ring again; and also is more non-

committal, and gives less hint about the turn of the story [than *The Return of the King*, which Unwin preferred]. The chapter titles have been chosen also to give away as little as possible in advance. But I am not set in my choice.

8 August 1953 Tolkien receives galley proofs of the foreword and table of contents. The foreword was devised before the decision to publish in three parts, and Tolkien now wonders if it (rather than an appendix to be published later) should contain a note on the pronunciation of strange words and names. (The note appears in p. 8 of the published volume.) He continues to hope that the 'Book of Mazarbul' pages can be included, without which 'the text as it stands is rather pointless'. He will attempt to re-draw and improve his Moria gate illustration, and will turn 'at once' to the delayed maps (the latter also promised 17 August).

13 August 1953 Tolkien returns corrected galleys 17–69 of *FR*. (N.B. I have noted occasions on which Tolkien received or returned proofs as they are recorded, incompletely, in the publisher's archive.)

18 August 1953 Tolkien returns corrected galleys 1–16 of *FR* with two pages of copy required for blocks (the runes on Gandalf's firework bundles, bk. 1, ch. 1, and the Ring inscription, bk. 1, ch. 2).

19 August 1953 FR is being put into page proof. Rayner Unwin asks Tolkien if he has any particular feelings about the placing of the maps. 'Possibly the large map might be used as an end paper and the small map of the Shire should perhaps be placed fairly soon after the commencement of the text.'

31 August 1953 Tolkien will bring printer's copy for *The Two Towers* to Unwin on 1 September. He has not yet completed the maps.

> I found that it needed a complete re-reading of the whole, and the making of a rough index of place-names (and distances); also I am bothered about shape and scale. . . .
>
> If I could have at least two colours in the maps it would be an enormous help.
>
> There is no danger now, after the thorough revision that I have just given it, of any major alteration in the text of Part II [*TT*]. I think we could dispense with galleys, if that is any advantage to speed and economy [galley proofs were made for all three volumes]. But I am a bit shaken in my faith in my own accuracy. In revising the text for place-names I have come across about 22 errors and in-consistencies unnoted in the proofs passed by me of Part I. However, they do not affect the line numbering, and can, I suppose, be left to page-proof.

9 September 1953 Beard sends reproduction drawings to Tolkien for approval.

23 September 1953 Tolkien replies to Beard: 'I am sorry that I have been such a long time holding on to the drawings, especially as they are not altogether satisfactory, I think. The fault must be divided. I should have done the original sketches more carefully, and given more explanations; but the execution of the copies is not in places very good.' His sketch of the Moria gate was made into a finished drawing by the printer's copyist without an understanding of its Elvish inscription. Tolkien agrees to the alteration of his original sketches, 'making the outer arms of the trees curve outside the pillars; but the third major leaf-curve on the right hand tree needs refining. The inscription, and the explanatory matter at the bottom (now in script italics) will need re-writing.' He does not like written italics in general, and the copyist's are 'not very good'. Tolkien intended the drawing to stop at the foot of the pillars, underneath which the explanation would be in typeset italics. 'If the words are to be made part of the block, then I think an upright form is in every way preferable; and I provide an example of the style and arrangement that I should like.' He asks (abandoning his white-on-black design) that the Moria gate illustration have a grey tint and very light grey tint, with the leaves and 'moon-curves' (i.e. crescent shapes) on the trees left white. The 'red letters', i.e. the Ring inscription in bk. 1, ch. 2, originally to be printed in red, are also not good enough. These were not made over but reproduced from Tolkien's original. He will supply a revision, though it still will not be good enough to represent 'elvish work'. The (copied) lettering of the title page inscription is satisfactory. 'A little of the lightness and style has gone in the process of regularizing the elvish letters at the foot; but the sketch will do.' However, it needs correction in two points (done before printing). The inscription on Balin's tomb (bk. 2, ch. 4), redrawn, 'is neater and firmer than the original; but I should have preferred a much closer copy. The style of the original has not been caught. The heavy strokes are now far too heavy, and irregularly so. . . . The characteristic thickening at some of the acute angles has been removed, making the letter-forms look much more "ordinary" and modern. In placing and weight the copy remains, to my mind, much to be preferred, in spite of its slight unsteadiness, which I hoped that a younger hand might have removed with more delicacy.'

29 September 1953 The printers have been asked to revise the blocks. Tolkien is sent page proofs of *FR* with corresponding galleys. The title page proof does not even approach the original design.

7 October 1953 Revised drawings are sent to Tolkien.

9 October 1953 Tolkien passes the 'much improved' drawings. He will bring the typescript of *The Return of the King* to London on 20 October (delayed to 3 December). It is not quite settled whether or not the 'epilogue' will be retained (eventually it was omitted) 'and what form and length the appendices, promised in the foreword, should take.' He is stumped by the maps,

> indeed in a panic. They are essential; and urgent; but I just cannot get them done. I have spent an enormous amount of time on them without profitable result. Lack of skill combined with being harried. Also the shape and proportions of 'The Shire' as described in the tale cannot (by me) be made to fit into shape of a page; nor at that size be contrived to be informative. . . .
>
> I feel that the maps ought to be done properly. . . . Even at a little cost there should be picturesque maps, providing more than a mere index to what is said in the text. I could do maps suitable to the text. It is the attempt to cut them down and omitting all their colour (verbal and other) to reduce them to black and white bareness, on a scale so small that hardly any names can appear, that has stumped me.

27 November 1953 Galley proofs of *The Two Towers* are sent to Tolkien.

1 December 1953 Proofs of *FR* preliminaries are sent to Tolkien. He is reading proof of *TT* and finds very few errors, at least in bk. 3.

3 December 1953 Further proofs of *FR* and *TT*, of miscellaneous paragraphs, the epilogue, and the foreword are sent to Tolkien.

4 January 1954 Rayner Unwin sends Tolkien a rough draft of the note about *TT* and *RK* that follows the text at the end of *FR*. He asks for the Shire map and a dust-jacket design as soon as possible.

22 January 1954 Tolkien returns corrected galleys 1–68 of *TT*. He has revised the manuscript of *RK* and will send it as soon as Rayner Unwin wishes. He tells Unwin: 'The matter for the extra 50 pages [appendices] I shall not be able to do just yet.' In response to the draft note sent by Unwin on 4 January, he has had second thoughts about the title 'The Two Towers'. 'It must if there is any real reference in it to Vol II refer to *Orthanc* and the *Tower of Cirith Ungol*. But since there is so much made of the basic opposition of the Dark Tower and Minas Tirith, that seems very misleading. There is, of course, actually no real connecting link between Books III and IV, when cut off and presented separately as a volume.'

25 January 1954 Tolkien is sent a proof of the general Middle-earth map, drawn in late 1953 by his son Christopher.

27 January 1954 Proofreader's queries are sent to Tolkien.

29 January 1954 Tolkien returns corrected galleys 69–118 of *TT*, queries on *FR* page proofs. He has completed the revision of *RK* but not the appendices.

2 February 1954 Tolkien is sent more proofreader's queries.

23 February 1954 Tolkien returns the proofreader's queries 'for which I am none the less grateful even though I have seldom accepted his suggestions'. He also returns, rewritten, the note for the last page of *FR*. He is unable to make a suitable Shire map, but his son Christopher has offered to do so. He is without time or inspiration to make a dust-jacket design. He approves a new proof of the Ring inscription, which 'sadly lacks any elvish precision or finesse. It would look better in *red* (as designed and intended); but the fault is mine: the thing is ill-done, and too large and sprawling. But I think it must suffice'. He also approves the proof of the general map though 'it has gone out of scale in places' (intended to be 2 cm. to 100 mi.), the red is slightly out of register, and the name 'Minas Tirith' is illegible. He sends copy for the note to follow the foreword in *FR*. He must give *RK* one more consideration before releasing it.

4 March 1954 Page proofs of *TT* are sent to Tolkien. At Rayner Unwin's suggestion, two pages are left blank for a synopsis of *FR* and *RK*.

16 March 1954 Tolkien returns the proof of the general map and sends Christopher Tolkien's drawing for the Shire map.

19 March 1954 Proofs of the note on pronunciation and final note for *FR*, and of other pages with blocks, are sent to Tolkien.

23 March 1954 Tolkien sends to Beard 'notions' for dust-jackets for *FR* and *TT*, 'I can hardly call them more, owing to their technical deficiencies.'

25 March 1954 Allen & Unwin like the central theme of Tolkien's dust-jacket design, but he has used too many colours. Rayner Unwin suggests using the same device on all three volumes, varying the colour of the background paper for each volume and setting the title in type rather than reproducing drawn lettering.

26 March 1954 Tolkien describes to Rayner Unwin his sketch for the dust-jacket of *RK* and remarks:

> ... I think the same device for each volume is, quite apart from expense, desirable: the whole thing is one book really, and it would be a mistake to over-emphasize the mechanically necessary divisions.
>
> I am not quite clear which is the variant [of the two 'notions' Tolkien sent 23 March] that you preferred. I hope it is the one with three subsidiary rings, since the symbolism of that is more suitable to the whole story than the one with a black centre and only the opposition of Gandalf indicated by the red-jewelled ring.
>
> As for the title lettering, could not that be in a simple form of Black Letter type, which accords better (I think) with the design and the elvish script than Roman?

Tolkien's design—which I have called throughout this bibliography the 'Ring and Eye device'—as printed on the dust-jackets of A5a consists of the One Ring, in gold, summoning the red, gold, and black Eye of Mordor against a black field within the One Ring; a smaller gold ring with a red gem, representing Narya the Great, the ring worn by Gandalf, in opposition from above; and the Ring inscription in red tengwar around the One Ring, terminating in flames. (See Plate VII.) Tolkien's preferred design included the other two of the 'three rings for the Elven-kings'.

29 March 1954 Tolkien returns the proofs sent him on 19 March, finds an error in the Ring verse (bk. 1, ch. 2), corrected before publication.

1 April 1954 Allen & Unwin choose the dust-jacket design with only one ring in

VII. *The Fellowship of the Ring* (A5a). Dust-jacket, with 'Ring and Eye' device.

opposition to the central Ring, partly because they like the look of it, and partly because of difficulties with Tolkien's three-ring design, which would need an additional colour in order to distinguish the rings. Black letter would be illegible, they feel. Rayner Unwin suggests 'some bold typeface that doesn't look too Roman but at the same time has a better display value than black letter.'

4 April 1954 Tolkien returns corrected galley proofs 1–192 of *RK*.

12 April 1954 Proofs of revised blocks for *FR* pp. 33 and 59, and revised proofs of *FR* pp. 1–32, are sent to Tolkien.

13 April 1954 Separations of dust-jacket drawings, made from Tolkien's sketch, are sent to the author with the remark that the lettering does not conform to the corrected Ring inscription.

15 April 1954 Tolkien approves the revised blocks for *FR*, but hopes that the Ring inscription will come out better in the book than in the proof 'in which the fine lines are blurred and shaggy.' He returns the proof of notes for the foreword, with deletions to relieve crowding and repetition. He finds '2 or 3' errors in the title page inscription. 'But I am afraid they must just remain—and I must bear the brunt of any later explanations or apologies to decipherers'. The errors, illustrated below, occur in the first impression of *FR* and *TT*, but were corrected for the first impression of *RK* and for the second impression of *FR* and *TT*.

Uncorrected inscription

Corrected inscription

15 April 1954 Tolkien returns the dust-jacket drawings. The lettering is correct, but the vowel marks are omitted from the tengwar, and the 'flames' need 'neatening'.

21 April 1954 The general map has been corrected to show 'Minas Tirith' more clearly.

27 April 1954 Ronald Eames, art editor at Allen & Unwin, suggests binding in a deep red cloth with a ring device stamped on the spine of each volume.

29 April 1954 Tolkien approves the binding design. The overall title (*The Lord of the Rings*) will be on the dust-jackets, only the volume titles will be on the binding spines.

4–6 May 1954 Tolkien is sent and approves final proofs of the general map.

7 May 1954 Tolkien returns corrected page proofs of *TT*. 'I have abandoned *hath doth* etc. as marks of the archaism of the language of the South, since I had used them so inconsistently and sporadically'. He encloses the synopsis for the beginning of *TT*.

8 May 1954 Tolkien sends Allen & Unwin the manuscript of *RK* to the end of the narrative. He has been giving attention to the appendices 'but cannot put [them] into final form until I know more or less precisely what room there is.' He must decide how much of the appended matter is wanted. 'Some readers no doubt will want little, others a lot.'

12 May 1954 *FR* has gone to press.

25 May 1954 A specimen binding case is sent to Tolkien.

26 May 1954 Tolkien approves the binding case.

31 May 1954 Eames proposes to print the *FR* dust-jacket on 'Caldecott' green paper, the *TT* jacket on 'Lobelia' blue, and the *RK* jacket on grey.

3 June 1954 Tolkien sees the dust-jackets in proof and writes to Eames that he thinks them ugly, especially the cover lettering, which 'has no affinity at all to "Black Letter", being not decorative but brutally emphatic.... A normal serifed uncial (capital) type would be indefinitely preferable, I think'. Eames had used Albertus, a 'chiseled' typeface designed in 1935–7 with Thirties' bold expressiveness. 'I also think [Tolkien continued] that the balance of the whole is wrong.... And the colours chosen are to my taste both ugly and unsuitable. To be effective, of course, the background should be black or very dark, and the same as the filling of the Ring. But at any rate I hope that something other than the blue, and especially the sick-green can be found.' However, 'what the jacket looks like is, I think, of much less importance now than issuing the book as soon as possible; and if I had had nothing to do with it, I should not much mind. But as the Ring-motif remains obviously mine (though made rather clumsier), I am likely to be suspected by the few who concern me of having planned the whole.'

4 June 1954 Eames will revise the dust-jackets using Perpetua, a roman typeface of classical design, in place of Albertus. The jackets for all three volumes now will be printed on grey paper.

9 June 1954 A duplicate proof of *TT* with queries is sent to Tolkien.

10–12 June 1954 Tolkien deals with additional proofreader's queries.

15 June 1954 Tolkien has received an advance copy of *FR*, which he finds 'very presentable indeed'. He remarks to Beard that 'the jacket is now much improved, and is rather striking. I like the grey paper used, and much prefer it to the other colours.'

21 June 1954 Revised page proofs of *TT* preliminaries are sent to Tolkien. Eames thinks that the Perpetua type on the revised dust-jackets looks thin, especially on the spine (and in comparison to Albertus).

5 July 1954 Galley proofs of *RK* are sent to Tolkien.

16 July 1954 Tolkien returns corrected proof of *TT* 'title page, synopses, etc.', also corrected *RK* galley proofs 'which seem very free of errors'.

29 July 1954 *FR* is published.

15 September 1954 Tolkien returns corrected galley proofs 1–97 of *RK*, encloses draft of a synopsis for *RK*.

17, 20 September 1954 Tolkien sends Allen & Unwin corrections for the second impression of *FR*.

18 September 1954 Tolkien has not yet completed the appendices for *RK*. 'My trouble is indecision (and conflicting advice) in selection from the too abundant matter. I have spent much ineffectual time on the attempt to satisfy the unfortunate promises of Vol. I, p. 8.' He hopes that his son Christopher will produce a map of the Gondor area.

22 October 1954 The printers are setting the family trees for *RK*. The 'Tale of Years' (Appendix B) wants shortening. Tolkien's deadline is 1 November. The map in particular is urgently needed.

11 November 1954 *TT* is published.

18 November 1954 Proofs of the family trees are sent to Tolkien.

6 December 1954 Corrections are made to *TT* for a second impression, and corrections to *FR* third impression (see below).

2 March 1955 Rayner Unwin pleads that Tolkien deliver the rest of the material for the appendices, or *RK* will have to be published without all the additional material.

4 March 1955 Galley proofs of (part of?) Appendix D are sent to Tolkien.

6 March 1955 Tolkien replies to Rayner Unwin's letter of 2 March:

I must accept your challenge. We must make do with what material I can produce by your return. I hope the map, which is really the most necessary, will be included.

I now wish that no appendices had been promised! For I think their appearance in truncated and compressed form will satisfy nobody: certainly not me; clearly from the (appalling mass of) letters I receive not those people who like that kind of thing—astonishingly many; while those who enjoy the book as an 'heroic romance' only and find 'unexplained vistas' part of the literary effect will neglect the appendices, very properly.

5–6 April 1955 Tolkien returns corrected galley proofs of *RK*.

14 April 1955 Tolkien sends corrections to page proofs of *RK*. He remarks to Rayner Unwin: 'The map is hell! I have not been as careful as I should in keeping track of distances. I think a large scale map simply reveals all the chinks in the armour, besides being obliged to differ somewhat from the printed small scale version, which was semi-pictorial. May have to abandon it for this trip!'

18 April 1955 Tolkien sends Allen & Unwin Christopher Tolkien's map of the Gondor area, drawn to a scale five times enlarged from the general map.

5 May 1955 Galley proofs of Appendices A, B, and E, and a revised proof of F, are sent to Tolkien.

18 May 1955 Proofs of the Gondor area map are sent to Tolkien.

19 May 1955 Tolkien checks the proof of the map and finds it short by 0.5 mm. in 60, or 3 mm. in total breadth. Tolkien and Beard later agreed that a new block might also be inaccurate, and to print the map as it was.

24 May 1955 Rayner Unwin informs Tolkien of a 'log-jam' in all printing-works.

26 May 1955 Tolkien finds few misprints of words in *RK*. The proofreader corrected even Tolkien's errors in Númenórean chronology.

2 July 1955 Tolkien receives page proofs of *RK* from Jarrold & Sons. Little correction seems to be needed. The printer has misunderstood Tolkien's intentions for the Angerthas table (Appendix E).

6 July 1955 Tolkien returns corrected page proofs of *RK*.

14 July 1955 Proofs of the second Angerthas table are sent to Tolkien.

15 July 1955 Tolkien explains to Allen & Unwin, at length, problems with the Angerthas table, sends alternatives.

18 July 1955 Final proofs of *RK* pp. 205–416, and queries, are sent to Tolkien.

23 July 1955 Tolkien returns final proofs of *RK*, corrected as well and as quickly as he can. He has not received corrected page proofs incorporating revisions sent months earlier. The head reader has old, unrevised text, and pages with marked queries have errors neither queried nor corrected. He is anxious about the Angerthas table coming out right.

20 October 1955 RK is published.

The second impression of *The Fellowship of the Ring* was published in December 1954, 2,500 copies printed by Jarrold & Sons, the printer of the first impression. The reprint was ordered by Allen & Unwin on 17 September 1954, and corrections to the text and the title page inscription were sent to Jarrold's a few days later. The publisher's records are clear that Allen & Unwin expected the printer to have kept the type of the first impression standing, from which moulds for plates were to be taken after the second impression. But by accident or misunderstanding, Jarrold's did not do so. Without informing Allen & Unwin of a problem, Jarrold's suggested that the book be reprinted by photo-offset from the first impression sheets; but Allen & Unwin preferred the quality of letterpress. The printer therefore had to reset the volume, and very quickly, to meet Allen & Unwin's need to replenish their stock after brisk sales. No one at Allen & Unwin seems to have known about the resetting, and Tolkien did not read a new proof. Jarrold's made the corrections given them, but in resetting introduced new errors, some of which have remained in print for many years. The following corrections were made in the second impression:

pp. [2–3], inscription corrected
p. 48, ll. 13–14: Proudfood > Proudfoot
p. 166, l. 41: Mind yours Ps and Qs > Mind your Ps and Qs
p. 197, l. 40: *far and free* > *fair and free*

In addition, at Tolkien's direction '*nought*' was changed to '*naught*', p. 220, l. 2. On p. 394, l. 2, '*únótime*' became '*únótime*' ('*únótimë*' in A5e.i).

Errors introduced in the second impression include:

p. 20, l. 20: [*first impression:*] mayoralty > [*second impression:*] mayorality
p. 29, ll. 12–13 after titling: *well-preserved* > *well*-preserved
p. 56, l. 7: Elven-rings > Elvin-rings
p. 72, l. 35: Gamgee > Gangee
p. 167, l. 30: Bree-dialect > Bee-dialect
p. 186, l. 15: South-gate > Sough-gate
p. 206, l. 17: bride-price > bride-piece
p. 212, l. 41: Bruinen > Buinen
p. 247, l. 25: *heard* > *hears*
p. 252, l. 19 after titling: Gandalf > Gandolf
p. 259, l. 30: Elrond the Halfelven > Elrond and Halfelven
p. 267, l. 36: of the Enemy > fo the Enemy
p. 269, l. 20: Dol Guldur > Dol Goldur
p. 275, l. 5: wolves > woves
p. 287, l. 39: into a strange country > in a strange country
p. 322, l. 18: Twenty other arms > Twenty others arms
p. 324, l. 5: tired as they were > tried as they were
p. 350, l. 21: tunic > turnic
p. 354, l. 1: *Elven-maid* > *Elvin-maid*
p. 392, l. 25: name a single strand > make a single strand
p. 416, ll. 1–2: Curse you and all halflings > Curse and all you halflings

The following errors (among others) appeared in both the first and second impressions of A5a.i:

p. 42, l. 30, 'I won't give my precious away. I tell you.' for 'I won't give my precious away, I tell you.'
p. 67, ll. 6–7, 'I wouldn't say' for 'It wouldn't say'

p. 89, l. 12, 'east of Great Sea' for 'east of the Great Sea'
p. 112, l. 24, 'sight of content' for 'sigh of content'
p. 144, l. 12, 'blue eyes' for 'blue eye'
p. 157, ll. 21–2, 'guarding from evil things, folk that are heedless' for 'guarding from evil things folk that are heedless'
p. 267, l. 23, '*thrakatalûk*' for '*thrakatulûk*'
p. 280, l. 16, 'white towers' for 'White Towers'
p. 321, l. 3, '*Open open!*' for '*Open, open!*'
p. 323, l. 39, 'take up' for 'take us'

The publisher's archive records, without fully detailing, eleven corrections submitted for the third impression of FR (January 1955, not seen). Beginning with the fourth impression, FR was printed from plates.

Errors noted in the first impression of *The Two Towers* include 'all the season of the year' for 'all the seasons of the year', p. 111, l. 34, and 'maylike' for 'may like', p. 350, l. 31. The note at the end of the volume, '*Here ends the second part . . .*', was added with the second impression (1955). Probably with the fourth impression (1956), 'fire and flood' was changed to 'fire and death', p. 118, l. 39. TT was printed from plates beginning with the fifth impression.

Errors noted in the first impression of *The Return of the King* include: 'beside his own, for, the sound' for 'beside his own, for the sound', p. 31, l. 25; 'as for others' for 'as for orders', p. 101, l. 22; and 'pit that open' for 'pit that opened', p. 209, l. 41. At least one error, 'he remote' for 'the remote', p. 274, l. 16, was corrected by 1960. RK was printed from plates beginning with the third impression.

Beginning in autumn 1957, A5a was sold both as separate volumes and as a set. A set of the regular trade edition, 1962 impressions, has been seen in a slipcase covered in light grey imitation leather with a printed label. In 1964 a deluxe set, printed 1963, the three volumes bound in black cloth with ribbon markers, was issued in a slipcase featuring a colour illustration by Pauline Baynes, a 'triptych' view of Middle-earth.

A book club edition was published in 1960 by the Readers Union, London, printed with the ninth? (partly corrected) impression of A5a, three volumes, bound in brown textured paper over boards, in grey dust-jackets printed in purple.

The poem 'Oliphaunt' from TT was included in *The Adventures of Tom Bombadil* (A6) and has been reprinted in anthologies. A separate broadside edition was printed at the Eden Press, Toronto, in September 1984, in an edition of fourteen copies. A separate 'board book' edition for very young children, with illustrations by Hank Hinton, was published in 1989 by Contemporary Books, Chicago. Other poems in LR also have been anthologized.

A dramatic adaptation of LR, in two series of six programmes each (FR, TT/RK), was broadcast on BBC radio, 14 November–18 December 1955 and 19 November–23 December 1956. A different series of ten weekly programmes adapted from LR was broadcast in the BBC Schools Broadcast series *Adventures in English*, 29 January–22 March 1956.

The Lord of the Rings attracted filmmakers' enquiries as early as 1957. An animated motion picture based on FR and part of TT was made by Ralph Bakshi and opened in cinemas on 15 November 1978. An animated television motion picture based largely upon RK was made by Rankin/Bass and was first broadcast in the United States on 11 May 1980. Both films were issued on laserdisc and videocassette.

LR has been adapted for the stage, at least as early as the adaptation by Joyce Biddell of Maidstone, Kent, in 1960. A popular solo dramatization has been performed by Rob Inglis, who has also recorded *LR* (see A5e note). Six poems from *LR* were set to music by Donald Swann (see B28 and section Fi).

Most of the extant manuscripts, typescripts, and galley proofs of *LR* are in the Department of Special Collections and University Archives, Marquette University Library, Milwaukee, Wisconsin. Additional manuscript materials, and illustrations for *LR* by Tolkien, are in the Bodleian Library, Oxford. A sentence from an unpublished version of Appendix E:II, on the Cirth, was quoted in Jim Allan, *A Speculation on* The Silmarillion ([Baltimore: T-K Graphics, 1977]), p. [15]. A 'fragment' of the Dwarves' Book of Mazarbul was reproduced, in black and white, in Nancy-Lou Patterson, 'Tree and Leaf: J. R. R. Tolkien and the Visual Image', *English Quarterly* (Canadian Council of Teachers of English), 7, no. 1 (Spring 1974), pp. 10–26. A page from the manuscript of *LR* was reproduced in Karen Sodlink, 'J. R. R. Tolkien: Manuscripts of a Fairy Tale Writer', *Marquette Journal*, Milwaukee, September 1981, pp. 8–10. Other illustrations of manuscript and proof pages for A5a, see Dii43, Dii46, and Dii87 note.

b. First American edition (1954–6):

i. THE FELLOWSHIP OF THE RING (1954):

[*1 line in certar, between double rules*] | The Fellowship | of the Ring | BEING THE FIRST PART OF | THE LORD OF THE RINGS | BY | J. R. R. TOLKIEN | Houghton Mifflin Company Boston | THE RIVERSIDE PRESS CAMBRIDGE | 1954 | [*2 lines in tengwar, between double rules*]

424 pp. + 1 plate (map). Collation: [1]^{8}2–26^{8}27^4. 22.2 × 14.2 cm.

[1] 'THE FELLOWSHIP OF THE RING'; [2] '[*1 line in certar, between double rules*] | THE LORD OF THE RINGS | BY J. R. R. TOLKIEN | PART I | THE FELLOWSHIP OF THE RING | PART II | THE TWO TOWERS | PART III | THE RETURN OF THE KING | [*2 lines in tengwar, between double rules*]'; [3] title; [4] '*Copyright, 1954, by J. R. R. Tolkien* | *All rights reserved including the right to reproduce* | *this book or parts thereof in any form.* | *First published in the United States 1954.* | *Books by J. R. R. Tolkien* | THE HOBBIT | FARMER GILES OF HAM | THE FELLOWSHIP OF THE RING | *Printed in Great Britain*'; [5] 'THE LORD OF THE RINGS | [*poem, "Three Rings for the Elven-kings" etc.*]'; [6] blank; [7]–8 foreword; [9] table of contents; [10] blank; 11–24 prologue; [25] map, *A Part of the Shire*, in black and red; [26] blank; [27] 'BOOK I | [*swelled rule*]'; [28] blank; 29–227 text and illustration; [228] blank; [229] 'BOOK II | [*swelled rule*]'; [230] blank; 231–423 text and illustrations; [424] blank. Map of Middle-earth, in black and red on folded leaf tipped onto back pastedown.

Illustrations, by Tolkien: Ring inscription, p. 59; Moria gate (redrawn by printer's artist), p. [319]; Balin's tomb inscription (redrawn by printer's artist), p. 333.

Wove paper. Bound in blue cloth over boards. Stamped on upper cover in gilt: 'THE | Fellowship | OF THE | Ring'. Stamped on spine in gilt: '[*within a frame, three rules at top and bottom, single rules at left and right:*] THE | Fellowship | OF THE | Ring | TOLKIEN | [*below the frame:*] H.M.CO.' Wove endpapers. No headbands. All edges trimmed. Top edge stained yellow-orange, fore- and bottom edges unstained.

Dust-jacket, wove paper. Printed on upper cover against a gold background with white speckles: '[*in red, framed on three sides by illustration:*] J. R. R. TOLKIEN | [*illustration by Walter Lorraine, of two entwined trees, a dragon, a hobbit with an umbrella, and other creatures and beings from the story, in dark brown, wraps around upper cover and spine; in red, against a round white panel within and overlapping the illustration:*] THE | Fellowship | OF THE | Ring | [*at bottom, in red:*] *An adventurous trip into | the looking-glass landscape of the hobbits*'. Printed on spine against a gold background: '[*illustration, in dark brown*] | [*in red:*] [*running down:*] THE Fellowship OF THE Ring | [*horizontal:*] TOLKIEN | [*illustration, in dark brown*] | [*running down, in red:*] Houghton [*parallel to the preceding word:*] Mifflin Co.' Photograph of Tolkien and note on Tolkien printed on lower cover in red. Printed on front flap in red: 'The | FELLOWSHIP | of the RING | J. R. R. TOLKIEN | [*blurb*]'. Printed on back flap in red: '[*blurb, continued*] | Jacket by | WALTER LORRAINE'.

Published 21 October 1954 at $5.00; 1,500 copies bound in the United States, sheets imported from Allen & Unwin.

Typeset as for A5a.i, except pp. [3–4], [424].

ii. THE TWO TOWERS (1955):

[*1 line in certar, between double rules*] | The Two Towers | BEING THE SECOND PART OF | THE LORD OF THE RINGS | BY | J. R. R. TOLKIEN | Houghton Mifflin Company Boston | THE RIVERSIDE PRESS CAMBRIDGE | 1955 | [*2 lines in tengwar, between double rules*]

352 pp. + 1 plate (map). Collation: [1]^{8}2–22^8. 22.0 × 14.3 cm.

[1–2] blank; [3] 'THE TWO TOWERS'; [4] '[*1 line in certar, between double rules*] | THE LORD OF THE RINGS | BY J. R. R. TOLKIEN | PART I | THE FELLOWSHIP OF THE RING | PART II | THE TWO TOWERS | PART III | THE RETURN OF THE KING | [*2 lines in tengwar, between double rules*]'; [5] title; [6] '*First published in 1954* | [*notice of restrictions under copyright*] | *Printed in Great Britain | in 11 on 12 point Imprint type | by Jarrold and Sons Limited | Norwich*'; [7] 'THE LORD OF THE RINGS | [*poem, "Three Rings for the Elven-kings" etc.*]'; [8] blank; 9–10 synopsis; 11 table of contents; [12] blank; [13] 'BOOK III | [*swelled rule*]'; [14] blank; 15–206 text; [207] 'BOOK IV | [*swelled rule*]'; [208] blank; 209–352 text. Map of Middle-earth, in black and red on folded leaf tipped onto recto, back free endpaper.

Wove paper. Bound in blue cloth over boards. Stamped on upper cover in gilt: '*The* Two | Towers'. Stamped on spine in gilt: '[*3 rules*] *The* Two | Towers | TOLKIEN | [*3 rules*] | H.M.CO.' Wove endpapers. No headbands. All edges trimmed. Top edge stained yellow-orange, fore- and bottom edges unstained.

Dust-jacket, wove paper. Printed on upper cover against a blue-green background with white speckles: '[*in brown, framed on three sides by illustration:*] J. R. R. TOLKIEN | [*illustration by Walter Lorraine as for A5b.i but in black, wraps around upper cover and spine; in brown, against a round white panel within and overlapping the illustration:*] *The* Two | Towers | [*at bottom, in brown:*] A new chronicle of the | fellowship of the Ring | "*No fiction I have read in the last | five years has given me more joy than* | THE FELLOWSHIP OF THE RING." W. H. Auden'. Printed on spine against a blue-green background with white speckles: '[*illustration*] | [*in brown:*] [*running down:*] *The* Two Towers | [*horizontal:*] TOLKIEN | [*illustration, in black*] | [*running down, in brown:*] Houghton [*parallel to the preceding word:*] Mifflin Co.' Quotation by W. H. Auden printed on lower cover in brown. Printed on front flap in brown: '$5.00 | The | TWO | TOWERS | J. R. R. TOLKIEN | [*blurb*]'. Printed on back flap in brown: '[*blurb, continued*] | Jacket by | WALTER LORRAINE'.

Published 21 April 1955 at $5.00; 1,000 copies bound in the United States, sheets imported from Allen & Unwin.

Typeset as for A5a.ii, except pp. [3], [5–6].

iii. THE RETURN OF THE KING (1956):

[*1 line in certar, between double rules*] | The Return of | the King | BEING THE THIRD PART OF | THE LORD OF THE RINGS | BY | J. R. R. TOLKIEN | Houghton Mifflin Company Boston | THE RIVERSIDE PRESS CAMBRIDGE | 1956 | [*2 lines in tengwar, between double rules*]

416 pp. + 1 plate (map). Collation: $[1–2]^83–26^8$. 22.2 × 14.1 cm.

[1–4] blank; [5] 'THE RETURN OF THE KING'; [6] '[*1 line in certar, between double rules*] | THE LORD OF THE RINGS | BY J. R. R. TOLKIEN | PART I | THE FELLOWSHIP OF THE RING | PART II | THE TWO TOWERS | PART III | THE RETURN OF THE KING | [*2 lines in tengwar, between double rules*]'; [7] title; [8] '*Books by J. R. R. Tolkien* | THE HOBBIT | FARMER GILES OF HAM | THE FELLOWSHIP OF THE RING | THE TWO TOWERS | *Printed in Great Britain*'; [9] 'THE LORD OF THE RINGS | [*poem, "Three Rings for the Elven-kings" etc.*].'; [10] blank; 11–13 synopsis; [14] blank; [15] table of contents; [16] blank; [17] 'BOOK V | [*swelled rule*]'; [18] blank; 19–169 text; [170] blank; [171] 'BOOK VI | [*swelled rule*]'; [172] blank; 173–311 text; [312] blank; 313–416 appendices; at foot of p. 416: 'PUBLISHER'S NOTE | We regret that it has not been possible to include as | an appendix to this edition the index of names an- | nounced in the Preface of *The Fellowship of the Ring*.' Map of Rohan, Gondor, and Mordor, in black and red on folded leaf tipped onto back pastedown.

Wove paper. Bound in blue cloth over boards. Stamped on upper cover in gilt: 'THE | Return | OF THE | King'. Stamped on spine in gilt: '[*3 rules*] | THE | Return | OF THE | King | TOLKIEN | [*3 rules*] | H.M.CO.' Wove endpapers. No headbands. All edges trimmed. Top edge stained yellow-orange, fore- and bottom edges unstained.

Dust-jacket, wove paper. Printed on upper cover against a grey background: '[*in red, framed on three sides by illustration:*] J. R. R. TOLKIEN | [*illustration by Walter Lorraine as for A5b.i, in red-brown, wraps around upper cover and spine; in red, against a round white panel within and overlapping the illustration:*] THE | Return | OF THE | King [*at bottom, in red:*] The final volume in | a trilogy acclaimed as a | modern epic, which includes | THE FELLOWSHIP OF THE RING | and THE TWO TOWERS'. Printed on spine against a grey background: '[*illustration, in red-brown*] | [*in red:*] [*running down:*] THE Return OF THE King | [*horizontal:*] TOLKIEN | [*illustration, in red-brown*] | [*running down, in red:*] Houghton [*parallel to the preceding word:*] Mifflin Co.' Blurb printed on lower cover. Printed on front flap: '$5.00 | The RETURN | of the KING | J. R. R. TOLKIEN | [*blurb*]'. Printed on back flap: '[*blurb, continued*] | Jacket by | WALTER LORRAINE'.

Published 5 January 1956 at $5.00; 5,000 copies bound in the United States, sheets imported from Allen & Unwin.

Typeset as for A5a.iii, except pp. [5], [7–8]. The title leaf is a cancellandum.

According to Paul Brooks, formerly of Houghton Mifflin, in his memoir *Two Park Street* (Boston: Houghton Mifflin, 1986), credit for publishing an American edition of *The Lord of the Rings* belongs largely to Anne Barrett, whose editorial report on *The Fellowship of the Ring* echoed that of Rayner Unwin to his father (A5a note). Barrett wrote: 'I think it is wonderful, but it has its drawbacks. Who will read 423 pages about an unfinished journey undertaken by mythical creatures with confusing names? Probably no one, but I still say it is wonderful and—with my heart in my mouth—*to publish.*'

The Lord of the Rings is reported to have been the Christmas Extra selection of the Science Fiction Book Club for 1960.

c. First (unauthorized) paperback edition (1965):

i. THE FELLOWSHIP OF THE RING

[*within open areas of illustration by Jack Gaughan:*] [*uncials, at top:*] THE FELLOWSHIP | OF THE RING | J. R. R. TOLKIEN | [*roman, at bottom:*] ACE BOOKS, INC. | 1120 Avenue of the Americas | New York 36, N. Y.

448 pp. Collation: 224 leaves. 17.8 × 10.5 cm.

[1] blurb, signed 'D. A. W.' (Donald A. Wollheim); [2] note on Tolkien; [3] title; [4] 'THE FELLOWSHIP OF THE RING | Complete & Unabridged | *Cover and title page by Jack Gaughan.* | Printed in U.S.A.'; [5] 'THE LORD OF THE RINGS | [*poem, "Three Rings for the Elven-kings" etc.*]'; [6] blank; [7] table of contents; [8] blank; 9–11 foreword; [12] blank; 13–27 prologue; [28] blank; 29 map, *A Part of the Shire*; [30] blank; [31] 'BOOK I'; [32] blank; 33–242 text and illustration; [243] 'BOOK II'; [244] blank; 245–448 text and illustrations.

Illustrations, by Tolkien (as for A5a.i): Ring inscription, p. 65; Moria gate, p. 339; Balin's tomb inscription, p. 354.

Wove paper. Bound in heavy wove wrappers. Covers and spine printed against a red background. Printed on upper cover : '[*at left:*] [*publisher's "a*/*ace" device, in black and white*] | [*in black:*] SCIENCE | FICTION | CLASSIC | A-4 | 75¢ | [*at right:*] J. R. R. TOLKIEN | [*in yellow:*] WINNER of the INTERNATIONAL FANTASY AWARD | [*in white:*] The Fellowship | of the Ring | [*in black:*] "Superb—one of the major achievements of epic | imagination in our lifetime, and your life is | the poorer if you have failed to read it." | —ANTHONY BOUCHER | [*colour illustration by Jack Gaughan, of five members of the Fellowship of the Ring standing on rocks*] | [*running up left edge of cover, in yellow, partly overlapping the illustration:*] Complete & Unabridged'. Printed on spine: '[*publisher's "a*/*ace" device, in black and white*] | [*in black:*] SCIENCE | FICTION | CLASSIC | A-4 | 75¢ | [*large asterisk, in yellow-green*] | [*running down, in white:*] The Fellowship of the Ring [*parallel to title, in yellow:*] J. R. R. TOLKIEN | [*followed by: 2 large asterisks, in yellow-green*]'. Printed on lower cover: '[*in white:*] The Fellowship of the Ring | [*flourish, in yellow-green*] | [*blurb, in black*] | [*large asterisk, in yellow-green*]'. All edges trimmed and stained orange.

Published May? 1965 at $0.75; 150,000 copies printed.

Reset, based on a corrected impression of A5a(–b).i, with further corrections, but continuing most of the errors noted for the earlier edition. The illustrations and Shire map were reproduced from A5a(–b).i. Omits the general map of Middle-earth.

ii. THE TWO TOWERS:

[*uncials:*] THE TWO | TOWERS | J. R. R. TOLKIEN | [*illustration by Jack Gaughan*] | [*roman:*] ACE BOOKS, INC. | 1120 Avenue of the Americas | New York, N.Y. 10036

384 pp. Collation: 192 leaves. 18.0 × 10.6 cm.

[1] '[*Ring inscription in tengwar, reproduced from A5b.i*] | THE LORD OF THE RINGS | [*poem, "Three Rings for the Elven-kings" etc.*].'; [2] note on Tolkien; [3] title; [4] 'THE TWO TOWERS | Complete & Unabridged | *Cover and title page by Jack Gaughan.* | Printed in U.S.A.'; [5] table of contents; [6] blank; 7–8 synopsis; [9] 'BOOK THREE | [*flourish*]'; [10] blank; 11–219 text; [220] blank; [221] 'BOOK FOUR | [*flourish*]'; [222] blank; 223–381 text; [382] 'CLASSICS OF GREAT SCIENCE FICTION | FROM ACE BOOKS | [*advertisement*]'; [383] advertisement of *World's Best Science Fiction: 1965*; [384] advertisement of *LR*.

Wove paper. Bound in heavy wove wrappers. Covers and spine printed against a yellow background. Printed on upper cover: '[*at left:*] [*publisher's "a/ace" device, in black and white*] | [*in black:*] SCIENCE | FICTION | CLASSIC | A-5 | 75¢ | [*at right:*] [in green:] LORD OF THE RINGS #2 | [*in black:*] J. R. R. TOLKIEN | [*in red-purple:*] The Two Towers | [*in black:*] "It is an extraordinary work—pure excitement, | unencumbered narrative, moral warmth, barefaced | rejoicing in beauty, but excitement most of all." | —NEW YORK TIMES | [*colour illustration by Jack Gaughan, of a Nazgûl flying on a winged horse over rocky terrain*] | [*running up left edge, in black, partly overlapping the illustration:*] Complete & Unabridged'. Printed on spine: '[*publisher's "a/ace" device, in black and white*] | [*in black:*] SCIENCE | FICTION | CLASSIC | A-5 | 75¢ | [*in green:*] LORD | OF THE | RINGS | #2 | [*running down:*] [*in red-purple:*] The Two Towers [*parallel to title, in black:*] J. R. R. TOLKIEN | [*followed by: 2 large asterisks, in orange*]'. Printed on lower cover: '[*in green:*] LORD OF THE RINGS #2 | [*in red-purple:*] The Two Towers | [*flourish, in orange*] | [*blurb, in black*] | [*large asterisk, in orange*]'. All edges trimmed and stained orange.

Published July? 1965 at $0.75; 150,000 copies printed.

Reset, based on a later impression of A5a(–b).ii (with 'fire and death'), with further corrections ('all the season of the year' > 'all the seasons of the year'; 'maylike' > 'may like'). Omits the general map of Middle-earth.

iii. THE RETURN OF THE KING:

[*uncials:*] THE RETURN | OF THE KING | J. R. R. TOLKIEN | [*illustration by Jack Gaughan*] | [*triple rule*] | [*roman:*] ACE BOOKS, INC. | 1120 Avenue of the Americas | New York, N.Y. 10036

448 pp. Collation: 224 leaves. 17.9 × 10.5 cm.

[1] blurb; [2] 'THE LORD OF THE RINGS | [*poem, "Three Rings for the Elven-kings" etc.*].'; [3] title; [4] 'THE RETURN OF THE KING | Complete & Unabridged | *Cover and title-page by Jack Gaughan.* | THE LORD OF THE RINGS | I. THE FELLOWSHIP OF THE RING (A-4) | II. THE TWO TOWERS (A-5) | III. THE RETURN OF THE KING (A-6) | Printed in U.S.A.'; [5] table of contents; [6] map of Rohan and Gondor, within a 'Greek key' frame; 7–10 synopsis; [11] 'BOOK FIVE | [*rule*]'; [12] blank; 13–181 text; [182] blank; [183] 'BOOK SIX | [*rule*]'; [184] map of Rohan, Gondor, and Mordor; 185–340 text; 341–444 appendices; [445] note on Tolkien; [446] 'CLASSICS OF GREAT SCIENCE FICTION | FROM ACE BOOKS | [*advertisement*]'; [447] advertisement of *World's Best Science Fiction: 1965*; [448] advertisement of *LR*.

Wove paper. Bound in heavy wove wrappers. Covers and spine printed against a grey-blue background. Printed on upper cover: '[*at left:*] [*publisher's "a/ace" device, in black and white*] | [*in black:*] SCIENCE | FICTION | CLASSIC | A-6 | 75¢ | [*at right:*] [*in yellow:*] LORD OF THE RINGS #3 | [*in black:*] J. R. R. TOLKIEN | [*in *white:*] The Return of | the King | [*in black:*] "An impressive achievement, unique | among the imaginative | works of our time." | —NEW YORK HERALD TRIBUNE | [*colour illustration by Jack Gaughan, of five members of the Fellowship of the Ring? and the figure of Sauron behind Barad-dûr?*] [*running up left edge, in yellow, partly overlapping the illustration:*] Complete & Unabridged'. Printed on spine: '[*publisher's "a/ace" device, in black and white*] | [*in black:*] SCIENCE | FICTION | CLASSIC | A-6 | 75¢ | [*in yellow:*] LORD | OF THE | RINGS | #3 | [*running down:*] [*in white:*] The Return of the King [*parallel to title, in black:*] J. R. R. TOLKIEN | [2 *large asterisks, in pink*]'. Printed on lower cover against a grey-blue background: '[*in yellow:*] LORD OF THE RINGS #3 | [*in white:*] The Return of the King | [*flourish, in pink*] | [*blurb, in black*] | [*large asterisk, in pink*]'. All edges trimmed and stained orange.

Published July? 1965 at $0.75; 150,000 copies printed.

Text proper reset, based on A5a(–b).iii, continuing the errors noted for that edition. The appendices were photographically reprinted (reduced) from A5a(–b).iii, with reset major section headings. References in the appendices are keyed, therefore, to the pagination of A5a–b, not to A5c. The map on p. [6] is a detail from the folded map in A5a(–b).i–ii. The map on p. [184] is a detail from the folded map in A5a(–b).iii.

The Lord of the Rings, like *The Hobbit*, was first published in America before the United States joined the international copyright convention, and when U.S. copyright law tended to 'protect' the American printing industry by limiting the importation of books printed abroad and by promoting domestic manufacture. Houghton Mifflin, Tolkien's American publisher, seemed to have been in technical violation of the law by having imported too many copies of *The Lord of the Rings* printed by Allen & Unwin. Ace Books took notice of Houghton Mifflin's sales and of the overseas production of the books (which are marked '*Printed in Great Britain*'), determined that *The Lord of the Rings* had fallen into the public domain in the United States, and launched their own edition in spring 1965.

Tolkien's authorized publishers were already aware that a challenge could be made to his American copyrights on technical grounds. They thought it unlikely that any reputable publisher would take advantage, but in early 1965 began to take steps to secure U.S. copyright beyond question. Tolkien was asked to provide new material for *The Lord of the Rings*, to create a new edition which could be copyrighted. The long-promised index also could be included, as well as new, brief introductions to the volumes if Tolkien could be persuaded to write them. In April 1965 rumour of the Ace Books edition reached Houghton Mifflin, and the matter of revision became urgent. A new edition was wanted not only to copyright, but to compete successfully against Ace Books' copies, which were cheaply priced. Houghton Mifflin began to investigate reprint houses and asked for Tolkien's new material by 1 July.

Tolkien wrote to Rayner Unwin on 25 May that he did not relish

the task of 're-editing' the *Lord of the Rings*. I think it will prove very difficult if not impossible to make any substantial changes in the general text. Volume I has now been gone through and the number of necessary or desirable corrections is very small. I am bound to say that my admiration for the tightness of the author's construction is somewhat increased. The poor fellow (who now seems to me only a remote friend) must have put a lot of work into it. I am hoping that alteration of the introductions, considerable modifications of the appendices and the inclusion of an index may prove sufficient for the purpose.

At first, when asked for the revision, Tolkien was distracted by other writings, including *Smith of Wootton Major* and his translation of *Sir Gawain and the Green Knight*. But his indignation over the Ace affair grew, and he produced what was required of him—if over a longer period of time than was asked. He also conducted a personal campaign against Ace Books in letters to American fans, remarking on the nature of theft. On 30 October 1965 he wrote to his grandson, Michael George Tolkien:

> My campaign in U.S.A. has gone well. 'Ace Books' are in quite a spot, and many institutions have banned all their products. They are selling their pirate edition quite well, but it is being discovered to be very badly and erroneously printed; and I am getting such an advt. from the rumpus that I expect my 'authorized' paper-back will in fact sell more copies than it would, if there had been no trouble or competition.

The 'War over Middle-earth' (as one writer put it) was fought in the popular press. The bibliography of the literature is astonishingly long, and most of the relevant articles and letters to editors are at least partly incorrect or are coloured by emotion. The most balanced argument appeared in the *Bulletin* of the Science Fiction Writers of America, November 1965—which, however, not surprisingly, came down on the side of the author. It was a 'war' over royalties, which Ace Books at first did not pay; but it was foremost a matter of principle, as Tolkien wrote as preface to the Ballantine Books *Lord of the Rings*:

> ... I feel that it [*LR*] is, while I am still alive, my property in justice unaffected by copyright laws. It seems to me a grave discourtesy, to say no more, to issue my book without even a polite note informing me of the project. ... However that may be, this paperback edition and no other has been published with my consent and co-operation. Those who approve of courtesy (at least) to living authors will purchase it and no other.

Within a year, Ace Books gave in to public pressure. They agreed to print no more copies of *The Lord of the Rings*, and they negotiated royalties to be paid to Tolkien. In early March 1966 Ace Books issued a news release which included a letter of 'amicable agreement' said to be by Tolkien but clearly written by someone else for his signature. If there was a war, this was its peace treaty.

One may note with irony that high prices are now paid by collectors for the Ace Books 'pirate' *Lord of the Rings*, its value driven by notoriety, while first impressions of the authorized paperback edition (A5d) may be had for pence.

Jack Gaughan is said to have painted all three covers for the Ace *LR* in a single weekend. He did not have time to read the book, but was 'talked through' his art by fantasy writer and critic Lin Carter. The runes in the background of his paintings for *LR* have no meaning.

d. Revised edition (1965):

i. THE FELLOWSHIP OF THE RING:

[*1 line in certar, between double rules*] | The Fellowship | of the Ring | BEING THE FIRST PART OF | THE LORD OF THE RINGS | with a new Foreword by the author | J. R. R. TOLKIEN | BALLANTINE BOOKS • NEW YORK | [*2 lines in tengwar, between double rules*]

528 pp. Collation: 264 leaves. 17.8 × 10.7 cm.

[i] '[*3 quotations, from the* New York Herald Tribune, Providence Sunday Journal,

and New York Times Book Review] | *This is the only complete and authorized* | *paperbound edition, containing all of the* | *original text and maps and a new* | *Foreword* | *by the author, J. R. R. Tolkien* | [*square brackets in original:*] [SEE NEXT PAGE]'; [ii–iii] blurb; [iv] '[*1 line in certar, between double rules*] | THE LORD OF THE RINGS | BY J. R. R. TOLKIEN | PART I | THE FELLOWSHIP OF THE RING | PART II | THE TWO TOWERS | PART III | THE RETURN OF THE KING | [2 *lines in tengwar, between double rules*]'; [v] title; [vi] 'Copyright © 1965 by J. R. R. Tolkien | THIS BOOK IS COPYRIGHT UNDER THE BERNE CONVENTION | PRINTED IN THE UNITED STATES OF AMERICA | This edition published by arrangement with Houghton Mifflin | Company | First Printing: October, 1965 | Published in the United States of America | BALLANTINE BOOKS, INC. | 101 Fifth Avenue, New York, New York 10003'; [vii] 'THE LORD OF THE RINGS | [*poem, "Three Rings for the Elven-kings" etc.*]'; viii–xiii foreword; [xiv] blank; [xv] table of contents; [xvi–xvii] map of Middle-earth; [xviii] blank; 19–36 prologue; 37–9 Note on the Shire Records; [40] map, *A Part of the Shire*; [41] 'BOOK I | [*swelled rule*]'; [42] blank; 43–286 text and illustration; [287] 'BOOK II'; [288] blank; 289–527 text and illustrations; [528] '*Available now from Ballantine Books!* | [*advertisement of H and LR*]'.

Illustrations, by Tolkien (as for A5a.i): Ring inscription, p. 80; Moria gate, p. 399; Balin's tomb inscription, p. 416.

Wove paper. Bound in heavy wove wrappers. Printed on upper cover against a colour illustration by Barbara Remington, the left one-third of a Middle-earth landscape: '[*running up edge at upper left, in white:*] BALLANTINE BOOKS U7040 [*to right of the preceding phrase, horizontal:*] [*publisher's "BB" device, in white and black*] [*in white:*] 95¢ [*at far right:*] 1 | [*at centre:*] THE AUTHORIZED EDITION | OF THE FAMOUS FANTASY TRILOGY | "THE LORD OF THE RINGS" | *Newly Revised, with a Special Foreword by the author* | ["*Gothic*" *lettering:*] J. R. R. TOLKIEN | [*roman:*] Part One | THE FELLOWSHIP | OF THE RING | [*against an orange panel:*] [*in black:*] HOUGHTON | MIFFLIN | COMPANY | [*in white:*] ["*dolphin*" *device*] | Dolphin | Edition | [*in black:*] WITH | BALLANTINE BOOKS'. Printed on spine: '[*in blue:*] U7040 | [*running down:*] [*in orange:*] THE FELLOWSHIP OF THE RING [*in black:*] ["*gear*" *ornament*] J. R. R. TOLKIEN | [*publisher's "BB" device, horizontal, in white and black*]'. Printed on lower cover: '[*blurb, in black with orange initial "I"*] | [*in black:*] [*quotation from* New York Herald Tribune Book Week] | [*against a yellow-green panel outlined in black:*] A STATEMENT FROM THE AUTHOR | "*This paperback edition, and no other,* | *has been published with my consent and* | *co-operation. Those who approve of* | *courtesy (at least) to living authors will* | *purchase it, and no other.*" | [*facsimile signature, "J. R. R. Tolkien"*] | [*below the panel:*] Printed in U.S.A.' All edges trimmed and stained orange.

Published October 1965 at $0.95; number of copies not known. 125,000 copies of each volume were printed in the United States, and another 10,000 in Canada, by 17 January 1966. 10,000 sets were sold by 17 January. One copy of A5e.i seen was inscribed by its owner on 14 October 1965.

Partly reset, revised, based on a corrected impression of A5a.i, with further corrections (e.g. 'mayorality' > 'mayoralty'; 'Bee-dialect' > 'Bree-dialect'). The following errors, among others, were continued from A5a.i:

p. 43, l. 15 after titling, '*well*-preserved' for '*well-preserved*'
p. 60, ll. 16–17, 'I won't give my precious away. I tell you.' for 'I won't give my precious away, I tell you.'

p. 90, l. 15, 'I wouldn't say' for 'It wouldn't say'
p. 184, l. 32, 'blue eyes' for 'blue eye'
p. 260, l. 36, 'bride-piece' for 'bride-price'
p. 268, l. 39, 'Buinen' for 'Bruinen'
p. 309, l. 21, *'hears'* for *'heard'*
p. 323, l. 27, 'Elrond and Halfelven' for 'Elrond the Halfelven'
p. 359, ll. 24–5, 'in a strange country' for 'into a strange country'
p. 401, ll. 2–3, *'Open open!'* for *'Open, open!'*
p. 404, l. 20, 'take up' for 'take us'
p. 440, l. 26, *'Elvin-maid'* for *'Elven-maid'*

Alterations (other than corrections to errors noted for A5a.i) and new errors made in A5d.i include:

A5d.i, pp. viii–xiii, a new foreword in place of the foreword of A5a–b, including a final paragraph (omitted in A5e.i) alluding to the Ace Books copyright dispute; p. x, ll. 8–9, 'or [*error, for* nor] to displease'; '*The Lord of the Rings* is now issued in a new form, and the opportunity has been taken of revising it. A number of errors and inconsistencies that still remained in the text have been corrected, and an attempt has been made to provide information on a few points which attentive readers have raised. I have considered all their comments and enquiries, and if some seem to have been passed over that may be because I have failed to keep my notes in order; but many enquiries could only be answered by additional appendices, or indeed by the production of an accessory volume containing much of the material that I did not include in the original edition, in particular more detailed linguistic information. In the meantime this edition offers this Foreword, an addition to the Prologue, some notes, and an index of the names of persons and places.' (p. xii; cf. A5e.i, 'issued in a new edition')
p. 24, ll. 15–21: There for a thousand years they were little troubled by wars, and they prospered and multiplied after the Dark Plague (S.R. 37) until the disaster of the Long Winter and the famine that followed it. Many thousands then perished, but the Days of Dearth (1158–60) were at the time of this tale long past and the Hobbits had again become accustomed to plenty. < A5a.i, p. 15, ll. 8–10: And thenceforward for a thousand years they lived in almost unbroken peace.
p. 24, ll. 26–8: Forty leagues it stretched from the Fox [*error, for* Far] Downs to the Brandywine Bridge, and [*error, omits* nearly] fifty from the western [*error, for* northern] moors < A5a.i, p. 15, ll. 14–16: Fifty leagues it stretched from the Westmarch under the Tower Hills to the Brandywine Bridge, and nearly fifty from the northern moors
p. 28, ll. 6–7: if they were accurate: they liked to have books < A5a.i, p. 18, l. 1: if they are accurate: they like to have books
p. 30, ll. 4–6: Boffins. Outside the Farthings were the East and West Marches: the Buckland [*error, omits page reference and semi-colon* (I 141–2);] and the West-march added to the Shire in S.R. 1462. ¶ The Shire < A5a.i, p. 18, l. 24–5: Boffins. ¶ The Shire
p. 34, l. 24: *We hate* [*error, for* hates] *it*
p. 36, l. 3: birthday (S.R. 1401). At this point < A5a.1, p. 24, l. 9: birthday. At that point
pp. 37–9, 'Note on the Shire Records' added, with an incorrect break between pp. 36–7
p. 49, l. 7: nasturtiums [*error, for* nasturtians]
p. 49, ll. 26–7: commodity, or < A5a.i, p. 34, l. 8: commodity or

p. 63, ll. 25–6: would only say *no doubt* < A5a.i, p. 45, l. 16: would say nothing, but *no doubt*

p. 72, ll. 8–15: but they were leaving Middle-earth and were no longer concerned with its troubles. There were, however, dwarves on the road in unusual numbers. The ancient East-West Road ran through the Shire to its end at the Grey Havens and dwarves had always used it on their way to their mines in the Blue Mountains. ¶ [*error, paragraph break*] They were [Tolkien intended the revision to read 'through the Shire over the Brandywine Bridge to its end at the Grey Havens', but accepted the misprinted text.] < A5a.i, p. 52, ll. 32–40: but they shook their heads and went away singing sadly to themselves. There were, however, dwarves in unusual numbers. ¶ The great West Road, of course, ran through the Shire over the Brandywine Bridge, and dwarves had always used it from time to time. They were

p. 80, the Ring inscription is inverted

p. 107, ll. 1–6: alder-trees. A mile or two further south they hastily crossed the great road from the Brandywine Bridge; they were now in the Tookland, and bending south-eastwards they made for the Green Hill Country. As they began to climb its first slopes they looked back and saw the lamps in Hobbiton far off twinkling in < A5a.i, p. 80, ll. 16–21: alder-trees. They were now in Tookland, and going southwards, but a mile or two further on they crossed the main road from Michel Delving to Bywater and Brandywine Bridge. Then they struck south-east and began to climb into the Green Hill Country south of Hobbiton. They could see the village twinkling down in

p. 107, ll. 22–3: Woodhall, and Stock, and the Bucklebury Ferry < A5a.i, p. 80, l. 34: Woodhall and the Bucklebury Ferry

p. 114, ll. 14–21: they came back to the road at the end of the long level over which it had run straight for some miles. At that point it bent left and went down into the Lowlands of the Yale, making for Stock; but a lane branched right, winding through a wood of ancient oak-trees on its way to Woodhall. ¶ [*error, paragraph break*] 'That is the way for us', said Frodo. ¶ Not far from the road-meeting they came < A5a.i, p. 86, ll. 11–15: they came to the end of the long level over which the road ran straight. At that point it bent somewhat southward, and began to wind again, as it entered a wood of ancient oak-trees. ¶ Not far from the edge of the road they came

p. 114, ll. 30–1: back to the lane < A5a.i, p. 86, l. 22: back to the road

p. 116, l. 5: hoofs in the lane < A5a.i, p. 87, l. 29: hoofs on the road

p. 116, l. 7: off the path < A5a.i, p. 87, l. 31: off the road

p. 116, l. 23: left the path < A5a.i, p. 88, l. 5: left the road

p. 116, l. 34: across the lane < A5a.i, p. 88, l. 14: across the road

p. 117, ll. 9–10: to wait. [*error, for* wait.'] ¶ The singing < A5a.i, p. 88, ll. 28–9: to wait by the road.' ¶ The singing

p. 117, ll. 33–4: amazement. 'Few of that fairest folk are ever seen < A5a.i, p. 89, ll. 10–11: amazement. 'I did not know that any of that fairest folk were ever seen

p. 118, l. 3: by the wayside < A5a.i, p. 89, l. 14: by the roadside

p. 118, l. 4: down the lane < A5a.i, p. 89, l. 15: down the road

p. 119, ll. 14–15: *omentielvo* < A5a.i, p. 90, l. 17: *omentielmo*

p. 119, l. 36: the lane went < A5a.i, p. 90, l. 36: the road went

p. 119, l. 39: from the path < A5a.i, p. 90, l. 38: from the road

p. 128, l. 19: make longer ones. At all cost < A5a.i, p. 97, l. 35: made longer ones. At all cost

p. 164, l. 24: felt sleep overwhelming him < A5a.i, p. 127, l. 30: felt the drowsiness attack him

p. 263, ll. 29–30: With a last effort, dropping his sword, Frodo [*error, for* Frodo, dropping his sword,] slipped < A5a.i, p. 208, ll. 27–8: With a last effort Frodo slipped

p. 264, l. 17 after titling: grass with his sword beneath him. Strider < A5a.i, p. 209, l. 14: grass. Strider

p. 268, l. 40–p. 269, l. 3: along the edge of the hills for many miles from the Bridge to the Ford of Bruinen. But I have not yet thought how we shall cross that water. < A5a.i, p. 212, ll. 42–3: along it for many leagues to the Ford. But I have not yet thought how we shall cross the water.

p. 270, ll. 29–30: The Road behind held on its way to the River Bruinen, but both < A5a.i, p. 214, ll. 16–17: The Road bent back again southward towards the River, but both

p. 277, l. 31: *root,* < A5a.i, p. 220, l. 10: *root:*

p. 277, l. 34: *groan,* < A5a.i, p. 220, l. 13: *groan.*

p. 278, ll. 19–22: the Road had left the Haarwell [*error, for* Hoarwell] far behind the river down in [*error, for* behind in] its narrow valley, and now clung close to the feet of the hills, rolling and winding lastward [*error, for* eastward] among woods < A5a.i, p. 220, ll. 34–6: the Road had turned away from the river down in its narrow valley, and now clung close to the feet of the hills, rolling and winding northward among woods

p. 278, l. 23: Nor far down the bank < A5a.i, p. 220, l. 38: Not far from the bank

p. 279, l. 30: its headstall flickered < A5a.i, p. 221, ll. 36–7: its bit and bridle flickered

p. 281, l. 3: the other four < A5a.i, p. 222, l. 37: the other Four

p. 283, ll. 3–5: the Road bent right and ran down towards the bottom of the valley, now making straight for the Bruinen. So far < A5a.i, p. 224, ll. 19–21: the Road turned right and ran steeply down towards the bottom of the valley, making once more for the river. So far

p. 299, ll. 31–5: of this [*error, for* his] close kindred. Young she was and yet not so. The braids of her dark hair were touched by no frost; her white arms and clear face were flawless and smooth, and the light of stars was in her bright eyes, grey as a cloudless night; yet < A5a.i, p. 239, ll. 24–8: of his close kindred. Young she was, and yet not so; for though the braids of her dark hair were touched by no frost and her white arms and clear face were hale and smooth, and the light of stars was in her bright eyes, grey as a cloudless night, yet

p. 344, l. 22: any man mounted him < A5a.i, p. 276, l. 8: any man bestrode him

p. 362, l. 38–p. 363, l. 2: fumbled inside. ¶ 'Here is your sword,' he said. 'But it was broken, you know. I took it to keep it safe but I've forgotten to ask if the smiths could mend it. No time now. So I thought < A5a.i, p. 290, ll. 26–8: fumbled inside. ¶ 'Your sword was broken, I believe,' he said hesitatingly to Frodo; 'and I thought

p. 389, l. 11: eten [*error, for* etten] < A5a.i, l. 18: eaten

p. 418, ll. 2–3: I think; the next word is blurred and burned: probably *room* < A5a.i, p. 335, ll. 30–1: I suppose, but it is written *gard,* followed probably by *room*

p. 418, l. 39: *Mirror mere. An* [*error, for* an] *orc shot him from behind a stone. We* [*error, for* we]

p. 443, footnote (to 'language', l. 35) added: 'See note in Appendix F: *Of the Elves.*'

p. 448, l. 39–p. 449, l. 1: the path that still went on along the west side < A5a.i, p. 360, l. 39: the old path on the west side

p. 449, l. 40: coiled two of them < A5a.i, p. 361, l. 30: coiled them

p. 449, l. 40–p. 450, l. 1: other side, drew back the last one, slung it < A5a.i, p. 361, ll. 31–2: other side, picked one up, slung it

p. 456, l. 33: *vanimelda* < A5a.i, *vanimalda*

p. 477, l. 27: if need be < A5a.i, p. 385, l. 5: if needs be

p. 489, l. 3: *súrinen!* [*error, for* súrinen]

p. 489, l. 4: *Yéni* [*error, for* yéni] *únótimë ve rámar aldaron,* [*error, for* aldaron!]

p. 489, l. 5: *yéni* [*error, for* Yéni] *ve lintë yuldar avánier* < A5a.i, p. 394, l. 3: *yéni ve linte yuldar vánier*

p. 489, l. 7: *Andúnë pella Vardo* < A5a.i, p. 394, l. 5: *Andúne pella Vardo*

p. 489, l. 11: *Tintallë* < A5a.i, p. 394, l. 9: *Tintalle*

p. 489, l. 12: *ortanë* [*error, for* ortanë,] < A5a.i, p. 394, l. 10: *ortane*

p. 489, l. 13: *ilyë tier undulávë lumbulë;* < A5a.i, p. 394, l. 11: *ilye tier unduláve lumbule,*

p. 489, l. 16: *oialë* < A5a.i, p. 394, l. 14: *oiale*

p. 489, l. 17: *ná* < A5a.i, p. 394, l. 15: *na*

p. 489, l. 18: *hiruvalyë* < A5a.i, p. 394, l. 16: *hiruvalye*

p. 489, l. 19: *elyë* < A5a.i, p. 394, l. 17: *elye*

p. 489, ll. 20–30: in the wind, long years numberless as the wings of trees! The long years [*error, for* The years] have passed like swift draughts of the sweet mead in lofty halls beyond the West beneath the blue vaults of Varda wherein the stars tremble in the song of her voice, holy and queenly. Who now shall refill the cup for me? For now the Kindler, Varda, the Queen of the Stars, from Mount Everwhite has uplifted her hands like clouds, and all paths are drowned deep in shadow; [Cf. *RGEO* (B28), 'Notes and Translations'.] < A5a.i, p. 394, ll. 18–25: in the wind! And numberless as the wings of trees are the years. The years have passed like sweet swift draughts of the white mead in halls beyond the West beneath the blue vaults of Varda, where the stars tremble in the song of her voice, holy and queenly. Who now shall refill the cup for me? For now the Kindler, Varda, the Queen of the Stars, from Mount Everwhite has uplifted her hands like clouds, and all paths are drowned in shadow,

The Ring inscription, p. 80, was printed correctly beginning with the fourth impression (March 1966). On p. 119, the revised 'omentielvo' was incorrectly changed to 'omentilmo' with the fifth (June 1966) or sixth (August 1966) impression; see Dick Plotz, letter to *Mythprint* (bulletin of The Mythopoeic Society), 10, no. 1 (July 1974), p. 3. The error 'Buinen' for 'Bruinen', p. 268, was corrected in the fifth or sixth impression. The revised 'avánier', p. 489, l. 5, was incorrectly changed to the earlier 'vánier' in the fifth or sixth impression. The errors 'this close kindred' for 'his close kindred', p. 299, and 'ortanë' for 'ortanë,' p. 489, were corrected no later than the sixth impression. The missing single quotation mark after 'wait.' on p. 117 was inserted after the forty-first (March 1973) and no later than the sixty-eighth (December 1978) impression. An appreciation by Peter S. Beagle, dated 14 July 1973, was later added to the preliminaries. The foreword was reset or repaginated more than once in later impressions.

Two different impressions of A5d.i were marked 'Eighth printing', one dated September 1966, the other, with earlier readings, dated March 1967. With the March 1984 impression, sometime after the seventy-ninth impression (June 1983), impression numbering was begun anew.

The maps, pp. [16–17] and [40], were redrawn, not by J. R. R. or Christopher Tolkien. *Circa* 1983, the general map of Middle-earth was replaced with the map drawn by Christopher Tolkien for *Unfinished Tales* (A17).

ii. THE TWO TOWERS:

[*1 line in certar, between double rules*] | The Two Towers | BEING THE SECOND PART OF | THE LORD OF THE RINGS | With a New Foreword by the Author |

J. R. R. TOLKIEN | BALLANTINE BOOKS • NEW YORK | [2 *lines in tengwar, inverted, between double rules*]

448 pp. Collation: 224 leaves. 17.7 × 10.7 cm.

[1] '[2 *quotations, from the* Boston Herald Traveler *and* New York Times Book Review] | *This is the only complete and authorized U.S.* | *paperbound edition of the trilogy, "The Lord* | *of the Rings," containing all of the original* | *text and maps, a new Foreword, additional* | *Prologue, Glossary, and Index by the author,* | J. R. R. Tolkien. | [*square brackets in original:*] [SEE NEXT PAGE]'; [2–3] blurb; [4] '[1 *line in certar, between double rules*] | THE LORD OF THE RINGS | BY J. R. R. TOLKIEN | PART I | THE FELLOWSHIP OF THE RING | PART II | THE TWO TOWERS | PART III | THE RETURN OF THE KING | [2 *lines in tengwar, between double rules*]'; [5] title; [6] 'Copyright © 1965 by J. R. R. Tolkien | THIS BOOK IS COPYRIGHT UNDER THE BERNE CONVENTION | PRINTED IN THE UNITED STATES OF AMERICA | This edition published by arrangement with Houghton Mifflin | Company | First Printing: November, 1965 | Published in the United States of America | BALLANTINE BOOKS, INC. | 101 Fifth Avenue, New York, New York 10003'; [7] 'THE LORD OF THE RINGS | [*poem, "Three Rings for the Elven-kings" etc.*]'; [8] blank; 9–10 synopsis; [11] table of contents; [12–13] map of Middle-earth; [14] blank; [15] 'BOOK III | [*swelled rule*]'; [16] blank; 17–262 text; [263] 'BOOK IV | [*swelled rule*]'; [264] blank; 265–447 text; [448] '*Available now from Ballantine Books!* | [*advertisement of H and LR*]'.

Wove paper. Bound in heavy wove wrappers. Printed on upper cover against a colour illustration by Barbara Remington, the centre one-third of a Middle-earth landscape: '[*running up edge at upper left, in white:*] BALLANTINE BOOKS U7041 | [*to right of the preceding phrase, horizontal:*] [*publisher's "BB" device, in white and black*] [*in white:*] 95¢ [*at far right:*] 2 | [*at centre:*] THE AUTHORIZED EDITION | OF THE FAMOUS FANTASY TRILOGY | "THE LORD OF THE RINGS" | *Newly Revised, with a Special Foreword by the author* | [*"Gothic" lettering:*] J. R. R. TOLKIEN | [*roman:*] *Part Two* | THE TWO TOWERS | [*against an orange panel:*] [*in black:*] HOUGHTON | MIFFLIN | COMPANY | [*in white:*] [*"dolphin" device*] | Dolphin | Edition | [*in black:*] WITH | BALLANTINE BOOKS'. Printed on spine: '[*in blue:*] U7041 | [*running down:*] [*in orange:*] THE TWO TOWERS [*in black:*] [*"gear" ornament*] J. R. R. TOLKIEN | [*publisher's "BB" device, horizontal, in white and black*]'. Printed on lower cover: '[*blurb, in black with orange initial "F"*] | [*in black:*] | [*quotation from* Time and Tide] | [*blurb*] | [*against a green panel outlined in black:*] A STATEMENT FROM THE AUTHOR | ABOUT THIS AMERICAN EDITION | "*This paperback edition, and no other,* | *has been published with my consent and* | *co-operation. Those who approve of* | *courtesy (at least) to living authors will* | *purchase it, and no other.*" | [*facsimile signature, "J. R. R. Tolkien"*] | [*below the panel:*] Printed in U.S.A.' All edges trimmed and stained orange.

Published October 1965 at $0.95; number of copies not known (see A5d.i).

Partly reset, revised, based on A5a.ii, with some corrections, but continuing the errors 'all the season of the year' for 'all the seasons of the year', p. 142, ll. 10–11, and 'maylike' for 'may like', p. 445, l. 15. Alterations (other than corrections to errors noted for A5a.ii) and new errors made in A5d.ii include:

p. 42, ll. 4–6: strange about you, stranger finds us swift and hard. Come! Who are you? Ranger. [*error, for* strange about you, Strider.' He bent his clear bright eyes again upon the Ranger. *with* Strider . . . the *replaced with a line from p.* 43]

p. 88, ll. 16–17: *Laurelindórinan* [*error, for* Laurelindórenan]

p. 88, l. 27: *Laurelindórinan* [*error, for* Laurelindórenan]

p. 88, l. 32: *Taurelilómëa-tumbalemorna Tumbaletaurë Lómëanor* < A5a.ii, p. 70, l. 42: *Taurililómëa-tumbalemorna Tumbaletaurëa Lómeanor*

p. 88, omits added footnote 'See Appendix F under *Ents.*' (cf. A5e.ii)

p. 90, l. 36: *Orod-na-Thôn!* < A5a.ii, p. 72, l. 26: *Orod-na-Thon!*

p. 91, l. 1: *Ambarona* [*error, for* Ambaróna] < A5a.ii, p. 72, l. 29: *Ambaróna*

p. 110, l. 24: *Carnimírië!* < A5a.ii, p. 87, l. 22: *Carnemírië!*

p. 110, l. 33: *Carnimírië!* < A5a.ii, p. 87, l. 29: *Carnemírië!*

p. 216, l. 13: spent the nights < A5a.ii, p. 170, l. 2: spent the nights

p. 216, l. 15: third day < A5a.ii, p. 170, l. 3: second day

p. 236, ll. 18–19: Remember Théodred at the Ford [*error, for* Fords] and the grave < A5a.ii, p. 185, l. 9: Remember the grave

p. 246, ll. 29–31 after titling: He had never met a hobbit before and did not know what kind of thing to say to you. But he had his eyes on you. [*error, for* But he had his eyes on you. *without the first sentence repeated from A5a.ii*]

p. 261, ll. 33–6: at my tail. Or that an heir of Elendil lives and stood beside me. If Wormtongue was not deceived by the armour of Rohan, he would remember Aragorn and the title that he claimed. That is < A5a.ii, p. 205, ll. 20–1: at my tail. That is

p. 302, l. 10: moors of the Noman-lands < A5a.ii, p. 239, ll. 9–10: moors of Nomen's Land

p. 308, l. 15 after titling: and thrust forward from its mouth < A5a.ii, p. 244, l. 13 after titling: and at its mouth

p. 312, ll. 19–23: hill at [*error, for* hill, at] some little height above a long trench-like [*error, for* trenchlike] valley that lay between it and the outer buttresses of the mountain [*error? for* the mountain-wall]. In the midst of the valley stood the black foundations of the western watchtower [*error, for* watch-tower]. By morning-light < A5a.ii, p. 247, ll. 20–3: hill and lay at some little height above the level of the plain. A long trench-like valley ran between it and the outer buttresses of the mountain-wall. In the morning-light

p. 312, ll. 26–30: Lithui; a [*error, for* and a] third that ran towards him. As it bent sharply round the tower, it entered a narrow defile and passed not far below the hollow where he stood. Westward, to his right, it turned < A5a.ii, p. 247, ll. 26–9: Lithui; and another that, bending sharply, ran close under the western watch-tower, and then passed along the valley at the foot of the hillside where the hobbits lay and not many feet below them. Soon it turned

p. 348, l. 12: Laurelindórinan [*error, for* Laurelindórenan]

p. 348, l. 31: Tol Brandir < A5a.ii, p. 275, l. 25: Tolbrandir

p. 349, ll. 12–13: *Laurelindórenan* < A5a.ii, p. 275, l. 40: *Laurelindórinan*

p. 430, l. 15: *A Elbereth!* < A5a.ii, p. 338, l. 39: *O Elbereth!*

p. 430, l. 18: *A Elbereth* < A5a.ii, p. 339, l. 1: *O Elbereth*

p. 430, l. 20: *nallon* < A5a.ii, p. 339, l. 3: *nallan*

The inverted title page inscription was corrected in the third (June 1966) or fourth (August 1966) impression. It was again inverted, now and then, in later impressions, which suggests that Ballantine Books retained at least two printing plates for that page. Beginning with the second impression (November 1965), the copyright page gave the date of the first impression as October 1965, which seems to be correct. The error on p. 42 was corrected no later than the seventh impression (October 1966). Sometime after the seventh impression, the reading 'Laurelindórinan' (for correct 'Laurelindórenan'), p. 348, was altered to even more incorrect 'Laurenlindórinan', and the error 'maylike' for 'may like', p. 445, was corrected. An appreciation by Peter S. Beagle, dated 14 July 1973, was later added to the preliminaries.

Sometime after the eighty-third impression (February 1987), impression numbering was begun anew.

The map, pp. [12–13], was redrawn, not by J. R. R. or Christopher Tolkien. *Circa* 1983, the general map of Middle-earth was replaced with the map drawn by Christopher Tolkien for *Unfinished Tales* (A17).

iii. THE RETURN OF THE KING:

[*1 line in certar, inverted, between double rules*] | The Return of | the King | BEING THE THIRD PART OF | THE LORD OF THE RINGS | with a New Foreword by the Author | J. R. R. TOLKIEN | BALLANTINE BOOKS • NEW YORK | [*2 lines in tengwar, between double rules*]

544 pp. Collation: 272 leaves. 17.8 × 10.7 cm.

[i] '[*2 quotations, from the* New York Herald Tribune Book Week *and the* Nation] | *This is the only complete and authorized U.S.* | *paperbound edition of the trilogy,* *"The Lord* | *of the Rings," containing all of the original* | *text and maps, a new* *Foreword, additional* | *Prologue, Glossary, and Index by the author,* | *J. R. R.* *Tolkien.* | [*square brackets in original:*] [SEE NEXT PAGE]'; [ii–iii] blurb; [iv] '[*1 line in certar, between double rules*] | THE LORD OF THE RINGS | BY J. R. R. TOLKIEN | PART I | THE FELLOWSHIP OF THE RING | PART II | THE TWO TOWERS | PART III | THE RETURN OF THE KING | [*2 lines in tengwar, between double rules*]'; [v] title; [vi] 'Copyright © 1965 by J. R. R. Tolkien | THIS BOOK IS COPYRIGHT UNDER THE BERNE CONVENTION | PRINTED IN THE UNITED STATES OF AMERICA | This edition published by arrangement with Houghton Mifflin | Company | First Printing: December, 1965 | Published in the United States of America | BALLANTINE BOOKS, INC. | 101 Fifth Avenue, New York, New York 10003'; [vii] 'THE LORD OF THE RINGS | [*swelled rule*] | [*poem, "Three Rings for the Elven-kings" etc.*].'; [viii] blank; ix–xii synopsis; [xiii] table of contents; [xiv–xv] map of Rohan, Gondor, and Mordor; [xvi] blank; [xvii] 'BOOK V | [*swelled rule*]'; [xviii] blank; 19–208 text; [209] 'BOOK VI'; [210] blank; 211–385 text; [386] blank; 387–520 appendices; 521–44 index.

Wove paper. Bound in heavy wove wrappers. Printed on upper cover against a colour illustration by Barbara Remington, the right one-third of a Middle-earth landscape: '[*running up edge at upper left, in white:*] BALLANTINE BOOKS U7042 | [*to right of the preceding phrase, horizontal:*] [*publisher's "BB" device, in white and black*] [*in white:*] 95¢ [*at far right:*] 3 | [*at centre:*] THE AUTHORIZED EDITION | OF THE FAMOUS FANTASY TRILOGY | "THE LORD OF THE RINGS" | *Newly Revised, with a Special Foreword by the author* | [*"Gothic" lettering:*] J. R. R. TOLKIEN | [*roman:*] Part Three | THE RETURN | OF THE KING | [*against an orange panel:*] [*in black:*] HOUGHTON | MIFFLIN | COMPANY | [*in white:*] [*"dolphin" device*] | Dolphin | Edition | [*in black:*] WITH | BALLANTINE BOOKS'. Printed on spine: '[*in blue:*] U7042 | [*running down:*] [*in red-orange:*] THE RETURN OF THE KING [*in black:*] [*"gear" ornament*] J. R. R. TOLKIEN | [*publisher's "BB" device, horizontal, in white and black*]'. Printed on lower cover: '[*blurb, in black with red initial "T"*] | [*in black:*] [*quotation from* New York Herald Tribune Book Week] | [*against a green panel outlined in black:*] A STATEMENT FROM THE AUTHOR | ABOUT THIS AMERICAN EDITION | *"This paperback edition, and no other,* | *has been published with my consent and* | *co-operation. Those who approve of* | *courtesy (at least) to living authors will* |

purchase it, and no other." | [*facsimile signature, "J. R. R. Tolkien"*] | [*below the panel:*] Printed in U.S.A.' All edges trimmed and stained orange.

Published October 1965 at $0.95; number of copies not known (see A5d.i).

Reset, revised, based on A5a.iii, with corrections, but continuing the errors 'beside his own, for, the sound' for 'beside his own, for the sound', p. 34, ll. 27–8, and 'as for others' for 'as for orders', p. 123, l. 21. Further alterations and errors made in A5d.iii include:

p. 25, ll. 31–3: shapely, fifty fathoms from its base to the pinnacle, where the banner of the Stewards floated a thousand < A5a.iii, p. 24, ll. 19–20: shapely it was, one hundred and fifty fathoms from base to pinnacle, where floated the banner of the Stewards

p. 40, l. 20: sea [*error, for* Sea]

p. 62, ll. 21–3: glinted. 'Did I not openly proclaim my title before the deson [*error, for* doors] of Edoras? What do you fear that I should say to him? [*error, reverses correct order of sentences* What do you fear that I should say to him? Did I not openly proclaim my title before the doors of Edoras?] Nay, < A5a.iii, p. 53, ll. 28–30: glinted. 'What do you fear that I should say: that I had a rascal of a rebel dwarf here that I would gladly exchange for a serviceable orc? Nay,

p. 62, ll. 38–9: till now. The eyes in Orthanc did not see through the armour of Théoden, but Sauron has not < A5a.iii, p. 53, l. 41: till now. But he has not

p. 69, ll. 18–19: Gate [*error, for* Door] of the Dead

p. 81, l. 4: Irensaga [*error, for* Írensaga]

p. 99, ll. 11–12: five birdlike forms < A5a.iii, p. 82, l. 19: huge birdlike forms

p. 120, l. 20: Sadly. 'The house of his spirit crumbles.' < A5a.iii, p. 99, ll. 5–6: Sadly. 'His house crumbles.'

p. 127, ll. 21–30 after titling: stay behind. He wondered, too, if the old King knew that he had been disobeyed and was angry. Perhaps not. There seemed to be some understanding between Dernhelm and Elfhelm, the marshal [*error, for* Marshal] who commanded the *éored* in which they were riding. He and all his men ignored Merry and presented not to hear if he spoke. He might have been just another bag that Dernhelm was carrying. Dernhelm was in [*error, for* no] comfort: he never spoke to anyone. Merry felt small, unwanted, and lonely. Now the time < A5a.iii, p. 104, ll. 19–20: stay behind. The king was not well pleased, and Dernhelm was no comfort: he seldom spoke a word. Now the time

p. 128, ll. 20–2: the voice of the marshal, Elfhelm. [*error, for* the voice of Elfhelm the Marshal] ¶ 'I am not a tree-root, Sir,' he said, 'nor a bag, but a < A5a.iii, p. 105, ll. 2–4: the voice of Elfhelm, captain of the company with which he was riding. ¶ 'I am not a tree-root, Captain,' he said, 'but a

p. 129, ll. 5–6: commands. Pack yourself up, Master Bag!' He vanished < A5a.iii, p. 105, l. 24: commands.' He vanished

p. 157, ll. 3–4: given to you, Steward of Gondor, to order < A5a.iii, p. 129, l. 7: given to you, nor to any other lord, to order

p. 176, ll. 14–15: hand in his and felt it warm with life returning. 'Awake! < A5a.iii, p. 144, l. 24: hand in his. 'Awake!

p. 188, l. 8: *Oft hope* < A5a.iii, p. 153, l. 30: *Hope oft*

p. 193, ll. 34–5: ride the sons of Elrond with the Dúnedain < A5a.iii, p. 158, l. 13: ride the Dúnedain

p. 193, ll. 38–9: some three thousand under the command of Elfhelm, should < A5a.iii, p. 158, l. 16: some three thousand, should

p. 223, omits added footnote to '*tarks*' (cf. A5e.iii)

p. 232, l. 13: evil Eye [*error, for* Evil Eye]

p. 247, l. 37: Urukhai < A5a.iii, p. 202, ll. 23–4: *Urukhai*

p. 284, ll. 10–21: beside their beds. ¶ 'The clothes that you wore on your way to Mordor,' said Gandalf. 'Even the orc-rags that you bore in the black land, Frodo, shall be preserved. No silks or [*error, for* and] linens, nor any armour or heraldry could be more honourable. But later I will find some other clothes, perhaps.' ¶ Then he held out his hands to them, and they saw that one shone with Light. [*error, for* light] 'What have you got there?' Frodo cried. 'Can it be—?' ¶ 'Yes, I have brought your two treasures. They were found on Sam when you were rescued. The Lady Galadnil's [*error, for* Galadriel's] gifts: your glass, Frodo, and your box, Sam. You will be glad to have these safe again.' ¶ When they were washed < A5a.iii, p. 230, ll. 37–41: beside their beds. ¶ 'The clothes that you journeyed in,' said Gandalf. 'No silks and linens, nor any armour or heraldry could be more honourable. But later we shall see.' ¶ When they were washed

p. 287, ll. 7–21: and then he laid before them two swords. ¶ 'I do not wish for any sword,' said Frodo. ¶ 'Tonight at least you should wear one,' said Gandalf. ¶ Then Frodo took the small sword that had belonged to Sam, and had been laid at his side in Cirith Ungol. 'Sting I gave to you Sam,' he said. ¶ 'No, master! Mr. Bilbo gave it to you, and it goes with his silver coat; he would not wish anyone else to wear it now.' ¶ Frodo gave way; and Gandalf, as if he were their esquire, knelt and girt the sword-belts about them, and then rising he set circlets of silver upon their heads. And when they were arrayed they went to the great feast; and they sat at the King's table with Gandalf, < A5a.iii, p. 233, ll. 1–3: and when the hobbits were made ready, and circlets of silver were set upon their heads, they went to the King's feast, and they sat at his table with Gandalf

p. 287, l. 24: But when, after the Standing Silence, wine < A5a.iii, p. 233, l. 6: But when wine

p. 291, l. 9 after titling: Morgulvale [*error, for* Morgul Vale]

p. 291, l. 28 after titling: Morgul-vale [*error, for* Morgul Vale]

p. 301, ll. 38–9: was bare save for a star upon his forehead bound by a slender fillet of silver. With him < A5a.iii, p. 244, ll. 25–6: was bare. With him

p. 302, ll. 37–9: Dúnedain of Arnor, Captain of the Host of the West, bearer of the Star of the North, wielder of < A5a.iii, p. 245, ll. 15–16: Dúnedain of the North, Captain of the Host of the West, wielder of

p. 303, l. 18: Eärnur < A5a.iii, p. 245, l. 20: Earnur

p. 304, ll. 7–8: blessed while the thrones of the Valar endure!' ¶ But when < A5a.iii, p. 246, l. 14–15: blessed!' ¶ But when

p. 304, l. 14: Faramir cried: < A5a.iii, p. 246, l. 20: Faramir said:

p. 306, ll. 18–20: passed; and the Riders of Rohan made ready, and rode away by the North-way; and it was lined [*error, for* passed; and on the eighth day of May the Riders of Rohan made ready, and rode off by the North-way, and with them went the sons of Elrond. All the road was lined]

p. 306, l. 21: Pelennor. And [*error, for* Then] all

p. 308, l. 16: I may [*error, for* shall] have life

p. 315, ll. 17–18: Léofa, and Walda, and Folca, and Folcwine, and Fengel < A5a.iii, p. 255, l. 23: Léof, and Walda, and Folca, and Fengel

p. 319, l. 14: gone seven days. I let him < A5a.iii, p. 258, l. 27: gone. I let him

p. 322, ll. 18–19: company, following the Isen, turned west and rode through the Gap into < A5a.iii, p. 260, l. 41–p. 261, l. 1: company came to the Isen, and crossed over it, and came into

p. 322, ll. 21–2: passed over the borders of Dunland. The Dunlendings < A5a.iii, p. 261, l. 2: passed by the borders of Dunland. And the Dunlendings

p. 322, ll. 28–30: would. ¶ On the sixth day since their parting from the King they journeyed < A5a.iii, p. 261, ll. 7–8: would; and as they went the summer wore away. ¶ After they had passed by Dunland and were come to places where few folk dwelt, and even birds and beasts were seldom to be seen, they journeyed

p. 322, l. 24: country at sundown they overtook < A5a.iii, p. 261, l. 13: country they overtook

p. 325, ll. 7–17: mean way.' ¶ Next day they went on into northern Dunland, where no men now dwelt, though it was a green and pleasant country. September came in with golden days and silver nights, and they rode at ease until they reached the Swanfleet river, and found the old ford, east of the falls where it went down suddenly into the lowlands. Far to the west in a haze lay the meres and eyots through which it would its way to the Greyflood: there countless swans housed in a land of reeds. ¶ So they passed into Eregion, and at last < A5a.iii, p. 263, ll. 8–9: mean way. ¶ September came in with golden days and silver nights. At last

p. 326, ll. 22–3: littered with papers < A5a.iii, p. 264, l. 6: littered with paper

p. 328, ll. 4–5: three books of lore < A5a.iii, p. 265, l. 14: some books of lore

p. 329, ll. 30–1: papers, and my diary too, and take < A5a.iii, p. 266, l. 29: papers and take

p. 348, l. 10: Whitfurrows < A5a.iii, p. 282, l. 4: Bamfurlong

p. 365, l. 7: Greenfields < A5a.iii, p. 295, ll. 34–5: Green Fields

p. 368, footnote: *sharkû* < A5a.iii, p. 298, footnote: *sharkū*

p. 383, l. 28: quay stood [*error, for* quay beside a great grey horse stood]

p. 383, ll. 85–6: saw that it was Gandalf; and on his hand he wore [*error, for* saw that Gandalf now wore openly on his hand]

The appendices were extensively revised for A5d.iii. Changes include:

p. 387, the opening paragraphs and footnotes of Appendix A were rewritten. A new (second) footnote reads: 'In this edition the dates have been revised, and some errors emended: most of these were accidents occurring in the course of typing and marking [*i.e.* typing and printing].'

p. 388, ll. 5–21, paragraph ('Fëanor was the greatest of the Eldar . . .') added

p. 388, ll. 22–3: There were three unions of the Eldar and the Edain: Lúthien < A5a.iii, p. 314, l. 5: There were only three unions of the High Elves and Men; Lúthien

p. 394, ll. 18–19: Aragorn II F.A. 120 < A5a.iii, p. 318, ll. 18–19: Aragorn II F.A. 100

p. 395, ll. 5–7: Calmacil 1304, Minalcor [*error, for* Minalcar] (regent 1240–1304), crowned as Rómendacil II 1304, died 1366, Valacar. < A5a.iii, p. 318, l. 32: Calmacil 1304, Rómendacil II 1366, Valacar.

p. 411, l. 7: loyalty [*error, for* royalty] of Arnor

p. 426, ll. 39–40: As Queen of Elves and Men she dwelt with Aragorn for six-score years < A5a.iii, p. 343, l. 5: As Queen of Elves and Men she dwelt with Aragorn for five-score years

p. 428, ll. 23–7: dwelt there alone under the fading trees until winter came. Galadriel had passed away and Celeborn also was gone, and the land was silent. ¶ 'There at last when the mallorn-leaves were falling, but spring had not yet come, [*footnote:* I, 434] she laid < A5a.iii, p. 344, ll. 17–19: dwelt there alone under the fading trees; for Galadriel also was gone, and the elven-leaves were withering. ¶ 'There at last she laid

p. 435, ll. 18–34, the notes on *Brytta*, *Walda*, and *Folca* are added between existing notes on *Fréaláf Hildeson* and *Folcwine* < A5a.iii, p. 349, ll. 39–40, *Brytta*, *Walda*, and *Folca* listed, without notes

p. 452, l. 25–p. 453, l. 4: remained. Most of these dwelt in Lindon west of the Ered Luin; but before the building of the Barad-dûr many of the Sindar passed eastward, and some established realms in the forests far away, where their people were mostly Silvan Elves. Thranduil, king in the north of Greenwood the Great, was one of these. In Lindon north of the Lune dwelt Gil-Galad [*error, for* Gil-galad], last heir of the kings of the Noldor in exile. He was acknowledged as High King of the Elves of the West. In Lindon south of the Lune dwelt for a time Celeborn, kinsman of Thingol; his wife was Galadriel, greatest of Elven women. She was sister of Finrod Felagund, Friend-of-Men, once king of Nargothrond, who gave his life to save Beren son of Barahir. ¶ Later some < A5a.iii, p. 363, ll. 21–7: remained. The exiled Noldor dwelt in Lindon, but many of the Sindar passed eastward and established realms in the forests far away. The chief of these were Thranduil in the north of Greenwood the Great, and Celeborn in the south of the forest. But the wife of Celeborn was Noldorin: Galadriel, sister of Felagund of the House of Finrod. ¶ Later some

p. 453, ll. 11–14: the two races. Celebrimbor was lord of Eregion and the greatest of their craftsmen; he was descended from Fëanor. ¶ Year < A5a.iii, p. 363, ll. 32–3: the two races. ¶ Year

p. 456, l. 23: 100 Elrond weds daughter of Celeborn. < A5a.iii, p. 366, l. 16: 100 Elrond weds Celebrían of Lórien.

p. 462, ll. 23–5: of Gondor ¶ 2968 Birth of Frodo. ¶ 2976 Denethor < A5a.iii, p. 370, ll. 46–7: of Gondor ¶ 2976 Denethor

p. 462, ll. 34–5: 2983 Faramir son of Denethor born. Birth of Samwise. ¶ 2984 Death < A5a.iii, p. 371, ll. 9–10: 2983 Faramir son of Denethor born. ¶ 2984 Death

p. 468, ll. 25–31: Woodmen. But after the passing of Galadriel in a few years Celeborn grew weary of his realm and went to Imladris to dwell with the sons of Elrond. In the Greenwood the Silvan Elves remained untroubled, but in Lórien there lingered sadly only a few of its former people, and there was no longer light or song in Caras' [*error, for* Caras] Galadon. ¶ At the same time < A5a.iii, p. 375, ll. 30–1: Woodmen. ¶ At the same time

p. 469, footnote (to divisional heading 'THE CHIEF DAYS . . .') added: Months and days are given according to the shire calendar [*error, for* Shire Calendar].

p. 469, ll. 19–20: 8 Éomer and Éowyn depart for Rohan with the sons of Elrond. 20 Elrond < A5a.iii, p. 376, l. 11: 8 Éomer and Éowyn depart for Rohan. 20 Elrond

p. 469, ll. 21–3: leaves Lórien. ¶ *June 14.* The sons of Elrond meet the escort and bring Arwen to Edoras. *16.* They set out for Gondor. *25.* King Elessar < A5a.iii, p. 376, ll. 12–13: leaves Lórien. ¶ *June 25.* King Elessar

p. 471, ll. 28–33: 1451 Elanor the Fair marries Fastred of Greenholm on the Far Downs. ¶ 1452 The Westmarch, from the Far Downs to the Tower Hills (*Emyn Beraid*), [footnote: I, 27; III, 400, note 2.] is added to the shire [*error, for* Shire] by the gift of the King. Many hobbits remove to it. ¶ 1454 Elfstan Fairbairn < A5a.iii, p. 377, ll. 37–8: 1451 Elanor the Fair marries Fastred of Greenholm. ¶ 1454 Elfstan Fairbairn

p. 471, ll. 34–40: 1455 Master Samwise becomes Mayor for the fifth time. [*error, omits* ¶ 1462 Master Samwise becomes Mayor for the sixth time.] At his request the Thain makes Fastred Warden of Westmarch. Fastred and Elanor make their dwelling at Undertowers on the Tower Hills, where their descendants, the Fairbairns of the Towers, dwelt for many generations. ¶ 1463 Faramir Took < A5a.iii, p. 377, l. 38–p. 378, l. 6: 1455 Master Samwise becomes Mayor for the fifth time. ¶ S.R. ¶ 1462 Master Samwise becomes Mayor for the sixth time. At his request the Thain makes Fastred and Elanor Wardens of the Westmarch (a region newly inhabited); they take up their dwelling on the slopes of the Tower Hills, where their descendants, the Fairbairns of Westmarch, dwell for many generations.

p. 472, ll. 21–5: Gondor. ¶ 1541 In this year [*footnote:* Fourth Age (Gondor) 120.] on March 1st came at last the Passing of King Elessar. It is said that the beds of Meriadoc and Peregrin were set beside the bed of the great king. Then < A5a.iii, p. 378, ll. 26–9: 1521 In this year came at last the Passing of King Elessar. It is said that the beds of Meriadoc and Peregrin were set beside the bed of the great King. Then

p. 490, l. 28: *lyg* < A5a.iii, p. 393, l. 32: *lŷg*

p. 496, ll. 39–43: The representation of the sounds here is the same as that employed in transcription and described on pp. 487–9, except that here *ch* represents the *ch* in English *church*; *j* represents the sound of English *j*, and *zh* the sound heard in *azure* and *occasion*, *n* [*error, for* ŋ] is used for *ng* in *sing*. < A5a.iii, p. 398, ll. 43–7: The representation of the sounds is not strictly phonetic, but is the same as that employed in transcription and described on pp. 391–5, except that here *ch* represents the *ch* in English *church*, and to distinguish it the back 'spirant' *ch* is represented by *kh*; *j* represents the sound of English *j*, and *zh* the sound heard in *azure* and *occasion*; ŋ is used for *ng* in *sing*.

p. 497, ll. 19–29, 'Note' ('The standard spelling of Quenya . . .') added between 'largely derived' and '*The additional letters.*' < A5a.iii, p. 399, ll. 7–8: largely derived. ¶ *The additional letters.*

p. 506, ll. 24–5: Lady Galadriel of the royal house of Finarphir and sister of Finrod Felagund, King of Nargothrond. < A5a.iii, p. 406, ll. 11–12: Lady Galadriel of the royal house of Finrod, father of Felagund, lord of Nargothrond.

p. 506, footnote (to '*Eldarin* form', l. 2) added: In Lórien at this period Sindarin was spoken. . . . But *Lórien, Caras Galador* [*error, for* Galadon], *Amrolt* [*error, for* Amroth], *Nimrodel* are probably of Silvan origin, adapted to Sindarin.

p. 507, ll. 40–4: 'Elfstone'. Most of the names of the other men and women of the Dúnedain, such as *Aragorn, Denethor, Gilraen* are of Sindarin form, being often the names of Elves or Men remembered in the songs and histories of the First Age (as *Beren Húnri* [*error, for* Beren, Húrin]). Some few are of mixed forms, as *Boromir.* < A5a.iii, p. 406, ll. 44–7: 'Elfstone'. The names of other lords of the Dúnedain, such as *Aragorn, Denethor, Faramir,* are of Sindarin form, being often the names of Elves or Men remembered in the songs and histories of the First Age.

On pp. 521–44, the index was added.

The certar inscription on the title page was corrected with the fourth or fifth impression (August 1966). The error 'Galadnil's' for 'Galadriel's', p. 284, was corrected after the thirty-seventh (March 1973) and no later than the sixty-first (November 1978) impression. Other changes were made to the appendices with the fourth or fifth impression, including:

p. 402, ll. 28–9: Aragorn indeed lived to be two hundred and ten < Aragorn indeed lived to be one hundred and ninety

p. 450, death date of 'Gimli Elf-friend': 3141 (F.A. 120) < 3121 (F.A. 100)

p. 457, l. 2: 1149 Reign of Atanatar Alcarin begins. < 1149 Reign of Atanamir Alcarin begins.

p. 471, l. 34–p. 472, l. 4, earlier readings commingled with revision: 1455 Master Samwise becomes Mayor for the fifth time. At his request the Thain makes Fastred Warden of Westmarch. Fastred and Elanor make their dwelling at Undertowers on the Tower Hills, where their descendants, the Fairbairns of the Towers, dwelt for many generations. ¶ 1462 Master Samwise becomes Mayor for the sixth time. At his request the Thain makes Fastred and Elanor Wardens of the Westmarch (a region newly inhabited); they take up their dwelling on the slopes of the Tower Hills, where their descendants, the Fairbairns of Westmarch, dwell for many generations. ¶ 1463 Faramir Took < p. 471, ll. 34–40: 1455 Master Samwise becomes Mayor for the fifth time. At his request the Thain makes Fastred Warden of Westmarch. Fastred and Elanor make their dwelling at Undertowers on the Tower Hills, where their descendants, the Fairbairns of the Towers, dwelt for many generations. ¶ 1463 Faramir Took

p. 476, 'Estella Bolger 1385' added to the Brandybuck family tree as the wife of Meriadoc.

The copyright page of A5d.iii later gave the date of the first impression as October 1965, which seems to be correct. An appreciation by Peter S. Beagle, dated 14 July 1973, was later added to the preliminaries.

Sometime after the seventy-eighth impression (July 1986), impression numbering was begun anew.

The map, pp. [14–15], was redrawn, not by J. R. R. or Christopher Tolkien. *Circa* 1983, the map was replaced with the general map of Middle-earth drawn by Christopher Tolkien for *Unfinished Tales* (A17).

The three cover illustrations of A5d together form a continuous landscape, also published by Ballantine Books as a poster. Cf. A3f note.

After the fortieth (March 1973) and no later than the forty-third (September 1973) impression of *FR*, the upper cover was changed to feature a colour illustration by Tolkien, detail from *The Hill: Hobbiton-across-the Water*. A colour photograph of Tolkien by Billett Potter was now printed on the lower cover. Probably with the seventy-second impression (April 1981), the cover was changed to feature a colour illustration by Darrell K. Sweet, *The West-Door of Moria*. After the new fifth (July 1985) and no later than the new seventh (July 1986) impression, the cover was changed to again feature *The Hill* by Tolkien. *Circa* September 1988, the cover was changed to feature a colour illustration by Michael Herring, of Frodo and Gandalf examining the Ring (the cover first seen, however, on the 'Ninth Printing: July 1987', with the cover art misidentified on the copyright page as *The Hills* [sic] by Tolkien); cf. A3cc note.

After the thirty-fourth (August 1972) and no later than the forty-first (September 1973) impression of *TT*, the upper cover was changed to feature a colour illustration by Tolkien, detail from *Fangorn Forest* (i.e. *Beleg Finds Gwindor in Taur-nu-Fuin*). A colour photograph of Tolkien by Billett Potter was now printed on the lower cover. After the sixty-fourth (December 1978) and no later than the sixty-ninth (April 1981) impression, the cover was changed to feature a colour illustration by Darrell K. Sweet, *The King at the Cross-roads*. After the eightieth (July 1985) and no later than the eighty-second (July 1986) impression, the cover was changed to again feature *Fangorn Forest* by Tolkien. *Circa* September 1988, the cover was changed to feature a colour illustration by Michael Herring, of Legolas and Gimli (the cover first seen, however, on a copy marked 'Eighty-third Printing: February 1987', with the cover art misidentified on the copyright page as *Fangorn* by Tolkien); cf. A3cc note.

With the fortieth impression (March 1973) of *RK*, the upper cover was changed to feature a colour illustration by Tolkien, detail from *Barad-dûr*. A colour photograph of Tolkien by Billett Potter was now printed on the lower cover. After the sixty-second (December 1978) and no later than the sixty-fifth (April 1981) impression, the cover was changed to feature a colour illustration by Darrell K. Sweet, *The White Sapling*. After the seventy-sixth (July 1985) but no later than the seventy-eighth (July 1986) impression, the cover was changed to again feature *Barad-dûr* by Tolkien. *Circa* September 1988, the cover was changed to feature a colour illustration by Michael Herring, of Aragorn, Gandalf, and three other figures (the cover first seen, however, on the 'Seventy-ninth Printing: April 1987', with the cover art misidentified on the copyright page as *Barad-Dûr* [sic] by Tolkien); cf. A3cc note.

A5d was sold as separate volumes and as a set. Three slipcases have been seen with copies of A5d bound in Remington-illustrated covers: (1) green embossed paper over boards, stamped on the spine in black: 'Authorized Edition | complete in three volumes'; (2) printed paper over boards, featuring the continuous cover illustration by Barbara Remington, in colour; and (3) printed paper over boards, featuring the Remington illustration, but as a line drawing. Copies of A5d with Tolkien-illustrated covers (first version) were sold with *H* (A3g) in a red (or blue, or gold) slipcase featuring heraldic devices by Tolkien. Later impressions of A5d were sold with A3g in slipcases complementary to their new covers.

From April? 1981 through 1984? A5d was sold as a 'Special Silver Jubilee Edition' to mark the twenty-fifth anniversary of the publication of *LR* in the United States.

A5d was published in Canada by Ballantine Books under licence from Allen & Unwin from 1965 though the end of 1966.

The Ballantine Books edition of *The Lord of the Rings* was published in response to the unauthorized paperback edition by Ace Books (see A5c note). Tolkien began to send material for a revised edition to Houghton Mifflin beginning in July 1965. His new foreword was ready by 21 July. On 28 July he sent Houghton Mifflin corrections, additions, and alterations to *FR*. He found inconsistencies between the maps of A5a and his text, and decided that it was easier for the most part to take the maps as 'correct' and adjust the narrative. But the Shire map, he warned,

> is most at fault and much needs correction (and some additions), and has caused a number of questions to be asked. The chief fault is that the ferry at Bucklebury and so Brandy Hall and Crickhollow have shifted about 3 miles too far north (about 4 mm.). This cannot be altered at this time, but it is unfortunate that Brandy Hall clearly on the river-bank is placed so that the main road runs in front of it instead of behind. [Cf. A5e note.]

On 31 July Tolkien sent Houghton Mifflin material for *TT*,

> mostly only corrections of errors (my own or compositors') that were in the first edition. (Some of these have been corrected in later impressions on this side; but I include them for completeness.) I do not find more than 3 points where any addition or alteration is possible or desirable.
>
> The first is on p. 192 [i.e. 193] where a statement about Saruman still survives that is (according to the completed story) quite untrue. The second on p. 205 (the point will be taken up again in Vol III p. 53) stops a small hole in the narrative: Aragorn was not at Orthanc in the earlier version of the chapter. If recognized, he would certainly have been addressed by Saruman. The third on p. 247 attempts to make my vision of the scene clearer: if I did not (or I do) retain a clear picture of what I was trying to describe, I should not get one from the present text.

By 7 September, Houghton Mifflin received corrections to *RK*.

See further, A5e note.

e. Second Allen & Unwin edition (1966):

i. THE FELLOWSHIP OF THE RING:

[*1 line in certar, between double rules*] | The Fellowship | of the Ring | BEING THE FIRST PART OF | THE LORD OF THE RINGS | BY | J. R. R. TOLKIEN | *London* | GEORGE ALLEN & UNWIN LTD | RUSKIN HOUSE MUSEUM STREET | [*2 lines in tengwar, between double rules*] iv, 424 pp. + 1 plate (map). Collation: [1–11^{16}12^{6}13^{16}]. 22.1 × 14.2 cm.

[i–ii] blank; [iii] 'THE FELLOWSHIP OF THE RING'; [iv] '[*1 line in certar, between double rules*] | THE LORD OF THE RINGS | BY J. R. R. TOLKIEN | PART I | THE FELLOWSHIP OF THE RING | PART II | THE TWO TOWERS | PART III | THE RETURN OF THE KING | [*2 lines in tengwar, between double rules*]'; [1] title; [2] '*First published in July 1954* | [*list of second through fifteenth impressions, 1954–66*] | *Second Edition 1966* | [*notice of restrictions under copyright*] | © *George Allen & Unwin Ltd, 1966* | *Printed in Great Britain* | *in 11 on 12 point Imprint type* | *by Jarrold & Sons Ltd,* | *Norwich*'; [3] 'THE LORD OF THE RINGS | [*poem, "Three Rings for the Elven-kings" etc.*]'; [4] blank; [5]–8 foreword; [9] table of contents; 10–25 prologue; [26] map, *A Part of the Shire*, in black and red; [27] 'BOOK I | [*swelled rule*]'; [28] blank; 29–227 text and illustration; [228] blank; [229] 'BOOK II | [*swelled rule*]'; [230] blank; 231–423 text and illustrations; [424] '[*publisher's square "St. George" device*] | GEORGE ALLEN & UNWIN LTD | [*19 addresses, London to Tokyo*]'. Map of Middle-earth, in black and red on folded leaf tipped onto recto, back free endpaper.

Illustrations, by Tolkien (as for A5a.i): Ring inscription, p. 59; Moria gate, p. [319]; Balin's tomb inscription, p. 333.

Wove paper. Bound in red cloth over boards. Stamped on spine in gilt: '[*within a ring:*] The | Fellowship | of the | Ring | [*below the ring:*] J. R. | TOLKIEN | GEORGE ALLEN | AND UNWIN'. Wove endpapers. No headbands. All edges trimmed. Top edge stained red, fore- and bottom edges unstained.

Dust-jacket, wove paper. Printed on upper cover against a grey-green background: 'TOLKIEN | [*rule, wraps around upper cover and spine*] | [*in white:*] The | Fellowship | of the Ring | [*rule, in black, wraps around upper cover and spine*] | [*"Ring and Eye" device in black, red, and gold*] | [*in white:*] REVISED EDITION'. Printed on spine against a grey-green background: 'J. R. R. | TOLKIEN | [*rule*] | [*in white:*] The | Fellowship | of the | Ring | [*in red:*] BEING THE | FIRST | PART OF | The Lord of | the Rings | [*rule, in black*] | [*semi-circle "flames", in red*] | [*in white:*] George | Allen | & | Unwin'. Printed on lower cover: 'J. R. R. TOLKIEN | [*advertisement of H, FGH, ATB, and TL, in black and red*] | [*in black:*] GEORGE ALLEN AND UNWIN LTD'. Printed on front flap: '[*blurb*] | Second Edition | The Fellowship of the Ring | J. R. R. Tolkien | G. Allen & Unwin Ltd | Price in U.K. | 25s net'. Printed on back flap: 'J. R. R. TOLKIEN | THE LORD OF THE RINGS | Med. 8vo. In three volumes 25s. net each. | De Luxe Boxed Edition set of three volumes £6 6s. net | VOLUME ONE | THE FELLOWSHIP OF THE RING | VOLUME TWO | THE TWO TOWERS | VOLUME THREE | THE RETURN OF THE KING | Printed in Great Britain'.

Partly reset, revised, based on a corrected impression of A5a.i, with further corrections. Continues the following errors, among others, from A5a.i:

p. 29, ll. 12–13 after titling, '*well*-preserved' for '*well-preserved*'
p. 42, l. 30, 'I won't give my precious away. I tell you.' for 'I won't give my precious away, I tell you.'
p. 56, l. 7, 'Elvin-rings' for 'Elven-rings'
p. 67, ll. 6–7, 'I wouldn't say' for 'It wouldn't say'
p. 112, l. 24, 'sight of content' for 'sigh of content'
p. 144, l. 12, 'blue eyes' for 'blue eye'
p. 167, l. 30, 'Bee-dialect' for 'Bree-dialect'
p. 186, l. 15, 'Sough-gate' for 'South-gate'

p. 206, l. 17, 'bride-piece' for 'bride-price'
p. 212, l. 41, 'Buinen' for 'Bruinen'
p. 247, l. 25, '*hears*' for '*heard*'
p. 252, l. 19 after titling, 'Gandolf' for 'Gandalf'
p. 259, l. 30, 'Elrond and Halfelven' for 'Elrond the Halfelven'
p. 267, l. 36, 'fo the Enemy' for 'of the Enemy'
p. 275, l. 5, 'woves' for 'wolves'
p. 287, l. 39, 'in a strange' for 'into a strange'
p. 321, l. 3, '*Open open!*' for '*Open, open!*'
p. 322, l. 18, 'Twenty others arms' for 'Twenty other arms'
p. 323, l. 39, 'take up' for 'take us'
p. 350, l. 21, 'turnic' for 'tunic'
p. 354, l. 1, '*Elvin-maid*' for '*Elven-maid*'

Alterations (other than corrections to errors noted for A5a.1) and new errors made in A5e.1 include:

pp. [5]–8, a new foreword; p. 6, l. 28, 'not [*error, for* nor] to displease'; p. 7, l. 24, 'author' (*error, for* 'author.'); '*The Lord of the Rings* is now issued in a new edition, and the opportunity has been taken of revising it. A number of errors and inconsistencies that still remained in the text have been corrected, and an attempt has been made to provide information on a few points which attentive readers have raised. I have considered all their comments and enquiries, and if some seem to have been passed over that may be because I have failed to keep my notes in order; but many enquiries could only be answered by additional appendices, or indeed by the production of an accessory volume containing much of the material that I did not include in the original edition, in particular more detailed linguistic information. In the meantime this edition offers this Foreword, an addition to the Prologue, some notes, and an index of the names of persons and places.' (p. 8; cf. A5d.i, 'issued in a new form')

p. 14, ll. 8–14: There for a thousand years they were little troubled by wars, and they prospered and multiplied after the Dark Plague (S.R. 37) until the disaster of the Long Winter and the famine that followed it. Many thousands then perished, but the Days of Dearth (1158–60) were at the time of this tale long past and the Hobbits had again become accustomed to plenty. < A5a.i, p. 15, ll. 8–10: And thenceforward for a thousand years they lived in almost unbroken peace.

p. 14, ll. 18–19: Forty leagues it stretched from the Far Downs to the Brandywine Bridge, and [*error, omits* nearly] fifty from the northern moors [Tolkien intended 'and nearly fifty' but accepted the misprint.] < A5a.i, p. 15, ll. 14–16: Fifty leagues it stretched from the Westmarch under the Tower Hills to the Brandywine Bridge, and nearly fifty from the northern moors

p. 17, l. 3: if they were accurate: they liked to have books < A5a.i, p. 18, l. 1: if they are accurate: they like to have books

p. 18, ll. 24–7: Boffins. Outside the Farthings were the East and West Marches: the Buckland (I 108) [*error, for* (I 108);] and the Westmarch added to the Shire in S.12 [*error, for* S.R.] 1462. ¶ The Shire < A5a.i, p. 18, l. 24–5: Boffins. ¶ The Shire

p. 23, l. 9: birthday (S.R. 1401). At this point < A5a.1, p. 24, l. 9: birthday. At that point

p. 23, l. 11–p. 25, 'Note on the Shire Records' is new

p. 34, l. 8: commodity, or < A5a.i, p. 34, l. 8: commodity or

p. 45, l. 16: would only say *no doubt* < A5a.i, p. 45, l. 16: would say nothing, but *no doubt*

p. 52, ll. 32–41: but they were leaving Middle-earth and were no longer concerned with its troubles. There were, however, dwarves on the road in unusual numbers. The ancient East-West Road ran through the Shire to its end at the Grey Havens, and dwarves had always used it on their way to their mines in the Blue Mountains. They were [Tolkien intended the revision 'through the Shire over the Brandywine Bridge to its end at the Grey Havens' but accepted the misprinted text as it appeared in A5d.i.] < A5a.i, p. 52, ll. 32–40: but they shook their heads and went away singing sadly to themselves. There were, however, dwarves in unusual numbers. ¶ The great West Road, of course, ran through the Shire over the Brandywine Bridge, and dwarves had always used it from time to time. They were

p. 80, ll. 16–21: alder-trees. A mile or two further south they hastily crossed the great road from the Brandywine Bridge; they were now in the Tookland and bending south-eastwards they made for the Green Hill Country. As they began to climb its first slopes they looked back and saw the lamps in Hobbiton far off twinkling in < A5a.i, p. 80, ll. 16–21: alder-trees. They were now in Tookland, and going southwards, but a mile or two further on they crossed the main road from Michel Delving to Bywater and Brandywine Bridge. Then they struck south-east and began to climb into the Green Hill Country south of Hobbiton. They could see the village twinkling down in

p. 80, l. 35: Woodhall [*error, for* Woodhall,] and Stock, and the Bucklebury Ferry < A5a.i, p. 80, l. 34: Woodhall and the Bucklebury Ferry

p. 86, ll. 10–15: they came back to the road at the end of the long level over which it had run straight for some miles. At that point it bent left and went down into the Lowlands of the Yale, making for Stock; but a lane branched right, winding through a wood of ancient oak-trees on its way to Woodhall. 'That is the way for us', said Frodo. ¶ Not far from the road-meeting they came < A5a.i, p. 86, ll. 11–15: they came to the end of the long level over which the road ran straight. At that point it bent somewhat southward, and began to wind again, as it entered a wood of ancient oak-trees. ¶ Not far from the edge of the road they came

p. 86, l. 22: back to the lane < A5a.i, p. 86, l. 22: back to the road

p. 87, l. 29: hoofs in the lane < A5a.i, p. 87, l. 29: hoofs on the road

p. 87, l. 31: off the path < A5a.i, p. 87, l. 31: off the road

p. 88, l. 5: left the path < A5a.i, p. 88, l. 5: left the road

p. 88, l. 14: across the lane < A5a.i, p. 88, l. 14: across the road

p. 88, ll. 28–9: to wait.' ¶ The singing < A5a.i, p. 88, ll. 28–9: to wait by the road.' ¶ The singing

p. 89, ll. 10–11: amazement. 'Few of that fairest folk are ever seen < A5a.i, p. 89, ll. 10–11: amazement. 'I did not know that any of that fairest folk were ever seen

p. 89, l. 14: by the wayside < A5a.i, p. 89, l. 14: by the roadside

p. 89, l. 15: down the lane < A5a.i, p. 89, l. 15: down the road

p. 90, l. 17: *omentielvo* < A5a.i, p. 90, l. 17: *omentielmo*

p. 90, l. 36: the lane went < A5a.i, p. 90, l. 36: the road went

p. 90, l. 38: from the path < A5a.i, p. 90, l. 38: from the road

p. 97, l. 35: make longer ones. At all cost < A5a.i, p. 97, l. 35: made longer ones. At all cost

p. 127, l. 30: felt sleep overwhelming him < A5a.i, p. 127, l. 30: felt the drowsiness attack him

p. 208, ll. 27–8: With a last effort Frodo, dropping his sword, slipped < A5a.i, p. 208, ll. 27–8: With a last effort Frodo slipped

p. 209, ll. 14–15 after titling: grass with his sword beneath him. Strider < A5a.i, p. 209, l. 14: grass. Strider

p. 212, l. 42–p. 213, l. 1: along the edge of the hills for many miles from the Bridge to the Ford of Bruinen. But I have not yet thought how we shall cross that water. <

A5a.i, p. 212, ll. 42–3: along it for many leagues to the Ford. But I have not yet thought how we shall cross the water.

p. 214, ll. 16–17: The Road behind held on its way to the River Bruinen, but both < A5a.i, p. 214, ll. 16–17: The Road bent back again southward towards the River, but both

p. 219, l. 25: *troll* [error, for troll,] < A5a.i, p. 219, l. 25: *troll.*

p. 220, l. 10: *root,* < A5a.i, p. 220, l. 10: *root:*

p. 220, l. 13: *groan,* < A5a.i, p. 220, l. 13: *groan.*

p. 220, ll. 34–5: the Road had left the Haarwell [error, for Hoarwell] far behind in its < A5a.i, p. 220, ll. 34–5: the Road had turned away from the river down in its

p. 220, l. 38: Nor far down the bank < A5a.i, p. 220, l. 38: Not far from the bank

p. 221, ll. 36–7: its headstall flickered < A5a.i, p. 221, ll. 36–7: its bit and bridle flickered

p. 222, l. 37: the other four < A5a.i, p. 222, l. 37: the other Four

p. 224, ll. 19–21: the Road bent right and ran down towards the bottom of the valley, now making straight for the Bruinen. So far < A5a.i, p. 224, ll. 19–21: the Road turned right and ran steeply down towards the bottom of the valley, making once more for the river. So far

p. 239, ll. 24–8: of this [error, for his] close kindred. Young she was and yet not so. The braids of her dark hair were touched by no frost, her [error, for frost; her] white arms and clear face were flawless and smooth, and the light of stars was in her bright eyes, grey as a cloudless night; yet < A5a.i, p. 239, ll. 24–8: of his close kindred. Young she was, and yet not so; for though the braids of her dark hair were touched by no frost and her white arms and clear face were hale and smooth, and the light of stars was in her bright eyes, grey as a cloudless night, yet

p. 276, l. 8: any man mounted him < A5a.i, p. 276, l. 8: any man bestrode him

p. 290, ll. 26–9: fumbled inside. ¶ 'Here is your sword,' he said. 'But it was broken, you know. I took it to keep it safe but I've forgotten to ask if the smiths could mend it. No time now. So I thought < A5a.i, p. 290, ll. 26–8: fumbled inside. ¶ 'Your sword was broken, I believe,' he said hesitatingly to Frodo; 'and I thought

p. 311, l. 18: etten < A5a.i, l. 18: eaten

p. 335, ll. 30–1: I think; the next word is blurred and burned: probably *room* < A5a.i, p. 335, ll. 30–1: I suppose, but it is written *gard*, followed probably by *room*

p. 356, footnote (to 'language', l. 36) added: 'See note in Appendix F: *Of the Elves.*'

p. 360, l. 39: the path that still went on along the west side < A5a.i, p. 360, l. 39: the old path on the west side

p. 361, l. 30: coiled two of them < A5a.i, p. 361, l. 30: coiled them

p. 361, ll. 31–2: other side, drew back the last one, slung it < A5a.i, p. 361, ll. 31–2: other side, picked one up, slung it

p. 367, l. 3: *vanimelda* < A5a.i, *vanimalda*

p. 385, l. 5: if need be < A5a.i, p. 385, l. 5: if needs be

p. 394, l. 1: *súinen,* < A5a.i, p. 394, l. 1: *súrinen!*

p. 394, l. 2: *Yéni* [error, for yéni] *únótimë ve rámar aldaron!* < A5a.i, p. 394, l. 2: *Yéni únótime ve rámar aldaron,*

p. 394, l. 3: *Yéni ve lintë yuldar avánier* < A5a.i, p. 394, l. 3: *yéni ve linte yuldar vánier*

p. 394, l. 5: *Andúnë pella, Vardo* < A5a.i, p. 394, l. 5: *Andúne pella Vardo*

p. 394, l. 9: *Tintallë* < A5a.i, p. 394, l. 9: *Tintalle*

p. 394, l. 10: *ortanë* [error, for ortanë,] < A5a.i, p. 394, l. 10: *ortane*

p. 394, l. 11: *ilyë tier undulávë lumbulë;* < A5a.i, p. 394, l. 11: *ilye tier unduláve lumbule,*

p. 394, l. 14: *oialë* < A5a.i, p. 394, l. 14: *oiale*
p. 394, l. 15: *ná* < A5a.i, p. 394, l. 15: *na*
p. 394, l. 16: *hiruvalyë* < A5a.i, p. 394, l. 16: *hiruvalye*
p. 394, l. 17: *elyë* < A5a.i, p. 394, l. 17: *elye*
p. 394, ll. 18–25: in the wind, long years numberless as the wings of trees! The long years [*error, for* The years] have passed like swift draughts of the sweet mead in lofty halls beyond the West, beneath the blue vaults of Varda wherein the stars tremble in the song of her voice, holy and queenly. Who now shall refill the cup for me? For now the Kindler, Varda, the Queen of the Stars, from Mount Everwhite has uplifted her hands like clouds, and all paths are drowned deep in shadow; [cf. *RGEO* (B28), 'Notes and Translations'] < A5a.i, p. 394, ll. 18–25: in the wind! And numberless as the wings of trees are the years. The years have passed like sweet swift draughts of the white mead in halls beyond the West beneath the blue vaults of Varda, where the stars tremble in the song of her voice, holy and queenly. Who now shall refill the cup for me? For now the Kindler, Varda, the Queen of the Stars, from Mount Everwhite has uplifted her hands like clouds, and all paths are drowned in shadow,

On the Shire map, p. [26], the black mark representing Buck Hill and Brandy Hall was moved to agree with the text on p. 110, l. 11.

Most of the errors noted for A5e.i were corrected in the second impression (1967). Further alterations made by Tolkien in the second impression include:

p. 16, l. 9: a green mound < [*first impression*]: a green hill
p. 18, l. 13: Though one Wizard < Though one wizard [A5a.i, p. 19, l. 13]
p. 18, ll. 24–7: Boffins. Outside the Farthings were the East and West Marches: the Buckland (I 108); and the Westmarch added to the Shire in S.12 [*error, for* S.R.] 1462. ¶ The Shire < Boffins. Outside the Farthings were the East and West Marches: the Buckland (I 108) [*error, for* (I 108);] and the Westmarch added to the Shire in S.12 [*error, for* S.R.] 1462. ¶ The Shire
p. 20, l. 2: 'nephew' < nephew
p. 21, l. 26: *pocketses* < *pockets* [A5a.i p. 22, l. 26]
p. 33, ll. 13–14: Gandalf the Wizard < Gandalf the wizard
p. 88, l. 30: elven-tongue < Elven-tongue
p. 89, l. 9: High Elves! < High-Elves!
p. 90, l. 18: high-elven speech < high elven-speech
p. 93, l. 35: affairs of Wizards < affairs of wizards
p. 97, l. 16: Ferry is east from Woodhall; but the hard road < Ferry is south-east from Woodhall; but the road
p. 97, l. 35: At all costs < At all cost
p. 99, l. 13: towards the south < towards the South
p. 100, l. 18: too much to the south < too much to the South
p. 100, ll. 38–9: he said. 'This is Bamfurlong; [*error, for* Bamfurlong,] old Farmer Maggot's land. That's his farm < he said. 'We are on old Farmer Maggot's land. That must be his farm
p. 145, l. 17: by the reed < by reed
p. 161, l. 15 after titling: Great Sea < Great Seas
p. 171, footnote (to 'Sunday', l. 8) added: See note, III 389
p. 184, l. 2: all those who < all those that
p. 193, l. 12: Stick-at-naught < Stick-at-nought
p. 235, l. 10: Firstborn < First-born
p. 241, l. 25: Dwarf-kingdom < dwarf-kingdom
p. 245, ll. 36–7: and of the interwoven words in elven-tongues, even < and the interwoven words in the Elven-tongue, even

p. 247, l. 13: Otherworld < otherworld
p. 254, l. 21: Dwarf-sires < dwarf-sires
p. 255, l. 21: Tale of the Ring < tale of the Ring
p. 256, l. 3: above the mouths < about the mouths
p. 259, l. 37: house of Elrond < House of Elrond
p. 266, l. 12: *an elven-script of Eregion* < *the Elven-script of Eregion*
p. 270, l. 28: a worthy Wizard < a worthy wizard
p. 284, l. 19: the Great < the great
p. 290, l. 3: Elvish smiths < elvish smiths
p. 296, l. 30: Zirakzigil < Zirak-zigil
p. 304, l. 26: mouths of Anduin < Mouths of Anduin
p. 331, l. 32: Michel Delving Mathom-house < Michel Delving Museum
p. 345, l. 17: *Elendil!* < Elendil!
p. 348, l. 3: Dwarf-kingdom < Dwarf kingdom
p. 355, l. 37: Galadhrim < Galadrim
p. 364, l. 31: Galadhrim < Galadrim
p. 365, l. 15: Galadhrim < Galadrim
p. 365, l. 37: Galadhrim < Galadrim
p. 368, l. 18 after titling: Galadhon < Galadon
p. 368, l. 19 after titling: Galadhrim < Galadrim
p. 370, l. 14: Galadhon < Galadon
p. 371, l. 26: Galadhrim < Galadrim
p. 374, ll. 7–8: with the Elven-folk; for few of these knew or would use the Westron tongue < with any of the Elven-folk; for few of these spoke any but their own silvan tongue
p. 376, l. 36: Galadhon < Galadon
p. 386, l. 14: Galadhrim < Galadrim
p. 387, l. 6: Galadhon < Galadon
p. 390, l. 34: Galadhrim < Galadrim
p. 391, l. 2: Galadhrim < Galadrim
p. 392, l. 17: Galadhrim < Galadrim
p. 394, ll. 32–3: hidden. To that fair land Frodo never came again. < hidden. Never did Frodo see that fair land again.

On *Galadon/Galadhon, Galadrim/Galadhrim*, see *Unfinished Tales*, p. 267 (A17a–e).

ii. THE TWO TOWERS:

[*1 line in certar, between double rules*] | The Two Towers | BEING THE SECOND PART OF | THE LORD OF THE RINGS | BY | J. R. R. TOLKIEN | *London* | GEORGE ALLEN & UNWIN LTD | RUSKIN HOUSE · MUSEUM STREET | [*2 lines in tengwar, between double rules*]

352 pp. + 1 plate (map). Collation: [1–11^{16}]. 22.1 × 14.2 cm.

[1–2] blank; [3] 'THE TWO TOWERS'; [4] '[*1 line in certar, between double rules*] | THE LORD OF THE RINGS | BY J. R. R. TOLKIEN | PART I | THE FELLOWSHIP OF THE RING | PART II | THE TWO TOWERS | PART III | THE RETURN OF THE KING | [*2 lines in tengwar, between double rules*]'; [5] title; [6] '*First published 1954* | [*list of second through twelfth impressions, 1955–66*] | *Second Edition 1966* | [*notice of restrictions under copyright*] | © *George Allen & Unwin, 1966* | *Printed in Great Britain* | *in 11 on 12 point Imprint type* | *by Jarrold & Sons Ltd,* | *Norwich*'; [7] 'THE LORD OF THE RINGS | [*poem, "Three Rings for the Elven-kings" etc.*]'; [8] blank; 9–10 synopsis; 11 table of contents; [12] blank; [13] 'BOOK III | [*swelled rule*]'; [14] blank; 15–206 text; [207] 'BOOK IV | [*swelled rule*]'; [208] blank; 209–352 text. Map of Middle-earth, in black and red on folded leaf tipped onto recto, back free endpaper.

Wove paper. Bound in red cloth over boards. Stamped on spine in gilt: '[*within a ring:*] The | Two | Towers | [*below the ring:*] J. R. R. | TOLKIEN | GEORGE ALLEN | AND UNWIN'. Wove endpapers. No headbands. All edges trimmed. Top edge stained red, fore- and bottom edges unstained.

Dust-jacket, wove paper. Printed on upper cover against a grey-green background: 'TOLKIEN | [*rule, wraps around upper cover and spine*] | [*in white:*] The | Two | Towers | [*rule, in black, wraps around upper cover and spine*] | [*"Ring and Eye" device in black, red, and gold*] | [*in white:*] REVISED EDITION'. Printed on spine against a grey-green background: 'J. R. R. | TOLKIEN | [*rule*] | [*in white:*] The | Two | Towers | [*in red:*] BEING THE | SECOND | PART OF | The Lord of | the Rings | [*rule, in black*] | [*semi-circle "flames", in red*] | [*in white:*] George | Allen | & | Unwin'. Printed on lower cover: 'J. R. R. TOLKIEN | [*advertisement of H, FGH, ATB, and TL, in black and red*] | [*in black:*] GEORGE ALLEN AND UNWIN LTD'. Printed on back flap: 'J. R. R. TOLKIEN | THE LORD OF THE RINGS | Med. 8vo. In three volumes 25s. net each. | De Luxe Boxed Edition set of three volumes £6 6s. net | VOLUME ONE | THE FELLOWSHIP OF THE RING | VOLUME TWO | THE TWO TOWERS | VOLUME THREE | THE RETURN OF THE KING | Printed in Great Britain'. Front flap varies, no priority determined: (1) '[*blurb*] | Second Edition | The Two Towers | J. R. R. Tolkien | G. Allen & Unwin Ltd | Price in U.K. | 25s net'; (2) '[*blurb*] | Second Edition | The Two Towers | ["The Return of the King", overprinted with a solid bar] | J. R. R. Tolkien | G. Allen & Unwin Ltd | Price in U.K. | 25s net'.

Partly reset, revised, based on a later impression of A5a.ii (with 'fire and death', p. 118, and the added note at the end of the volume), with the error on p. 332 corrected, but continuing the errors 'all the season of the year' for 'all the seasons of the year', p. 111, l. 34, and 'maylike' for 'may like', p. 350, l. 31. Further alterations and new errors made in A5e.ii include:

p. 70, l. 28: *Laurelindórenan!* < A5a.ii, p. 70, l. 28: *Laurelindórinan!*
p. 70, l. 37: *Laurelindórenan!* < A5a.ii, p. 70, l. 37: *Laurelindórinan!*
p. 70, l. 42: *Taurelilómëa-tumbalemorna Tumbaletaurëa Lómëanor* < A5a.ii, p. 70, l. 42: *Taurililómëa-tumbalemorna Tumbaletaurëa Lómeanor*
p. 70, footnote (to the preceding Elvish phrase) added: See Appendix F under *Ents.*
p. 72, l. 26: *Orod-na-Thôn!* < A5a.ii, p. 72, l. 26: *Orod-na-Thon!*
p. 72, l. 29: *Ambarona* [*error, for* Ambaróna] < A5a.ii, p. 72, l. 29: *Ambaróna*
p. 87, l. 22: *Carnimírië!* < A5a.ii, p. 87, l. 22: *Carnemírië!*
p. 87, l. 29: *Carnimírië!* < A5a.ii, p. 87, l. 29: *Carnemírië!*
p. 170, l. 2: spent the nights < A5a.ii, p. 170, l. 2: spent the nights
p. 170, l. 3: third day < A5a.ii, p. 170, l. 3: second day
p. 185, ll. 8–9: Remember Théodred at the Ford [*error, for* Fords] and the grave < A5a.ii, p. 185, l. 9: Remember the grave
p. 193, l. 27 after titling: He had his eyes on you. < A5a.ii, p. 193, ll. 26–8 after titling: He had never met a hobbit before and did not know what kind of thing to say to you. But he had his eyes on you.
p. 205, ll. 20–3: at my tail. Or that an heir of Elendil lives and stood beside me. If Wormtongue was not deceived by the armour of Rohan, he would remember

Aragorn and the title that he claimed. That is < A5a.ii, p. 205, ll. 20–1: at my tail. That is

p. 239, ll. 9–10: moors of the Noman-lands < A5a.ii, p. 239, ll. 9–10: moors of Nomen's Land

p. 244, ll. 13–14 after titling: and thrust forward from its mouth < A5a.ii, p. 244, l. 13 after titling: and at its mouth

p. 247, l. 20–3: hill, at some little height above a long trenchlike valley that lay between it and the outer buttresses of the mountains [*error? for* mountain-wall]. In the midst of the valley stood the black foundations of the western watch-tower. By morning-light < A5a.ii, p. 247, ll. 20–3: hill and lay at some little height above the level of the plain. A long trench-like valley ran between it and the outer buttresses of the mountain-wall. In the morning-light

p. 247, ll. 27–30: and a third that ran towards him. As it bent sharply round the tower, it entered a narrow defile and passed not far below the hollow where he stood. Westward, to his right, it turned < A5a.ii, p. 247, ll. 26–9: and another that, bending sharply, ran close under the western watch-tower, and then passed along the valley at the foot of the hillside where the hobbits lay and not many feet below them. Soon it turned

p. 275, l. 10: Laurelindórenan < A5a.ii, p. 275, l. 10: Laurelindórinan

p. 275, l. 25: Tol Brandir < A5a.ii, p. 275, l. 25: Tolbrandir

p. 275, l. 40: *Laurelindórenan* < A5a.ii, p. 275, l. 40: *Laurelindórinan*

p. 338, l. 39: A Elbereth! < A5a.ii, p. 338, l. 39: O Elbereth!

p. 339, l. 1: *A Elbereth* < A5a.ii, p. 339, l. 1: *O Elbereth*

p. 339, l. 3: *nallon* < A5a.ii, p. 339, l. 3: *nallan*

Most of the errors noted for A5e.ii were corrected in the second impression (1967). Further alterations made by Tolkien in the second impression include:

p. 37, l. 12: laughed the Rider < [*first impression:*] laughed the rider

p. 37, l. 20: said the Rider < said the rider

p. 37, l. 38: Greyhame < Grayhame

p. 49, ll. 2–3: both be questioned < each be questioned

p. 49, l. 28: you'd all have run < you'ld all have run

p. 63, l. 19: the Mark < Rohan

p. 75, l. 33: Galadhon < Galadon

p. 75, l. 39: business of Wizards: Wizards are < business of wizards: wizards are

p. 76, l. 17: Saruman is a Wizard < Saruman is a wizard

p. 76, l. 18: history of Wizards < history of wizards

p. 111, l. 33: *simbelmynë* < Simbelmynë

p. 119, l. 37: Lady of Rohan < lady of Rohan

p. 122, l. 3: Marshal of the Mark < marshal of the Mark

p. 127, ll. 16–17: House of Eorl < house of Eorl

p. 128, l. 6: House of Eorl < house of Eorl

p. 132, l. 29: shield-wall < shieldwall

p. 136, l. 8: best Riders < best riders

p. 142, l. 39: *Elendil, Elendil!* < Elendil, Elendil!'

p. 157, ll. 7–10: Some men I sent with Grimbold of Westfold to join Erkenbrand. Some I set to make this burial. They have now followed your marshal, Elfhelm. I sent him with many Riders to Edoras. < [p. 157, ll. 7–9:] Some of them I sent to join Erkenbrand; some I set to this labour that you see, and they by now have gone back to Edoras. Many others also I sent thither before to guard your house.

p. 159, l. 35: chief of Wizards < chief of wizards

p. 169, l. 27: of Barad-dûr, Lugbúrz < of Mordor, or Lugbúrz

p. 175, ll. 13–14: was already dark < was getting dark

p. 175, l. 33: there is a Wizard < there is a wizard

p. 184, l. 5: House of Eorl < house of Eorl

p. 185, l. 26: House of Eorl < house of Eorl

p. 186, l. 2: House of Eorl < house of Eorl

p. 189, ll. 30–1: It is not a thing, I guess, that Saruman < It is not a thing that Saruman

p. 190, l. 22: I guess that < I fancy that

p. 194, l. 3: all Wizards < all wizards

p. 196, l. 6: *affairs of Wizards* < *affairs of wizards*

p. 196, l. 9: affairs of Wizards < affairs of wizards

p. 199, l. 21: affairs of Wizards < affairs of wizards

p. 200, l. 2: Stone < stone

p. 200, ll. 14–16: did not at once guess the nature of the Stone. Then I was weary, and as I lay pondering it, sleep overcame me. Now I know! < did not guess the nature of the stone until it was too late. Only now have I become sure of it.

p. 200, l. 25: Stone < stone

p. 200, l. 32: Stone < stone

p. 202, l. 40: *palantíri* < *Palantíri*

p. 203, ll. 13–17: We had not yet given thought to the fate of the *palantíri* of Gondor in its ruinous wars. By Men they were almost forgotten. Even in Gondor they were a secret known only to a few; in Arnor they were remembered only in a rhyme of lore among the Dúnedain. < It was not known to us that any of the *palantíri* had escaped the ruin of Gondor. Outside the Council it was not even remembered among Elves or Men that such things had ever been, save only in a Rhyme of Lore preserved among Aragorn's folk.

p. 203, l. 23: Stones < stones

p. 203, ll. 25–8: The three others were far away in the North. In the house of Elrond it is told that they were at Annúminas, and Amon Sûl, and Elendil's stone was on the Tower Hills < The others were far away. Few now know where, for no rhyme says. But in the House of Elrond it is told that they were at Annúminas, and Amon Sûl, and on the Tower Hills

p. 203, ll. 30–1: Each *palantír* replied to each, but all those in Gondor were ever open to the view of Osgiliath. < Each *palantír* spoke to each, but at Osgiliath they could survey them all together at one time.

p. 203, ll. 38–9: where the lost Stones of Arnor and Gondor now lie, buried < where all those other stones now lie, broken, or buried

p. 205, l. 6: Stone < stone

p. 205, l. 8: Stone < stone

p. 206, l. 3: house of Eorl < House of Eorl

p. 216, l. 1: Vale of Anduin < vale of Anduin

p. 217, l. 22: Elf-country < elf-country

p. 220, l. 15: my Precious, my Precious < my precious, my precious

p. 220, l. 17: Precious < precious

p. 220, l. 19: Precious < precious

p. 241, l. 15: the sea < the Sea

p. 244, l. 10 after titling: Núrnen < Nûrnen

p. 252, l. 14: *palantír* < *Palantír*

p. 254, l. 3: were very close < was very close

p. 263, l. 40: Elvish waybread < elvish waybread

p. 303, l. 12 after titling: Valley of Living Death < valley of Living Death

p. 332, ll. 12–13: The Cleft, Cirith Ungol < The cleft, Cirith Ungol

p. 339, l. 2: *palan-diriel* < *palan-díriel*
p. 339, l. 4: *tiro* < *tíro*
p. 341, l. 22: Ring < ring
p. 349, l. 13: Great Siege < great Siege

Two different impressions of A5e.ii were marked 'ninth impression', the first published in 1974 at £3.75, the second, with revised text, published in 1978 at £4.95. The latter is probably the tenth impression, marked in error; but a 'tenth impression' was also published in 1978.

iii. THE RETURN OF THE KING:

[*1 line in certar, between double rules*] | The Return of | the King | BEING THE THIRD PART OF | THE LORD OF THE RINGS | BY | J. R. R. TOLKIEN | *London* | GEORGE ALLEN & UNWIN LTD | RUSKIN HOUSE MUSEUM STREET | [*2 lines in tengwar, between double rules*]

[5]–440 pp. + 1 plate (map). Collation: $[1-12^{16}13^{10}14^{16}]$. 22.1 × 14.1 cm.

[5] 'THE RETURN OF THE KING'; [6] '[*1 line in certar, between double rules*] | THE LORD OF THE RINGS | BY J. R. R. TOLKIEN | PART I | THE FELLOWSHIP OF THE RING | PART II | THE TWO TOWERS | PART III | THE RETURN OF THE KING | [*2 lines in tengwar, between double rules*]'; [7] title; [8] 'First published October 1955 | [*list of second through eleventh impressions, 1955–65*] | Second Edition 1966 | [*notice of restrictions under copyright*] | © George Allen & Unwin Ltd, 1966 | Printed in Great Britain | in 11 on 12 point Imprint type | by Jarrold & Sons Ltd, | Norwich'; [9] 'THE LORD OF THE RINGS | [*poem, "Three Rings for the Elven-kings" etc.*]'; [10] blank; 11–13 synopsis; [14] blank; 15 table of contents; [16] blank; [17] 'BOOK V | [*swelled rule*]'; [18] blank; 19–169 text; [170] blank; [171] 'BOOK VI | [*swelled rule*]'; [172] blank; 173–311 text; [312] blank; 313–416 appendices; 417–40 index. Map of Rohan, Gondor, and Mordor, in black and red on folded leaf tipped onto recto, back free endpaper.

Wove paper. Bound in red cloth over boards. Stamped on spine in gilt: '[*within a ring:*] The | Return | of the | King | [*below the ring:*] J. R. R. | TOLKIEN | GEORGE ALLEN | AND UNWIN'. Wove endpapers. No headbands. All edges trimmed. Top edge stained red, fore- and bottom edges unstained.

Dust-jacket, wove paper. Printed on upper cover against a grey-green background: 'TOLKIEN | [*rule, wraps around upper cover and spine*] | [*in white:*] The | Return of | the King | [*rule, in black, wraps around upper cover and spine*] | ["*Ring and Eye*" *device in black, red, and gold*] | [*in white:*] REVISED EDITION'. Printed on spine against a grey-green background: 'J. R. R. | TOLKIEN | [*rule*] | [*in white:*] The | Return | of the | King | [*in red:*] BEING THE | THIRD | PART OF | The Lord of | the Rings | [*rule, in black*] | [*semi-circle "flames", in red*] | [*in white:*] George | Allen | & | Unwin'. Printed on lower cover: 'J. R. R. TOLKIEN | [*advertisement of* H, FGH, ATB, *and* TL, *in black and red*] | [*in black:*] GEORGE ALLEN AND UNWIN LTD'. Printed on back flap: 'J. R. R. TOLKIEN | THE LORD OF THE RINGS | Med. 8vo. In three volumes 25s. net each. | De Luxe Boxed Edition set of three volumes £6 6s. net | VOLUME ONE | THE FELLOWSHIP OF THE RING | VOLUME TWO | THE TWO TOWERS | VOLUME THREE | THE RETURN OF THE KING | Printed in Great Britain'. Front flap varies, no priority determined: (1) '[*blurb*] | Second Edition | The Return of the King | J. R. R. Tolkien | G. Allen & Unwin Ltd | Price in U.K. | 25s net'; (2) '[*blurb*] | Second Edition | The Return of the King |

[*"The Two Towers"*, *overprinted with a solid bar*] | J. R. R. Tolkien | G. Allen & Unwin Ltd | Price in U.K. | 25s net'.

Partly reset, revised, based on A5a.iii, with at least one correction ('pit that open' > 'pit that opened', p. 209, l. 41), but continuing the errors 'beside his own, for, the sound' for 'beside his own, for the sound', p. 31, l. 25, and 'as for others' for 'as for orders', p. 101, l. 22. Further alterations and new errors made in A5e.iii include:

p. 24, ll. 19–20: shapely, fifty fathoms from its base to the pinnacle, where the banner of the Stewards floated a thousand < A5a.iii, p. 24, ll. 19–20: shapely it was, one hundred and fifty fathoms from base to pinnacle, where floated the banner of the Stewards

p. 36, l. 8: Sea < A5a.iii, p. 36, l. 8: sea

p. 53, ll. 28–9: glinted. 'Did I not openly proclaim my title before the doors of Edoras? What do you fear that I should say to him? [*error, reverses correct order of sentences:* What do you fear that I should say to him? Did I not openly proclaim my title before the doors of Edoras?] Nay, < A5a.iii, p. 53, ll. 28–30: glinted. 'What do you fear that I should say: that I had a rascal of a rebel dwarf here that I would gladly exchange for a serviceable orc? Nay,

p. 53, l. 41: till now. The eyes in Orthanc did not see through the armour of Théoden, but Sauron has not < A5a.iii, p. 53, l. 41: till now. But he has not

p. 59, l. 11: Gate [*error, for* Door] of the Dead

p. 68, l. 4: Írensaga < A5a.iii, p. 68, l. 4: Irensaga

p. 82, l. 19: five birdlike forms < A5a.iii, p. 82, l. 19: huge birdlike forms

p. 99, ll. 5–6: Sadly. 'The house of his spirit crumbles.' < A5a.iii, p. 99, ll. 5–6: Sadly. 'His house crumbles.'

p. 104, ll. 19–26 after titling: stay behind. He wondered, too, if the old King knew that he had been disobeyed and was angry. Perhaps not. There seemed to be some understanding between Dernhelm and Elfhelm, the marshal [*error, for* Marshal] who commanded the *éored* in which they were riding. He and all his men ignored Merry and presented not to hear if he spoke. He might have been just another bag that Dernhelm was carrying. Dernhelm was no comfort: he never spoke to anyone. Merry felt small, unwanted, and lonely. Now the time < A5a.iii, p. 104, ll. 19–20: stay behind. The king was not well pleased, and Dernhelm was no comfort: he seldom spoke a word. Now the time

p. 105, ll. 8–9: the voice of the marshal, Elfhelm. [*error, for* the voice of Elfhelm the Marshal] ¶ 'I am not a tree-root, Sir,' he said, 'nor a bag, but a < A5a.iii, p. 105, ll. 2–4: the voice of Elfhelm, captain of the company with which he was riding. ¶ 'I am not a tree-root, Captain,' he said, 'but a

p. 105, ll. 29–30: commands. Pack yourself up, Master Bag!' He vanished < A5a.iii, p. 105, l. 24: commands.' He vanished

p. 129, l. 7: given to you, Steward of Gondor, to order < A5a.iii, p. 129, l. 7: given to you, nor to any other lord, to order

p. 144, ll. 24–5: hand in his and felt it warm with life returning. 'Awake! < A5a.iii, p. 144, l. 24: hand in his. 'Awake!

p. 153, l. 30: *Oft hope* < A5a.iii, p. 153, l. 30: *Hope oft*

p. 158, l. 13–14: ride the sons of Elrond with the Dúnedain < A5a.iii, p. 158, l. 13: ride the Dúnedain

p. 158, ll. 16–17: some three thousand under the command of Elfhelm, should < A5a.iii, p. 158, l. 16: some three thousand, should

p. 182, footnote (to '*tarks*', l. 29) added: See App. F, 409

p. 189, l. 42: evil Eye [*error, for* Evil Eye]

p. 202, ll. 23–4: Urukhai < A5a.iii, p. 202, ll. 23–4: *Urukhai*

p. 230, l. 38–p. 231, l. 3: beside their beds. ¶ 'The clothes that you wore on your way to Mordor,' said Gandalf. 'Even the orc-rags that you bore in the black land, Frodo, shall be preserved. No silks and linens, nor any armour or heraldry could be more honourable. But later I will find some other clothes, perhaps.' ¶ Then he held out his hands to them, and they saw that one shone with light. 'What have you got there?' Frodo cried. 'Can it be—?' ¶ 'Yes, I have brought your two treasures. They were found on Sam when you were rescued. The Lady Galadriel's gifts: your glass, Frodo, and your box, Sam. You will be glad to have these safe again.' ¶ When they were washed < A5a.iii, p. 230, ll. 37–41: beside their beds. ¶ 'The clothes that you journeyed in,' said Gandalf. 'No silks and linens, nor any armour or heraldry could be more honourable. But later we shall see.' ¶ When they were washed

p. 233, ll. 5–17: and then he laid before them two swords. ¶ 'I do not wish for any sword,' said Frodo. ¶ 'Tonight at least you should wear one,' said Gandalf. ¶ Then Frodo took the small sword that had belonged to Sam, and had been laid at his side in Cirith Ungol. 'Sting I gave to you Sam,' he said. ¶ 'No, master! Mr. Bilbo gave it to you, and it goes with his silver coat; he would not wish anyone else to wear it now.' ¶ Frodo gave way; and Gandalf, as if he were their esquire, knelt and girt the sword-belts about them, and then rising he set circlets of silver upon their heads. And when they were arrayed they went to the great feast; and they sat at the King's table with Gandalf, < A5a.iii, p. 233, ll. 1–3: and when the hobbits were made ready, and circlets of silver were set upon their heads, they went to the King's feast, and they sat at his table with Gandalf

p. 233, l. 20: But when, after the Standing Silence, wine < A5a.iii, p. 233, l. 6: But when wine

p. 236, ll. 7–8 after titling: Morgul-vale [*error, for* Morgul Vale]

p. 236, l. 25 after titling: Morgul-vale [*error, for* Morgul Vale]

p. 244, ll. 25–6: was bare save for a star upon his forehead bound by a slender fillet of silver. With him < A5a.iii, p. 244, ll. 25–6: was bare. With him

p. 245, ll. 15–16: Dúnedain of Arnor, Captain of the Host of the West, bearer of the Star of the North, wielder of < A5a.iii, p. 245, ll. 15–16: Dúnedain of the North, Captain of the Host of the West, wielder of

p. 245, l. 30: Eärnur < A5a.iii, p. 245, l. 30: Earnur

p. 246, ll. 14–16: blessed while the thrones of the Valar endure!' ¶ But when < A5a.iii, p. 246, l. 14–15: blessed! ¶ But when

p. 246, l. 21: Faramir cried: < A5a.iii, p. 246, l. 20: Faramir said:

p. 247, l. 28: Morgul-vale [*error, for* Morgul Vale]

p. 248, ll. 7–9: passed; and on the eighth day of May the Riders of Rohan made ready, and rode off by the North-way, and with them went the sons of Elrond. All the road was lined < A5a.iii, p. 248, ll. 7–8: passed; and the Riders of Rohan made ready, and rode away by the North-way; and it was lined

p. 248, l. 11: Pelennor. Then all < A5a.iii, p. 248, l. 10: Pelennor. And all

p. 249, l. 31: I shall have life < A5a.iii, p. 249, ll. 29–30: I may have life

p. 255, ll. 23–4: Léofa, and Walda, and Folca, and Folcwine, and Fengel < A5a.iii, p. 255, l. 23: Léof, and Walda, and Folca, and Fengel

p. 258, l. 27: gone seven days. I let him < A5a.iii, p. 258, l. 27: gone. I let him

p. 260, l. 41–p. 261, l. 1: company following [*error, for* company following] the Isen, turned west and rode through the Gap into < A5a.iii, p. 260, l. 41–p. 261, l. 1: company came to the Isen, and crossed over it, and came into

p. 261, ll. 2–3: passed over the borders of Dunland. The Dunlendings < A5a.iii, p. 261, l. 2: passed by the borders of Dunland. And the Dunlendings

p. 261, ll. 7–8: would. ¶ On the sixth day since their parting from the King they journeyed < A5a.iii, p. 261, ll. 7–8: would; and as they went the summer wore away. ¶ After they had passed by Dunland and were come to places where few folk dwelt, and even birds and beasts were seldom to be seen, they journeyed

p. 261, l. 11: country at sundown they overtook < A5a.iii, p. 261, l. 13: country they overtook

p. 263, ll. 6–14: mean way. [*error, for* way.'] ¶ Next day they went on into northern Dunland, where no men now dwelt, though it was a green and pleasant country. September came in with golden days and silver nights, and they rode at ease until they reached the Swanfleet river, and found the old ford, east of the falls where it went down suddenly into the lowlands. Far to the west in a haze lay the meres and eyots through which it would its way to the Greyflood: there countless swans housed in a land of reeds. ¶ So they passed into Eregion, and at last < A5a.iii, p. 263, ll. 8–9: mean way. ¶ September came in with golden days and silver nights. At last

p. 264, l. 9: littered with papers < A5a.iii, p. 264, l. 6: littered with paper

p. 265, l. 17: three books of lore < A5a.iii, p. 265, l. 14: some books of lore

p. 266, l. 32–3: papers, and my diary too, and take < A5a.iii, p. 266, l. 29: papers and take

p. 282, l. 4: Whitfurrows < A5a.iii, p. 282, l. 4: Bamfurlong

p. 295, ll. 34–5: Greenfields < A5a.iii, p. 295, ll. 34–5: Green Fields

p. 298, footnote: *sharkû* < A5a.iii, p. 298, footnote: *sharkū*

p. 310, l. 15: quay beside a great grey horse stood < A5a.iii, p. 310, l. 15: quay stood

p. 310, ll. 17–18: saw that Gandalf now wore openly upon [*error, for* on] his hand < A5a.iii, p. 210, ll. 16–17: saw that it was Gandalf; and on his hand he wore

The appendices were reset for A5e.iii, with extensive revision. Changes include:

p. 313, the opening paragraphs and footnotes of Appendix A were rewritten. A new (second) footnote reads: 'In this edition the dates have been revised, and some errors emended: most of these were accidents occurring in the course of typing and printing.'

p. 313, l. 31–p. 314, l. 12 (excepting footnotes, p. 313), paragraph ('Fëanor was the greatest of the Eldar . . .') added

p. 314, l. 13: There were three unions of the Eldar and the Edain: Lúthien < A5a.iii, p. 314, l. 5: There were only three unions of the High Elves and Men; Lúthien

p. 318, ll. 20–1: Aragorn II F.A. 120 < A5a.iii, p. 318, ll. 18–19: Aragorn II F.A. 100

p. 318, ll. 34–7: Calmacil 1304, Minalcar (regent 1240–1304), crowned as Rómendacil II 1304, died 1366, Valacar. < A5a.iii, p. 318, l. 32: Calmacil 1304, Rómendacil II 1366, Valacar.

p. 324, l. 19: the endings of their king [*error, for* ending of their kings]

p. 330, l. 40: loyalty [*error, for* royalty] of Arnor

p. 343, l. 11: As Queen of Elves and Men she dwelt with Aragorn for six-score years < A5a.iii, p. 343, l. 5: As Queen of Elves and Men she dwelt with Aragorn for five-score years

p. 344, ll. 23–7: dwelt there alone under the fading trees until winter came. Galadriel had passed away and Celeborn also was gone, and the land was silent. ¶ 'There at last when the mallorn-leaves were falling, but spring had not yet come, [*footnote:* I, 349] she laid herself to rest upon Cerin Amroth < A5a.iii, p. 344, ll. 17–19: dwelt there alone under the fading trees; for Galadriel also was gone, and the elven-leaves were withering. ¶ 'There at last she laid

p. 349, l. 38–p. 350, l. 11, the notes on *Brytta*, *Walda*, and *Folca* are added between existing notes on *Fréaláf* Hildeson and *Folcwine* < A5a.iii, p. 349, ll. 38–40, *Brytta*, *Walda*, and *Folca* listed, without notes

p. 363, l. 12: domination [*error, for* dominion] of Men

p. 363, ll. 21–32: remained. Most of these dwelt in Lindon west of the Ered Luin; but before the building of the Barad-dûr many of the Sindar passed eastward, and some established realms in the forests far away, where their people were mostly Silvan Elves. Thranduil, king in the north of Greenwood the Great, was one of these. In Lindon north of the Lune dwelt Gil-galad, last heir of the kings of the Noldor in exile. He was acknowledged as High King of the Elves of the West. In Lindon south of the Lune dwelt for a time Celeborn, kinsman of Thingol; his wife was Galadriel, greatest of Elven women. She was sister of Finrod Felagund, Friend-of-Men, once king of Nargothrond, who gave his life to save Beren son of Barahir. ¶ Later some < A5a.iii, p. 363, ll. 21–7: remained. The exiled Noldor dwelt in Lindon, but many of the Sindar passed eastward and established realms in the forests far away. The chief of these were Thranduil in the north of Greenwood the Great, and Celeborn in the south of the forest. But the wife of Celeborn was Noldorin: Galadriel, sister of Felagund of the House of Finrod. ¶ Later some

p. 363, l. 37–p. 364, l. 1: two races. Celebrimbor was lord of Eregion and the greatest of their craftsmen; he was descended from Fëanor. ¶ Year < A5a.iii, p. 363, ll. 32–3: two races. ¶ Year

p. 366, ll. 4–5: Círdan. Gil-galad before he died gave his ring to Elrond; Círdan later surrendered his to Mithrandir. < A5a.iii, p. 365, l. 43–p. 366, l. 1 (excepting footnote, p. 365): The ring of Gil-galad was given by him to Elrond; but Círdan surrendered his to Mithrandir.

p. 366, l. 19: 109 Elrond weds daughter of Celeborn. < A5a.iii, p. 366, l. 16: 100 Elrond weds Celebrían of Lórien.

p. 366, l. 20: 130 Birth of Elladan and Elrohir < A5a.iii, p. 366, l. 17: 139 Birth of Elladan and Elrohir

p. 368, l. 5: The Dwarves of Lórien flee south. [*error, for* The Dwarves flee from Moria. Many of the Silvan Elves of Lórien flee south.]

p. 371, ll. 5–6: errantries. As Thorongil he serves < A5a.iii, p. 370, ll. 45–6: errantries. He serves

p. 371, ll. 7–9: of Gondor ¶ 2968 Birth of Frodo. ¶ 2976 Denethor < A5a.iii, p. 370, ll. 46–7: of Gondor ¶ 2976 Denethor

p. 371, ll. 17–18: 2983 Faramir son of Denethor born. Birth of Samwise. ¶ 2984 Death < A5a.iii, p. 371, ll. 9–10: 2983 Faramir son of Denethor born. ¶ 2984 Death

p. 375, ll. 38–43: Woodmen. But after the passing of Galadriel in a few years Celeborn grew weary of his realm and went to Imladris to dwell with the sons of Elrond. In the Greenwood the Silvan Elves remained untroubled, but in Lórien there lingered sadly only a few of its former people, and there was no longer light or song in Caras Galadon. ¶ At the same time < A5a.iii, p. 375, ll. 30–1: Woodmen. ¶ At the same time

p. 376, footnote (to divisional heading 'THE CHIEF DAYS...') added: Months and days are given according to the Shire Calendar.

p. 376, ll. 24–5: 8 Éomer and Éowyn depart for Rohan with the sons of Elrond. 20 Elrond < A5a.iii, p. 376, l. 11: 8 Éomer and Éowyn depart for Rohan. 20 Elrond

p. 376, ll. 26–9: leaves Lórien. ¶ *June 14*. The sons of Elrond meet the escort and bring Arwen to Edoras. *16*. They set out for Gondor. *25*. King Elessar < A5a.iii, p. 376, ll. 12–13: leaves Lórien. ¶ *June 25*. King Elessar

p. 378, ll. 10–14: 1451 Elanor the Fair marries Fastred of Greenholm on the Far Downs. ¶ 1452 The Westmarch, from the Far Downs to the Tower Hills (*Emyn Beraid*), [*footnote:* I, 17; III, 322, note 2.] is added to the Shire by the gift of the King. Many hobbits remove to it. ¶ 1454 Elfstan Fairbairn < A5a.iii, p. 377, ll. 37–8: 1451 Elanor the Fair marries Fastred of Greenholm. ¶ 1454 Elfstan Fairbairn

p. 378, ll. 15–20: 1455 Master Samwise becomes Mayor for the fifth time. [*error, omits* ¶ 1462 Master Samwise becomes Mayor for the sixth time.] At his request the Thain makes Fastred Warden of Westmarch. Fastred and Elanor make their dwelling at Undertowers on the Tower Hills, where their descendants, the Fairbairns of the Towers, dwelt for many generations. ¶ 1463 Faramir Took < A5a.iii, p. 377, l. 38–p. 378, l. 6 (excepting footnote on p. 377): 1455 Master Samwise becomes Mayor for the fifth time. ¶ S.R. ¶ 1462 Master Samwise becomes Mayor for the sixth time. At his request the Thain makes Fastred and Elanor Wardens of the Westmarch (a region newly inhabited); they take up their dwelling on the slopes of the Tower Hills, where their descendants, the Fairbairns of Westmarch, dwell for many generations.

p. 378, ll. 40–3: Gondor. ¶ 1541 In this year [*footnote:* Fourth Age (Gondor) 120.] on March 1st came at last the Passing of King Elessar. It is said that the beds of Meriadoc and Peregrin were set beside the bed of the great king. Then < A5a.iii, p. 378, ll. 26–9: 1521 In this year came at last the Passing of King Elessar. It is said that the beds of Meriadoc and Peregrin were set beside the bed of the great King. Then

p. 392, l. 17: in Adûnaic and Westron, as in < A5a.iii, p. 392, l. 17: in Adûnaic, as in

p. 392, ll. 27–8: occuring [*error, for* occurring] in Westron [*error, for* Westron,] Dwarvish and Orkish < A5a.iii, p. 392, l. 27: occurring in Dwarvish and Orkish

p. 392, l. 45: a sound like that often heard < A5a.iii, p. 392, l. 45: a sound like that heard

p. 393, ll. 11–12: except initially and finally < A5a.iii, p. 393, l. 11: except finally

p. 393, l. 32: *lyg* < A5a.iii, p. 393, l. 32: *lŷg*

p. 398, ll. 43–5: The representation of the sounds here is the same as that employed in transcription and described above, except that here *ch* represents the *ch* in English *church*; *j* represents the sound of English *j*, and *zh* the sound heard in *azure* and *occasion*. < A5a.iii, p. 398, ll. 43–7: The representation of the sounds is not strictly phonetic, but is the same as that employed in transcription and described on pp. 391–5, except that here *ch* represents the *ch* in English *church*, and to distinguish it the back 'spirant' *ch* is represented by *kh*; *j* represents the sound of English *j*, and *zh* the sound heard in *azure* and *occasion*; ŋ is used for *ng* in *sing*.

p. 399, ll. 6–14, 'Note' ('The standard spelling of Quenya...') added between 'largely derived' and '*The additional letters.*' < A5a.iii, p. 399, ll. 7–8: largely derived. ¶ *The additional letters.*

p. 405, l. 18: Drúdan [*error, for* Drúadan] Forest

p. 405, footnote (to '*Eldarin* form', l. 2) added: In Lórien at this period Sindarin was spoken.... But *Lórien, Caras Galadon, Amroth, Nimrodel* are probably of Silvan origin, adapted to Sindarin.

p. 406, ll. 14–5: Lady Galadriel of the royal house of Finarphir and sister of Finrod Felagund, King of Nargothrond. < A5a.iii, p. 406, ll. 11–12: Lady Galadriel of the royal house of Finrod, father of Felagund, lord of Nargothrond.

p. 406, l. 22: *Antani* [*error, for* Atani]

p. 406, ll. 44–8 (footnote): 'Elfstone'. Most of the names of the other men and women of the Dúnedain, such as *Aragorn, Denethor, Gilraen* are of Sindarin form, being often the names of Elves or Men remembered in the songs and histories of the First Age (as *Beren Húrin* [*error, for* Beren, Húrin]). Some few are of mixed forms, as *Boromir.* < A5a.iii, p. 406, ll. 44–7: 'Elfstone'. The names of other lords of the Dúnedain, such as *Aragorn, Denethor, Faramir,* are of Sindarin form, being often the names of Elves or Men remembered in the songs and histories of the First Age.

p. 409, l. 17: *Fanghorn* [*error, for* Fangorn]

p. 409, ll. 36–9: Orkish. In this jargon *tark*, 'man of Gondor', was a debased form of *tarkil*, a Quenya word used in Westron for one of Númenórean descent; see III, 182. ¶ It is said < A5a.iii, p. 409, ll. 36–7: Orkish. ¶ It is said

p. 416, l. 7: The [*error, for* Their] dominion
p. 415, l. 20: Aluë [*error, for* Aulë]
On pp. 417–40, the index was added.

Most of the errors noted for A5e.iii were corrected in the second impression (1967). Further alterations made by Tolkien in the second impression include:

p. 25, l. 7: Guards < [*first impression:*] guards
p. 31, l. 37: *Isildur's Bane* < *Isildur's bane*
p. 53, l. 9: Shire-folk < Shirefolk
p. 56, l. 19: Nay, lady < Nay, Lady
p. 63, l. 27: rose at once < rose in haste
p. 76, l. 17: Riders of renown < riders of renown
p. 89, l. 18: winged Shadows < winged shadows
p. 106, l. 6: father of Horsemen < father of horsemen
p. 124, l. 14: Great Battle < great battle
p. 128, l. 17: the Hallows < the hallows
p. 132, ll. 30–1: long ago I guessed that here in the White Tower, one at least of the Seven Seeing Stones < long have I known that here in the White Tower, as at Orthanc, one of the Seven Stones
p. 132, l. 32: Denethor did not presume [*error, for* Denethor would not presume; *see* UT *(A17), p. 413, n. 11*]
p. 132, l. 35: deceived: far too often, I guess, since Boromor [*error, for* Boromir] departed < deceived: more than once, I guess, since Boromir departed
p. 137, l. 20: banner of the Kings < banner of the kings
p. 137, l. 21: Elendil's House < Elendil's house
p. 137, ll. 32–3: North Kingdom < North-kingdom
p. 139, l. 16: I am *Elessar*, the Elfstone, and *Envinyatar*, the Renewer < I am Elessar, the Elfstone, and the Renewer
p. 143, l. 19: *house of Eorl* < *House of Eorl*
p. 163, ll. 26–7: The two vast iron doors of the Black Gate under its frowning arch were fast closed. < The three vast doors of the Black Gate under their frowning arches were fast closed.
p. 165, l. 28: first the short sword that Sam < first a short sword such as Sam
p. 167, ll. 27–8: leaped up. The great doors of the Black Gate swung < leaped up. All the doors of the Morannon swung
p. 174, l. 23: Cleft < cleft
p. 175, l. 8: Cleft < cleft
p. 182, l. 14 up: *tark's* < *tark's*
p. 196, ll. 23–4: Vale of Anduin < vale of Anduin
p. 224, l. 14: *Precious* < *precious*
p. 237, l. 13: In this house, lady < In this house, Lady
p. 244, ll. 30–1: beside her. 'Those are *Periain*, out of < beside her. 'They are Periannath, out of
p. 249, l. 9: Vale of Anduin < vale of Anduin
p. 253, l. 19: Lady in the Golden Wood < Lady of the Golden Wood

Since the death of J. R. R. Tolkien in 1973, his son and literary executor Christopher Tolkien has made numerous corrections to *LR*, including, in *FR*, 'bride-piece' > 'bride- price'; in *TT*, 'Deeping Coomb' > 'Deeping-coomb'; and in *RK* (pagination for A5e.iii):

p. 164, l. 24: the door of the Black Gate < the middle door of the Black Gate

p. 324, l. 4: There were fifteen Chieftains, before the sixteenth and last was born < There were fourteen Chieftains, before the fifteenth and last was born

p. 324, l. 19: the ending of their kings the waning was swifter in Gondor, and < the endings of their king the waning was swifter in Gondor; and

p. 351, l. 5: chief Marshal < chief marshal

p. 351, l. 26: became a Marshal < became a marshal

p. 361, death date of 'Gimli Elf-friend': 3141 (F.A. 120) < 3121 (F.A. 100)

p. 366, l. 19: 109 Elrond weds Celebrían, daughter of Celeborn. < 109 Elrond weds daughter of Celeborn.

p. 368, l. 47: Southfarthing < South-farthing

p. 388, l. 29: Eastfarthing < East-farthing

p. 392, l. 30: *s* in spoken Quenya < *s* in Quenya spoken

p. 405, l. 41: cited in I, ii, chs 6, 7, 8 < cited in I, chs 6, 7, 8

p. 405, ll. 42–3: *Caras Galadhon* < *Caras Galadon*

p. 406, l. 14: Finarfin < Finarphir

p. 416, l. 3: Finarfin < Finrod

Some corrections appeared first in the three-volume Unwin Paperbacks edition (A5j). Most corrections were carried into the various later editions and impressions of *LR*. At least one new error was introduced in *RK* (A5e.iii) when resetting for correction: 'the Tower of the Dome of Osgiliath' for 'the Tower of the Stone of Osgiliath', p. 327, l. 7.

Published 27 October 1966 at 25s. per volume; number of copies not known.

Maps drawn by Christopher Tolkien, as for A5a except with revision to Shire map.

The revisions to *LR* were to be used first for the authorized paperback, which Ballantine Books rushed into print (see A5d note), then for new hardcover editions by Houghton Mifflin, and then for new editions by Allen & Unwin. But by mid-December 1965 the British edition was needed urgently. By January 1966, all changes in the Ballantine edition, except for the appendices, were transferred to Houghton Mifflin's master set of proofs and sent to Allen & Unwin. But Tolkien's original revisions to the appendices were lost, and Allen & Unwin had to reset based on the printed Ballantine Books text. 'It is unfortunate that the emended sheets for the Appendices are not available,' Tolkien wrote to Allen & Unwin,

> since I was very hard pressed for time at this point. Emendation of the Appendices though desirable, in view of my own reconsiderations and criticisms by keen-eyed critics, required much work and calculation; and I appear, by reference to the B [Ballantine] text, not in my check-copy to have taken the same care as elsewhere to distinguish between changes sent to HM [Houghton Mifflin], those suggested but reserved for possible inclusion in a new AU [Allen & Unwin] edition, and those few discovered as necessary after I had sent the sheets to USA. In consequence some of the work has had to be done again. I have taken the B[allantine] text as basic, and have in general contented myself with correcting errors in it, avoiding the introduction of serious discrepancies between B and a new AU.

He prepared revisions to the index, then noted on 26 February 1966: 'Closer scrutiny has revealed many more errors, several omissions, and some confused entries [in the Ballantine Books edition index]. I have in the event done much alteration and correction—making, I think, the index more useful and informative within its limits.'

Tolkien continued to revise *LR* into the summer of 1966, after the first impression of the new Allen & Unwin edition had been completed. His later revisions were incorporated in the second impression of A5e. See further, Åke Jönsson (Bertenstam), 'The Kings' Reckoning: Did Tolkien Reckon Correct?' *Beyond Bree* (newsletter of the American Mensa Tolkien Special Interest Group), November 1985, pp. 5–6; Julian C. Bradfield, 'Changes in *The Lord of the Rings*, Appendices D & E between the First and Second Allen & Unwin Editions (1955, 1966)', *Beyond Bree*, October 1984, p. 3, with a note by Nancy Martsch; Louis Epstein, 'Index Difference Roundup', *Frodo Fortnightly*, nos. 141 (19 September 1982)–154 (20 March 1983); Nancy Martsch, 'A Discrepancy in the Took Family Tree', *Beyond Bree*, April 1988, p. 7; Donald O'Brien, 'More Differences between the Allen & Unwin and the Ballantine Editions of *The Lord of the Rings*', *Beyond Bree*, October 1986, p. 9; and Christina Scull, 'A Preliminary Study of Variations in Editions of *The Lord of the Rings*', *Beyond Bree*, April 1985, pp. 3–6, and August 1985, pp. 1–6, with a comment by Robert Acker.

'De Luxe Boxed Edition' on the dust-jackets refers to A5a, not A5e.

With the seventh impression (1973) of each volume, the dust-jackets were changed to feature a larger 'Ring and Eye' device. Copies with these jackets were sold separately or in a slipcase, printed paper over boards featuring the 'Ring and Eye' device, brown cloth over boards top and bottom. The dust-jackets were changed again with the sixteenth impression (1987) of *FR* and the fourteenth impression (1987) of *TT* and *RK*, now under the Unwin Hyman imprint, to feature colour illustrations by Tolkien: *FR*, *The Forest of Lothlorien in Spring*; *TT*, *Fangorn Forest* (i.e. *Beleg Finds Gwindor in Taur-nu-Fuin*); *RK*, *Dunharrow*. A5e was later issued as a set in a dark green imitation leather box stamped in gilt, and with *H* (A3r) and *Silm* (A15a) as *The Tolkien Library* (see A3r note). A5e was published by HarperCollins beginning in 1991, in dust-jackets illustrated by John Howe.

In 1971 Methuen, Toronto, published a three-volume paperback edition, re-printed (reduced) from the typesetting of A5e, wrappers featuring colour illustrations by Pauline Baynes from her *Map of Middle-earth* (Eii4). On the lower cover of each volume is the statement over Tolkien's signature: 'I welcome the publication in Canada of this edition of *The Lord of the Rings*'.

In 1972 A5e was reprinted by Bookcase Shop, Taipei, under licence by George Allen & Unwin, in three volumes.

A book club edition was published by Book Club Associates, London, in 1987, three volumes reprinted from the Unwin Hyman edition.

A selection from the final chapter of *LR* was privately printed in 1990 by Edith McKeon Abbott, 'At the Sign of the Pilcrow', Brookline, Massachusetts, as a memorial to her father.

LR was adapted for radio and broadcast on the BBC Third Programme in 1955 and 1956. Another adaptation, by Brian Sibley and Michael Bakewell with music by Stephen Oliver, was first broadcast on BBC Radio 4 in twenty-six weekly parts beginning 8 March 1981, and was issued by the BBC in 1987 on thirteen audio cassettes. *The Adventures of Frodo*, selections from *LR* read by Michael Hordern, originally produced for BBC Schools Radio, were issued by the BBC in 1987 on two audio cassettes. A 1979 dramatization by Bernard Mayes was issued by Jabber-wocky on twelve audio cassettes and was broadcast ('The Mind's Eye', 'Radio 2000') on American radio.

An unabridged recording of *FR*, *TT*, *RK*, and Appendix A (*Annals of the Kings and Rulers*), made by Rob Inglis, was issued in 1991 on forty-one audio cassettes by Recorded Books, Prince Frederick, Maryland, and (except Appendix A) by Isis Audio Books, Oxford.

f. Second Houghton Mifflin edition (1967):

i. THE FELLOWSHIP OF THE RING:

[*1 line in certar, between double rules*] | The Fellowship | of the Ring | BEING THE FIRST PART OF | THE LORD OF THE RINGS | BY | J. R. R. TOLKIEN | *Second Edition* | HOUGHTON MIFFLIN COMPANY BOSTON | [*black letter:*] The Riverside Press Cambridge | [*roman:*] 1967 | [*2 lines in tengwar, between double rules*]

iv, 428 pp. + 1 plate (map). Collation: $[1-11^{16}12^{8}13-14^{16}]$. 22.0 × 14.3 cm.

Contents as for A5e.i, except pp. [1] title, as above; [2] 'FIRST PRINTING W | COPYRIGHT © 1966 BY GEORGE ALLEN & UNWIN LTD. | ALL RIGHTS RESERVED INCLUDING THE RIGHT TO | REPRODUCE THIS BOOK OR PARTS THEREOF IN ANY FORM | LIBRARY OF CONGRESS CATALOG CARD NUMBER: 67-12274 | PRINTED IN THE UNITED STATES OF AMERICA'; and [424–8] blank. Map of Middle-earth, in black and red on folded leaf tipped onto recto, back free endpaper. The Shire map, p. [26], is printed in black only.

Illustrations as for A5e.i.

Wove paper. Bound in black cloth over boards. 'Ring and Eye' device stamped on upper cover in copper and gilt, against a blind-stamped panel. Stamped on spine in gilt: '[*against a blind-stamped panel:*] TOLKIEN | [*against a blind-stamped panel:*] The | Fellow- | ship | of the | Ring | [*against a blind-stamped panel:*] HMCO'. Wove endpapers. Yellow/purple headbands. All edges trimmed. Top edge stained orange, fore- and bottom edges unstained.

Dust-jacket, wove paper. Wraparound abstract illustration by Robert Quackenbush in orange and black. Printed on upper cover against the illustration: '[*against an orange panel:*] [*in gold, within a frame of black runes between 2 black double rule frames:*] The | Fellowship | of the Ring | BEING THE FIRST PART OF | THE LORD OF THE RINGS | J. R. R. TOLKIEN | [*below the panel, in black:*] REVISED EDITION'. The runes repeated at left and right read (as at the head of the title page): 'THE LORD OF THE RINGS TRANSLATED FROM THE RED BOOK'. The runes repeated at top and bottom read: 'TRANSLATED FROM THE RED BOOK'. Printed on spine in gold, against the illustration: '[*against an orange panel:*] The | Fellowship | of the Ring | J. R. R. TOLKIEN | [*below the panel:*] HOUGHTON | MIFFLIN CO.' 'Ring and Eye' device printed on lower cover in black, gold, and orange, against an orange panel, against the illustration. Printed on front flap: '$6.00 | [*in red-brown:*] The Lord | of the | Rings | J. R. R. TOLKIEN | [*in black:*] Second Edition, Revised | With a New Foreword by the Author | "*Here are beauties which pierce like swords | or burn like cold iron.*"—C. S. Lewis | [*blurb*] | 0267'. Printed on back flap: '[*blurb, continued*] | [*note on Tolkien*] | Jacket by Robert Quackenbush | HOUGHTON MIFFLIN COMPANY | 2 Park Street | Boston, Massachusetts | 02107'.

Typeset as for A5e.i, first impression, except pp. [1–2], [424]. Maps as for A5e.

ii. THE TWO TOWERS:

[*1 line in certar, between double rules*] | The Two Towers | BEING THE SECOND PART OF | THE LORD OF THE RINGS | BY | J. R. R. TOLKIEN | *Second Edition* | HOUGHTON MIFFLIN COMPANY BOSTON | [*black letter:*] The Riverside Press Cambridge | [*roman:*] 1967 | [*2 lines in tengwar, between double rules*]

352 pp. + 1 plate (map). Collation: [1–11¹⁶]. 22.0 × 14.3 cm.

Contents as for A5e.ii, except pp. [5] title, as above; and [6] 'FIRST PRINTING W | COPYRIGHT © 1966 BY GEORGE ALLEN & UNWIN LTD. | ALL RIGHTS RESERVED INCLUDING THE RIGHT TO | REPRODUCE THIS BOOK OR PARTS THEREOF IN ANY FORM | LIBRARY OF CONGRESS CATALOG CARD NUMBER: 67-12276 | PRINTED IN THE UNITED STATES OF AMERICA'. Map of Middle-earth, in black and red on folded leaf tipped onto recto, back free endpaper.

Wove paper. Bound in black cloth over boards. 'Ring and Eye' device stamped on upper cover in red and gilt, against a blind-stamped panel. Stamped on spine in gilt: '[*against a blind-stamped panel:*] TOLKIEN | [*against a blind-stamped panel:*] The | Two | Towers | [*against a blind-stamped panel:*] HMCO'. Wove endpapers. Yellow/ purple headbands. All edges trimmed. Top edge stained salmon red, fore- and bottom edges unstained.

Dust-jacket, wove paper. Wraparound abstract illustration by Robert Quackenbush in red and black. Printed on upper cover against the illustration: '[*against a red panel:*] [*in gold, within a frame of black runes between 2 black double rule frames:*] The | Two Towers | BEING THE SECOND PART OF | THE LORD OF THE RINGS | J. R. R. TOLKIEN | [*below the panel, in red:*] REVISED EDITION'. Runes as for A5f.i. Printed on spine in gold, against the illustration: '[*against a red panel:*] The | Two Towers | J. R. R. TOLKIEN | [*below the panel:*] HOUGHTON | MIFFLIN CO.' 'Ring and Eye' device printed on lower cover in black, gold, and red, against a red panel, against the illustration. Printed on front flap: '$6.00 | [*in red-brown:*] The Lord | of the | Rings | J. R. R. TOLKIEN | [*in black:*] Second Edition, Revised | With a New Foreword by the Author | "*Here are beauties which pierce like swords | or burn like cold iron.*"—C. S. Lewis | [*blurb*] | 0267'. Printed on back flap: '[*blurb, continued*] | [*note on Tolkien*] | Jacket by Robert Quackenbush | HOUGHTON MIFFLIN COMPANY | 2 Park Street | Boston, Massachusetts | 02107'.

Typeset as for A5e.ii, first impression, except pp. [5–6].

iii. THE RETURN OF THE KING:

[*1 line in certar, between double rules*] | The Return of | the King | BEING THE THIRD PART OF | THE LORD OF THE RINGS | BY | J. R. R. TOLKIEN | *Second Edition* | HOUGHTON MIFFLIN COMPANY BOSTON | [*black letter:*] The Riverside Press Cambridge | [*roman:*] 1967 | [*2 lines in tengwar, between double rules*]

[5]–444 pp. + 1 plate (map). Collation: [1–12¹⁶13¹²14¹⁶]. 22.1 × 14.3 cm.

Contents as for A5e.iii, except pp. [7] title, as above; [8] 'FIRST PRINTING W | COPYRIGHT © 1966 BY GEORGE ALLEN & UNWIN LTD. | ALL RIGHTS RESERVED INCLUDING THE RIGHT TO | REPRODUCE THIS BOOK OR PARTS THEREOF IN ANY FORM | LIBRARY OF CONGRESS CATALOG CARD NUMBER: 67-12275 | PRINTED IN THE UNITED STATES OF AMERICA'; and [441–4] blank. Map of Rohan, Gondor, and Mordor, in black and red on folded leaf tipped onto recto, back free endpaper.

Wove paper. Bound in black cloth over boards. 'Ring and Eye' device stamped on upper cover in purple and gilt, against a blind-stamped panel. Stamped on spine in gilt: '[*against a blind-stamped panel:*] TOLKIEN | [*against a blind-stamped panel:*]

The | Return | of | the | King | [*against a blind-stamped panel:*] HMCO'. Wove endpapers. Yellow/purple headbands. All edges trimmed. Top edge stained purple, fore- and bottom edges unstained.

Dust-jacket, wove paper. Wraparound abstract illustration by Robert Quackenbush in purple and black. Printed on upper cover against the illustration: '[*against a purple panel:*] [*in gold, within a frame of black runes between 2 black double rule frames:*] The Return | of the | King | BEING THE THIRD PART OF | THE LORD OF THE RINGS | J. R. R. TOLKIEN | [*below the panel, in purple:*] REVISED EDITION'. Runes as for A5f.i. Printed on spine in gold, against the illustration: '[*against a purple panel:*] The Return | of the | King | J. R. R. TOLKIEN | [*below the panel:*] HOUGHTON | MIFFLIN CO.' 'Ring and Eye' device printed on lower cover in black, gold, and purple, against a purple panel. Printed on front flap: '$6.00 | [*in purple:*] The Lord | of the | Rings | J. R. R. TOLKIEN | [*in black:*] Second Edition, Revised | With a New Foreword by the Author | *"Here are beauties which pierce like swords | or burn like cold iron."*—C. S. Lewis | [*blurb*] | 0267'. Printed on back flap: '[*blurb, continued*] | [*note on Tolkien*] | Jacket by Robert Quackenbush | HOUGHTON MIFFLIN COMPANY | 2 Park Street | Boston, Massachusetts | 02107'.

Typeset as for A5e.iii, first impression, except pp. [7–8].

Published 27 February 1967 at $6.00 per volume, $17.50 the set; 13,300 copies of each volume printed.

Sold as separate volumes and as a set in slipcase, black paper over boards with light red label affixed to left side (open end toward viewer). Printed on label in gold, within a frame of black runes between 2 black double rule frames: 'The Lord | of the | Rings | J. R. R. TOLKIEN | HOUGHTON MIFFLIN COMPANY'.
    Also published as a set by the Book-of-the-Month Club.
    In 1981 copies of the seventeenth impression of A5f were issued as a 'Silver Anniversary edition' to mark the twenty-fifth anniversary of the publication of *LR* in the United States. These volumes are bound in silver imitation leather, stamped in black and red, in a slipcase, black cloth over boards.
    In 1984 The Easton Press, Norwalk, Connecticut, reprinted A5f as a special bonus for subscribers to Easton Press series of finely-bound books. The three Easton volumes are bound in dark green leather over boards, stamped with a design of gilt rules and runes by George Herrick, with gold watered silk endleaves and a gold ribbon marker. Each volume has a colour frontispiece by Michael Hague.

g. First British (one-volume) paperback edition (1968):

[*1 line in certar, between double rules*] | THE LORD OF | THE RINGS | *by* | J. R. R. TOLKIEN | *Part I* | THE FELLOWSHIP OF THE RING | *Part II* | THE TWO TOWERS | *Part III* | THE RETURN OF THE KING | *London* | GEORGE ALLEN AND UNWIN LTD | RUSKIN HOUSE MUSEUM STREET | [*2 lines in tengwar, between double rules*]

1080 pp. Collation: 540 leaves. 21.0 × 14.0 cm.

[1] 'THE LORD OF THE RINGS'; [2] blank; [3] title; [4] 'THE LORD OF THE RINGS | *The Fellowship of the Ring* first published 1954 (fifteen | impressions); second edition 1966 (three impressions) | © George Allen & Unwin Ltd 1966 | *The Two Towers* first published 1954 (twelve impressions); | second edition 1966 (three impressions) | © George Allen & Unwin Ltd 1966 | *The Return of the King* first published 1955 (eleven impres- | sions); second edition 1966 (three impressions) | ©

George Allen & Unwin Ltd 1966 | First published in one volume 1968 | © *George Allen & Unwin Ltd 1968* | [*notice of restrictions under copyright*] | SBN 04 823087 1 | [*notice of conditions of sale*] | Cover illustration by Pauline Baynes | PRINTED IN GREAT BRITAIN | *in 10 on 11 point Pilgrim type* | *by* HAZELL WATSON & VINEY LTD | AYLESBURY, BUCKS'; [5] poem, 'Three Rings for the Elven-kings' etc.; [6] key map of Middle-earth, with locations of enlarged sections and additional maps; [7]–10 foreword; [11]–12 table of contents; [13]–28 prologue; [29] 'THE FELLOWSHIP | OF THE RING | [*swelled rule*] | *being the first part of* | *The Lord of the Rings*'; [30] map, *A Part of the Shire*; [31] 'BOOK I | [*swelled rule*]'; [32] sectional map 1; [33]–231 text and illustration; [232] blank; [233] 'BOOK II | [*swelled rule*]'; [234] sectional map 2; [235]–427 text and illustrations; [428] blank; [429] 'THE TWO TOWERS | [*swelled rule*] | *being the second part of* | *The Lord of the Rings*'; [430] blank; [431] 'BOOK III | [*swelled rule*]'; [432] sectional map 3; [433]–624 text; [625] 'BOOK IV | [*swelled rule*]'; [626] sectional map 4; [627]–770 text; [771] 'THE RETURN OF | THE KING | [*swelled rule*] | *being the third part of* | *The Lord of the Rings*'; [772] blank; [773] 'BOOK V | [*swelled rule*]'; [774–5] map of Rohan, Gondor, and Mordor; [776] blank; [777]–927 text; [928] blank; [929] 'BOOK VI | [*swelled rule*]'; [930] sectional map 5; [931]–1069 text; [1070]–7 appendix, 'A Part of the Tale of Aragorn and Arwen'; [1078] blank; [1079] 'Other books by J. R. R. Tolkien | [*advertisements*] | LONDON : GEORGE ALLEN AND UNWIN LTD'; [1080] '[*publisher's square "St. George" device*] | GEORGE ALLEN & UNWIN LTD | [*21 addresses, London to Tokyo*]'.

Illustrations, by Tolkien (as for A5a.i): Ring inscription, p. 63; Moria gate, p. [323]; Balin's tomb inscription, p. 337.

Wove paper. Bound in heavy wove wrappers. Printed on upper cover in red shadowed in black, against a colour illustration by Pauline Baynes, of the Shire and mountains beyond, framed by trees and strange creatures: 'THE | LORD | OF THE | RINGS'. Printed on spine against a yellow background: 'THE LORD | OF THE | RINGS | [*rule*] | [*running down, in orange shadowed in black:*] TOLKIEN | [*horizontal, in black:*] [*rule*] | 30s net | GEORGE ALLEN | AND UNWIN'. Colour illustration by Pauline Baynes, of Minas Tirith and Mt. Doom, framed by trees and strange creatures, printed on lower cover. Printed on lower cover in red shadowed in black, against a colour illustration by Pauline Baynes, of Minas Tirith and Mt. Doom, framed by trees and strange creatures: 'TOLKIEN'. All edges trimmed and unstained.

Published 10 October 1968 at 30s.; 50,000 copies printed.

Reset, based on A5e as corrected for the second impression. Paragraph added to foreword, p. 10: 'This one-volume, paperback edition of *The Lord of the Rings* contains the complete text of the revised edition of 1966. The index and all but one of the numerous appendices [i.e. 'A Part of the Tale of Aragorn and Arwen' from Appendix A] have been omitted. Though they contain much information that has proved very interesting to many readers, only a small part is necessary to the reading of the tale. They may still be found in the standard hardback edition where they occupy the last 130 pages of *The Return of the King*.' Errors were introduced in the resetting, e.g. 'some promises' for 'such promises', p. 24, l. 19.

Maps as for A5e, the general map of Middle-earth printed here as a key map and enlarged sections.

The cover illustrations are two-thirds of the triptych painted by Pauline Baynes for the slipcase of the 1964 deluxe edition (see A5a note).

The imprint changed to 'Unwin Paperbacks' in 1978. For a few impressions,

1978–83, the final two lines of 'Namárië' were lost. In May 1979 the cover was changed to feature a scene (Black Riders) from the Ralph Bakshi animated film of *LR* (A5a note). In January 1992, as published by HarperCollins, the cover was changed to feature a painting by John Howe, of Gandalf.

A book club edition was published in 1971 by Book Club Associates, London, bound in light brown textured paper over boards, in a dust-jacket similar to the cover of A5g. Reprinted several times.

h. 'India paper edition' (1969):

[*1 line in certar, between double rules*] | [*in red:*] THE LORD | OF | THE RINGS | [*in black:*] J. R. R. Tolkien | *London* | GEORGE ALLEN AND UNWIN LTD | [*2 lines in tengwar, between double rules*]

1200 pp. + 2 leaves (maps). Collation: [1–36^{16}37^{8}38^{16}]. 22.2 × 14.1 cm.

[1] 'THE LORD OF THE RINGS'; [2] '*Part I* | THE FELLOWSHIP OF THE RING | *Part II* | THE TWO TOWERS | *Part III* | THE RETURN OF THE KING'; [3] title; [4] 'THE LORD OF THE RINGS | *The Fellowship of the Ring* first published 1954 (fifteen | impressions); second edition 1966 (three impressions) | © George Allen & Unwin Ltd 1966 | *The Two Towers* first published 1954 (twelve impressions); | second edition 1966 (three impressions) | © George Allen & Unwin Ltd 1966 | *The Return of the King* first published 1955 (eleven impres- | sions); second edition 1966 (three impressions) | © George Allen & Unwin Ltd 1966 | First published in one volume 1968 (three impressions) | © George Allen & Unwin Ltd 1968 | This India paper edition first published 1969 | © George Allen & Unwin Ltd 1969 | [*notice of restrictions under copyright*] | SBN 0 04 823091 X | PRINTED IN GREAT BRITAIN | *in 10 on 11 point Pilgrim type* | by HAZELL WATSON & VINEY LTD | AYLESBURY, BUCKS'; [5] poem, 'Three Rings for the Elven-kings' etc.; [6]–8 table of contents; [9]–12 foreword; [13]–28 prologue; [29] 'THE FELLOWSHIP | OF THE RING | [*swelled rule*] | *being the first part of* | *The Lord of the Rings*'; [30] map, *A Part of the Shire*, in black and red; [31] 'BOOK I | [*swelled rule*]'; [32] blank; [33]–231 text and illustration; [232] blank; [233] 'BOOK II | [*swelled rule*]'; [234] blank; [235]–427 text and illustrations; [428] blank; [429] 'THE TWO TOWERS | [*swelled rule*] | *being the second part of* | *The Lord of the Rings*'; [430] blank; [431] 'BOOK III | [*swelled rule*]'; [432] blank; [433]–624 text; [625] 'BOOK IV | [*swelled rule*]'; [626] blank; [627]–770 text; [771–2] blank; [773] 'THE RETURN OF | THE KING | [*swelled rule*] | *being the third part of* | *The Lord of the Rings*'; [774] blank; [775] 'BOOK V | [*swelled rule*]'; [776] blank; [777]–927 text; [928] blank; [929] 'BOOK VI | [*swelled rule*]'; [930] blank; [931]–1069 text; [1070]–1172 appendices; [1173]–93 index; [1194] blank; [1195] '[*publisher's "St. George" device*] | GEORGE ALLEN & UNWIN LTD | [*21 addresses, London to Toronto*]'; [1196–1200] blank. The Ring inscription, p. 63, is printed in red. Map of Rohan, Gondor, and Mordor, in black and red on folded leaf tipped onto p. [771]. Map of Middle-earth, in black and red on folded leaf tipped onto recto, back free endpaper.

Illustrations, by Tolkien (as for A5a.i): Ring inscription, p. 63; Moria gate, p. [323]; Balin's tomb inscription, p. 337.

Wove India paper, watermarked 'Oxford India'. Bound in black cloth over boards. Illustration by Tolkien, of a Númenórean throne with 'Elendil' in tengwar, stamped on upper cover in gilt, silver, and green. Stamped on spine in gilt, within a gilt single rule frame: '[*2 rules*] | J. R. R. | Tolkien | [*dash*] | THE | LORD | OF | THE | RINGS |

[*8 rules*] | George | Allen | & | Unwin'. Mottled black and grey wove endpapers. Light green/white headbands. All edges trimmed and speckled light green.

Slipcase, black textured paper over boards.

Published 13 November 1969 at 126s.; number of copies not known.

Typeset chiefly as for A5g. Reset full appendices and index, based on A5e. Paragraph added to foreword, p. 12: 'The heraldic device on the binding of this edition represents the ancient throne of Elendil; it bears his monogram L. ND. L. For the significance of the design above the throne see the Index under Tree and Star [i.e. "Star, as emblem"]. The green jewel at the bottom represents the coming of the new King, Elessar.' Errors were introduced in the resetting, e.g. 'they spoke a little' for 'they spoke little', p. 1166, l. 21; 'The dominion' for 'Their dominion', p. 1172, l. 2. In the index entry 'Star, as emblem', p. 1193, col. 1, '(2) and (4) had six [rays]' (A5e.iii) was altered to '(2) and (4) had five [rays]'.

Corrected and further altered in later impressions; see A5e note.

Maps as for A5e.

The binding decoration is a simplified version of a design made by Tolkien for the binding of *The Return of the King* but never used. An erupting mountain and the 'long arm of Sauron' were to be stamped in the upper background, but could not be accommodated to the process. The silver inscription between the wings and the throne was originally written too delicately for the purpose.

Later issued in a box rather than a slipcase.

i. Ballantine Books trade paperback edition (1970):

i. THE FELLOWSHIP OF THE RING:

[*1 line in certar, between double rules*] | The Fellowship | of the Ring | BEING THE FIRST PART OF | THE LORD OF THE RINGS | with a new Foreword by the author | J. R. R. TOLKIEN | BALLANTINE BOOKS • NEW YORK | [*2 lines in tengwar, between double rules*]

528 pp. Collation: 264 leaves. 20.9 × 13.7 cm.

Contents as for A5d.i, except pp. [vi] 'Copyright © 1965 by J. R. R. Tolkien | THIS BOOK IS COPYRIGHT UNDER THE BERNE CONVENTION. ALL RIGHTS RESERVED | SBN 345-02020-0-750 | First Printing, Special Edition: September, 1970 | Published in the United States of America | BALLANTINE BOOKS, INC. | 101 Fifth Avenue, New York, N.Y. 10003 | An INTEXT Publisher'; and [528] advertisement of *H, LR, TR*.

Illustrations as for A5d.i.

Wove paper. Bound in heavy wove wrappers. Printed on upper cover: '[*in red:*] J. R. R. TOLKIEN | THE LORD OF THE RINGS | [*in green:*] Volume I | THE FELLOWSHIP OF THE RING | [*colour illustration by Pauline Baynes, of Hobbiton*]'. Printed on spine: '[*publisher's "BB" device in white and black*] | [*running down:*] [*in red:*] J. R. R. TOLKIEN [*in green:*] THE FELLOWSHIP OF THE RING Volume I'. All edges trimmed and unstained.

ii. THE TWO TOWERS:

[*1 line in certar, between double rules*] | The Two Towers | BEING THE SECOND PART OF | THE LORD OF THE RINGS | with a New Foreword by the Author |

J. R. R. TOLKIEN | BALLANTINE BOOKS • NEW YORK | [*2 lines in tengwar, between double rules*]

448 pp. Collation: 224 leaves. 20.9 × 13.7 cm.

Contents as for A5d.ii, except pp. [6] 'Copyright © 1965 by J. R. R. Tolkien | THIS BOOK IS COPYRIGHT UNDER THE BERNE CONVENTION. ALL RIGHTS RESERVED | SBN 345-02020-0-750 | First Printing, Special Edition: September, 1970 | Published in the United States of America | BALLANTINE BOOKS, INC. | 101 Fifth Avenue, New York, N.Y. 10003 | An INTEXT Publisher'; and [448] advertisement of *H, LR, TR, Smith of Wootton Major and Farmer Giles of Ham*, and *RGEO*.

Wove paper. Bound in heavy wove wrappers. Printed on upper cover: '[*in red:*] J. R. R. TOLKIEN | THE LORD OF THE RINGS | [*in gold:*] Volume II | THE TWO TOWERS | [*colour illustration by Pauline Baynes, of Minas Tirith*]'. Printed on spine: '[*publisher's "BB" device, in white and black*] | [*running down:*] [*in red:*] J. R. R. TOLKIEN [*in gold:*] THE TWO TOWERS Volume II'. All edges trimmed and unstained.

iii. THE RETURN OF THE KING:

[*1 line in certar, between double rules*] | The Return of | the King | BEING THE THIRD PART OF | THE LORD OF THE RINGS | with a New Foreword by the Author | J. R. R. TOLKIEN | BALLANTINE BOOKS • NEW YORK | [*2 lines in tengwar, between double rules*]

544 pp. Collation: 272 leaves. 20.9 × 13.7 cm.

Contents as for A5d.iii, except p. [vi] 'Copyright © 1965 by J. R. R. Tolkien | THIS BOOK IS COPYRIGHT UNDER THE BERNE CONVENTION. ALL RIGHTS RESERVED | SBN 345-02020-0-750 | First Printing, Special Edition: September, 1970 | Published in the United States of America | BALLANTINE BOOKS, INC. | 101 Fifth Avenue, New York, N.Y. 10003 | An INTEXT Publisher'.

Wove paper. Bound in heavy wove wrappers. Printed on upper cover: '[*in red:*] J. R. R. TOLKIEN | THE LORD OF THE RINGS | [*in blue:*] Volume III | THE RETURN OF THE KING | [*colour illustration by Pauline Baynes, of the Towers of the Teeth*]'. Printed on spine: '[*publisher's "BB" device, in white and black*] | [*running down:*] [*in red:*] J. R. R. TOLKIEN [*in blue:*] THE RETURN OF THE KING Volume III'. All edges trimmed and unstained.

Slipcase, paper over boards. Printed on left and right sides: '[*in white against a green panel:*] TOLKIEN | [*colour illustration by Pauline Baynes,* A Map of Middle-earth *(cf. Eii4), its top and bottom panels omitted*]'. Colour illustration by Baynes, of the Fellowship of the Ring (the top panel of *A Map of Middle-earth*), printed on top side. Printed on spine: 'THE | LORD | OF | THE | RINGS | TRILOGY | Volume I | THE FELLOWSHIP OF THE RING | Volume II | THE TWO TOWERS | Volume III | THE RETURN OF THE KING | Ballantine Books'.

Published September 1970 at $7.50 the set; number of copies not known.

Typeset as for A5d, except copyright pages and advertisements. Photographically enlarged.
  The cover illustrations by Pauline Baynes are from *A Map of Middle-earth*, published here before the publication of the poster map (Eii4).

j. New British (three-volume) paperback edition (1974):

i. THE FELLOWSHIP OF THE RING:

[*1 line in certar, between double rules*] | The Fellowship | of the Ring | Being the First Part of | *The Lord of the Rings* | J. R. R. TOLKIEN | UNWIN BOOKS | [*2 lines in tengwar, between double rules*]

ii, 398 pp. Collation: 200 leaves. 19.6 × 13.1 cm.

[i–ii] blank; [1] '[*publisher's alternating black/white "U" devices*] | UNWIN BOOKS | The Fellowship of the Ring | [*blurb*]'; [2] '[*1 line in certar, between double rules*] | *The Lord of the Rings* | J. R. R. TOLKIEN | Part I | The Fellowship of the Ring | Part II | The Two Towers | Part III | The Return of the King | [*2 lines in tengwar, between double rules*]'; [3] title; [4] 'First published in July 1954 | Fifteenth impression 1966 | Second edition 1966 | Seventh impression 1973 | Unwin Books edition 1974 | [*notice of restrictions under copyright*] | © George Allen & Unwin Ltd 1966, 1974 | ISBN 0 04 823112 6 | UNWIN BOOKS | George Allen & Unwin Ltd | Ruskin House, Museum Street | London W.C.1 | Printed in Great Britain | in 9 point Plantin type | by Cox & Wyman Ltd | London, Reading and Fakenham'; [5] 'The Lord of the Rings | [*poem, "Three Rings for the Elven-kings" etc.*].'; [6] blank; [7]–10 foreword; [11] table of contents; [12] blank; [13]–26 prologue; [27] blank; [28] map, *A Part of the Shire*; [29]–385 text; [386] blank; [387] key map of Middle-earth; [388–91] sectional maps; [392] blank; [393] '[*publisher's square "St. George" device*] | GEORGE ALLEN & UNWIN LTD | [*25 addresses, London to Barbados*]'; [394–8] blank.

Illustrations, by Tolkien (as for A5a.i): Ring inscription, p. 56; Moria gate, p. [291]; Balin's tomb inscription, p. 304.

Wove paper. Bound in heavy wove wrappers. Wraparound colour illustration by Tolkien, detail from *Rivendell*. Printed below the illustration: publisher's wrap-around alternating green/dark green 'U' devices, with 'UNWIN BOOKS' in green at lower left on upper and lower covers, against a dark green background. Printed on upper cover in blue outlined in white, against the illustration: 'The | Fellowship | of the Ring | TOLKIEN'. Printed on spine, running down, in blue outlined in white, against the illustration: 'TOLKIEN The Fellowship [*parallel to first part of title:*] of the Ring'. Printed on inside upper cover: 'PRICE NET £0.65p | IN U.K. ONLY'. All edges trimmed and unstained.

ii. THE TWO TOWERS:

[*1 line in certar, between double rules*] | The Two Towers | Being the Second Part of | *The Lord of the Rings* | J. R. R. TOLKIEN | UNWIN BOOKS | [*2 lines in tengwar, between double rules*]

320 pp. Collation: 160 leaves. 19.6 × 12.9 cm.

[1] '[*publisher's alternating black/white "U" devices*] | UNWIN BOOKS | The Two Towers | [*blurb*]'; [2] '[*1 line in certar, between double rules*] | *The Lord of the Rings* | J. R. R. TOLKIEN | Part I | The Fellowship of the Ring | Part II | The Two Towers | Part III | The Return of the King | [*2 lines in tengwar, between double rules*]'; [3] title; [4] 'First published in 1954 | Twelfth impression 1966 | Second edition 1966 | Seventh impression 1973 | Unwin Books edition 1974 | [*notice of restrictions under copyright*] | © George Allen & Unwin Ltd 1966, 1974 | ISBN 0 04 823113 4 | UNWIN BOOKS | George Allen & Unwin Ltd | Ruskin House, Museum Street |

London W.C.1 | Printed in Great Britain | in 9 point Plantin type | by Cox & Wyman Ltd | London, Reading and Fakenham'; [5] 'The Lord of the Rings | [*poem, "Three Rings for the Elven-kings" etc.*]'; [6] blank; [7]–8 synopsis; [9] table of contents; [10] blank; [11]–313 text; [314] blank; [315] key map of Middle-earth; [316–19] sectional maps; [320] blank.

Wove paper. Bound in heavy wove wrappers. Wraparound colour illustration by Tolkien, detail from *Taniquetil*. Printed below the illustration: publisher's wraparound alternating yellow-green/blue-purple 'U' devices, with 'UNWIN BOOKS' in yellow-green at lower left on upper and lower covers, against a blue-purple background. Printed on upper cover in blue outlined in white, against the illustration: 'The Two | Towers | TOLKIEN'. Printed on spine, running down, in blue outlined in white, against the illustration: 'TOLKIEN The Two Towers'. Printed on inside upper cover: 'PRICE NET | £0.65p | IN U.K. ONLY'. All edges trimmed and unstained.

iii. THE RETURN OF THE KING:

[*1 line in certar, between double rules*] | The Return | of the King | Being the Third Part of | *The Lord of the Rings* | J. R. R. TOLKIEN | UNWIN BOOKS | [*2 lines in tengwar, between double rules*]

416 pp. Collation: 208 leaves. 19.7 × 12.9 cm.

[1] '[*publisher's alternating black/white "U" devices*] | UNWIN BOOKS | The Return of the King | [*blurb*]'; [2] '[*1 line in certar, between double rules*] | *The Lord of the Rings* | J. R. R. TOLKIEN | Part I | The Fellowship of the Ring | Part II | The Two Towers | Part III | The Return of the King | [*2 lines in tengwar, between double rules*]'; [3] title; [4] 'First published October 1955 | Eleventh impression 1965 | Second edition 1966 | Seventh impression 1973 | Unwin Books edition 1974 | [*notice of restrictions under copyright*] | © George Allen & Unwin Ltd 1966, 1974 | ISBN 0 04 823114 2 | UNWIN BOOKS | George Allen & Unwin Ltd | Ruskin House, Museum Street | London W.C.1 | Printed in Great Britain | in 9 point Plantin type | by Cox & Wyman Ltd | London, Reading and Fakenham'; [5] 'The Lord of the Rings | [*poem, "Three Rings for the Elven-kings" etc.*]'; [6] blank; [7]–9 synopsis; [10] blank; [11] table of contents; [12–13] map of Rohan, Gondor, and Mordor; [14] blank; [15]–275 text; [276]–387 appendices; [388]–411 indexes; [412] key map of Middle-earth; [413–16] sectional maps.

Wove paper. Bound in heavy wove wrappers. Wraparound colour illustration by Tolkien, detail from *Bilbo Woke Up with the Early Morning Sun in His Eyes*. Printed below the illustration: publisher's wraparound alternating yellow-green/red-purple 'U' devices, with 'UNWIN BOOKS' in yellow-green at lower left on upper and lower covers,, against a red-purple background. Printed on upper cover in blue outlined in white, against the illustration: 'The | Return | of the King | TOLKIEN'. Printed on spine, running down, in blue outlined in white, against the illustration: 'TOLKIEN The Return [*parallel with first part of title:*] of the King'. Printed on inside upper cover: 'PRICE NET | £0.65p | IN U.K. ONLY'. All edges trimmed and unstained.

Published August? 1974 at £0.65 per volume; 100,000 copies printed.

Reset, based on a corrected impression of A5e. Numerous errors were introduced. Extensively corrected in the third (1975), fourth (1976), and especially fifth (1977) impressions; see A5e note. Most notable among textual changes is the progression, p. 376, ll. 21–2, 'Finarphir' (first and second impressions) > 'Finarphin' (third impression) > 'Finarfin' (fourth impression) as Christopher Tolkien determined the final text of *The Silmarillion* (A15).

Maps as for A5e.

The first impression of A5j was entirely for export. The price of the second impression (also 100,000 copies), the first for domestic sale, was raised to £0.75 per volume due to an increase in the cost of paper.

With the fourth impression (1976) the covers were changed to feature the 'Ring and Eye' device in black, red-orange, and orange, with white lettering, against a green (*FR*), dark blue (*TT*), or brown (*RK*) background.

The second and third impressions were sold as separate volumes and as sets in a paper sleeve featuring a colour illustration by Tolkien, *Fangorn Forest* (i.e. *Beleg Finds Gwindor in Taur-nu-Fuin*). The fourth and fifth impressions were sold as separate volumes or as sets in a paper slipcase featuring the cover art.

k. 'Collector's edition' (1974):

[*1 line in certar, between double rules, in grey*] | [*uncials:*] [*in black:*] J. R. R. TOLKIEN | [*in red:*] THE LORD | OF THE | RINGS | [*in black:*] COLLECTOR'S EDITION | [*roman:*] BOSTON | [*uncials:*] HOUGHTON MIFFLIN COMPANY | 1974 | [*2 lines in tengwar, between double rules, in grey*]

iv, 26, [2], 27–424, 11–352, 15–442 pp. + 1 plate (map). Collation: [1–34^{16}35^{8}36–38^{16}]. 23.4 × 15.4 cm.

First section: [i] [*uncials, in red:*] THE LORD | OF THE | RINGS'; [ii] blank; [iii] title; [iv] 'FIRST PRINTING *Collector's Edition* H | COPYRIGHT © 1965 BY J. R. R. TOLKIEN | COPYRIGHT © 1966 BY GEORGE ALLEN & UNWIN LTD. | [*notice of restrictions*] | ISBN 0-395-19395-8 | PRINTED IN THE UNITED STATES OF AMERICA'; [1] 'THE LORD OF THE RINGS | [*poem, "Three Rings for the Elven-kings" etc.*]'; [2] blank; 3–6 foreword; 7–9 table of contents; 10–25 prologue; 26 map, *A Part of the Shire*; [27] '[*1 line in certar, between double rules, in grey*] | [*uncials:*] [*in black:*] PART I | [*in red:*] THE FELLOWSHIP | OF THE RING'; [28] blank; [28+1] '[*1 line in certar, between double rules, in grey*] | [*uncials, in black:*] BOOK ONE'; [28+2] blank; 29–227 text; [228] blank; [229] '[*1 line in certar, between double rules, in grey*] | [*uncials, in black:*] BOOK TWO'; [230] blank; 231–423 text; [424] blank. *Second section:* [11] '[*1 line in certar, between double rules, in grey*] | [*uncials:*] [*in black:*] PART II | [*in red:*] THE TWO TOWERS'; [12] blank; [13] '[*1 line in certar, between double rules, in grey*] | [*uncials, in black:*] BOOK THREE'; [14] blank; 15–206 text; [207] '[*1 line in certar, between double rules, in grey*] | [*uncials, in black:*] BOOK FOUR'; [208] blank; 209–352 text. *Third section:* [15] '[*1 line in certar, between double rules, in grey*] | [*uncials:*] [*in black:*] PART III | [*in red:*] THE RETURN | OF THE KING'; [16] blank; [17] '[*1 line in certar, between double rules, in grey*] | [*uncials, in black:*] BOOK FIVE'; [18] blank; 19–169 text; [170] blank; [171] '[*1 line in certar, between double rules, in grey*] | [*uncials, in black:*] BOOK SIX'; [172] blank; 173–311 text; [312] blank; 313–416 appendices; 417–40 index; [441–2] blank. Folios and running heads, chapter titles, and headings for appendix sections and index printed in red. Map of Middle-earth, printed in black and red on folded leaf, tipped onto recto, back free endpaper.

Illustrations, by Tolkien (as for A5a.i): Ring inscription, p. 59; Moria gate, p. [319]; Balin's tomb inscription, p. 333.

Wove paper. Bound in red imitation leather over boards. Stamped on upper cover:

two stylized trees, after Tolkien's Moria Gate decorations, placed horizontally above and below gilt emblem of Fingolfin, with blue stars, dots, and circles and green dots and diamonds. Stamped on spine, lettering in uncials: '[*in gilt:*] TOLKIEN | [*rule*] | [*3 diamonds, in green, each with a blue dot in its centre*] | [*in gilt:*] [*rule*] | THE LORD | OF THE | RINGS | [*stylized tree, in gilt, with blue stars and circles and green dots*] | [*rule, in gilt*] | [*3 diamonds, in green, each with a blue dot in its centre*] | [*in gilt:*] [*rule*] | [*between 2 green diamonds, each with a blue dot in its centre:*] HMCO'. Lower cover stamped like upper cover, except with one less star at the top of the emblem. Red and black 'marbled' wove endpapers. Red/yellow headbands. All edges trimmed and unstained.

Slipcase, red imitation leather.

Published 1 November 1974 at $35.00; 20,000 copies printed.

Typeset as for A5f, the three volumes combined into one, except reset title leaf, table of contents, divisional titles, folios, and running heads, and with synopses omitted.
  Cf. revised impression, A5r.

l. Folio Society edition (1977):

i. THE FELLOWSHIP OF THE RING:

J. R. R. TOLKIEN | [*uncials:*] THE FELLOWSHIP | OF THE RING | [*roman:*] being the First Part of | *The Lord of the Rings* | Illustrations by | INGAHILD GRATHMER | drawn by | ERIC FRASER | LONDON | THE FOLIO SOCIETY | 1977

464 pp. Collation: [1–12^{16}13^{8}14^{16}]. 22.2 × 14.2 cm.

[1] 'THE FELLOWSHIP OF THE RING'; [2] illustration; [3] title; [4] '© *Text copyright George Allen & Unwin Ltd 1954* | © *Illustrations copyright The Folio Society Ltd 1977* | *The text of this edition is used by kind permission* | *of George Allen & Unwin Ltd* | PRINTED IN GREAT BRITAIN | *by W & J Mackay Limited, Chatham*'; [5] 'THE LORD OF THE RINGS | [*poem, "Three Rings for the Elven-kings" etc.*]'; [6] blank; [7]–9 table of contents; [10] list of frontispiece illustrations; [11]–31 prologue; [32] blank; [33] illustration; [34] blank; [35]–250 text of Book One and illustrations; [251] illustration; [252] blank; [253]–459 text of Book Two and illustrations; [460] 'SET IN 11 POINT BARBOU LEADED 1 POINT | WITH LIBRA FOR DISPLAY | AND PRINTED BY W & J MACKAY LIMITED | IN QUARTER BASIL WITH SCHOLCO | COLORETA CLOTH SIDES | BLOCKED WITH A SPECIAL DESIGN | BY JEFF CLEMENTS'; [461–4] blank.

Illustrations by Tolkien (as for A5a.i): Ring inscription, p. 67; Moria gate, p. [349]; Balin's tomb inscription, p. 364.

Wove paper. Bound in grey cloth over boards, light grey leather spine. 'Labyrinth' decoration by Jeff Clements stamped on upper cover in gilt. Stamped on spine in gilt: '[*"labyrinth" decoration*] | [*dash*] | [*running up:*] J. R. R. Tolkien [*parallel to name:*] The Fellowship of the Ring'. Wove endpapers: map of The Shire, in blue and white, on front endsheet; map of Middle-earth, with inset map of north Gondor and west Mordor, in blue and white, on back endsheet. White headband. All edges trimmed. Top edge stained grey, fore- and bottom edges unstained.

ii. THE TWO TOWERS:

J. R. R. TOLKIEN | [*uncials:*] THE | TWO TOWERS | [*roman:*] being the Second Part of | *The Lord of the Rings* | Illustrations by | INGAHILD GRATHMER | drawn by | ERIC FRASER | LONDON | THE FOLIO SOCIETY | 1977

376 pp. Collation: [1–11^{16}12^{12}]. 22.1 × 14.2 cm.

[1] 'THE TWO TOWERS'; [2] illustration; [3] title; [4] '© *Text copyright George Allen & Unwin Ltd 1954* | © *Illustrations copyright The Folio Society Ltd 1977* | *The text of this edition is used by kind permission* | *of George Allen & Unwin Ltd.* | PRINTED IN GREAT BRITAIN | *by W & J Mackay Ltd, Chatham*'; [5] 'THE LORD OF THE RINGS | [*poem, "Three Rings for the Elven-kings" etc.*]'; [6] blank; [7] table of contents; [8] list of frontispiece illustrations; [9]–10 synopsis; [11] illustration; [12] blank; [13]–215 text of Book Three and illustrations; [216] blank; [217] illustration; [218] blank; [219]–372 text of Book Four and illustrations; [373] 'SET IN 11 POINT BARBOU LEADED 1 POINT | WITH LIBRA FOR DISPLAY | AND PRINTED BY W & J MACKAY LIMITED | IN QUARTER BASIL WITH SCHOLCO | COLORETA CLOTH SIDES | BLOCKED WITH A SPECIAL DESIGN | BY JEFF CLEMENTS'; [374–6] blank.

Wove paper. Bound in grey cloth over boards, light grey leather spine. 'Labyrinth' decoration by Jeff Clements stamped on upper cover in gilt. Stamped on spine in gilt: '[*"labyrinth" decoration*] | [*2 dashes*] | [*running up:*] J. R. R. Tolkien [*parallel to name:*] The Two Towers'. Wove endpapers, as for A5l.i. White headband. All edges trimmed. Top edge stained grey, fore- and bottom edges unstained.

iii. THE RETURN OF THE KING:

J. R. R. TOLKIEN | [*uncials:*] THE RETURN OF | THE KING | [*roman:*] being the Third Part of | *The Lord of the Rings* | Illustrations by | INGAHILD GRATHMER | drawn by | ERIC FRASER | LONDON | THE FOLIO SOCIETY | 1977

488 pp. Collation: [1–14^{16}15^{4}16^{16}]. 22.1 × 14.2 cm.

[1] 'THE RETURN OF THE KING'; [2] illustration; [3] title; [4] '© *Text copyright George Allen & Unwin Ltd 1955* | © *Illustrations copyright The Folio Society Ltd 1977* | *The text of this edition is used by kind permission* | *of George Allen & Unwin Ltd* | PRINTED IN GREAT BRITAIN | *by W & J Mackay Ltd, Chatham*'; [5] 'THE LORD OF THE RINGS | [*poem, "Three Rings for the Elven-kings" etc.*]'; [6] list of frontispiece illustrations; [7]–8 table of contents; [9]–11 synopsis; [12] blank; [13] illustration; [14] blank; [15]–177 text of Book Five and illustrations; [178] blank; [179] illustration; [180] blank; [181]–330 text of Book Six and illustrations; [331]– 462 appendices; [463]–87 index; [488] 'SET IN 11 POINT BARBOU LEADED 1 POINT | WITH LIBRA FOR DISPLAY | AND PRINTED BY W & J MACKAY LIMITED | IN QUARTER BASIL WITH SCHOLCO | COLORETA CLOTH SIDES | BLOCKED WITH A SPECIAL DESIGN | BY JEFF CLEMENTS'.

Wove paper. Bound in grey cloth over boards, light grey leather spine. 'Labyrinth' decoration by Jeff Clements stamped on upper cover in gilt. Stamped on spine in gilt: '[*"labyrinth" decoration*] | [*3 dashes*] | [*running up:*] J. R. R. Tolkien [*parallel to name:*] The Return of the King'. Wove endpapers: map of Middle-earth, with inset map of north Gondor and west Mordor, printed in blue and white on front endsheet; map of The Shire printed in blue and white on back endsheet. White headband. All edges trimmed. Top edge stained grey, fore- and bottom edges unstained.

Slipcase, paper over boards, black paper top and bottom, grey 'leather' paper sides.

Published May? 1977 at £29.50? the set; number of copies not known.

Reset, based on a corrected impression of A5e. Tolkien's illustrations in *FR* and the Angerthas table in *RK* were reproduced from A5e. The maps were redrawn, giving the river Anduin two more tributaries in the Brown Lands, and mislabelling the river Glanduin 'Glandin'.

'Ingahild Grathmer' is H.M. Queen Margrethe II of Denmark. Cf. section G, Danish 1.

Reprinted in May 1990, bound in cream 'elephant hide' stamped in gilt, silver, and red with a cover decoration of multiple rings, in red slipcase.

m. Houghton Mifflin trade paperback edition (1978):

i. THE FELLOWSHIP OF THE RING:

[*1 line in certar, between double rules*] | The Fellowship | of the Ring | BEING THE FIRST PART OF | THE LORD OF THE RINGS | BY | J. R. R. TOLKIEN | SECOND EDITION | Houghton Mifflin Company Boston | 1978 | [*2 lines in tengwar, between double rules*]

iv, 428 pp. Collation: 216 leaves. 20.8 × 13.5 cm.

[i–ii] blank; [iii] 'THE FELLOWSHIP OF THE RING'; [iv] '[*1 line in certar, between double rules*] | THE LORD OF THE RINGS | BY J. R. R. TOLKIEN | PART I | THE FELLOWSHIP OF THE RING | PART II | THE TWO TOWERS | PART III | THE RETURN OF THE KING | [*2 lines in tengwar, between double rules*]'; [1] title; [2] 'COPYRIGHT © 1965 BY J. R. R. TOLKIEN | ALL RIGHTS RESERVED INCLUDING THE RIGHT TO | REPRODUCE THIS BOOK OR PARTS THEREOF IN ANY FORM | LIBRARY OF CONGRESS CATALOG CARD NUMBER: 67-12274 | ISBN: 0-395-08254-4 | ISBN: 0-395-27223-8 PBK | PRINTED IN THE UNITED STATES OF AMERICA | [*printing code, beginning "M", ending "1"*]'; [3] 'THE LORD OF THE RINGS | [*poem, "Three Rings for the Elven-kings" etc.*]'; [4] blank; [5]–8 foreword; [9] table of contents; 10–25 prologue; [26] map, *A Part of the Shire*; [27] 'BOOK I | [*swelled rule*]'; [28] blank; 29–227 text; [228] blank; [229] 'BOOK II | [*swelled rule*]'; [230] blank; 231–423 text; [424–5] blank; [426–7] map of Middle-earth; [428] blank.

Illustrations, by Tolkien (as for A5a.i): Ring inscription, p. 59; Moria gate, p. [319]; Balin's tomb inscription, p. 333.

Wove paper. Bound in heavy wove wrappers. Covers and spine printed against a gold background. Printed on upper cover: '[*in red:*] Being the First Part of | THE LORD OF THE RINGS | [*facsimile signature, "J. R. R. Tolkien", in black*] | [*in red:*] THE | FELLOWSHIP | OF THE RING | [*"Ring and Eye" device, in black*] | [*in red:*] REVISED EDITION'. Printed on spine: '[*in red:*] THE | [*running down:*] FELLOW-SHIP [*parallel to the preceding word:*] OF THE RING | [*"Ring and Eye" device, horizontal, in black*] | [*running down, in red:*] J. R. R. TOLKIEN [*parallel to name:*] HOUGHTON MIFFLIN COMPANY | [*publisher's "dolphin" device, horizontal, in red*]'. Printed on lower cover: '[*in red:*] "Here are beauties which pierce like swords | or burn like cold iron."—C. S. LEWIS | [*in black:*] [*blurb*] | ISBN 0-395-27223-8 | [*rule*] | 6-97078 | HOUGHTON MIFFLIN COMPANY © 1978'. All edges trimmed and unstained.

i. THE TWO TOWERS:

[*1 line in certar, between double rules*] | The Two Towers | BEING THE SECOND PART OF | THE LORD OF THE RINGS | BY | J. R. R. TOLKIEN | SECOND EDITION | Houghton Mifflin Company Boston | 1978 | [*2 lines in tengwar, between double rules*]

5–356 pp. Collation: 176 leaves. 20.8 × 13.5 cm.

[5] 'THE TWO TOWERS'; [6] '[*1 line in certar, between double rules*] | THE LORD OF THE RINGS | BY J. R. R. TOLKIEN | PART I | THE FELLOWSHIP OF THE RING | PART II | THE TWO TOWERS | PART III | THE RETURN OF THE KING | [*2 lines in tengwar, between double rules*]'; [7] title; [8] 'COPYRIGHT © 1965 BY J. R. R. TOLKIEN | ALL RIGHTS RESERVED INCLUDING THE RIGHT TO | REPRODUCE THIS BOOK OR PARTS THEREOF IN ANY FORM | LIBRARY OF CONGRESS CATALOG CARD NUMBER: 67-12276 | ISBN: 0-395-08255-2 | ISBN: 0-395-27222-X PBK | PRINTED IN THE UNITED STATES OF AMERICA | [*printing code, beginning "M", ending "1"*]'; [9] 'THE LORD OF THE RINGS | [*poem, "Three Rings for the Elven-kings" etc.*]'; 10–11 synopsis; 12 table of contents; [13] 'BOOK III | [*swelled rule*]'; [14] blank; 15–206 text; [207] 'BOOK IV | [*swelled rule*]'; [208] blank; 209–352 text; [353] blank; [354–5] map of Middle-earth; [356] blank.

Wove paper. Bound in heavy wove wrappers. Covers and spine printed against a gold background. Printed on upper cover: '[*in red:*] Being the Second Part of | THE LORD OF THE RINGS | [*facsimile signature, "J. R. R. Tolkien", in black*] | [*in red:*] THE TWO | TOWERS | [*"Ring and Eye" device, in black*] | [*in red:*] REVISED EDITION'. Printed on spine: '[*running down, in red:*] THE TWO [*parallel to first part of title:*] TOWERS | [*"Ring and Eye" device, horizontal, in black*] | [*running down, in red:*] J. R. R. TOLKIEN [*parallel to name:*] HOUGHTON MIFFLIN COMPANY | [*publisher's "dolphin" device, horizontal, in red*]'. Printed on lower cover: '[*in red:*] "Here are beauties which pierce like swords | or burn like cold iron."—C. S. LEWIS | [*in black:*] [*blurb*] | ISBN 0-395-27222-X | [*rule*] | 6-97079 | HOUGHTON MIFFLIN COMPANY © 1978'. All edges trimmed and unstained.

iii. THE RETURN OF THE KING:

[*1 line in certar, between double rules*] | The Return of | the King | BEING THE THIRD PART OF | THE LORD OF THE RINGS | BY | J. R. R. TOLKIEN | SECOND EDITION | Houghton Mifflin Company Boston | 1978 | [*2 lines in tengwar, between double rules*]

3–450 pp. Collation: 224 leaves. 20.8 × 13.5 cm.

[3–4] blank; [5] 'THE RETURN OF THE KING'; [6] '[*1 line in certar, between double rules*] | THE LORD OF THE RINGS | BY J. R. R. TOLKIEN | PART I | THE FELLOWSHIP OF THE RING | PART II | THE TWO TOWERS | PART III | THE RETURN OF THE KING | [*2 lines in tengwar, between double rules*]'; [7] title; [8] 'COPYRIGHT © 1965 BY J. R. R. TOLKIEN | ALL RIGHTS RESERVED INCLUDING THE RIGHT TO | REPRODUCE THIS BOOK OR PARTS THEREOF IN ANY FORM | LIBRARY OF CONGRESS CATALOG CARD NUMBER: 67-12275 | ISBN: 0-395-08256-0 | ISBN: 0-395-27221-1 PBK | PRINTED IN THE UNITED STATES OF AMERICA | [*printing code, beginning "M", ending "1"*]'; [9] 'THE LORD OF THE RINGS | [*poem, "Three Rings for the Elven-kings" etc.*]'; [10] blank; 11–13 synopsis; [14] blank; 15 table of contents; [16] blank; [17] 'BOOK V | [*swelled rule*]'; [18] blank; 19–169 text; [170] blank; [171] 'BOOK VI | [*swelled rule*]'; [172] blank; 173–311 text; [312] blank; 313–416 appendices; 417–40 index; [441–7] blank; [448–9] map of Rohan, Gondor, and Mordor; [450] blank.

Wove paper. Bound in heavy wove wrappers. Covers and spine printed against a gold background. Printed on upper cover: '[*in red:*] Being the Third Part of | THE

LORD OF THE RINGS | [*facsimile signature, "J. R. R. Tolkien", in black*] | [*in red:*] THE RETURN | OF THE KING | [*"Ring and Eye" device, in black*] | [*in red:*] REVISED EDITION'. Printed on spine: '[*running down, in red:*] THE RETURN [*parallel to first part of title:*] OF THE KING | [*"Ring and Eye" device, horizontal, in black*] | [*running down, in red:*] J. R. R. TOLKIEN [*parallel to name:*] HOUGHTON MIFFLIN COMPANY | [*publisher's "dolphin" device, horizontal, in red*]'. Printed on lower cover: '[*in red:*] "Here are beauties which pierce like swords | or burn like cold iron."—C. S. LEWIS | [*in black:*] [*blurb*] | ISBN 0-395-27221-1 | [*rule*] | 6–97080 | HOUGHTON MIFFLIN COMPANY © 1978'. All edges trimmed and unstained.

Slipcase, paper over boards. Sides and spine printed against a red background. Printed on left side (open end of case toward viewer): '[*facsimile signature, "J. R. R. Tolkien"*] | [*in gold:*] THE | LORD | OF THE | RINGS | [*in black:*] HOUGHTON MIFFLIN COMPANY © 1978'. Printed on right side as for left side, except without a copyright statement. Printed on spine: '[*"Ring and Eye" device, in black and gold*] | [*in black:*] ISBN 0-395-27220-3 | [*rule*] | 6-97081'. Top and bottom printed solid red.

Published 28 October 1978 at $13.95 the set; 40,000 copies printed.

Typeset as for A5f, except the title and copyright pages.
  Maps as for A5e, here all integral leaves.
  Later sold in a slipcase with *H*; see A3t note.

n. 'Third edition' (1979):

i. THE FELLOWSHIP OF THE RING:

'[*1 line in certar, between double rules*] | The Fellowship | of the Ring | Being the First Part of | *The Lord of the Rings* | J. R. R. TOLKIEN | London | UNWIN PAPERBACKS | Boston Sydney | [*2 lines in tengwar, between double rules*]

536 pp. Collation: 268 leaves. 17.7 × 11.1 cm.

[1] blurb; [2] blank; [3] 'THE FELLOWSHIP OF THE RING'; [4] '[*1 line in certar, between double rules*] | *The Lord of the Rings* | J. R. R. Tolkien | Part I | The Fellowship of the Ring | Part II | The Two Towers | Part III | The Return of the King | *also by J. R. R. Tolkien* | [*8 titles, beginning with H, ending with TL*] | *with Donald Swann* | THE ROAD GOES EVER ON | [*2 lines in tengwar, between double rules*]'; [5] title; [6] 'First published in Great Britain by George Allen & Unwin | 1954 | Reprinted fifteen times | Second edition 1966 | Reprinted seven times | First published in Unwin Paperbacks 1974 | Reprinted five times | Third edition 1979 | [*notice of restrictions under copyright*] | UNWIN® PAPERBACKS | 40 Museum Street, London WC1A 1LU | © George Allen & Unwin (Publishers) Ltd 1966, 1974, 1979 | [*within a single rule frame:*] [*British Library Cataloguing in Publication Data*] | ISBN 0-04-823155-X | [*below the frame:*] Typeset in 10 on 11 point Times and | Printed in Great Britain by | Cox & Wyman Ltd, London, Reading and Fakenham'; [7] 'The Lord of the Rings | [*poem, "Three Rings for the Elven-kings" etc.*]'; [8] blank; [9]–13 foreword; [14] blank; [15] table of contents; [16] blank; [17]–36 preface; [37] blank; [38] map, *A Part of the Shire*; [39]–529 text; [530] blank; [531] key map of Middle-earth; [532–5] sectional maps; [536] 'Also in Unwin Paperbacks | [*advertisement of* The Complete Guide to Middle-earth *by Robert Foster and* J. R. R. Tolkien: A Biography *by Humphrey Carpenter*]'.

Illustrations, by Tolkien (as for A5a.i): Ring inscription, p. 77; Moria gate, p. [398]; Balin's tomb inscription, p. 416.

Wove paper. Bound in heavy wove wrappers. Covers and spine printed against a dark green background. Printed on upper cover: '[*in orange:*] TOLKIEN | [*in white:*] THE LORD OF THE RINGS | [*in black:*] 1 The Fellowship of the Ring | [*"Ring and Eye" device, in red, orange, and black, within and extending beyond a black single rule frame, against and extending beyond a white panel*] | [*publisher's "unwin/ UNWIN PAPERBACKS" device, in orange, white, and black*]'. Printed on spine, running down: '[*in orange:*] TOLKIEN [*in white:*] THE LORD OF THE RINGS [*parallel to title, in black:*] 1 The Fellowship of the Ring [*followed by: publisher's "unwin/UNWIN PAPERBACKS" device, in orange, white, and black*]'. Printed on lower cover within a black single rule frame, against a white panel: '[*in orange:*] The first part of J. R. R. Tolkien's three book | *The Lord of the Rings.* | [*5 quotations, from the* Sunday Times, Sunday Telegraph, Observer, New Statesman, *and* Guardian, *in black and red*] | [*in black:*] [*at left:*] UNITED KINGDOM £0.95 | AUSTRALIA \$2.95 (Recommended) | CANADA \$2.75 [*at right:*] TOLKIEN/ FANTASY | ISBN 0 04 823155 X'. All edges trimmed and unstained.

ii. THE TWO TOWERS:

[*1 line in certar, between double rules*] | The Two Towers | Being the Second Part of | *The Lord of the Rings* | J. R. R. TOLKIEN | London | UNWIN PAPERBACKS | Boston Sydney | [*2 lines in tengwar, between double rules*]

448 pp. Collation: 224 leaves. 17.9 × 11.1 cm.

[1] blurb; [2] '[*1 line in certar, between double rules*] | *The Lord of the Rings* | J. R. R. Tolkien | Part I | The Fellowship of the Ring | Part II | The Two Towers | Part III | The Return of the King | *also by J. R. R. Tolkien* | [*8 titles, beginning with* H, *ending with* TL] | *with Donald Swann* | THE ROAD GOES EVER ON | [*2 lines in tengwar, between double rules*]'; [3] title; [4] 'First published in Great Britain by George Allen & Unwin 1954 | Reprinted twelve times | Second edition 1966 | Reprinted seven times | First published in Unwin Paperbacks 1974 | Reprinted four times | Third edition 1979 | [*notice of restrictions under copyright*] | UNWIN® PAPERBACKS | 40 Museum Street, London WC1A 1LU | © George Allen & Unwin (Publishers) Ltd 1966, 1974, 1979 | [*within a single rule frame:*] [*British Library Cataloguing in Publication Data*] | ISBN 0-04-823156-8 | [*below the frame:*] Typeset in 10 on 11 point Times and | printed in Great Britain by Cox & Wyman Ltd, | London, Reading and Fakenham'; [5] 'The Lord of the Rings | [*poem, "Three Rings for the Elven-kings" etc.*]'; [6] blank; [7]–8 synopsis; [9] table of contents; [10] blank; [11]–442 text; [443] key map of Middle-earth; [444–7] sectional maps; [448] 'Also by J. R. R. Tolkien | [*advertisement of* H *and* Silm] | Also in Unwin Paperbacks | [*advertisement of Foster,* The Complete Guide to Middle-earth]'.

Wove paper. Bound in heavy wove wrappers. Covers and spine printed against a dark blue background. Printed on upper cover: '[*in orange:*] TOLKIEN | [*in white:*] THE LORD OF THE RINGS | [*in black:*] 2 The Two Towers | [*"Ring and Eye" device, in red, orange, and black, within and extending beyond a black single rule frame, against and extending beyond a white panel*] | [*publisher's "unwin/UNWIN PAPERBACKS" device, in orange, white, and black*]'. Printed on spine, running down: '[*in orange:*] TOLKIEN [*in white:*] THE LORD OF THE RINGS [*parallel to title, in black:*] 2 The Two Towers [*publisher's "unwin/UNWIN PAPERBACKS" device, in orange, white, and black*]'. Printed on lower cover within a black single rule frame, against a white panel: '[*in orange:*] The second part of J. R. R. Tolkien's three book | *The Lord of the Rings.* | [*3 quotations, from the* Sunday Times, Sunday Telegraph, *and* Observer, *in black and red*] | [*in black:*] [*at left:*] UNITED

KINGDOM £0.95 | AUSTRALIA $2.95 (Recommended) | CANADA $2.75 [*at right:*] TOLKIEN/FANTASY | ISBN 0 04 823156 8'. All edges trimmed and unstained.

iii. THE RETURN OF THE KING:

'[*1 line in certar, between double rules*] | The Return | of the King | Being the Third Part of | *The Lord of the Rings* | J. R. R. TOLKIEN | London | UNWIN PAPERBACKS | Boston Sydney | [*2 lines in tengwar, between double rules*]

560 pp. Collation: 280 leaves. 17.9 × 11.1 cm.

[1] blurb; [2] '[*1 line in certar, between double rules*] | *The Lord of the Rings* | J. R. R. Tolkien | Part I | The Fellowship of the Ring | Part II | The Two Towers | Part III | The Return of the King | *also by J. R. R. Tolkien* | [*8 titles, beginning with* H, *ending with* TL] | *with Donald Swann* | THE ROAD GOES EVER ON | [*2 lines in tengwar, between double rules*]'; [3] title; [4] 'First published in Great Britain by George Allen & Unwin 1955 | Reprinted eleven times | Second edition 1966 | Reprinted seven times | First published in Unwin Paperbacks 1974 | Reprinted four times | Third edition 1979 | [*notice of restrictions under copyright*] | UNWIN® PAPERBACKS | 40 Museum Street, London WC1A 1LU | © George Allen & Unwin (Publishers) Ltd 1966, 1974, 1979 | [*within a single rule frame:*] [*British Library Cataloguing in Publication Data*] | ISBN 0-04-823157-6 | [*below the frame:*] Typeset in 10 on 11 point Times and | printed in Great Britain by Cox & Wyman Ltd, | London, Reading and Fakenham'; [5] 'The Lord of the Rings | [*poem, "Three Rings for the Elven-kings" etc.*]'; [6] blank; [7]–10 synopsis; [11] table of contents; [12–13] map of Rohan, Gondor, and Mordor; [14] blank; [15]–378 text; [379]–530 appendices; [531]–56 index; [557] key map of Middle-earth; [558–60] sectional maps (continued onto inside lower cover).

Wove paper. Bound in heavy wove wrappers. Covers and spine printed against a tan background. Printed on upper cover: '[*in orange:*] TOLKIEN | [*in white:*] THE LORD OF THE RINGS | [*in black:*] 3 The Return of the King | [*"Ring and Eye" device, in red, orange, and black, within and extending beyond a black single rule frame, against and extending beyond a white panel*] | [*publisher's "unwin/UNWIN PAPERBACKS" device, in orange, white, and black*]'. Printed on spine, running down: '[*in orange:*] TOLKIEN [*in white:*] THE LORD OF THE RINGS [*parallel to title, in black:*] 3 The Return of the King [*publisher's "unwin/UNWIN PAPER-BACKS" device, in orange, white, and black*]'. Printed on lower cover within a black single rule frame, against a white panel: '[*in orange:*] The third part of J. R. R. Tolkien's three book | *The Lord of the Rings.* | [*5 quotations, from the* Sunday Times, Sunday Telegraph, *London* Times, Daily Telegraph, *and* Guardian, *in black and red*] | [*in black:*] [*at left:*] UNITED KINGDOM £0.95 | AUSTRALIA $2.95 (Recommended) | CANADA $2.75 [*at right:*] TOLKIEN/FANTASY | ISBN 0 04 823157 6'. All edges trimmed and unstained.

Published 12 March? 1979 at £0.95 per volume, and as set, price not known; number of copies not known.

Sold as separate volumes and as a boxed set. Printed on right side of box (flap A toward viewer) against a dark green background: '[*in red:*] TOLKIEN | [*in white:*] The Lord of | the Rings | [*colour photograph of Tolkien, overprinted by:*] [*in black:*] Picture © John Wyatt'. Printed on left side as for right side, except without copyright statement. Printed on top and bottom against a gold background: '[*in red:*] Tolkien'. Printed on flap A against a dark green background: '[*in red:*]

TOLKIEN | [*in white:*] The Lord of | the Rings | [*publisher's "unwin" device, in white, red, and black, outlined in white*]'. Printed on flap B against a dark green background: '[*in red:*] 3 | books | Tolkien | [*in white:*] The Fellowship | of the Ring | The Two Towers | The Return of the King | [*in red:*] 3 | books | [*in white:*] UNWIN PAPERBACKS | 0 04 823160 1 | Printed in the United Kingdom'.

Reset, based on a corrected impression of A5e. Paragraph added to foreword, p. 13, including: 'This latest edition has been reset and minor corrections have been made throughout. The text is based on the revised edition of 1966 in which a number of errors and inconsistencies that still remained in the text were corrected, and an attempt was made to provide information on a few points which attentive readers had raised.'
      Maps as for A5e.
      A5n was later sold, 20 October 1980, as a '25th Anniversary Collection', in a slipcase, silver paper over boards, accompanied by a souvenir booklet by Humphrey Carpenter (see Dii43). It was also later sold with *H* (A3n) in the set *Stories from the Third Age*, and with *H* (A3n) and *Silm* (A15f) as *The Middle-earth Collection*; see A3n note.
      The Unwin Paperbacks 'fourth edition' (1981) is a reprint of A5n, issued in wrappers with the Pauline Baynes 'triptych' Middle-earth landscape (see A5a note). The general map of Middle-earth was replaced with the new map drawn by Christopher Tolkien for *UT* (A17). Later issued in a slipcase, printed paper over boards, featuring the Baynes 'triptych'. Reissued in March 1986 by Unwin Paperbacks under the 'Unicorn' imprint, with new cover illustrations by Roger Garland, a continuous Middle-earth landscape. In 1990 the covers were changed to feature illustrations by Ted Nasmith. Beginning in 1991, the edition was published by HarperCollins, with cover illustrations by John Howe.

o. 'Unicorn' edition (1983):

[*1 line in certar, between double rules*] | The Lord of the Rings | J. R. R. TOLKIEN | Part 1: The Fellowship of the Ring | Part 2: The Two Towers | Part 3: The Return of the King | *Complete with the Index and full Appendices* | [*publisher's 'Unicorn' device*] | London | UNWIN PAPERBACKS | Boston Sydney | [*2 lines in tengwar, between double rules*]

8, [2], 9–1198 pp. Collation: 600 leaves. 19.7 × 12.8 cm.

[1] blurb; [2] '*also by J. R. R. Tolkien* | [*13 titles, beginning with* ATB, *ending with* UT] | *with Donald Swan* [*sic*] | THE ROAD GOES EVER ON'; [3] title; [4] '*The Fellowship of the Ring* first published in Great Britain | by George Allen & Unwin 1954 | First edition reprinted fifteen times: second edition 1966 reprinted | eleven times | *The Two Towers* first published in Great Britain by George | Allen & Unwin 1954 | First edition reprinted twelve times: second edition 1966 | reprinted ten times | *The Return of the King* first published in Great Britain by | George Allen & Unwin 1955 | First edition reprinted eleven times: second edition 1966 | reprinted ten times | First published in a one volume paperback 1968 | Reprinted seventeen times | First published as one volume in Unwin Paperbacks 1978 | Reprinted twice | Third edition 1983 | This book is copyright under the Berne Convention. No reproduction | without permission. All rights reserved. | [*3 publisher's addresses, London to North Sydney*] | *The Fellowship of the Ring* © George Allen & Unwin | (Publishers) Ltd 1966 | *The Two Towers* © George Allen & Unwin (Publishers) Ltd 1966 | *The Return of the King* © George Allen & Unwin | (Publishers) Ltd 1966 | *The Lord of the Rings* one paperback volume © George Allen & | Unwin (Publishers) Ltd 1968, 1978, 1983 | [*rule*] | [*British Library Cataloguing in Publication Data*] | [*rule*] |

Printed in Great Britain by | Hazell Watson & Viney Ltd, Aylesbury, Bucks'; [5] poem, 'Three Rings for the Elven-kings' etc.; [6]–8 table of contents; [8+1] blank; [8+2] key map, *The West of Middle-earth at the End of the Third Age*, with locations of enlarged sections and additional maps; [9]–12 foreword; [13]–28 prologue; [29] 'THE FELLOWSHIP | OF THE RING | [*swelled rule*] | *being the first part of* | *The Lord of the Rings*'; [30] map, *A Part of the Shire*; [31] 'BOOK I | [*swelled rule*]'; [32] sectional map 1; [33]–231 text; [232] blank; [233] 'BOOK II | [*swelled rule*]'; [234] sectional map 2; [235]–427 text; [428] blank; [429] 'THE TWO TOWERS | [*swelled rule*] | *being the second part of* | *The Lord of the Rings*'; [430] blank; [431] 'BOOK III | [*swelled rule*]'; [432] sectional map 3; [433]–624 text; [625] 'BOOK IV | [*swelled rule*]'; [626] sectional map 4; [627]–770 text; [771] 'THE RETURN OF | THE KING | [*swelled rule*] | *being the third part of* | *The Lord of the Rings*'; [772] blank; [773] 'BOOK V | [*swelled rule*]'; [774–5] map of Rohan, Gondor, and Mordor; [776] blank; [777]–927 text; [928] blank; [929] 'BOOK VI | [*swelled rule*]'; [930] sectional map 5; [931]–1069 text; [1070]–172 appendices; [1173]–93 index; [1194] blank; [1195] Unwin Paperbacks advertisement of books by and about Tolkien; [1196] '*Also published in Unicorn by J. R. R. Tolkien* | [*advertisement of* Silm, UT]'; [1197] '*Also published in Unicorn* | [*advertisement of 5 titles, beginning with* Beagle, The Last Unicorn, *ending with* Chant, Red Moon and Black Mountain]'; [1198] publisher's order form.

Illustrations, by Tolkien (as for A5a.i): Ring inscription, p. 63; Moria gate, p. [323]; Balin's tomb inscription, p. 337.

Wove paper. Bound in heavy wove wrappers. Covers and spine printed against a black background. Printed on upper cover within a red single rule frame interrupted at top by a red ellipse: '[*publisher's "Unicorn" device, in white, within the ellipse*] | [*colour illustration by Roger Garland, of Barad-dûr*] | [*in white, against the illustration:*] THE LORD OF | THE RINGS | J. R. R. Tolkien'. Printed on spine, running down: '[*in white:*] THE LORD OF THE RINGS [*parallel to the title:*] J. R. R. Tolkien [*in red:*] ONE VOLUME EDITION WITH [*parallel to the preceding four words:*] THE INDEX AND APPENDICES [*followed by: publisher's "unwin" device, in red, white, and black against a white panel*]'. Printed on lower cover within a red single rule frame interrupted at top by a red ellipse: '[*publisher's "Unicorn" device, in white, within the ellipse*] | [*against a grey panel:*] [*in black:*] ONE VOLUME EDITION WITH | THE INDEX AND APPENDICES | [*2 quotations, by Richard Hughes and C. S. Lewis*] | [*at left:*] *Cover illustration by* | *Roger Garland* | UNICORN | UNWIN PAPERBACKS | FICTION/FANTASY | £5.95 [*at right, against a white panel:*] GB £ NET +005.95 | ISBN 0-04-823229-7 | [*bar codes*]'. All edges trimmed and unstained.

Published 21 February 1983 at £5.95; number of copies not known.

Substantially a corrected reprint of A5g, with the appendices of A5h. Paragraph added to foreword, p. 12: 'This new one volume paperback edition of *The Lord of the Rings* contains the complete text of the revised edition of 1966 together with the Index and Appendices which were previously omitted.'

The general map of Middle-earth is the version redrawn by Christopher Tolkien for *UT* (A17). Shire map and map of Rohan, Gondor, and Mordor as for A5e.

p. Reset book club edition (1986):

i. THE FELLOWSHIP OF THE RING:

[*1 line in certar, between double rules*] | The Fellowship | of the Ring | BEING THE

FIRST PART OF | THE LORD OF THE RINGS | BY | J. R. R. TOLKIEN | HOUGHTON MIFFLIN COMPANY BOSTON | [2 *lines in tengwar, between double rules*]

448 pp. Collation: gatherings not distinct. 20.8 × 13.7 cm.

[1] 'THE FELLOWSHIP OF THE RING'; [2] '[*1 line in certar, between double rules*] | THE LORD OF THE RINGS | BY J. R. R. TOLKIEN | PART I | THE FELLOWSHIP OF THE RING | PART II | THE TWO TOWERS | PART III | THE RETURN OF THE KING | [*2 lines in tengwar, between double rules*]'; [3] title; [4] 'Copyright © 1954, 1965 by J. R. R. Tolkien | Copyright © renewed 1982 by Christopher R. Tolkien, | Michael H. R. Tolkien, John F. R. Tolkien and Priscilla M. A. R. Tolkien | [*notice of restrictions under copyright*] | Printed in the United States of America'; [5] 'THE LORD OF THE RINGS | [*poem, "Three Rings for the Elven-kings" etc.*]'; [6] blank; [7] 'THE FELLOWSHIP OF THE RING'; [8] blank; [9]–12 foreword; [12] table of contents; [14]–29 prologue; [30] map, *A Part of the Shire*; [31] 'BOOK I | [*swelled rule*]'; [32] blank; [33]–239 text; [240] blank; [241] 'BOOK II | [*swelled rule*]'; [242] blank; [243]–444 text; [445–48] blank. Printing code, 'Q41', printed in gutter, p. 443.

Illustrations, by Tolkien (as for A5a.i): Ring inscription, p. 65; Moria gate, p. [335]; Balin's tomb inscription, p. 350.

Wove paper. Bound in smooth black paper over boards, textured black paper spine. 'Ring and Eye' device stamped on upper cover in gilt. Stamped on spine in gilt: '[*running down:*] 'J. R. R. Tolkien [*diamond with centre dot*] The Fellowship of the Ring | [*horizontal:*] [*diamond with centre dot*] | HMCO'. Wove endpapers: map of Middle-earth by Christopher Tolkien, but with names set in type, printed in black and red on front endsheet; map of Rohan, Gondor, and Mordor by Christopher Tolkien, but with names set in type, printed in black and red on back endsheet. No headbands. Top edge trimmed, fore- and bottom edges untrimmed. All edges unstained.

Dust-jacket, wove paper. Covers and spine printed against a tan background. Printed on upper cover: '[*in brown:*] Being the First Part of | THE LORD OF THE RINGS | [*facsimile signature, "J. R. R. Tolkien", in black*] | [*in brown:*] THE | FELLOWSHIP | OF THE RING | [*"Ring and Eye" device, in black and orange*] | [*in brown:*] REVISED EDITION'. Printed on spine: '[*in brown:*] THE | [*running down:*] FELLOWSHIP [*parallel to the preceding word:*] OF THE RING | [*"Ring and Eye" device, horizontal, in black and orange*] | [*running down, in black:*] J. R. R. TOLKIEN [*parallel to name:*] HOUGHTON MIFFLIN COMPANY'. Printed on lower cover: '10259'. Printed on front flap: ' "Here are beauties which pierce like swords | or burn like cold iron."—C. S. LEWIS | [*blurb*] | Book Club | Edition'. Printed on back flap: '[*blurb, continued*] | [*note on Tolkien*] | HOUGHTON MIFFLIN COMPANY © 1978 | PRINTED IN THE U.S.A.'

ii. THE TWO TOWERS:

[*1 line in certar, between double rules*] | The Two Towers | BEING THE SECOND PART OF | THE LORD OF THE RINGS | BY | J. R. R. TOLKIEN | HOUGHTON MIFFLIN COMPANY BOSTON | [2 *lines in tengwar, between double rules*]

352 pp. Collation: gatherings not distinct. 20.8 × 13.7 cm.

[1] 'THE TWO TOWERS'; [2] '[*1 line in certar, between double rules*] | THE LORD OF THE RINGS | BY J. R. R. TOLKIEN | PART I | THE FELLOWSHIP OF THE

RING | PART II | THE TWO TOWERS | PART III | THE RETURN OF THE KING | [2 *lines in tengwar, between double rules*]'; [3] title; [4] 'Copyright © 1954, 1965 by J. R. R. Tolkien | Copyright © renewed 1982 by Christopher R. Tolkien, | Michael H. R. Tolkien, John F. R. Tolkien and Priscilla M. A. R. Tolkien | [*notice of restrictions under copyright*] | Printed in the United States of America'; [5] 'THE LORD OF THE RINGS | [*poem, "Three Rings for the Elven-kings" etc.*].'; [6] blank; [7] 'THE TWO TOWERS'; [8] blank; [9]–10 synopsis; [11] table of contents; [12] blank; [13] 'BOOK III | [*swelled rule*]'; [14] blank; 15–206 text; [207] 'BOOK IV | [*swelled rule*]'; [208] blank; 209–350 text; [351–2] blank. Printing code, 'Q41', printed in gutter, p. 349.

Wove paper. Bound in smooth grey paper over boards, textured black paper spine. 'Ring and Eye' device stamped on upper cover in gilt. Stamped on spine in gilt: '[*running down:*] 'J. R. R. Tolkien [*diamond with centre dot*] The Two Towers | [*horizontal:*] [*diamond with centre dot*] | HMCO'. Endpapers as for A5p.i. No headbands. Top edge trimmed, fore- and bottom edges untrimmed. All edges unstained.

Dust-jacket, wove paper. Covers and spine printed against a tan background. Printed on upper cover: '[*in brown:*] Being the Second Part of | THE LORD OF THE RINGS | [*facsimile signature, "J. R. R. Tolkien", in black and gold*] | [*in brown:*] THE TWO | TOWERS | [*"Ring and Eye" device, in black*] | [*in brown:*] REVISED EDITION'. Printed on spine: '[*running down, in brown:*] THE TWO [*parallel to first part of title:*] TOWERS | [*"Ring and Eye" device, horizontal, in black and gold*] | [*running down, in black:*] J. R. R. TOLKIEN [*parallel to name:*] HOUGHTON MIFFLIN COMPANY'. Printed on lower cover: '10260'. Printed on front flap: '"Here are beauties which pierce like swords | or burn like cold iron."—C. S. LEWIS | [*blurb*] | Book Club | Edition'. Printed on back flap: '[*blurb, continued*] | [*note on Tolkien*] | HOUGHTON MIFFLIN COMPANY © 1978 | PRINTED IN THE U.S.A.'

iii. THE RETURN OF THE KING:

[1 *line in certar, between double rules*] | The Return of | the King | BEING THE THIRD PART OF | THE LORD OF THE RINGS | BY | J. R. R. TOLKIEN | HOUGHTON MIFFLIN COMPANY BOSTON | [2 *lines in tengwar, between double rules*]

448 pp. Collation: gatherings not distinct. 20.8 × 13.7 cm.

[1] 'THE RETURN OF THE KING'; [2] '[1 *line in certar, between double rules*] | THE LORD OF THE RINGS | BY J. R. R. TOLKIEN | PART I | THE FELLOWSHIP OF THE RING | PART II | THE TWO TOWERS | PART III | THE RETURN OF THE KING | [2 *lines in tengwar, between double rules*]'; [3] title; [4] 'Copyright © 1955, 1965 by J. R. R. Tolkien | Copyright © renewed 1983 by Christopher R. Tolkien, | Michael H. R. Tolkien, John F. R. Tolkien and Priscilla M. A. R. Tolkien | [*notice of restrictions under copyright*] | Printed in the United States of America'; [5] 'THE LORD OF THE RINGS | [*poem, "Three Rings for the Elven-kings" etc.*].'; [6] blank; [7] 'THE RETURN OF THE KING'; [8] blank; [9]–11 synopsis; [12] blank; [13]–14 table of contents; [15] 'BOOK V | [*swelled rule*]'; [16] blank; [17]–171 text; [172] blank; [173] 'BOOK VI | [*swelled rule*]'; [174] blank; [175]–316 text; [317]–424 appendices; [425]–47 indexes; [448] blank. Printing code, 'Q41', printed in gutter, p. 446.

Wove paper. Bound in light grey paper over boards, textured black paper spine.

'Ring and Eye' device stamped on upper cover in gilt. Stamped on spine in gilt: '[*running down:*] 'J. R. R. Tolkien [*diamond with centre dot*] The Return of the King [*diamond with centre dot*] | [*horizontal:*] HMCO'. Endpapers as for A5p.i. No headbands. Top edge trimmed, fore- and bottom edges untrimmed. All edges unstained.

Dust-jacket, wove paper. Covers and spine printed against a tan background. Printed on upper cover: '[*in brown:*] Being the Third Part of | THE LORD OF THE RINGS | [*facsimile signature, "J. R. R. Tolkien", in black*] | [*in brown:*] THE RETURN | OF THE KING | [*"Ring and Eye" device, in black and purple*] | [*in brown:*] REVISED EDITION'. Printed on spine: '[*running down, in brown:*] THE RETURN [*parallel to first part of title:*] OF THE KING | [*"Ring and Eye" device, horizontal, in black and purple*] | [*running down, in black:*] J. R. R. TOLKIEN [*parallel to name:*] HOUGHTON MIFFLIN COMPANY'. Printed on lower cover: '10261'. Printed on front flap: ' "Here are beauties which pierce like swords | or burn like cold iron."—C. S. LEWIS | [*blurb*] | *Book Club* | *Edition*'. Printed on back flap: '[*blurb, continued*] | [*note on Tolkien*] | HOUGHTON MIFFLIN COMPANY © 1978 | PRINTED IN THE U.S.A.'

Published by the Science Fiction Book Club in early October 1986 at $5.98? per volume or $15.98? per set; number of copies not known.

Reset. The text agrees with (uncorrected) A5f.
    Maps as for A5e.

q. Houghton Mifflin edition, revised impression (1987):

i. THE FELLOWSHIP OF THE RING:

[*1 line in certar, between double rules*] | The Fellowship | of the Ring | BEING THE FIRST PART OF | THE LORD OF THE RINGS | BY | J. R. R. TOLKIEN | *Second Edition* | HOUGHTON MIFFLIN COMPANY | BOSTON | [*2 lines in tengwar, between double rules*]

viii, 424 pp. + 1 plate (map). Collation: gatherings not distinct. 21.9 × 14.1 cm.

[i] 'THE FELLOWSHIP OF THE RING'; [ii] '[*1 line in certar, between double rules*] | THE LORD OF THE RINGS | BY J. R. R. TOLKIEN | PART I | THE FELLOWSHIP OF THE RING | PART II | THE TWO TOWERS | PART III | THE RETURN OF THE KING | [*2 lines in tengwar, between double rules*]'; [iii] title; [iv] 'Copyright © 1954, 1965 by J. R. R. Tolkien | Copyright © renewed 1982 by Christopher R. Tolkien, | Michael H. R. Tolkien, John F. R. Tolkien | and Priscilla M. A. R. Tolkien | "Note on the Text" copyright © 1986 by Houghton Mifflin Company | [*notice of restrictions under copyright*] | *Library of Congress Catalog Card Number: 67-12274* | ISBN 0-395-08254-4 | ISBN 0-395-27223-8 (pbk.) | Printed in the United States of America | [*printing code, beginning "Q", ending "19"*] | The text of this edition incorporates all corrections | and revisions intended by its author and, taken with the | other two volumes, constitutes an authoritative edition | of The Lord of the Rings, uniform with that published | in Great Britain by Allen & Unwin.'; [v]–viii note on the text, by Douglas A. Anderson; [1] 'THE FELLOWSHIP OF THE RING'; [2] blank; [3] 'THE LORD OF THE RINGS | [*poem, "Three Rings for the Elven-kings" etc.*]'; [4] blank; [5]–8 foreword; [9] table of contents; 10–25 prologue; [26] map, *A Part of the Shire*; [27] 'BOOK I | [*swelled rule*]'; [28] blank; 29–227 text; [228] blank; [229] 'BOOK II | [*swelled rule*]'; [230] blank; 231–423 text; [424–8] blank. Map of Middle-earth, printed in black and red on folded leaf tipped onto recto, back free endpaper.

Illustrations, by Tolkien (as for A5a.i): Ring inscription, p. 63; Moria gate, p. [323]; Balin's tomb inscription, p. 337.

Wove paper. Bound in black cloth over boards. 'Ring and Eye' device stamped on upper cover in copper and gilt. Stamped on spine, running down: '[*in gilt:*] 'TOLKIEN [*diamond with centre dot, in copper*] [*in gilt:*] The Fellowship of the Ring [*diamond with centre dot, in copper*] [*in gilt:*] HMCO'. Orange wove endpapers. Black/white headbands. All edges trimmed. Top edge stained orange, fore- and bottom edges unstained.

ii. THE TWO TOWERS:

[*1 line in certar, between double rules*] | The Two Towers | BEING THE SECOND PART OF | THE LORD OF THE RINGS | BY | J. R. R. TOLKIEN | *Second Edition* | HOUGHTON MIFFLIN COMPANY | BOSTON | [*2 lines in tengwar, between double rules*]

352 pp. + 1 plate (map). Collation: gatherings not distinct. 22.0 × 14.2 cm.

[1–2] blank; [3] 'THE TWO TOWERS'; [4] '[*1 line in certar, between double rules*] | THE LORD OF THE RINGS | BY J. R. R. TOLKIEN | PART I | THE FELLOWSHIP OF THE RING | PART II | THE TWO TOWERS | PART III | THE RETURN OF THE KING | [*2 lines in tengwar, between double rules*]'; [5] title; [6] 'Copyright © 1954, 1965 by J. R. R. Tolkien | Copyright © renewed 1982 by Christopher R. Tolkien, | Michael H. R. Tolkien, John F. R. Tolkien | and Priscilla M. A. R. Tolkien | [*notice of restrictions under copyright*] | *Library of Congress Catalog Card Number: 67-12276* | ISBN 0-395-08255-2 | ISBN 0-395-27222-X (pbk.) | Printed in the United States of America | [*printing code, beginning "Q", ending "18"*] | The text of this edition incorporates all corrections | and revisions intended by its author and, taken with the | other two volumes, constitutes an authoritative edition | of *The Lord of the Rings*, uniform with that published | in Great Britain by Allen & Unwin.'; [7] 'THE LORD OF THE RINGS | [*poem, "Three Rings for the Elven-kings" etc.*]'; [8] blank; 9–10 synopsis; 11 table of contents; [12] blank; [13] 'BOOK III | [*swelled rule*]'; [14] blank; 15–206 text; [207] 'BOOK IV | [*swelled rule*]'; [208] blank; 209–352 text. Map of Middle-earth, printed in black and red on folded leaf tipped onto recto, back free endpaper.

Wove paper. Bound in black cloth over boards. 'Ring and Eye' device stamped on upper cover in green and gilt. Stamped on spine, running down: '[*in gilt:*] 'TOLKIEN [*diamond with centre dot, in green*] [*in gilt:*] The Two Towers [*diamond with centre dot, in green*] [*in gilt:*] HMCO'. Yellow-green wove endpapers. Black/white headbands. All edges trimmed. Top edge stained light green, fore- and bottom edges unstained.

iii. THE RETURN OF THE KING:

[*1 line in certar, between double rules*] | The Return of | the King | BEING THE THIRD PART OF | THE LORD OF THE RINGS | BY | J. R. R. TOLKIEN | *Second Edition* | HOUGHTON MIFFLIN COMPANY | BOSTON | [*2 lines in tengwar, between double rules*]

440 pp. + 1 plate (map). Collation: gatherings not distinct. 22.1 × 14.2 cm.

[1–2] blank; [3] 'THE RETURN OF THE KING'; [4] '[*1 line in certar, between double rules*] | THE LORD OF THE RINGS | BY J. R. R. TOLKIEN | PART I | THE FELLOWSHIP OF THE RING | PART II | THE TWO TOWERS | PART III | THE

RETURN OF THE KING | [*2 lines in tengwar, between double rules*]'; [5] title; [8] 'Copyright © 1955, 1965 by J. R. R. Tolkien | Copyright © renewed 1983 by Christopher R. Tolkien, | Michael H. R. Tolkien, John F. R. Tolkien | and Priscilla M. A. R. Tolkien | [*notice of restrictions under copyright*] | Library of Congress Catalog Card Number: 67-12275 | ISBN 0-395-08256-0 | ISBN 0-395-27222-2 (pbk.) | Printed in the United States of America | [*printing code, beginning "Q", ending "18"*] | The text of this edition incorporates all corrections | and revisions intended by its author and, taken with the | other two volumes, constitutes an authoritative edition | of *The Lord of the Rings*, uniform with that published | in Great Britain by Allen & Unwin.'; [7] 'THE LORD OF THE RINGS | [*poem, "Three Rings for the Elven-kings" etc.*]'; [8] blank; [9] 'THE RETURN OF THE KING'; [10] blank; 11–13 synopsis; [14] blank; 15 table of contents; [16] blank; [17] 'BOOK V | [*swelled rule*]'; [18] blank; 19–169 text; [170] blank; [171] 'BOOK VI | [*swelled rule*]'; [172] blank; 173–311 text; [312] blank; 313–416 appendices; 417–40 index. Map of Rohan, Gondor, and Mordor, printed in black and red on folded leaf tipped onto recto, back free endpaper.

Wove paper. Bound in black cloth over boards. 'Ring and Eye' device stamped on upper cover in red-purple and gilt.

Stamped on spine, running down: '[*in gilt:*] TOLKIEN [*diamond with centre dot, in red-purple*] [*in gilt:*] The Return of the King [*diamond with centre dot, in red-purple*] [*in gilt:*] HMCO'. Light purple wove endpapers. Black/white headbands. All edges trimmed. Top edge stained purple, fore- and bottom edges unstained.

Issued without dust-jackets.

Slipcase, paper over boards. Printed on left and right sides against a cream background: '[*facsimile signature, "J. R. R. Tolkien"*] | [*in red:*] THE | LORD | OF THE | RINGS | [*in black:*] HOUGHTON MIFFLIN COMPANY © 1978'. All other sides printed solid cream.

Published April 1987 at $43.35 the set; number of copies not known.

Typeset chiefly as for A5e as later corrected. Noted, p. viii: 'This new reprinting of the three volumes of *The Lord of the Rings* is photo-offset from the most recent reprinting of the three-volume British hardcover edition, which has been until now the most authoritative text available. Additionally this new reprinting contains some further corrections, and integrates the errant Ballantine branch of revision ... into the main branch of textual descent'. However, with some errors still continued, e.g. 'woves' for 'wolves', *FR* p. 275, l. 5; 'Aragorn indeed lived to be one hundred and ninety' for 'Aragorn indeed lived to be two hundred and ten', *RK* p. 324, ll. 21–2.

   Note 4, p. viii, describes the general map of Middle-earth in vols. 1 and 2 as the revised version drawn by Christopher Tolkien for *UT* (A17), but the earlier map (as for A5e) was inserted in A5q instead. Shire map and map of Rohan, Gondor, and Mordor as for A5e.

   The second impression (1988, *FR* marked as twentieth impression, *TT* and *RK* marked as nineteenth impression) was printed on heavier paper, bound in brown cloth over boards, and issued in dust-jackets featuring colour illustrations by Alan Lee. Sold as separate volumes or as a set in a slipcase featuring the Lee jacket illustrations, which together form a Middle-earth landscape.

r. 'Collector's edition', revised impression (1987):

[*1 line in certar, between double rules, in grey*] | [*uncials:*] [*in black:*] J.R.R. TOLKIEN | [*in red:*] THE LORD | OF THE | RINGS | [*in black:*] COLLECTOR'S

EDITION | [*roman:*] BOSTON | [*uncials:*] HOUGHTON MIFFLIN COMPANY | [*2 lines in tengwar, between double rules, in grey*]

x, 26, [2], 27–424, 11–352, 15–452 pp. + 1 plate (map). Collation: [1–38^{16}]. 23.5 × 15.2 cm.

First section: [i] '[*uncials, in red:*] THE LORD | OF THE | RINGS'; [ii] blank; [iii] title; [iv] '"Note on the Text": | Copyright © 1987 by Houghton Mifflin Company. | "The Fellowship of the Ring" and "The Two Towers": | Copyright © 1954, 1965 by J. R. R. Tolkien. | Copyright © renewed 1982 by Christopher R. Tolkien, | Michael H. R. Tolkien, John F. R. Tolkien | and Priscilla M. A. R. Tolkien. | "The Return of the King": | Copyright © 1955, 1965 by J. R. R. Tolkien. | Copyright © renewed 1983 by Christopher R. Tolkien, | Michael H. R. Tolkien, John F. R. Tolkien | and Priscilla M. A. R. Tolkien. | [*notice of restrictions under copyright*] | ISBN 0-395-19395-8 | Printed in the United States of America | Collector's Edition | [*printing code, beginning "A", ending "13"*] | The text of this edition incorporates all corrections | and revisions intended by its author constitutes an authoritative edition | of *The Lord of the Rings*, uniform with that published | in Great Britain by Allen & Unwin.'; [v]–viii note on the text, by Douglas A. Anderson; [ix] '[*uncials, in red:*] THE LORD | OF THE | RINGS'; [x] blank; [1] 'THE LORD OF THE RINGS | [*poem, "Three Rings for the Elven-kings" etc.*].'; [2] blank; 3–6 foreword; 7–9 table of contents; 10–25 prologue; 26 map, *A Part of the Shire*; [27] '[*1 line in certar, between double rules, in grey*] | [*uncials:*] [*in black:*] PART I | [*in red:*] THE FELLOWSHIP | OF THE RING'; [28] blank; [28+1] '[*1 line in certar, between double rules, in grey*] | [*uncials, in black:*] BOOK ONE'; [28+2] blank; 29–227 text; [228] blank; [229] '[*1 line in certar, between double rules, in grey*] | [*uncials, in black:*] BOOK TWO'; [230] blank; 231–423 text; [424] blank. *Second section:* [11] '[*1 line in certar, between double rules, in grey*] | [*uncials:*] [*in black:*] PART II | [*in red:*] THE TWO TOWERS'; [12] blank; [13] '[*1 line in certar, between double rules, in grey*] | [*uncials, in black:*] BOOK THREE'; [14] blank; 15–206 text; [207] '[*1 line in certar, between double rules, in grey*] | [*uncials, in black:*] BOOK FOUR'; [208] blank; 209–352 text. *Third section:* [15] '[*1 line in certar, between double rules, in grey*] | [*uncials:*] [*in black:*] PART III | [*in red:*] THE RETURN | OF THE KING'; [16] blank; [17] '[*1 line in certar, between double rules, in grey*] | [*uncials, in black:*] BOOK FIVE'; [18] blank; 19–169 text; [170] blank; [171] '[*1 line in certar, between double rules, in grey*] | [*uncials, in black:*] BOOK SIX'; [172] blank; 173–311 text; [312] blank; 313–416 appendices; 417–40 index; [441–52] blank. Folios and running heads, chapter titles, and headings for appendix sections and index printed in red. Map of Middle-earth, printed in black and red on folded leaf tipped onto recto back free endpaper.

Illustrations, by Tolkien (as for A5a.i): Ring inscription, p. 63; Moria gate, p. [323]; Balin's tomb inscription, p. 337.

Wove paper. Binding and slipcase as for A5k.

Published April 1987 at $50.00; number of copies not known.

Typeset chiefly as for A5k, with corrections. Cf. A5q. Includes 'Note on the Text' by Douglas A. Anderson.

    Maps as for A5q.

s. Houghton Mifflin trade paperback edition, revised impression (1988):

i. THE FELLOWSHIP OF THE RING:

[*1 line in certar, between double rules*] | The Fellowship | of the Ring | BEING THE

FIRST PART OF | THE LORD OF THE RINGS | BY | J. R. R. TOLKIEN | [*publisher's 'dolphin' device*] | *Second Edition* | HOUGHTON MIFFLIN COMPANY | BOSTON | [*2 lines in tengwar, between double rules*]

viii, 424 pp. Collation: 216 leaves. 20.9 × 13.5 cm.

[i] 'THE FELLOWSHIP OF THE RING'; [ii] '[*1 line in certar, between double rules*] | THE LORD OF THE RINGS | BY J. R. R. TOLKIEN | PART I | THE FELLOWSHIP OF THE RING | PART II | THE TWO TOWERS | PART III | THE RETURN OF THE KING | [*2 lines in tengwar, between double rules*]'; [iii] title; [iv] 'Fellowship of the Ring | Copyright © 1954, 1965 by J. R. R. Tolkien | Copyright © renewed 1982 by Christopher R. Tolkien, | Michael H. R. Tolkien, John F. R. Tolkien | and Priscilla M. A. R. Tolkien | "Note on the Text" copyright © 1986 by Houghton | Mifflin Company | All rights reserved | For information about permission to reproduce | selections from this book, write to Permissions, | Houghton Mifflin Company, 2 Park Street, Boston, | Massachusetts 02108. | *Library of Congress Catalog Card Number:* 67-12274 | ISBN 0-395-48931-8 | ISBN 0-395-27223-8 (pbk.) | Printed in the United States of America | [*printing code, beginning "BTA", ending "7"*] | The text of this edition incorporates all corrections | and revisions intended by its author and, taken with the | other two volumes, constitutes an authoritative edition | of *The Lord of the Rings*, uniform with that published | in Great Britain by Allen & Unwin.'; [v]–viii note on the text, by Douglas A. Anderson; [1] 'THE FELLOWSHIP OF THE RING'; [2–3] map of Middle-earth; [4] 'THE LORD OF THE RINGS | [*poem, "Three Rings for the Elven-kings" etc.*]'; [5]–8 foreword; [9] table of contents; 10–25 prologue; [26] map, *A Part of the Shire*; [27] 'BOOK I | [*swelled rule*]'; [28] blank; 29–227 text; [228] blank; [229] 'BOOK II | [*swelled rule*]'; [230] blank; 231–423 text; [424] blank.

Illustrations, by Tolkien (as for A5a.i): Ring inscription, p. 63; Moria gate, p. [323]; Balin's tomb inscription, p. 337.

Wove paper. Bound in heavy wove wrappers. Covers and spine printed against a pale green background. Printed on upper cover against a panel of diagonal black and white rules, within a decorative frame in grey, light green, and white with the Ring inscription in runes ('ONE RING TO RULE THEM ALL, ONE RING TO FIND THEM, ONE RING TO BRING THEM ALL AND IN THE DARKNESS BIND THEM'): '[*3 coloured panels outlined in black, against a 12-sided white panel outlined in black:*] [*against the first, light blue-green panel:*] THE | [*against the second, dark grey panel:*] [*initial "F" in white outlined in black, against a blue-green panel outlined in black, against a white panel outlined in black*] [*in white outlined in black:*] ELLOWSHIP | [*in black, descender of "f" extending beyond the panels:*] of [*in white outlined in black:*] THE RING | [*in white outlined in black, against the third, blue-green panel:*] J. R. R. TOLKIEN | [*in black, against 2 coloured panels outlined in black, against an 8-sided white panel outlined in black:*] [*against the first, light blue-green panel:*] Being the first part of | [*against the second, dark blue-green panel:*] THE LORD OF THE RINGS'. Printed on spine: '[*running down:*] [*in dark blue-green outlined in black:*] THE FELLOWSHIP [*parallel to the first part of the title:*] OF THE RING [*followed by, in white outlined in black:*] J. R. R. TOLKIEN | [*in black:*] [*publisher's "dolphin" device, horizontal*] | [*running down:*] HOUGHTON [*parallel to first part of name:*] MIFFLIN'. Printed on lower cover: '[*at left:*] 6-97078 [*at right, against a white panel:*] ISBN 0-395-27223-8'. All edges trimmed and unstained.

Dust-jacket, wove paper. Covers, spine, and flaps printed against a pale grey background. Colour illustration by Alan Lee, left third of a Middle-earth landscape with a flying Nazgûl, printed on upper cover within a decorative frame as on upper cover of binding. Lettering against panels on upper cover as on upper cover of binding, except that the topmost coloured panel is blue-grey and partly overlaps the frame, the second coloured panel is grey with initial 'F' against a blue-grey panel, and the remaining coloured panels are blue-grey. Printed on spine: '[*running down:*] [*in blue-grey outlined in black:*] THE FELLOWSHIP [*parallel to first part of title:*] OF THE RING [*followed by, in grey outlined in black:*] J. R. R. TOLKIEN | [*in black:*] [*publisher's "dolphin" device, horizontal*] | [*running down:*] HOUGHTON [*parallel to the first part of the name:*] MIFFLIN'. Printed on lower cover: 'FANTASY | [*blurb, in black with initial "I" in grey outlined in black*] | [*in black:*] [2 quotations, by W. H. Auden and C. S. Lewis] | [*at left:*] 6-97078 [*at right, against a white panel:*] ISBN 0-395-27223-8'. Printed on front flap: 'FPT>>$7.95 | [*blurb*] | 10077088 | ISBN 0-395-27223-8'. Printed on back flap: '[*note on Tolkien*] | *Front-of-jacket design: Rita Marshall* | *Front-of-jacket illustration: Alan Lee* | HOUGHTON MIFFLIN COMPANY | TWO PARK STREET | BOSTON, MASSACHUSETTS 02108'.

ii. THE TWO TOWERS:

[*1 line in certar, between double rules*] | The Two Towers | BEING THE SECOND PART OF | THE LORD OF THE RINGS | BY | J. R. R. TOLKIEN | [*publisher's 'dolphin' device*] | *Second Edition* | HOUGHTON MIFFLIN COMPANY | BOSTON | [*2 lines in tengwar, between double rules*]

360 pp. Collation: 180 leaves. 20.9 × 13.5 cm.

[1] 'THE TWO TOWERS'; [2–3] map of Middle-earth; [4] '[*1 line in certar, between double rules*] | THE LORD OF THE RINGS | BY J. R. R. TOLKIEN | PART I | THE FELLOWSHIP OF THE RING | PART II | THE TWO TOWERS | PART III | THE RETURN OF THE KING | [*2 lines in tengwar, between double rules*]'; [5] title; [6] 'The Two Towers | Copyright © 1954, 1965 by J. R. R. Tolkien | Copyright © renewed 1982 by Christopher R. Tolkien, | Michael H. R. Tolkien, John F. R. Tolkien | and Priscilla M. A. R. Tolkien | All rights reserved | For information about permission to reproduce | selections from this book, write to Permissions, | Houghton Mifflin Company, 2 Park Street, Boston, | Massachusetts 02108. | *Library of Congress Catalog Card Number: 67-12276* | ISBN 0-395-48933-4 | ISBN 0-395-27222-X (pbk.) | Printed in the United States of America | [*printing code, beginning "BTA", ending "7"*] | The text of this edition incorporates all corrections | and revisions intended by its author and, taken with the | other two volumes, constitutes an authoritative edition | of *The Lord of the Rings*, uniform with that published | in Great Britain by Allen & Unwin.'; [7] 'THE LORD OF THE RINGS | [*poem, "Three Rings for the Elven-kings" etc.*]'; [8] blank; 9–10 synopsis; 11 table of contents; [12] blank; [13] 'BOOK III | [*swelled rule*]'; [14] blank; 15–206 text; [207] 'BOOK IV | [*swelled rule*]'; [208] blank; 209–352 text.

Wove paper. Bound in heavy wove wrappers. Covers and spine printed against a pale pink background. Printed on upper cover against a panel of diagonal black and white rules, within a decorative frame in grey, light pink, and white with the Ring inscription in runes: '[*3 coloured panels outlined in black, against a 12-sided white panel outlined in black:*] [*against the first, light copper panel:*] THE | [*against the second, dark grey panel:*] [*initial "T" in white outlined in black, against a copper panel outlined in black, against a white panel outlined in black*] [*in white outlined in black:*] WO TOWERS | [*in white outlined in black, against the third, copper panel:*] J. R. R. TOLKIEN | [*in black, against 2 coloured panels outlined in black, against an*

8-sided white panel outlined in black:] [*against the first, dark copper panel:*] Being the second part of | [*against the second, dark copper panel:*] THE LORD OF THE RINGS'. Printed on spine: '[*running down:*] [*in copper outlined in black:*] THE TWO TOWERS [*in white outlined in black:*] J. R. R. TOLKIEN | [*in black:*] [*publisher's "dolphin" device, horizontal*] | [*running down:*] HOUGHTON [*parallel to first part of name:*] MIFFLIN'. Printed on lower cover: '[*at left:*] 6-97079 [*at right, against a white panel:*] ISBN 0-395-27222-X'. All edges trimmed and unstained.

Dust-jacket, wove paper. Covers, spine, and flaps printed against a pale grey background. Colour illustration by Alan Lee, centre third of a Middle-earth landscape with a flying Nazgûl, printed on upper cover within a decorative frame as on upper cover of binding, against a pale grey background. Lettering against panels on upper cover as on upper cover of binding, except that the topmost coloured panel is light copper and partly overlaps the frame, the second coloured panel is grey with initial 'T' against a light copper panel, and the remaining coloured panels are light copper. Printed on spine: '[*running down:*] [*in copper outlined in black:*] THE TWO TOWERS [*followed by, in grey outlined in black:*] J. R. R. TOLKIEN | [*in black:*] [*publisher's device, horizontal*] | [*running down:*] HOUGHTON [*parallel to the first part of the name:*] MIFFLIN'. Printed on lower cover: 'FANTASY | [*blurb, in black with initial "I" in copper outlined in black*] | [*in black:*] [*2 quotations, by W. H. Auden and C. S. Lewis*] | [*at left:*] 6–97079 [*at right, against a white panel:*] ISBN 0-395-27222-X'. Printed on front flap: 'FPT>>$7.95 | [*blurb*] | 10077088 | ISBN 0-395-27222-X'. Printed on back flap: '[*note on Tolkien*] | *Front-of-jacket design: Rita Marshall* | *Front-of-jacket illustration: Alan Lee* | HOUGHTON MIFFLIN COMPANY | TWO PARK STREET | BOSTON, MASSACHUSETTS 02108'.

iii. THE RETURN OF THE KING:

[*1 line in certar, between double rules*] | The Return of | the King | BEING THE THIRD PART OF | THE LORD OF THE RINGS | BY | J. R. R. TOLKIEN | [*publisher's 'dolphin' device*] | *Second Edition* | HOUGHTON MIFFLIN COMPANY | BOSTON | [*2 lines in tengwar, between double rules*]

456 pp. Collation: 228 leaves. 20.9 × 13.5 cm.

[1–2] blank; [3] 'THE RETURN OF THE KING'; [4] '[*1 line in certar, between double rules*] | THE LORD OF THE RINGS | BY J. R. R. TOLKIEN | PART I | THE FELLOWSHIP OF THE RING | PART II | THE TWO TOWERS | PART III | THE RETURN OF THE KING | [*2 lines in tengwar, between double rules*]'; [5] title; [6] 'The Return of the King | Copyright © 1955, 1965 by J. R. R. Tolkien | Copyright © renewed 1983 by Christopher R. Tolkien, | Michael H. R. Tolkien, John F. R. Tolkien | and Priscilla M. A. R. Tolkien | All rights reserved | For information about permission to reproduce | selections from this book, write to Permissions, | Houghton Mifflin Company, 2 Park Street, Boston, | Massachusetts 02108. | *Library of Congress Catalog Card Number: 67-12275* | ISBN 0-395-48930-X | ISBN 0-395-27221-1 (pbk.) | Printed in the United States of America | [*printing code, beginning "BTA", ending "7"*] | The text of this edition incorporates all corrections | and revisions intended by its author and, taken with the | other two volumes, constitutes an authoritative edition | of *The Lord of the Rings*, uniform with that published | in Great Britain by Allen & Unwin.'; [7] 'THE LORD OF THE RINGS | [*poem, "Three Rings for the Elven-kings" etc.*]'; [8] blank; [9] 'THE RETURN OF THE KING'; [10] blank; 11–13 synopsis; [14] blank; 15 table of contents; [16] blank; [17] 'BOOK V | [*swelled rule*]'; [18] blank; 19–169 text; [170]

blank; [171] 'BOOK VI | [*swelled rule*]'; [172] blank; 173–311 text; [312] blank; 313–416 appendices; 417–40 index; [441–5] blank; [446–7] map of Rohan, Gondor, and Mordor; [448–56] blank.

Wove paper. Bound in heavy wove wrappers. Covers and spine printed against a pale blue-grey background. Printed on upper cover against a panel of diagonal black and white rules, within a decorative frame in grey, blue-grey, and white with the Ring inscription in runes: '[*3 coloured panels outlined in black, against a 12-sided white panel outlined in black:*] [*against the first, light grey-blue panel:*] THE | [*against the second, dark grey panel:*] [*initial "R" in white outlined in black, against a grey-blue panel outlined in black, against a white panel outlined in black*] [*in white outlined in black:*] ETURN | [*in black, descender of "f" extending beyond the panels:*] of [*in white outlined in black:*] OF THE KING | [*in white outlined in black, against the third, grey-blue panel:*] J. R. R. TOLKIEN | [*in black, against 2 coloured panels outlined in black, against an 8-sided white panel outlined in black:*] [*against the first, light grey-blue panel:*] Being the third part of | [*against a dark grey-blue panel outlined in black:*] THE LORD OF THE RINGS'. Printed on spine: '[*running down:*] [*in grey-blue outlined in black:*] THE RETURN [*parallel to first part of title:*] OF THE KING [*followed by, in white outlined in black:*] J. R. R. TOLKIEN | [*in black:*] [*publisher's "dolphin" device, horizontal*] | [*running down:*] HOUGHTON [*parallel to first part of name:*] MIFFLIN'. Printed on lower cover: '[*at left:*] 6-97080 [*at right, against a white panel:*] ISBN 0-395-27221-1'. All edges trimmed and unstained.

Dust-jacket, wove paper. Covers, spine, and flaps printed against a pale grey background. Colour illustration by Alan Lee, right third of a Middle-earth landscape with a flying Nazgûl, printed on upper cover within a decorative frame as on upper cover of binding. Lettering against panels on upper cover as on upper cover of binding, except that the topmost coloured panel is light purple and partly overlaps the frame, the second coloured panel is grey with initial 'R' against a light purple panel, and the remaining coloured panels are light purple. Printed on spine: '[*running down:*] [*in light purple outlined in black:*] THE RETURN [*parallel to the first part of the title:*] OF THE KING [*followed by, in grey outlined in black:*] J. R. R. TOLKIEN | [*in black:*] [*publisher's "dolphin" device, horizontal*] | [*running down:*] HOUGHTON [*parallel to the first part of the name:*] MIFFLIN'. Printed on lower cover: 'FANTASY | [*blurb, in black with initial "I" in light purple outlined in black*] | [*in black:*] [*2 quotations, by W. H. Auden and C. S. Lewis*] | [*at left:*] 6-97080 [*at right, against a white panel:*] ISBN 0-395-27221-1'. Printed on front flap: 'FPT>>$7.95 | [*blurb*] | 10077088 | ISBN 0-395-27221-1'. Printed on back flap: '[*note on Tolkien*] | *Front-of-jacket design: Rita Marshall* | *Front-of-jacket illustration: Alan Lee* | HOUGHTON MIFFLIN COMPANY | TWO PARK STREET | BOSTON, MASSACHUSETTS 02108'.

Published 2 October 1988 at $7.95 per volume (with dust-jackets), and (without dust-jackets) with *H* (A3t) at $29.95 the set; 40,000 copies of each volume printed.

Sold as separate volumes and as a set in slipcase, printed paper over boards. Wraparound colour illustration by Alan Lee, of a Middle-earth landscape with a flying Nazgûl (as on jackets but less cropped), outlined at top and bottom in white, between solid black bands which extend to top and bottom of slipcase. Printed on left and right sides against bands and illustration: '[*2 coloured panels outlined in black, against an 8-sided white panel outlined in black:*] [*in white outlined in black, against the first, red panel:*] THE HOBBIT | [*against the second, grey panel:*] [*in black, against a copper panel outlined in black, against a white panel outlined in black on three sides and set into the grey panel at left:*] AND [*followed by:*] [*in white outlined in black:*] THE LORD | [*in black, descender of "f" extending beyond the panels:*] of [*in white outlined in black:*] THE RINGS | [*at foot of side, in white outlined in black, against a copper panel outlined in black, against a white panel outlined in black:*] J. R. R. TOLKIEN'.

Typeset chiefly as for A5q, except title and copyright pages.
  Maps as for A5q.

t. Unwin Hyman one-volume trade hardcover edition (1988):

[*1 line in certar, between double rules*] | THE LORD | OF | THE RINGS | J. R. R. Tolkien | Part 1: The Fellowship of the Ring | Part 2: The Two Towers | Part 3: The Return of the King | UNWIN | [*publisher's 'man drawing a circle' device*] | HYMAN | LONDON SYDNEY WELLINGTON | [*2 lines in tengwar, between double rules*]

1200 pp. Collation: $[1-9^{32}10^{24}11-19^{32}]$. 22.1 × 14.0 cm.

Contents as for A5h, except pp. [2] '[*1 line in certar, between double rules*] | *also by* J. R. R. Tolkien | [*21 titles, beginning with* ATB, *ending with* UT] | With Donald Swann | THE ROAD GOES EVER ON | [*2 lines in tengwar, between double rules*]'; [3] title, as above; [4] 'The Fellowship of the Ring first published in Great Britain by George Allen | & Unwin 1954 | First edition reprinted fifteen times: second edition 1966 reprinted eighteen | times | The Two Towers first published in Great Britain by George Allen & Unwin | 1954 | First edition reprinted twelve times: second edition 1966 reprinted sixteen | times | The Return of the King first published in Great Britain by George Allen & | Unwin 1955 | First edition reprinted eleven times: second edition 1966 reprinted sixteen | times | The Fellowship of the Ring © George Allen & Unwin (Publishers) Ltd 1966 | The Two Towers © George Allen & Unwin (Publishers) Ltd 1966 | The Return of the King © George Allen & Unwin (Publishers) Ltd 1966 | First published in one volume 1968. This edition of The Lord of the Rings | © George Allen & Unwin (Publishers) Ltd 1968, Unwin Hyman Limited 1988 | [*notice of restrictions*] | [*3 publisher's addresses, London to Wellington*] | Printed and bound in Great Britain at The Bath Press, Avon.'; and [1194–1200] blank.

Illustrations as for A5h.

Wove paper. Bound in blue textured paper over boards. Stamped on spine in gilt: 'J. R. R. | TOLKIEN | THE | LORD | OF THE | RINGS | [*"JRRT" monogram*] | ONE VOLUME EDITION | WITH THE | INDEX AND APPENDICES | UNWIN | [*publisher's "man drawing a circle" device*] | HYMAN'. Wove endpapers. Dark blue/white headbands. Dark blue ribbon marker. All edges trimmed and unstained.

Dust jacket, wove paper. Colour illustration by Roger Garland, *Barad-dûr*, printed on upper cover. Stamped on upper cover in gilt against the illustration: 'THE LORD | OF THE RINGS | J. R. R. TOLKIEN'. Stamped or printed on spine against a blue background: '[*stamped in gilt:*] J. R. R. | TOLKIEN | THE | LORD | OF THE | RINGS | [*"JRRT" monogram*] | [*printed:*] [*in white:*] ONE VOLUME EDITION | WITH THE | INDEX AND APPENDICES | [*detail from colour illustration on upper cover, within a stamped gilt double rule frame*] | [*printed in white:*] UNWIN | [*publisher's "man drawing a circle" device*] | HYMAN'. Stamped or printed on lower cover against a blue background: '[*"JRRT" monogram, stamped in gilt*] | [*printed in black, against a white panel:*] ISBN 0-04-440305-4 | [*bar code*]'. Printed on front flap: '[*blurb*] | £17.50 net UK'. Printed on back flap: '[*4 quotations, from the* Evening Standard, Daily Telegraph, *and* Sunday Times, *and by* C. S. Lewis] |

Jacket illustration by Roger Garland | Jacket design by The Pinpoint Design Company'.

Published 13 October 1988 at £17.50; number of copies not known.

Typeset as for A5h, except pp. [2–4]. The final paragraph of the foreword, erroneously retained from A5h, describes the binding of the India paper edition (A5h).

No maps of Middle-earth are included except *A Part of the Shire*, drawn by Christopher Tolkien as for A5e.

In January 1992, as published by HarperCollins, the dust-jacket was changed to feature a painting by John Howe, of Gandalf.

u. Reset book club edition (1990):

[*1 line in certar, between double rules*] | [*within 3 concentric single rule frames, alternating thin-thick-thin:*] THE LORD OF | THE RINGS | [*rule*] [*diamond*] [*rule*] | J. R. R. Tolkien | [*below the frame:*] Part 1: The Fellowship of the Ring | Part 2: The Two Towers | Part 3: The Return of the King | GUILD PUBLISHING | LONDON · NEW YORK · SYDNEY · TORONTO | [*2 lines in tengwar, between double rules*]

1248 pp. Collation: 624 leaves. 19.7 × 12.6 cm.

[1] 'THE LORD OF THE RINGS'; [2] 'ALSO BY J. R. R. TOLKIEN | [*8 titles, beginning with* H, *ending with* SGPO] | With Donald Swann | *The Road Goes Ever On*'; [3] title; [4] 'This edition published 1990 by | Guild Publishing | by arrangement with George Allen & Unwin Ltd | *The Fellowship of the Ring* first published in Great Britain by | George Allen & Unwin 1954 | *The Two Towers* first published in Great Britain by George | Allen & Unwin 1954 | *The Return of the King* first published in Great Britain by | George Allen & Unwin 1955 | [*notice of restrictions under copyright*] | *The Fellowship of the Ring* © George Allen & Unwin | (Publishers) Ltd 1966 | *The Two Towers* © George Allen & Unwin (Publishers) Ltd | 1966 | *The Return of the King* © George Allen & Unwin | (Publishers) Ltd 1966 | CN 1579 | Printed in Great Britain by | Mackays of Chatham PLC, Chatham, Kent'; [5] poem, 'Three Rings for the Elven-kings' etc.; [6] '[*key map of Middle-earth*] | *The Maps of Middle-earth* | [*notes on map sections and on Shire map*]'; 7–10 foreword; 11–13 table of contents; 14–32 prologue; [33] 'THE FELLOWSHIP | OF THE RING | [*swelled rule*] | *being the first part of* | *The Lord of the Rings*'; [34] map, *A Part of the Shire*; [35] 'BOOK I | [*swelled rule*]'; [36] sectional map 1; 37–268 text; [269] 'BOOK II | [*swelled rule*]'; [270] sectional map 2; 271–494 text; [495] 'THE TWO TOWERS | [*swelled rule*] | *being the third* [sic] *part of* | *The Lord of the Rings*'; [496] blank; [497] BOOK III | [*swelled rule*]'; [498] sectional map 3; 499–723 text; [724] blank; [725] 'BOOK IV | [*swelled rule*]'; [726] sectional map 4; 727–891 text; [892] blank; [893] 'THE RETURN OF | THE KING | [*swelled rule*] | *being the third part of The Lord of the* | *Rings*'; [894] blank; [895] 'BOOK V | [*swelled rule*]'; [896–7] map of Rohan, Gondor, and Mordor; [898] blank; 899–1235 text; 1236–44 appendix, 'A Part of the Tale of Aragorn and Arwen'; [1245–8] blank.

Illustrations, by Tolkien (as for A5a.i): Ring inscription, p. 73; Moria gate, p. [374]; Balin's tomb inscription, p. 390.

Wove paper. Mottled blue-green-grey paper over boards, dark green imitation leather spine with raised bands. Gilt vertical rule stamped on leatherette on upper and lower covers. Stamped on upper cover in gilt, within a thin gilt single rule frame, against a dark grey panel outlined by a thick gilt rule: 'THE LORD OF | THE

RINGS | [*rule*] [*diamond*] [*rule*] | J. R. R. Tolkien'. Stamped on spine in gilt: '[*thick rule*] | THE LORD | OF THE | RINGS | [*2 thick rules*] | [*thin rule*] | J. R. R. | TOLKIEN | [*thin rule*] | [*2 thick rules*] | [*thin rule*] | GUILD | CLASSICS | [*thin rule*] | [*2 thick rules*] | [*publisher's "gp" device within a decorative frame*] | [*thick rule*]'. Wove mottled blue-green-grey endpapers. Green/white headbands. Dark green ribbon marker. All edges trimmed and unstained.

Published December? 1990 at £10.95; number of copies not known.

Reset, based on (uncorrected) A5f.
   Maps as for A5e.

v. Large-print edition (1990):

i. THE FELLOWSHIP OF THE RING:

[*1 line in certar, between double rules*] | The Fellowship of | the Ring | Being the First Part of | THE LORD OF THE | RINGS | J. R. R. TOLKIEN | [*publisher's 'ISIS CLEAR TYPE CLASSIC' device*] | [*2 lines in tengwar, between double rules*]

xxxiv, 526 pp. Collation: [1–16¹⁶17⁸18¹⁶]. 23.2 × 15.6 cm.

[i] 'THE FELLOWSHIP OF THE RING'; [ii] 'Other titles available in this series: | ISIS Clear Print | THE TWO TOWERS | THE RETURN OF THE KING | Windrush Large Print | THE HOBBIT | ISIS Audio | THE FELLOWSHIP OF THE RING | THE TWO TOWERS | THE RETURN OF THE KING'; [iii] title; [iv] 'Copyright © George Allen & Unwin (Publishers) Ltd, 1966 | First published in Great Britain 1954 by George Allen & Unwin | Published in Large Print 1990 by Clio Press, 55 St Thomas' | Street, Oxford, OX1 1JG, by arrangement with Unwin Hyman | Ltd and Houghton Mifflin Co. | All rights reserved | [*British Library Cataloguing in Publication Data*] | ISBN 1-85089-414-0 | Printed and bound by Hartnolls Ltd., Bodmin, Cornwall | Cover designed by CGS Studios, Cheltenham'; [v] 'THE LORD OF THE RINGS | [*poem, "Three Rings for the Elven-kings" etc.*].'; [vi] blank; [vii–xi] foreword; [xii] blank; [xiii] table of contents; [xiv] blank; [xv–xxxiv] prologue; [1] 'BOOK I'; [2] blank; 3–261 text; [262] blank; [263] 'BOOK II'; [264] blank; 265–513 text; [514] blank; [515–23] publisher's advertisements; [524–6] blank. Map, *The West of Middle-earth at the End of the Third Age*, in red and black on folded leaf tipped in at p. [515].

Illustrations, by Tolkien (as for A5a.i): Ring inscription, p. 42; Moria gate, p. 380; Balin's tomb inscription, p. 397.

Wove paper. Bound in white cloth over boards. Printed or stamped on upper cover: '[*printed in black:*] [*publisher's "ISIS CLEAR TYPE CLASSIC" device*] | The Fellowship | of the Ring | [*printed in red:*] Being the first part of The Lord of the Rings | ["Ring and Eye" device, printed in red and black and stamped in gilt] | [*printed in black:*] J. R. R. TOLKIEN'. Printed on spine in black: '[*publisher's "ISIS CLEAR TYPE CLASSIC" device*] | [*running down:*] The Fellowship of the Ring [*parallel to the title:*] J. R. R. TOLKIEN'. Printed on lower cover in black: '[*blurb*] | ISBN 1 85089 414 0'. Wove endpapers. No headbands. All edges trimmed and unstained.

ii. THE TWO TOWERS:

[*1 line in certar, between double rules*] | The Two Towers | Being the Second Part of | THE LORD OF THE | RINGS | J. R. R. TOLKIEN | [*publisher's 'ISIS CLEAR TYPE CLASSIC' device*] | [*2 lines in tengwar, between double rules*] x, 438 pp. Collation: [1–14^{16}]. 23.3 × 15.6 cm.

[i] 'THE TWO TOWERS'; [ii] 'Other titles available in this series: | ISIS Clear Print | THE FELLOWSHIP OF THE RING | THE RETURN OF THE KING | Windrush Large Print | THE HOBBIT | ISIS Audio | THE FELLOWSHIP OF THE RING | THE TWO TOWERS | THE RETURN OF THE KING'; [iii] title; [iv] 'Copyright © George Allen & Unwin (Publishers) Ltd, 1966 | First published in Great Britain 1954 by George Allen & Unwin | Published in Large Print 1990 by Clio Press, 55 St Thomas' | Street, Oxford, OX1 1JG, by arrangement with Unwin Hyman | Ltd and Houghton Mifflin Co. | All rights reserved | [*British Library Cataloguing in Publication Data*] | ISBN 1-85089-419-1 | Printed and bound by Hartnolls Ltd., Bodmin, Cornwall | Cover designed by CGS Studios, Cheltenham'; [v] 'THE LORD OF THE RINGS | [*poem, "Three Rings for the Elven-kings" etc.*].'; [vi] blank; [vii–viii] synopsis; [ix] table of contents; [x] blank; [1] 'BOOK III'; [2] blank; 3–250 text; [251] 'BOOK IV'; [252] blank; 253–438 text. Map, *The West of Middle-earth at the End of the Third Age*, in red and black on folded leaf tipped onto recto, back free endpaper.

Wove paper. Bound in white cloth over boards. Printed or stamped on upper cover: '[*printed in black:*] [*publisher's "ISIS CLEAR TYPE CLASSIC" device*] | The | Two Towers | [*printed in red:*] *Being the second part of The Lord of the Rings* | [*"Ring and Eye" device, printed in red and black and stamped in gilt*] | [*printed in black:*] J. R. R. TOLKIEN'. Printed on spine in black: '[*publisher's "ISIS CLEAR TYPE CLASSIC" device*] | [*running down:*] The Two Towers [*parallel to the title:*] J. R. R. TOLKIEN'. Printed on lower cover in black: '[*blurb*] | ISBN 1 85089 419 1'. Wove endpapers. No headbands. All edges trimmed and unstained.

iii. THE RETURN OF THE KING:

[*1 line in certar, between double rules*] | The Return of | the King | Being the Third Part of | THE LORD OF THE | RINGS | J. R. R. TOLKIEN | [*publisher's 'ISIS CLEAR TYPE CLASSIC' device*] | [*2 lines in tengwar, between double rules*]

xii, 548 pp. Collation: [1–15^{16}16^{8}17–18^{16}]. 23.3 × 15.4 cm.

[i] 'THE RETURN OF THE KING'; [ii] 'Other titles available in this series: | ISIS Clear Print | THE FELLOWSHIP OF THE RING | THE TWO TOWERS | Windrush Large Print | THE HOBBIT | ISIS Audio | THE TWO TOWERS | THE FELLOWSHIP OF THE RING | THE RETURN OF THE KING'; [iii] title; [iv] 'Copyright © George Allen & Unwin (Publishers) Ltd, 1966 | First published in Great Britain 1955 by George Allen & Unwin | (Publishers) Ltd | Published in Large Print 1990 by Clio Press, 55 St Thomas' | Street, Oxford, OX1 1JG, by arrangement with Unwin Hyman | Ltd and Houghton Mifflin Co. | All rights reserved | [*British Library Cataloguing in Publication Data*] | ISBN 1-85089-429-8 | Printed and bound by Hartnolls Ltd., Bodmin, Cornwall | Cover designed by CGS Studios, Cheltenham'; [v] 'THE LORD OF THE RINGS | [*poem, "Three Rings for the Elven-kings" etc.*].'; [vi] blank; [vii–x] synopsis; [xi–xii] table of contents; [1] 'BOOK V'; [2] blank; 3–198 text; [199] 'BOOK VI'; [200] blank; 201–382 text; 383–544 appendices; [545] blank; [546–8] publisher's advertisements. Map of Rohan, Gondor, and Mordor, in red and black on folded leaf tipped in at p. [545].

Wove paper. Bound in white cloth over boards. Printed or stamped on upper cover: '[*printed in black:*] [*publisher's "ISIS CLEAR TYPE CLASSIC" device*] | The Return of | the King | [*printed in red:*] *Being the third part of The Lord of the Rings* | [*"Ring and Eye" device, printed in red and black and stamped in gilt*] | [*printed in black:*] J. R. R. TOLKIEN'. Printed on spine in black: '[*publisher's "ISIS CLEAR TYPE CLASSIC" device*] | [*running down:*] The Return of the King [*parallel to the title:*] J. R. R. TOLKIEN'. Printed on lower cover in black: '[*blurb*] | ISBN 1 85089 429 8'. Wove endpapers. No headbands. All edges trimmed and unstained.

Published December 1990 at £19.45 (£14.95 to libraries) per volume; 1,250 copies of each volume printed.

Reset, based on a later, corrected impression of A5e. In the appendices, the family trees, the Shire calendar, and the tengwar and Angerthas tables were photographically reproduced from A5e.

The general map of Middle-earth is the version redrawn by Christopher Tolkien for *UT* (A17). Shire map and map of Rohan, Gondor, and Mordor as for A5e.

w. New (trade) edition (1991):

[*1 line in certar, between double rules*] | ['*JRRT' device, in white and black*] | [*in black:*] TOLKIEN | THE | LORD | OF THE | RINGS | J R R TOLKIEN | *Illustrated by Alan Lee* | [*publisher's 'fire and water' device*] | HarperCollins*Publishers* | [*2 lines in tengwar, between double rules*]

1200 pp. + 50 plates. Collation: [1–4¹⁶5⁸6¹⁶7–10⁸11–12¹⁶13–17⁸18–20¹⁶21–3⁸ 24¹⁶25⁸26–7¹⁶28–31⁸32¹⁶33–9⁸40¹⁶41–50⁸51–5¹⁶]. 24.5 × 16.2 cm.

[i–ii] blank; [1] 'THE | LORD | OF THE | RINGS'; [2] '*also by* J. R. R. Tolkien | [*23 titles, beginning with* ATB, *ending with* The War of the Ring] | With Donald Swann | THE ROAD GOES EVER ON'; [3] title; [4] 'HarperCollins*Publishers* | 77–85 Fulham Palace Road, | Hammersmith, London W6 8JB | THE FELLOWSHIP OF THE RING first published by George Allen & Unwin | 1954, second edition published 1966 | THE TWO TOWERS first published by George Allen & Unwin 1954, | second edition published 1966 | THE RETURN OF THE KING first published by George Allen & Unwin | 1955, second edition published 1966 | THE FELLOWSHIP OF THE RING © George Allen & Unwin (Publishers) Ltd | 1954, 1966 | THE TWO TOWERS © George Allen & Unwin (Publishers) Ltd 1954, | 1966 | THE RETURN OF THE KING © George Allen & Unwin (Publishers) Ltd | 1954, 1966 | First published in a single volume 1968 | Illustrations © Alan Lee 1991 | [*at left, "JRRT" device; at right:*] ™©1990 Frank Richard Williamson and Christopher Reuel | Tolkien, executors of the estate of the late John Ronald | Reuel Tolkien | [*below the preceding:*] A CIP catalogue record for this book | is available from the British Library | ISBN 0-261-10230-3 | Printed in Hong Kong | [*notice of restrictions*]'; [5] poem, 'Three Rings for the Elven-kings' etc.; [6]–8 table of contents; [9]–12 foreword; [13]–28 prologue; [29] 'THE FELLOWSHIP | OF THE RING | [*rule*] | *Being the first part of* | THE LORD OF THE RINGS | [*Tolkien centenary device, with blank centre*]'; [30] map, *A Part of the Shire*; [31] '[*1 line in certar, between double rules*] | BOOK I | [*2 lines in tengwar, between double rules*]'; [32] blank; [33]–231 text; [232] blank; [233] '[*1 line in certar, between double rules*] | BOOK II | [*2 lines in tengwar, between double rules*]'; [234] blank; [235]–427 text; [428] blank; [429] 'THE TWO | TOWERS | [*rule*] | *Being the second part of* | THE LORD OF THE RINGS | [*Tolkien centenary device, with blank centre*]'; [430] blank; [431] '[*1 line in certar, between double rules*] | BOOK III | [*2 lines in tengwar, between double rules*]'; [432] blank; [433]–624 text; [625] '[*1 line in certar, between double rules*] | BOOK IV | [*2 lines in tengwar, between double rules*]'; [626] blank; [627]–770 text; [771–2] blank; [773] 'THE RETURN OF | THE KING | [*rule*] | *Being the third part of* | THE LORD OF THE RINGS | [*Tolkien* *centenary device, with blank centre*]'; [774] blank; [775] '[*1 line in certar, between double rules*] | BOOK V | [*2 lines in tengwar, between double rules*]'; [776] blank; [777]–927 text; [928] blank; [929] '[*1 line in certar, between double rules*] | BOOK VI | [*2 lines in tengwar, between double rules*]'; [930] blank; [931]–1069 text; [1070]–1172 appendices; [1173]–93 index; [1194–5] map of Rohan, Gondor, and Mordor; [1196] key map, *The West of Middle-earth at the End of the Third Age*; [1197–1200] sectional maps. Colour plates by Alan Lee inserted facing pp. [1], [33], 64, 96, 128, 144, 176, [192], 208, 224, 240, 272, 304, 320, 336, 352, 268, 284, 416, 448, 480, 496, 512, [528], 560, 576, 608, 640, 656, 672, 688, 704, 736, 752, 768, 784, 800, 816, 832, 848, 880, 896, 929, 944, 960, 976, 992, 1008, 1024, 1040.

Illustrations by Tolkien (as for A5a.i): Ring inscription, p. 63; Moria gate, p. [323]; Balin's tomb inscription, p. 337.

Wove paper. Bound in brown cloth over boards. 'JRRT' monogram stamped on upper cover in gilt. Stamped on spine in gilt: 'J R R | TOLKIEN | [*"JRRT" device (reversed, brown on gilt)*] | THE | LORD | OF THE | RINGS | ILLUSTRATED BY | ALAN LEE | [*publisher's "fire and water" device*] | Harper | Collins'. Tan wove endpapers. Red headbands. Red ribbon marker. All edges trimmed and unstained.

Dust jacket, wove paper. Printed or stamped on upper cover: '[*wraparound repeated inscription in certar, from the top of the title page, printed in black against a gilt-stamped background*] | [*wraparound thin rule, printed in black*] | [*wraparound thick rule, printed in black*] | [*printed colour illustration by Alan Lee, of Frodo, Sam, and Gollum above the Gate of Mordor; within the illustration, against an oval white panel outlined by a thick-thin gilt-stamped rule, the panel and rule partly overlapped by the illustration:*] [*stamped in gilt:*] J R R | TOLKIEN | [*printed in red:*] THE LORD | OF THE RINGS | [*printed in black:*] Illustrated by | ALAN LEE | [*below the illustration:*] [*wraparound thick rule, printed in black*] | [*wraparound thin rule, printed in black*] | [*wraparound repeated inscription in certar, as at top of cover, printed in black against a gilt-stamped background*]'. Printed on spine, between wraparound inscription and rules at top and bottom: '[*against a black panel within a single rule frame:*] [*"JRRT" device, in black and white*] | [*in white:*] TOLKIEN | [*below the frame:*] [*in red:*] J R R | TOLKIEN | [*in black:*] THE LORD | OF THE RINGS | [*in red:*] | Illustrated by | ALAN LEE | [*colour illustration by Alan Lee, detail from illustration of the battle of Helm's Deep (plate facing p. 560), outlined in red, within a single rule oval*] | [*publisher's "fire and water" device, in red and blue*] | [*in black:*] Harper | Collins'. Printed or stamped on lower cover, between wraparound inscription and rules at top and bottom, against colour illustration by Alan Lee, detail from illustration of a Middle-earth landscape (plate facing p. 576): '[*Tolkien centenary device, printed in red, white, and black and stamped in gilt*] | [*against a white panel, in black:*] ISBN 0-261-10230-3 | [*bar code*]'. Printed on front flap: '[*"JRRT" device*] | [*poem, "Three Rings for the Elven-kings" etc., in red*] | [*blurb, in black with initial "I" in red*] | [*in black:*] This edition contains fifty full colour illustrations specially | commissioned from artist Alan Lee to commemorate the | centenary of J. R. R. Tolkien's birth. It also includes Tolkien's | appendices and maps. | 0-044-480679 £30.00'. Printed on back flap: '[*photograph of Tolkien*] | [*note on Tolkien, in black with initial "J" in red*] | [*in black:*] The Lord of the Rings was first published in three | volumes between 1954 and 1955, to great acclaim. | [*4 quotations, by Bernard Levin, W. H. Auden, and C. S. Lewis, and from the* Sunday Times] | [*note on Lee*] | HarperCollins*Publishers*'.

Published 19 September 1991 at £30.00; 38,000 copies printed. A5w, x, y, and z were printed simultaneously in Great Britain.

Typeset chiefly as for A5h. The final paragraph of the foreword, erroneously retained from A5h, describes the binding of the India paper edition (A5h).

The general map of Middle-earth is the version redrawn by Christopher Tolkien for *UT* (A17). Shire map and map of Rohan, Gondor, and Mordor as for A5e.

Published in a book club edition in 1991 by Book Club Associates, 27,000 copies printed with A5w–z.

x. New Houghton Mifflin (limited) edition (1991):

[*1 line in certar, between double rules*] | [*publisher's 'JRRT' device, in white and black*] | [*in black:*] TOLKIEN | THE | LORD | OF THE | RINGS | J R R | TOLKIEN | *Illustrated by Alan Lee* | [*publisher's 'dolphin' device*] | Boston | Houghton Mifflin Company | 1991 | [*2 lines in tengwar, between double rules*]

Pagination, collation, and size as for A5w.

Contents as for A5w, except pp. [i] '[*Tolkien centenary device*] | THE LORD | OF THE RINGS | J R R | TOLKIEN | *Illustrated with fifty original paintings* | *by Alan Lee* | This specially bound and slipcased edition of | *The Lord of the Rings* has been published to celebrate the | centenary of J. R. R. Tolkien's birth on January 3, 1892. | This edition has been limited to 250 copies | for Houghton Mifflin Company, Boston, | each one numbered and signed by the artist. | THIS COPY NUMBER | [*dotted line, with copy number and edition added in pen, e.g.* "174/250"] | [*dotted line, with the artist's signature added in pen*]'; [3] title, as above; and [4] 'Illustrations copyright © 1991 by Alan Lee | "The Fellowship of the Ring" and "The Two Towers": | Copyright © 1954, 1965 by J. R. R. Tolkien. | Copyright © renewed 1982 by Christopher R. Tolkien, | Michael H. R. Tolkien, John F. R. Tolkien | and Priscilla M. A. R. Tolkien. | "The Return of the King": | Copyright © 1955, 1965 by J. R. R. Tolkien. | Copyright © renewed 1983 by Christopher R. Tolkien, | Michael H. R. Tolkien, John F. R. Tolkien | and Priscilla M. A. R. Tolkien. | ALL RIGHTS RESERVED. | For information about permission to reproduce selections from this | book, write to Permissions, Houghton Mifflin Company, 2 Park Street, | Boston, Massachusetts 02108. | CIP data is available. | ISBN 0 395 60423 0 | Printed in Hong Kong | The text of this edition incorporates all corrections and revisions | intended by its author and constitutes an authoritative edition of The | Lord of the Rings, uniform with that published in Great Britain by | HarperCollins*Publishers*. | [*at left*, "*JRRT*" *device with trademark symbol; at right:*] is a trademark of Frank Richard Williamson | and Christopher Reuel Tolkien, executors of | the Estate of the late John Ronald Reuel Tolkien.'

Illustrations by Tolkien as for A5w. Illustrations by Lee as for A5w, except that the first plate faces p. [i].

Wove paper. Bound in grey-blue cloth over boards, dark blue leather spine. Vertical rule stamped on leather on upper and lower covers, in silver. 'JRRT' monogram stamped on upper cover in silver. Stamped on spine in silver: 'J R R | TOLKIEN | [*"JRRT" device (reversed blue on silver)*] | THE | LORD | OF THE | RINGS | *Illustrated by* | ALAN LEE | [*publisher's "dolphin" device*] | HOUGHTON | MIFFLIN'. Blue, grey, white 'marbled' endpapers. Dark blue/silver headbands. Red ribbon marker. All edges trimmed and silvered.

Slipcase, grey-blue cloth over boards. Publisher's 'JRRT' device stamped on left and right sides in silver.

Published 12 November 1991 at $250.00; 250 copies printed.

Typeset as for A5w, except pp. [i], [3–4].
  Maps as for A5w.

y. New Houghton Mifflin (trade) edition (1991):

[*1 line in certar, between double rules*] | ['*JRRT' device, in white and black*] | [*in black:*] TOLKIEN | THE | LORD | OF THE | RINGS | J R R | TOLKIEN | *Illustrated by Alan Lee* | [*publisher's 'dolphin' device*] | Boston | Houghton Mifflin Company | 1991 | [*2 lines in tengwar, between double rules*]

1200 pp. + 50 plates. Collation as for A5w. 24.5 × 16.2 cm.

Contents as for A5x, except pp. [i–ii] (limitation statement) omitted.

Illustrations as for A5w.

Wove paper. Binding as for A5w, except imprint at foot of spine: '[*publisher's "dolphin" device*] | HOUGHTON | MIFFLIN'.

Dust jacket, wove paper. Printed or stamped on upper cover: '[*wraparound repeated inscription in certar, from the top of the title page, printed in black against a gilt-stamped background*] | [*wraparound thin rule, printed in black*] | [*wraparound thick rule, printed in black*] | [*stamped in gilt within a gilt-stamped single rule frame, against a grey-blue panel, against a printed colour illustration by Alan Lee, of Frodo, Sam, and Gollum above the Gate of Mordor:*] J R R TOLKIEN | [*rule*] | THE LORD OF | [*rule*] | THE RINGS | [*rule*] | illustrated by ALAN LEE | [*below the illustration:*] [*wraparound thick rule, printed in black*] | [*wraparound thin rule, printed in black*] | [*wraparound repeated inscription in certar, as at top of cover, printed in black against a gilt-stamped background*]'. Printed or stamped on spine against a grey-blue background, between wraparound inscription and rules at top and bottom: '[*printed against a black panel outlined in white:*] ["*JRRT*" *device, in black and white*] | [*in white:*] TOLKIEN | [*below the outlined panel:*] [*stamped in gilt within a gilt-stamped single rule frame:*] J R R TOLKIEN | [*rule*] | THE LORD OF | [*rule*] | THE RINGS | [*rule*] | illustrated by ALAN LEE | [*printed below the frame:*] [*colour illustration by Alan Lee, detail from illustration of the battle of Helm's Deep (plate facing p. 560), outlined in white*]'. Printed or stamped on lower cover, between wraparound inscription and rules at top and bottom, against colour illustration by Alan Lee, detail from illustration of a Middle-earth landscape (plate facing p. 576): '[*Tolkien centenary device, printed in grey-blue, white, and black and stamped in gilt*] | [*in black:*] [*at left:*] 6-97047 [*at right, against a white panel:*] ISBN 0-395-59511-8 | [*bar codes*]'. Printed on front flap: '$60.00 | ["*JRRT*" *device*] | [*blurb*] | 1091'. Printed on back flap: '[*photograph of Tolkien*] | [*note on Tolkien*] | [*note on Lee*] | [*3 quotations, by C. S. Lewis, Naomi Mitchison, and Dan Wickenden*] | Jacket paintings copyright © 1991 by Alan Lee. | Houghton Mifflin Company | 2 Park Street, Boston, Massachusetts 02108'.

Published 12 November 1991 at $60.00; 25,000 copies printed.

Typeset as for A5x, except p. [i] blank.
  Maps as for A5x.

z. New (limited) edition (1991):

[*1 line in certar, between double rules*] | ['*JRRT' device, in white and black*] | [*in black:*] TOLKIEN | THE | LORD | OF THE | RINGS | J R R | TOLKIEN | *Illustrated by Alan Lee* | [*publisher's 'fire and water' device*] | HarperCollins*Publishers* | [*2 lines in tengwar, between double rules*] ii, 1200 pp. + 50 plates. Collation: [π1 1–4^{16}5^{8}6^{16}7–10^{8}11–12^{16}13–17^{8}18–20^{16} 21–3^{8}24^{16}25^{8}26–7^{16}28–31^{8}32^{16}33–9^{8}40^{16}41–50^{8}51–5^{16}]. 24.4 × 16.2 cm.

Contents as for A5w, except pp. [i] '[*Tolkien centenary device*] | THE LORD | OF THE RINGS | J R R | TOLKIEN | *Illustrated with fifty original paintings* | *by Alan Lee* | This specially bound and slipcased edition of | *The Lord of the Rings* has been published to celebrate the | centenary of J. R. R. Tolkien's birth on January 3, 1892. | This edition has been limited to 250 copies | for HarperCollins*Publishers*, London | each one numbered and signed by the artist. | THIS COPY NUMBER | [*dotted line, with copy number and edition added in pen, e.g.* "226/250"] | [*dotted line, with the artist's signature added in pen*]'; and [4] 'HarperCollins*Publishers* | 77–85 Fulham Palace Road, | Hammersmith, London W6 8JB | This special Limited Edition | Published by HarperCollins*Publishers* 1991 | THE FELLOWSHIP OF THE RING first published by George Allen & Unwin | 1954, second edition published 1966 | THE TWO TOWERS first published by George Allen & Unwin 1954, | second edition published 1966 | THE RETURN OF THE KING first published by George Allen & Unwin | 1955, second edition published 1966 | THE FELLOWSHIP OF THE RING © George Allen & Unwin (Publishers) Ltd | 1954, 1966 | THE TWO TOWERS © George Allen & Unwin (Publishers) Ltd 1954, | 1966 | THE RETURN OF THE KING © George Allen & Unwin (Publishers) Ltd | 1954, 1966 | First published in a single volume 1968 | Illustrations © Alan Lee 1991 | [*at left, "JRRT" device; at right:*] ™©1990 Frank Richad [*sic*] Williamson and Christopher Reuel | Tolkien, executors of the estate of the late John Ronald | Reuel Tolkien | [*below the preceding:*] A CIP catalogue record for this book | is available from the British Library | ISBN 0 261 10274 5 | Printed in Hong Kong | [*notice of restrictions*]'.

Illustrations as for A5x.

Wove paper. Binding as for A5x, except imprint at foot of spine: '[*publisher's "fire and water" device*] | Harper | Collins'.

Slipcase as for A5x.

Published 12 December 1991 at £150; 250 copies printed.

Typeset as for A5w, except pp. [i], [4].
    Maps as for A5w.
    An additional 200 copies of A5z were printed for Australia, identical except for a variant limitation statement.

A6   THE ADVENTURES OF TOM BOMBADIL   1962

a. First edition:

J. R. R. TOLKIEN | THE ADVENTURES | OF TOM BOMBADIL | *and other verses* | *from* The Red Book | [*illustration, in black and orange*] | [*in black:*] WITH ILLUSTRATIONS BY | PAULINE BAYNES | [*illustration, in black and orange*] | [*in black:*] London | GEORGE ALLEN & UNWIN LTD | RUSKIN HOUSE MUSEUM STREET

64 pp. Collation: [1–4^8]. 22.2 × 14.1 cm.

[1] 'THE ADVENTURES | OF TOM BOMBADIL'; [2] illustration, in black and orange; [3] title; [4] 'FIRST PUBLISHED IN 1962 | [*notice of restrictions under copyright*] | © *George Allen & Unwin Ltd* 1962 | PRINTED IN GREAT BRITAIN | *in* 12 *point Garamond type* | BY JARROLD AND SONS LTD | NORWICH'; [5]

table of contents; [6] illustration; 7–9 preface; [10] illustration; 11–[64] text and illustrations. Illustrations on pp. [14], [22], [26], [35], 38, 42, 47, [50], 51, [55] also printed in black and orange.

Order of poems: 'The Adventures of Tom Bombadil'; 'Bombadil Goes Boating'; 'Errantry'; 'Princess Mee'; 'The Man in the Moon Stayed Up Too Late'; 'The Man in the Moon Came Down Too Soon'; 'The Stone Troll'; 'Perry-the-Winkle'; 'The Mewlips'; 'Oliphaunt'; 'Cat'; 'Fastitocalon'; 'Shadow-Bride'; 'The Hoard'; 'The Sea-Bell'; 'The Last Ship'.

Wove paper. Bound in paper over boards. Wraparound colour illustration by Pauline Baynes, of Tom Bombadil, a mariner, and birds, fishes, shells, etc. against a background of earth, sea, and sky. Printed on upper cover within open area of illustration: 'J. R. R. TOLKIEN | The Adventures | of | Tom Bombadil | ILLUS-TRATED BY | PAULINE BAYNES'. Printed on spine, running up, against the illustration: 'J. R. R. TOLKIEN Tom Bombadil'. Wove endpapers. No headbands. All edges trimmed and unstained.

Dust-jacket, wove paper. Covers identical with binding. Printed on front flap: '[*blurb*] | GEORGE ALLEN AND UNWIN | 40 *Museum Street* | London, W.C.1 | *Adventures of Tom Bombadil* | J. R. R. Tolkien | George Allen & Unwin Ltd. | 13s 6d net | in U.K. only'. Printed on back flap: 'J. R. R. TOLKIEN | THE LORD OF THE RINGS | THE FELLOWSHIP OF THE RING | THE TWO TOWERS | THE RETURN OF THE KING | [*blurb*] | FARMER GILES OF HAM | *Also illustrated by Pauline Baynes* | THE HOBBIT | *Illustrated by the author* [quotation from the Times Literary Supplement] | *Printed in Great Britain*'.

Published 22 November 1962 at 13s. 6d.; 10,000 copies planned (December 1961).

On 16 December 1937 Tolkien wrote to Stanley Unwin enclosing a copy of his poem 'The Adventures of Tom Bombadil', which had appeared in the *Oxford Magazine* in 1934 (C27). He asked: 'Do you think Tom Bombadil, the spirit of the (vanishing) Oxford and Berkshire countryside, could be made into the hero of a story [as a successor to *The Hobbit*]?' Unwin put this question in turn to his young son, Rayner, who reported:

> I think that *Tom Bombadil* would make quite a good story, but as *The Hobbit* has already been very successful I think the story of Old Took's great grand-uncle, Bullroarer, who rode a horse and charged the goblins of Mount Gram in the battle of the Green Fields and knocked King Golfimbil's [*sic*] head off with a wooden club would be better. This story could be a continuation of *The Hobbit*, for Bilbo could tell it to Gandalf and Balin in his hobbit hole when they visited him.

Neither Rayner's preference nor a prose tale of Tom Bombadil was written, but the character was introduced into *The Lord of the Rings*.

In a staff memo of October 1937 Stanley Unwin noted that Tolkien had 'a great deal of verse of one kind and another which would probably be worth looking at.' But more than two decades passed before Allen & Unwin published a collection of his poetry. In 1961 his aunt, Jane Neave, asked him to 'get out a small book with Tom Bombadil at the heart of it, the sort of size of book that we old 'uns can afford to buy for Christmas presents' (quoted in *Biography*, p. 244). Though Tolkien did not feel inclined to write any more about the character, he thought that his original poem 'might make a pretty booklet of the kind you [Aunt Jane] would like if each verse could be illustrated by Pauline Baynes', who had so successfully illustrated *Farmer Giles of Ham* (letter of 4 October 1961). In a letter of 11 October 1961 to Rayner Unwin he suggested the book as 'an interim amusement', i.e. between *The Lord of the Rings* and the still unfinished *Silmarillion*, 'and also . . . a gift-book not so costly to avuncular or auntly pockets'. 'The Adventures of Tom Bombadil', he thought, was very pictorial, and might do well with Baynes' illustrations. Unwin agreed, hoping for a work as long as *Farmer Giles* which could be published as a companion piece. But the poem ran to only 127 lines, and Tolkien had in mind a very small book 'with very little letter press and lots of pictures, rather like a Beatrix Potter with a difference' (letter to Rayner Unwin, 15 November 1961, referring to Potter's children's books sized for small hands). Unwin suggested that 'Tom Bombadil' appear together with other 'occasional verses', 'not just the ones contained in *The Lord of the Rings* and *The Hobbit*, but ones like "Errantry". It would not need a great number, but enough to make a book and not a pamphlet' (letter to Tolkien, 2 November 1961).

On 15 November Tolkien reported to Unwin that he had had copies made of 'any poems that might conceivably see the light or (somewhat tidied up) be presented again [having been previously published]. The harvest is not rich, for one thing there is not much that really goes together with Tom Bombadil'. With his letter he sent copies of 'Errantry' (revised from C24), 'The Man in the Moon Came Down Too Soon' (revised from *A Northern Venture*, B4), 'Perry-the-Winkle' (revised from an unpublished poem, 'The Bumpus', see C22), 'The Dragon's Visit' (cf. C29), 'The Sea-Bell' (revised from 'Looney', C26), and 'The Hoard' (revised from 'Iumonna Gold Galdre Bewunden', C31). On 18 November Tolkien sent Unwin another poem, which had never been printed 'and very likely does not deserve to be': 'Princess Mee' (cf. 'Princess Ni' in *Leeds University Verse*, B5). The poems were sent to Pauline Baynes to read 'and see if she catches fire', Unwin wrote to Tolkien on 18 November. 'If she does I see no reason why we should not work out a little volume but I think it would be wise to include most, if not all, those you have sent us as very small books tend to look horribly expensive.' By 6 December Baynes had agreed to illustrate the book, though she does not seem to have been formally offered the commission until May 1962.

Production began at once, despite Tolkien's misgivings about the incompatibility of some of the poems to one another and about 'the vaguer, more subjective and least successful piece labelled The Sea-Bell' (letter to Rayner Unwin, 8 December 1961). On 12 January 1962 Unwin sent Tolkien a specimen page with an estimate for a sixty-four-page book. On 5 February 1962 Tolkien wrote to Unwin that he had again 'raked over my collection of old verses; there are some that might be made use of with a thorough re-handling.' With this letter he sent four more poems: 'Firiel' (C25), 'The Trees of Kortirion' (see *BLT1*, A21, pp. 39–43), 'Shadow-Bride', and 'Knocking at the Door' (C30). 'I think—apart from the question of whether it is good or bad in itself— "Firiel" might go with the others that I have sent. "The Trees" is too long and too ambitious, and even if considered good enough would probably upset the boat. I wonder, if a few more things are really required, whether one or two of the pieces taken from my collection and put into *The Lord of the Rings*, could not be included.' As examples of the latter he cited 'Oliphaunt' and 'The Ostler's Cat', i.e. 'The Man in the Moon Stayed Up Too Late'. Unwin agreed that 'The Trees of Kortirion' did not fit with the rest of the poems, and he did not object to including pieces from *The Lord of the Rings*. Christopher Tolkien has speculated that his father was revising 'The Little House of Lost Play' (A21) for *The Adventures of Tom Bombadil*, but it was not included.

On 12 April 1962 Tolkien wrote to Rayner Unwin that he had 'given every moment that I could spare to the "poems"' but that he had 'lost all confidence in these things, and all judgement, and unless Pauline Baynes can be inspired by them, I cannot see them making a "book". I do not see why she should be inspired, though I fervently hope that she will be. Some of the things may be good in their way, and all of them privately amuse me; but elderly hobbits are easily pleased.' He had now made an arrangement of sixteen poems, presumably the selection finally published—now including, therefore, 'The Man in the Moon Stayed Up Too Late', 'The Stone Troll', and 'Oliphaunt' from *The Lord of the Rings* and the bestiary poems 'Cat' (written in 1956 to amuse his granddaughter, Joan Anne) and 'Fastitocalon' (cf. the poem by the same title in the *Stapeldon Magazine*, C20). 'The Dragon's Visit' was excluded from the published book, 'Knocking at the Door' was revised as 'The Mewlips', and 'Firiel', revised, became 'The Last Ship'. Tolkien also wrote a new poem, 'Bombadil Goes Boating', which further integrated that character with the world of *The Lord of the Rings*. 'I am afraid it [the new poem] largely tickles my pedantic fancy,' Tolkien wrote to Unwin on 12 April, 'because of its echo of the Norse Niblung matter (the otter's whisker); and because one of the lines comes straight, incredible though that may seem, from *The Ancrene Wisse*', an edition of which he had just completed (B25).

> I have placed the 16 items in an order: roughly Bilboish, Samlike [after two characters in *LR*], and Dubious. Some kind of order will be necessary, for the scheme of illustration and decoration. But I am not wedded to this arrangement. I am open to criticisms of it—and of any of the items; and to rejections. Miss Baynes is free to re-arrange things to fit her work, if she wishes.
>
> Some kind of foreword might possibly be required. The enclosed is not intended for that purpose! Though one or two of its points might be made more simply. But I found it easier, and more amusing (for myself) to represent to you in the form of a ridiculous editorial fiction what I have done to the verses, and what their references now are. Actually, although a fiction, the relative age, order of writing, and references of the items are pretty nearly represented as they really were.

Rayner Unwin was also amused by the 'foreword', which related the verses to hobbits and *The Lord of the Rings* and which with corrections made in early May 1962 became the finished preface.

The poems were set in type and rough proofs were made for Pauline Baynes' use. Tolkien received galley proofs on 18 June and returned them corrected on 21 June. The illustrations were complete by late August. On 27 August Rayner Unwin sent six full-page illustrations to Tolkien so that he could choose one to be omitted. He chose to exclude the picture for 'The Hoard', criticizing the appearance of the young warrior and the position of the dragon; but in the event, all six illustrations were published. (Baynes took Tolkien's criticism into account when re-illustrating 'The Hoard' for *Poems and Stories* [A16].) Tolkien received proofs of the binding and dust-jacket and a mock-up of the book in mid-September and a finished copy at the end of October. He was disappointed with the binding/jacket illustration now that it was divided into covers and spine, and now that he saw that its orientation should have been reversed, with Tom Bombadil on the front and the ship sailing left, to the west. He was also unhappy with the slab-serif lettering of the cover title, but it was too late to change the design within Allen & Unwin's tight publication schedule.

Only one side of each sheet of the four gatherings of the book was printed in two colours. Pauline Baynes' full-page illustration of cats, meant to accompany 'Cat', was placed on p. [50] to take advantage of the added colour; in this position, however, in the first impression it does not face 'Cat' (text on p. [48]) but bisects 'Fastitocalon' (pp. 49, 51). On 26 October 1962 Rayner Unwin remarked in a letter to Tolkien that 'there is obviously too heavy a weight of illustrations on pages 50 and 51, but this was inevitable as we printed the second colour only on one [side of each] sheet. In the event of a reprint would we have your permission to move the order of the poems a little so as to get the picture of the cat on the same opening as the poem and away from the large Fastitocalon drawing?' Tolkien agreed; and since Allen & Unwin sold approximately 5,000 copies of *ATB* before publication, a second impression was needed immediately and the change was put into effect. 'Cat' was moved to p. [51] and 'Fastitocalon' to pp. 48–9, leaving the Baynes 'cats' in place. The tailpiece to 'Fastitocalon', which in the first impression had orange licks of flame above the campfire wood, was relocated from p. 51, [4_2r], to p. 49, [4_1r], i.e. to the side of the fourth sheet without added colour, and so became fire-less. The table of contents was also altered, to reflect the new order of poems and pagination; but the references to nos. 11 and 12 in the preface were not corrected. See further, John D. Rateliff and Wayne G. Hammond, ' "Fastitocalon" and "Cat": A Problem in Sequencing', *Beyond Bree* (newsletter of the American Mensa Tolkien Special Interest Group), August 1987, pp. 1–2, and additional comment by David Bratman, *Beyond Bree*, September 1987, p. 6.

An error in the last line of 'The Sea-Bell', p. 60, 'men that meet' for 'men that I meet', was corrected sometime after the second impression (1962).

The Adventures of Tom Bombadil was also published in *The Tolkien Reader* (A8), *Farmer Giles of Ham [and] The Adventures of Tom Bombadil* (A12), and *Poems and Stories* (A16). Poems in *ATB* are often reprinted in anthologies.

b. First American edition (1963):

J. R. R. TOLKIEN | THE ADVENTURES | OF TOM BOMBADIL | *and other verses* | *from The Red Book* | [*illustration, in black and orange*] | [*in black:*] WITH ILLUSTRATIONS BY | PAULINE BAYNES | [*illustration in black and orange*] | [*in black:*] [*black letter:*] The Riverside Press Cambridge | [*roman:*] HOUGHTON MIFFLIN COMPANY BOSTON | 1963

64 pp. Collation: [1–4⁸]. 22.1 × 14.0 cm.

[1] 'THE ADVENTURES | OF TOM BOMBADIL'; [2] 'ALSO BY J. R. R. TOLKIEN | [*illustration, in black and orange*] | [6 titles, beginning with H, *ending with* RK, *in black*]'; [3] title; [4] '*First Printing* | *First American Edition 1963* | *Copyright* © *1962 by George Allen & Unwin Ltd.* | *All rights reserved including the right to repro-* | *duce this book or parts thereof in any form* | *Library of Congress Catalog Card Number: 63-10658* | *Printed in the U.S.A.*'; [5] table of contents; [6] illustration; 7–9 preface; [10] illustration; 11–[64] text and illustrations. Illustrations on pp. [14], [22], [26], [35], 38, 42, 47, [50], [55] also printed in black and orange.

Order of poems: 'The Adventures of Tom Bombadil'; 'Bombadil Goes Boating'; 'Errantry'; 'Princess Mee'; 'The Man in the Moon Stayed Up Too Late'; 'The Man in the Moon Came Down Too Soon'; 'The Stone Troll'; 'Perry-the-Winkle'; 'The Mewlips'; 'Oliphaunt'; 'Fastitocalon'; 'Cat'; 'Shadow-Bride'; 'The Hoard'; 'The Sea-Bell'; 'The Last Ship'.

Wove paper. Binding as for A6a, except printed on spine, against the illustration; '[*running up:*] J. R. R. TOLKIEN Tom Bombadil | [*horizontal:*] HMCo.' Wove endpapers. No headbands. All edges trimmed and unstained.

Dust-jacket, wove paper. Covers and spine identical with binding. Printed on front flap: '$3.50 | J. R. R. TOLKIEN | The Adventures | of | Tom Bombadil | ILLUSTRATED BY | PAULINE BAYNES | [*blurb*]'. Blurb continued on back flap.

Published 22 October 1963 at $3.50; 5,000 copies printed.

Typeset as for A6a, except pp. [2–5], and with the order of poems as for the second impression of A6a. The revised order is reflected in the reset table of contents. Illustrations as for A6a, second impression.

On 3 October 1978 Houghton Mifflin published a new 'first' impression of *ATB*, with the title page dated 1978 and the printing code on the copyright page beginning 'A' and ending '1', but with no resetting of text, in a similar binding except with a squared rather than rounded spine and with a blurb and other text on the lower cover.

c. New edition, hardcover copies (1990):

J. R. R. TOLKIEN | THE ADVENTURES | OF TOM BOMBADIL | and other verses | from The Red Book | With illustrations by Roger Garland | [*publisher's 'man drawing a circle' device*] | UNWIN | PAPERBACKS [*sic*] | LONDON SYDNEY WELLINGTON

xiv, 82 pp. Collation: 48 leaves. 19.6 × 12.9 cm.

[i–ii] blank; [iii] 'THE ADVENTURES | OF TOM BOMBADIL'; [iv] 'By J. R. R. Tolkien | [*13 titles, beginning with* H, *ending with* UT] | and, edited by Christopher Tolkien, | *The History of Middle-earth* | [*7 titles, beginning with* The Book of Lost Tales, *ending with* The War of the Ring]'; [v] title; [vi] 'Reset New Format 1990 | This new reset format first published in Great Britain by | Unwin Hyman, an imprint of Unwin Hyman Limited, 1990 | © Unwin Hyman Limited 1990 | [*notice of restrictions*] | [*3 publisher's addresses, London to Wellington*] | A CIP catalogue record for this book is available | from the British Library. | Paperback ISBN 0-04-440726-2 | Hardback ISBN 0-04-440727-0 | [*at left, publisher's "JRRT" device; at right, two lines:*] © Frank Richard Williamson and Christopher Reuel Tolkien, | executors of the Estate of the late John Ronald Reuel Tolkien | Set in 11½ on 14 point Bembo by | Nene Phototypesetters Ltd, Northampton | and printed in Great Britain by | Cox and Wyman Ltd, Reading'; [vii–xii] preface; [xiii] 'THE ADVENTURES | OF TOM BOMBADIL'; [xiv] blank; 1–75 text and illustrations; [76] blank; [77] advertisement of 'The Complete Tolkien Catalogue'; [78] blank; [79] '*Books by J. R. R. Tolkien in Unwin Paperbacks* | [*order form*]'; [80–2] blank.

Wove paper. Bound in black textured paper over boards. Stamped on spine in gilt: '[*running down:*] The Adventures Of Tom Bombadil J. R. R. TOLKIEN | [*horizontal:*] UNWIN | [*publisher's "man drawing a circle" device*] | HYMAN'. Wove pastedowns; no free endpapers. No headbands. All edges trimmed and unstained.

Dust-jacket, wove paper. Printed on upper cover in white, against a colour illustration by Garland, of Tom Bombadil by a stream. Printed against the illustration, in white: 'J. R. R. TOLKIEN | The Adventures | Of Tom Bombadil | Illustrated by Roger Garland | [*publisher's "JRRT" device*]'. Printed on spine: '[*running down:*] [*in green:*] The Adventures Of Tom Bombadil [*in black:*] J. R. R. TOLKIEN | [*horizontal:*] UNWIN | [*publisher's "man drawing a circle" device*] | HYMAN'. Printed on lower cover: '[*colour illustration, of water lilies, detail from upper cover illustration*] | [*in black within a black single rule frame:*] ISBN 0-04-440727-0 | [*bar code*]'. Printed on front flap: "*something close to genius'* | Anthony Thwaite, THE LISTENER | [*blurb*] | [*illustration by Garland, of Bombadil falling in the water, from p. 1*] | [*at left, publisher's "JRRT" device; at right:*] £8.99 net U.K.' Printed on back flap: '[*note on Tolkien*] | [*note on Garland*] | Jacket illustration by Roger Garland'.

Published 23 August 1990 at £8.99; 1,000 copies printed, simultaneous with A6d.

Reset, continuing the error in the preface. Order of poems as for A6a, second impression.

d. New edition, paperback copies (1990):

Sheets, pagination, collation as for A6c. 19.6 × 12.7 cm.

Bound in heavy wove wrappers. Upper cover as for the upper jacket of A6c. Printed on spine: '[*running down:*] [*in green:*] The Adventures Of Tom Bombadil [*in black:*] J. R. R. TOLKIEN | [*horizontal, publisher's "man drawing a circle" device*]'. Printed on lower cover: '[*colour illustration, of two dragonflies, adapted from upper cover illustration*] | [*in black:*] 'something close to genius' | Anthony Thwaite, THE LISTENER | [*blurb*] | [*at left:*] [*publisher's "JRRT" device*] | Cover illustration by Roger Garland | UNWIN PAPERBACKS | CHILDREN/FANTASY | £3.99 net U.K. [*at right, within a single rule frame:*] ISBN 0-04-440726-2 | [*bar code*]'. All edges trimmed and unstained.

Published 23 August 1990 at £3.99; 10,000 copies printed, simultaneous with A6c.

e. New American edition (1991):

J. R. R. TOLKIEN | THE ADVENTURES | OF TOM BOMBADIL | and other verses | from The Red Book | With illustrations by Roger Garland | [*publisher's 'dolphin' device*] | Houghton Mifflin Company | Boston 1991

xiv, 82 pp. Collation: 48 leaves. 19.6 × 12.9 cm.

[i–ii] blank; [iii] 'THE ADVENTURES | OF TOM BOMBADIL'; [iv] 'By J. R. R. Tolkien | [*15 titles, beginning with* H, *ending with* Bilbo's Last Song] | and, edited by Christopher Tolkien, | *The History of Middle-earth* | [*7 titles, beginning with* The Book of Lost Tales, *ending with* The War of the Ring]'; [v] title; [vi] '[*on adhesive label:*] THE ADVENTURES OF TOM BOMBADIL | Copyright © 1962, 1990 Unwin Hyman Ltd. | Copyright © renewed 1990 by Christopher R. Tolkien | John F. R. Tolkien And Priscilla M. A. R. Tolkien | First American edition 1991 | Originally published in Great Britain in 1990 by Unwin Hyman Ltd. | All rights reserved. For information about permission to reproduce | selections from this book, write to Permissions, Houghton Mifflin | Company, 2 Park Street, Boston, Massachusetts 02108. | ISBN 0-395-57647-4 | Printed in Great Britian [*sic*] | [*printing code, beginning "10", ending "1"*] | [*below the label, printed directly on the paper:*] [*at left, "JRRT" device; at right:*] is a trademark of Frank Richard Williamson and | Christopher Reuel Tolkien, executors of the Estate of | the late John Ronald Reuel Tolkien.'; [vii–xii] preface; [xiii] 'THE ADVENTURES | OF TOM BOMBADIL'; [xiv] blank; 1–75 text and illustrations; [76] blank; [77] advertisement of *H*; [78] blank; [79] advertisement of *LR*; [80–2] blank.

Wove paper. Bound in black textured paper over boards. Stamped on spine in gilt: '[*running down:*] The Adventures Of Tom Bombadil J. R. R. TOLKIEN | [*horizontal:*] [*publisher's "dolphin" device*] | HMCo'. Wove pastedowns; no free endpapers. No headbands. All edges trimmed and unstained.

Dust-jacket, wove paper. Upper cover as for A6c. Printed on spine: '[*running down:*] [*in green:*] The Adventures Of Tom Bombadil [*in black:*] J. R. R. TOLKIEN | [*horizontal:*] [*publisher's "dolphin" device*] | HMCo'. Printed on lower cover: '[*colour illustration, of water lilies, detail from upper cover illustration*] | [*in black:*] [*at left:*] 5-97097 [*at right:*] ISBN 0-395-57647-4 | [*bar codes*]'. Printed on front flap: '$13.95 | [*blurb*] | [*illustration by Garland, of Tom Bombadil falling in the water, from p. 1*] | [*"JRRT" device*] 0491'. Printed on back flap: '[*note on Tolkien*] | [*note on Garland*] | Jacket art © 1990 by Unwin Hyman Limited | Jacket illustration by Roger Garland'.

Published 29 April 1991 at $13.95; 5,000 copies printed.

Typeset as for A6c, except pp. [iv–vi], [77], [79]. Illustrations as for A6c.

A7   TREE AND LEAF   1964

a. First edition, paperback copies:

J. R. R. TOLKIEN | TREE AND LEAF | *[facsimile signature, 'J. R. R. Tolkien']* | LONDON · UNWIN BOOKS

96 pp. Collation: 48 leaves. 18.4 × 12.1 cm.

[1] '*[publisher's "U books" device, in white and black]* | *[in black:]* TREE AND LEAF | *[blurb]*'; [2] 'BY J. R. R. TOLKIEN | The Hobbit | Farmer Giles of Ham | The Lord of the Rings | The Adventures of Tom Bombadil'; [3] title; [4] 'First published in this edition 1964 | *[notice of restrictions under copyright]* | *This edition* © *George Allen & Unwin Ltd.*, 1964 | UNWIN BOOKS | *George Allen & Unwin Ltd* | *Ruskin House, Museum Street* | *London, W.C.1* | PRINTED IN GREAT BRITAIN | *in* 10 *on* 12 *point Plantin type* | BY C. TINLING AND CO. LTD | LIVERPOOL, LONDON AND PRESCOT'; [5] introductory note; [6] blank; [7] table of contents; [8] blank; [9] 'ON FAIRY-STORIES'; [10] blank; [11]–63 text; 64–70 notes; [71] 'LEAF BY NIGGLE'; [72] blank; [73]–92 text; [93] '*[publisher's open "St. George" device]* | GEORGE ALLEN & UNWIN LTD | *[19 addresses, London to Toronto]*; [94] advertisement of *LR*; [95] advertisement of *ATB* and *FGH*; [96] advertisement of *H* and Davis and Wrenn, eds., *English and Medieval Studies.*

Wove paper. Bound in heavy wove wrappers. Printed on upper cover: '*[in purple:]* J. R. R. TOLKIEN | *[at left:]* *[in black:]* TREE | and | LEAF | *[in purple:]* Unwin | Books | *[in yellow-green:]* 5s. net | in U.K. only *[at right, illustration by Tolkien,* The Tree of Amalion, *in black, against and partly extending beyond a five-sided yellow-green panel]*'. Printed on spine: '*[running up, above device:]* *[in black:]* TREE and LEAF *[in purple:]* J. R. R. TOLKIEN | *[horizontal:]* *[publisher's "U books" device, in white and yellow-green]* | *[in yellow-green:]* 54'. Printed on lower cover: '*[at right:]* *[in yellow-green:]* UNWIN BOOKS *[publisher's "U books" device, in white and yellow-green]* | *[running up, in yellow-green:]* Cover illustration: Drawing by author *[at left, in black, list of 55 titles published in Unwin Books, beginning with* Russell, On Education, *ending with* Africa's Freedom]'. All edges trimmed and unstained.

Published 28 May 1964 at 5s.; number of copies not known.

On 27 October 1955, soon after the final volume of *The Lord of the Rings* was published, Rayner Unwin wrote to Tolkien about plans for future books. He felt that 'On Fairy-Stories', Tolkien's Andrew Lang Lecture published in *Essays Presented to Charles Williams* (B19), could be reprinted as a small book by itself if expanded by fifty percent and framed more as a long essay than as a lecture. The idea seems to have languished for nearly eight years, until revived (probably by Unwin) in spring 1963. In a letter to Tolkien of 3 July 1963 Unwin proposed that 'On Fairy-Stories' be included in Allen & Unwin's paperback 'U Books' series. He now suggested that the work could be published with minimal revision, or expanded if Tolkien could find new material and time to incorporate it, or published together with Tolkien's story 'Leaf by Niggle' from the *Dublin Review* (C32). On 5 October 1963 Tolkien sent Allen & Unwin 'the items required from me', additions and changes to 'On

Fairy-Stories', 'Leaf by Niggle' without change, and an introductory note to the new book, with the hope that the note was neither too solemn nor written with too little solemnity. He suggested the collective title *Tree and Leaf* 'with reference to the passage at the top of page 73 in the Essay, and to the key-word *effoliation* at the end, p. 84'. The passage on p. 73 (of *Essays Presented to Charles Williams*) includes 'the countless foliage of the Tree of Tales, with which the Forest of Days is carpeted'.

Unwin asked Tolkien to suggest a suitable cover illustration: perhaps one from Andrew Lang's fairy-tale books, or a tree or leaf from some medieval illuminated manuscript, or a tree drawn by Tolkien himself. Tolkien replied on 23 December 1963: 'Mediæval MSS are not (in my not very extensive experience) good on trees. I have among my "papers" more than one version of a mythical "tree", which crops up regularly at those times when I feel driven to pattern-designing. They are elaborated and coloured and more suitable for embroidery than printing; and the tree bears besides various shapes of leaves many flowers small and large signifying poems and major legends.' This was *The Tree of Amalion*, reproduced in *Pictures* (Ei2) as no. 41. Tolkien sent Unwin a 'hasty reduction of this pattern' (4.25 × 3.25 in.), which he offered to do again, larger and more carefully, if it was found suitable, 'unless you think it had better be given to someone of more skill & firmer line.' On 31 December Unwin asked Tolkien to redraw the tree to about double the size, more elongated, and with his initials. Tolkien sent the final version, 8.5 × 5 in., on 8 January 1964. His initials 'JRRT' are unobtrusively worked into the ragged baseline of the drawing at lower right. (See Plate VIII.)

Tolkien received proofs of *Tree and Leaf* on 1 February 1964 and returned them corrected on 3 February. He received a proof of the dust-jacket for the library issue (A7b) on or about 5 February, and a proof of the paperback cover on or before 22 February.

Tolkien states (or understates) in his introductory note to *Tree and Leaf* that 'On Fairy-Stories' was reprinted from *Essays Presented to Charles Williams* 'with only a few minor alterations'. The two versions differ in the respects detailed below (in addition to minor typographical errors in *TL*). Printed copies of *EPCW* and *TL* have been compared with each other and with manuscripts and proofs in the Bodleian Library. All of the alterations (distinct from changes in error) are authorial, except 'to-day' > 'today' *passim* and the minor changes in punctuation, *TL* pp. 53, l. 14, and 58, l. 26, evidently the publisher's preferences.

Essays Presented to Charles Williams, p. [38], first three paragraphs of text:

This essay was originally intended to be one of the Andrew Lang lectures at St. Andrews, and it was, in abbreviated form, delivered there in 1940. To be invited to lecture in St. Andrews is a high compliment to any man; to be allowed to speak about fairy-stories is (for an Englishman in Scotland) a perilous honour. I felt like a conjuror who finds himself, by some mistake, called upon to give a display of magic before the court of an elf-king. After producing his rabbit, such a clumsy performer may consider himself lucky, if he is allowed to go home in his proper shape, or indeed to go home at all. There are dungeons in fairyland for the overbold.

And overbold I fear I may be accounted, because I am a reader and lover of fairy-stories, but not a student of them, as Andrew Lang was. I have not the learning, nor the still more necessary wisdom, which the subject demands. The land of fairy-story is wide and deep and high, and is filled with many things: all manner of beasts and birds are found there; shoreless seas and stars uncounted; beauty that is an enchantment, and an ever-present peril; both sorrow and joy as sharp as swords. In that land a man may (perhaps) count himself fortunate to

VIII. *Tree and Leaf* (A7a). Paperback cover, with *The Tree of Amalion* by J. R. R. Tolkien.

have wandered, but its very richness and strangeness make dumb the traveller who would report it. And while he is there it is dangerous for him to ask too many questions, lest the gates shut and the keys be lost. The fairy gold too often turns to withered leaves when it is brought away. All that I can ask is that you, knowing these things, will receive my withered leaves, as a token that my hand at least once held a little of the gold.

But there are some questions that one who is to speak about fairy-stories cannot help asking, whatever the folk of Faërie think of him or do to him. For instance: What are fairy-stories? What is their origin? What is the use of them? I will try to give answers to these questions, or rather the broken hints of answers to them that I have gleaned—primarily from the stories themselves: such few of their multitude as I know.

> *Tree and Leaf,* A7a–b, p. [11], first three paragraphs of text:

I propose to speak about fairy-stories, though I am aware that this is a rash adventure. Faërie is a perilous land, and in it are pitfalls for the unwary and dungeons for the overbold. And overbold I may be accounted, for though I have been a lover of fairy-stories since I learned to read, and have at times thought about them, I have not studied them professionally. I have been hardly more than a wandering explorer (or trespasser) in the land, full of wonder but not of information.

The realm of fairy-story is wide and deep and high and filled with many things: all manner of beasts and birds are found there; shoreless seas and stars uncounted; beauty that is an enchantment, and an ever-present peril; both joy and sorrow as sharp as swords. In that realm a man may, perhaps, count himself fortunate to have wandered, but its very richness and strangeness tie the tongue of a traveller who would report them. And while he is there it is dangerous for him to ask too many questions, lest the gates should be shut and the keys be lost.

There are, however, some questions that one who is to speak about fairy-stories must expect to answer, or attempt to answer, whatever the folk of Faërie may think of his impertinence. For instance: What are fairy-stories? What is their origin? What is the use of them? I will try to give answers to these questions, or such hints of answers to them as I have gleaned—primarily from the stories themselves, the few of all their multitude that I know.

EPCW, p. [38], l. 35–p. 39, l. 3: It is in this case no good hastening to the *Oxford English Dictionary,* because it will not tell you. It contains no reference to the combination *fairy-story,* and is unhelpful on the subject of *fairies* generally: volume F was not edited by a Scotsman. > *TL,* p. [11], l. 25–p. 12, l. 1: In this case you will turn to the *Oxford English Dictionary* in vain. It contains no reference to the combination *fairy-story,* and is unhelpful on the subject of *fairies* generally.

EPCW, p. 39, ll. 8–9: Not too narrow for a lecture (it is large enough for fifty), but too narrow > *TL,* p. 12, ll. 7–8: Not too narrow for an essay; it is wide enough for many books, but too narrow

EPCW, p. 39, l. 34: deny that that notion > *TL,* p. 12, l. 33, incorrectly reads: deny that the notion

EPCW, p. 41, l. 14: the only one before A.D. 1400 > *TL,* p. 14, l. 25, corrects: the only one before A.D. 1450

EPCW, p. 43, l. 12: nor explained away. > *TL,* p. 16, ll. 31–2, adds sentence: nor explained away. Of this seriousness the medieval *Sir Gawain and the Green Knight* is an admirable example.

EPCW, p. 48, l. 38: living moment > *TL,* p. 23, l. 19, incorrectly reads: living monument

EPCW, p. 53, l. 32: descending from Olympus > *TL*, p. 29, l. 9, incorrectly reads: descended from Olympus

EPCW, p. 54, ll. 18–19: had warned the archbishop > *TL*, p. 29, ll. 28–9: had warned the Archbishop

EPCW, p. 56, l. 22: golden Frey > *TL*, p. 32, l. 6, reads, without the author's direction to change: Golden Frey

EPCW, p. 56, ll. 25–6 > *TL*, p. 32, ll. 9–10, line break omitted

EPCW, p. 56, l. 37: *Machandelboom* > *TL*, p. 32, ll. 20–1, incorrectly reads: *Machandelbloom*

EPCW, p. 57, ll. 36–7: And with that I think we come to the children, and with them to the last and most important of the three questions: what, if any, > *TL*, p. 33, ll. 26–7: I will now turn to children, and so come to the last and most important of the three questions: what, if any,

EPCW, p. 57, ll. 38–9: It is often now assumed > *TL*, p. 33, l. 28: It is usually assumed

EPCW, p. 59, ll. 20–2: they have been ruined. All children's books are on a strict judgement poor books. Books written entirely for children are poor even as children's books. > *TL*, p. 35, ll. 21–2, omits the two sentences after 'they have been ruined'

EPCW, p. 62, l. 28: no special childish 'wish to believe' > *TL*, p. 39, l. 10, incorrectly omits word: no special 'wish to believe'

EPCW, p. 65, l. 40–p. 66, l. 1: Eloi and Morlocks: pretty children > *TL*, p. 42, ll. 32–3, incorrectly omits colon: Eloi and Morlocks pretty children

EPCW, p. 66, l. 9: and the sciences. > *TL*, p. 43, ll. 6–10, adds two sentences: and the sciences. Though it may be better for them to read some things, especially fairy-stories, that are beyond their measure rather than short of it. Their books like their clothes should allow for growth, and their books at any rate should encourage it.

EPCW, p. 66, l. 34: opinion in this > *TL*, p. 44, l. 2, incorrectly reads: opinion on this

EPCW, p. 69, ll. 3–4: represent Fantasy or Magic > *TL*, p. 46, ll. 20–1: represent either Fantasy or Magic

EPCW, p. 72, l. 31: their nations > *TL*, p. 50, l. 22, incorrectly reads: their notions

EPCW, p. 72, l. 38: As for the disabilities of age, that possibly is true. But it is > *TL*, p. 50, ll. 29–31: As for old age, whether personal or belonging to the times in which we live, it may be true, as is often supposed, that this imposes disabilities (cf. p. 36). But it is

EPCW, p. 73, ll. 2–3: stage-plays. (Andrew Lang is, I fear, an example of this). The study > *TL*, p. 51, l. 2, omits sentence: stage-plays. The study

EPCW, p. 73, l. 16: for some eye this very year > *TL*, p. 51, l. 15, incorrectly omits word: for some this very year

EPCW, p. 73, l. 19–p. 74, l. 12:

We do not, or need not, despair of painting because all lines must be either straight or curved. The combinations may not be infinite (for we are not), but they are innumerable.

It remains true, nevertheless, that we must not in our day be too curious, too anxious to be original. For we *are* older: certainly older than our known ancestors. The days are gone, as Chesterton said, when red, blue, and yellow could be invented blindingly in a black and white world. Gone also are the days when from blue and yellow green was made, unique as a new colour. We are far advanced into Chesterton's third stage with its special danger: the danger of becoming knowing, esoteric, privileged, or pretentious; the stage in which red and green are mixed. In this way a rich russet may (perhaps) be produced. Some will call it a drab brown (and they may be right); but in deft blendings it may be a subtle thing, combining the richness of red and the coolness of green. But in any case we cannot go much further, in the vain desire to be more 'original'. If we add another colour the result is likely to be much like mud, or a mere dead slime. Or if we turn from colour-allegory to fantastic beasts: Fantasy can produce many mythical monsters: of man and horse, the centaur; of lion and eagle, the griffin. But as Chesterton says: 'The offspring of the Missing Link and a mule mated with the child of a manx-cat and a penguin would not outrun the centaur and the griffin, it would merely lack all the interesting features of man and beast and bird: it would not be wilder but much tamer, not fantastic but merely shapeless.'

This stage was indeed reached long ago; even in fairy-tales it is sometimes found (not in good ones). But before we reach it, there is need of renewal and return. We must hark back, to purple and brown, to dragons and centaurs, and so maybe recover camelopards and green; even (who knows) we may see again yellow, blue, and red, and look upon horses, sheep, and dogs! This recovery fairy-stories help us to make. In that sense only, a taste for them may make (or keep) us childish.

> *TL*, p. 51, l. 18–p. 52, l. 2:

We do not, or need not, despair of drawing because all lines must be either curved or straight, nor of painting because there are only three 'primary' colours. We may indeed be older now, in so far as we are heirs in enjoyment or in practice of many generations of ancestors in the arts. In this inheritance of wealth there may be a danger of boredom or of anxiety to be original, and that may lead to a distaste for fine drawing, delicate pattern, and 'pretty' colours, or else to mere manipulation and over-elaboration of old material, clever and heartless. But the true road of escape from such weariness is not to be found in the wilfully awkward, clumsy, or misshapen, not in making all things dark or unremittingly violent; nor in the mixing of colours on though [i.e. through] subtlety to drabness, and the fantastical complication of shapes to the point of silliness and on towards delirium. Before we reach such states we need recovery. We should look at green again, and be startled anew (but not blinded) by blue and yellow and red. We should meet the centaur and the dragon, and then perhaps suddenly behold, like the ancient shepherds, sheep, and dogs, and horses—and wolves. This recovery fairy-stories help us to make. In that sense only a taste for them may make us, or keep us, childish.

EPCW, p. 75, l. 19: clay, stone, and wood > *TL*, p. 53, l. 14: clay, stone and wood

EPCW, p. 75, l. 37: some consideration > *TL*, p. 53, l. 32, incorrectly reads: some considerations

EPCW, p. 76, l. 3: misusers of Escape are fond > *TL*, p. 54, ll. 3–4, incorrectly omits two words: misusers are fond

EPCW, p. 76, l. 17: Fuehrer's > *TL*, p. 54, l. 17: Führer's

EPCW, p. 78, l. 27: 'Scientifiction' > *TL*, p. 57, l. 7: Science fiction

EPCW, p. 78, ll. 33–6, ellipsis in original: Later he adds: 'why is the stockbroker less beautiful than an Homeric warrior or an Egyptian priest? Because he is less incorporated with life: he is not inevitable but accidental. . . . The full Victorian panoply > *TL*, p. 56, ll. 29–30, omits the first two sentences of the quotation: Later he adds: 'The full Victorian panoply

EPCW, p. 78, ll. 36–7: expressed something essential > *TL*, p. 56, l. 31, incorrectly reads: expressed essential

EPCW, p. 79, l. 27: into our time when > *TL*, p. 58, l. 3: into our time, when

EPCW, p. 79, l. 32: aimlessness of the internal-combustion engine > *TL*, p. 58, l. 8: extravagance of the internal-combustion engine

EPCW, p. 80, l. 10: ancient: but > *TL*, p. 58, l. 26: ancient; but

EPCW, p. 81, l. 13: fairy-stories > *TL*, p. 60, l. 1, incorrectly reads: fairy-tales

EPCW, p. 82, l. 34: satiric twist > *TL*, p. 61, l. 27, incorrectly reads: satirical twist

EPCW, p. 83, ll. 8–9: that question 'Is it true?' > *TL*, p. 62, l. 9: that question, 'Is it true?'

EPCW, p. 83, ll. 16–18: matter. I am a Christian, and so at least should not be suspected of wilful irreverence. Knowing my own ignorance and dullness, it is perhaps presumptuous > *TL*, p. 62, l. 16, omits twenty-one words: matter. It is presumptuous

EPCW, p. 83, ll. 30–1: self-contained significance; and at the same time powerfully symbolic and allegorical; and among > *TL*, p. 62, ll. 27–8: self-contained significance; and among

EPCW, p. 83, ll. 32–3: conceivable eucatastrophe. The Birth of Christ > *TL*, p. 62, ll. 28–31, adds sentence: conceivable eucatastrophe. But this story has entered History and the primary world; the desire and aspiration of sub-creation has been raised to the fulfilment of Creation. The Birth of Christ

EPCW, p. 83, n. 1: The Gospels are not artistic in themselves; the Art is here in the story itself, not in the telling. For the Author of the story was not the evangelists. 'Even the world itself could not contain the books that should be written', if that story had been fully written down. > *TL*, p. 62, n. 2: The Art is here in the story itself rather than in the telling; for the Author of the story was not the evangelists.

EPCW, p. 88, l. 42–p. 89, l. 4 (final paragraph of note G): It is a curious result of the application of evolutionary hypothesis concerning Man's animal body to his whole being, that it tends to produce both arrogance and servility. Man has merely succeeded (it seems) in dominating other animals by force and chicane, not by hereditary right. He is a tyrant not a king. A cat may look at a king; but let no cat look at a tyrant! As for men taking animal form, or animals doing human things, this is dangerous indecent nonsense, insulting to the *Herrenvolk*. But strong or proud men talk of breeding other men like their cattle, and for similar purposes. For a self-chosen *Herrenvolk* always ends by becoming the slaves of a gang, a *Herrenbande*. > *TL*, p. 69, omits this paragraph

EPCW, p. 89, l. 29: 'Picture Post' > *TL*, p. 69, l. 36: *Picture Post*

In addition, the text between the first three paragraphs and the epilogue was divided into five sections, with the sub-headings: 'Fairy-story', 'Origins', 'Children', 'Fantasy', and 'Recovery, Escape, Consolation'; and the internal page references were altered to accord with the resetting.

Later, when Tolkien compared the Allen & Unwin setting with the proofs of A7c, he found a large number of faults in the British edition which he marked in a copy of A7a now in the Bodleian Library. Most of these are minor typographical errors or inconsistencies of punctuation. The reading 'Lang was using belief', A7a–b p. 36, l. 14, agrees with the *EPCW* text; the reading noted by Tolkien as correct, 'Lang was using *belief*', appears in A7c and A19. Tolkien also marked two corrections which have not yet been made in any edition of *TL*: [A7a–b] p. 17, l. 19, 'fifty years ago' > 'seventy years ago'; and p. 59, l. 24, 'human stories' > 'Human-stories'.

The introductory note to A7a–d purports to correct, to 1938, the date of Tolkien's presentation of 'On Fairy-Stories' as an Andrew Lang Lecture, given in *Essays Presented to Charles Williams* as 1940. The lecture was actually delivered on 8 March 1939, as noted in Christopher Tolkien's preface to A7e–g.

'Leaf by Niggle' in A7a–b differs from the *Dublin Review* (C32) text in the use of single rather than double quotation marks, in the absence of a full stop after 'Mr' and 'Mrs', and in the following respects:

TL, p. 74, l. 25: One day, Niggle stood a little way off < C32, p. 47, l. 14: One day Niggle stood a little way off

TL, p. 81, ll. 14–15: he began to have a feeling of—well satisfaction < C32, p. 52, ll. 35–6: he began to have a feeling of—well, satisfaction

TL, p. 82, l. 35: mostly of the easier sort, and < C32, p. 54, l. 2: mostly of the easier sort; and

TL, p. 88, l. 15: the lake that glimmered, far away and < C32: the lake that glimmered far away and

TL, p. 91, ll. 3–4: None for this old-fashioned stuff < C32: None for his old-fashioned stuff

TL, p. 92, l. 7: give the region a name < C32: give the new region a name

In all cases, the author's final typescript agrees with C32. In his copy of A7a, p. 81, Tolkien corrected in manuscript 'well satisfaction' to 'well, satisfaction'. He also marked two additional corrections (or one correction and an alteration): 'Parish often wondered about looking at trees' (also the reading of C32) > 'Parish often wandered about looking at trees', p. 87, ll. 26–7; and 'No practical or economic use' > 'No practical or economic *use*', p. 90, l. 20. The former was corrected in A7c and in *Poems and Stories* (A16).

Tree and Leaf was also published in *The Tolkien Reader* (A8), *Tree and Leaf, Smith of Wootton Major, [and] The Homecoming of Beorhtnoth Beorhthelm's Son* (A13), and *Poems and Stories* (A16). 'Leaf by Niggle' was published, in addition, in *Smith of Wootton Major and Leaf by Niggle* (A20), and has appeared in anthologies. 'On Fairy-Stories' is frequently quoted in criticism of fantasy literature.

Pertinent notes and correspondence on the publication of *LBN* in *TL*, photocopies of *OFS* and *LBN* with autograph revisions for their publication in *TL*, and a copy of *TL* with manuscript corrections by Tolkien are in the Bodleian Library, Oxford.

b. First edition, hardcover copies (1964):

J. R. R. TOLKIEN | TREE AND LEAF | [*facsimile signature, 'J. R. R. Tolkien'*] | LONDON | GEORGE ALLEN & UNWIN LTD

96 pp. Collation: [A]^{8}B–F^8. 18.4 × 12.3 cm.

Contents as for A7a, except pp. [1] 'TREE AND LEAF | [*blurb*]'; [3] title, as above; and [4] 'First published in this edition 1964 | [*notice of restrictions under copyright*] | This edition © George Allen & Unwin Ltd., 1964 | PRINTED IN GREAT BRITAIN | in 10 on 12 point Plantin type | BY C. TINLING AND CO. LTD | LIVERPOOL, LONDON AND PRESCOT'.

Wove paper. Bound in dark green textured paper over boards. Stamped on spine in gilt: '[*running up, above imprint:*] TREE AND LEAF *Tolkien* | [*horizontal:*] GEORGE | ALLEN | AND | UNWIN'. Wove endpapers. No headbands. All edges trimmed. Top edge stained dark green, fore- and bottom edges unstained.

Dust-jacket, light green laid paper, watermarked 'Abbey Mills'. Printed on upper cover: '*J. R. R. Tolkien* | [*decorative swelled rule, in green*] | [*in black:*] TREE | [*decorative swelled rule, in green*] | [*in black:*] and | [*decorative swelled rule, in green*] | [*in black:*] LEAF | [*in green:*] [*decorative swelled rule*] | GEORGE ALLEN AND UNWIN LTD'. Printed on spine: '[*running up, above imprint:*] *Tolkien TREE AND LEAF* | [*horizontal, in green:*] GEORGE | ALLEN | AND | UNWIN'. Printed on lower cover: 'TOLKIEN | [*advertisement of* H, LR, ATB, FGH] | GEORGE ALLEN & UNWIN LTD'. Printed on front flap: '[*blurb*] | *Tree and Leaf* | J. R. R. Tolkien | George Allen & Unwin Ltd. | 10s. 6d. net | in U.K. only'. Printed on back flap: '*Printed in Great Britain*'.

Published 28 May 1964 at 10s. 6d.; number of copies not known.

Typeset as for A7a, except pp. [1], [3–4]. A hardcover issue for libraries.

c. First American edition (1965):

TREE AND LEAF | J. R. R. TOLKIEN | [*publisher's 'tree/HMCO' device, in dark grey*] | [*in black:*] HOUGHTON MIFFLIN COMPANY BOSTON | [*black letter:*] The Riverside Press Cambridge | [*roman:*] 1965

[2], viii, 118 pp. Collation: [1–4^{16}]. 20.6 × 13.3 cm.

[preliminary 1–2] blank; [i] 'TREE AND LEAF'; [ii] 'BY J. R. R. TOLKIEN | THE HOBBIT | FARMER GILES OF HAM | THE LORD OF THE RINGS: | *The Fellowship of the Ring* | *The Two Towers* | *The Return of the King* | THE ADVENTURES OF TOM BOMBADIL | TREE AND LEAF'; [iii] title; [iv] 'FIRST PRINTING W | FIRST AMERICAN EDITION 1965 | COPYRIGHT © 1964 BY GEORGE ALLEN & UNWIN LTD. | ALL RIGHTS RESERVED INCLUDING THE RIGHT TO | REPRODUCE THIS BOOK OR PARTS THEREOF IN ANY FORM | LIBRARY OF CONGRESS CATALOG CARD NUMBER: 65-10533 | PRINTED IN THE UNITED STATES OF AMERICA'; [v] table of contents; [vi] blank; [vii]–viii introductory note; [1] 'ON FAIRY-STORIES'; [2] blank; [3]–73 text; [74] blank; [75]–84 notes; [85] 'LEAF BY NIGGLE'; [86] blank; [87]–112 text; [113–18] blank.

Wove paper. Bound in dark blue cloth over boards. Stamped on upper cover in gilt: 'TREE AND LEAF'. Stamped on spine, running down, in gilt: 'TOLKIEN — TREE AND LEAF — HMCO'. Dark blue-green wove endpapers. Yellow/blue headbands. All edges trimmed. Top edge stained orange, fore- and bottom edges unstained.

Dust-jacket, laid paper. Illustration by Robert Quackenbush, of a tree, printed on upper cover and spine, in black, dark blue, and red. Lettered on upper cover within the illustration: 'TREE | AND | LEAF | J. R. R. TOLKIEN'. Lettered on spine, running down, against the illustration: 'TREE AND LEAF J. R. R. TOLKIEN HMCO'. Printed on lower cover: 'J. R. R. TOLKIEN | [*advertisement of* H, LR, ATB]'. Printed on front flap: '$4.00 | Tree | and | Leaf | J. R. R. Tolkien | [*blurb*]'. Printed on back flap: '[*note on Tolkien*] | Jacket by Robert Quackenbush'.

Published 3 March 1965 at $4.00; 4,500 copies printed.

Reset, based on A7a–b, continuing the following readings:

   p. 5, l. 20, 'the notion' for 'that notion'
   p. 19, l. 21, 'living monument' for 'living moment'
   p. 27, ll. 7–8, 'descended from Olympus' for 'descending from Olympus'
   p. 31, 'Golden Frey' for 'golden Frey'
   p. 40, ll. 9–10, 'no special "wish to believe"' for 'no special childish "wish to believe"'
   p. 46, l. 21, 'opinion on this' for 'opinion in this'
   p. 55, ll. 17–18, 'their notions' for 'their nations'

p. 56, l. 22, 'for some this very year' for 'for some eye this very year'
p. 60, l. 2, 'some considerations' for 'some consideration'
p. 60, l. 9, 'misusers are fond' for 'misusers of Escape are fond'
p. 68, l. 6, 'fairy-tales' for 'fairy-stories'
p. 69, ll. 28–9, 'satirical twist' for 'satiric twist'

Four errors were corrected in A7c:

p. 31, l. 20: *Machandelbloom* > *Machandelboom*
p. 36, l. 19: Lang was using belief > Lang was using *belief*
p. 45, ll. 8–9, restores colon: Eloi and Morlocks: pretty children
p. 63, l. 32: expressed essential > expressed something essential

The text of 'Leaf by Niggle' agrees with A7a-b, except with 'a feeling of—well, satisfaction' on p. 98, l. 11, in agreement with C32, and 'Parish often wandered about looking at trees', p. 106, l. 20.

Titles in the 'U Books' series (see A7a note) were normally published in the United States by Barnes & Noble, but Allen & Unwin offered *Tree and Leaf* to Houghton Mifflin, the American publisher of *The Hobbit* and *The Lord of the Rings*, with the hope that Houghton Mifflin would publish the work in cloth while allowing Barnes & Noble to publish it in paperback. In the event, only a hardcover edition was published in the United States, by Houghton Mifflin.

In a letter to Joy Hill of 11 September 1964, Tolkien remarked that the block designed for p. iii of the proofs of the American edition was 'a ghastly thing, like a cross between a fat sea-anemone and a pollarded spanish chestnut, plastered with lettering of indecent ugliness.' His complaint seems strange, if it was directed at the device that appears on p. [iii] (the title page) of the published book: a stylized tree with 'HMCO' in classical roman capital letters. Probably he was referring to the dust-jacket illustration, with 'TREE AND LEAF' 'cut into' the trunk of a (woodcut?) tree, which may have appeared on p. iii of the proofs Tolkien received on 8 September 1964.

d. Second edition (1975):

J. R. R. TOLKIEN | TREE AND LEAF | *London* | GEORGE ALLEN & UNWIN LTD | RUSKIN HOUSE MUSEUM STREET

96 pp. Collation: [1–6^8]. 19.8 × 12.7 cm.

[1] 'TREE AND LEAF'; [2] 'BY J. R. R. TOLKIEN | [*6 titles, beginning with* H, *ending with* SGPO]'; [3] title; [4] 'First published in this edition 1964 | [*list of second through ninth impressions, 1966–74*] | Reset Tenth Impression 1975 | [*notice of restrictions under copyright*] | This edition © George Allen & Unwin Ltd, 1964 | ISBN 0 04 824020 6 | Printed in Great Britain | by Cox and Wyman Ltd, London, Fakenham and Reading'; [5]–6 introductory note; [7] table of contents; [8] blank; [9]–66 text of 'On Fairy-Stories'; 66–73 notes; [74] blank; [75]–95 text of 'Leaf by Niggle'; [96] blank.

Wove paper. Bound in dark green textured paper over boards. Stamped on spine, running down, in gilt: 'TREE AND LEAF *Tolkien* GEORGE ALLEN [*parallel to the preceding two words:*] & UNWIN'. Wove endpapers. No headbands. All edges trimmed. Top edge stained dark green, fore- and bottom edges unstained.

Dust-jacket, yellow-green laid paper, watermarked 'Abbey Mills'. Printed on upper cover: 'J. R. R. Tolkien | [*in dark red:*] TREE | AND | LEAF | [*in black:*] GEORGE ALLEN & UNWIN'. Printed on spine, running down: '[*in dark red:*] TREE AND

LEAF [*in black:*] Tolkien GEORGE ALLEN [*parallel to the preceding two words:*] & UNWIN'. Printed on lower cover: 'J. R. R. Tolkien | [*advertisement of* H, LR, ATB, FGH, SWM, *in dark red*]'. Printed on front flap in dark red: '[*blurb*] | [*5 quotations, from the* Cambridge Review, *K. M. Briggs, the* School Librarian, New York Times, *and* Birmingham Post] | *Tenth Impression, reset* | PRICE NET | £2·50 | IN UK ONLY'. Printed on back flap in dark red: 'J. R. R. Tolkien | Sir Gawain and the Green Knight | Pearl, Sir Orfeo | [*blurb*] | ISBN 0 04 824013 3 | *Printed in Great Britain*'.

Published July? 1975 at £2.50; number of copies not known. British Library copy acquired 28 July 1975.

Reset, based on A7a–b. Some minor typographical errors were corrected. The following readings were continued from A7a–b:

p. 11, l. 1, 'the notion' for 'that notion'
p. 22, l. 21, 'living monument' for 'living moment'
p. 28, l. 28, 'descended from Olympus' for 'descending from Olympus'
p. 31, l. 35, 'Golden Frey' for 'golden Frey'
p. 32, l. 15, '*Machandelbloom*' for '*Machandelboom*'
p. 36, ll. 17–18, 'Lang was using belief' for 'Lang was using *belief*'
p. 39, l. 19, 'no special "wish to believe"' for 'no special childish "wish to believe"'
p. 43, ll. 20–1, 'Eloi and Morlocks pretty children' for 'Eloi and Morlocks: pretty children'
p. 44, l. 26, 'opinion on this' for 'opinion in this'
p. 51, l. 36, 'their notions' for 'their nations'
p. 52, ll. 29–30, 'for some this very year' for 'for some eye this very year'
p. 55, l. 22, 'some considerations' for 'some consideration'
p. 55, l. 29, 'misusers are fond' for 'misusers of Escape are fond'
p. 58, l. 31, 'expressed essential' for 'expressed something essential'
p. 62, l. 8, 'fairy-tales' for 'fairy-stories'
p. 63, l. 31, 'satirical twist' for 'satiric twist'

The text of 'Leaf by Niggle' agrees with A7a–b, except 'the lake that glimmered, far away, and', p. 91, ll. 25–6, at variance with both A7a–b and C32.

e. 'Second', i.e. third edition, hardcover copies (1988):

J. R. R. TOLKIEN | [*rule*] | TREE AND LEAF | including the poem *Mythopoeia* | [*rule*] | With an Introduction by | CHRISTOPHER TOLKIEN | UNWIN | [*publisher's 'man drawing a circle' device*] | HYMAN | LONDON SYDNEY WELLINGTON

ii, 8, [2], [9]–108 pp. Collation: [1–2^{16}3^{8}4^{16}]. 19.7 × 12.8 cm.

[i–ii] blank; [1] 'TREE AND LEAF'; [2] 'by J. R. R. TOLKIEN | [*25 titles, beginning with* H, *ending with* Pictures]'; [3] title; [4] 'First published 1964 | Reprinted eight times | Reset tenth impression 1975 | Reprinted twice | This second edition 1988 | This second edition published in Great Britain by the Trade Division of | Unwin Hyman Limited, in 1988. | This edition, including *Mythopoeia*, © The Tolkien Trust, 1988. | *Tree and Leaf* © George Allen & Unwin Ltd, 1964. | [*notice of restrictions*] | [*3 publisher's addresses, London to Wellington*] | [*rule*] | [*British Library Cataloguing in Publication Data*] | [*rule*] | Printed in Great Britain by | Biddles Ltd, Guildford and Kings Lynn'; [5]–8 preface, by Christopher Tolkien; [8+ 1] table of contents; [8+2] blank; [9]–66 text of 'On Fairy-Stories'; 66–73 notes;

[74] blank; [75]–95 text of 'Leaf by Niggle'; [96] blank; [97]–101 text of 'Mythopoeia'; [102–8] blank.

Wove paper. Bound in dark green textured paper over boards. Stamped on spine in gilt: '[*running down:*] J. R. R. TOLKIEN [*vertical rule*] TREE AND LEAF | [*horizontal:*] UNWIN | [*publisher's "man drawing a circle" device*] | HYMAN'. Wove endpapers. No headbands. All edges trimmed and unstained.

Dust-jacket, wove paper. Covers and spine stamped or printed against a dark green background. Stamped on upper cover in gilt: 'J. R. R. TOLKIEN | [*rule*] | TREE AND LEAF | including the poem *Mythopoeia* | [*illustration by Tolkien*, The Tree of Amalion] | [*rule*] | With an Introduction by | CHRISTOPHER TOLKIEN'. Stamped or printed on spine: '[*running down, stamped in gilt:*] J. R. R. TOLKIEN [*vertical rule*] TREE AND LEAF | [*horizontal, printed in white:*] UNWIN | [*publisher's "man drawing a circle" device*] | HYMAN'. Printed on lower cover in dark green, against a white panel: 'ISBN 0-04-440254-6 | [*bar code*]'. Printed on front flap in dark green: '[*blurb*] | £7.95 net U.K.' Four quotations, from the *Cambridge Review* and *New York Times*, *Folklore* (K. M. Briggs), and the *Birmingham Post*, printed on back flap in dark green.

Published 25 August 1988 at £7.95; 2,000 copies printed.

Typeset as for A7d, except new preliminaries (pp. [1]–8, [8+1]); reset but textually unaltered p. 9, ll. 28–30, p. 10, ll. 24 to bottom, and p. 67, l. 12 (to repair marred lines in the copy of A7d used for photo-offset reprinting); and new pp. [97]–101. The contents leaf was not included in the pagination so that pp. [9]–95 of A7e–f could remain as set for A7d. J. R. R. Tolkien's introductory note for A7a–d is quoted in full in A7e within the preface by Christopher Tolkien.

The text of 'Mythopoeia' as printed in A7e is 'that of the final version exactly as it stands in the manuscript' (preface, p. 8). In this form it differs in capitalization and punctuation from extracts earlier printed in *Biography* (B32) and *The Inklings* (B33) and in an essay by Stephen Medcalf, 'The Coincidence of Myth and Fact', in *Ways of Reading the Bible*, ed. Michael Wadsworth (Brighton: Harvester Press; Totowa, N.J.: Barnes & Noble, 1981), p. 56. The text also differs in the penultimate line of the fifth stanza, 'The right has not decayed' for 'That right'.

Two likely typographical errors are 'one' for 'once', p. 98, l. 33; and 'dreadly' for 'deadly', p. 99, l. 18.

'Mythopoeia' was inspired by a conversation by J. R. R. Tolkien with C. S. Lewis and Hugo Dyson on 19 September 1931. The poem developed through seven versions.

f. 'Second', i.e. third edition, paperback copies (1988):

J. R. R. TOLKIEN | [*rule*] | TREE AND LEAF | including the poem *Mythopoeia* | [*rule*] | With an Introduction by | CHRISTOPHER TOLKIEN | [*publisher's 'man drawing a circle' device*] | UNWIN | PAPERBACKS | LONDON SYDNEY WELLINGTON

ii, 108 pp. Collation: [1–2^{16}3^{8}4^{16}]. 19.8 × 13.0 cm.

Contents as for A7e, except pp. [1] blurb; [2] '*Books by J. R. R. Tolkien in Unwin Paperbacks* | *The Hobbit* | *The Illustrated Hobbit* | *The Lord of the Rings: one volume* | *The Fellowship of the Ring* | *The Two Towers* | *The Return of the King* | *Tolkien boxed set* | (*The Lord of the Rings, 3 volumes, & The Hobbit*) | [*9 additional titles, beginning with* Silm, *ending with* Sir Gawain and the Green Knight]'; [3] title, as above; and [4] 'First published 1964 | Reprinted eight times |

Reset tenth impression 1975 | Reprinted twice | This second edition 1988 | This second edition published in Great Britain by Unwin® Paperbacks, | an imprint of Unwin Hyman Limited, in 1988. | This edition, including *Mythopoeia*, © The Tolkien Trust, 1988. | *Tree and Leaf* © George Allen & Unwin Ltd, 1964. | [*notice of restrictions*] | [*3 publisher's addresses, London to Wellington*] | [*rule*] | [*British Library Cataloguing in Publication Data*] | [*rule*] | Printed in Great Britain by | Biddles Ltd, Guildford and Kings Lynn'.

Wove paper. Bound in heavy wove wrappers. Covers and spine stamped or printed against a dark green background. Upper cover as for A7e. Stamped or printed on spine: '[*running down, stamped in gilt:*] J. R. R. TOLKIEN [*vertical rule*] TREE AND LEAF | [*publisher's "man drawing a circle" device, horizontal, printed in white*]'. Printed on lower cover: '[*in white:*] [*blurb*] | [*2 quotations, from the* Cambridge Review *and* New York Times] | [*at left:*] Cover illustration | by J. R. R. Tolkien | UNWIN PAPERBACKS | TOLKIEN/FANTASY | £3.95 net UK [*at right, in dark green, against a white panel:*] ISBN 0-04-440253-8 [*3 parallel lines*] | [*bar codes*]'. All edges trimmed and unstained.

Published 25 August 1988 at £3.95; 10,000 copies printed.

Typeset as for A7e, except pp. [1–4].

g. Second American edition (1989):

J. R. R. TOLKIEN | [*rule*] | TREE AND LEAF | including the poem *Mythopoeia* | [*rule*] | *with an Introduction by* | CHRISTOPHER TOLKIEN | [*publisher's 'dolphin' device*] | HOUGHTON MIFFLIN COMPANY | BOSTON 1989

ii, 110 pp. Collation: signatures not distinct. 20.2 × 12.6 cm.

[i] 'TREE AND LEAF'; [ii] 'by J. R. R. TOLKIEN | [*25 titles, beginning with* H, *ending with* Pictures]'; [1] title; [2] '*Tree and Leaf* copyright © 1964 *by George Allen & Unwin Ltd.* | This edition, including *Mythopoeia*, copyright © 1988 by The Tolkien Trust | All rights reserved | For information about permission to reproduce selections from | this book, write to Permissions, Houghton Mifflin Company, | 2 Park Street, Boston, Massachusetts 02018. | [*Library of Congress Cataloging-in-Publication Data*] | PRINTED IN THE UNITED STATES OF AMERICA | [*printing code, beginning* "Q", *ending* "1"]'; [3] table of contents; [4] blank; [5]–8 introduction, by Christopher Tolkien; [9]–66 text of 'On Fairy-Stories'; 66–73 notes; [74] blank; [75]–95 text of 'Leaf by Niggle'; [96] blank; [97]–101 text of 'Mythopoeia'; [102–10] blank.

Wove paper. Bound in black cloth over boards. Stamped on spine in copper: '[*running down:*] J. R. R. TOLKIEN [*vertical rule*] TREE AND LEAF HOUGHTON MIFFLIN COMPANY | [*publisher's "dolphin" device, horizontal*]'. Cream wove endpapers. Black headbands. All edges trimmed and unstained.

Dust-jacket, wove paper. Covers and spine stamped or printed against a dark blue-green background. Stamped on upper cover in copper: 'J. R. R. TOLKIEN | [*rule*] | TREE AND LEAF | including the poem *Mythopoeia* | [*illustration by Tolkien, The Tree of Amalion*] | [*rule*] | With an Introduction by | CHRISTOPHER TOLKIEN'. Stamped on spine in copper: '[*running down:*] J. R. R. TOLKIEN [*vertical rule*] TREE AND LEAF HOUGHTON MIFFLIN | [*publisher's "dolphin" device, horizontal*]'. Printed on lower cover: '[*in black against a rough-edged white panel:*] TREE AND LEAF | [*ragged rule*] | [*blurb*] | [*below the panel:*] [*at left, in white:*] 6-97019 [*at right, in black against a white panel:*] ISBN 0-395-50232-2 | [*bar *codes*]'. Printed on front flap in black, with dark green initial 'F' beginning blurb: 'FPT>$12.95 | [*blurb*] | 07127089 | ISBN 0-395-50232-2'. Printed on back flap: '[*note on J. R. R. Tolkien*] | [*note on Christopher Tolkien*] | Houghton Mifflin Company | Two Park Street, Boston, Massachusetts 02108'.

Published 13 July 1989 at $12.95; 4,000 copies printed.

Typeset as for A7e, except pp. [1–2], and with p. [5] title '*Introduction*' (as on the jacket and title page) rather than '*Preface*'. The preliminaries were reimposed.

A8   **THE TOLKIEN READER**   1966

a. First edition:

THE | TOLKIEN | READER | by | J. R. R. TOLKIEN | BALLANTINE BOOKS • NEW YORK

xvi, 24, 84, 87–112, 5–80, 5–66 pp. Collation: 144 leaves. 17.6 × 10.7 cm.

First section: [i] 'J. R. R. Tolkien | [*blurb*]'; [ii] 'BY J. R. R. TOLKIEN | [*8 titles, beginning with* H, *ending with* TL] | [*note on availability of hardcover and paperbound editions*]'; [iii] title; [iv] 'Copyright © 1966 by J. R. R. Tolkien | TOLKIEN'S MAGIC RING, by Peter Beagle, first appeared in *Holiday* | Magazine, Copyright © 1966 by Curtis Publishing Co. | THE HOMECOMING OF BEORHTNOTH BEORHTHELM'S SON, first appeared in *Essays and Studies for 1953*, Copyright © 1953 by the | English Association. | TREE AND LEAF © 1964 by George Allen & Unwin Ltd. | FARMER GILES OF HAM © 1949 by George Allen & Unwin Ltd. | THE ADVENTURES OF TOM BOMBADIL © 1962 by George Allen & | Unwin Ltd. | Publication of this volume is made possible by arrangement with | Houghton Mifflin Company, and with the kind permission of the | author and of George Allen & Unwin Ltd. | First Edition: September, 1966 | Printed in the United States of America | BALLANTINE BOOKS, INC. | 101 Fifth Avenue, New York, New York 10003'; [v] table of contents; [vi] blank; [vii–viii] publisher's note; ix–xvi 'Tolkien's Magic Ring' by Peter S. Beagle. *Second section:* [1] 'THE | HOMECOMING | OF | BEORHTNOTH | BEORHTHELM'S SON | [*illustration*]'; [2] blank; 3–24 text. *Third section:* [1] 'TREE AND LEAF | [*illustration*] | ON FAIRY STORIES | *page 3* | LEAF BY NIGGLE | *page 87*'; [2] introductory note; [3]–84 text of 'On Fairy-Stories'; [87]–112 text of 'Leaf by Niggle'. *Fourth section:* [5] 'FARMER GILES | OF HAM | [*black letter:*] Aegidii Ahenobarbi Julii Agricole de Hammo | Domini de Domito | Aule Draconarie Comitis | Regni Minimi Regis et Basilei | mira facinora et mirabilis | exortus | [*roman:*] or in the vulgar tongue | *The Rise and Wonderful Adventures of* | *Farmer Giles, Lord of Tame,* | *Count of Worminghall* | *and King of* | *the Little Kingdom* | [*illustration*] | [*black letter:*] To C. H. Wilkinson'; [6] blank; 7–8 foreword; 9–[79] text and illustrations; [80] blank. *Fifth section:* [5] 'J. R. R. TOLKIEN | THE ADVENTURES | OF TOM BOMBADIL | *and other verses* | *from The Red Book* | [*illustration*] | WITH ILLUSTRATIONS BY | PAULINE BAYNES | [*illustration*] | [*black letter:*] The Riverside Press Cambridge | [*roman:*] HOUGHTON MIFFLIN COMPANY BOSTON'; [6] blank; 7–9 preface; [10] illustration; 11–[64] text and illustrations; [65] 'NOW IN BALLANTINE BOOKS | [*advertisement of Agee and Evans*, Let Us Now Praise Famous Men]'; [66] '*Now available from Ballantine Books:* | [*advertisement of four novels by Anthony Burgess*]'.

Wove paper. Bound in heavy wove wrappers. Printed on upper cover, against an oval white panel outlined in dark blue, against a colour illustration by Pauline Baynes, of Tom Bombadil, birds, and fish (detail from left half of binding/jacket illustration of *ATB* [A6]): 'U7038 [*publisher's "BB" device, in white and dark blue*] [*in black:*] 95¢ | [*in pink:*] THE | TOLKIEN READER | [*in black:*] *Stories, poems and an essay by the author of* | *"The Hobbit" and "The Lord of the Rings"* | [*"Gothic" lettering, in dark blue:*] J. R. R. TOLKIEN | [*roman, in black:*] A BALLANTINE BOOK'. Printed on spine: 'U7038 | 95¢ | [*running down:*] [*in pink:*] THE TOLKIEN READER [*in dark blue:*] J. R. R. TOLKIEN | [*publisher's "BB" device, horizontal, in white and black*]'. Printed on lower cover, within open area of colour illustration by Pauline Baynes, of a mariner, a bell, and fish (detail from right half of binding/jacket illustration of A6): '[*in pink:*] J. R. R. TOLKIEN'S | [*in black:*] *devoted following in America has* | *expanded into a multitude. Now, for all* | *hobbit fanciers and Tolkien collectors,* | *here is a rich treasury of his shorter* | *fiction, from the publishers of the* | *Authorized Edition of "The Hobbit"* | *and "The Lord of the Rings."* | Printed in U.S.A.' All edges trimmed and stained orange.

Published September 1966 at $0.95; number of copies not known.

Contains: 'The Homecoming of Beorhtnoth Beorhthelm's Son'; *Tree and Leaf*; *Farmer Giles of Ham*; and *The Adventures of Tom Bombadil*. *HBBS* was reset from *Essays and Studies* (B22). *TL* was photographically reprinted from A7c, except with the title page, the introductory note, and the heading on p. [75] reset, and with preliminary matter and pp. [85–6] omitted. The statement on p. 84, 'Pages 85 and 86, illustrations in hard cover editions [i.e. the Houghton Mifflin edition, A7c], have been deleted', is erroneous: in A7c, p. [85] is a divisional title and p. [86] is blank. *FGH* was photographically reprinted from A4b, except with the preliminaries shortened to one page (partial title page and dedication combined, the section here beginning with p. [5]), and the plates omitted. *ATB* was photographically reprinted from A6b, except with the preliminaries shortened (the section here beginning with p. [5]). All illustrations are by Pauline Baynes, reprinted from A4 and A6.

In early 1966 Ballantine Books proposed a 'Tolkien reader' which might contain *Farmer Giles of Ham*, *The Adventures of Tom Bombadil*, and *Tree and Leaf*, as well as other shorter writings by Tolkien and various essays and articles about him. 'English and Welsh' (B27), an essay by Tolkien on *Beowulf* (probably the British Academy lecture, A2), and 'Mr. Bliss' (A18) were considered but not included. On 29 March 1966 Rayner Unwin suggested to Tolkien that Ballantine Books would be unwise to include his academic works in a popular anthology, and he wished to reserve Tolkien's more important unpublished short works, especially 'Smith of Wootton Major', for a book of two or three stories to be published by Allen & Unwin. Tolkien does not seem to have expressed an opinion on 'English and Welsh' and 'Beowulf'—unless his silence in the Tolkien-Allen & Unwin correspondence expresses his disapproval of their inclusion—but he did not object entirely to Ballantine Books having an academic work in their anthology. He wrote to Rayner Unwin on 25 April 1966: 'If the Reader is to be of use (e.g. stopping people attributing views to me that I don't hold), I personally should wish to include the poem "The Homecoming of Beorhtnoth", with the accompanying essay on "Heroism"—this is very germane to the general division of sympathy exhibited in *The Lord of the Rings*.' He also thought that one or two poems from *Songs for the Philologists* (B15, which a 'nosy bibliographer' had just unearthed) 'might do for the Reader. It includes, for instance, a translation into Anglo Saxon of "The Mermaid" ... which proved quite popular in its time.' But by 10 May 1966 Tolkien decided that none of these rhymes would be suitable.

W. H. Auden was approached to write an introduction to *The Tolkien Reader*, but was too busy. Clyde S. Kilby of Wheaton College, Illinois, who had visited Tolkien in 1964 and 1966 (see his *Tolkien &* The Silmarillion, Dii34), and Dick Plotz, president of the Tolkien Society of America, were also considered for the task. In the event, the anthology was 'introduced' with an essay on Tolkien by Peter S. Beagle reprinted from *Holiday* magazine, and included no other writings about Tolkien.

Ballantine Books set Part II of *HBBS* to fit the short measure of the paperback page, hyphenating at will, and thus altered some of the line breaks of the verse drama from the form Tolkien had intended (as it was printed in *Essays and Studies*). A note, in what appears to be Tolkien's hand, was pencilled in an Allen & Unwin file copy of *The Tolkien Reader*: 'This is verse!' With the ninth impression of *TR* (May 1970), Part II of *HBBS* was completely reset, correcting the ends of 79 lines.

The error in the final line of 'The Sea-Bell' from A6, 'men that meet' for 'men that I meet', was continued in early impressions of *The Tolkien Reader*, corrected probably after the fifth impression (November 1967), not later than the ninth impression (May 1970).

The wrappers of A8a were altered later, notably with the twenty-second impression when the Baynes illustration on the upper cover was reduced to a smaller detail against a white background. Still later, the Baynes illustration on the lower cover was replaced with type.

b. Second edition ('Twenty-ninth' impression, 1978):

THE | TOLKIEN | READER | by | J. R. R. TOLKIEN | BALLANTINE BOOKS • NEW YORK

xviii, 254 pp. Collation: 136 leaves. 17.6 × 10.6 cm.

[i] 'J. R. R. TOLKIEN | [*blurb*]'; [ii] 'THE AUTHORIZED EDITIONS | *of the Works of J. R. R. Tolkien* | THE HOBBIT | *The Lord of the Rings Trilogy* | *Part I* | THE FELLOWSHIP OF THE RING | *Part II* | THE TWO TOWERS | *Part III* | THE RETURN OF THE KING | THE TOLKIEN READER | SMITH OF WOOTTON MAJOR | AND FARMER GILES OF HAM | [*note on Tolkien*]'; [iii] title; [iv] 'Copyright © 1966 by J. R. R. Tolkien | All rights reserved. Published in the United States by | Ballantine Books, a division of Random House, Inc., | New York. | ISBN 0-345-27681-7 | TOLKIEN'S MAGIC RING by Peter Beagle, | first appeared in Holiday Magazine. Copyright © 1966 | by Curtis Publishing Co. | THE HOMECOMING OF BEORHTNOTH | BEORHTHELM'S SON, first appeared in *Essays and | Studies for 1953*. Copyright © 1953 by the | English Association. | TREE AND LEAF © 1964 by George Allen & Unwin Ltd. | FARMER GILES OF HAM © 1949 by George Allen & | Unwin Ltd. | THE ADVENTURES OF TOM BOMBADIL © 1962 | by George Allen & Unwin Ltd. | Cover and illustrations by Pauline Baynes | This edition published by arrangement with Houghton | Mifflin Company, and with the kind permission of the | author and of George Allen & Unwin Ltd. | Manufactured in the United States of America | First Ballantine Books Edition: September 1966 | Twenty-ninth Printing: January 1978'; v table of contents; [vi] blank; vii–viii publisher's note; ix–xvii 'Tolkien's Magic Ring' by Peter S. Beagle, with note on Beagle on p. xvii; [xviii] blank; [1] 'The | Homecoming | of | Beorhtnoth | Beorhthelm's Son | [*illustration*]'; [2] blank; 3–27 text; [28] blank; [29] 'Tree and Leaf | [*illustration*] | On Fairy-Stories | *page 33* | Leaf by Niggle | *page 100*'; [30] blank; 31–2 introductory note; 33–90 text of *TL*; 91–9 notes; 100–20 text of *LBN*; [121] 'Farmer Giles | of Ham | [*black letter:*] Aegidii Ahenobarbi Julii Agricole de Hammo | Domini de Domito | Aule Draconarie Comitis | Regni Minimi

Regis et Basilei | mira facinora et mirabilis | exortus | [*roman:*] or in the vulgar tongue | *The Rise and Wonderful Adventures of* | *Farmer Giles, Lord of Tame,* | *Count of Worminghall* | *and King of* | *the Little Kingdom* | [*illustration*] | [*black letter:*] To C. H. Wilkinson'; [122] blank; 123–4 foreword; 125–87 text and illustrations; [188] blank; [189] 'The Adventures | of Tom Bombadil | *and other verses* | *from The Red Book* | [*illustration*] | *with illustrations by* | *Pauline Baynes* | [*illustration*]'; [190] blank; 191–4 preface; [195] illustration; [196] blank; 197–251 text and illustrations; [252] '[*uncials, at left:*] STEP THIS WAY | TO THE LAND OF | ENCHANTMENT . . . | J. R. R. TOLKIEN'S | MIDDLE EARTH! [*illustration, at right*] | Available at your book store or use this coupon. | [*publisher's order form*]'; [253] advertisement of *Biography*; [254] '[*within a thick-thin rule frame:*] J. R. R. TOLKIEN: | MAN | AND MYTH | [*below the frame, advertisement of 5 titles, beginning with* Carpenter, Tolkien: A Biography, *ending with* J. R. R. Tolkien: Man and Myth Boxed Set]'.

Wove paper. Bound in heavy wove wrappers. Printed on upper cover: '[*publisher's "BB" device, in white and black*] [*in black:*] Ballantine/Fantasy 27681/$2.25 | The | TOLKIEN READER | [*rule*] | STORIES, POEMS AND COMMENTARY BY THE | AUTHOR OF "THE HOBBIT," "THE LORD OF THE RINGS" TRILOGY | AND "THE SILMARILLION" | [*rule*] | J. R. R. Tolkien | [*colour illustration by Pauline Baynes, lower part of upper cover illustration of A8a*]'. Printed on spine: '[*publisher's "BB" device, in white and black*] | [*in black:*] Fantasy | [*running down:*] The TOLKIEN READER J. R. R. Tolkien 345-27681-7-225'. Printed on lower cover against colour illustration by Pauline Baynes as for A8a: '[*blurb*] | [*at lower left, running up, in white:*] Cover printed in USA'. All edges trimmed. Top edge stained light orange, fore- and bottom edges unstained.

Published January 1978 at $2.25; number of copies not known.

Reset. The note at the end of 'On Fairy-Stories', p. 99, 'illustrations in hard cover editions have been deleted', was altered but remains erroneous. Illustrations as for A8a.

A9   SMITH OF WOOTTON MAJOR   1967

a. First edition:

Smith | *of Wootton Major* | BY | J. R. R. TOLKIEN | ILLUSTRATIONS BY PAULINE BAYNES | *London* | GEORGE ALLEN & UNWIN LTD | [*illustration, extends upward to left and right of imprint*]

64 pp. Collation: [1–4⁸]. 14.7 × 10.5 cm.

[1] '*Smith of Wootton Major*'; [2] illustration; [3] title; [4] '*First Published in 1967* | [*notice of restrictions under copyright*] | © *George Allen & Unwin Ltd.*, 1967 | *Printed in Great Britain* | *in 11 point Garamond type* | *by Unwin Brothers Ltd* | *Woking and London*'; 5–[62] text and illustrations; [63] blank; [64] '*Other titles by J. R. R. Tolkien* | [8 *titles, beginning with* LR, *ending with* TL] | [*open swelled rule*] | GEORGE ALLEN AND UNWIN LTD'.

Wove paper. Bound in paper over boards. Two bindings, priority as follows:

(1) Wraparound illustration by Pauline Baynes, of Smith in Faery, printed in black, red, olive-green, and white. The black bleeds to all edges and wraps around the spine. Printed on upper cover in white, against the illustration: 'J. R. R.

TOLKIEN | *Smith* | *of Wootton Major*'. Printed on spine in white, against the illustration: '[*running up:*] SMITH OF WOOTTON MAJOR [*parallel with the title:*] J. R. R. TOLKIEN | [*horizontal:*] G | A | & | U'.

(2) Wraparound illustration as for (1), but printed in black, pink, olive-green, and white. The black is here confined to the covers, and the edges are white. The spine is also white except for the pink fantastic creatures of the wraparound illustration. Upper cover printed as for (1). Printed on spine in black: '[*above the illustration, running up:*] SMITH OF WOOTTON MAJOR [*parallel with the title:*] J. R. R. TOLKIEN | [*horizontal, below the illustration:*] G | A | & | U'. Binding 2 was introduced probably because the black spine and edges of binding 1 too readily showed wear.

Both bindings have wove endpapers, no headbands, all sheet edges trimmed and unstained.

Issued without dust-jacket.

Published 9 November 1967 at 7s. 6d.; number of copies not known, but within a week of publication more than 20,000 copies were shipped to bookshops by Allen & Unwin.

In 1964 Tolkien was invited to write a preface to a new edition of 'The Golden Key' by George MacDonald, to be published by Pantheon Books of New York. He conveyed his agreement in a letter to editor Michael di Capua, 7 September 1964 (see further, *Letters* no. 262), and began work at the end of January 1965. He intended the preface to explain the meaning of *Fairy* by means of a brief story about a cook and a cake (see excerpt, *Biography*, pp. 242–3); but the story grew and took on a life of its own, and the preface was abandoned.

Tolkien first called his tale 'The Great Cake'. Its later title, 'Smith of Wootton Major', was meant to suggest an early work by P. G. Wodehouse or a story in the *Boys' Own Paper*. Tolkien sent 'Smith' to Rayner Unwin, who liked it but felt that it was too short to be published on its own. Tolkien replied, in a letter of 20 May 1965, that there was nothing suitable among his papers to publish as companions to 'Smith'. Early in 1966 Tolkien's shorter works were collected by Ballantine Books in *The Tolkien Reader* (A8). Rayner Unwin reserved 'Smith', however, still hoping that it could be published in a small collection by Allen & Unwin. On 26 October 1966 Tolkien read 'Smith' to an audience of more than 800 at Blackfriars, Oxford (see *Letters* no. 290).

On 26 April 1967 Unwin reported to Tolkien that Allen & Unwin had sold 'Smith of Wootton Major' to *Redbook* magazine for their Christmas number. Now it seemed to Unwin that once 'Smith' was published in an American magazine the pressure would become intense in the United States to have it in a more permanent form. He suggested that Allen & Unwin anticipate demand (and Houghton Mifflin's interest in an American edition) by publishing 'Smith', without companions, as a Christmas gift book with illustrations by Pauline Baynes, or by incorporating the story in the next reprint of *Tree and Leaf* (A7) 'as a further example of the variety of leaves that the tree will produce'. On balance, he preferred the former option. Throughout May he corresponded with Baynes about the illustrations. By mid-July the illustrations were ready, and Unwin considered printing them in two colours. Tolkien, however, wanted the drawings to appear in simple black and white, like Baynes' successful illustrations for *Farmer Giles of Ham*.

Tolkien was sent page proofs on 6 August 1967 and returned them corrected on 9 August. On 15 August he objected to the placement of three of the illustrations, two of which were moved to his satisfaction; the third, the frontispiece, had been designed as part of the title spread and could not be moved. He received copies of the finished book on 30 October.

The Golden Key was published in 1967 by Farrar, Straus, and Giroux of New York, for whom Michael di Capua now worked. Instead of a preface by Tolkien the book included an afterword by W. H. Auden, and was illustrated by Maurice Sendak.

'Smith of Wootton Major' was published on 23 November 1967 in *Redbook*, New York, the December 1967 issue, pp. 58–61, 101, 103–7 and editorial mention, p. 6. Pauline Baynes' illustrations were omitted in favour of colour pictures in a contemporary style by Milton Glaser (one reprinted as no. 357 in *The Push Pin Style* [Palo Alto, Calif.: Communications Arts Magazine, 1970]). The story was also published in *Smith of Wootton Major and Farmer Giles of Ham* (A10), *Tree and Leaf, Smith of Wootton Major, [and] The Homecoming of Beorhtnoth Beorhthelm's Son* (A13), *Poems and Stories* (A16), and *Smith of Wootton Major and Leaf by Niggle* (A20). A9a was reprinted *circa* 1969–70 by Yumi Shobo Ltd., Tokyo, in a slipcase with a 16-page booklet, 'Notes on Smith of Wootton Major' by Yoko Inokuma.

b. First American edition (1967):

Smith | *of Wootton Major* | BY | J. R. R. TOLKIEN | ILLUSTRATIONS BY PAULINE BAYNES | *Boston* | HOUGHTON MIFFLIN COMPANY | 1967 | [*illustration, extends upward to left and right of imprint*]

64 pp. Collation: [1–4⁸]. 16.2 × 10.8 cm.

[1] 'SMITH OF WOOTTON MAJOR'; [2] illustration; [3] title; [4] '*First Printing H* | *Copyright* © *1967 by George Allen & Unwin Ltd.* | *All rights reserved including the right* | *to reproduce this book or parts thereof in any form* | *Printed in the United States of America*'; 5–[62] text and illustrations; [63–4] blank.

Wove paper. Bound in yellow-green cloth over boards. Illustration of Smith and Ned, after the illustration by Pauline Baynes on p. [62], stamped on upper cover in green. Stamped on spine, running down, in gilt, against three green panels: 'J. R. R. TOLKIEN SMITH OF WOOTTON MAJOR HMCO'. Buff wove endpapers. No headbands. All edges trimmed. Top edge stained orange, fore- and bottom edges unstained.

Dust-jacket, wove paper. Printed on upper cover: '[*calligraphic script:*] J. R. R. TOLKIEN | [*illustration by Pauline Baynes, of Smith in Faery, coloured version of the illustration on p. [25]*] | [*in olive green:*] SMITH OF | WOOTTON MAJOR | [*in black italic type:*] Illustrated by Pauline Baynes'. Printed on spine, running down: '[*calligraphic script:*] [*in black:*] TOLKIEN [*in olive green:*] SMITH OF WOOTTON MAJOR [*in black type:*] HMCO'. Printed on lower cover in white, against a photograph of Tolkien: 'SOWM 6-97076'. Printed on front flap: '$1.95 | [*blurb*] [*to left of blurb, running down edge:*] 1167'. Printed on back flap: '[*note on Tolkien*] | Photograph of J. R. R. Tolkien | by Roger Hill | [*illustration by Baynes, of Smith and Ned, as on p. [62], in yellow-brown*] | [*in olive-green:*] HOUGHTON MIFFLIN COMPANY | 2 Park Street | Boston, Massachusetts | 02107'.

Published 24 November 1967 at $1.95; 30,000 copies printed.

Typeset as for A9a. Illustrations as for A9a.

c. Second edition (1975):

J. R. R. TOLKIEN | SMITH | OF | WOOTTON MAJOR | WITH ILLUSTRA-TIONS BY | PAULINE BAYNES | [*illustration*] | London | GEORGE ALLEN & UNWIN LTD | Ruskin House Museum Street

64 pp. Collation: [1–4⁸]. 22.3 × 14.2 cm.

[1] blank; [2] 'BY J. R. R. TOLKIEN | [9 *titles, beginning with* LR, *ending with* SGPO]'; [3] 'SMITH | OF | WOOTTON MAJOR'; [4] illustration; [5] title; [6] '*First Published 1967* | [*list of second through seventh impressions, 1967–74*] | *Second Edition 1975* | [*notice of restrictions under copyright*] | © *George Allen & Unwin Ltd., 1967, 1975* | ISBN 0 04 823121 5 | *Printed in Great Britain* | *in 14 point Bembo type* | *by* W & J *Mackay Limited, Chatham*'; 7–[62] text and illustrations; [63–4] blank.

Wove paper. Bound in paper over boards. Wraparound colour illustration by Pauline Baynes, two views of Smith in Faery. Printed on upper cover within open area of illustration: 'J. R. R. TOLKIEN | Smith of | Wootton Major | ILLUS-TRATED BY | PAULINE BAYNES'. Printed on spine, running up, against the illustration: 'J. R. R. TOLKIEN Smith of Wootton Major'. Printed on lower cover against the illustration: 'PRICE NET | £1.95 | IN U.K. ONLY'. Wove endpapers. No headbands. All edges trimmed and unstained.

Issued without dust-jacket.

Published July 1975 at £1.95; number of copies not known.

Reset. Illustrations as for A9a–b.

d. Second American edition (1978):

J. R. R. TOLKIEN | SMITH | OF | WOOTTON MAJOR | WITH ILLUSTRA-TIONS BY | PAULINE BAYNES | [*illustration*] | HOUGHTON MIFFLIN COMPANY BOSTON | 1978

ii, 62 pp. Collation: [1–2¹⁶]. 22.1 × 13.9 cm.

[i] 'SMITH | OF | WOOTTON MAJOR'; [ii] blank; [1] 'BOOKS BY J. R. R. TOLKIEN | [*10 titles, beginning with* LR, *ending with* SGPO] | *The Father Christmas Letters* | (*edited by Baillie Tolkien*) | *The Silmarillion* | (*edited by Christopher Tolkien*) | WITH DONALD SWANN | *The Road Goes Ever On*'; [2] illustration; [3] title; [4] '*Copyright* © *1967, 1975 by George Allen & Unwin Ltd.* | [*notice of restrictions*] | ISBN 0-395-26800-1 | *Printed in the United States of America* | [*printing code, beginning* "A", *ending* "1"]'; [5] 'SMITH | OF | WOOTTON MAJOR'; [6] blank; 7–[62] text and illustrations.

Wove paper. Bound in paper over boards. Wraparound colour illustration by Pauline Baynes, as for A9c. Printed on upper cover within open space in the illustration: 'J. R. R. TOLKIEN | Smith of | Wootton Major | ILLUSTRATED BY | PAULINE BAYNES'. Printed on spine, running up, against the illustration: 'J. R. R. TOLKIEN Smith of Wootton Major'. Printed on lower cover against a pink panel, against the illustration: '[*blurb*] | [*note on Tolkien*] | [*at left:*] HOUGHTON MIFFLIN COMPANY © 1978 | $4.95 [*at right:*] ISBN 0-395-26800-1 | [*rule*] | 6-97062'. Wove endpapers. No headbands. All edges trimmed and unstained.

Issued without dust-jacket.

Published 3 October 1978 at $4.95; 10,000 copies printed.

Typeset as for A9c. Illustrations as for A9c.

e. New edition, hardcover copies (1990):

J. R. R. TOLKIEN | SMITH | OF | WOOTTON MAJOR | With illustrations by Roger Garland | UNWIN HYMAN | London

x, 86 pp. Collation: 48 leaves. 19.6 × 12.9 cm.

[i–ii] blank; [iii] 'SMITH | OF | WOOTTON MAJOR | [*illustration*]'; [iv] blank; [v] 'By J. R. R. Tolkien | [*13 titles, beginning with* H, *ending with* UT] | and, edited by Christopher Tolkien, | *The History of Middle-earth* | [*7 titles, beginning with* The Book of Lost Tales, *ending with* The War of the Ring]'; [vi] illustration; [vii] title; [viii] 'First published in 1967 | [*list of second through seventh impressions, 1967–74*] | Second edition 1975 | Reset New Format 1990 | This new reset format first published in Great Britain by | Unwin Hyman, an imprint of Unwin Hyman Limited, 1990 | © Unwin Hyman Limited 1990 | [*notice of restrictions*] | [*3 publisher's addresses, London to Wellington*] | A CIP catalogue record for this book is available | from the British Library. | Paperback ISBN 0-04-440722-X | Hardback ISBN 0-04-440725-4 | [*at left, publisher's "JRRT" device; at right, two lines:*] © Frank Richard Williamson and Christopher Reuel Tolkien, | executors of the Estate of the late John Ronald Reuel Tolkien | Set in 14 on 18 point Bembo by | Nene Phototypesetters Ltd, Northampton | and printed in Great Britain by | Cox and Wyman Ltd, Reading'; [ix] 'SMITH | OF | WOOTTON MAJOR | [*illustration*]'; [x] blank; 1–74 text and illustrations; [75–6] blank; [77] advertisement of *H*; [78] blank; [79] advertisement of *LR*; [80] blank; [81] advertisement of 'The Complete Tolkien Catalogue'; [82] blank; [83] '*Books by J. R. R. Tolkien in Unwin Paperbacks* | [*order form*]'; [84–6] blank.

Wove paper. Bound in black textured paper over boards. Stamped on spine in gilt: '[*running down:*] Smith Of Wootton Major J. R. R. TOLKIEN | [*horizontal:*] UNWIN | [*publisher's "man drawing a circle" device*] | HYMAN'. Wove pastedowns; no free endpapers. No headbands. All edges trimmed and unstained.

Dust-jacket, wove paper. Printed on upper cover in white, against a colour illustration by Garland, of Smith at work, above a man and horse in a mountain landscape, within and overlapping an architectural frame: 'J. R. R. TOLKIEN | Smith Of | Wootton Major | Illustrated by Roger Garland | [*publisher's "JRRT" device*]'. Printed on spine: '[*running down:*] [*in dark blue:*] Smith Of Wootton Major [*in black:*] J. R. R. TOLKIEN | [*horizontal:*] UNWIN | [*publisher's "man drawing a circle" device*] | HYMAN'. Printed on lower cover: '[*colour illustration, of a blue bird, detail from upper cover illustration*] | [*in black within a black single rule frame:*] ISBN 0-04-440725-4 | [*bar code*]'. Printed on front flap: '[*blurb*] | [2 *quotations, from the* Times Educational Supplement *and* New Statesman] | [*illustration, of Smith walking in Faery, from p. 1*] | [*publisher's "JRRT" device*] £8.99 net U.K.' Printed on back flap: '[*note on Tolkien*] | [*note on Garland*] | Jacket illustration by Roger Garland'.

Published 23 August 1990 at £8.99; 1,000 copies printed, simultaneous with A9f.

Reset, with new illustrations.

f. New edition, paperback copies (1990):

Sheets, pagination, collation as for A9d. 19.6 × 12.7 cm.

Bound in heavy wove wrappers. Upper cover as for the upper jacket of A9d. Printed on spine: '[*running down:*] [*in dark blue:*] Smith Of Wootton Major [*in black:*] J. R. R. TOLKIEN | [*horizontal, publisher's "man drawing a circle" device*]'. Printed on lower cover: '[*colour illustration, of a man and horse in a mountain landscape, detail from upper cover illustration*] | [*in black:*] [*blurb*] | [2 *quotations, from the* Times Educational Supplement *and* New Statesman] | [*at left:*] [*publisher's "JRRT" device*] | Cover illustration by Roger Garland | UNWIN PAPERBACKS |

CHILDREN/FANTASY | £3.99 net U.K. [*at right, within a single rule frame:*] ISBN 0-04-440722-X | [*bar code*]'. All edges trimmed and unstained.

Published 23 August 1990 at £3.99; 10,000 copies printed, simultaneous with A9e.

g. New American edition (1991):

J. R. R. TOLKIEN | SMITH | OF | WOOTTON MAJOR | With illustrations by Roger Garland | [*publisher's 'dolphin' device*] | Houghton Mifflin Company | Boston 1991

x, 86 pp. Collation: 48 leaves. 19.6 × 12.9 cm.

[i–ii] blank; [iii] 'SMITH | OF | WOOTTON MAJOR | [*illustration*]'; [iv] blank; [v] 'By J. R. R. Tolkien | [*15 titles, beginning with* H, *ending with* Bilbo's Last Song] | and, edited by Christopher Tolkien, | *The History of Middle-earth* | [*7 titles, beginning with* The Book of Lost Tales, *ending with* The War of the Ring]'; [vi] illustration; [vii] title; [viii] 'New reset format copyright © 1990 by Unwin Hyman Limited | First American edition 1991 | Originally published in Great Britain in 1990 by Unwin Hyman Ltd. | All rights reserved. For information about permission to reproduce | selections from this book, write to Permissions, Houghton Mifflin | Company, 2 Park Street, Boston, Massachusetts 02108 | ISBN 0-395-57646-6 | Printed in Great Britain | [*printing code, beginning* "10", *ending* "1"] | [*at left,* "JRRT" *device; at right:*] is a trademark of Frank Richard Williamson and | Christopher Reuel Tolkien, executors of the Estate of | the late John Ronald Reuel Tolkien.'; [ix] 'SMITH | OF | WOOTTON MAJOR | [*illustration*]'; [x] blank; 1–74 text and illustrations; [75–6] blank; [77] advertisement of *H*; [78] blank; [79] advertisement of *LR*; [80–6] blank.

Wove paper. Bound in black textured paper over boards. Stamped on spine in gilt: '[*running down:*] Smith Of Wootton Major J. R. R. TOLKIEN | [*horizontal:*] [*publisher's "dolphin" device*] | HMCo'. Wove pastedowns; no free endpapers. No headbands. All edges trimmed and unstained.

Dust-jacket, wove paper. Upper cover as for A9d. Printed on spine: '[*running down:*] [*in dark blue:*] Smith Of Wootton Major [*in black:*] J. R. R. TOLKIEN | [*horizontal:*] [*publisher's "dolphin" device*] | HMCo'. Printed on lower cover: '[*colour illustration, of a blue bird, detail from upper cover illustration*] | [*in black:*] [*at left:*] 5-97096 [*at right:*] ISBN 0-395-57646-6 | [*bar codes*]'. Printed on front flap: '$13.95 | [*blurb*] | [*illustration, of Smith walking in Faery, from p. 1*] | ["JRRT" *device*] 0491'. Printed on back flap: '[*note on Tolkien*] | [*note on Garland*] | Jacket art © 1990 by Unwin Hyman Limited | Jacket illustration by Roger Garland'.

Published 29 April 1991 at $13.95; 5,000 copies printed.

Typeset as for A9e–f, except pp. [v], [vii–viii], [81], [83]. Illustrations as for A9e–f.

A10   **SMITH OF WOOTTON MAJOR AND**   1969
FARMER GILES OF HAM

a. First combined edition:

Smith | *of Wootton Major* | and | *Farmer Giles* | *of Ham* | by | J. R. R. TOLKIEN | Illustrations | by | Pauline Diana Baynes | BALLANTINE BOOKS · NEW YORK

160 pp. Collation: 80 leaves. 17.8 × 10.6 cm.

[1] '*About* SMITH OF WOOTTON MAJOR: | [*quotation from* New York Times Book Review]'; [2] '*Other books by J. R. R. Tolkien:* | [*7 titles, beginning with* H, *ending with* RGEO] | *All available in Ballantine editions.*'; [3] title; [4] '*Smith of Wootton Major* | Copyright © 1967 by George Allen & Unwin Ltd. | *Farmer Giles of Ham* | Copyright © 1949 by George Allen & Unwin Ltd. | All rights reserved including the right to reproduce | this book or parts thereof in any form. | This edition published by arrangement with | Houghton Mifflin Co. | First Printing: March, 1969 | Printed in the United States of America | BALLANTINE BOOKS, INC. | 101 Fifth Avenue, New York, N.Y. 10003'; [5] table of contents; [6] illustration; [7] '*Smith* | *of Wootton Major* | [*illustration*]'; [8] blank; 9–59 text and illustrations; [60] blank; [61] '*Farmer Giles* | *of Ham* | [*black letter:*] Aegidii Ahenobarbi Julii Agricole de Hammo | Domini de Domito | Aule Draconarie Comitis | Regni Minimi Regis et Basilei | mira facinora et mirabilis | exortus | [*roman:*] or in the vulgar tongue | *The Rise and Wonderful Adventures of* | *Farmer Giles, Lord of Tame,* | *Count of Worminghall* | *and King of* | *the Little Kingdom* | [*decoration*]'; [62] blank; 63 '[*black letter:*] To C. H. Wilkinson | [*illustration*]'; 64 illustration; 65–7 foreword; [68] blank; 69–156 text and illustrations; [157] note on Tolkien; [158] blank; [159] 'The great masterpieces of fantasy by | J. R. R. TOLKIEN | [*advertisement of works by Tolkien*]'; [160] advertisement of Porter, *In Wildness is the Preservation of the World.*

Wove paper. Bound in heavy wove wrappers. Printed on upper cover: '[*at upper left:*] [*publisher's "BB" device, in white and black*] [*in black:*] 95¢ | [*below device, running up:*] A BALLANTINE BOOK 01538 | [*at centre of cover, horizontal:*] *By the author of "THE HOBBIT"* | [*calligraphic script:*] J. R. R. TOLKIEN | [*illustration by Pauline Baynes for* SWM, *of Smith in Faery, coloured version of the illustration on p. 27*] | [*against a dark yellow-green panel:*] [*in black:*] [*type:*] HOUGHTON | MIFFLIN | COMPANY | [*in white:*] [*Houghton Mifflin "dolphin" device*] | *Dolphin* | *Edition* | [*in black:*] WITH | BALLANTINE BOOKS | [*below panel:*] [*calligraphic script:*] SMITH of WOOTTON MAJOR | & FARMER GILES of HAM | [*italic type:*] *Illustrated by Pauline Baynes*'. Printed on spine: '[*publisher's "BB" device, in white and black*] | [*running down:*] [*calligraphic script:*] J. R. R. TOLKIEN SMITH of WOOTTON MAJOR [*parallel to first title:*] & FARMER GILES of HAM [*followed by, in type:*] 345-01538-095'. Printed on lower cover in black: '[*within open area of illustration by Baynes printed in brown, as for the upper dust-jacket of A4a:*] *SMITH OF WOOTTON MAJOR* | *and* | *FARMER GILES OF HAM* | *by* | *J. R. R. Tolkien* | *Author of* | *"The Lord of the Rings"* | [*below illustration:*] Cover printed in U.S.A.' All edges trimmed and unstained.

Published March 1969 at $0.95; number of copies not known.

Reset. On p. 28, l. 2, the text reads 'eleven mariners' for 'elven mariners', uncorrected through at least the tenth impression, January 1974. The latter reading is correct, though the accompanying illustration in fact shows eleven mariners. On p. 37, l. 26, 'you own folk' is misprinted for 'your own folk'. Illustrations as for A9 and A4, excluding the first full-page illustration of A4a–e.

With the eleventh impression (August 1975), the cover was changed to feature a colour illustration by the Brothers Hildebrandt, of Farmer Giles and Chrysophylax.

b. New combined edition (1984):

[*title page spread:*] [*left page:*] J. R. R. TOLKIEN | SMITH | OF | WOOTTON MAJOR | WITH ILLUSTRATIONS BY | PAULINE BAYNES | [*illustration*] [*right page:*] FARMER GILES | OF HAM | [*black letter:*] Aegidii Ahenobarbi Julii

Agricole de Hammo | Domini de Domito | Aule Draconarie Comitis | Regni Minimi Regis et Basilei | mira facinora et mirabilis exortus | [*roman:*] or in the vulgar tongue | *The Rise and Wonderful Adventures* | *of Farmer Giles, Lord of Tame* | *Count of Worminghall and* | *King of the Little Kingdom* | EMBELLISHED BY | PAULINE BAYNES | [*decoration*] | NELSON DOUBLEDAY, INC. | GARDEN CITY, NEW YORK

viii, 120 pp. Collation: [1–8⁸]. 20.8 × 13.8 cm.

[i] 'SMITH | OF | WOOTTON MAJOR | *and* | FARMER GILES | OF HAM'; [ii–iii] title; [iv] 'SMITH OF WOOTTON MAJOR | *Copyright* © *1967, 1975 by George Allen & Unwin Ltd.* | FARMER GILES OF HAM | *Copyright* © *1976 by* | *George Allen & Unwin (Publishers) Ltd.* | [*notice of restrictions*] | *Printed in the United States of America*'; [v] table of contents; [vi] blank; [vii] 'SMITH | OF | WOOTTON MAJOR | *and* | FARMER GILES | OF HAM'; [viii] blank; [1] 'SMITH | OF | WOOTTON MAJOR'; [2] illustration; [3]–43 text and illustrations; [44] blank; [45] 'FARMER GILES | OF HAM'; [46] blank; [47]–8 foreword; [49]–117 text and illustrations ([116] is blank); [118–20] blank. Printing code, 'O13', printed in gutter, p. 114.

Wove paper. Bound in yellow-gold paper over boards. Stamped in black on spine: '[*running down:*] SMITH OF WOOTTON MAJOR [*parallel to preceding title:*] & FARMER GILES OF HAM [*followed by:*] J. R. R. Tolkien | [*horizontal:*] NELSON | DOUBLEDAY'. Wove endpapers. Illustrations by Pauline Baynes for *Farmer Giles of Ham* printed in black, grey-blue, and yellow-brown on endpapers: on front pastedown and verso, back free endpaper, the dragon Chrysophylax attacking; on recto, front free endpaper and back pastedown, Chrysophylax unhorsing Farmer Giles. No headbands. Top edge trimmed, fore- and bottom edges untrimmed. All edges unstained.

Dust-jacket, wove paper. Printed on upper cover against a colour illustration by Daniel R. Horne, of a dragon and a decorated cake under a tree: '[*in white:*] J. R. R. Tolkien | [*in yellow-green:*] SMITH OF WOOTTON MAJOR | & FARMER GILES OF HAM'. Printed on spine against a blue-purple background: '[*running down, in yellow-green:*] SMITH OF WOOTTON MAJOR [*parallel to preceding title:*] & FARMER GILES OF HAM [*followed by, in white:*] J. R. R. Tolkien | [*horizontal:*] NELSON | DOUBLEDAY'. Printed on lower cover against a white panel, against a blue-purple background: '4020'. Printed on front flap: '[*in yellow outlined in black:*] SMITH OF WOOTTON MAJOR | & FARMER GILES OF HAM | [*in blue:*] J. R. R. Tolkien | [*in black:*] [*blurb*] | *Book Club* | *Edition*'. Printed on back flap: '[*blurb, continued*] | Jacket painting by | Daniel R. Horne | PRINTED IN THE U.S.A.' Published by the Science Fiction Book Club, late March 1984? at $3.98?; number of copies not known.

Reset. Illustrations as for A9 and A4, except that the coloured illustrations for *FGH* are printed on the endpapers.

A11   BILBO'S LAST SONG   1974

a. First edition:

BILBO'S LAST SONG | (At the Grey Havens) | [*poem*] | J. R. R. Tolkien

Poster, printed one side only. 60.0 × 40.2 cm.

Wove paper. Poem printed in black against a colour photograph by Robert Strindberg, of a river scene. Printed against the illustration at lower left, in yellow-green: 'TEXT COPYRIGHT © 1974 BY M. JOY HILL | PHOTOGRAPH © 1974 BY ROBERT STRINDBERG'.

Published by Houghton Mifflin, Boston, 2 April 1974 at $2.50; 105,000 copies printed.

The final line of the poem correctly reads 'I see the Star above your mast!'

It is not known when Tolkien wrote 'Bilbo's Last Song'. It was not, at least, the last poem he wrote. His friend and secretary, Joy Hill, found it written in an exercise book while putting his library in order when he moved to Bournemouth. Tolkien presented the poem to her, with its copyright, on 3 September 1970, as a token of gratitude.

b. First British edition (1974):

BILBO'S LAST SONG | (At the Grey Havens) | [*poem*] | J. R. R. Tolkien

Poster, printed one side only. 76.2 × 50.5 cm.

Wove paper. Poem printed in black against a colour illustration by Pauline Baynes, of Sam, Merry, and Pippin watching the Last Ship sail away (at the end of *The Lord of the Rings*). Printed below the illustration: 'Illustration © Pauline Baynes 1974. Text © M. Joy Hill 1974. First published by George Allen & Unwin Ltd 1974. ISBN 0 04 912005 0 Printed in Great Britain by Jolly & Barber Ltd, Rugby.'

Published 26 September 1974 at £0.80; number of copies not known.

Reset, with a new illustration. The final line of the poem incorrectly reads: 'I see the Star above my [*for* your] mast!'.

This version was 'published' in the United States as a double-sided jigsaw puzzle (with *A Map of Middle-earth* by Pauline Baynes) by International Polygonics, New York, 1976.

c. New edition (1990):

BILBO'S LAST SONG | (At the Grey Havens) | J. R. R. Tolkien | Illustrated by Pauline Baynes | [*colour illustration*] | UNWIN | [*publisher's 'man drawing a circle' device*] | HYMAN | LONDON SYDNEY WELLINGTON

32 pp. Collation: [1–2⁸]. 25.3 × 20.3 cm.

[1] title; [2] '[*3 publisher's addresses, London to Wellington*] | Conceived designed and produced by Signpost Books Ltd. | 44 Uxbridge Street, London W8 7TG | Copyright in this format © 1990 Signpost Books Ltd. | Text copyright © 1974 M. Joy Hill | Illustrations copyright © 1990 Pauline Baynes | Editor: Felicity Trotman | The quotations are taken from the second hardback | edition of *The Lord of the Rings* (© George Allen | & Unwin (Publishers) Ltd., 1966) and the fourth | hardback edition of *The Hobbit* (© George Allen | & Unwin Ltd., 1978) and are reproduced by kind | permission of Unwin Hyman Ltd. | A CIP catalogue record for this book is available from | The British Library | Set in Optima Classified | Printed and bound in Hong Kong | [*colour illustrations*]'; 3–27 text and colour illustrations; 28 blank; 29 poem, 'Bilbo's Last Song', with facsimile signature 'J. R. R. Tolkien'; 30–2 notes on the pictures.

Wove paper. Bound in paper over boards. Covers and spine printed against a dark green background. Printed on upper cover: '[*within a white double rule frame:*] [*in white:*] BILBO'S LAST | SONG | [*colour illustration by Pauline Baynes, of the procession from Rivendell, from p. 11*] | [*in white:*] J. R. R. TOLKIEN | [*interrupting the frame:*] Illustrated by Pauline Baynes'. Printed on spine, running down, in white: 'BILBO'S LAST SONG J. R. R. TOLKIEN UNWIN HYMAN'. Printed on lower cover against a white panel: 'ISBN 0-04-440728-9 | [*bar code*]'. Wove endpapers; colour illustration by Baynes, of the procession from Rivendell, printed on each spread of pastedown and free endpaper. No headbands. All edges trimmed and unstained.

Dust-jacket, wove paper. Covers and spine identical to binding. Printed on front flap: '[*blurb*] | £6.95'. Printed on back flap: '[*note on Tolkien*] | [*note on Baynes*] | Cover design by Ned Hoste/2H'.

Published 13 September 1990 at £6.95; 6,000 copies printed.

Reset, newly illustrated, in book form.

Three series of illustrations run parallel through the book. The first, at top on rectos (except p. [3], facing the text of the poem on the opposite verso), tells the story of Bilbo Baggins' last days at Rivendell, his procession with Elrond, Galadriel, et al. to the Grey Havens, his farewell to his hobbit friends, and his sailing to the Undying Lands, as told in the final chapters of *The Lord of the Rings*. The second series, which divides the pages into upper and lower sections, depicts a pensive or sleepy Bilbo, remembering his past adventures. The third series, at the foot of each page, tells the story of *The Hobbit*.

Published in Canada in 1990 by Riverwood, Sharon, Ontario.

A British book club edition was published in 1990, identical to A11c except with no price printed on the dust-jacket.

d. New American edition (1990):

BILBO'S LAST SONG | (At the Grey Havens) | J. R. R. Tolkien | Illustrated by Pauline Baynes | [*colour illustration*] | Houghton Mifflin Company Boston 1990

32 pp. Collation: [1–2⁸]. 25.3 × 20.3 cm.

Contents as for A11c, except pp. [1] title, as above; and [2]: 'First American Edition 1990 | Conceived, designed, and produced by Signpost Books Ltd. | 44 Uxbridge Street, London W8 7TG | Copyright in this format © 1990 Signpost Books Ltd. | Text copyright © 1974 M. Joy Hill | Illustrations copyright © 1990 Pauline Baynes | All rights reserved | For information about permission to reproduce selections | from this book, write to Permissions, Houghton Mifflin | Company, 2 Park Street, Boston, Massachusetts 02108. | [*Library of Congress Cataloging in Publication Data*] | Editor: Felicity Trotman | The quotations are taken from the second hardback edition of The | Lord of the Rings (© George Allen & Unwin Ltd., 1966) and the | fourth hardback edition of *The Hobbit* (© George Allen & Unwin | Ltd., 1978) and are reproduced by kind permission of Unwin | Hyman Ltd. | Set in Optima Classified | Printed and bound in Hong Kong | [*colour illustrations*]'.

Wove paper. Bound in paper over boards. Covers and spine printed against a dark green background. Upper cover as for A11c. Printed on spine in white: '[*running down:*] Houghton Mifflin | [*publisher's "dolphin" device, horizontal*]'. Printed on lower cover against a white panel: 'ISBN 0-395-53810-6 | [*bar codes*]'. Wove endpapers; colour illustration by Baynes, of the procession from Rivendell, printed on each spread of pastedown and free endpaper. No headbands. All edges trimmed and unstained.

Dust-jacket, wove paper. Covers and spine printed against a dark green background.

Upper cover as for A11c. Printed on spine in white: '[*running down:*] BILBO'S LAST SONG J. R. R. TOLKIEN Houghton Mifflin | [*publisher's "dolphin" device, horizontal*]'. Printed on lower cover: '[*at left, in white:*] 6–97104 [*at right, in black, against a white panel:*] ISBN 0-395-53810-6 | [*bar codes*]'. Printed on front flap: '$14.95 | [*blurb*] | 0990'. Printed on back flap: '[*note on Tolkien*] | [*note on Baynes*] | Cover design by Ned Hoste/2H'.

Published 14 November 1990 at $14.95; 10,000 copies printed.

Typeset as for A11c, except pp. [1–2]. Illustrations as for A11c.

e. First British paperback edition (1992):

BILBO'S LAST SONG | (At the Grey Havens) | J. R. R. Tolkien | Illustrated by Pauline Baynes | [*colour illustration*] | RED FOX

32 pp. Collation: [1–2^8]. 25.5 × 20.2 cm.

Contents as for A11c, except pp. [1] title, as above; and [2] 'A Red Fox Book | Published by Random Century Children's Books | 20 Vauxhall Bridge Road, London SW1V 2SA | A division of the Random Century Group | London Melbourne Sydney Auckland | Johannesburg and agencies throughout the world | First published in Great Britain by Unwin Hyman Ltd 1990 | Red Fox edition 1992 | Copyright in this format © Signpost Books Ltd | Text copyright © M. Joy Hill 1974 | Illustrations copyright © Pauline Baynes 1990 | Editor: Felicity Trotman | The quotations are taken from the second hardback edition of THE LORD OF THE RINGS | (© George Allen & Unwin (Publishers) Ltd., 1966) and the fourth hardback edition of | THE HOBBIT (© George Allen & Unwin (Publishers) Ltd., 1978) and are reproduced by kind | permission of Harper Collins Publishers. | [*note on conditions of sale*] | Printed in Hong Kong | ISBN 0 09 991020 9 | [*colour illustrations*]'.

Wove paper. Bound in heavy wove wrappers. Covers and spine printed against a dark green background. Upper cover as for A11c. Printed on spine, running down, in white: 'BILBO'S LAST SONG J. R. R. Tolkien Arrow Books'. Printed on lower cover: '[*in white, within a white double rule frame:*] [*blurb*] | [*2 quotations, from the* School Librarian *and* Publishers Weekly] | [*note on Tolkien*] | 1992 is the centenary of the birth of J R R Tolkien, and | BILBO'S LAST SONG appears for the first time in paperback. | [*in black, against white and grey panels outlined in black, interrupting the frame:*] [*against the white panel:*] ISBN 0-09-991020-9 | [*bar code*] | [*rule, dividing the panels*] | [*against the light grey panel:*] UK £3.99'. All edges trimmed and unstained.

Published 19 March 1992 at £3.99; 15,150 copies printed.

Typeset as for A11c, except pp. [1–2]. Illustrations as for A11c.

f. First American paperback edition (1992):

BILBO'S LAST SONG | (At the Grey Havens) | J. R. R. Tolkien | Illustrated by Pauline Baynes | [*colour illustration*] | DRAGONFLY BOOKS • ALFRED A. KNOPF | New York

32 pp. Collation: [1–2^8]. 25.4 × 20.0 cm.

Contents as for A11c, except pp. [1] title, as above; and [2]: 'A DRAGONFLY BOOK PUBLISHED BY ALFRED A. KNOPF, INC. | Text copyright © 1974 M. Joy Hill | Illustrations copyright © 1990 Pauline Baynes | [*notice of restrictions under copyright*] | Library of Congress Catalog Card Number: 89-48659 | ISBN: 0-679-

82710-2 | First Dragonfly Books edition: March 1992 | Manufactured in Hong Kong | *[printing code, beginning "10", ending "1"]* | The quotations are taken from the second hardback | edition of *The Lord of the Rings* (© George Allen | & Unwin Ltd., 1966) and the fourth | hardback edition of *The Hobbit* (© George Allen | & Unwin Ltd., 1978) and are reproduced by kind | permission of Unwin Hyman Ltd. | *[colour illustrations]*'.

Wove paper. Bound in heavy wove wrappers. Covers and spine printed against a dark green background. Printed on upper cover: '*[at upper right, publisher's "fly-book" device, in light pink]* *[at centre:]* *[in yellow:]* J. R. R. TOLKIEN | *[in white:]* *[flourish]* *[3 leaf ornaments]* *[flourish]* | *[in yellow:]* BILBO'S LAST SONG | *[colour illustration by Pauline Baynes, of the procession from Rivendell, framed by two trees (the complete illustration from p. 11), against an irregular white panel]* | *[in light pink:]* illustrated by pauline baynes'. Printed on spine, running down, in white: 'Tolkien / Baynes BILBO'S LAST SONG Knopf'. Printed on lower cover: '*[publisher's "fly-book" device, in light pink]* | *[in yellow:]* "RIVETING!"* | *[in white:]* *[flourish]* *[3 leaf ornaments]* *[flourish]* | *[in yellow:]* *[blurb]* | "A must for all fans of Tolkien's vast, epic fantasy." | —*Publishers Weekly** | *[in white:]* *[flourish]* *[3 leaf ornaments]* *[flourish]* | *[note on Tolkien, in yellow]* | *[at left, in black against a white panel:]* *[2 bar codes]* | ISBN 0-679-82710-2 *[at right, in light pink:]* A DRAGONFLY BOOK™ | Alfred A. Knopf · New York | $6.99 U.S. Printed in Hong Kong'. All edges trimmed and unstained.

Published 2 March 1992 at $6.99; number of copies not known.

Typeset as for A11c, except pp. [1–2]. Illustrations as for A11c.

A12   FARMER GILES OF HAM   1975
          [AND] THE ADVENTURES OF TOM BOMBADIL

Farmer Giles | of Ham | The Adventures | of Tom Bombadil | J. R. R. TOLKIEN | UNWIN BOOKS

144 pp. Collation: 72 leaves. 19.6 × 12.7 cm.

[1] '*[publisher's alternating black/white "U" devices]* | UNWIN BOOKS | Farmer Giles of Ham | The Adventures of Tom Bombadil | *[blurbs]*'; [2] 'by J. R. R. Tolkien | *[8 titles, beginning with H, ending with SGPO]*'; [3] title; [4] '*Farmer Giles of Ham* first published in 1949 | Eleventh impression 1974 | *The Adventures of Tom Bombadil* first published in 1961 | Eighth impression 1974 | Unwin Books Edition 1975 | *[notice of restrictions under copyright]* | © George Allen & Unwin Ltd, 1949, 1961, 1975 | UNWIN BOOKS | George Allen & Unwin Ltd | Ruskin House, Museum Street | London WC1A 1LU | Printed in Great Britain | in 11 on 13 pt Plantin type | by Cox & Wyman Ltd | London, Reading and Fakenham'; [5] table of contents; [6] illustration; [7] 'Farmer Giles | of Ham | *[black letter:]* Aegidii Ahenobarbi Julii Agricole de Hammo | Domini de Domito | Aule Draconarie Comitis | Regni Minimi Regis et Basilei | mira facinora et mirabilis | exortus | *[roman:]* or in the vulgar tongue | *The Rise and Wonderful Adventures of* | *Farmer Giles, Lord of Tame* | *Count of Worminghall and* | *King of the Little Kingdom* | embellished by Pauline Diana Baynes | *[illustration]*'; [8] '*[black letter:]* To C. H. Wilkinson | *[illustration]*'; [9]–10 foreword and illustrations; [11]–[76] text and illustrations; [77] 'The Adventures | of Tom Bombadil | *and other verses* | *from The Red Book* | *[illustration]* | with illustrations by Pauline Baynes | *[illustration]* | *[illustration]*'; [78]–82 preface, with illustrations on p. [82]; [83]–144 text and illustrations.

Wove paper. Bound in heavy wove wrappers. Covers and spine printed against a green background. Printed on upper cover: '[*in white:*] TOLKIEN | [*in purple:*] Farmer Giles | of Ham | [*colour illustration, of a hanging sword, after the drawing by Pauline Baynes for* FGH, *p. [8]*] | [*in purple:*] The | Adventures | of | Tom | Bombadil | [*colour illustration, of a bird and leafy branches, half-enclosing "Bombadil"*] | [*publisher's wraparound, alternating green/dark green "U" devices, partly overlapped by "Bombadil" and the lower illustration*] | [*in dark green:*] UNWIN BOOKS'. Printed on spine: '[*running down:*] [*in white:*] TOLKIEN [*in purple:*] Farmer Giles of Ham [*parallel to first title:*] The Adventures of Tom Bombadil | [*publisher's "U" device*]'. Lower cover identical with upper cover, except that 'TOLKIEN' is omitted and the remainder, except the wraparound devices and 'UNWIN BOOKS', is raised on the page. Printed inside upper cover: 'PRICE NET | £1·00 | IN U.K. ONLY'. All edges trimmed and unstained.

Published 30 October 1975 at £1.00; number of copies not known.

Issued separately or in a set with *The Hobbit* (A5n) and *Tree and Leaf, Smith of Wootton Major [and] The Homecoming of Beorhtnoth Beorhthelm's Son* (A13), 2 September 1976; slipcase, see A5n.

Reset. Illustrations as for A4 and A6, except that all are printed in black and white.

   With the third impression (1979) the cover was changed to feature a colour illustration of Chrysophylax, after the drawing by Pauline Baynes for *Farmer Giles of Ham* (A12, p. 42).

A13   TREE AND LEAF, SMITH OF WOOTTON MAJOR   1975
[AND] THE HOMECOMING OF BEORHTNOTH
BEORHTHELM'S SON

Tree and Leaf | Smith of | Wootton Major | The Homecoming | of Beorhtnoth | Beorhthelm's Son | J. R. R. TOLKIEN | UNWIN BOOKS

176 pp. Collation: 88 leaves. 19.6 × 12.8 cm.

[1] '[*publisher's alternating black/white "U" devices*] | Tree and Leaf Smith of Wootton Major | The Homecoming of Beorhtnoth Beorhthelm's Son | [blurbs]'; [2] 'by J. R. R. Tolkien | [*8 titles, beginning with* H, *ending with* SGPO]'; [3] title; [4] '*Tree and Leaf* first published 1964 | Ninth impression 1974 | Second (Reset) Edition 1975 | *Smith of Wootton Major* first published 1967 | Seventh impression 1974 | Second (Reset) Edition 1975 | *The Homecoming of Beorhnoth Beorhthelm's Son* | first published by George Allen & Unwin Ltd 1975 | Unwin Books Edition 1975 | [*notice of restrictions under copyright*] | © George Allen & Unwin Ltd 1964, 1967, 1975 | ISBN 0 04 820015 8 | UNWIN BOOKS | George Allen & Unwin Ltd | Ruskin House Museum Street | London WC1A 1LU | Printed in Great Britain | in 10 point Plantin type | by Cox & Wyman Ltd, | London, Reading and Fakenham'; [5] table of contents; [6] blank; [7] 'Tree and Leaf'; [8] blank; [9]–10 introductory note; [11]–79 text of 'On Fairy-Stories'; [80]–102 text of 'Leaf by Niggle'; [103] 'Smith of | Wootton Major'; [104] illustration; [105] 'Smith of | Wootton Major | Illustrations by Pauline Baynes | [*illustration*]'; [106] blank; [107]–46 text and illustrations; [147] 'The Homecoming | of Beorhtnoth | Beorhthelm's Son'; [148] blank; [149]–75 text; [176] '[*publisher's alternating black/white "U" devices*] | UNWIN BOOKS | [*advertisement of* LR, H, *and* Farmer Giles of Ham and The Adventures of Tom Bombadil]'.

Wove paper. Bound in heavy wove wrappers. Covers and spine printed against a dark blue-green background. Printed on upper cover: '[*in white:*] TOLKIEN | [*in orange, enclosed on three sides by colour illustration after Tolkien, of two trees with various kinds of leaves:*] Tree | and Leaf | Smith of | Wootton Major | The | Homecoming | of | Beorhtnoth | [*publisher's wraparound, alternating gold/green "U" devices, partly overlapped by "Beorhtnoth" and the illustration*] | [*in gold:*] UNWIN BOOKS'. Printed on spine, running down: '[*in white:*] TOLKIEN [*partly against illustrations extending onto spine from upper and lower covers, and partly against the publisher's "U" device:*] Tree and Leaf/Smith of Wootton Major [*parallel with the preceding titles:*] The Homecoming of Beorhtnoth'. Lower cover identical with upper cover, except that 'TOLKIEN' is omitted. Printed inside upper cover: 'PRICE NET | £1·00 | IN U.K. ONLY'. All edges trimmed and unstained.

Published 30 October 1975 at £1.00; number of copies not known.

Issued separately or in a set with *The Hobbit* (A5n) and *Farmer Giles of Ham [and] The Adventures of Tom Bombadil* (A12), 2 September 1976; slipcase, see A5n.

Reset. Illustrations for *SWM* as for A9.
   With the third impression (1979), the cover was changed to feature an illustration of a tree by J. R. R. Tolkien (cf. Ei2, no. 41 [colour, upper left]).

A14   **THE FATHER CHRISTMAS LETTERS**   1976

a. First edition:

J. R. R. TOLKIEN | THE | FATHER | CHRISTMAS | LETTERS | *Edited by* Baillie Tolkien | [*colour illustration, extends across title spread*] | London | George Allen & Unwin Ltd | RUSKIN HOUSE · MUSEUM STREET

48 pp. Collation: [1–3⁸]. 27.6 × 21.9 cm.

[1] 'THE | FATHER | CHRISTMAS | LETTERS | [*decoration*]'; [2] 'J. R. R. TOLKIEN | [*10 titles, beginning with* LR, *ending with* SGPO] | With Donald Swann | The Road Goes Ever On | [*left half of illustration*]'; [3] title; [4] illustrations; [5–7] introduction and illustrations; [8–45] text and illustrations; [46–7] appendix, with alphabets; [48] 'First published in 1976 | [*notice of restrictions under copyright*] | © George Allen & Unwin (Publishers) Ltd 1976 | ISBN 0 04 823130 4 | Printed in Great Britain | by Westerham Press'. All illustrations are by J. R. R. Tolkien, in colour except pp. [12], [46–7].

Wove paper. Bound in paper over boards. Covers and spine are printed against a dark green background. Printed on upper cover: '[*in red:*] J. R. R. TOLKIEN | [*in white:*] The Father | Christmas Letters | [*colour illustration by Tolkien, of Father Christmas and the northern lights, from p. [10]*]'. Printed on spine, running down: '[*in red:*] J. R. R. TOLKIEN [*in white:*] The Father Christmas Letters [*in black, against a white panel:*] GEORGE ALLEN [*parallel to the preceding two words:*] & UNWIN'. Colour illustration by Tolkien, *Polar Bear had Fallen from Top to Bottom upon His Nose* (from p. [15]), printed on lower cover. Circular gold label affixed to lower cover, printed in black: 'PRICE NET | £2.50 | In U.K. Only'. Wove endpapers. No headbands. All edges trimmed and unstained.

Issued without dust-jacket.

Published 2 September 1976 at £2.50; 50,000 copies printed.

Contains most of the letters J. R. R. Tolkien, as 'Father Christmas', wrote and illustrated for his children, beginning in 1920 when his first son, John, was three, and continuing until 1943. The letters through 1939 are transcribed. Some of the manuscripts and 'almost all of the pictures' are reproduced, most of them in colour.

Published in Canada in 1976 by Methuen, Toronto.

A book club edition was published in 1976 by Book Club Associates, London, in similar binding and dust-jacket.

b. First American edition (1976):

J. R. R. TOLKIEN | THE | FATHER | CHRISTMAS | LETTERS | *Edited by* Baillie Tolkien | [*colour illustration, extends across title spread*] | Boston | Houghton Mifflin Company 1976 | Copyright © George Allen & Unwin Ltd 1976

48 pp. Collation: [1–3^8]. 27.3 × 21.5 cm.

Contents as for A14a, except pp. [2] 'J. R. R. TOLKIEN | [*10 titles, beginning with* LR, *ending with* SGPO] | With Donald Swann | *The Road Goes Ever On*] | [*left half of illustration*] | [*notice of restrictions under copyright*] | ISBN 0 395 24981 3'; and [3] title, as above.

Wove paper. Bound in beige cloth over boards. Illustration, *By Elf Messenger* (after illustration by Tolkien, p. [4]), printed on upper cover in red and green. Printed on spine, running down: '[*five-dot ornament, in red*] [*in green*] J. R. R. TOLKIEN [*five-dot ornament, in red*] [*in green:*] THE FATHER CHRISTMAS LETTERS [*five-dot ornament, in red*] [*in green:*] HMCO [*five-dot ornament, in red*]'. Wove endpapers. No headbands. All edges trimmed and unstained.

Dust-jacket, wove paper. Covers as for covers of A14a, except printed against the illustration on the lower cover: 'ISBN 0-395-24981-3 | [*rule*] | 6-97066'. Printed on spine, running down, against a dark green background: '[*in red:*] J. R. R. TOLKIEN [*in white:*] The Father Christmas Letters [*in red, against a white panel:*] Houghton Mifflin [*parallel to the preceding two words:*] Company'. Printed on front flap: '$8.95 | [*blurb*] [*to left of blurb, running down:*] 1076'. Printed on back flap: '[*blurb, continued*] | HOUGHTON MIFFLIN COMPANY | 2 Park Street | Boston, Massachusetts 02107'.

Published 19 October 1976 at $8.95; 40,000 copies printed. A second impression of 25,000 copies was printed before publication.

Typeset as for A14a, except pp. [2–3]. Illustrations as for A14a.

c. First paperback edition (1978):

J. R. R. TOLKIEN | THE | FATHER | CHRISTMAS | LETTERS | *Edited by* Baillie Tolkien | [*colour illustration, extends across title spread*] | London | UNWIN® PAPERBACKS | Boston Sydney

48 pp. Collation: [1–2^{12}]. 24.4 × 18.6 cm.

Contents as for A14a, except pp. [1] 'THE | FATHER | CHRISTMAS | LETTERS | [*illustration*] | [*blurb*]'; [2] 'J. R. R. TOLKIEN | [*11 titles, beginning with* LR, *ending with* SGPO] | With Donald Swann | *The Road Goes Ever On* | [*left half of illustration extending across title spread*]'; [3] title, as above; and [48] 'First published in Great Britain by George Allen & Unwin 1976 | First published in Unwin Paperbacks 1978 | [*notice of restrictions under copyright*] | UNWIN® PAPERBACKS | 40 Museum Street, London WC1A 1LU | © George Allen & Unwin (Publishers) Ltd 1976, 1978 | [*British Library Cataloguing in Publication Data, within a single rule frame*] | Printed in Great Britain by William Clowes & Sons, Limited | London, Beccles and Colchester'.

Wove paper. Bound in heavy wove wrappers. Printed on upper cover against a mottled cream background: '[*in red:*] The | Father Christmas | Letters | [*in blue:*] J. R. R. Tolkien | [*colour illustrations by Tolkien, of Father Christmas and two "stamps", from pp. [4], [7], [20]*] | [*publisher's "unwin/UNWIN PAPERBACKS" device, in red, white, and black*]'. Spine printed in mottled cream, no lettering. Printed on lower cover within a single rule frame, against a mottled cream background: '[*blurb*] | [*4 quotations, from* Woman's Own, Country Life, Books for Your Children, *and the London* Sunday Times] | [*at left:*] UNITED KINGDOM £1.50 [*at right:*] TOLKIEN/CHILDREN'S | 0 04 823148 7'. All edges trimmed and unstained.

Published September 1978 at £1.50; number of copies not known.

Typeset as for A14a, except pp. [1–3], [48]. Illustrations as for A14a, except some illustrations reduced to fit the smaller format.

A14c was reprinted in 1990 by Unwin Paperbacks, marked as if the first Unwin Paperbacks edition, with colour illustration by Tolkien, *Polar Bear had Fallen from Top to Bottom upon His Nose*, on the upper cover.

d. First American paperback edition (1979):

J. R. R. TOLKIEN | THE | FATHER | CHRISTMAS | LETTERS | *Edited by* Baillie Tolkien | [*colour illustration, extends across title spread*] | HOUGHTON MIFFLIN COMPANY BOSTON 1979

48 pp. Collation: 24 leaves. 27.2 × 21.1 cm.

Contents as for A14a, except pp. [2] 'J. R. R. TOLKIEN | [*10 titles, beginning with* LR, *ending with* SGPO] | With Donald Swann | *The Road Goes Ever On* | [*left half of illustration*] | Copyright © George Allen & Unwin (Publishers) Ltd. 1976 | [*notice of restrictions under copyright*] | ISBN 0-395-24981-3 | ISBN 0-395-28262-4 (pbk.) | [*printing code, beginning "N", ending "1"*]'; [3] title, as above; and [48] blank.

Wove paper. Bound in heavy wove wrappers. Covers as for A14a, except 'ISBN 0-395-28262-4 | [*rule*] | 6–97083 | HOUGHTON MIFFLIN COMPANY © 1979' printed on lower cover against the illustration, and circular label affixed to lower cover, printed: '$4.95'. Printed on spine in red, against a white background: '[*running down:*] J. R. R. TOLKIEN THE FATHER CHRISTMAS LETTERS HOUGHTON MIFFLIN COMPANY | [*publisher's "dolphin" device, horizontal*]'. All edges trimmed and unstained.

Published 18 October 1979 at $4.95; 30,000 copies printed.

A14d was reprinted in 1991 by Houghton Mifflin, with colour illustration by Tolkien, *Polar Bear had Fallen from Top to Bottom upon His Nose*, on the upper wrapper.

A15   THE SILMARILLION   1977

a. First edition (British), export copies:

[*2 lines in tengwar, between double rules*] | J. R. R. TOLKIEN | The Silmarillion | edited by | CHRISTOPHER TOLKIEN | London | GEORGE ALLEN & UNWIN | Boston Sydney | [*2 lines in tengwar, between double rules*]

368 pp. + 1 plate (map). Collation: [1–4^{16}(4$_{12}$+χ1)5–10^{16}11^{8}12^{16}]. 22.0 × 14.1 cm.

[1–2] blank; [3] 'THE SILMARILLION'; [4] '[*2 lines in tengwar, between double rules*] | J. R. R. TOLKIEN | QUENTA SILMARILLION | (The History of the Silmarils) | together with | AINULINDALË | (The Music of the Ainur) | and | VALAQUENTA | (Account of the Valar) | To which is appended | AKALLABÊTH | (The Downfall of Númenor) | and | OF THE RINGS OF POWER AND | THE THIRD AGE | [*2 lines in tengwar, between double rules*]'; [5] title; [6] '*First published in 1977* | [*notice of restrictions under copyright*] | © *George Allen & Unwin (Publishers) Ltd, 1977* | ISBN 0 04 823139 8 | *Printed in Great Britain* | *in 11 on 12 point Imprint type* | *by William Clowes & Sons, Limited* | *London, Beccles and Colchester*'; 7–9 foreword; [10] blank; 11–12 table of contents; [13] 'AINULINDALË | [*swelled rule*]'; [14] blank; 15–22 text; [23] 'VALAQUENTA | [*swelled rule*]'; [24] blank; 25–32 text; [33] 'QUENTA SILMARILLION | [*swelled rule*] | *The History of the* | *Silmarils*'; [34] blank; 35–121 text; [121+1] map, *The Realms of the Noldor and the Sindar*, in black and red; [121+2] blank; 122–255 text; [256] blank; [257] 'AKALLABÊTH | [*swelled rule*]'; [258] blank; 259–82 text; [283] 'OF THE | RINGS OF POWER | AND THE | THIRD AGE | [*swelled rule*]'; [284] blank; 285–304 text; [305–9] genealogical tables; 310–11 note on pronunciation; [312] blank; 313–54 index; 355–65 appendix; [366–8] blank. *Map of Beleriand and the Lands to the North*, in black and red on folded leaf tipped onto blank p. [387], or onto recto, back free endpaper; no priority determined.

Wove paper. Bound in dark blue cloth, or dark blue textured paper, over boards; no priority determined. Stamped on spine in gilt: '[*decoration after Tolkien, heraldic device of Lúthien Tinúviel*] | The | Silmarillion | J. R. R. | TOLKIEN | GEORGE ALLEN | AND UNWIN'. Wove endpapers. Dark blue/white headbands (copies with stained top edge) or no headbands (copies with unstained top edge). All edges trimmed. Top edge stained dark blue (copies with headbands) or unstained (copies with no headbands), fore- and bottom edges unstained.

Dust-jacket, wove paper. Covers and spine printed against a dark blue (copies with stained top edge) or dark blue-purple (copies with top edge unstained) background, no priority determined. Printed on upper cover: '[*in red outlined in white:*] The | Silmarillion | [*colour illustration by Tolkien, heraldic device of Lúthien Tinúviel, outlined in white*] | [*in white:*] TOLKIEN'. Printed on spine: '[*running down:*] [*in red outlined in white:*] The Silmarillion [*in white:*] TOLKIEN | [*horizontal, in red:*] GEORGE ALLEN | & UNWIN'. Five colour illustrations by Tolkien, heraldic devices, outlined in white. Blurb printed on front flap. Printed on back flap: '[*blurb, continued*] | *Emblems designed by J. R. R. Tolkien* | *Front cover:* Lúthien Tinúviel | *Back cover:* Fingolfin Eärendil | Idril Celebrindal | Elwë Fëanor | ISBN 0 04 823139 8 | *Printed in Great Britain*'.

Published 15 September 1977 at £4.95; number of copies, see below.

Also sold with *H* (A3r) and *LR* (A5e) in a set, *The Tolkien Library*; see A3r.

Maps and genealogical tables drawn and lettered by Christopher Tolkien.

The title page inscription (also printed on p. [4]) reads: 'The tales of the First Age when Morgoth dwelt in Middle-earth and the Elves made war upon him for the recovery of the Silmarils: to which are appended the Downfall of Númenor and the history of the Rings of Power and the Third Age in which these tales come to their end'.

Includes the following errors:

p. 168, l. 22, 'Leithien' for 'Leithian'
p. 196, l. 9, 'makers of fire' for 'masters of fire'

p. 248, l. 11, 'besides him' for 'beside him'

p. 267, l. 37, 'nineteenth king' for 'twentieth king'

p. 267, l. 38, 'Adûnakhor' for 'Adûnakhôr'

p. 268, l. 5, 'twenty-second king' for 'twenty-third king'

p. 270, l. 6, 'three and twenty' for 'four and twenty'

p. 313, l. 33 after titling, '*Adûnakhor*' for '*Adûnakhôr*', 'nineteenth King' for 'twentieth King'

p. 317, l. 23 (entry for *Ar-Gimilzôr*), 'Twenty-second King' for 'Twenty-third King'

p. 317, l. 37 (entry for *Ar-Pharazôn*), 'twenty-fourth and last King' for 'twenty-fifth and last King'

p. 321, l. 24 (entry for *Caranthir*), '142–3' for '143'

p. 330, l. 4, '*Fëanor*' for '*Fëanor.*'

p. 336, l. 12, 'Nauglamîr' for 'Nauglamír'

p. 336, l. 31 (entry for *Ilúvatar*), '65–6' for '66'

p. 349, l. 33 (entry for *Taniquetil*), '281' for '282'

p. 350, l. 5 (entry for *Tar-Palantir*), 'Twenty-third King' for 'Twenty-fourth King'

p. 350, l. 42 (entry for *Thargelion*), '142' for '143'

p. 352, l. 39 (entry for *Ulmo*), '*Lord of Waters and King of the Sea*' for '*Lord of Waters* and *King of the Sea*'

p. 355, l. 17 after titling (entry for *alda*), '*Galadon*' for '*Galadhon*', '*Galadrim*' for '*Galadhrim*'

p. 357, l. 8, 'Treebeard's song' for 'Quickbeam's song'

p. 357, l. 18, 'appears to mean' for 'means'

p. 365, l. 21, 'deep dale in Moria' for 'deep dale in Mordor'

The misprints on pp. 330 and 352 were corrected in a later impression or impressions.

The Silmarillion was Tolkien's life's-work, begun in 1914 with a vision of Eärendel the star-mariner, and continued until his death. It was already well developed when it came to the attention of George Allen & Unwin in October 1937. *The Hobbit* had just been published with success, and Stanley Unwin had warned Tolkien that the public would soon be clamouring for more of the same. Tolkien replied in a letter of 15 October 1937 that though he could not think of anything more to say about hobbits

> I have only too much to say, and much already written, about the world into which the hobbit intruded. You can, of course, see any of it, and say what you like about it, if and when you wish. I should rather like an opinion, other than that of Mr C. S. Lewis and my children, whether it has any value in itself, or as a marketable commodity, apart from hobbits. But if it is true that *The Hobbit* has come to stay and more will be wanted, I will start the process of thought, and try to get some idea of a theme drawn from this material for treatment in a similar style and for a similar audience—possibly including actual hobbits.

Tolkien appears to have met with Unwin on 27 October to discuss possibilities for a new book. In a memo of late October 1937 Unwin noted that Tolkien had (so Unwin thought) practically ready for publication 'a volume of short fairy stories in various styles', e.g. 'Roverandum' and 'Farmer Giles of Ham' (cf. A4a); 'the typescript of a History of the Gnomes [Elves], and stories arising from it'; *Mr. Bliss*; '*The Lost Road*, a partly written novel of which we could see the opening chapters'; 'a great deal of verse of one kind and another which would probably be worth looking at'; and '*Beowulf* [i.e. a Modern English translation] upon which he has as yet done very little'.

On 15 November Tolkien met with Unwin in London and delivered for his consideration the manuscripts of 'Farmer Giles of Ham', *Mr. Bliss*, *The Lost Road*, 'The Lay of Leithian', the prose 'Quenta Silmarillion', the 'Ainulindalë', the 'Ambarkanta', and the 'Akallabêth'. The 'Lay' was recorded by the publisher simply as a 'Long Poem', and the latter four works collectively as 'The Gnomes Material'. The manuscripts were disordered, and Tolkien apparently did not make clear how his 'Silmarillion' poetry and prose works related to one another. Christopher Tolkien has speculated that 'the Gnomes material' was set aside by the publisher as too peculiar and difficult. 'The Lay of Leithian', also known as 'The Gest(e) of Beren and Lúthien', alone among the 'Silmarillion' manuscripts was given to Edward Crankshaw, a publisher's reader. Crankshaw reported with not a little confusion on 10 December 1937:

> I am rather at a loss to know what to do with this—it doesn't even seem to have an author!—or any indication of sources, etc. Publisher's readers are rightly supposed to be of moderate intelligence and reading; but I confess my reading has not extended to early Celtic Gestes, and I don't even know whether this is a famous Geste or not, or, for that matter, whether it is authentic. I presume it is, as the unspecified versifier has included some pages of a prose-version (which is far superior).
>
> In any case, authenticity apart, it seems to boil down to one thing: would there be any market for a long, involved, romantic verse-tale of Celtic elves and mortals? I think not. Especially as this particular verse is of a very thin, if not always downright bad, quality, and the tale in this retelling has been spread out almost to nothingness.

The (later) 'prose-version' had been attached by Tolkien in order to complete the story of the unfinished 'Lay'. Crankshaw felt that 'it has something of that mad, bright-eyed beauty that perplexes all Anglo-Saxons in the face of Celtic art (and that they can only stand in very small doses, like the Immortal Hour, or a very few chapters of Lord Dunsany); and of course it has the charm of something primitive, downright, and strange. All this is gone in the verse-version. . . .'

On 15 December Stanley Unwin returned the 'Silmarillion' manuscripts to Tolkien, and wrote: 'As you yourself surmised, it is going to be very difficult to do anything with *The Geste of Beren and Luthien* in verse form, but our reader is much impressed with the pages of a prose version which accompanied it.' He then quoted only the approving part of Crankshaw's report, and added: '*The Silmarillion* contains plenty of wonderful material; in fact it is a mine to be explored in writing further books like *The Hobbit* rather than a book in itself.' Tolkien replied on 16 December that he was pleased that his work had not been 'rejected with scorn'.

> I have suffered a sense of fear and bereavement, quite ridiculous, since I let this private and beloved nonsense out; and I think if it had seemed to you to be nonsense I should have felt really crushed. I do not mind about the verse-form, which in spite of certain virtuous passages has grave defects; for it is only for me the rough material. But I shall certainly now hope one day to be able, or to be able to afford, to publish *The Silmarillion*! . . .
>
> I did not think any of the stuff I dropped on you filled the bill. But I did want to know whether any of the stuff had any exterior non-personal value. I think it is plain that quite apart from it, a sequel or successor to *The Hobbit* is called for. But I am sure you will sympathize when I say that the construction of elaborate and consistent mythology (and two languages) rather occupies the mind, and the Silmarils are in my heart. So that goodness knows what will happen.

'Beyond question,' Christopher Tolkien has remarked (*Lays*, p. 366), 'Stanley Unwin's object was to save my father's feelings, while (relying on the reader's report—which concerned [only] the poem) rejecting the material submitted, and to persuade him to write a book that would continue the success of *The Hobbit*. But the result was that my father was entirely misled.... He thought ... [*The Silmarillion*] had been read and rejected, whereas it had merely been rejected.'

Tolkien immediately began to write 'a new story about Hobbits' (letter to C. A. Furth, 19 December 1937), and after several false starts found his way. But his story grew beyond Unwin's expectations, into the epic *The Lord of the Rings* (A5). It derived, in the first instance, from *The Hobbit*, drawing from that book the race of Hobbits, a magic ring, and a handful of characters. But it was built chiefly on the languages, history, geography, and cosmology of *The Silmarillion*, which by now had developed for more than twenty years. In *The Hobbit* the *legendarium* is only glimpsed; in *The Lord of the Rings* it is pervasive, providing depth and purpose. 'The Silmarils'—the matter of Middle-earth—were indeed in Tolkien's heart; and *vice versa*, he had put his heart into *The Silmarillion*. It was dear to him, and he wanted it published.

Near the end of 1949, when he was finishing *The Lord of the Rings*, Tolkien was introduced to Milton Waldman, an editor with the London publisher Collins. Waldman expressed interest in both *The Lord of the Rings* and *The Silmarillion*, and Tolkien considered leaving Allen & Unwin for a publisher who seemed more willing to take the whole 'saga of the Jewels and the Rings', which he thought of as one work, not two. Collins, as stationers and printers as well as publishers, had a greater allowance of paper than most firms in post-war Britain, so were in a good position to publish Tolkien's epic—as well as *The Hobbit*, if they could acquire that lucrative property from Allen & Unwin. Tolkien needed only to consider his legal and moral obligations. He wrote to Waldman on 5 February 1950 (in draft):

> I believe myself to have no *legal* obligation to Allen and Unwin, since the clause in *The Hobbit* contract with regard to offering the next book seems to have been satisfied either (a) by their rejection of *The Silmarillion* or (b) by their eventual acceptance and publication of *Farmer Giles*. I should (as you note) be glad to leave them, as I have found them in various ways unsatisfactory. But I have friendly personal relations with Stanley ... and with his second son Rayner.... Sir Stanley has long been aware that *The Lord of the Rings* has outgrown its function, and is not pleased since he sees no money in it for anyone (so he said); but he is anxious to see the final result all the same. If this constitutes a moral obligation then I have one: at least to explain the situation.

On 24 February he wrote to Stanley Unwin that *The Silmarillion* had

> bubbled up, infiltrated, and probably spoiled everything (that even remotely approached 'Faery') which I have tried to write since. It was kept out of *Farmer Giles* with an effort, but stopped the continuation. Its shadow was deep on the later parts of *The Hobbit*. It has captured *The Lord of the Rings*, so that that has become simply its continuation and completion, requiring the *Silmarillion* to be fully intelligible—without a lot of references and explanations that clutter it in one or two places.
>
> Ridiculous and tiresome as you may think me, I want to publish them both— *The Silmarillion* and *The Lord of the Rings*—in conjunction or in connexion. 'I want to'—it would be wiser to say 'I should like to', since a little packet of, say, a million words, of matter set out *in extenso* that Anglo-Saxons (or the English-speaking public) can only endure in moderation, is not very likely to see the light, even if paper were available at will.

All the same that is what I should like. Or I will let it all be. I cannot contemplate any drastic re-writing or compression. . . .

Unwin replied by suggesting that the two works be divided into three or four self-contained volumes. But Tolkien was in a mood to be uncompromising, and indeed to discourage Allen & Unwin from further interest. On 3 April Unwin unwisely sent Tolkien his son Rayner's frank opinion that '*really* relevant material from *The Silmarillion* could be incorporated into *The Lord of the Rings*', and if this could not be done, the latter book should be published and *The Silmarillion* dropped after a second look. Tolkien's letter of reply, 14 April 1950, was polite but angry and direct. He asked for a decision, Yes or No, whether Allen & Unwin would take both works together. Stanley Unwin could answer only No, not having seen a final manuscript and considering the substantial cost of publishing a book of so great a length.

Tolkien now dealt with Collins. It was hoped that typesetting could begin in autumn 1950. But Milton Waldman lived in Italy except for visits to London in spring and autumn, and no one else at Collins was familiar with Tolkien's books. The relationship between author and publisher was further strained by Collins' suggestion that *The Lord of the Rings* wanted cutting. The length of *The Silmarillion* as projected by Tolkien (in the event, greatly overestimated) was also worrisome. In late 1951, apparently at Waldman's request, Tolkien wrote a letter of some ten thousand words to explain his saga and demonstrate the interdependency of *The Silmarillion* and *The Lord of the Rings* (see *Letters* no. 131). By March 1952 he still had no contract with Collins. He felt that his time had been wasted, and he demanded that *The Lord of the Rings* be published immediately. But his book was long, the cost of paper had soared, and Collins withdrew.

Tolkien and Allen & Unwin, in the meantime, had not completely severed relations. *Farmer Giles of Ham* was still in print, and *The Hobbit* had gone into a second edition (see A3c). Now, in the summer of 1952, Rayner Unwin made friendly overtures, and Tolkien responded. Years were becoming precious, he said, and he was now willing to have *The Lord of the Rings* published by itself (see A5a note). That work appeared at last in three volumes in 1954–5. Immediately after the final volume was published, Rayner Unwin began to encourage Tolkien to complete *The Silmarillion*.

The correspondence that followed, for almost twenty years, between Tolkien and his publisher with regard to *The Silmarillion* is a tale of hope and frustration. Rayner Unwin was ever encouraging, while Tolkien was ever apologetic that he had little or no time to apply to the book. On 8 December 1955, for example, Tolkien wrote: 'I hope in this vacation to begin surveying the "Silmarillion"; though evil fate has plumped a doctorate thesis on me.' And on 29 February 1956: 'I am much harrassed with professional concerns, and I have not had a chance of turning, as is my chief desire, to the *Silmarillion*. It needs prolonged concentration.' And on 1 February 1957: 'I have not got near *The Silmarillion* for months.' And so forth. He had many duties while he held his professorship, and later he was much concerned with translations of his books, with copyright matters, with offers of film adaptations, and with other writings and new editions. He did work on the saga in his last years, but made slow progress. Joy Hill of Allen & Unwin wrote on 4 January 1973 to an American fan that Tolkien had not looked at the manuscript for well over a year, and a date of completion could not be predicted (see *Mythprint* [bulletin of The Mythopoeic Society], 7, no. 5 [May 1973], p. 7).

Some critics have said that Tolkien did not truly want to let go of *The Silmarillion*, because it was a living part of him. There may be some truth to this. Joy Hill suggested that the full manuscript would be held back while Tolkien lived because income from its publication would bring large death duties on his estate. For whatever reason, in the end he did not complete it, and delegated his son Christopher, after the author himself the person most intimately familiar with *The Silmarillion*, to put it in a form suitable for publication.

In 1974 Rayner Unwin remarked to a meeting of The Tolkien Society that it would take at least three years to complete work on *The Silmarillion*. In the event, a final typescript was completed by Christopher Tolkien, with the assistance of Guy Gavriel Kay, by late 1976. The work as prepared for publication is a single text selected and arranged from J. R. R. Tolkien's many-layered, often revised and rewritten manuscripts 'in such a way as seemed . . . to produce the most coherent and internally self-consistent narrative' (foreword, p. 8). Maps, genealogies of Elves and Men, a note on pronunciation, an index, and a list of elements in Elvish names are provided by Christopher Tolkien, but not the further 'burden' (as he then felt) of commentary. Page proofs were ready in March 1977. At this time also the index was completed. The book was ready for press on 29 April 1977.

The first print order was for 100,000 copies. By the end of May 1977 booksellers' orders included 65,000 from overseas, and the print run was increased to 300,000. Later the order was raised to 325,000, and in September to 375,000. Several firms were commissioned to print the book, at one time four printers, working in blocks of 50,000 copies, to insure against a feared industrial action stopping production. The total of 375,000 copies before publication includes both export (Clowes) and domestic (Billings) copies as well as book club copies with the Book Club Associates imprint (printed by Clowes, in a similar binding and jacket). The initial impression seems to have been 200,000 copies (export and domestic combined), with two later impressions of 50,000 each and 75,000 for the book club. But with apparently continuous production, virtually identical sheets, and simultaneous (or near-simultaneous) publication of all copies worldwide, it seems pointless to make much of a distinction.

The dust-jacket illustration was originally to have been J. R. R. Tolkien's *Lake Mithrim* (Ei2, no. 32), in blue, white, and gold, but on consideration it was found too delicate and was replaced with Lúthien's heraldic device, which is more striking and more symbolic of the book.

A small number of copies of the Clowes impression were specially bound in dark blue leather, upper cover and spine stamped in gilt, for presentation by the publisher. One thousand copies of the Clowes impression were reserved for publication in 1982; see A15h.

The Silmarillion was later published in Britain by HarperCollins, with new impression numbering. In January 1992 its dust-jacket was changed to feature a painting by John Howe, of the fall of Gondolin. HarperCollins also issued copies of the second Allen & Unwin impression, unchanged except with the new HarperCollins jacket.

See further, *The Silmarillion [by] J. R. R. Tolkien: A Brief Account of the Book and Its Making* by Christopher Tolkien (Boston: Houghton Mifflin, 1977; reprinted in *Mallorn* [journal of The Tolkien Society], no. 14 [1980], pp. 3–5, 7–8); and Christopher Tolkien's comments in *Unfinished Tales* (A17) and 'The History of Middle-earth' (A21 etc.).

Christopher Tolkien has also made two audio recordings of *The Silmarillion*:

The Silmarillion: Of Beren and Lúthien. New York: Caedmon Records, 1977. LP no. TC 1564; cassette no. CDL 51564. Reissued 1977 by Caedmon in *The J. R. R. Tolkien Soundbook*, LPs SBR 101, cassettes SBC 101, including booklet and poster map from *Silm*. A reading of the greater part of ch. 19, with a few omissions. Sleeve notes and colour sleeve illustration, *Map of Beleriand and the Lands to the North*, by Christopher Tolkien.

Of the Darkening of Valinor and Of the Flight of the Noldor from The Silmarillion. New York: Caedmon Records, 1978. LP no. TC 1579; cassette no. CDL 51579. A reading of chs. 8 and 9. Sleeve notes by Christopher Tolkien. Colour sleeve illustration, *Taniquetil*, by J. R. R. Tolkien.

Pertinent manuscripts and typescripts are in the Bodleian Library, Oxford.

b. First edition (British), domestic copies (1977):

[*2 lines in tengwar, between double rules*] | J. R. R. TOLKIEN | The Silmarillion | edited by | CHRISTOPHER TOLKIEN | London | GEORGE ALLEN & UNWIN | Boston Sydney | [*2 lines in tengwar, between double rules*]

368 pp. + 1 plate (map). Collation: $[1-7^8(7_4+\chi 1)8-23^8]$. 22.1 × 13.9 cm.

[1–2] blank; [3] 'THE SILMARILLION'; [4] '[*2 lines in tengwar, between double rules*] | J. R. R. TOLKIEN | QUENTA SILMARILLION | (The History of the Silmarils) | together with | AINULINDALË | (The Music of the Ainur) | and | VALAQUENTA | (Account of the Valar) | To which is appended | AKALLABÊTH | (The Downfall of Númenor) | and | OF THE RINGS OF POWER AND | THE THIRD AGE | [*2 lines in tengwar, between double rules*]'; [5] title; [6] '*First published in 1977* | [*notice of restrictions under copyright*] | © *George Allen & Unwin (Publishers) Ltd, 1977* | ISBN 0 04 823139 8 | *Printed in Great Britain by offset lithography by* | *Billing & Sons Ltd, Guildford, London and Worcester*'; 7–9 foreword; [10] blank; 11–12 table of contents; [13] 'AINULINDALË | [*swelled rule*]'; [14] blank; 15–22 text; [23] 'VALAQUENTA | [*swelled rule*]'; [24] blank; 25–32 text; [33] 'QUENTA SILMARILLION | [*swelled rule*] | *The History of the* | *Silmarils*'; [34] blank; 35–120 text; [120+1] map, *The Realms of the Noldor and the Sindar*, in black and red; [120+2] blank; 121–255 text; [256] blank; [257] 'AKALLABÊTH | [*swelled rule*]'; [258] blank; 259–82 text; [283] 'OF THE | RINGS OF POWER | AND THE | THIRD AGE | [*swelled rule*]'; [284] blank; 285–304 text; [305–9] genealogical tables; 310–11 note on pronunciation; [312] blank; 313–54 index; 355–65 appendix; [366–8] blank. *Map of Beleriand and the Lands to the North*, in black and red on folded leaf tipped onto blank p. [387].

Wove paper. Bound in dark blue cloth over boards. Spine stamped as for A15a. Wove endpapers. No headbands. All edges trimmed. Top edge stained dark blue, fore- and bottom edges unstained.

Dust-jacket, wove paper. Covers and spine printed as for A15a, against a dark blue-purple background. Printed on front flap: '[*blurb*] | PRICE NET | £4.95 | IN U.K. ONLY'. Back flap printed as for A15a.

Published 15 September 1977 at £4.95; number of copies, see A15a note.

Typeset as for A15a, except p. [6]. Maps and genealogical tables drawn and lettered as for A15a.

Also published by Bookcase Shop, Taiwan, November 1977, authorized by Allen & Unwin, with altered copyright page, bound in tan cloth over boards, with a dust-jacket similar to the one for A15a–b.

c. First edition (American, 1977):

[*2 lines in tengwar, between double rules*] | J. R. R. TOLKIEN | The Silmarillion | edited by | CHRISTOPHER TOLKIEN | HOUGHTON MIFFLIN COMPANY | BOSTON | 1977 | [*2 lines in tengwar, between double rules*]

120, [2], 121–366 pp. + 1 plate (map). Collation: [1–7^{16}8^{8}9–12^{16}]. 22.7 × 15.1 cm.

[1] 'THE SILMARILLION'; [2] blank; [3] 'BOOKS BY J. R. R. TOLKIEN | [*10 titles, beginning with* LR, *ending with* SGPO] | The Father Christmas Letters | (edited by Baillie Tolkien) | The Silmarillion | (edited by Christopher Tolkien) | WITH DONALD SWANN | The Road Goes Ever On'; [4] '[*2 lines in tengwar, between double rules*] | J. R. R. TOLKIEN | QUENTA SILMARILLION | (The History of the Silmarils) | together with | AINULINDALË | (The Music of the Ainur) | and | VALAQUENTA | (Account of the Valar) | To which is appended | AKALLABÊTH | (The Downfall of Númenor) | and | OF THE RINGS OF POWER AND | THE THIRD AGE | [*2 lines in tengwar, between double rules*]'; [5] title; [6] 'FIRST PRINTING | First American Edition | Copyright © 1977 by George Allen & Unwin (Publishers) Ltd | [*notice of restrictions under copyright*] | [*rule*] | [*Library of Congress Cataloging in Publication Data*] | [*rule*] | Printed in the United States of America | [*printing code, beginning "W", ending "1"*]'; 7–9 foreword; [10] blank; 11–[12] table of contents; [13] 'AINULINDALË | [*swelled rule*]'; [14] blank; 15–22 text; [23] 'VALAQUENTA | [*swelled rule*]'; [24] blank; 25–32 text; [33] 'QUENTA SILMARILLION | [*swelled rule*] | The History of the | Silmarils'; [34] blank; 35–120 text; [120+1] map, *The Realms of the Noldor and the Sindar*, in black and dark grey; [120+2] blank; [*in black:*] 121–255 text; [256] blank; [257] 'AKALLABÊTH | [*swelled rule*]'; [258] blank; 259–82 text; [283] 'OF THE | RINGS OF POWER | AND THE | THIRD AGE | [*swelled rule*]'; [284] blank; 285–304 text; [305–9] genealogical tables; 310–11 note on pronunciation; [312] blank; 313–54 index; 355–65 appendix; [366] blank. *Map of Beleriand and the Lands to the North*, in black and red on folded leaf tipped onto recto, back free endpaper.

Wove paper. Bound in green cloth over boards. Heraldic device of Fingolfin, after Tolkien, stamped on upper cover in copper or gilt; no priority determined (see below). Stamped on spine: '[*2 identical heraldic devices of Fingolfin, connected by a vertical rule, in copper or gilt; to right of the rule, running down, in silver:*] The Silmarillion [*parallel to the title, to left of the rule, in silver:*] J. R. R. TOLKIEN | [*below the second heraldic device, horizontal, in copper or gilt:*] HMCO'. Wove endpapers. Red/yellow headbands. All edges trimmed. Top edge stained red, fore- and bottom edges unstained.

Dust-jacket, wove paper. Printed on upper cover: 'J. R. R. Tolkien | [*within a black single rule frame:*] [*in white, against an illustration (for* The Hobbit) *by Tolkien, coloured by H. E. Riddett,* The Mountain-path:] The | SILMARILLION'. Printed on spine: '[*running down:*] [*in red-brown:*] The SILMARILLION [*in black:*] J. R. R. Tolkien | [*horizontal:*] HOUGHTON | MIFFLIN | COMPANY'. Printed on lower cover within a single rule frame: 'Photo: Roger Hill | [*photograph of Tolkien*] | ISBN 0-395-25730-1 | [*rule*] | 6-97065'. Printed on front flap: '$10.95 | [*blurb; to left of blurb, running up:*] 0977'. Printed on back flap: '[*blurb, continued*] | [*note on Tolkien*] | JACKET DRAWING BY J. R. R. TOLKIEN | COLORED BY H. E. RIDDETT | JACKET DESIGN BY LOUISE NOBLE | HOUGHTON MIFFLIN COMPANY | 2 Park Street | Boston, Massachusetts 02107'.

Published 15 September 1977 at $10.95; 325,000 copies printed.

Typeset as for A15a–b, except pp. [3] (with misprint '*Father Giles*' for '*Farmer Giles*'), [5–6], 11 (italic word *page* omitted), [12] (reset, with added list of maps), 313 (headed 'Index of Names' instead of 'Index'). Maps and genealogical tables drawn and lettered as for A15a–b.

    Five combinations of sheets and binding have been noted, probably no priority (though publisher's advance copy as [1]):

(1) no loss of text on p. 229; printed on distinctly white paper; binding stamped in copper and silver

(2) loss of text on p. 229 at right edge of type block; printed on distinctly white paper; binding stamped in copper and silver

(3) loss of text on p. 229 at right edge of type block; printed on distinctly white paper; binding stamped in gold and silver

(4) loss of text on p. 229 at right edge of type block; printed on paper more distinctly ivory than (1)–(3); binding stamped in gold and silver

(5) no loss of text on p. 229 at right edge of type block; binding stamped in gold and silver

Like Allen & Unwin, Houghton Mifflin used more than one printer for its 'first impression' of *The Silmarillion*. More than one set of printing plates is clearly indicated by the variation on p. 229 described above. Bindings with copper stamping seem to have been shipped primarily to the western United States. Publisher's records indicate a first impression of 325,000, followed by three more impressions (50,000; 50,000; 100,000) before publication.

Also published by the Book-of-the-Month Club.

d. Reset American book club edition (1978):

[2 *lines in tengwar, between double rules*] | J. R. R. TOLKIEN | The Silmarillion | edited by | CHRISTOPHER TOLKIEN | HOUGHTON MIFFLIN COMPANY BOSTON | [2 *lines in tengwar, between double rules*]

xii, 372 pp. Collation: [1–16^{12}]. 20.8 × 13.8 cm.

[i] 'THE SILMARILLION'; [ii] blank; [iii] 'BOOKS BY J. R. R. TOLKIEN | [*10 titles, beginning with* LR, *ending with* SGPO] | The Father Christmas Letters | (edited by Baillie Tolkien) | The Silmarillion | (edited by Christopher Tolkien) | WITH DONALD SWANN | The Road Goes Ever On'; [iv] '[2 *lines in tengwar, between double rules*] | J. R. R. TOLKIEN | QUENTA SILMARILLION | (The History of the Silmarils) | together with | AINULINDALË | (The Music of the Ainur) | and | VALAQUENTA | (Account of the Valar) | To which is appended | AKALLABÊTH | (The Downfall of Númenor) | and | OF THE RINGS OF POWER AND | THE THIRD AGE | [2 *lines in tengwar, between double rules*]'; [v] title; [vi] 'Copyright © 1977 by George Allen & Unwin (Publishers) Ltd | [*notice of restrictions under copyright*] | Printed in the United States of America]; vii–ix foreword; [x] blank; [xi]–xii table of contents; [1] 'AINULINDALË | [*swelled rule*]'; [2] blank; [3]–10 text; [11] 'VALAQUENTA | [*swelled rule*]'; [12] blank; [13]–20 text; [21] 'QUENTA SILMARILLION | [*swelled rule*] | The History of the | Silmarils'; [22] blank; [23]–253 text, with map, *The realms of the Noldor and the Sindar*, on p. [115]; [254] blank; [255] 'AKALLABÊTH | [*swelled rule*]'; [256] blank; [257]–80 text; [281] 'OF THE | RINGS OF POWER | AND THE | THIRD AGE | [*swelled rule*]'; [282] blank; [283]–303 text; [304–8] genealogical tables; [309]–10 note on pronunciation; [311]–56 index; [357]–68 appendix; [369–72] blank. Printing code, 'I 16', printed in gutter, p. 367.

Wove paper. Bound in green cloth over boards. Heraldic device of Fingolfin, after Tolkien, stamped on upper cover in yellow-green. Stamped on spine in yellow-green: '[2 *identical heraldic devices of Fingolfin, connected by a vertical rule; to the right of the rule, running down:*] The Silmarillion [*parallel to the title, to the left of the rule:*] J. R. R. TOLKIEN | [*below the second device, horizontal:*] HMCO'. Wove endpapers; *Map of Beleriand and the Lands to the North* printed in black and dark red on each endsheet. No headbands. Top edge trimmed, fore- and bottom edges untrimmed. All edges unstained.

Dust-jacket, wove paper. Covers and spine as for A15c. Printed on front flap: '[*blurb*] | *Book Club* | *Edition*'. Printed on back flap: '[*blurb, continued*] | [*note on Tolkien*] | JACKET DRAWING BY J. R. R. TOLKIEN | COLORED BY H. E. RIDDETT | JACKET DESIGN BY LOUISE NOBLE | *Printed in the U.S.A.* | 1590'.

Published by the Science Fiction Book Club, mid- to late April 1978? at $6.98?; number of copies not known.

Reset, based on A15a–c, continuing most of the errors noted for that typesetting. Page references in the index changed to accord with the new setting. Maps and genealogical tables drawn and lettered as for A15a–c.

e. Reset British book club edition (1978):

[2 *lines in tengwar, between double rules*] | J. R. R. TOLKIEN | The Silmarillion | edited by | CHRISTOPHER TOLKIEN | BOOK CLUB ASSOCIATES LONDON | [2 *lines in tengwar, between double rules*]

416 pp. Collation: 208 leaves. 19.7 × 12.7 cm.

[1] 'THE SILMARILLION'; [2] '[2 *lines in tengwar, between double rules*] | J. R. R. TOLKIEN | QUENTA SILMARILLION | (The History of the Silmarils) | together with | AINULINDALË | (The Music of the Ainur) | and | VALAQUENTA | (Account of the Valar) | To which is appended | AKALLABÊTH | (The Downfall of Númenor) | and | OF THE RINGS OF POWER AND | THE THIRD AGE | [2 *lines in tengwar, between double rules*]'; [3] title; [4] '*This edition published 1978 by* | *Book Club Associates* | *by arrangement with* | *George Allen & Unwin (Publishers) Ltd.* | [*notice of restrictions under copyright*] | © *George Allen & Unwin (Publishers) Ltd, 1977* | Printed in Great Britain by | Richard Clay (The Chaucer Press), Ltd., | Bungay, Suffolk'; [5–6] table of contents; [7]–9 foreword; [10–11] *Map of Beleriand and the Lands to the North*; [12] blank; [13] 'AINULINDALË | [*swelled rule*]'; [14] blank; [15]–23 text; [24] blank; [25] 'VALAQUENTA | [*swelled rule*]'; [26] blank; [27]–35 text; [36] blank; [37] 'QUENTA SILMARILLION | [*swelled rule*] | *The History of the* | *Silmarils*'; [38] blank; [39]–289 text, with map, *The Realms of the Noldor and the Sindar*, on p. [147]; [290] blank; [291] 'AKALLABÊTH'; [292] blank; [293]–319 text; [320] blank; [321] 'OF THE | RINGS OF POWER | AND THE | THIRD AGE | [*swelled rule*]'; [322] blank; [323]–45 text; [346] blank; [347]–51 genealogical tables; [352] blank; [353]–4 note on pronunciation; [355]–402 index; [403]–14 appendix; [415–16] blank.

Wove paper. Bound in light wine red textured paper over boards. Stamped on spine in gilt: '[*running down:*] J. R. R. TOLKIEN [*star*] The Silmarillion | [*publisher's "bca" device, horizontal*]'. Wove endpapers. No headbands. All edges trimmed and unstained.

Dust-jacket, wove paper. Covers and spine printed as for A15a, with dark blue background, except with publisher's 'bca' device at foot of spine in red. Blurb printed on front flap. Printed on back flap: '[*blurb, continued*] | *Emblems designed by J. R. R. Tolkien* | *Front cover:* | Lúthien Tinúviel | *Back cover:* | Fingolfin Eärendil | Idril Celebrindal | Elwë Fëanor | CN 2505 | [*rule*] | *Originally published at* £4.95'.

Published in 1978; date of publication, price, and number of copies not known.

Reset, based on A15a–c, continuing most of the errors noted for that typesetting. Page references in the index changed to accord with the new setting. Maps and genealogical tables drawn and lettered as for A15a–c.

Another impression of this typesetting was published in 1981 by Guild Publishing, London, bound in dark wine red imitation leather, gilt.

f. First paperback edition (1979):

[*2 lines in tengwar, between double rules*] | The Silmarillion | J. R. R. TOLKIEN | Edited by Christopher Tolkien | London | UNWIN PAPERBACKS | Boston Sydney | [*2 lines in tengwar, between double rules*]

448 pp. Collation: 224 leaves. 17.7 × 10.9 cm.

[1] blurb; [2] '*also by J. R. R. Tolkien* | THE HOBBIT | THE LORD OF THE RINGS | 1 THE FELLOWSHIP OF THE RING | 2 THE TWO TOWERS | 3 THE RETURN OF THE KING | [*5 titles, beginning with* ATB, *ending with* SGPO] | *with Donald Swann* | THE ROAD GOES EVER ON'; [3] 'THE SILMARILLION'; [4] '[*2 lines in tengwar, between double rules*] | J. R. R. TOLKIEN | QUENTA SILMARIL-LION | (The History of the Silmarils) | together with | AINULINDALË | (The Music of the Ainur) | and | VALAQUENTA | (Account of the Valar) | To which is appended | AKALLABÊTH | (The Downfall of Númenor) | and | OF THE RINGS OF POWER | AND THE THIRD AGE | [*2 lines in tengwar, between double rules*]'; [5] title; [6] 'First published in Great Britain by George Allen & Unwin 1977 | First published in Unwin Paperbacks 1979 | [*notice of restrictions under copyright*] | UNWIN® PAPERBACKS | 40 Museum Street, London WC1A 1LU | © George Allen & Unwin (Publishers) Ltd 1977, 1979 | [*within a single rule frame:*] [*British Library Cataloguing in Publication Data*] | ISBN 0-04-823153-3 | [*below the frame:*] Typeset in 10 on 11 point Times | and printed in Great Britain | by Cox & Wyman Ltd, London, Reading and Fakenham'; [7]–9 foreword; [10] blank; [11]–12 table of contents; [13] 'AINULINDALË'; [14] blank; [15]–24 text; [25] 'VALA-QUENTA'; [26] blank; [27]–35 text; [36] blank; [37] 'QUENTA SILMARILLION | *The History of the* | *Silmarils*'; [38] blank; [39]–307 text, with map, *The Realms of the Noldor and the Sindar*, on p. [154]; [308] blank; [309] 'AKALLABÊTH'; [310] blank; [311]–39 text; [340] blank; [341] 'OF THE RINGS OF POWER | AND THE THIRD AGE'; [342] blank; [343]–67 text; [368] blank; [369–73] genealogical tables; [374] blank; [375]–6 note on pronunciation; [377]–426 index; [427]–39 appendix; [440–1] *Map of Beleriand and the Lands to the North*; [442] blank; [443] '[*within a single rule frame:*] Also by J. R. R. Tolkien | [*advertisements of* H, LR, ATB, RGEO]'; [444] blank; [445] '[*within a single rule frame:*] Also in Unwin Paperbacks | [*advertisements of Foster,* The Complete Guide to Middle-earth, *and Carpenter,* J. R. R. Tolkien: A Biography]'; [446–8] blank.

Wove paper. Bound in heavy wove wrappers. Covers and spine printed against a blue background. Printed on upper cover: '[*in red:*] TOLKIEN | [*in white:*] The | Silmarillion | [*colour illustration by Tolkien, heraldic device of Lúthien Tinúviel, outlined in white*] | [*publisher's "unwin/UNWIN PAPERBACKS" device, in red, white, and black*]'. Printed on spine, running down: '[*in red:*] TOLKIEN [*in white:*] The Silmarillion [*publisher's "unwin/UNWIN PAPERBACKS" device, in red, white, and black*]'. Printed on lower cover within a red single rule frame, against a white panel: '[*9 quotations, beginning with the* Guardian, *ending with the* Sydney Morning Herald] | [*at left:*] UNITED KINGDOM £1.25 | AUSTRALIA $3.95 (Recommended) | CANADA $2.75 [*at right:*] TOLKIEN/FANTASY | ISBN 0 04 823153 3'. All edges trimmed and unstained.

Published March 1979 at £1.25; number of copies not known.

Reset, based on A15a–c, continuing most of the errors noted for that typesetting:

p. 202, l. 7, 'Leithien' for 'Leithian'
p. 236, ll. 9–10, 'makers of fire' for 'masters of fire'
p. 298, l. 35, 'besides him' for 'beside him'
p. 322, l. 2, 'nineteenth king' for 'twentieth king'
p. 322, l. 4, 'Adûnakhor' for 'Adûnakhôr'
p. 322, l. 13, 'twenty-second king' for 'twenty-third king'
p. 324, l. 32, 'three and twenty' for 'four and twenty'
p. 378, l. 3, '*Adûnakhor*' for '*Adûnakhôr*'
p. 378, ll. 3–4, 'nineteenth King' for 'twentieth King'
p. 382, l. 4, 'Twenty-second King' for 'Twenty-third King'
p. 382, l. 21, 'twenty-fourth and last King' for 'twenty-fifth and last King'
p. 404, ll. 15–16, 'Nauglamîr' for 'Nauglamír'
p. 420, l. 33, 'Twenty-third King' for 'Twenty-fourth King'
p. 429, l. 33, 'appears to mean' for 'means'
p. 438, l. 40–1, 'deep dale in Moria' for 'deep dale in Mordor'

The page references in the index changed to agree with the new setting, but contain new errors. Most of the errors noted above were corrected in later impressions.

Maps and genealogical tables drawn and lettered as for A15a–c.

Later published by HarperCollins. In January 1992 the cover was changed to feature a painting by John Howe, of the fall of Gondolin.

g. First American paperback edition (1979):

[2 *lines in tengwar, between double rules*] | J. R. R. TOLKIEN | The Silmarillion | edited by | CHRISTOPHER TOLKIEN | BALLANTINE BOOKS • NEW YORK | [2 *lines in tengwar, between double rules*]

xvi, 464 pp. Collation: 240 leaves. 17.8 × 10.6 cm.

[i] 'THE SILMARILLION | FOR J. R. R. TOLKIEN IT WAS THE | SUPREME WORK OF A LIFETIME! | FOR HIS ADORING READERS IT IS A | REASON TO REJOICE! | [*rule*] | [4 *quotations, from the* Baltimore Sunday Sun, Seattle Times, Los Angeles Times, *and* Wall Street Journal]'; [ii] '[2 *lines in tengwar, between double rules*] | J. R. R. TOLKIEN | QUENTA SILMARILLION | (The History of the Silmarils) | together with | AINULINDALË | (The Music of the Ainur) | and | VALAQUENTA | (Account of the Valar) | To which is appended | AKALLABÊTH | (The Downfall of Númenor) | and | OF THE RINGS OF POWER AND | THE THIRD AGE | [2 *lines in tengwar, between double rules*]'; [iii] title; [iv] 'Copyright © 1977 by George Allen & Unwin (Publishers) | Ltd. This book is copyright under the Berne Convention. | [*notice of restrictions*] | Library of Congress Catalog Card Number: 77 8025 | ISBN 0-345-27255-2 | This edition published by arrangement with | Houghton Mifflin Company | Manufactured in the United States of America | First Ballantine Books Edition: March 1979'; v–vi table of contents; [vii] 'BELERIAND AND THE LANDS TO | THE NORTH | [*rule*]'; [viii–ix] map; [x] blank; xi–xiv foreword; [xv] 'The Silmarillion'; [xvi] blank; [1] 'AINULINDALË | [*swelled rule*]'; [2] blank; 3–13 text; [14] blank; [15] 'VALAQUENTA | [*swelled rule*]'; [16] blank; 17–26 text; [27] 'QUENTA | SILMARILLION | *The History of the* | *Silmarils* [*swelled rule*]'; [28] blank; 29–316 text, with map, *The Realms of the Noldor and the Sindar*, on p. [143]; [317] 'AKALLABÊTH | [*swelled rule*]'; [318] blank; 319–49 text; [350] blank; [351] 'OF THE | RINGS OF POWER | AND

THE | THIRD AGE | [*swelled rule*]'; [352] blank; 353–78 text; 379–83 genealogical tables; 384–5 note on pronunciation; [386] blank; [387] 'INDEX | OF NAMES | [*swelled rule*]'; [388] blank; 389–442 index of names; [443] 'APPENDIX | [*swelled rule*]'; [444] blank; 445–58 appendix; [459] '[*within a thick-thin rule frame:*] BESTSELLERS | By J. R. R. TOLKIEN | Today's best-loved author of fantasy. | [*below the frame:*] Available at your bookstore or use this coupon. | [*publisher's order form*]'; [460] advertisement for Carpenter, *Tolkien*; [461] '[*at left, in uncials:*] STEP THIS WAY | TO THE LAND OF | ENCHANTMENT . . . | J. R. R. TOLKIEN'S | MIDDLE EARTH! [*at right, illustration*] | [*in roman:*] Available at your bookstore or use this coupon. | [*publisher's order form for Tolkien-related posters*]'; [462] blank; [463] '[*within a thick-thin rule frame:*] J. R. R. TOLKIEN: | MAN | AND MYTH | [*below the frame:*] [*advertisement for 5 titles, beginning with* Carpenter, Tolkien: A Biography, *ending with* J. R. R. Tolkien: Man and Myth *boxed set*] | [*at left, publisher's "BB" device; at right:*] Ballantine Books LG-7'; [464] blank.

Wove paper. Bound in heavy wove wrappers. Printed on upper cover: '[*in red-brown:*] AMERICA'S #1 BESTSELLER! | [*rule, in black*] | [*in red-brown:*] ONE MILLION SOLD IN HARDCOVER! | [*in light green outlined and shadowed in black:*] The [*in black:*] J. R. R. Tolkien's | [*in light green outlined and shadowed in black:*] SILMARILLION | [*illustration (for* The Hobbit) *by Tolkien, coloured by* H. E. Riddett, The Mountain-path, *within a black single rule frame*] | [*at lower right, running down, in black:*] Ballantine/Novel/27255/$2.95 | [*publisher's "BB" device, horizontal, in white and black*]'. Printed on spine: '[*publisher's "BB" device, in white and black*] | [*in black:*] Novel | [*running down:*] [*in light green outlined and shadowed in black:*] The SILMARILLION [*in black:*] J. R. R. Tolkien 345-27255-2-295'. Printed on lower cover: '[*in red-brown:*] THE LONG-AWAITED BOOK FROM | J. R. R. Tolkien, | THE MASTER OF FANTASY. | [*in black:*] [*rule*] | Here is his story of the creation of the world—the | ancient dream that sets the stage for | [*underlined:*] THE HOBBIT [*not underlined:*] AND [*underlined:*] THE LORD OF THE RINGS. | [*rule*] | [*3 quotations, from the* Philadelphia Inquirer, *by Richard Adams, and from* Time, *separated by rules*] | [*rule*] | [*at lower right, running down:*] Cover printed in USA'. All edges trimmed and unstained.

Published March 1979 at $2.95. *Publishers Weekly*, 5 March 1979, reported 2,515,000 copies printed before publication.

Reset, based on A15a–c, continuing most of the errors noted for that typesetting:

   p. 239, l. 29, 'makers of fire' for 'masters of fire'
   p. 307, l. 2, 'besides him' for 'beside him'
   p. 330, ll. 27–8, 'nineteenth king' for 'twentieth king'
   p. 330, l. 29, 'Adûnakhor' for 'Adûnakhôr'
   p. 330, l. 39, 'twenty-second king' for 'twenty-third king'
   p. 333, ll. 23–4, 'three and twenty' for 'four and twenty'
   p. 390, l. 5, '*Adûnakhor*' for '*Adûnakhôr*'
   p. 390, ll. 5–6, 'nineteenth King' for 'twentieth King'
   p. 394, l. 25, 'Twenty-second King' for 'Twenty-third King'
   p. 395, l. 1, 'twenty-fourth and last King' for 'twenty-fifth and last King'
   p. 410, l. 31, '*Fëanor* Chapters' for '*Fëanor.* Chapters'
   p. 436, l. 22, 'Twenty-third King' for 'Twenty-fourth King' p. 440, ll. 5–6, '*Lord of Waters and King of the Sea*' for '*Lord of Waters* and *King of the Sea*'
   p. 445, l. 21 after titling, '*Galadon*' for '*Galadhon*'
   p. 445, l. 22 after titling, '*Galadrim*' for '*Galadhrim*'

> p. 447, l. 32, 'Treebeard's song' for 'Quickbeam's song'
> p. 448, l. 2, 'appears to mean' for 'means'
> p. 458, l. 3, 'deep dale in Moria' for 'deep dale in Mordor'

The page references in the index changed to agree with the new setting.

Maps and genealogical tables drawn and lettered as for A15a–c.

With the second impression (January 1982), the cover was changed to feature an illustration by Darrell K. Sweet.

h. Limited edition (1982):

[2 *lines in tengwar, between double rules*] | J. R. R. TOLKIEN | The Silmarillion | edited by | CHRISTOPHER TOLKIEN | London | GEORGE ALLEN & UNWIN | Boston Sydney | [2 *lines in tengwar, between double rules*]

2, [2], 3–368 pp. + 1 plate (map). Collation: [$1^{16}(1_1+\chi1)2-4^{16}\chi1\ 5-10^{16}11^812^{16}$]. 22.0 × 14.1 cm.

[1–2] blank; [2+1] '[*within a thick-thin rule frame:*] FIRST EDITION PLATE | This is copy number [*numeral(s) added in pen*] of the first | one thousand copies off the | press of the first edition of | The Silmarillion | by J. R. R. Tolkien | reserved for later publication | in this collector's edition | [*signature of Christopher Tolkien, in signed copies*] | ["*JRRT*" *monogram*]'; [2+2] blank; [3] 'THE SILMARILLION'; [4] '[2 *lines in tengwar, between double rules*] | J. R. R. TOLKIEN | QUENTA SILMARIL-LION | (The History of the Silmarils) | together with | AINULINDALË | (The Music of the Ainur) | and | VALAQUENTA | (Account of the Valar) | To which is appended | AKALLABÊTH | (The Downfall of Númenor) | and | OF THE RINGS OF POWER AND | THE THIRD AGE | [2 *lines in tengwar, between double rules*]'; [5] title; [6] '*First published in 1977* | [*notice of restrictions under copyright*] | © *George Allen & Unwin (Publishers) Ltd, 1977* | ISBN 0 04 823129 8 | *Printed in Great Britain* | *in 11 on 12 point Imprint type* | *by William Clowes & Sons, Limited* | *London, Beccles and Colchester*'; 7–9 foreword; [10] blank; 11–12 table of contents; [13] 'AINULINDALË | [*swelled rule*]'; [14] blank; 15–128 text; [128+1] map, *The Realms of the Noldor and the Sindar*, in black and red; [128+2] blank; 129–304 text; [305–9] genealogical tables; 310–11 note on pronunciation; [312] blank; 313–54 index; 355–65 appendix; [366–8] blank. *Map of Beleriand and the Lands to the North*, in black and red on folded leaf tipped onto back pastedown.

Wove paper. Bound in dark red morocco leather over boards. 'JRRT' monogram, within a single-rule frame, stamped on upper cover in gilt. Stamped on spine in gilt between blind-stamped bands: '[*band*] | The | Silmarillion | [*band*] | J. R. R. | TOLKIEN | [3 *bands*] | GEORGE ALLEN | AND UNWIN'. Heraldic device of Lúthien Tinúviel, after Tolkien, stamped in blind on lower cover. Grey-tan wove endpapers. Red/yellow headbands. Dark red ribbon marker. All edges trimmed. Top edge gilt, fore- and bottom edges plain.

Slipcase, red cloth over boards, open edges tipped in dark red morocco leather.

Published 15 September 1982 at £100 (signed copies) or £75 (unsigned copies). According to the publisher's prospectus, 1,000 sets of sheets, 'the first one thousand to leave the press of the first impression', were to be bound identically in red morocco, the first 100 signed by Christopher Tolkien. However, Allen & Unwin do not seem to have bound all 1,000 sets of sheets, and some originally unsigned copies were later converted to signed copies. All 100 signed copies appear to have been sold.

The publisher issued two prospectuses, one directed to the general public and one, evidently, to the book trade. Both announce publication on 15 September 1982 to coincide with the fifth anniversary of the first publication of *The Silmarillion*. Some copies were delayed, however, probably in binding. The Hammond signed copy, no. 9, was received no earlier than late March 1983, the earliest Allen & Unwin could fill the order. But the Scull copy, unsigned, was purchased by her only a few weeks after the official publication date. The bottom edge was not gilded as announced, Tolkien's monogram was stamped from a die, not 'inlaid', and in other respects both prospectuses were incorrect or imprecise. At least in their prospectus directed to the public, Allen & Unwin offered a free copy of *Pictures by J. R. R. Tolkien* with each order.

i. 'Second edition', 'Unicorn' paperback (1983):

[*2 lines in tengwar, between double rules*] | The Silmarillion | J. R. R. TOLKIEN | *edited by* | CHRISTOPHER TOLKIEN | [*publisher's 'Unicorn' device*] | London | UNWIN PAPERBACKS | Boston Sydney | [*2 lines in tengwar, between double rules*]

448 pp. Collation: 224 leaves. 19.6 × 13.2 cm.

Contents as for A15f, except pp. [2] '*also by J. R. R. Tolkien* | [*15 titles, beginning with* ATB, *ending with* UT] | *with Donald Swann* | THE ROAD GOES EVER ON'; [5] title, as above; [6] 'First published in Great Britain by George Allen & Unwin 1977 | First published in Unwin Paperbacks 1979 | Reprinted 1979 | Second edition 1983 | This book is copyright under the Berne Convention. No reproduction | without permission. All rights reserved. | [*3 publisher's addresses, London to North Sydney*] | © George Allen & Unwin (Publishers) Ltd 1977, 1979, 1983 | [*rule*] | [*British Library Cataloging in Publication Data*] | [*rule*] | Set in 10 on 11 point Times | and printed in Great Britain | by Cox and Wyman Ltd, Reading'; [443] Unwin Paperbacks advertisement of books by and about Tolkien; [444] '*Also published in Unicorn* | [*advertisement of* LR]'; [445] advertisement of UT; [446] advertisement of Beagle, *The Last Unicorn*, Dunsany, *The King of Elfland's Daughter*, and Frith, *Asgard*; [447] advertisement of Chant, *Red Moon and Black Mountain*, and Beagle, *A Fine and Private Place*; [448] publisher's order form.

Wove paper. Bound in heavy wove wrappers. Covers and spine printed against a black background. Printed on upper cover within a red single rule frame interrupted at top by a red ellipse: '[*publisher's "unicorn" device, in white, within the ellipse*] | [*in white, against a colour illustration by Roger Garland*, The Haven of the Swans, *fantastic swan-prowed ships in a harbour:*] THE | SILMARILLION | J. R. R. Tolkien'. Printed on spine, running down: '[*in white:*] THE SILMARILLION [*parallel to the title:*] J. R. R. Tolkien [*followed by: publisher's "unwin" device in red, white, and black outlined in white*]'. Printed on lower cover within a red single rule frame interrupted at top by a red ellipse: '[*publisher's "unicorn" device, in white, within the ellipse*] | [*against a grey panel:*] [*in black:*] [*5 quotations, from the* Guardian, Financial Times, Washington Post, Toronto Globe & Mail, *and* Sydney Morning Herald] | [*at left:*] Cover illustration by | Roger Garland | UNICORN | UNWIN PAPERBACKS | FICTION/FANTASY | £2.95 [*at right, against a white panel outlined in black:*] GB £ NET +002.95 | ISBN 0-04-823230-0 | [*bar codes*]'. All edges trimmed and unstained.

Published 21 February 1983 at £2.95; number of copies not known.

Typeset as for A15f, with most of the errors noted for that edition corrected, continuing only 'Leithien' for 'Leithian', p. 202, l. 7; 'makers of fire' for 'masters of fire', p. 236, ll. 9–10; and 'twenty-second king' for 'twenty-third king', p. 322, l. 13. Maps and genealogical tables drawn and lettered as for A15a–c.

j. Houghton Mifflin trade paperback edition (1983):

[2 *lines in tengwar, between double rules*] | J. R. R. TOLKIEN | The Silmarillion | edited by | CHRISTOPHER TOLKIEN | HOUGHTON MIFFLIN COMPANY BOSTON | [2 *lines in tengwar, between double rules*]

120, [2], 121–366 pp. Collation: 184 leaves. 20.8 × 13.9 cm.

Contents as for A15c, except pp. [3] 'BOOKS BY J. R. R. TOLKIEN | [9 *titles, beginning with* LR, *ending with* TL] | Sir Gawain and the Green Knight, | Pearl *and* Sir Orfeo | (translation) | The Father Christmas Letters | (edited by Baillie Tolkien) | The Silmarillion | (edited by Christopher Tolkien) | Unfinished Tales | (edited by Christopher Tolkien) | The Letters of J. R. R. Tolkien | (selected and edited by Humphrey Carpenter) | Mr. Bliss | Finn and Hengest | (edited by Alan Bliss) | WITH DONALD SWANN | The Road Goes Ever On'; [5] title, as above; and [6] 'Copyright © 1977 by George Allen & Unwin (Publishers) Ltd | [*notice of restrictions under copyright*] | [*rule*] | [*Library of Congress Cataloging in Publications Data*] | [*rule*] | Printed in the United States of America | [*printing code, beginning* "V", *ending* "1"] | Houghton Mifflin Company paperback 1983'.

Wove paper. Bound in heavy wove wrappers. Covers and spine printed against a metallic red background. Printed on upper cover: '[*in white:*] THE | SILMARIL-LION | J. R. R. TOLKIEN | [*colour illustration by Tolkien, heraldic device of Elwë*]'. Printed on spine: '[*running down, in white:*] THE SILMARILLION | [*colour illustration as on cover*] | [*in white:*] TOLKIEN | [*horizontal:*] HOUGHTON | MIFFLIN | COMPANY | [*publisher's "dolphin" device*]'. Printed on lower cover: '[*in white:*] FANTASY FPT >>$7.95 | OVER A MILLION COPIES SOLD IN HARDCOVER! | [*blurb*] | [*note on Tolkien*] | [*in black:*] HOUGHTON MIFFLIN COMPANY © 1983 | HOUGHTON MIFFLIN COMPANY, 2 PARK STREET, BOSTON, MASSACHUSETTS 02108 | [*at left:*] 09077083 | [*rule*] | 6–97087 [*at right, against a white panel:*] ISBN 0–395–34646–0'. *Map of Beleriand and the Lands to the North*, divided in half, printed on inner covers. All edges trimmed and unstained.

Published 7 September 1983 at $7.95; 15,000 copies printed.

Typeset as for A15a–c, except pp. [3], [6], and with all errors noted for that setting corrected except 'asssembled' for 'assembled', p. 190, l. 17; 'makers of fire' for 'masters of fire', p. 196, l. 9; and 'twenty-second king' for 'twenty-third king', p. 268, l. 5. Maps and genealogical tables drawn and lettered as for A15a–c.

  With the second impression, 1991? the cover was changed to feature colour illustrations by Tolkien, of a flowering tree and details from friezes (Ei2, no. 42).

k. New reset book club edition (1990):

[2 *lines in tengwar, between double rules*] | [*within 3 concentric single rule frames, alternating thin-thick-thin:*] THE | SILMARILLION | [*rule*] [*diamond*] [*rule*] | J. R. R. Tolkien | [*below the frames:*] GUILD PUBLISHING | LONDON · NEW YORK · SYDNEY · TORONTO | [2 *lines in tengwar, between double rules*]

416 pp. Collation: signatures not distinct. 19.7 × 12.6 cm.

[1] 'THE SILMARILLION'; [2] '[2 *lines in tengwar, between double rules*] | J. R. R. TOLKIEN | QUENTA SILMARILLION | (The History of the Silmarils) | together with | AINULINDALË | (The Music of the Ainur) | and | VALAQUENTA | (Account of the Valar) | To which is appended | AKALLABÊTH | (The Downfall of Númenor) | and | OF THE RINGS OF POWER AND | THE THIRD AGE | [2 *lines in tengwar,*

between double rules]'; [3] title; [4] 'This edition published 1990 by | Guild Publishing | by arrangement | with George Allen & Unwin (Publishers) Ltd | © George Allen & Unwin (Publishers) Ltd, 1977 | [*notice of restrictions under copyright*] | CN 2102 | Printed and bound in Great Britain by | Mackays of Chatham PLC, Chatham, Kent'; 5–6 table of contents; 7–9 foreword; [10–11] *Map of Beleriand and the Lands to the North*; [12] blank; 13 'AINULINDALË | [*swelled rule*]'; [14] blank; [15]–23 text; [24] blank; 25 'VALAQUENTA | [*swelled rule*]'; [26] blank; 27–34 text; 35 'QUENTA SILMARILLION | [*swelled rule*] | The History of the Silmarils'; [36] blank; 37–290 text, with map, *The Realms of the Noldor and the Sindar*, on p. 146; 291 'AKALLABÊTH'; [292] blank; 293–320 text; [321] 'OF THE | RINGS OF POWER | AND THE | THIRD AGE | [*swelled rule*]'; [322] blank; 323–46 text; 347–51 genealogical tables; [352] blank; 353–4 note on pronunciation; 355–403 index; 404–16 appendix on elements of Quenya and Sindarin names.

Wove paper. Mottled blue-green-grey paper over boards, dark green imitation leather spine with raised bands. Gilt vertical rule stamped on leatherette on upper and lower covers. Stamped on upper cover in gilt, within a thin gilt single rule frame, against a dark grey panel outlined by a thick gilt rule: 'THE | SILMARILLION | [*rule*] [*diamond*] [*rule*] | J. R. R. Tolkien'. Stamped on spine in gilt: '[*thick rule*] | THE | SILMARILLION | [*2 thick rules*] | [*thin rule*] | J. R. R. | TOLKIEN | [*thin rule*] | [*2 thick rules*] | [*thin rule*] | GUILD | CLASSICS | [*thin rule*] | [*2 thick rules*] | [*publisher's "gp" device, within a decorative frame*] | [*thick rule*]'. Wove mottled blue-green-grey endpapers. Green/white headbands. Dark green ribbon marker. All edges trimmed and unstained.

Published December? 1990 at £7.95; number of copies not known.

Reset, based on A15a–c, continuing most of the errors noted for that typesetting. Page references in the index changed to accord with the new setting. Maps and genealogical tables drawn and lettered as for A15a–c.

A16   POEMS AND STORIES   1980

[*in orange:*] Poems and Stories | [*in black:*] J. R. R. TOLKIEN | Illustrated by PAULINE BAYNES | London | GEORGE ALLEN & UNWIN | Boston Sydney

244 pp. Collation: [1–20⁸21⁴22⁸]. 22.1 × 14.3 cm.

[1] '[*in orange, within a decorative orange, grey, and white frame surmounted by an illustration in brown, orange, and grey:*] Poems and Stories'; [2] blank; [3] title; [4] '*Poems and Stories* first published in Great Britain 1980 | *The Adventures of Tom Bombadil* first published in Great Britain | 1961. Reprinted seven times | First published in Unwin Paperbacks 1975. Reprinted twice | *The Homecoming of Beorhtnoth Beorhthelm's Son* first published in | Great Britain 1975 | First published in Unwin Paperbacks 1975. Reprinted twice | *On Fairy-Stories* and *Leaf by Niggle* first published in Great | Britain 1964. Reprinted eight times | First published in Unwin Paperbacks 1979 | *Farmer Giles of Ham* first published in Great Britain 1949. | Reprinted ten times | First published in Unwin Paperbacks 1979 | *Smith of Wootton Major* first published in Great Britain 1967. | Reprinted eight times | First published in Unwin Paperbacks 1979 | [*notice of restrictions under copyright*] GEORGE ALLEN & UNWIN LTD | 40 Museum Street, London WC1A 1LU | © George Allen & Unwin (Publishers) Ltd, 1949, 1961, | 1964, 1967, 1975, 1980 | [*within a single rule frame:*] [*British Library Cataloguing in Publication data*] | ISBN 0-04-823174-6 | Typeset in

12 on 13 point Garamond by Bedford Typesetters Ltd | and printed in Great Britain | by W & J Mackay Limited, Chatham'; [5] table of contents; [6] illustration, in brown; [7] '[*in orange, within a brown single rule frame surmounted by an illustration in brown, orange, grey, and black:*] The | Adventures of | Tom Bombadil'; [8] illustration; 9–12 preface to *ATB*; 13–70 text and illustrations; [71] blank; [72–3] illustration, in white and orange; [74] illustration, in brown; [75] '[*in orange, within a brown single rule frame surmounted by an illustration in brown, orange, grey, and black:*] The | Homecoming of | Beorhtnoth | Beorhthelm's Son'; [76] blank; 77–109 text and illustrations; [110–11] illustration, in white and orange; [112] illustration, in brown; [113] '[*in orange, within a brown, 3-sided single rule frame surmounted by an illustration in brown, orange, grey, and black:*] On Fairy-Stories'; [114] blank; 115 introductory note; 116–88 text; [189] blank; [190–1] illustration, in white and orange; [192] illustration, in brown; [193] '[*in orange, within a brown single rule frame surmounted by an illustration in brown, orange, and black:*] Leaf by Niggle'; [194] blank; 195–220 text and illustrations; [221] blank; [222–3] illustration, in white and orange; [224–5] illustration, in brown; [225] '[*in orange, within a brown single rule frame surmounted by an illustration in brown, orange, grey, and black:*] Farmer | Giles of Ham'; [226] blank; 227–8 foreword; 229–99 text and illustrations; [300–1] illustration, in white and orange; [302–3] illustration, in brown; [303] '[*in orange, within a brown single rule frame surmounted by an illustration in brown, orange, and black:*] Smith of | Wootton Major'; [304] blank; 305–42 text and illustrations; [343] illustration; [344] blank. All headings printed in orange. Numerous illustrations with orange colour added.

Wove paper. Bound in black cloth over boards. Illustration, after *The Tree of Amalion* by Tolkien, stamped on upper cover in gilt and green. Stamped on spine in gilt, within a gilt single rule frame: '[*2 rules*] | J. R. R. | Tolkien | [*dash*] | POEMS | AND | STORIES | [*8 rules*] | George | Allen | & | Unwin'. Green/white headbands. Grey and black mottled wove endpapers. All edges trimmed and speckled green.

Some copies issued in unprinted white tissue dust-jacket.

Black paper box. Label affixed to lid, printed: '[*double rule*] | [*in red:*] POEMS | and | STORIES | [*in black:*] J. R. R. Tolkien | DE LUXE EDITION | [*double rule*]'.

Published 29 May 1980 at £17.50; 10,000? copies printed.

Contains: *The Adventures of Tom Bombadil*, 'The Homecoming of Beorhtnoth Beorhthelm's Son', 'On Fairy-Stories', 'Leaf by Niggle', 'Farmer Giles of Ham', and 'Smith of Wootton Major', all reset. Most of the illustrations were reprinted from the original editions of *ATB* (A6), *FGH* (A4), and *SWM* (A9). The illustrations are predominantly brown, usually in combination with orange and black.

In 'On Fairy-Stories' the following readings were continued from A7d (i.e. no corrections):

p. 118, l. 7, 'the notion' for 'that notion'

p. 130, ll. 26–7, 'living monument' for 'living moment'

p. 137, l. 22, 'descended from Olympus' for 'descending from Olympus'

p. 141, l. 6, 'Golden Frey' for 'golden Frey'

p. 141, l. 23, '*Machandelbloom*' for '*Machandelboom*'

p. 146, l. 6, 'Lang was using belief' for 'Lang was using *belief*'

p. 149, l. 18, 'no special "wish to believe"' for 'no special childish "wish to believe"'

p. 153, ll. 31–2, 'Eloi and Morlocks pretty children' for 'Eloi and Morlocks: pretty children'

p. 155, l. 14, 'opinion on this' for 'opinion in this'
p. 163, ll. 13–14, 'their notions' for 'their nations'
p. 164, ll. 25–6, 'for some this very year' for 'for some eye this very year'
p. 167, l. 27, 'some considerations' for 'some consideration'
p. 167, l. 35, 'misusers are fond' for 'misusers of Escape are fond'
p. 171, l. 29, 'expressed essential' for 'expressed something essential'
p. 175, l. 7, 'fairy-tales' for 'fairy-stories'
p. 176, l. 30, 'satirical twist' for 'satiric twist'

The text of 'Leaf by Niggle' agrees with A7a–b, except 'Parish often wandered about looking at trees', p. 214, ll. 22–3.

A17   UNFINISHED TALES   1980

a. First edition:

[*2 lines in tengwar, between double rules*] | Unfinished Tales | of Númenor and Middle-earth | *by* | J. R. R. TOLKIEN | *edited with introduction, commentary, index and maps by* | CHRISTOPHER TOLKIEN | London | GEORGE ALLEN & UNWIN | Boston Sydney | [*3 lines in tengwar, between double rules*]

viii, 472 pp. + 1 plate (map). Collation: [1–11⁸χ112–30⁸]. 22.2 × 14.2 cm.

[i] 'UNFINISHED TALES'; [ii] '[*2 lines in tengwar, between double rules*] | PART I | THE FIRST AGE | PART II | THE SECOND AGE | PART III | THE THIRD AGE | PART IV | THE DRÚEDAIN, THE ISTARI, THE PALANTÍRI | [*3 lines in tengwar, between double rules*]'; [iii] title; [iv] 'First published in 1980 | [*notice of restrictions under copyright*] | GEORGE ALLEN & UNWIN LTD | 40 Museum Street, London WC1A 1LU | © George Allen & Unwin (Publishers) Ltd, 1980 | [*within a single rule frame:*] [*British Library Cataloguing in Publication Data*] | ISBN 0-04-823179-7 | Typeset in 11 on 12 point Imprint by Bedford Typesetters Ltd | and printed in Great Britain | by Unwin Brothers Ltd, Old Woking, Surrey'; [v–vi] table of contents; [vii] note; [viii] blank; [1]–14 introduction; [15] 'PART ONE | [*swelled rule*] | THE FIRST AGE'; [16] blank; 17–162 text, with sketch map on p. 149; [163] 'PART TWO | [*swelled rule*] | THE SECOND AGE'; [164] blank; [165]–8 text; [168+1] map, *Númenórë*, in black and red; [168+2] blank; 169–267 text, with genealogical table, 'The earlier generations of the Line of Elros', on p. [210]; [268] blank; [269] 'PART THREE | [*swelled rule*] | THE THIRD AGE'; [270] blank; [271]–373 text; [374] blank; [375] 'PART FOUR'; [376] blank; [377]–415 text; [416]–72 index. Map, *The West of Middle-earth at the End of the Third Age*, in black and red on folded leaf tipped onto back pastedown.

Wove paper. Bound in wine red cloth over boards. Stamped on spine in gilt: '[*"JRRT" monogram*] | Unfinished | Tales | J. R. R. | TOLKIEN | GEORGE ALLEN | AND UNWIN'. Wove endpapers. No headbands. All edges trimmed. Top edge stained wine red, fore- and bottom edges unstained.

Dust-jacket, wove paper. Printed on upper cover against a dark brown background: '[*in white:*] TOLKIEN | [*in blue outlined in white:*] Unfinished | [*connected to a white rule at left and right:*] Tales | [*illustration after Tolkien, of a Númenórean helmet, in red, green, blue, and black outlined in white, extending onto front flap*]'. Printed on spine against a dark brown background: '[*running down:*] [*in white:*] TOLKIEN [*in blue outlined in white:*] Unfinished Tales | [*horizontal, in white:*] GEORGE ALLEN | & UNWIN'. Lower cover printed solid dark brown. Blurb printed on front flap in dark brown, above extension of cover illustration. Ivory label affixed to front flap, printed in black: 'A&U | £7·50'. Printed on back flap in dark brown: '[*note on the cover illustration*] | ISBN 0 04 823179 7 | *Printed in Great Britain*'. The blue ink on the dust-jacket is not light fast, and is usually found faded.

Published 2 October 1980 at £7.50; number of copies not known, but the first three impressions together equalled 44,000 copies.

Maps and genealogical table drawn and lettered by Christopher Tolkien. The map of Middle-earth is drawn to a larger scale than the earlier general map (in A5), and with 'minor defects' corrected.

Additional or variant writings by J. R. R. Tolkien related to *The Silmarillion*, *The Hobbit*, and *The Lord of the Rings*. The works are narrative or descriptive, and 'unfinished', as Christopher Tolkien explains in his introduction, 'to a greater or lesser degree, and in different senses of the word.' The book contains: 'Of Tuor and His Coming to Gondolin'; 'Narn i Hîn Húrin'; 'A Description of the Island of Númenor'; 'Aldarion and Erendis: The Mariner's Wife'; 'The Line of Elros: Kings of Númenor'; 'The History of Galadriel and Celeborn and of Amroth King of Lórien', with notes on the Silvan Elves, on the boundaries of Lórien, on the port of Lond Daer, and on the names of Celeborn and Galadriel; 'The Disaster of the Gladden Fields', with a note on Númenórean linear measures; 'Cirion and Eorl and the Friendship of Gondor and Rohan'; 'The Quest of Erebor'; 'The Hunt for the Ring'; 'The Battle of the Fords of Isen'; 'The Drúedain'; 'The Istari'; and 'The Palantíri'.

The title page inscription (also printed on p. [ii]) reads: 'In this book of Unfinished Tales by John Ronald Reuel Tolkien which was brought together by Christopher Tolkien, his son, are told many things of men and elves in Númenor and in Middle-earth, from the Elder Days in Beleriand to the War of the Ring and an account is given of the Drúedain, of Istari, and the Palantiri.'

Includes, among others, the errors:

p. 318, l. 21, '*Eynd*' for '*Enyd*'
p. 351, l. 32, 'Halflngs' for 'Halflings'
p. 383, l. 20, 'values of the White Mountains' for 'vales of the White Mountains'
p. 391, l. 9, 'unwearingly' for 'unwearyingly'

Pertinent manuscripts and typescripts are in the Bodleian Library, Oxford.

b. First American edition (1980):

[*2 lines in tengwar, between double rules*] | Unfinished Tales | of Númenor and Middle-earth | *by* | J. R. R. TOLKIEN | *edited with introduction, commentary, index and maps by* | CHRISTOPHER TOLKIEN | HOUGHTON MIFFLIN COMPANY BOSTON | 1980 | [*3 lines in tengwar, between double rules*]

viii, 472 pp. + 1 plate (map). Collation: [1–15¹⁶]. 22.8 × 15.0 cm.

[i] 'UNFINISHED TALES'; [ii] '[*2 lines in tengwar, between double rules*] | PART I | THE FIRST AGE | PART II | THE SECOND AGE | PART III | THE THIRD AGE | PART IV | THE DRÚEDAIN, THE ISTARI, THE PALANTÍRI | [*3 lines in tengwar, between double rules*]'; [iii] title; [iv] 'BOOKS BY J. R. R. TOLKIEN | [*10 titles, beginning with* LR, *ending with* SGPO] | The Father Christmas Letters | (edited by Baillie Tolkien) | The Silmarillion | (edited by Christopher Tolkien) | Unfinished Tales | (edited by Christopher Tolkien) | WITH DONALD SWANN | The Road Goes Ever On | First American Edition | Copyright © 1980 by George Allen & Unwin (publishers) Ltd | [*notice of restrictions under copyright*] | ISBN: 0-395-29917-9 |

Library of Congress Catalogue Card Number: 80-83072 | Printed in the United States of America | [*printing code, beginning "W", ending "1"*]'; [v–vi] table of contents; [vii] note; [viii] map, *Númenórë*; [1]–14 introduction; [15] 'PART ONE | [*swelled rule*] | THE FIRST AGE'; [16] blank; 17–162 text, with sketch map on p. 149; [163] 'PART TWO | [*swelled rule*] | THE SECOND AGE'; [164] blank; [165]–267 text, with genealogical table, 'The earlier generations of the Line of Elros', on p. [210]; [268] blank; [269] 'PART THREE | [*swelled rule*] | THE THIRD AGE'; [270] blank; [271]–373 text; [374] blank; [375] 'PART FOUR'; [376] blank; [377]–415 text; [416]–72 index. Map, *The West of Middle-earth at the End of the Third Age*, in black and red on folded leaf tipped onto recto, back free endpaper.

Wove paper. Bound in yellow-green cloth over boards. Heraldic device of Gil-galad, after Tolkien, stamped on upper cover in silver and green. Stamped on spine: '[*2 identical heraldic devices of Gil-galad connected by a vertical rule, in green; to right of the rule, running down, in silver:*] Unfinished Tales [*parallel to the title, to left of the rule, in silver:*] J. R. R. TOLKIEN | [*below the second heraldic device, horizontal, in green:*] HMCO'. Wove endpapers. Gold headbands. All edges trimmed. Top edge stained orange, fore- and bottom edges unstained.

Dust-jacket, wove paper. Covers and spine printed against a gold background. Printed on upper cover: 'Edited with an Introduction, Commentary, | Index, and Maps by Christopher Tolkien | [*in dark blue outlined in white:*] Unfinished | Tales [*in red-brown outlined in white:*] J · R · R · | Tolkien | [*colour illustration by Tolkien, of a Númenórean helmet*]'. Printed on spine, running down: '[*colour illustration as on cover*] | [*in dark blue outlined in white:*] Unfinished Tales [*parallel to the title:*] [*in red-brown outlined in white:*] J · R · R · Tolkien [*in black:*] HOUGHTON [*parallel to the preceding word:*] MIFFLIN [*parallel to the preceding word:*] COMPANY'. Printed on lower cover: '[*note on the cover illustration*] | [*against a white panel:*] ISBN 0-395-29917-9 | 6-97069'. Printed on front flap: '$15.00 | [*blurb*] | [*note on Christopher Tolkien; to left of note, running down:*] 1180'. Printed on back flap: 'OTHER BOOKS BY J. R. R. TOLKIEN | [*10 titles, beginning with LR, ending with SGPO*] | The Father Christmas Letters | (edited by Baillie Tolkien) | The Silmarillion | (edited by Christopher Tolkien) | Unfinished Tales | (edited by Christopher Tolkien) | The Letters of J. R. R. Tolkien | (selected and edited by Humphrey Carpenter) | Mr. Bliss | Finn and Hengest | (edited by Alan Bliss) | WITH DONALD SWANN | The Road Goes Ever On | JACKET DESIGN BY LOUISE NOBLE | HOUGHTON MIFFLIN COMPANY | 2 Park Street, Boston, Massachusetts 02107 | HOUGHTON MIFFLIN COMPANY © 1980'.

Published 18 November 1980 at $15.00. 80,000 copies printed.

Typeset as for A17a, except pp. [iii–iv], with the thick swelled rules used in A17a on divisional title pages for parts 1–3 replaced by slimmer swelled rules, with a swelled rule added on the divisional title page for part 4 (absent in A17a). Maps and genealogical table drawn and lettered as for A17a.

   Also published by the Book-of-the-Month Club.

c. Reset book club edition (1981):

[*2 lines in tengwar, between double rules*] | Unfinished Tales | of Númenor and Middle-earth | by | J. R. R. TOLKIEN | *edited with introduction, commentary, index and maps by* | CHRISTOPHER TOLKIEN | HOUGHTON MIFFLIN COMPANY BOSTON | [*3 lines in tengwar, between double rules*]

xxiv, 488 pp. Collation: [1–16^{16}]. 20.8 × 13.7–13.8 cm. (width varies).

[i] 'UNFINISHED TALES'; [ii] '[*2 lines in tengwar, between double rules*] | PART I | THE FIRST AGE | PART II | THE SECOND AGE | PART III | THE THIRD AGE | PART IV | THE DRÚEDAIN, THE ISTARI, THE PALANTÍRI | [*3 lines in tengwar, between double rules*]'; [iii] title; [iv] 'Copyright © 1980 by George Allen & Unwin (publishers) Ltd | [*notice of restrictions under copyright*] | Printed in the United States of America'; [v]–vii table of contents; [viii] blank; [ix] note; [x] map, *Númenórë*; [xii]–xxiv introduction; [1] 'PART ONE | [*swelled rule*] | THE FIRST AGE'; [2] blank; [3]–154 text, with sketch map on p. 141; [155] 'PART TWO | [*swelled rule*] | THE SECOND AGE'; [156] blank; [157]–265 text, with genealogical table, 'The earlier generations of the Line of Elros', on p. 203; [266] blank; [267] 'PART THREE | [*swelled rule*] | THE THIRD AGE'; [268] blank; [269]–378 text; [379] 'PART FOUR | [*swelled rule*]'; [380] blank; [381]–422 text; [423]–83 index; [484–8] blank. Printing code, 'L25', printed in gutter, p. 482.

Wove paper. Bound in tan paper over boards, brown cloth spine. Stamped on spine in red: '[*2 identical heraldic devices of Gil-galad connected by a vertical rule; to right of the rule, running down:*] Unfinished Tales [*parallel to the title, to left of the rule:*] J. R. R. TOLKIEN | [*below the second heraldic device, horizontal:*] HMCO'. Wove endpapers; map, *The West of Middle-earth at the End of the Third Age*, printed in black and dark red on each endpaper. No headbands. Top edge trimmed, fore- and bottom edges untrimmed. All edges unstained.

Dust-jacket, wove paper. Covers and spine printed against a gold background. Printed on upper cover: 'Edited with an Introduction, Commentary, | Index, and Maps by Christopher Tolkien | [*in purple outlined in white:*] Unfinished | Tales [*in red-brown outlined in white:*] J · R · R · | Tolkien | [*colour illustration by Tolkien, of a Númenórean helmet*]'. Printed on spine, running down: '[*colour illustration as on cover*] | [*in purple outlined in white:*] Unfinished Tales [*parallel to the title:*] [*in red-brown outlined in white:*] J · R · R · Tolkien [*in black:*] HOUGHTON [*parallel to the preceding word:*] MIFFLIN [*parallel to the preceding word:*] COMPANY'. Printed on lower cover: '[*note on the cover illustration*] | [*against a white panel:*] 5671'. Printed on front flap: '[*blurb*] | [*note on Christopher Tolkien*] | Book Club | Edition'. Printed on back flap: 'JACKET DESIGN BY LOUISE NOBLE | PRINTED IN THE U.S.A. | HOUGHTON MIFFLIN COMPANY © 1980'.

Published by the Science Fiction Book Club in early June 1981? at $6.50?; number of copies not known.

Reset, based on A17a–b, continuing most of the typographical errors of that typesetting. Maps and genealogical table drawn and lettered as for A17a–b.

d. First paperback edition (1982):

[*2 lines in tengwar, between double rules*] | Unfinished Tales | of Númenor and Middle-earth | J. R. R. TOLKIEN | *edited with introduction, commentary, index and maps by* | CHRISTOPHER TOLKIEN | [*publisher's 'unicorn' device*] | London | UNWIN PAPERBACKS | Boston Sydney | [*3 lines in tengwar, between double rules*]

x, 486 pp. Collation: 243 leaves. 19.8 × 13.0 cm.

[i] blurb; [ii] blank; [iii] 'UNFINISHED TALES'; [iv] '[*2 lines in tengwar, between double rules*] | Part I | The First Age | Part II | The Second Age | Part III | The Third Age | Part IV | The Drúedain, the Istari, the Palantíri | *also by J. R. R. Tolkien* | [*15 titles, beginning with* ATB, *ending with* TT] | *with Donald Swann* | THE ROAD GOES EVER ON | [*3 lines in tengwar, between double rules*]'; [v] title; [vi] 'First published in

Great Britain by George Allen & Unwin 1980 | Reprinted three times | First published by Unwin Paperbacks 1982 | This book is copyright under the Berne Convention. No reproduction | without permission. All rights reserved. | [*3 publisher's addresses, London to North Sydney*] | © George Allen & Unwin (Publishers) Ltd, 1980, 1982 | ISBN 0 04 823208 4 | Typeset in Imprint by Bedford Typesetters Ltd | and printed in Great Britain by | Hazell Watson and Viney Ltd, Aylesbury, Bucks'; [vii–viii] table of contents; [ix] note; [x] blank; [1]–14 introduction; [15] 'PART ONE | [*swelled rule*] | THE FIRST AGE'; [16] blank; 17–162 text, with sketch map on p. 149; [163] 'PART TWO | [*swelled rule*] | THE SECOND AGE'; [164] map, *Númenórë*; [165]–267 text, with genealogical table, 'The earlier generations of the Line of Elros', on p. [210]; [268] blank; [269] 'PART THREE | [*swelled rule*] | THE THIRD AGE'; [270] blank; [271]–373 text; [374] blank; [375] 'PART FOUR'; [376] blank; [377]–415 text; [416]–72 index; [473–4] blank; [475] key map, *The West of Middle-earth at the End of the Third Age*; [476–9] sectional maps; [480] blank; [481] Unwin Paperbacks advertisement of books by and about Tolkien; [482] advertisement of *LR*; [483] advertisement of *H* and *Silm*; [484] '*Also published in Unicorn* | [*advertisement of* Beagle, The Last Unicorn, *Dunsany*, The King of Elfland's Daughter, *Frith*, Asgard, *and* Beagle, A Fine and Private Place]'; [485] publisher's order form; [486] blank.

Wove paper. Bound in heavy wove wrappers. Covers and spine printed against a black background. Printed on upper cover within a red single rule frame interrupted at top by a red ellipse: '[*publisher's "unicorn" device in white, within the ellipse*] | [*in white, against a colour illustration by Roger Garland,* Glaurung, the dragon of Morgoth:] | UNFINISHED | TALES | J. R. R. Tolkien'. Printed on spine, running down: '[*in white:*] UNFINISHED TALES [*parallel to the title:*] J. R. R. Tolkien [*followed by: publisher's "unwin" device in red, white, and black within a white single rule frame*]'. Printed on lower cover within a red single rule frame interrupted at top by a red ellipse: '[*publisher's "unicorn" device in white, within the ellipse*] | [*against a grey panel, in black:*] [2 quotations, from the Sunday Times *and* Sunday Telegraph] | [*blurb*] | Cover illustration by Roger Garland | [*at left:*] UNICORN | UNWIN PAPERBACKS | FICTION/FANTASY | £2.95 [*at right, against a white panel:*] GB £ NET +002.95 | ISBN 0-04-823208-4 | [*bar codes*]'. All edges trimmed and unstained.

Published 13 September 1982 at £2.95; 15,000? copies printed.

Typeset as for A17a, except pp. [i], [v–vi], [481–5], and with corrections. Continues some typographical errors from A17a, e.g. 'Halflngs' for 'Halflings', p. 351, l. 32. Maps and genealogical table drawn and lettered as for A17a–b.

e. First American (trade) paperback edition (1982):

[*2 lines in tengwar, between double rules*] | Unfinished Tales | of Númenor and Middle-earth | by | J. R. R. TOLKIEN | *edited with introduction, commentary, index and maps by* | CHRISTOPHER TOLKIEN | HOUGHTON MIFFLIN COMPANY BOSTON | [*3 lines in tengwar, between double rules*]

viii, 472 pp. Collation: 240 leaves. 20.9 × 13.9 cm.

Contents as for A17b, except pp. [iii] title, as above; and [iv] 'BOOKS BY J. R. R. TOLKIEN | [*10 titles, beginning with* LR, *ending with* SGPO] | The Father Christmas Letters (edited by Baillie Tolkien) | The Silmarillion | (edited by Christopher Tolkien) | Unfinished Tales | (edited by Christopher Tolkien) | WITH DONALD SWANN | The Road Goes Ever On | Copyright © 1980 by George Allen & Unwin (publishers) Ltd | [*notice of restrictions under copyright*] | ISBN: 0-395-29917-9 | ISBN: 0-395-32441-6 pbk. | Library of Congress Catalogue Card Number: 80-83072 | Printed in the United States of America | [*printing code, beginning "V", ending "1"*] | Houghton Mifflin Company paperback 1982'.

Wove paper. Bound in heavy wove wrappers. Covers and spine printed against a gold background. Printed on upper cover: '[*in red-brown:*] SIX MONTHS ON | BEST SELLER LISTS | [*rule, in dark blue*] | [*in black:*] Edited with an Introduction, Commentary, | Index, and Maps by Christopher Tolkien | [*in dark blue outlined in white:*] Unfinished | Tales [*in red-brown outlined in white:*] J·R·R· | Tolkien | [*colour illustration by Tolkien, of a Númenórean helmet*]'. Printed on spine: '[*running down:*] [*colour illustration, as on upper cover*] [*in dark blue outlined in white:*] Unfinished Tales [*parallel to the title:*] [*in red-brown outlined in white:*] J·R·R· TOLKIEN [*in black:*] HOUGHTON [*parallel to the preceding word:*] MIFFLIN [*parallel to the preceding word:*] COMPANY | [*publisher's "dolphin" device, horizontal*]'. Printed on lower cover: 'FICTION FPT >>$8.25 | [*blurb*] | [*note on Christopher Tolkien*] | [*in red-brown:*] HOUGHTON MIFFLIN COM-PANY © 1982 | [*in dark blue:*] HOUGHTON MIFFLIN COMPANY, 2 PARK STREET, BOSTON, MASSACHUSETTS 02108 | [*in black:*] [*at left:*] 09080082 | 6-97094 [*at right, against a white panel:*] ISBN 0-395-32441-6'. Map, *The West of Middle-earth at the End of the Third Age*, divided in half, printed on inner covers. All edges trimmed and unstained.

Published 30 September 1982 at $8.25; 30,000 copies printed.

Typeset as for A17b, except pp. [iii–iv]. Maps and genealogical table drawn and lettered as for A17a–b.

f. Ballantine Books edition (1988):

[*2 lines in tengwar, between double rules*] | UNFINISHED | TALES OF | NÚMENOR AND | MIDDLE-EARTH | by | J. R. R. TOLKIEN | edited with introduction, commentary, | and index by | CHRISTOPHER TOLKIEN | BALLANTINE BOOKS • NEW YORK | [*3 lines in tengwar, between double rules*]

xiv, 498 pp. Collation: 256 leaves. 17.5 × 10.5 cm.

[i] '[*within a double rule frame:*] HEREIN LIE THE SECRETS OF | THE WORLD OF MIDDLE-EARTH | [*blurb*]'; [ii] '[*2 lines in tengwar, between double rules*] | By J. R. R. Tolkien | Published by Ballantine Books: | [*10 titles, beginning with H, ending with* Smith of Wootton Major & Farmer Giles of Ham] | *By Humphrey Carpenter:* | Tolkien: The Authorized Biography | *By Paul H. Kocher:* | Master of Middle-earth: | The Fiction of J. R. R. Tolkien | *By Robert Foster:* | The Complete Guide to Middle-earth: | From The Hobbit to The Silmarillion | [*3 lines in tengwar, between double rules*]'; [iii] title; [iv] 'Copyright © 1980 by George Allen & Unwin (publishers) Ltd | All rights reserved under International and Pan-American Copy-right | Conventions. Published in the United States of America by Ballantine | Books, a division of Random House, Inc., New York. | [*notice of restrictions under copyright*] | Library of Congress Catalog Card Number: 80-83072 | ISBN 0-345-35711-6 | First published by Houghton Mifflin Company. Reprinted by permission | of Houghton Mifflin Company. | Manufactured in the United States of America | First Ballantine Books Edition: September 1988 | Maps by Shelly Shapiro'; v–vi table of contents; [vii] note; [viii] blank; [ix] map, *Númenórë*, by Christopher Tolkien; [x–xi] map of Third Age Middle-earth, by Shelly Shapiro, with inset map of The Shire; [xii–xiii] map of Gondor and Mordor, by Shelly Shapiro; [xiv] blank; 1–15 introduction; [16] blank; [17] 'PART ONE | [*swelled rule*] | THE FIRST AGE'; [18] blank; 19–170 text, with sketch map on p. 157; [171] 'PART TWO |

[*swelled rule*] | THE SECOND AGE'; [172] map, 'Númenórë', by Shelly Shapiro; 173–280 text, with genealogical table, 'The earlier generations of the Line of Elros', on p. 221; [281] 'PART THREE | [*swelled rule*] | THE THIRD AGE'; [282] blank; 283–390 text; [391] 'PART FOUR | [*swelled rule*]'; [392] blank; 393–433 text; 434–93 index; [494] blank; [495] '[*3 lines and blurb between thick-thin rules at left and right:*] J. R. R. TOLKIEN'S | Epic Fantasy Classic | The Lord of the Rings | [*blurb*] | [*publisher's order form*]'; [496–8] blank.

Wove paper. Bound in heavy wove wrappers. Printed or stamped on upper cover against a cream background: '[*printed in black:*] WITH NOTES AND AN INTRO-DUCTION BY CHRISTOPHER TOLKIEN | [*rule*] | [*stamped in gilt:*] J. R. R. | TOLKIEN | [*printed:*] [*in black:*] [*rule*] | The Lost Lore of Middle-earth | [*rule*] | [*in dark green:*] UNFINISHED | TALES | [*colour illustration by Michael Herring, of a hooded figure (Morgoth?) seated on a carved throne, surrounded by a wolf (Carcharoth?), an Orc (?), and a snake, all contained within an archway; printed at upper right, partly overlapping the illustration, in black within a gold ring:*] Fifty Years | of Tolkien— | Share the | Fantasy | [*at lower left of cover:*] [*running up:*] Ballantine/Fantasy/35711/U.S. $5.95 | [*below the preceding line, publisher's "BB" device in white and black*]'. Printed on spine against a cream background: '[*publisher's "BB" device, in white and black*] | [*in black:*] Fantasy | [*running down, between black rules:*] J. R. R. TOLKIEN | [*in gold:*] · | [*colour illustration as on upper cover, horizontal*] | [*running down, in dark green:*] UNFINISHED [*parallel to the preceding word:*] TALES | [*horizontal, in black:*] U.S. 595 | [*rule*] | 345- | 35711-6'. Printed on lower cover against a cream background: '[*blurb, in black and dark green*] | [*in black:*] [*against a white panel:*] [*bar codes*] | ISBN 0-345-35711-6 [*to right of panel, running down:*] Cover printed in USA'. Printed on inside front cover, running down: 'ISBN 0-345-35711-6 [*bar code*]'. All edges trimmed and stained yellow.

Published September 1988 at $5.95; number of copies not known.

Reset, based on A17a–b, continuing the errors: '*Eynd*' for '*Enyd*', p. 318, l. 21; 'Halflngs' for 'Halflings', p. 351, l. 32; 'values of the White Mountains' for 'vales of the White Mountains', p. 383, l. 20; and 'unwearingly' for 'unwearyingly', p. 391, l. 9. Maps and genealogical table as for A17a–b, with added new maps.

A18   **MR. BLISS**   **1982**

a. First edition:

[*facsimile of manuscript title:*] Mr. Bliss | [*colour illustration by Tolkien*] | [*in type:*] J. R. R. TOLKIEN | London | GEORGE ALLEN & UNWIN | Boston Sydney

112 pp. Collation: [1–7⁸]. 14.8 × 20.9 cm.

[1–4] blank ([1–2] pasted down); [5] title; [6] '© Christopher Reuel Tolkien and Frank Richard Williamson as | Executors of the Estate of J. R. R. Tolkien. 1982 | This book is copyright under the Berne Convention. No reproduction without permission. All rights reserved. | [*3 publisher's addresses, London to North Sydney*] | First published in 1982 | The manuscript of *Mr. Bliss* is owned by Marquette University, Milwaukee, | Wisconsin, U.S.A. The Manuscript is held in the Department of Special | Collections and University Archives. The Publishers gratefully acknowledge | the assistance of Marquette University in the publication of this work. | [*rule*] | [*British Library Cataloguing in Publication Data*] ISBN 0-04-823215-7 | [*rule*] | Colour reproduction by Vidicolor Ltd., Hemel Hempstead, Herts. | Printed and bound in Great Britain by W. S. Cowell Ltd., Ipswich.'; [7–107] reproduction of Tolkien's illustrated manuscript of *Mr. Bliss* in colour facsimile on rectos, and on versos when appropriate, transcriptions of the text in type between single rules; [108] blank; [109] 'A list of books by J. R. R. Tolkien | [*2-column list of books by or about Tolkien published by Allen & Unwin, beginning with* H, *ending with Shippey,* The Road to Middle Earth (*sic*)]'; [110–12] blank ([111–12] pasted down).

Wove paper, mechanically tinted. Bound in paper over boards. Covers and spine printed against a light peach background. Printed on upper cover against a light grey panel, within a black single rule frame: '[*facsimile of manuscript title, in dark blue:*] Mr. Bliss | [*colour illustration by Tolkien, of Mr. Bliss in his motor car*] | [*in dark green type:*] J. R. R. TOLKIEN'. Printed on spine, running down: 'MR. BLISS J. R. R. TOLKIEN GEORGE ALLEN & UNWIN'. Page 10 of the manuscript ('So he turned sharp to the right . . .') is reproduced in colour on the lower cover, within a black single rule frame. No endpapers or headbands. All edges trimmed and unstained.

Dust-jacket, wove paper. Covers and spine printed as for the binding, except that the panel on the upper cover is light green-grey, the general background colour is a darker peach, and a round gold label is affixed to the lower cover at lower left, printed in black: 'PRICE NET | £4.95 | IN UK ONLY'. Printed on front flap: '[*blurb*] | *Each page of J. R. R. Tolkien's original* | *manuscript is reproduced in facsimile* | *with a facing printed text.*' Printed on back flap: 'ISBN 0 04 823215 7 | *Printed in Great Britain*'.

Published 20 September 1982 at £4.95; 50,000? copies printed.

The title lettering on p. [5], on the binding, and on the dust-jacket is from the first, unnumbered page of the manuscript. The illustration (Mr. Bliss in his motor-car) following the title is from p. 9 of the manuscript.

Mr. Bliss, Tolkien's strange comic story of a man, a motor-car, three bears, and a 'girabbit' (giraffe-rabbit), was devised *circa* summer 1928, when its telling was recorded in a diary kept by the middle Tolkien son, Michael. According to Mrs. Michael Tolkien, *Mr. Bliss* was inspired by young Christopher Tolkien's toy car, not, as stated by Humphrey Carpenter in *Biography*, the family car purchased in 1932 and Tolkien's mishaps while driving it. The bears of the story are the teddy bears that belonged to Tolkien's three sons. According to Christopher Tolkien, the handwriting of the manuscript suggests that it was written out in the nineteen-thirties. Jared C. Lobdell assigned it to 1928–32; see his 'Mr Bliss: Notes on the Manuscript and Story', *Selections from the Marquette J. R. R. Tolkien Collection* (Milwaukee: Marquette University Library, 1987), pp. [5–10].

Tolkien submitted his illustrated manuscript of *Mr. Bliss* to George Allen & Unwin in late 1936, while *The Hobbit* was in production. C. A. Furth, production manager for Allen & Unwin, admired Tolkien's calligraphy and art but foresaw difficulties in their printing. *Mr. Bliss*, he wrote to Tolkien on 7 January 1937, was 'in a class which it shares with *Alice in Wonderland* and the extremely few comparable books. The difficulty [in publishing *Mr. Bliss*] is solely a technical one, but it seems at the moment serious.' Estimates were prepared, and a specimen of lettering obtained from a calligrapher in the style of Tolkien's own writing. 'But it is questionable', wrote Furth, 'whether a simpler lettering or an attractive type would not be more readable for children?' If 5,000 copies were printed, and the book were bound only in stiff wrappers with the title printed on the cover in two colours, the minimum sale price per copy might be 3s. 6d., which Furth thought unusually high for a book of only '56 little pages'. The high estimate was due mainly to the cost of colour separations.

The manuscript was returned to Tolkien, who wrote to Furth on 17 January that he did not imagine that *Mr. Bliss* was worth so much trouble. 'The pictures seem to me mostly only to prove that the author cannot draw', he complained. But he offered to try to make them easier to reproduce. He thought that he might find odd moments to work on the book, having been freed from the burden of examining for two years. He liked the calligrapher's lettering, and favoured 'something of the kind' rather than another style, or a typeface, and 'the retention of the mixture of text and picture on one page (if possible) to retain something of the free and easy air of a ms. book.' He seems to have met with Furth in mid-February to discuss (if not resolve) the book's technical problems.

In the meantime, *The Hobbit* moved closer to publication (see A3a note) and Allen & Unwin looked to the future. No one, Furth assured Tolkien on 4 September 1937, 'would be more delighted than we if after *The Hobbit* we might come out with *Mr. Bliss*.' But Tolkien had 'no immediate chance' to revise *Mr. Bliss* for publication, he wrote to Furth on 5 September. 'My research fellowship is rather exigent. But there might be odd moments, if I felt at all sure of what is required for (reasonably cheap) reproductions. It would not be difficult to copy the existing MS.—probably on a larger scale—in watercolours (or in a few cases black-and-white), as per *Hobbit* illustrations, with story in a simple script. But would you not require the colour scheme limited?'

The manuscript was submitted again on 15 November 1937, together with *The Silmarillion* and other candidates to succeed *The Hobbit* (see A15a note). It was returned to Tolkien on 15 February 1938 with instructions for revising the illustrations. Furth suggested that he redraw a little larger and in three colours and black, the black to be photographed and the colours copied by hand onto printing cylinders. Tolkien replied on 17 February:

> I am sorry you have had so much trouble with [*Mr. Bliss*]. . . . I wish you could find someone to redraw the pictures properly. I don't believe I am capable of it. I have at any rate no time now—it is easier to write a story at odd moments than draw (though neither are easy).
>
> It would be easy to abjure ink (or pencil). But the *three* colours is rather a blight. *Green* is essential; the bears require *brown*. What can one do deprived of *two* of red, blue, yellow? What is the objection to the [Beatrix] 'Potter' style with shiny paper? Children like it. Is it too costly?

Furth agreed on 19 February that Tolkien's drawings could be reproduced probably as they were by the 'Potter process', i.e. colour halftones, but the publisher had felt that the glossy paper required for halftones would be objectionable. 'However, if you really find that children do not mind it, would you return *Mr. Bliss* at your convenience and we will work out some figures by that process.'

The manuscript did not immediately return to Allen & Unwin, though it was not forgotten. During late summer 1938 *Mr. Bliss* was briefly considered as Tolkien's next book after *The Hobbit*, to appear sometime in 1939 (it was too late for Christmas 1938 sales); and on 2 February 1939 Tolkien promoted it in a letter to C. A. Furth. But the publisher was still faced, on the one hand, with an exorbitant cost to reproduce Tolkien's coloured pictures, and on the other with the need to sell a children's book at a low price.

In 1957 Tolkien sold the manuscript of *Mr. Bliss*, together with manuscripts of *The Hobbit*, *Farmer Giles of Ham*, and *The Lord of the Rings*, to Marquette University in Milwaukee, Wisconsin. By late 1964 the story came to the attention of Clyde S. Kilby of Wheaton College, Wheaton, Illinois, who had met Tolkien earlier that year and corresponded with him about *Mr. Bliss*. At first Tolkien was prepared to consider its publication in the United States; but he came to dislike the story except as a private joke, and decided that it would be best for his reputation if published posthumously. Allen & Unwin maintained an interest in *Mr. Bliss*, which tended to discourage would-be publishers. Only after Tolkien's death in 1973, when several American firms had inquired about the book, was it published at last, nearly a half-century after it was first submitted, by Allen & Unwin in Britain and Houghton Mifflin in the United States. Any problems of illegible handwriting were solved by printing transcriptions facing the manuscript.

Pages 9–10 of the manuscript were reproduced in the *Milwaukee Sentinel*, 17 December 1966, p. 10.

Portions of the manuscript, and two preliminary sketches, were described by T. J. R. Santoski in *Catalogue of an Exhibit of the Manuscripts of J R R T* (Ei3; Milwaukee: Marquette University, Memorial Library, Department of Special Collections and University Archives, 1983), pp. 8–10. Minor differences between the manuscript and the printed transcriptions of the text are detailed in Donald O'Brien, 'The Transcription of J. R. R. Tolkien's *Mr. Bliss*', *Beyond Bree* (newsletter of the American Mensa Tolkien Special Interest Group), July 1987, pp. 1–4.

A book club edition was published in 1982 by Book Club Associates, London, in similar binding and dust-jacket.

b. First American edition (1983):

[*facsimile of manuscript title:*] Mr. Bliss | [*colour illustration by Tolkien*] | [*in type:*] J. R. R. TOLKIEN | Boston | HOUGHTON MIFFLIN COMPANY | 1983

112 pp. Collation: $[1-3^{12}4^{8}5^{12}]$. 14.5 × 20.8 cm.

[1] blank; [2] 2 rules; [3] 'Mr. Bliss' (reproduction of first, unnumbered page of Tolkien's manuscript); [4] 'BOOKS BY J. R. R. TOLKIEN | [*10 titles, beginning with* LR, *ending with* SGPO] | The Father Christmas Letters | (edited by Baillie Tolkien) | The Silmarillion | (edited by Christopher Tolkien) | Pictures by J. R. R. Tolkien | Unfinished Tales | (edited by Christopher Tolkien) | Letters of J. R. R. Tolkien | (edited by Humphrey Carpenter) | Finn and Hengest: The Fragment and the Episode | (edited by Alan Bliss) | *With Donald Swann* | The Road Goes Ever On'; [5] title; [6] 'First American Edition 1983 | Copyright © 1982 by Christopher Reuel Tolkien and Frank Richard Williamson | as Executors of the Estate of J. R. R. Tolkien | [*notice of restrictions under copyright*] | [*rule*] | [*Library of Congress Cataloging in Publication Data*] | [*rule*] | Printed in the United States of America | [*printing code, beginning "H", ending "1"*] | The manuscript of *Mr. Bliss* is owned by Marquette University, Milwaukee, | Wisconsin, U.S.A. The Manuscript is held in the Department of Special Collections | and University Archives. The Publishers gratefully acknowledge the assistance | of Marquette University in the publication of this work.'; [7–107] reproduction of Tolkien's illustrated manuscript of *Mr. Bliss* in colour facsimile on rectos, and on versos when appropriate, transcriptions of the text in type between single rules; [108] blank; [109] blurb, between single rules; [110–12] blank.

Wove paper, mechanically tinted. Bound in dark green cloth over boards. Stamped on spine, running down, in gilt: 'MR. BLISS J. R. R. Tolkien HMCO'. 'Oatmeal' endpapers. No headbands. All edges trimmed and unstained.

Dust-jacket, wove paper. Covers and spine printed as for the binding of A18a, except that the panel on the upper cover is light green-grey, the general background colour is a darker peach, and below the frame on the lower cover is printed in black: '6-97095 [*against a white panel:*] ISBN 0-395-32936-1'. Printed on front flap: 'FPT ISBN

0-395-32936-1 >$11.95 | [*blurb*] | 01114583'. Printed on back flap: '[*blurb, continued*] | HOUGHTON MIFFLIN COMPANY | 2 Park Street, Boston, Massachusetts 02108'.

Published 17 January 1983 at $11.95; 25,000 copies printed.

Typeset as for A18a, except pp. [2], [4–6], [109]. Illustrations as for A18a.

A book club edition was also published in 1983, bound in printed paper over boards as for A18a, marked '*Book Club Edition*' on lower cover, without dust-jacket.

| A19 | THE MONSTERS AND THE CRITICS AND OTHER ESSAYS | 1983 |

a. First edition:

J. R. R. TOLKIEN | THE MONSTERS AND | THE CRITICS | and Other Essays | Edited by Christopher Tolkien | London | GEORGE ALLEN & UNWIN | Boston Sydney

viii, 240 pp. Collation: [1–6¹⁶7¹²8¹⁶]. 22.1 × 14.1 cm.

[i–ii] blank; [iii] 'THE MONSTERS AND THE CRITICS | AND OTHER ESSAYS'; [iv] blank; [v] title; [vi] '© Frank Richard Williamson and Christopher Reuel Tolkien as | Executors of the Estate of J. R. R. Tolkien, 1983 | This book is copyright under the Berne Convention. No reproduction | without permission. All rights reserved. | [*3 publisher's addresses, London to North Sydney*] | First published in 1983 | [*rule*] | [*British Library Cataloguing in Publication Data*] | [*rule*] | Set in 11 on 13 point Baskerville by Bedford Typesetters Ltd | and printed in Great Britain by Mackays of Chatham'; [vii] table of contents; [viii] blank; [1]–4 foreword; [5]–240 text.

Wove paper. Bound in dark blue textured paper over boards. Stamped on spine, running down, in gilt: 'J. R. R. TOLKIEN The Monsters and the Critics [*parallel to first part of title:*] and Other Essays [*following the title:*] GEORGE ALLEN [*parallel to the preceding two words:*] & UNWIN'. Wove endpapers. No headbands. All edges trimmed. Top edge stained dark blue, fore- and bottom edges unstained.

Dust-jacket, wove paper. Printed on upper cover against a dark blue background: '[*in white:*] J. R. R. TOLKIEN | [*rule, in white*] [*in light peach:*] The [*rule, in white*] | [*in light peach:*] Monsters | and the Critics | and Other Essays | [*rule, in white*]'. Printed on spine against a dark blue background: '[*running down:*] [*in white:*] J. R. R. TOLKIEN [*in light peach:*] The Monsters and the Critics [*parallel to first part of title:*] and Other Essays | [*horizontal, in white:*] GEORGE ALLEN | & UNWIN'. Lower cover printed solid dark blue. Blurb printed on front flap in dark blue. Printed on back flap in dark blue: 'ISBN 0 04 809019 0 | *Printed in Great Britain*'.

Published 3 March 1983 at £9.95; 5,000 copies planned.

Contains: 'Beowulf: The Monsters and the Critics'; 'On Translating Beowulf'; 'Sir Gawain and the Green Knight' (lecture); 'On Fairy-Stories'; 'English and Welsh'; 'A Secret Vice'; and 'Valedictory Address to the University of Oxford'. 'Beowulf: The Monsters and the Critics,' pp. [5]–48, was reprinted from *Proceedings of the British Academy* (see A2). 'On Translating Beowulf,' pp. [49]–71, was first published as prefatory remarks in *Beowulf and the Finnesburg Fragment* (B17). 'Sir Gawain and the Green Knight,' pp. [72]–108, was delivered by Tolkien on 15 April 1953 at the University of Glasgow, as the W. P. Ker Memorial Lecture, and was published here for the first time. 'On Fairy-Stories,' pp. [109]–61, was reprinted from *Tree and Leaf*, continuing the following readings from A7d:

p. 110, l. 31, 'the notion' for 'that notion'
p. 138, l. 31, 'opinion on this' for 'opinion in this'
p. 144, l. 36, 'their notions' for 'their nations'
p. 145, ll. 24–5, 'for some this very year' for 'for some eye this very year'
p. 147, l. 37, 'some considerations' for 'some consideration'
p. 153, l. 16, 'fairy-tales' for 'fairy-stories'
p. 154, l. 31, 'satirical twist' for 'satiric twist'

Nine corrections were made to *OFS*:

p. 120, l. 19: living monument > living moment
p. 125, l. 25: descended from Olympus > descending from Olympus
p. 128, l. 11: Golden Frey > golden Frey
p. 132, l. 1: Lang was using belief > Lang was using *belief*
p. 128, l. 26: *Machandelbloom* > *Machandelboom*
p. 134, ll. 19–20: no special 'wish to believe' > no special childish 'wish to believe'
p. 137, ll. 32–3, restores colon: Eloi and Morlocks: pretty children
p. 148, ll. 4–5: misusers are fond > misusers of Escape are fond
p. 150, l. 35: expressed essential > expressed something essential

'English and Welsh,' pp. [162]–97, was reprinted from *Angles and Britons* (B27). 'A Secret Vice,' pp. [198]–223, an address, dated by Christopher Tolkien as given in 1931 and titled in manuscript 'A Hobby for the Home,' was published here for the first time. Two errors noted: 'Men' for 'Man', p. 221, l. 39; 'fána' for 'fáne', p. 222, l. 3. 'Valedictory Address to the University of Oxford,' pp. [224]–40, was published here from a different manuscript, with alterations, than that published in *J. R. R. Tolkien: Scholar and Storyteller* (B34).

Pertinent manuscripts and typescripts are in the Bodleian Library, Oxford.

b. First American edition (1984):

J. R. R. TOLKIEN | THE MONSTERS AND | THE CRITICS | and Other Essays | Edited by Christopher Tolkien | Houghton Mifflin Company | *Boston* | 1984

viii, 248 pp. Collation: gatherings not distinct. 22.1 × 13.9 cm.

[i] 'THE MONSTERS AND THE CRITICS | AND OTHER ESSAYS'; [ii] blank; [iii] title; [iv] 'Copyright © 1983 by Frank Richard Williamson and Christopher Reuel Tolkien | as Executors of the Estate of J. R. R. Tolkien | [*notice of restrictions under copyright*] | [*Library of Congress Cataloging in Publication Data*] | Printed in the United States of America | [*printing code, beginning "Q", ending "1"*]'; [v] table of contents; [vi] blank; [vii] 'THE MONSTERS AND THE CRITICS | AND OTHER ESSAYS'; [viii] blank; [1]–4 foreword; [5]–240 text; [241–8] blank.

Wove paper. Bound in blue-purple paper over boards, dark blue cloth spine. Stamped on spine in gilt: '[*running down:*] THE MONSTERS AND THE CRITICS [*parallel to first part of title:*] AND OTHER ESSAYS · J. R. R. TOLKIEN | [*horizontal:*] HMCO'. Wove endpapers. Dark blue headbands. All edges trimmed and unstained.

Dust-jacket, wove paper. Covers and spine as for the jacket of A19a, except that the cover and spine titles are printed in cream, the spine imprint is 'HOUGHTON | MIFFLIN | COMPANY' in dark blue against a white panel, and on the lower cover is printed, against a dark blue background: '[*in white:*] 6-97096 [*in dark blue, against a white panel:*] ISBN 0-395-35635-0'. Printed on front flap in dark blue: 'FPT ISBN 0-395-35635-0 >$15.95 | [*blurb*] | 04154584'. Printed on back flap in dark blue:

'[*note on Tolkien*] | HOUGHTON MIFFLIN COMPANY © 1984 | HOUGHTON MIFFLIN COMPANY | 2 Park Street | Boston, Massachusetts 02108'.

Published 15 April 1984 at $15.95; 4,000 copies printed.

Typeset as for A19a.

| A20 | SMITH OF WOOTTON MAJOR AND LEAF BY NIGGLE | 1983 |

J. R. R. TOLKIEN | SMITH OF | WOOTTON MAJOR | and | LEAF BY NIGGLE | WITH ILLUSTRATIONS BY | PAULINE BAYNES | London | UNWIN PAPER-BACKS | Boston Sydney

x, 86 pp. Collation: 48 leaves. 17.7 × 11.0 cm.

[i] blurb; [ii] blank; [iii] 'SMITH OF | WOOTTON MAJOR | and | LEAF BY NIGGLE'; [iv] blank; [v] *also by J. R. R. Tolkien* | [*15 titles, beginning with* ATB, *ending with* UT] | *with Donald Swann* | The Road Goes Ever On'; [vi] blank; [vii] title; [viii] '*Smith of Wootton Major* first published in Great | Britain by George Allen & Unwin 1967 | Reprinted six times | *Leaf by Niggle* first published in book form in | *Tree and Leaf* in Great Britain by George Allen | & Unwin 1964 | Reprinted eight times | *Smith of Wootton Major* and *Leaf by Niggle* | first published in Unwin Paper-backs with | *The Homecoming of Beorhtnoth Beorhthelm's Son* 1975 | Reprinted 1977, 1979, 1982 | This edition first published in Unwin Paperbacks | 1983 | This book is copyright under the Berne Convention. | No reproduction without permission. All rights reserved. | [*3 publisher's addresses, London to North Sydney*] | © George Allen & Unwin (Publishers) Ltd, 1964, 1967, 1975, 1983 | ISBN 0-04-823232-7 | Set in 12 on 14 point Bembo by V&M Graphics Ltd, Aylesbury, Bucks | and printed in Great Britain by Cox and Wyman Ltd, Reading'; [ix] blank; [x] illustration; 1–[47] text of *SWM* and illustrations; [48] blank; [49] 'LEAF BY NIGGLE'; [50] blank; 51–78 text; [79–80] blank; [81] Unwin Paperbacks advertisement of books by and about Tolkien; [82] advertisement of *H*, *LR*; [83] publisher's order form; [84–6] blank.

Wove paper. Bound in heavy wove wrappers. Printed on upper cover, against a colour illustration by Pauline Baynes, of Smith in Faery (detail of upper cover illustration of A9c): '[*in open area:*] J. R. R. TOLKIEN | Smith of | Wootton Major | Illustrated by | Pauline Baynes | [*publisher's "unwin" device, in red, white, and black*]'. Printed on spine, running down, against a blue-green background: 'Smith of Wootton Major J. R. R. TOLKIEN [*publisher's "unwin" device, in red, white, and black*]'. Printed on lower cover against a blue-green background: '[*blurb*] | [*2 quotations, from the* Times Educational Supplement *and* New Statesman, *in black and white*] | [*at left:*] UNWIN | PAPERBACKS | CHILDREN/ | FANTASY | £1.50 [*at right, against a white panel outlined in black:*] GB £ NET +001.50 | ISBN 0-04-823232-7 | [*bar codes*]'. All edges trimmed and unstained. Copies of the first impression were later issued in a binding as above, except with 'Baines' misprinted for 'Baynes' on the upper cover; cf. A4e.

Published 13 June 1983 at £1.50; number of copies not known.

Reset. The text of *LBN* agrees with A7d. Illustrations for *SWM* as for A10.

A21–A29 *The History of Middle-earth*

'The History of Middle-earth' is an account of Tolkien's vast *legendarium*: the body of tales, languages, geography, and other lore from which sprang *The Lord of the Rings* and *The Silmarillion*, and into which *The Hobbit* 'intruded'. Selections from

Tolkien's variant manuscripts are printed to show their complex evolution, together with commentary and notes by Christopher Tolkien. The series encompasses J. R. R. Tolkien's invented mythology from *The Book of Lost Tales* (begun 1916–17), through *The Lord of the Rings*, to the author's last, inconclusive work on 'The Silmarillion' and associated writings before his death in 1973.

The lists of errors in A21–A29 are not complete. Additional errors have been remarked by Christopher Tolkien and Charles E. Noad, and are known to me; but most of these are trivial, such as inevitably occur in typesettings as complex as 'The History of Middle-earth'. I have listed only those errors (as far as I am aware of them) which to me do not seem trivial or easily detected, in particular errors to texts by J. R. R. Tolkien (as distinct from commentary).

Pertinent manuscripts and typescripts are in the Bodleian Library, Oxford, and (*The Lord of the Rings* only) in the Department of Special Collections and University Archives of the Marquette University Library, Milwaukee, Wisconsin.

A21   THE BOOK OF LOST TALES, PART ONE   1983

a. First edition:

[*2 lines in tengwar, between double rules*] | J. R. R. TOLKIEN | THE | BOOK OF LOST TALES | PART I | Edited by Christopher Tolkien | London | GEORGE ALLEN & UNWIN | Boston Sydney | [*3 lines in tengwar, between double rules*]

vi, 298 pp. + 1 plate. Collation: [1–8¹⁶9⁸10¹⁶]. 22.2 × 14.2 cm.

[i] 'THE BOOK OF LOST TALES | Part I'; [ii] '[*2 lines in tengwar, between double rules*] | THE HISTORY OF MIDDLE-EARTH | I | THE BOOK OF LOST TALES, PART ONE | II | THE BOOK OF LOST TALES, PART TWO | (in preparation) | III | THE LAYS OF BELERIAND | (in preparation) | [*3 lines in tengwar, between double rules*]'; [iii] title; [iv] '© George Allen & Unwin (Publishers) Ltd 1983 | This book is copyright under the Berne Convention. No reproduction | without permission. All rights reserved. | [*3 publisher's addresses, London to North Sydney*] | First published in 1983 | [*rule*] | [*British Library Cataloguing in Publication Data*] | [*rule*] | Set in 11 on 12 point Imprint by Bedford Typesetters Ltd | and printed in Great Britain | by Mackays of Chatham'; [v] table of contents; [vi] blank; [1]–11 foreword; [12] blank; [13]–245 text and illustration; [246]–73 appendix; [274]–5 glossary; [276]–97 index; [298] blank.

Illustrations, by Tolkien: *I Vene Kemen* ('World-Ship'), halftone on plate facing p. [i], also printed in line on p. [84]; 'the earliest map', p. 81.

Wove paper. Bound in dark blue cloth over boards. Stamped on spine in gilt: '[*double rule*] | 1 | [*double rule*] | [*running down:*] THE BOOK OF LOST TALES J. R. R. TOLKIEN | [*horizontal:*] GEORGE | ALLEN | & | UNWIN'. Wove endpapers. No headbands. All edges trimmed. Top edge stained dark blue, fore- and bottom edges unstained.

Dust-jacket, wove paper. Covers and spine printed against a dark blue background. Printed on upper cover within a gold double rule frame interrupted at top by 'THE HISTORY OF MIDDLE-EARTH' in gold: '[*in white:*] CHRISTOPHER TOLKIEN | [*"JRRT" monogram, in gold*] | [*in white:*] THE BOOK OF | LOST TALES | [*in gold:*] [*rule*] 1 [*rule*] | [*in white and gold:*] J. R. R. TOLKIEN'. Printed on spine: '[*in gold:*] [*double rule*] | 1 | [*double rule*] | [*running down, in white:*] THE BOOK OF LOST TALES J. R. R. TOLKIEN | [*horizontal, in gold:*] GEORGE | ALLEN | & | UNWIN'.

'JRRT' monogram printed on lower cover in gold, within a gold double rule frame. Blurb printed on front flap. Label affixed to front flap, printed: 'A&U | £12·50'. Printed on back flap: 'Jacket design by Marilyn Carvell | ISBN 0 04 823238 6 | *Printed in Great Britain*'.

Published 27 October 1983 at £12.50; 5,000 copies printed.

The first volume of 'The History of Middle-earth'. Contains: 'The Cottage of Lost Play', with texts of the poems 'You & Me and the Cottage of Lost Play'/'Mar Vanwa Tyaliéva, The   Cottage of Lost Play'/'The Little House of Lost Play: Mar Vanwa Tyaliéva' and 'Kortirion among the Trees'/'The Trees of Kortirion', and a draft for the final paragraph of Appendix F to *The Lord of the Rings* (A5); 'The Music of the Ainur'; 'The Coming of the Valar and the Building of Valinor', with the poem 'Habbanan beneath the Stars'; 'The Chaining of Melko', with the poems 'Tinfang Warble' and 'Over Old Hills and Far Away'; 'The Coming of the Elves and the Making of Kôr', with the poems 'Kôr: In a City Lost and Dead' and 'A Song of Aryador'; 'The Theft of Melko and the Darkening of Valinor'; 'The Flight of the Noldoli'; 'The Tale of the Sun and Moon', with the poem 'Why the Man in the Moon Came Down Too Soon' (cf. B4); 'The Hiding of Valinor'; and 'Gilfanon's Tale: The Travail of the Noldoli and the Coming of Mankind'.

The title page inscription (also printed on p. [ii]) reads: 'This is the first part of the book of the lost tales of Elfenesse which Eriol the mariner learned from the Elves of Tol Eressea the Lonely Isle in the western ocean and afterwards wrote in the Golden Book of Tavrobel. Herein are told the tales of Valinor from the music of the Ainur to the exile of the Noldoli and the hiding of Valinor.'

The text contains several minor errors, e.g.:

p. 7, l. 22, 'limitation book-backs' for 'imitation book-backs'
p. 40, poem l. 13, 'windling' for 'winding'
p. 46, l. 12, 'pendant' for 'pendent'
p. 61, l. 22, 'Ówen' with added bar above O, for 'Ówen'
p. 132, l. 20, 'Nóleme' for 'Nólemë'
p. 137, l. 13, 'p. 175' for 'p. 125'
p. 177, l. 25, 'Meässë' for 'Meássë'
p. 190, l. 12, 'flickleness' for 'fickleness'
p. 196, l. 44, 'Úr' for 'Ûr'
p. 221, l. 17, 'p. 4' for 'p. 15'
p. 274, l. 37 (entry for *or . . . or*), '127, 214' for '127, 192, 214'
p. 296, l. 4, '*Valwë* Father of Vairë wife of Lindo' for '*Valwë* Father of Lindo'

In addition, in the table of contents, p. [v], the line 'Notes 244' is misaligned; and on p. 204, the text of 'Why the Man in the Moon Came Down Too Soon' is incorrectly described as 'the earlier published form'. Some errors were corrected in later impressions.

A book club edition was published in 1983 by Guild Publishing (Book Club Associates), London, in similar binding and dust-jacket, 1,000? copies printed with a later Allen & Unwin impression.

b. First American edition (imported sheets, 1984):

[*2 lines in tengwar, between double rules*] | J. R. R. TOLKIEN | THE | BOOK OF LOST TALES | PART I | Edited by Christopher Tolkien | Boston | HOUGHTON MIFFLIN COMPANY | 1984 | [*3 lines in tengwar, between double rules*]

vi, 298 pp. + 1 plate. Collation: [1–8^{16}9^{8}10^{16}]. 22.0 × 14.1 cm.

Contents as for A21a, except pp. [iii] title, as above; [iv] 'First American edition 1984 | Copyright © 1983 George Allen & Unwin (Publishers) Ltd | [*notice of restrictions under copyright*] | [*rule*] | [*Library of Congress Cataloging in Publication Data*] | [*rule*] | Printed in Great Britain | [*printing code, beginning "10", ending "1"*]'.

Illustrations as for A21a.

Wove paper. Bound in black cloth over boards. Stamped on spine in gilt: '[*thick rule*] | [*thin rule*] | J. R. R. | TOLKIEN | [*running down:*] THE BOOK OF LOST TALES | [*horizontal:*] HMCO | [*thin rule*] | [*thick rule*]'. Orange-tan wove endpapers. Black headbands. All edges trimmed and unstained.

Dust-jacket, wove paper. Covers and spine printed against a metallic green background. Printed on upper cover: '[*in white:*] THE HISTORY OF MIDDLE-EARTH | CHRISTOPHER TOLKIEN | [*in silver:*] THE [*"JRRT" monogram, in gold*] | [*in silver:*] BOOK | OF LOST | TALES | [*in gold:*] PART ONE | [*in silver:*] J · R · R · TOLKIEN'. Printed on spine: '[*in gold:*] [*"JRRT" monogram*] | TOLKIEN | [*running down, in silver:*] THE BOOK OF LOST TALES | [*horizontal, in gold:*] | HOUGHTON | MIFFLIN | COMPANY'. Printed on lower cover: '[*quotation by Glen H. GoodKnight, in silver and gold*] | [*in white:*] 6–97082 [*in black, against a white panel:*] ISBN 0-395-35439-0'. Printed on front flap: 'FPT ISBN 0-395-35439-0 >$14.95 | [*blurb*] | 01144584'. Printed on back flap: '[*note on Christopher Tolkien*] | HOUGHTON MIFFLIN COMPANY © 1984 | HOUGHTON MIFFLIN COMPANY | 2 Park Street, Boston, Massachusetts 02108'.

Published 22 February 1984 at $16.95; 4,000 copies printed.

Typeset as for A21a, except pp. [iii–iv].

   Two different sets of sheets, representing two distinct impressions, each marked as the 'First American Edition', were sold as such by Houghton Mifflin. Priority of manufacture can be assigned to A21b (uncorrected text), but A21b and A21c were published simultaneously. Houghton Mifflin initially ordered 4,000 sets of sheets from Allen & Unwin, but as U.S. advance orders rose to more than 18,500 by December 1983, Houghton Mifflin printed 30,000 copies domestically in addition to the 4,000 imported.

c. First American edition (corrected U.S. sheets, 1984):

[*2 lines in tengwar, between double rules*] | J. R. R. TOLKIEN | THE | BOOK OF LOST TALES | PART I | Edited by Christopher Tolkien | HOUGHTON MIFFLIN COMPANY | BOSTON | [*3 lines in tengwar, between double rules*]

vi, 298 pp. Collation: [1–3^{16}4^{8}5–10^{16}]. 22.0 × 14.1 cm.

Contents as for A21b, except pp. [iii] title, as above; [iv] 'First American edition 1984 | Copyright © 1983 by Frank Richard Williamson and Christopher Reuel Tolkien | as Executors of the Estate of J. R. R. Tolkien | [*notice of restrictions under copyright*] | [*Library of Congress Cataloging in Publication Data*] | Printed in the United States of America | [*printing code, beginning "S", ending "1"*]'; [12] illustration.

Illustrations as for A21a, except that *I Vene Kemen* is printed as a halftone on an integral leaf (p. [12]), as well as in line on p. [84].

Paper, binding, and dust-jacket as for A21b.

Published 22 February 1984 at $16.95; 30,000 copies printed. Cf. A21b.

Typeset as for A21b, except pp. [iii–v], and with most of the errors noted for A21a (and other errors) corrected. The errors on pp. 190 and 274 were continued. In the table of contents, p. [v], the line 'Notes 244' is correctly aligned with the titling for ch. X.

A book club edition was published in 1984 by the Science Fiction Book Club with the Houghton Mifflin imprint, reprinted from the corrected setting, bound in black paper over boards and black cloth spine, dust-jacket similar to that of A21b–c.

d. First paperback edition (1985):

[2 *lines in tengwar, between double rules*] | J. R. R. TOLKIEN | THE | BOOK OF LOST TALES | PART I | Edited by Christopher Tolkien | London | UNWIN PAPERBACKS | Boston Sydney | [3 *lines in tengwar, between double rules*]

vi, 298 pp. Collation: 152 leaves. 19.7 × 12.9 cm.

Contents as for A21a, except pp. [i] blurb; [iii] title, as above; [iv] 'First published in Great Britain by George Allen & Unwin 1983 | Fourth impression 1984 | First published by Unwin Paperbacks 1985 | This book is copyright under the Berne Convention. No reproduction | without permission. All rights reserved. | [3 *publisher's addresses, London to North Sydney*] | © George Allen & Unwin (Publishers) Ltd 1983, 1985 | [*rule*] | [*British Library Cataloguing in Publication Data*] | [*rule*] | Set in Imprint by Bedford Typesetters Ltd | and printed by | Cox and Wyman Ltd, Reading'.

Illustrations, by Tolkien: *I Vene Kemen* ('World-Ship'), printed in line only, p. [84]; 'the earliest map', p. 81.

Wove paper. Bound in heavy wove wrappers. Covers and spine printed against a black background. Printed on upper cover within a red single rule frame interrupted at top by a red ellipse: '[*publisher's "Unicorn" device, within the ellipse, in white*] | [*in white, against a colour illustration by Roger Garland,* The Tale of the Sun and Moon, *the blazing galleon of the Sun at the gates of Valinor:*] THE BOOK OF | LOST TALES 1 | J. R. R. Tolkien'. Printed on spine, running down: '[*in white:*] THE BOOK OF LOST TALES 1 [*parallel to the title:*] J. R. R. Tolkien [*followed by: publisher's "unwin" device, in red, white, and black within a white single rule frame*]'. Printed on lower cover within a thick red single rule frame interrupted at the top by a thin red single rule frame: '[*within the thin rule frame, in white:*] THE HISTORY OF MIDDLE-EARTH | CHRISTOPHER TOLKIEN | [*below the thin rule frame, against a grey panel:*] [*in black:*] [*blurb*] [3 *quotations, from* Mythlore, *the* Daily Telegraph, *and the* Birmingham Post] | [*at left:*] Cover illustration: *The Tale of the Sun* | *and Moon,* by Roger Garland. | UNICORN | UNWIN PAPERBACKS | FICTION/FANTASY | £2.95 U.K. | $6.95 IN CANADA [*at right, against a white panel:*] GB £ NET +002.95 | ISBN 0-04-823281-5 | [*bar codes*]'. All edges trimmed and unstained.

Published 4 March 1985 at £2.95; 25,000 copies printed.

Typeset as for A21a, except pp. [i], [iii–iv], and with the errors noted for A21a (and other errors) corrected. The text introducing 'Why the Man in the Moon Came Down Too Soon', p. 204, was corrected and slightly enlarged.

e. First American (trade) paperback edition (1986):

[2 *lines in tengwar, between double rules*] | J. R. R. TOLKIEN | THE | BOOK OF LOST TALES | PART I | Edited by Christopher Tolkien | HOUGHTON MIFFLIN COMPANY | BOSTON | [3 *lines in tengwar, between double rules*]

vi, 298 pp. Collation: 152 leaves. 22.1 × 14.2 cm.

Contents as for A21c, except pp. [ii] '[*2 lines in tengwar, between double rules*] | THE HISTORY OF MIDDLE-EARTH | I | THE BOOK OF LOST TALES, PART ONE | II | THE BOOK OF LOST TALES, PART TWO | III | THE LAYS OF BELERIAND | IV | THE SHAPING OF MIDDLE-EARTH | THE QUENTA, THE AMBARKANTA AND THE ANNALS | (in preparation) | [*3 lines in tengwar, between double rules*]'; [iv] 'Copyright © 1983 by Frank Richard Williamson and Christopher Reuel Tolkien | as Executors of the Estate of J. R. R. Tolkien | [*notice of restrictions under copyright*] | [*Library of Congress Cataloging in Publication Data*] | Printed in the United States of America | [*printing code, beginning "S", ending "1"*] | Houghton Mifflin Company paperback, 1986'.

Illustrations, by Tolkien: *I Vene Kemen* ('World-Ship'), printed in line only, p. [84]; 'the earliest map', p. 81.

Wove paper. Bound in heavy wove wrappers. Covers and spine printed against a green background. Printed on upper cover: '[*in white:*] THE HISTORY OF MIDDLE-EARTH | VOLUME I • CHRISTOPHER TOLKIEN | [*in silver:*] THE ["*JRRT*" monogram, in gold] | [*in silver:*] BOOK | OF LOST | TALES | PART ONE | J · R · R · TOLKIEN'. Printed on spine: '[*in white:*] VOLUME I | ["*JRRT*" monogram, in gold] | [*in silver:*] TOLKIEN | [*running down:*] THE BOOK OF LOST TALES | [*horizontal:*] PART ONE | [*in white:*] HOUGHTON | MIFFLIN | COMPANY'. Printed on lower cover: '[*in white:*] FICTION FPT >>$8.95 | THE HISTORY OF MIDDLE-EARTH | [*list of vols. I–IV in the series, in white and silver*] | ["*JRRT*" monogram, in gold] | [*in silver:*] [*quotation from the* Baltimore Sun] | © HOUGHTON MIFFLIN COMPANY | HOUGHTON MIFFLIN COMPANY, 2 Park Street, Boston, Massachusetts 02108 | [*at left, in white:*] 02087086 | [*rule*] | 6-97099 [*at right, in green, against a white panel:*] ISBN 0-395-40927-6'. All edges trimmed and unstained.

Published 20 February 1986 at $8.95; 20,000 copies printed.

Typeset as for A21c, except pp. [ii], [iv].

f. Ballantine Books edition (1992):

THE BOOK | OF | LOST | TALES | Part I | J. R. R. Tolkien | *Edited by* Christopher Tolkien | [*publisher's 'DEL REY' device*] | A Del Rey Book | BALLANTINE BOOKS • NEW YORK

xxii, 346 pp. Collation: 188 leaves. 17.4 × 10.6 cm.

[i] 'THE COMING OF | THE VALAR | [*quotation*]'; [ii] 'By J. R. R. Tolkien | *Published by Ballantine Books:* | [*12 titles, beginning with* H, *ending with* Smith of Wootton Major & Farmer Giles of Ham] | *By Humphrey Carpenter:* | Tolkien: The Authorized Biography | *By Paul H. Kocher:* | Master of Middle-earth: | The Fiction of J. R. R. Tolkien | *By Robert Foster:* | The Complete Guide to Middle-earth: | From *The Hobbit* to *The Silmarillion*'; [iii] title; [iv] '[*note on condition of sale*] | A Del Rey Book | Published by Ballantine Books | Copyright © 1983 by Frank Richard Williamson and Christopher | Reuel Tolkien as Executors of the Estate of J. R. R. Tolkien | All rights reserved under International and Pan-American | Copyright Conventions. Published in the United States of | America by Ballantine Books, a division of Random House, | Inc., New York. | For information about permission to reproduce selections from | this book, write to Permissions, Houghton Mifflin Company, | 2 Park Street, Boston, Massachusetts 02108. | Library of Congress Catalog Card Number: 83-12782 | ISBN 0-345-37521-1 | First published in the United States by Houghton Mifflin Com- | pany. Reprinted by special arrangement wiht [*sic*] Houghton Mifflin | Company. | Manufactured in the United States of America | First Ballantine Books

Edition: June 1992'; [v] table of contents; [vi] blank; vii–xxi foreword; [xxii] illustration; 1–279 text and illustrations; 280–318 appendix; 319–21 glossary; 322–45 index; [346] '[*3 lines and blurb between thick-thin rules at left and right:*] J. R. R. TOLKIEN'S | Epic Fantasy Classic | The Lord of the Rings | [*blurb*] | [*order form*]'.

Illustrations, by Tolkien: *I Vene Kemen* ('World-Ship'), twice printed (in line), pp. [xxii] and 87; 'the earliest map', p. 83.

Wove paper. Bound in heavy wove wrappers. Wraparound colour illustration by John Howe, of a dragon, a Balrog, and the forces of Melko before Gondolin. Printed on upper cover against the illustration: '[*against a light blue panel framed on three sides by the illustration:*] J. R. R. | TOLKIEN | THE BOOK | OF LOST TALES 1 | [*at foot of cover:*] [*in white:*] [*publisher's "DEL REY/dragon/FANTASY" device*] Ballantine/ 37521/U.S. $5.99 [*against a red panel outlined in white:*] ["*JRRT*" *device, in light orange and white*] | [*in white:*] TOLKIEN'. Printed on spine against the illustration: '[*publisher's "DEL REY" device, in black and white*] | [*in white:*] Fantasy | [*running down:*] [*against an orange panel outlined in black:*] J. R. R. TOLKIEN [*in blue, against a light blue panel outlined in black, joined at left to the preceding outlined panel:*] THE BOOK OF LOST TALES 1 | [*below the panels, horizontal, in white:*] U.S. 599 | [*rule*] | 345- | 37521-1'. Printed on lower cover against the illustration: '[*against a light blue panel framed on three sides by the illustration:*] [*in blue:*] THE HISTORY OF MIDDLE-EARTH | Edited by CHRISTOPHER TOLKIEN | [*blurb, in black*] | [*below the frame:*] [*in white:*] 1 | [*2 quotations, from the* Daily Telegraph *and* Mythlore] | [*in black:*] [*at left, running down:*] Cover printed in USA [*parallel to the preceding four words:*] Cover Art by John Howe [*at right, against a white panel:*] ISBN 0-345-37521-1 | [*bar codes*]'. All edges trimmed and unstained.

Published June 1992 at $5.99; number of copies not known.

Reset, based on A21a–b, with most of the errors for that typesetting corrected. 'The Man in the Moon Came Down Too Soon' is still described, p. 230, as the 'earlier published form', and the error '*Valwë* Father of Vairë wife of Lindo' for '*Valwë* Father of Lindo', was continued, p. 343, l. 39.

A22   THE BOOK OF LOST TALES, PART TWO   1984

a. First edition:

[*2 lines in tengwar, between double rules*] | J. R. R. TOLKIEN | THE | BOOK OF LOST TALES | PART II | Edited by Christopher Tolkien | London | GEORGE ALLEN & UNWIN | Boston Sydney | [*3 lines in tengwar, between double rules*]

vi, 386 pp. + 1 plate. Collation: [1–11^{16}12^{4}13^{16}]. 22.1 × 14.2 cm.

[i] 'THE BOOK OF LOST TALES | Part II'; [ii] '[*2 lines in tengwar, between double rules*] | THE HISTORY OF MIDDLE-EARTH | I | THE BOOK OF LOST TALES, PART ONE | II | THE BOOK OF LOST TALES, PART TWO | III | THE LAYS OF BELERIAND | (in preparation) | IV | THE SHAPING OF MIDDLE-EARTH | THE QUENTA, THE AMBARKANTA AND THE ANNALS | (in preparation) | [*3 lines in tengwar, between double rules*]'; [iii] title; [iv] '© George Allen & Unwin (Publishers) Ltd 1984 | This book is copyright under the Berne Convention. No reproduction | without permission. All rights reserved. | [*3 publisher's addresses, London to North Sydney*] | First published in 1984 | [*rule*] | [*British Library Cataloguing in Publication Data*] | [*rule*] | Set in 11 on 12 point Imprint by Bedford Typesetters Ltd | and printed in Great Britain | by Mackays of Chatham'; [v] table of contents; [vi] blank; [1]

preface; [2] blank; [3]–334 text; [335]–49 appendix; [350]–2 glossary; [353]–85 index; [386] blank.

Illustrations, by Tolkien, on plate inserted between pp. 26–7: manuscript page from 'The Tale of Tinúviel', manuscript page from 'The Fall of Gondolin'.

Wove paper. Bound in wine red textured paper over boards. Stamped on spine in gilt: '[*double rule*] | 2 | [*double rule*] | [*running down:*] THE BOOK OF LOST TALES [*parallel to the preceding 5 words:*] Part II | [*running down:*] J. R. R. TOLKIEN | [*horizontal:*] GEORGE | ALLEN | & | UNWIN'. Wove endpapers. No headbands. All edges trimmed. Top edge stained light wine red, fore- and bottom edges unstained.

Dust-jacket, wove paper. Covers and spine printed against a brown background. Printed on upper cover within a gold double rule frame interrupted at top by 'THE HISTORY OF MIDDLE-EARTH' in gold: '[*in white:*] CHRISTOPHER TOLKIEN | [*"JRRT" monogram, in gold*] | [*in white:*] THE BOOK OF | LOST TALES | [*in gold:*] [*rule*] Part II [*rule*] | [*in white and gold:*] J. R. R. TOLKIEN'. Printed on spine: '[*in gold:*] [*double rule*] | 2 | [*double rule*] | [*running down, in white:*] THE BOOK OF LOST TALES [*parallel to the preceding 5 words:*] Part II [*followed by:*] J. R. R. TOLKIEN | [*horizontal, in gold:*] GEORGE | ALLEN | & | UNWIN'. 'JRRT' monogram printed on lower cover in gold, within a gold double rule frame. Blurb printed on front flap in brown. Label affixed to front flap, printed: 'A&U | £12·50'. Printed on back flap in brown: 'ISBN 0 04 823265 3 | *Printed in Great Britain*'.

Published 16 August 1984 at £12.50; 7,500? copies printed.

The second volume of 'The History of Middle-earth'. Contains: 'The Tale of Tinúviel'; 'Turambar and the Foalókë' ('The Tale of Turambar'); 'The Fall of Gondolin' ('Tuor and the Exiles of Gondolin'); 'The Nauglafring' ('Tale of the Necklace' or 'Necklace of the Dwarves'); 'The Tale of Eärendel', with the poems 'Éalá Éarendel Engla Beorhtast' (originally 'The Voyage of Éarendel the Evening Star', later 'The Last Voyage of Éarendel'), 'The Bidding of the Minstrel' ('The Lay of Éarendel'), 'The Shores of Faery' (cf. B32), and, in two versions, 'The Happy Mariners' (cf. B4); and 'The History of Eriol or Ælfwine and the End of the Tales', with three related poems, 'Prelude', 'The Town of Dreams', and 'The City of Present Sorrows' (in different drafts with the overall title *The Sorrowful City* or *The Town of Dreams and the City of Present Sorrow*), the poem 'The Song of Eriol', and the narrative 'Ælfwine of England'. The appendix extends the glossary of names in *BLT1*.

The title page inscription (also printed on p. [ii]) reads: 'This is the second part of the book of the lost tales of Elfinesse which Eriol the mariner learned from the Elves of Tol Eressea the lonely isle in the western ocean and afterwards wrote in the Golden Book of Tavrobel: herein are told the tales of Beren and Tinúviel, the Turambar and fall of Gondolin, and of the necklace of the Dwarves.'

A book club edition was published in 1984 by Guild Publishing, London, in similar binding and dust-jacket, 1,000 copies printed apparently with the Allen & Unwin first impression, in addition to the 7,500? copies for trade publication.

b. First American edition (1984):

[2 *lines in tengwar, between double rules*] | J. R. R. TOLKIEN | THE | BOOK OF LOST TALES | PART II | Edited by Christopher Tolkien | BOSTON | HOUGHTON MIFFLIN COMPANY | 1984 | [3 *lines in tengwar, between double rules*]

vi, 26, [2], 27–392 pp. Collation: [1–11^{16}12^{8}13^{16}]. 21.8 × 14.0 cm.

[i] 'THE BOOK OF LOST TALES | Part II'; [ii] '[2 *lines in tengwar, between double*

rules] | THE HISTORY OF MIDDLE-EARTH | I | THE BOOK OF LOST TALES, PART ONE | II | THE BOOK OF LOST TALES, PART TWO | III | THE LAYS OF BELERIAND | (in preparation) | IV | THE SHAPING OF MIDDLE-EARTH | THE QUENTA, THE AMBARKANTA AND THE ANNALS | (in preparation) | [*3 lines in tengwar, between double rules*]'; [iii] title; [iv] 'Copyright © 1984 by | Frank Richard Williamson and Christopher Reuel Tolkien | as Executors of the Estate of J. R. R. Tolkien | [*notice of restrictions under copyright*] | [*Library of Congress Cataloging in Publication Data*] | Printed in the United States of America | [*printing code, beginning "V", ending "1"*]'; [v] table of contents; [vi] blank; [1] preface; [2] blank; [3]–26 text; [26+1] illustration, manuscript page from 'The Tale of Tinúviel'; [26+2] illustration, manuscript page from 'The Fall of Gondolin'; 27–334 text; [335]–49 appendix; [350]–2 glossary; [353]–85 index; [386–92] blank.

Illustrations as for A22a, but printed on an integral leaf.

Wove paper. Bound in black cloth over boards. Stamped on spine in gilt: '[*thick rule*] | [*thin rule*] | J. R. R. | TOLKIEN | [*running down:*] THE BOOK OF LOST TALES | [*horizontal:*] II | HMCO | [*thin rule*] | [*thick rule*]'. Orange-tan wove endpapers. Black headbands. All edges trimmed and unstained.

Dust-jacket, wove paper. Covers and spine printed against a metallic red background. Printed on upper cover: '[*in white:*] THE HISTORY OF MIDDLE-EARTH | CHRISTOPHER TOLKIEN | [*in silver:*] THE [*"JRRT" monogram, in gold*] | [*in silver:*] BOOK | OF LOST | TALES | [*in white:*] PART TWO | [*in silver:*] J·R·R· TOLKIEN'. Printed on spine: '[*in white:*] PART TWO | [*in gold:*] [*"JRRT" monogram*] | [*in white:*] TOLKIEN | [*running down, in silver:*] THE BOOK OF LOST TALES | [*horizontal, in white:*] HOUGHTON | MIFFLIN | COMPANY'. Printed on lower cover: '[*2 quotations, from the* Baltimore Sun *and* Publishers Weekly, *in silver and black*] | [*in white:*] 6-97097 [*in black, against a white panel:*] ISBN 0-395-36614-3'. Printed on front flap: 'FPT ISBN 0-395-36614-3 >$16.95 | [*blurb*] | 11164584'. Printed on back flap: '[*note on Christopher Tolkien*] | HOUGHTON MIFFLIN COMPANY © 1984 | HOUGHTON MIFFLIN COMPANY | 2 Park Street, Boston, Massachusetts 02108'.

Published 26 November 1984 at $16.95; 22,500 copies printed.

Typeset as for A22a, except pp. [iii–iv].
    Also published by the Book-of-the-Month Club.

c. First paperback edition (1986):

[*2 lines in tengwar, between double rules*] | J. R. R. TOLKIEN | THE | BOOK OF LOST TALES | PART II | Edited by Christopher Tolkien | London | UNWIN PAPERBACKS | Boston Sydney | [*3 lines in tengwar, between double rules*]

viii, 392 pp. Collation: 200 leaves. 19.7 × 12.9 cm.

[i] blurb; [ii] blank; [iii] 'THE | BOOK OF LOST TALES | PART II'; [iv] '[*2 lines in tengwar, between double rules*] | THE HISTORY OF MIDDLE-EARTH | I | THE BOOK OF LOST TALES, PART ONE | II | THE BOOK OF LOST TALES, PART TWO | III | THE LAYS OF BELERIAND | IV | THE SHAPING OF MIDDLE-EARTH | THE QUENTA, THE AMBARKANTA AND THE ANNALS | [*3 lines in tengwar, between double rules*]'; [v] title; [vi] 'First published in Great Britain by George Allen & Unwin 1984 | First published by Unwin Paperbacks 1986 | This book is copyright under the Berne Convention. No reproduction | without permission. All rights reserved. | [*4 publisher's addresses, London to Wellington*] | © George Allen &

Unwin (Publishers) Ltd 1984, 1986 | [*rule*] | [*British Library Cataloguing in Publication Data*] | [*rule*] | Printed in Great Britain by Cox & Wyman Ltd | Reading'; [vii] table of contents; [viii] blank; [1] preface; [2] blank; [3]–334 text; [335]–49 appendix; [350]–2 glossary; [353]–85 index; [386] blank; [387] '*Also by J. R. R. Tolkien* | [*advertisement of* BLT1]'; [388] advertisement of *Silm*; [389] advertisement of *UT*; [390] advertisement of *LR*; [391] advertisement of *H*; [392] '*Also by J. R. R. Tolkien* | [*publisher's order form*]'.

Omits illustrations.

Wove paper. Bound in heavy wove wrappers. Covers and spine printed against a black background. Printed on upper cover within a blue single rule frame interrupted at top by a blue ellipse: '[*publisher's "Unicorn" device, within the ellipse, in white*] | [*in white, against a colour illustration by Roger Garland,* The Fall of Gondolin, *dragons and a siege engine before the walls of Gondolin:*] THE BOOK OF | LOST TALES 2 | J. R. R. Tolkien'. Printed on spine: '[*publisher's "Unicorn" device, in white and blue*] | [*running down:*] [*in white:*] THE BOOK OF LOST TALES 2 [*parallel to the title:*] J. R. R. Tolkien [*followed by publisher's "unwin" device, in blue, white, and black within a white single rule frame*]'. Printed on lower cover within a thick blue single rule frame interrupted at top by a thin blue single rule frame: '[*within the thin rule frame, in white:*] THE HISTORY OF MIDDLE-EARTH | CHRISTOPHER TOLKIEN | [*below the thin rule frame, in black, against a grey panel:*] [*blurb*] | [5 *quotations from the* Financial Times, British Book News, Amon Hen, Yorkshire Post, *and* New York Times Book Review] | [*at left:*] Cover illustration: | *The Fall of Gondolin,* | by Roger Garland. | UNICORN | UNWIN PAPERBACKS | FICTION/ FANTASY | £3.50 U.K. | $6.95 IN CANADA [*at right, against a white panel:*] GB £ NET +003.50 | ISBN 0-04-823338-2 | [*bar codes*]'. All edges trimmed and unstained.

Published 28 July 1986 at £3.50; 25,000 copies printed.

Typeset as for A22a, except pp. [i], [iv–vi], [387–92].

d. First American (trade) paperback edition (1986):

[2 *lines in tengwar, between double rules*] | J. R. R. TOLKIEN | THE | BOOK OF LOST TALES | PART II | Edited by Christopher Tolkien | BOSTON | HOUGHTON MIFFLIN COMPANY | [3 *lines in tengwar, between double rules*]

vi, 26, [2], 27–392 pp. Collation: 199 leaves. 21.9 × 14.0 cm.

Contents as for A22b, except pp. [ii] '[2 *lines in tengwar, between double rules*] | THE HISTORY OF MIDDLE-EARTH | I | THE BOOK OF LOST TALES, PART ONE | II | THE BOOK OF LOST TALES, PART TWO | III | THE LAYS OF BELERIAND | IV | THE SHAPING OF MIDDLE-EARTH | THE QUENTA, THE AMBARKANTA AND THE ANNALS | [3 *lines in tengwar, between double rules*]'; [iii] title, as above; [iv] 'Copyright © 1984 by | Frank Richard Williamson and Christopher Reuel Tolkien | as Executors of the Estate of J. R. R. Tolkien | [*notice of restrictions under copyright*] | [*Library of Congress Cataloging in Publication Data*] | Printed in the United States of America | [*printing code, beginning "V", ending "3"*] | Houghton Mifflin Company paperback, 1986'.

Illustrations as for A22b.

Wove paper. Bound in heavy wove wrappers. Covers and spine printed against a red background. Printed on upper cover: '[*in white:*] THE HISTORY OF MIDDLE-EARTH | VOLUME II • CHRISTOPHER TOLKIEN | [*in silver:*] THE [*"JRRT" monogram, in gold*] | [*in silver:*] BOOK | OF LOST | TALES | [*in white:*] PART TWO | [*in silver:*] J · R · R · TOLKIEN'. Printed on spine: '[*in white:*] VOLUME II | ["*JRRT*" *monogram, in gold*] | [*in silver:*] TOLKIEN | [*running down:*] THE BOOK OF LOST TALES | [*horizontal, in white:*] PART TWO | [*publisher's "dolphin" device*] | HOUGHTON | MIFFLIN | COMPANY'. Printed on lower cover: '[*in white:*] FICTION FPT >>$8.95 | THE HISTORY OF MIDDLE-EARTH | [*in white and silver:*] [*list of vols. I–IV in the series*] | VOLUME V In Preparation | ["*JRRT*" *monogram, in gold*] | [*in silver:*] [*quotation from the* Baltimore Sun] | HOUGHTON MIFFLIN COMPANY © 1986 | HOUGHTON MIFFLIN COMPANY, 2 Park Street, Boston, Massachusetts 02108 | [*at left, in white:*] 11087086 | [*rule*] | 6-97089 [*at right, in black, against a white panel:*] ISBN 0-395-42640-5'. All edges trimmed and unstained.

Published 10 November 1986 at $8.95; 12,500 copies printed.

Typeset as for A22b, except pp. [ii–iv]. The printing code on p. [iv] indicates that the trade paperback was printed from the third Houghton Mifflin hardcover impression.

e. Ballantine Books edition (1992):

THE BOOK | OF | LOST | TALES | Part II | J. R. R. Tolkien | Edited by Christopher Tolkien | [*publisher's 'DEL REY' device*] | A Del Rey Book | BALLANTINE BOOKS • NEW YORK

viii, 392 pp. Collation: 200 leaves. 17.5 × 10.5 cm.

[i] 'DEATH OF A DRAGON | [*quotation*]'; [ii] 'By J. R. R. Tolkien | *Published by Ballantine Books:* | [*12 titles, beginning with* H, *ending with* Smith of Wootton Major & Farmer Giles of Ham] | *By Humphrey Carpenter:* | Tolkien: The Authorized Biography | *By Paul H. Kocher:* | Master of Middle-earth: | The Fiction of J. R. R. Tolkien | *By Robert Foster:* | The Complete Guide to Middle-earth: | From *The Hobbit* to *The Silmarillion*'; [iii] title; [iv] '[*note on condition of sale*] | A Del Rey Book | Published by Ballantine Books | Copyright © 1984 by Frank Richard Williamson and Christopher Reuel | Tolkien as Executors of the Estate of J. R. R. Tolkien | All rights reserved under International and Pan-American Copyright | Conventions. Published in the United States of America by Ballantine | Books, a division of Random House, Inc., New York. | For information about permission to reproduce selections from this | book, write to Permissions, Houghton Mifflin Company, 2 Park Street, | Boston, Massachusetts 02108. | Library of Congress Catalog Card Number: 83-12782 | ISBN 0-345-37522-X | First published in the United States by Houghton Mifflin Company. | Reprinted by special arrangement with Houghton Mifflin Company. | Manufactured in the United States of America | First Ballantine Books Edition: June 1992'; [v] table of contents; [vi] blank; vii–viii preface; 1–340 text and illustrations; 341–57 appendix; 358–60 glossary; 361–91 index; [392] '[*3 lines and blurb between thick-thin rules at left and right:*] J. R. R. TOLKIEN'S | Epic Fantasy Classic | The Lord of the Rings | [*blurb*] | [*order form*]'.

Illustrations as for A22a, except printed on an integral leaf (pp. 25–6).

Wove paper. Bound in heavy wove wrappers. Wraparound colour illustration by John Howe, of the galleon of the sun at the gates of Valinor. Printed on upper cover against the illustration: '[*against an orange-yellow panel framed on three sides by the illustration:*] J. R. R. | TOLKIEN | THE BOOK | OF LOST TALES 2 | [*at foot of cover:*] [*in white:*] [*publisher's "DEL REY/dragon/FANTASY" device*] Ballantine/ 37522/U.S. $5.99 [*against a red panel outlined in white:*] ["*JRRT*" *device, in light orange and white*] | [*in white:*] TOLKIEN'. Printed on spine against the illustration:

'[*publisher's "DEL REY" device, in black and white*] | [*in white:*] Fantasy | [*running down:*] [*against an orange-yellow panel outlined in black:*] J. R. R. TOLKIEN [*in dark blue, against an orange panel outlined in black, joined at left to the preceding outlined panel:*] THE BOOK OF LOST TALES 2 | [*below the panels, horizontal, in white:*] U.S. 599 | [*rule*] | 345- | 37522-X'. Printed on lower cover against the illustration: '[*against an orange-yellow panel framed on three sides by the illustration:*] [*in dark blue:*] THE HISTORY OF MIDDLE-EARTH | Edited by CHRISTOPHER TOLKIEN | [*blurb, in black*] | [*below the frame:*] [*in white:*] 2 | [*2 quotations, from the* New York Times Book Review *and* British Book News] | [*at left, running down:*] Cover printed in USA [*parallel to the preceding four words:*] Cover Art by John Howe [*at right, in black against a white panel:*] ISBN 0-345-37522-X | [*bar codes*]'. All edges trimmed and unstained.

Published June 1992 at $5.99; number of copies not known.

Reset.

A23   THE LAYS OF BELERIAND   1985

a. First edition:

[*2 lines in tengwar, between double rules*] | J. R. R. TOLKIEN | THE LAYS | OF | BELERIAND | Edited by Christopher Tolkien | London | GEORGE ALLEN & UNWIN | Boston Sydney | [*3 lines in tengwar, between double rules*]

vi, 394 pp. + 1 plate. Collation: [1–$11^{16}12^813^{16}$]. 22.2 × 14.3 cm.

[i] 'THE LAYS OF BELERIAND | The opening of Canto 2 in the *Lay of Leithian* recommenced'; [ii] '[*2 lines in tengwar, between double rules*] | THE HISTORY OF MIDDLE-EARTH | I | THE BOOK OF LOST TALES, PART ONE | II | THE BOOK OF LOST TALES, PART TWO | III | THE LAYS OF BELERIAND | IV | THE SHAPING OF MIDDLE-EARTH | THE QUENTA, THE AMBARKANTA AND THE ANNALS | (in preparation) | [*3 lines in tengwar, between double rules*]'; [iii] title; [iv] '© George Allen & Unwin (Publishers) Ltd 1985 | The text of the commentary by C. S. Lewis on | *The Lay of Leithian* © C. S. Lewis PTE Limited 1985 | This book is copyright under the Berne Convention. No reproduction | without permission. All rights reserved. | [*3 publisher's addresses, London to North Sydney*] | First published in 1985 | ISBN 0 04 823277 7 | Set in 11 on 12 point Imprint by Bedford Typesetters Ltd | and printed in Great Britain | by Mackays of Chatham'; [v–vi] table of contents; [1]–2 preface; [3]–367 text and illustrations; [368]–72 glossary; [373]–93 index; [394] blank.

Colour illustration, by Tolkien, on plate facing p. [i]: manuscript page of 'the opening of Canto 2 in the *Lay of Leithian* recommenced'. Black and white illustrations, by Tolkien: p. [15], two manuscript pages from 'The Lay of the Children of Húrin'; p. [299], manuscript ll. 3994–4027 from 'The Lay of Leithian'.

Wove paper. Bound in dark green textured paper over boards. Stamped on spine in gilt: '[*double rule*] | 3 | [*double rule*] | [*running down:*] THE LAYS OF BELERIAND J. R. R. TOLKIEN | [*horizontal:*] GEORGE | ALLEN | & | UNWIN'. Wove endpapers. No headbands. All edges trimmed. Top edge stained dark green, fore- and bottom edges unstained.

Dust-jacket, wove paper. Covers and spine printed against a green background. Printed on upper cover, within a gold double rule frame interrupted at top by 'THE

HISTORY OF MIDDLE-EARTH' in gold: '[*in white:*] CHRISTOPHER TOLKIEN | [*"JRRT" monogram, in gold*] | [*in white:*] THE LAYS OF | BELERIAND | [*in white and gold:*] J. R. R. TOLKIEN'. Printed on spine: '[*in gold:*] [*double rule*] | 3 | [*double rule*] | [*running down, in white:*] THE LAYS OF BELERIAND J. R. R. TOLKIEN | [*horizontal, in gold:*] GEORGE | ALLEN | & | UNWIN'. Printed on lower cover: '[*"JRRT" monogram, within a double rule frame, in gold*] | [*in green, against a white panel obscuring the lower right corner of the frame:*] ISBN 0-04-823277-7 | [*bar code*]'. Printed on front flap in green: '[*blurb*] | Price net | £14.95 | in U.K. only'. Printed on back flap in green: 'ISBN 0 04 823277 7'.

Published 22 August 1985 at £14.95; 6,000 copies printed.

The third volume of 'The History of Middle-earth.' Contains: 'The Lay of the Children of Húrin'; 'The Flight of the Noldoli from Valinor'; a fragment of an alliterative 'Lay of Eärendel'; parts of 'The Lay of the Fall of Gondolin'; and 'The Lay of Leithian'. Also contains a 'Commentary on "The Lay of Leithian"' by C. S. Lewis, and a note by Christopher Tolkien on the original submission to Allen & Unwin of 'The Lay of Leithian' and *The Silmarillion* in 1937.

The title page inscription (also printed on p. [ii]) reads: 'In the first part of this book is given the Lay of the Children of Húrin by John Ronald Reuel Tolkien in which is set forth in part the Tale of Turin: in the second part is the Lay of Leithian which is the Gest of Beren and Lúthien as far as the encounter of Beren with Carcharoth at the gate of Angband.'

The text contains several minor errors, e.g.:

p. 157, poem l. 11, 'fron sun to sea' for 'from sun to sea'
p. 240, poem l. 2447, 'than gasping woe' for 'then gasping woe'
p. 280, poem l. 3473, 'howling undermoon' for 'howling under moon'
p. 310, l. 20, 'hated by Thingol as p. 270' for 'hated by Thingol'
p. 332, poem l. 42, 'more then these' for 'more than these'
p. 339, poem l. 331, 'laid' for 'lain'

A book club edition was published in 1986 by Guild Publishing, London, in similar binding and dust-jacket, 2,000 copies printed with the Allen & Unwin second impression.

b. First American edition (1985):

[*2 lines in tengwar, between double rules*] | J. R. R. TOLKIEN | THE LAYS | OF | BELERIAND | Edited by Christopher Tolkien | BOSTON | HOUGHTON MIFFLIN COMPANY | 1985 | [*3 lines in tengwar, between double rules*]

vi, 394 pp. Collation: gatherings not distinct. 22.0 × 14.1 cm.

Contents as for A23a, except pp. [i] 'THE LAYS OF BELERIAND | [*illustration*] | The opening of Canto 2 in the *Lay of Leithian* recommenced'; [iii] title, as above; [iv] 'The text of the commentary by C. S. Lewis on The Lay of Leithian | © C. S. Lewis PTE Limited 1985 | Copyright © 1985 by Frank Richard Williamson and Christopher Reuel Tolkien | as Executors of the Estate of J. R. R. Tolkien. | [*notice of restrictions under copyright*] | [*Library of Congress Cataloging in Publication Data*] | Printed in the United States of America | [*printing code, beginning "V", ending "1"*]'.

Illustrations as for A23a, except that the illustration 'the opening of Canto 2 in the *Lay of Leithian* recommenced' is printed in black and white on an integral leaf (p. [i]).

Wove paper. Bound in black cloth over boards. Stamped on spine in gilt: '[*thick rule*] | [*thin rule*] | J. R. R. | TOLKIEN | [*running down:*] THE LAYS OF BELERIAND | [*horizontal:*] HMCO | [*thin rule*] | [*thick rule*]'. Orange-tan wove endpapers. Black headbands. All edges trimmed and unstained.

Dust-jacket, wove paper. Covers and spine printed against a metallic blue background. Printed on upper cover: '[*in white:*] THE HISTORY OF MIDDLE-EARTH | CHRISTOPHER TOLKIEN | VOLUME III | [*at left, in silver:*] THE | LAYS OF [*at right, "JRRT" monogram, in gold*] | [*below the preceding, in silver:*] BELERIAND | J · R · R · TOLKIEN'. Printed on spine: '[*in white:*] VOLUME III | ["*JRRT*" *monogram, in gold*] | [*in silver:*] TOLKIEN | [*running down:*] THE LAYS OF BELERIAND | [*horizontal, in white:*] HOUGHTON | MIFFLIN | COMPANY'. Printed on lower cover: '[*in white:*] THE HISTORY OF MIDDLE-EARTH | [*list of vols. I–IV in the series, in white and silver*] | ["*JRRT*" *monogram, in gold*] | [*quotation from the* Baltimore Sun, *in silver*] | [*in white:*] 6-97098 [*in black, against a white panel:*] ISBN 0-395-39429-5'. Printed on front flap: 'FPT >$16.95 | [*blurb*] | 11164585 | ISBN 0-395-39429-5'. Printed on back flap: '[*blurb, continued*] | [*note on Christopher Tolkien*] | HOUGHTON MIFFLIN COMPANY © 1985 | HOUGHTON MIFFLIN COMPANY | 2 Park Street, Boston, Massachusetts 02108'.

Published 20 November 1985 at $16.95; 20,000 copies printed.

Typeset as for A23a, except pp. [iii–vi]. The table of contents was reset, with numerous but unimportant differences in wording, capitalization, and italicization.

c. First paperback edition (1987):

[*2 lines in tengwar, between double rules*] | [*within a hairline-thick-thin rule frame:*] THE LAYS OF | BELERIAND | J. R. R. TOLKIEN | [*below the frame:*] Edited by Christopher Tolkien | UNWIN PAPERBACKS | London Sydney | [*3 lines in tengwar, between double rules*]

vi, 394 pp. Collation: 200 leaves. 19.7 × 12.9 cm.

Contents as for A23a, except pp. [i] blurb; [ii] '[*2 lines in tengwar, between double rules*] | THE HISTORY OF MIDDLE-EARTH | I | THE BOOK OF LOST TALES, PART ONE | II | THE BOOK OF LOST TALES, PART TWO | III | THE LAYS OF BELERIAND | IV | THE SHAPING OF MIDDLE-EARTH | THE QUENTA, THE AMBARKANTA AND THE ANNALS | V | THE LOST ROAD | VI | RETURN OF THE SHADOW | [*3 lines in tengwar, between double rules*]'; [iii] title, as above; [iv] 'First published by George Allen & Unwin (Publishers) Ltd, 1985. | First published by Unwin ®Paperbacks, an imprint of Unwin Hyman | Limited, 1987. | © George Allen & Unwin (Publishers) Ltd 1985 | The text of the commentary by C. S. Lewis on *The Lay of Leithian* | © C. S. Lewis PTE Limited 1985 | [*notice of restrictions*] | [*4 publisher's addresses, London (Denmark House) to Wellington*] | [*rule*] | [*British Library Cataloguing in Publication Data*] | [*rule*] | Printed in Great Britain by | Cox & Wyman Ltd, Reading'.

Illustrations, by Tolkien: p. [15], two manuscript pages from 'The Lay of the Children of Húrin'; p. [299], manuscript ll. 3994–4027 from 'The Lay of Leithian'. Omits the illustration 'The opening of Canto 2 in the *Lay of Leithian* recommenced'.

Wove paper. Bound in heavy wove wrappers. Printed on upper cover within a black thick-thin rule frame, against a tan panel, against a colour illustration by Roger Garland, *Thû*, a great wolf: '[*in red:*] THE LAYS OF | BELERIAND | [*in black:*]

J. R. R. TOLKIEN'. Printed on spine, running down: '[*in red:*] THE LAYS OF [*parallel to the preceding words:*] BELERIAND [*followed by:*] [*in black:*] J. R. R. TOLKIEN [*publisher's "unwin" device, in red, white, and black*]'. Printed on lower cover: '[*2 quotations, from the* Daily Mail *and* Mallorn, *in black*] | [*in red:*] THE HISTORY OF MIDDLE EARTH [*sic, no hyphen*] | CHRISTOPHER TOLKIEN | [*in black:*] [*blurb*] | [*at left:*] Cover illustration by Roger Garland | UNWIN PAPERBACKS | FICTION/FANTASY | £3.95 [*at right, within a single rule frame:*] ISBN 0-04-440018-7 [*3 parallel rules*] | [*bar codes*]'. All edges trimmed and unstained.

Published 24 September 1987 at £3.95; 24,000 copies printed.

Typeset as for A23a, except pp. [i–iv].
    An additional 6,000 copies were printed with the first impression for distribution in Canada by Methuen, with altered wrappers.

d. First American (trade) paperback edition (1988):

[*2 lines in tengwar, between double rules*] | J. R. R. TOLKIEN | THE LAYS | OF | BELERIAND | Edited by Christopher Tolkien | [*publisher's 'dolphin' device*] | BOSTON | HOUGHTON MIFFLIN COMPANY | [*3 lines in tengwar, between double rules*]

vi, 394 pp. Collation: 200 leaves. 21.9 × 13.8 cm.

Contents as for A23b, except pp. [ii] '[*2 lines in tengwar, between double rules*] | THE HISTORY OF MIDDLE-EARTH | I | THE BOOK OF LOST TALES, PART ONE | II | THE BOOK OF LOST TALES, PART TWO | III | THE LAYS OF BELERIAND | IV | THE SHAPING OF MIDDLE-EARTH | THE QUENTA, THE AMBARKANTA AND THE ANNALS | V | THE LOST ROAD AND OTHER WRITINGS | VI | THE RETURN OF THE SHADOW | THE HISTORY OF THE LORD OF THE RINGS, | PART ONE | [*3 lines in tengwar, between double rules*]'; [iii] title, as above; [iv] 'The text of the commentary by C. S. Lewis on The Lay of Leithian | © C. S. Lewis PTE Limited 1985 | Copyright © 1985 by Frank Richard Williamson and Christopher Reuel Tolkien | as Executors of the Estate of J. R. R. Tolkien | All rights reserved. | For information about permission to reproduce selections from | this book, write to Permissions, Houghton Mifflin Company, | 2 Park Street, Boston, Massachusetts 02108. | [*Library of Congress Cataloging in Publication Data*] | Printed in the United States of America | [*printing code, beginning "V", ending "3"*]'.

Illustrations as for A23b.

Wove paper. Bound in heavy wove wrappers. Covers and spine printed against a metallic blue background. Printed on upper cover: '[*in white:*] THE HISTORY OF MIDDLE-EARTH | CHRISTOPHER TOLKIEN | VOLUME III | [*at left, in silver:*] THE | LAYS OF [*at right, "JRRT" monogram, in gold*] | [*below the preceding, in silver:*] BELERIAND | J · R · R · TOLKIEN'. Printed on spine: '[*in white:*] VOLUME III | [*"JRRT" monogram, in gold*] | [*in silver:*] TOLKIEN | [*running down:*] THE LAYS OF BELERIAND | [*horizontal, in white:*] | [*publisher's "dolphin" device*] | HOUGHTON | MIFFLIN | COMPANY'. Printed on lower cover: '[*in white:*] FANTASY FPT>>$9.95 | THE HISTORY OF MIDDLE-EARTH | [*list of vols. I–VI in the series*] | [*blurb*] | [*2 quotations, from the* New York City (*sic*) Tribune *and* Booklist] | [*at left:*] 10097088 | [*rule*] | 6-97044 [*at right, in black, against a white panel:*] ISBN 0-395-48683-1'. All edges trimmed and unstained.

Published 28 October 1988 at $9.95; 7,500 copies printed.

Typeset as for A23b, except pp. [ii–iv].

The printing code on p. [iv] indicates that the trade paperback edition was printed from the third Houghton Mifflin hardcover impression.

A24   THE SHAPING OF MIDDLE-EARTH   1986

a. First edition:

[*2 lines in tengwar, between double rules*] | J. R. R. TOLKIEN | THE SHAPING OF | MIDDLE-EARTH | THE QUENTA, THE AMBARKANTA | AND THE ANNALS | together with | the earliest 'Silmarillion' and the first Map | Edited by Christopher Tolkien | London | GEORGE ALLEN & UNWIN | Boston Sydney | [*3 lines in tengwar, between double rules*]

viii, 392 pp. + 2 plates. Collation: [1–7^{16}8^{4}9–12^{16}13^{4}14^{16}]. 22.2 × 14.3 cm.

[i–ii] blank; [iii] 'THE SHAPING OF MIDDLE-EARTH'; [iv] '[*2 lines in tengwar, between double rules*] | THE HISTORY OF MIDDLE-EARTH | I | THE BOOK OF LOST TALES, PART ONE | II | THE BOOK OF LOST TALES, PART TWO | III | THE LAYS OF BELERIAND | IV | THE SHAPING OF MIDDLE-EARTH | THE QUENTA, THE AMBARKANTA AND | THE ANNALS | V | THE LOST ROAD | AND OTHER WRITINGS | [*3 lines in tengwar, between double rules*]'; [v] title; [vi] '© George Allen & Unwin (Publishers) Ltd 1986 | This book is copyright under the Berne Convention. No reproduction | without permission. All rights reserved. | [*3 publisher's addresses, London to North Sydney*] | First published in 1986 | [*rule*] | [*British Library Cataloguing in Publication Data*] | [*rule*] | Set in 11 on 12 point Imprint by Bedford Typesetters Ltd | and printed in Great Britain | by Mackays of Chatham'; [vii] table of contents; [viii] blank; [1]–2 preface; [3]–341 text and illustrations; [342]–80 index; [381–92] blank.

Colour illustrations, by Tolkien, on 2 plates inserted between pp. 220–1: 'The Northern Half of the First "Silmarillion" Map' and 'The Southern Half of the First "Silmarillion" Map'. Black and white illustrations, by Tolkien: 'The Westward Extension', p. 228; 'The Eastward Extension', p. 231; 'Ambarkanta' Diagram I, p. 243; 'Ambarkanta' Diagram II, p. 245; 'Ambarkanta' Diagram III, p. 247; 'Ambarkanta' Map IV, p. 249; 'Ambarkanta' Map V, p. 251.

Wove paper. Bound in black textured paper over boards. Stamped on spine in gilt: '[*double rule*] | 4 | [*double rule*] | [*running down:*] THE SHAPING OF MIDDLE-EARTH J. R. R. TOLKIEN | [*horizontal:*] ALLEN | & | UNWIN'. Wove endpapers. No headbands. All edges trimmed. Top edge stained black, fore- and bottom edges unstained.

Dust-jacket, wove paper. Covers and spine printed against a red-purple background. Three variants seen, issued simultaneously; upper cover, spine, and back flap are printed the same for each variant. Printed on upper cover within a gold double rule frame interrupted at top by 'THE HISTORY OF MIDDLE-EARTH' in gold: '[*in white:*] CHRISTOPHER TOLKIEN | [*"JRRT" monogram, in gold*] | [*in white:*] THE SHAPING | OF | MIDDLE-EARTH | [*in gold:*] [*rule*] 4 [*rule*] | [*in white and gold:*] J. R. R. TOLKIEN'. Printed on spine: '[*in gold:*] [*double rule*] | 4 | [*double rule*] | [*running down, in white:*] THE SHAPING OF MIDDLE-EARTH J. R. R. TOLKIEN | [*horizontal, in gold:*] ALLEN | & | UNWIN'. Printed on back flap in red-purple: 'ISBN: 0 04 823279 3'. Printed on lower cover against a red-purple background: variant 1, '["*JRRT" monogram, in gold, within a gold double rule frame*] | [*in purple, against a white panel obscuring the lower right corner of the frame:*] ISBN 0-04-823279-3 | [*bar code*]'; variant 2, 'JRRT' monogram, in gold, within a gold double rule frame, with bar code printed on an adhesive label; variant 3, 'JRRT' monogram, in gold, within a gold double rule frame. Printed on front flap in red-purple: variant 1, '[*blurb*] | Price net | £14.95 | in U.K. only'; variant 2, blurb, with paper price label; variant 3, blurb only. The jacket without printed price (variants 2 and 3) was intended for book club use. Allen & Unwin seem to have printed more volumes than jackets for their own edition, and more jackets than volumes for the book club edition.

Published 21 August 1986 at £14.95; 6,000 copies printed.

The fourth volume of 'The History of Middle-earth'. Contains: prose fragments following the 'Lost Tales'; the 'earliest "Silmarillion"' ('Sketch of the Mythology'); the 'Quenta' ('Quenta Noldorinwa', the second version of 'The Silmarillion'), with the poem 'The Horns of Ylmir' (earlier 'The Tides' and 'Sea Chant of an Elder Day', cf. B32); the 'Ambarkanta' ('Of the Fashion of the World'); the 'earliest Annals of Valinor'; and the 'earliest Annals of Beleriand'.

The title page inscription (printed also on p. [iv]) reads: 'Herein are the Quenta Noldorinwa, the History of Gnomes; the Ambarakanta or Shape of the World by Rúmil; the Annals of Valinor and the Annals of Beleriand by Pengolod the Wise of Gondolin; with maps of the world in the Elder Days and translations made by Aelfwine the Mariner of England into the tongue of his own land'.

Two errors in J. R. R. Tolkien's text are especially notable: 'living fire combined in the light' for 'living fire combined of the light', p. 14, l. 23; and '*black magics from the Gnomes*' for '*black magics of the Gnomes*', p. 125, l. 2.

Christopher Tolkien notes in *The Lost Road* (A25), p. 3, that the reproduction of the 'Westward Extension' map in *Shaping*, p. 231, was 'reinforced' (presumably photographically), giving an erroneously dark (if clearer) appearance compared with the 'Eastward Extension' as reproduced. The latter, and 'Diagram III' and 'Map V', were reproduced from photocopies of the faintly pencilled originals, the other black and white map and diagrams from photographs. A detail of 'Map V', redrawn by Christopher Tolkien, was printed in *The Lost Road*, p. 270.

Cedric Chivers, Bath, bound 150 copies of the first impression for libraries, probably run on rather than part of the 6,000 copies recorded for trade publication.

A book club edition was published in 1986 by Guild Publishing, in similar binding and dust-jacket, 4,000 copies printed separately by Allen & Unwin after the first impression with their imprint.

b. First American edition (1986):

[*2 lines in tengwar, between double rules*] | J. R. R. TOLKIEN | THE SHAPING OF | MIDDLE-EARTH | THE QUENTA, THE AMBARKANTA | AND THE ANNALS | together with | the earliest 'Silmarillion' and the first Map | Edited by Christopher Tolkien | BOSTON | HOUGHTON MIFFLIN COMPANY | 1986 | [*3 lines in tengwar, between double rules*]

viii, 220, [2], 221–390 pp. Collation: [1–2^{16}3^{8}4–13^{16}]. 22.0 × 14.2 cm.

[i–ii] blank; [iii] 'THE SHAPING OF MIDDLE-EARTH'; [iv] '[*2 lines in tengwar, between double rules*] | THE HISTORY OF MIDDLE-EARTH | I | THE BOOK OF LOST TALES, PART ONE | II | THE BOOK OF LOST TALES, PART TWO | III | THE LAYS OF BELERIAND | IV | THE SHAPING OF MIDDLE-EARTH | THE

QUENTA, THE AMBARKANTA AND | THE ANNALS | V | THE LOST ROAD | AND OTHER WRITINGS | (in preparation) | [*3 lines in tengwar, between double rules*]'; [v] title; [vi] 'Copyright © 1986 by Frank Richard Williamson and Christopher Reuel Tolkien | as Executors of the Estate of J. R. R. Tolkien | [*notice of restrictions under copyright*] | [*Library of Congress Cataloging in Publication Data*] | Printed in the United States of America | [*printing code, beginning "S", ending "1"*]'; [vii] table of contents; [viii] blank; [1]–2 preface; [3]–220 text; [220+1] illustration by Tolkien, 'The Northern Half of the First "Silmarillion" Map'; [220+ 2] illustration by Tolkien, 'The Southern Half of the First "Silmarillion" Map'; 221– 341 text and illustrations; [342]–80 index; [381–90] blank.

Illustrations as for A24a, except that the 'First "Silmarillion" Map' is printed in black and white, on one integral leaf.

Wove paper. Bound in black cloth over boards. Stamped on spine in gilt: '[*thick rule*] | [*thin rule*] | J. R. R. | TOLKIEN | [*running down:*] THE SHAPING OF MIDDLE-EARTH | [*horizontal:*] HMCO | [*thin rule*] | [*thick rule*]'. Orange-tan wove endpapers. Black headbands. All edges trimmed and unstained.

Dust-jacket, wove paper. Covers and spine printed against a metallic blue-purple background. Printed on upper cover: '[*in white:*] THE HISTORY OF MIDDLE-EARTH | VOLUME IV • CHRISTOPHER TOLKIEN | [*in silver:*] THE [*"JRRT" monogram, in gold*] | [*in silver:*] SHAPING OF | MIDDLE-EARTH | THE QUENTA, THE AMBARKANTA | and THE ANNALS | J·R·R· TOLKIEN'. Printed on spine: '[*in white:*] VOLUME IV | [*"JRRT" monogram, in gold*] | [*in silver:*] TOLKIEN | [*running down:*] THE SHAPING OF MIDDLE-EARTH | [*horizontal, in white:*] | HOUGHTON | MIFFLIN | COMPANY'. Printed on lower cover: '[*in white:*] THE HISTORY OF MIDDLE-EARTH | [*list of vols. I–IV in the series, in white and silver*] | [*in white:*] VOLUME V [*in silver:*] In Preparation | [*"JRRT" monogram, in gold*] [*quotation from the* Baltimore Sun, *in silver*] | [*in white:*] 6–97088 [*in black, against a white panel:*] ISBN 0-395-42501-8'. Printed on front flap: 'FPT >$16.95 | [*blurb*] | 11164586 | ISBN 0-395-42501-8'. Printed on back flap: 'Praise from reviewers | for the previous volumes in the series | [*3 quotations, from the* New York Tribune, *by Atanielle Annyn Noel, and from* Christian Century] | [*rule*] | [*note on Christopher Tolkien*] | HOUGHTON MIFFLIN COMPANY © 1986 | HOUGHTON MIFFLIN COMPANY | 2 Park Street, Boston, Massachusetts 02108'.

Published in 14 November 1986 at $16.95; 17,500 copies printed.

Typeset as for A24a, except pp. [iv–vi], [215]. On the latter page, two paragraphs were reset, with 'names in red ink' changed to 'names that were written in red ink' to accommodate the printing of the 'First "Silmarillion" Map' in black and white on pp. [220+1–2].

c. First paperback edition (1988):

[*2 lines in tengwar, between double rules*] | J. R. R. TOLKIEN | THE SHAPING OF | MIDDLE-EARTH | THE QUENTA, THE AMBARKANTA | AND THE ANNALS | together with | the earliest 'Silmarillion' and the first Map | Edited by Christopher Tolkien | [*publisher's 'man drawing a circle' device*] | UNWIN | PAPERBACKS | LONDON SYDNEY WELLINGTON | [*3 lines in tengwar, between double rules*]

viii, 392 pp. + 2 plates. Collation: 200 leaves. 19.7 × 12.8 cm.

[i] blurb; [ii] blank; [iii] 'THE SHAPING OF MIDDLE-EARTH'; [iv] '[2 *lines in tengwar, between double rules*] | THE HISTORY OF MIDDLE-EARTH | I | THE BOOK OF LOST TALES, PART ONE | II | THE BOOK OF LOST TALES, PART TWO | III | THE LAYS OF BELERIAND | IV | THE SHAPING OF MIDDLE-EARTH | THE QUENTA, THE AMBARKANTA AND | THE ANNALS | V | THE LOST ROAD | AND OTHER WRITINGS | [3 *lines in tengwar, between double rules*]'; [v] title; [vi] 'First published in Great Britain by the Trade Division of | Unwin Hyman Limited, 1986 | First published in paperback by Unwin® Paperbacks, an imprint of | Unwin Hyman Limited, in 1988. | © Unwin Hyman Ltd 1988 | [*notice of restrictions*] | [*notice of condition of sale*] | [3 *publisher's addresses, London to Wellington*] | [*rule*] | [*British Library Cataloguing in Publication Data*] | [*rule*] | Printed and bound in Great Britain by | Cox & Wyman Ltd, Reading'; [vii] table of contents; [viii] blank; [1]–2 preface; [3]–341 text and illustrations; [342]–80 index; [381] blank; [382] advertisement of *H*; [383] advertisement of *LR*; [384] advertisement of *Silm*; [385] advertisement of *UT*; [386] advertisement of *BLT1*; [387] advertisement of *BLT2*; [388] advertisement of *Lays*; [389] advertisement of Foster, *The Complete Guide to Middle-earth*; [390] advertisement of Carpenter, *Biography*; [391] 'Books by J. R. R. Tolkien in Unwin Paperbacks | [*order form*]'; [392] blank.

Illustrations as for A24a, except that the colour plates are inserted between pp. 224–5.

Wove paper. Bound in heavy wove wrappers. Printed on upper cover within a black thick-thin rule frame, against a light tan panel, against a colour illustration by Roger Garland, *Eärendil and Elwing*, a sea bird flying up to a celestial ship: '[*in purple:*] THE SHAPING | OF | MIDDLE-EARTH | [*in black:*] J. R. R. TOLKIEN'. Printed on spine: '[*running down:*] [*in purple:*] THE SHAPING OF [*parallel to the preceding words:*] MIDDLE-EARTH [*followed by, in black:*] J. R. R. TOLKIEN | [*publisher's "man drawing a circle" device, horizontal*]'. Printed on lower cover: '[*in purple:*] THE HISTORY OF MIDDLE-EARTH | [*in black:*] edited by Christopher Tolkien | [*blurb*] | [*quotation from* Vector] | [*at left:*] *Cover illustration by Roger Garland* | UNWIN PAPERBACKS | FICTION/FANTASY | £4.95 net U.K. [*at right:*] ISBN 0-04-440150-7 [3 *parallel rules*] | [*bar codes*]'. All edges trimmed and unstained.

Published 22 September 1988 at £4.95; 20,000 copies printed.

Typeset as for A24a, except pp. [i], [v–vi], [382–91].

A25   THE LOST ROAD AND OTHER WRITINGS   1987

a. First edition:

[2 *lines in tengwar, between double rules*] | J. R. R. TOLKIEN | THE LOST ROAD | AND OTHER WRITINGS | Language and Legend | before | 'The Lord of the Rings' | Edited by Christopher Tolkien | UNWIN HYMAN | London Sydney | [3 *lines in tengwar, between double rules*]

viii, 456 pp. Collation: [1–14¹⁶15⁸]. 22.3 × 14.3 cm.

[i–ii] blank; [iii] 'THE LOST ROAD | AND OTHER WRITINGS'; [iv] '[2 *lines in tengwar, between double rules*] | THE HISTORY OF MIDDLE-EARTH | I | THE BOOK OF LOST TALES, PART ONE | II | THE BOOK OF LOST TALES, PART TWO | III | THE LAYS OF BELERIAND | IV | THE SHAPING OF MIDDLE-

EARTH | THE QUENTA, THE AMBARKANTA AND | THE ANNALS | V | THE LOST ROAD | AND OTHER WRITINGS | VI | THE RETURN OF THE SHADOW | THE HISTORY OF THE LORD OF THE RINGS, PART ONE | (in preparation) | [3 *lines in tengwar, between double rules*]'; [v] title; [vi] 'First published in Great Britain by Unwin Hyman, an | imprint of Unwin Hyman Limited, 1987 | © Unwin Hyman Ltd 1987 | [*notice of restrictions*] | [*4 publisher's addresses, London (Denmark House) to Wellington*] | [*rule*] | [*British Library Cataloguing in Publication Data*] | [*rule*] | Set in 11 on 12 pt Imprint by Bedford Typesetters Ltd | and printed in Great Britain | by Mackays of Chatham'; [vii]–viii table of contents; [1]–3 preface; [4] blank; [5] 'PART ONE | [*swelled rule*] | THE FALL OF | NUMENOR | AND | THE LOST ROAD'; [6] blank; [7]–104 text; [105] 'PART TWO | [*swelled rule*] | VALINOR AND | MIDDLE-EARTH | BEFORE | THE LORD OF | THE RINGS'; [106] blank; [107]–338 text and illustrations; [339] 'PART THREE | [*swelled rule*] | THE | ETYMOLOGIES'; [340] blank; [341]–400 text; [401] 'APPENDIX | [*swelled rule*] | THE GENEALOGIES | THE LIST OF | NAMES | AND | THE SECOND | 'SILMARILLION' | MAP'; [402] blank; [403]–13 text and illustrations; [414] blank; [415]–55 index; [456] blank.

Illustrations, by Tolkien: three manuscript 'genealogical' tables, 'The Tree of Tongues', outlining the descent of languages in Tolkien's invention, pp. 169, 170, 196; a fourth manuscript table, 'The Peoples of the Elves', p. 197. Also contains two sketch maps by Christopher Tolkien, pp. 270–1; and a second 'Silmarillion' map (cf. A24), redrawn by Christopher Tolkien from his father's heavily-altered original, pp. 408–[11].

Wove paper. Bound in dark blue textured paper over boards. Stamped on spine in gilt: '[*double rule*] | 5 | [*double rule*] | [*running down:*] THE LOST ROAD and other writings J. R. R. TOLKIEN | [*horizontal:*] UNWIN | HYMAN'. Wove endpapers. No headbands. All edges trimmed and unstained.

Dust-jacket, wove paper. Covers and spine printed against a blue background. Printed on upper cover within a gold double rule frame interrupted at top by 'THE HISTORY OF MIDDLE-EARTH' in gold: '[*in white:*] CHRISTOPHER TOLKIEN | [*"JRRT" monogram, in gold*] | [*in white:*] THE | LOST ROAD | and other writings | [*in gold:*] [*rule*] 5 [*rule*] | [*in gold and white:*] J. R. R. TOLKIEN'. Printed on spine: '[*in gold:*] [*double rule*] | 5 | [*double rule*] | [*running down, in white:*] THE LOST ROAD and other writings J. R. R. TOLKIEN | [*horizontal, in gold:*] UNWIN | HYMAN'. Printed on lower cover: '[*"JRRT" monogram, in gold, within a gold double rule frame*] | [*in blue, against a white panel obscuring the lower right corner of the frame:*] ISBN 0-04-823349-8 | [*bar code*]'. Printed on front flap in blue: '[*blurb*] | Autumn 1987 | Price net | £16.95 | in U.K. only'. Printed on back flap in blue: 'ISBN 004 823349 8'.

Published 27 August 1987 at £16.95; 6,000 copies printed.

The fifth volume of 'The History of Middle-earth'. Contains: versions of 'The Fall of Númenor'; *The Lost Road*, with the poem 'The Nameless Land' and later versions ('The Song of Ælfwine on Seeing the Uprising of Eärendel'); the 'later Annals of Valinor'; the 'later Annals of Beleriand'; the 'Ainulindalë'; the 'Lhammas' (or 'Account of Tongues'); the 'Quenta Silmarillion' (the third version of 'The Silmarillion'); and the 'Etymologies'.

The title page inscription (also printed on p. [iv]) reads: 'Herein are collected the oldest tale of the downfall of Númenor; the story of the Lost Road into the West; the Annals of Valinor and the Annals of Beleriand in a later form; the Ainulindalë or music of the Ainur; the Lhammas or account of tongues; the Quenta Silmarillion or history of the Silmarils; and the history of many words and names'.

Error, p. 99, l. 3 (l. 11 of 'The Nameless Land'): 'singing clear' for 'singing sheer'.

The origin of *The Lost Road* as a time-travel story to match one on space travel by C. S. Lewis is described by Tolkien in *Letters* no. 257. Chapters of the book were submitted to Allen & Unwin for consideration on 15 November 1937 (see A15a note). The publisher's reader reported, 17 December 1937, that as far as he could judge on the basis of a fragment of the text, it was 'a hopeless proposition. It is immensely interesting as a revelation of the personal enthusiasms of a very unusual mind, and there are passages of beautiful descriptive prose.' He thought it 'difficult to imagine this novel when completed receiving any sort of recognition except in academic circles. . . . Perhaps the whole should be seen, but one could not hold out to the author a promise of popular success or large sales as an inducement to finish it.' Stanley Unwin returned the typescript of *The Lost Road* to Tolkien on 20 December 1937 with the polite remark that 'it is difficult to judge from this fragment whether it would make any popular appeal'. C. S. Lewis's space-travel story, the popular *Out of the Silent Planet*, was submitted to Allen & Unwin in 1938, and was rejected for similar reasons.

A book club edition was published in 1985 by Guild Publishing, London, in similar binding and dust-jacket, 2,500 copies printed with the Unwin Hyman first impression in addition to the 6,000 copies for trade publication.

Cedric Chivers, Bath, bound 150 copies of the Unwin Hyman first impression for libraries, printed in addition to the 6,000 copies for trade publication.

b. First American edition (1987):

[*2 lines in tengwar, between double rules*] | J. R. R. TOLKIEN | THE LOST ROAD | AND OTHER WRITINGS | Language and Legend | before | 'The Lord of the Rings' | Edited by Christopher Tolkien | BOSTON | HOUGHTON MIFFLIN COMPANY | 1987 | [*3 lines in tengwar, between double rules*]

viii, 456 pp. Collation: [1–2^{16}3^{8}4–15^{16}]. 22.1 × 14.2 cm.

Contents as for A25a, except pp. [v] title, as above; [vi] 'Copyright © 1987 by Frank Richard Williamson and Christopher Reuel Tolkien | as Executors of the Estate of J. R. R. Tolkien | [*notice of restrictions under copyright*] | [*Library of Congress Cataloging in Publication Data*] | Printed in the United States of America | [*printing code, beginning "S", ending "1"*]'.

Illustrations as for A25a.

Wove paper. Bound in black cloth over boards. Stamped on spine in gilt: '[*thick rule*] | [*thin rule*] | J. R. R. | TOLKIEN | [*running down:*] THE LOST ROAD [*parallel to preceding three words*] AND OTHER WRITINGS | [*horizontal:*] HMCO | [*thin rule*] | [*thick rule*]'. Orange-tan wove endpapers. Black headbands. All edges trimmed and unstained.

Dust-jacket, wove paper. Covers and spine printed against a metallic blue-grey background. Printed on upper cover: '[*in white:*] THE HISTORY OF MIDDLE-EARTH | VOLUME V • CHRISTOPHER TOLKIEN | [*at right, "JRRT" mono-gram, in gold; to left of and below monogram, in silver:*] THE | LOST | ROAD | AND OTHER WRITINGS | J·R·R· TOLKIEN'. Printed on spine: '[*in white:*] VOLUME V | [*"JRRT" monogram, in gold*] | [*in silver:*] TOLKIEN | [*running down:*] THE LOST ROAD | [*horizontal, in white:*] | HOUGHTON | MIFFLIN | COMPANY'. Printed on lower cover: '[*in white:*] THE HISTORY OF MIDDLE-

EARTH | [*list of vols. I–V in the series, in white and silver*] | [*in white:*] VOLUME VI [*in silver:*] In Preparation | [*quotation from* Mythprint, *in silver*] | [*in white:*] 6-97048 [*in black, against a white panel:*] ISBN 0-395-45519-7'. Printed on front flap: 'FPT >$18.95 | [*blurb*] | 11184587 | ISBN 0-395-45519-7'. Printed on back flap: '[*note on Christopher Tolkien*] | HOUGHTON MIFFLIN COMPANY © 1987 | HOUGHTON MIFFLIN COMPANY | 2 Park Street, Boston, Massachusetts 02108'.

Published in 30 November 1987 at $16.95; 15,000 copies printed.

Typeset as for A25a, except pp. [v]–viii. The table of contents was reset with no alteration of text.

c. First paperback edition (1989):

[*2 lines in tengwar, between double rules*] | J. R. R. TOLKIEN | THE LOST ROAD | AND OTHER WRITINGS | Language and Legend | before | 'The Lord of the Rings' | Edited by Christopher Tolkien | [*publisher's 'man drawing a circle' device*] | UNWIN | PAPERBACKS | LONDON SYDNEY WELLINGTON | [*3 lines in tengwar, between double rules*]

vi, 456 pp. Collation: 231 leaves. 19.7 × 12.9 cm.

Contents as for A25a, except pp. [i] blurb; [ii] '[*2 lines in tengwar, between double rules*] | THE HISTORY OF MIDDLE-EARTH | I | THE BOOK OF LOST TALES, PART ONE | II | THE BOOK OF LOST TALES, PART TWO | III | THE LAYS OF BELERIAND | IV | THE SHAPING OF MIDDLE-EARTH | THE QUENTA, THE AMBARKANTA AND | THE ANNALS | V | THE LOST ROAD | AND OTHER WRITINGS | VI | THE RETURN OF THE SHADOW | THE HISTORY OF THE LORD OF THE RINGS, PART ONE | (in preparation) | VII | TREASON OF ISENGARD | [*3 lines in tengwar, between double rules*]'; [iii] title, as above; [iv] 'First published in Great Britain by Unwin Hyman, an | imprint of Unwin Hyman Limited, 1987 | First published in paperback by Unwin® Paperbacks, an imprint of | Unwin Hyman Limited, in 1989 | © Unwin Hyman Ltd 1987 | [*notice of restrictions*] | [*notice of condition of sale*] | [*3 publisher's addresses, London to Wellington*] | [*rule*] | [*British Library Cataloguing in Publication Data*] | [*rule*] | Set in 11 on 12 pt Imprint by Bedford Typesetters Ltd. | Printed & bound in Finland by | Werner Söderström Oy'; [v]–vi table of contents.

Illustrations as for A25a.

Wove paper. Bound in heavy wove wrappers. Printed on upper cover within a black thick-thin rule frame, against a tan panel, against a colour illustration by Roger Garland, *The Haven of Moriondë,* an Elf overlooking a harbour: '[*in purple:*] THE | LOST ROAD | [*in black:*] J. R. R. TOLKIEN'. Printed on spine: [*running down:*] [*in purple:*] THE LOST ROAD [*in black:*] J. R. R. TOLKIEN | [*publisher's "man drawing a circle" device, horizontal*]'. Printed on lower cover: '[*in purple:*] THE HISTORY OF MIDDLE-EARTH | [*in black:*] edited by Christopher Tolkien | [*blurb*] | [*at left:*] *Cover illustration:* | *The Haven of Moriondë,* | *by Roger Garland* | UNWIN PAPERBACKS | FICTION/FANTASY | £4.99 net U.K. [*at right:*] ISBN 0-04-440398-4 | [*bar code*]'. All edges trimmed and unstained.

Published 21 September 1989 at £4.99; 15,000 copies printed.

Typeset as for A25a, except pp. [i–iv], and with p. 99, l. 3 corrected.

a. First edition:

[*2 lines in tengwar, between double rules*] | J. R. R. TOLKIEN | THE RETURN OF | THE SHADOW | The History of | The Lord of the Rings | Part One | Christopher Tolkien | UNWIN HYMAN | London | [*3 lines in tengwar, between double rules*]

xii, 500 pp. + 1 plate. Collation: [1–16^{16}]. 22.1 × 14.0 cm.

[i–ii] blank; [iii] 'THE RETURN OF THE SHADOW | THE HISTORY OF THE LORD OF THE RINGS, PART ONE'; [iv] '[*2 lines in tengwar, between double rules*] | THE HISTORY OF MIDDLE-EARTH | I | THE BOOK OF LOST TALES, PART ONE | II | THE BOOK OF LOST TALES, PART TWO | III | THE LAYS OF BELERIAND | IV | THE SHAPING OF MIDDLE-EARTH | THE QUENTA, THE AMBARKANTA AND | THE ANNALS | V | THE LOST ROAD | AND OTHER WRITINGS | VI | THE RETURN OF THE SHADOW | THE HISTORY OF THE LORD OF THE RINGS, PART ONE | VII | THE HISTORY OF THE LORD OF THE RINGS, PART TWO | *(in preparation)* | [*3 lines in tengwar, between double rules*]'; [v] title; [vi] 'First published in Great Britain by Unwin Hyman, an | imprint of Unwin Hyman Limited, 1988 | © Unwin Hyman Ltd 1988 | [*notice of restrictions*] | [*3 publisher's addresses, London to Wellington*] | [*rule*] | [*British Library Cataloguing in Publication Data*] | [*rule*] | Set in 11 on 12 pt Imprint by Bedford Typesetters Ltd | and printed in Great Britain | by Mackays of Chatham'; [vii] '*To* | *RAYNER UNWIN*'; [viii] blank; [ix] quotation from a letter by Tolkien to W. H. Auden, 7 June 1955; [x] blank; [xi]–xii table of contents and (p. xii) list of illustrations; [1]–7 foreword; [8] blank; [9] 'THE FIRST PHASE'; [10] blank; [11]– 229 text and illustration; [230] blank; [231] 'THE SECOND PHASE'; [232] blank; [233]–305 text and illustrations; [306] blank; [307] 'THE THIRD PHASE'; [308] blank; [309]–87 text and illustrations; [388] blank; [389] 'THE STORY | CON- TINUED'; [390] blank; [391]–467 text and illustrations; [468]–97 index; [498– 500] blank.

Illustrations, by Tolkien: sketch map of The Shire, colour plate facing p. [iii]; p. 12, the original opening manuscript page of *LR*; p. 257, manuscript page, 'the original description of the writing on the Ring'; p. 259, manuscript page including 'the Ring- verse, and the emergence of the Ruling Ring in the narrative'; sketch plan of Bree, p. 335; p. 383, manuscript page, 'the emergence of Treebeard'; 'the earliest [sketch] map of the lands south of the map of Wilderland in *The Hobbit*', p. 439; p. 450 (not 447 as cited in the list of illustrations), manuscript page including the inscription of the West Gate of Moria. Also contains two sketch maps by Christopher Tolkien, p. 201.

Wove paper. Bound in black textured paper over boards. Stamped on spine in gilt: '[*double rule*] | 6 | [*double rule*] | [*running down:*] THE RETURN OF THE SHADOW J. R. R. TOLKIEN | [*horizontal:*] UNWIN | [*publisher's "man drawing a circle" device*] | HYMAN'. Wove endpapers. No headbands. All edges trimmed and unstained.

Dust-jacket, wove paper. Covers and spine printed against a black background. Printed on upper cover within a gold double rule frame interrupted at top by 'THE HISTORY OF MIDDLE-EARTH' in gold: '[*in white:*] CHRISTOPHER TOLKIEN | [*"JRRT" monogram, in gold*] | [*in white:*] THE RETURN | OF THE SHADOW | the history of | THE LORD OF THE RINGS | Part One | [*in gold:*] [*rule*] 6 [*rule*] | [*in white and gold:*] J. R. R. TOLKIEN'. Printed on spine: '[*in gold:*] [*double rule*] | 6 |

[*double rule*] | [*running down, in white:*] THE RETURN OF THE SHADOW | J. R. R. TOLKIEN | [*horizontal, in gold:*] UNWIN | [*publisher's "man drawing a circle" device*] | HYMAN'. Printed on lower cover: '[*"JRRT" monogram, within a double rule frame, in gold*] | [*in black, against a white panel obscuring the lower right corner of the frame:*] ISBN 0-04-440162-0 | [*bar code*]'. Printed on front flap: '[*blurb*] | Autumn 1988 | £17.95 net U.K.'

Published 25 August 1988 at £17.95; 5,000 copies printed.

The sixth volume of 'The History of Middle-earth'. Contains portions of the manuscripts of *The Lord of the Rings*, bk. 1, ch. 1 through bk. 2, ch. 4 (as the books and chapters were later constituted). Includes the 'germ' of the poem 'The Adventures of Tom Bombadil' (C27); 'The Root of the Boot', reprinted from *Songs for the Philologists* (B15); and 'The Cat and the Fiddle', reprinted from *Yorkshire Poetry* (C16). Also contains excerpts from an unpublished letter from Tolkien to Stanley Unwin, 15 September 1939.

The title page inscription (printed also on p. [iv]) reads: 'In *The Return of the Shadow* are traced the first forms of the story of *The Lord of the Rings*: herein the journey of the hobbit who bore the great ring, at first named Bingo but afterwards Frodo, is followed from Hobbiton in the Shire through the Old Forest to Weathertop and Rivendell and ends in this volume before the tomb of Balin the Dwarf-lord of Moria'.

Errors include: p. xii, last line, '447' for '450'; p. 32, ll. 11–12 are repeated as ll. 15–16 in place of the text 'Bingo's last words, "I am leaving after dinner", were corrected on the manuscript to "I am leaving now."'

Cedric Chivers, Bath, bound 120 copies of the Unwin Hyman first impression for libraries, printed in addition to the 5,000 copies recorded for trade publication.

Copies of the Unwin Hyman edition, without alteration, were sold to book club members, probably beginning with a later impression.

b. First American edition (1988):

[*2 lines in tengwar, between double rules*] | J. R. R. TOLKIEN | THE RETURN OF | THE SHADOW | The History of | The Lord of the Rings | Part One | Christopher Tolkien | [*publisher's device*] | BOSTON | HOUGHTON MIFFLIN COMPANY | 1988 | [*3 lines in tengwar, between double rules*]

x, 502 pp. + 1 plate. Collation: $[1–16^{16}]$. 22.1 × 14.1 cm.

[i] 'THE RETURN OF THE SHADOW | THE HISTORY OF THE LORD OF THE RINGS, PART ONE'; [ii] '[*2 lines in tengwar, between double rules*] | THE HISTORY OF MIDDLE-EARTH | I | THE BOOK OF LOST TALES, PART ONE | II | THE BOOK OF LOST TALES, PART TWO | III | THE LAYS OF BELERIAND | IV | THE SHAPING OF MIDDLE-EARTH | THE QUENTA, THE AMBAR-KANTA AND | THE ANNALS | V | THE LOST ROAD | AND OTHER WRITINGS | VI | THE RETURN OF THE SHADOW | THE HISTORY OF THE LORD OF THE RINGS, PART ONE | VII | THE HISTORY OF THE LORD OF THE RINGS, PART TWO | *(in preparation)* | [*3 lines in tengwar, between double rules*]'; [iii] title; [iv] 'Copyright © 1988 by Frank Richard Williamson and Christopher Reuel Tolkien | as Executors of the Estate of J. R. R. Tolkien | All rights reserved | For information about permission to reproduce selections from | this book, write to Permissions, Houghton Mifflin Company, | 2 Park Street, Boston, Massachusetts 02108. | [*Library of Congress Cataloging in Publication Data*] | Printed in the United States of America | [*printing code, beginning "S", ending "1"*]';

[v] '*To* | *RAYNER UNWIN*'; [vi] blank; [vii] quotation from a letter by Tolkien to W.H. Auden, 7 June 1955; [viii] blank; [ix]–x table of contents and (p. x) list of illustrations; [1]–7 foreword; [8] blank; [9] 'THE FIRST PHASE'; [10] blank; [11]–229 text and illustration; [230] blank; [231] 'THE SECOND PHASE'; [232] blank; [233]–305 text and illustrations; [306] blank; [307] 'THE THIRD PHASE'; [308] blank; [309]–87 text and illustrations; [388] blank; [389] 'THE STORY | CONTINUED'; [390] blank; [391]–467 text and illustrations; [468]–97 index; [498–502] blank.

Illustrations as for A26a, except that the colour plate faces p. [i].

Wove paper. Bound in black cloth over boards. Stamped on spine in gilt: '[*thick rule*] | [*thin rule*] | J. R. R. | TOLKIEN | [*running down:*] THE RETURN OF [*parallel with preceding three words:*] THE SHADOW | [*horizontal:*] [*publisher's "dolphin" device*] | HMCO | [*thin rule*] | [*thick rule*]'. Orange-tan wove endpapers. Black headbands. All edges trimmed and unstained.

Dust-jacket, wove paper. Printed on upper cover against a colour illustration by Alan Lee, of Bag End: '[*against a light grey panel:*] [*in grey:*] THE HISTORY OF MIDDLE-EARTH | VOLUME VI • CHRISTOPHER TOLKIEN | THE RETURN | [*rule, in white*] | [*in grey:*] OF | [*rule, in white*] | [*in grey:*] THE SHADOW | THE HISTORY OF THE LORD OF THE RINGS | PART ONE | [*below the panel:*] [*"JRRT" monogram, in grey*] | [*in grey, against a light grey panel:*] J. R. R. TOLKIEN'. Printed on spine: 'VOLUME VI | [*"JRRT" monogram*] | TOLKIEN | [*running down:*] THE RETURN OF THE SHADOW | [*horizontal:*] HOUGHTON | MIFFLIN | COMPANY'. Printed on lower cover: 'THE HISTORY OF MIDDLE-EARTH | [*list of vols. I–VI in the series*] | VOLUME VII In Preparation | [*"JRRT" monogram*] | [*quotations from* Publishers Weekly, *the* Hartford Courant, *and* Mythprint] | 6-97045 ISBN 0-395-49863-5'. Printed on front flap: 'FPT>$19.95 | [*blurb*] | 10194588 | ISBN 0-395-49863-5'. Printed on back flap: '[*note on Christopher Tolkien*] | FRONT JACKET ILLUSTRATION: ALAN LEE | HOUGHTON MIFFLIN COMPANY © 1988 | HOUGHTON MIFFLIN COMPANY | Two Park Street, Boston, Massachusetts 02108'.

Planned for publication 5 January 1989, but put on sale in October 1988, at $19.95; 20,000 copies printed.

Typeset as for A26a, except pp. [iii–iv], with the reference to p. 450 corrected in the list of illustrations, and with the correct text on p. 32.

c. First paperback edition (1990):

[*2 lines in tengwar, between double rules*] | J. R. R. TOLKIEN | THE RETURN OF | THE SHADOW | The History of | The Lord of the Rings | Part One | Christopher Tolkien | [*publisher's 'man drawing a circle' device*] | UNWIN | PAPERBACKS | LONDON SYDNEY WELLINGTON | [*3 lines in tengwar, between double rules*]

xii, 500 pp. Collation: 256 leaves. 19.5 × 12.8 cm.

[i] blank; [ii] illustration; [iii] 'THE RETURN OF THE SHADOW | THE HISTORY OF THE LORD OF THE RINGS, PART ONE'; [iv] '[*2 lines in tengwar, between double rules*] | THE HISTORY OF MIDDLE-EARTH | I | THE BOOK OF LOST TALES, PART ONE | II | THE BOOK OF LOST TALES, PART TWO | III | THE LAYS OF BELERIAND | IV | THE SHAPING OF MIDDLE-EARTH | THE QUENTA, THE AMBARKANTA AND | THE ANNALS | V | THE LOST ROAD | AND OTHER WRITINGS | VI | THE RETURN OF THE SHADOW | THE

HISTORY OF THE LORD OF THE RINGS, PART ONE | VII | THE HISTORY OF THE LORD OF THE RINGS, PART TWO | *(in preparation)* | [*3 lines in tengwar, between double rules*]'; [v] title; [vi] 'First published in Great Britain by Unwin Hyman, an | imprint of Unwin Hyman Limited, 1988 | First published in paperback by | Unwin® Paperbacks, an imprint of | Unwin Hyman Limited, 1990 | © Unwin Hyman 1988 | [*notice of restrictions under copyright*] | [*3 publisher's addresses, London to Wellington*] | [*at left, "JRRT" device with circled trademark symbol; at right:*] © Frank Richard Williamson and Christopher Reuel Tolkien, | executors of the Estate of the late John Ronald Reuel Tolkien | [*rule*] | [*British Library Cataloguing in Publication Data*] | [*rule*] | Set in 11 on 12 pt Imprint by Bedford Typesetters Ltd | and printed and bound in Great Britain | by Cox & Wyman Limited, Reading'; [vii] 'To | RAYNER UNWIN'; [viii] blank; [ix] quotation from a letter by Tolkien to W. H. Auden, 7 June 1955; [x] blank; [xi]–xii table of contents and (p. xii) list of illustrations; [1]–7 foreword; [8] blank; [9] 'THE FIRST PHASE'; [10] blank; [11]–229 text and illustration; [230] blank; [231] 'THE SECOND PHASE'; [232] blank; [233]–305 text and illustrations; [306] blank; [307] 'THE THIRD PHASE'; [308] blank; [309]–87 text and illustrations; [388] blank; [389] 'THE STORY | CONTINUED'; [390] blank; [391]–467 text and illustrations; [468]–97 index; [498] blank; [499] advertisement for *The Complete Tolkien Catalogue*; [500] '*Books by J. R. R. Tolkien in Unwin Paperbacks* | [*order form*]'.

Illustrations as for A26a, except that the sketch map of The Shire is printed as a black and white illustration on p. [ii].

Wove paper. Bound in heavy wove wrappers. Printed on upper cover against a colour illustration by Roger Garland, *The Return of the Shadow*, figures in a boat watched by a cloaked, blue-skinned figure: '[*against a green, 12-sided panel outlined in orange:*] [*in yellow:*] J. R. R. TOLKIEN | [*in white:*] [*rule*] | THE HISTORY OF | THE LORD | OF THE RINGS | [*in light orange:*] PART ONE | [*in white:*] [*rule*] | THE RETURN OF | THE SHADOW | [*below the panel, in lower right corner, "JRRT" device, in white*]'. Printed on spine: '[*running down:*] [*in dark red:*] THE RETURN [*parallel to the preceding words:*] OF THE SHADOW [*followed by, in black:*] J. R. R. TOLKIEN | [*publisher's "man drawing a circle" device, horizontal*]'. Printed on lower cover: '[*within an orange, 12-sided single rule frame:*] THE HISTORY OF MIDDLE-EARTH | — Volume 6 — | edited by Christopher Tolkien | [*below the frame, within another orange, 12-sided single rule frame:*] J. R. R. TOLKIEN | [*rule*] | [*in dark red:*] THE HISTORY OF | THE LORD OF THE RINGS | [*in dark blue:*] PART ONE | [*in black:*] [*rule*] | THE RETURN OF THE SHADOW | [*blurb*] | [*below the frame:*] [*"JRRT" device with circled trademark symbol*] [*at left:*] Cover design by The Pinpoint Design Company | Cover illustration by Roger Garland | UNWIN PAPERBACKS | TOLKIEN/FICTION | £5.50 net U.K. [*at right:*] ISBN 0-04-440669-X | [*bar code*]'. All edges trimmed and unstained.

Published 28 June 1990 at £4.99; 25,000 copies printed.

Typeset as for A26a, except pp. [v–vi], [499–500], with the reference to p. 450 corrected in the list of illustrations, and with the correct text on p. 32.

A27   THE TREASON OF ISENGARD   1989

a. First edition:

[*2 lines in tengwar, between double rules*] | J. R. R. TOLKIEN | THE TREASON OF | ISENGARD | The History of | The Lord of the Rings | Part Two | Christopher

Tolkien | UNWIN HYMAN | London | [*3 lines in tengwar, between double rules*]

viii, 504 pp. + 1 plate. Collation: [1–16^{16}]. 22.1 × 14.2 cm.

[i] 'THE TREASON OF ISENGARD | THE HISTORY OF THE LORD OF THE RINGS, PART TWO'; [ii] '[*2 lines in tengwar, between double rules*] | THE HISTORY OF MIDDLE–EARTH | I | THE BOOK OF LOST TALES, PART ONE | II | THE BOOK OF LOST TALES, PART TWO | III | THE LAYS OF BELERIAND | IV | THE SHAPING OF MIDDLE-EARTH | THE QUENTA, THE AMBAR-KANTA AND | THE ANNALS | V | THE LOST ROAD | AND OTHER WRITINGS | VI | THE RETURN OF THE SHADOW | THE HISTORY OF THE LORD OF THE RINGS, PART ONE | VII | THE TREASON OF ISENGARD | THE HISTORY OF THE LORD OF THE RINGS, PART TWO | VIII | THE HISTORY OF THE LORD OF THE RINGS, PART THREE | *(in preparation)* | [*3 lines in tengwar, between double rules*]'; [iii] title; [iv] 'First published in Great Britain by Unwin Hyman, an | imprint of Unwin Hyman Limited, 1989 | © Unwin Hyman Limited 1989 | [*notice of restrictions*] | [*3 publisher's addresses, London to Wellington*] | [*rule*] | British Library Cataloguing in Publication Data | [*blank space*] | [*rule*] | Set in 11 on 12 pt Sabon by | Nene Phototypesetters Ltd, Northampton | and printed in Great Britain by | Mackays of Chatham Ltd'; [v]–vi table of contents; [vii] list of illustrations; [viii] blank; [1]–4 foreword; [5]–451 text and illustrations; [452]–65 appendix on runes; [466]–504 index.

Illustrations, by Tolkien: *Orthanc (1)*, colour plate facing p. [i]; 'The West Gate of Moria: the earliest drawing of the inscription and signs', p. 182; runic inscription on Balin's tomb, p. 186; p. 342, manuscript page, including 'Sketch for the Gate of Minas Morgul'; p. 383, part of manuscript page, including 'Sketch-plan of the scene of the Breaking of the Fellowship'. Also contains, by Christopher Tolkien: key and sections of 'The First Map of *The Lord of the Rings*', pp. 297, 302, 303, 305, 308, 309, 314, 317, 319; calligraphic text on runes, pp. 460–5.

Wove paper. Bound in red textured paper over boards. Stamped on spine in gilt: '[*double rule*] | 7 | [*double rule*] | [*running down:*] THE TREASON OF ISENGARD J. R. R. TOLKIEN | [*horizontal:*] UNWIN | [*publisher's "man drawing a circle" device*] | HYMAN'. Wove endpapers. No headbands. All edges trimmed and unstained.

Dust-jacket, wove paper. Covers and spine printed against a red background. Printed on upper cover within a gold double rule frame interrupted at top by 'THE HISTORY OF MIDDLE-EARTH' in white: '[*in white:*] CHRISTOPHER TOLKIEN | [*"JRRT" monogram, in gold*] | [*in white:*] THE TREASON | OF ISENGARD | [*in gold:*] [*rule*] 7 [*rule*] | [*in white and gold:*] J. R. R. TOLKIEN'. Printed on spine: '[*in gold:*] [*double rule*] | 7 | [*double rule*] | [*running down, in white:*] THE TREASON OF ISENGARD J. R. R. TOLKIEN | [*horizontal, in gold:*] UNWIN | [*publisher's "man drawing a circle" device*] | HYMAN'. Printed on lower cover: '[*"JRRT" monogram, within a double rule frame, in gold*] | [*in black, against a white panel obscuring the lower right corner of the frame:*] ISBN 0-04-440396-8 | [*bar code*]'. Printed on front flap: '[*blurb, in red*] | [*in black:*] £17.95 | NET U.K.'

Published 7 September 1989 at £17.95; 5,000 copies printed.

The seventh volume of 'The History of Middle-earth'. Contains portions of the manuscripts of *The Lord of the Rings* from further revisions to bk. 1, ch. 1, through drafts of bk. 3, ch. 6. Includes a history of the related poems 'Errantry' and the 'Eärendillinwë' (Bilbo's song at Rivendell, *LR*, bk. 2, ch. 1).

The title page inscription (printed also on p. [ii]) reads: 'In The Treason of Isengard the story of the Fellowship of the Ring is traced from Rivendell through Moria and the land of Lothlórien to the day of its ending at Calembel beside Anduin the great river. Then is told of the return of Gandalf Mithrandir, of the meeting of the hobbits with Fangorn, and of the war upon the Riders of Rohan by the traitor Saruman.'

An additional 3,000 copies of the first impression were printed for sale to book club members, identical to A27a except with no price printed on the dust-jacket.

b. First American edition (1989):

[*2 lines in tengwar, between double rules*] | J. R. R. TOLKIEN | THE TREASON OF | ISENGARD | The History of | The Lord of the Rings | Part Two | Christopher Tolkien | [*publisher's 'dolphin' device*] | Boston | Houghton Mifflin Company | 1989 | [*3 lines in tengwar, between double rules*]

viii, 504 pp. + 1 plate. Collation: [1–16^{16}]. 21.8 × 14.1 cm.

Contents as for A27a, except pp. [iii] title, as above; [iv] 'Copyright © 1989 by Frank Richard Williamson and Christopher Reuel Tolkien as | Executors of the Estate of J. R. R. Tolkien | All rights reserved | For information about permission to reproduce selections from | this book, write to Permissions, Houghton Mifflin Company, | 2 Park Street, Boston, Massachusetts 02108. | [*Library of Congress Cataloging in Publication Data*] | Printed in the United States of America | [*printing code, beginning "Q", ending "1"*]'

Illustrations as for A27a.

Wove paper. Bound in black cloth over boards. Stamped on spine in gilt: '[*thick rule*] | [*thin rule*] | J. R. R. | TOLKIEN | [*running down:*] THE TREASON OF ISENGARD | [*horizontal:*] [*publisher's "dolphin" device*] | HMCO | [*thin rule*] | [*thick rule*]'. Orange-tan wove endpapers. Black headbands. All edges trimmed and unstained.

Dust-jacket, wove paper. Printed on upper cover against a colour illustration by Alan Lee, of Orthanc: '[*against a light grey panel:*] [*in grey:*] THE HISTORY OF MIDDLE-EARTH | VOLUME VII • CHRISTOPHER TOLKIEN | THE TREASON | [*rule, in white*] | [*in grey:*] OF | [*rule, in white*] | [*in grey:*] ISENGARD | THE HISTORY OF THE LORD OF THE RINGS | PART TWO | [*below the panel:*] ["*JRRT*" *monogram, in grey*] | [*in grey, against a light grey panel:*] J. R. R. TOLKIEN'. Printed on spine in grey: 'VOLUME VII | ["*JRRT*" *monogram*] | TOLKIEN | [*running down:*] THE TREASON OF ISENGARD | [*horizontal:*] HOUGHTON | MIFFLIN | COMPANY'. Printed on lower cover: 'THE HISTORY OF MIDDLE-EARTH | [*list of vols. I–VII in the series*] | VOLUME VIII In Preparation | [*4 quotations, from* Publishers Weekly, Mythprint, *the Decatur Daily, and the* Hartford Courant] | [*at left:*] 6-97039 [*at right:*] ISBN 0-395-51562-9 | [*bar codes*]'. Printed on front flap: '$19.95 | [*blurb*] | 1189'. Printed on back flap: '[*note on Christopher Tolkien*] | Jacket illustration: Alan Lee © 1989 | Houghton Mifflin Company | 2 Park Street, Boston, Massachusetts 02108'.

Published 30 November 1989 at $19.95; 12,500 copies printed.

Typeset as for A27a, except pp. [iii–iv].

c. First paperback edition (1990):

['*JRRT*' *device, in white and black*] | TOLKIEN | TREASON OF | ISENGARD | The History of | The Lord of the Rings | Part Two | CHRISTOPHER TOLKIEN | [*publisher's 'fire and water' device*] | Grafton | *An Imprint of* HarperCollins*Publishers* viii, 504 pp. + 1 plate. Collation: 256 leaves. 19.6 × 13.0 cm.

[i] 'THE TREASON OF ISENGARD | THE HISTORY OF THE LORD OF THE RINGS, PART TWO | [*illustration*]'; [ii] 'THE HISTORY OF MIDDLE-EARTH | I | THE BOOK OF LOST TALES, PART ONE | II | THE BOOK OF LOST TALES, PART TWO | III | THE LAYS OF BELERIAND | IV | THE SHAPING OF MIDDLE-EARTH | V | THE LOST ROAD | AND OTHER WRITINGS | VI | THE RETURN OF THE SHADOW | THE HISTORY OF THE LORD OF THE RINGS, PART ONE | VII | THE TREASON OF ISENGARD | THE HISTORY OF THE LORD OF THE RINGS, PART TWO | VIII | SAURON DEFEATED | THE HISTORY OF THE LORD OF THE RINGS, PART THREE'; [iii] title; [iv] 'Grafton | An Imprint of HarperCollins*Publishers* | 77–85 Fulham Palace Road, | Hammersmith, London W6 8JB | Published by Grafton 1992 | [*printing code, beginning "9", ending "1"*] | © Unwin Hyman Limited 1989 | [*at left, "JRRT" device with circled trademark symbol; at right:*] © 1990 Frank Richard Williamson | and Christopher Reuel Tolkien, | executors of the estate of the late | John Ronald Reuel Tolkien | ISBN 0 261 10220 6 | Printed in Great Britain by | HarperCollins Manufacturing Glasgow | [*notice of restrictions*] | [*notice of condition of sale*]'; [v]–vi table of contents; [vii] list of illustrations; [viii] blank; [1]–4 foreword; [5]–451 text and illustrations; [452]–65 appendix on runes; [466]–504 index.

Illustrations as for A27a, except that *Orthanc (1)* is printed in black and white on p. [i].

Wove paper. Bound in heavy wove wrappers. Printed on upper cover against a blue-purple, 12-sided panel outlined in green, against a colour illustration by Roger Garland, of the funeral of Boromir: '[*in light blue:*] J R R TOLKIEN | [*in white:*] [*rule*] | THE HISTORY OF | THE LORD | OF THE RINGS | [*in light blue:*] PART TWO | [*in white:*] [*rule*] | *THE TREASON OF* | *ISENGARD*'. Printed on spine: '[*against a black panel within a single rule frame:*] ["*JRRT*" *device, in black and white*] | [*in white:*] TOLKIEN | [*below the frame:*] [*running down:*] [*in dark red:*] THE TREASON [*parallel to the preceding words:*] OF ISENGARD [*followed by, in black:*] J R R TOLKIEN | [*horizontal:*] [*publisher's "fire and water" device, in red and blue*] | [*in black:*] Grafton'. Printed on lower cover: '[*within an orange, 12-sided single rule frame:*] THE HISTORY OF MIDDLE-EARTH | — *Volume 7* — | edited by Christopher Tolkien | [*below the frame, within another orange, 12-sided single rule frame:*] J R R TOLKIEN | [*rule*] | [*in dark red:*] THE HISTORY OF | THE LORD OF THE RINGS | [*in blue-purple:*] PART TWO | [*in black:*] [*rule*] | *THE TREASON OF ISENGARD* | [*blurb*] | [*below the frame:*] [*at left:*] TOLKIEN/NON-FICTION | Front cover illustration by | Roger Garland | UNITED KINGDOM £5.99 | NEW ZEALAND $17.95 RRP INC. GST | AUSTRALIA $14.95 (recommended) | CANADA $11.95 [*at right:*] ISBN 0-261-10220-6 [*3 parallel rules*] | [*bar codes*]'. All edges trimmed and unstained.

Published 2 January 1992 at £5.99; number of copies not known.

Typeset as for A27a, except pp. [ii–iv].

A28   **THE WAR OF THE RING**   1990

a. First edition:

[*2 lines in tengwar, between double rules*] | J. R. R. TOLKIEN | THE WAR OF | THE RING | The History of | The Lord of the Rings | Part Three | Christopher Tolkien | UNWIN HYMAN | London | [*3 lines in tengwar, between double rules*] xii, 476 pp. + 1 plate. Collation: [1–14¹⁶15⁴16¹⁶]. 22.1 × 14.0 cm.

[i] 'THE WAR OF THE RING | THE HISTORY OF THE LORD OF THE RINGS, PART THREE'; [ii] '[2 *lines in tengwar, between double rules*] | THE HISTORY OF MIDDLE-EARTH | I | THE BOOK OF LOST TALES, PART ONE | II | THE BOOK OF LOST TALES, PART TWO | III | THE LAYS OF BELERIAND | IV | THE SHAPING OF MIDDLE-EARTH | THE QUENTA, THE AMBARKANTA AND | THE ANNALS | V | THE LOST ROAD | AND OTHER WRITINGS | VI | THE RETURN OF THE SHADOW | THE HISTORY OF THE LORD OF THE RINGS, PART ONE | VII | THE TREASON OF ISENGARD | THE HISTORY OF THE LORD OF THE RINGS, PART TWO | VIII | THE WAR OF THE RING | THE HISTORY OF THE LORD OF THE RINGS, PART THREE | IX | *(in preparation)* | [3 *lines in tengwar, between double rules*]'; [iii] title; [iv] 'First published in Great Britain by Unwin Hyman, | an imprint of Unwin Hyman Limited, 1990 | © Unwin Hyman 1990 | [*notice of restrictions*] | [3 *publisher's addresses, London to Wellington*] | [*rule*] | British Library Cataloguing in Publication Data | [*rule*] | Set in 11 on 12 pt Sabon by | Nene Phototypesetters Ltd, Northampton | and printed in Great Britain by | The University Press, Cambridge'; [v]–vi table of contents; [vii] list of illustrations; [viii] blank; [ix]–xi foreword; [xii] blank; [1] PART ONE | [*swelled rule*] | THE FALL OF | SARUMAN'; [2] blank; [3]–81 text and illustrations; [82] blank; [83] 'PART TWO | [*swelled rule*] | THE RING GOES EAST'; [84] blank; [85]–226 text and illustrations; [227] 'PART THREE | [*swelled rule*] | MINAS TIRITH'; [228] blank; [229]–439 text and illustrations; [440]–76 index.

Illustrations, by Tolkien: *Dunharrow* (cf. Ei2, no. 29), recto of colour plate inserted before p. [i]; manuscript page with sketch, *Shelob's Lair* (cf. Ei2, no. 28), verso of colour plate; *Orthanc (2), (3), (4)*, p. 33; *Isengard & Orthanc (5)*, p. 34; p. 90, page from the first manuscript of 'The Taming of Sméagol'; portions of two manuscript pages, with early sketches of Kirith Ungol, p. 108; p. 114, manuscript page with sketch of Kirith Ungol; map of Minas Morghul and the Cross-roads, p. 181; p. 201, manuscript page with plan of Shelob's lair; p. 204, manuscript page with sketch of Kirith Ungol; sketch of Shelob's lair, p. 225; p. 239, manuscript page with sketch of Dunharrow; p. 258, manuscript page with sketch map of Harrowdale; p. 261, manuscript page with the earliest sketch of Minas Tirith; p. 280, manuscript page with sketches of Minas Tirith and Mindolluin; sketch plan of Minas Tirith, p. 290; p. 314, manuscript page with sketches of the Starkhorn, Dwimorberg, and Irensaga. Also contains maps by Christopher Tolkien: Frodo's journey to the Morannon, p. 117; the White Mountains and South Gondor, p. 269; West and East halves of the 'second map' of Middle-earth, pp. 434, 435. The order of the colour illustrations as described above is the reverse of that called for both in the list of illustrations and in references to the 'frontispieces', pp. 193 and 250.

Wove paper. Bound in dark green textured paper over boards. Stamped on spine in gilt: '[*double rule*] | 8 | [*double rule*] | [*running down:*] THE WAR OF [*parallel to the preceding three words:*] THE RING [*followed by:*] J. R. R. TOLKIEN | [*horizontal:*] UNWIN | [*publisher's "man drawing a circle" device*] | HYMAN'. Wove endpapers. No headbands. All edges trimmed and unstained.

Dust-jacket, wove paper. Covers and spine printed against a dark green background. Printed on upper cover within a gold double rule frame interrupted at top by 'THE HISTORY OF MIDDLE-EARTH' in gold: '[*in white:*] CHRISTOPHER TOLKIEN | ["*JRRT*" monogram, in gold] | [*in white:*] THE WAR | OF THE RING | [*in gold:*] [*rule*] 8 [*rule*] | [*in white and gold:*] J. R. R. TOLKIEN'. Printed on spine: '[*in gold:*] [*double rule*] | 8 | [*double rule*] | [*running down, in white:*] THE WAR OF [*parallel* to *the preceding three words:*] THE RING [*followed by:*] J. R. R. TOLKIEN | [*horizontal, in gold:*] UNWIN | [*publisher's "man drawing a circle" device*] | HYMAN'. Printed on lower cover: '[*"JRRT" monogram, within a double rule frame, in gold*] | [*in black, against a white panel obscuring the lower right corner of the frame:*] ISBN 0-04-440685-1 | [*bar code*]'. Printed on front flap: '[*blurb*] | [*at left:*] [*"JRRT" device with circled trademark symbol*] [*at right:*] £17.95 | NET UK'.

Published September 1990 at £17.95; 4,000 copies printed.

The eighth volume of 'The History of Middle-earth'. Contains portions of the manuscripts of *The Lord of the Rings* from bk. 3, ch. 7 through bk. 5.

The title page inscription (printed also on p. [ii]) reads: 'In *The War of the Ring* is traced the story of the victory at Helm's Deep and the drowning of Isengard by the Ents. Then is told of the journey of Frodo with Samwise and Gollum to the Morannon, of the meeting with Faramir, and the stairs of Kirith Ungol, of the Battle of the Pelennor Fields, and of the coming of Aragorn in the fleet of Umbar.'

An additional 3,500 copies of the first impression were printed for sale to book club members, identical to A28a except with no price printed on the dust-jacket.

Morley Books, Leeds, bound 100 copies for libraries. The publisher's records are not clear whether these were run on with or reserved from the 4,000 copies recorded for trade publication.

b. First American edition (1990):

[*2 lines in tengwar, between double rules*] | J. R. R. TOLKIEN | THE WAR OF | THE RING | The History of | The Lord of the Rings | Part Three | Christopher Tolkien | [*publisher's 'dolphin' device*] | Boston | Houghton Mifflin Company | 1990 | [*3 lines in tengwar, between double rules*]

xii, 484 pp. + 1 plate. Collation: [1–13^{16}14^{8}15–16^{16}]. 21.9 × 14.0 cm.

Contents as for A28a, except pp. [iii] title, as above; [iv] 'Copyright © 1990 by Frank Richard Williamson and Christopher Reuel Tolkien | as Executors of the Estate of J. R. R. Tolkien | All rights reserved | For information about permission to reproduce selections from | this book, write to Permissions, Houghton Mifflin Company, | 2 Park Street, Boston, Massachusetts 02108. | [*Library of Congress Cataloging in Publication Data*] | Printed in the United States of America | [*printing code, beginning "HAD", ending "1"*] | [*"JRRT" device with trademark symbol in oval*] | is a trademark of Frank Richard Williamson and Christopher Reuel Tolkien, | executors of the Estate of the late John Ronald Reuel Tolkien'; [477–84] blank.

Illustrations as for A28a.

Wove paper. Bound in black cloth over boards. Stamped on spine in gilt: '[*thick rule*] | [*thin rule*] | J. R. | TOLKIEN | [*running down:*] THE TREASON OF ISENGARD | [*horizontal:*] [*publisher's "dolphin" device*] | HMCO | [*thin rule*] | [*thick rule*]'. Orange-tan wove endpapers. Black headbands. All edges trimmed and unstained.

Dust-jacket, wove paper. Printed on upper cover against a colour illustration by Alan Lee, of the Battle of Helm's Deep: '[*in dark blue, against a light grey panel:*] THE HISTORY OF MIDDLE-EARTH | VOLUME VIII • CHRISTOPHER TOLKIEN | THE WAR OF | THE RING | THE HISTORY OF THE LORD OF THE RINGS | PART THREE | [*below the panel:*] [*"JRRT" monogram, in white*] | [*in dark blue, against a light grey panel:*] J. R. R. TOLKIEN'. Printed on spine in dark blue: 'VOLUME VIII | [*"JRRT" monogram*] | TOLKIEN | [*running down:*]

THE WAR OF THE RING | [*horizontal:*] HOUGHTON | MIFFLIN | COMPANY'.
Printed on lower cover against a light grey background: '[*in dark blue:*] THE
HISTORY OF MIDDLE-EARTH | [*list of vols. I–VIII in the series*] | VOLUME IX •
In Preparation | [*4 quotations, from the* Salisbury (N.C.) Post, Publishers Weekly,
Hartford Courant, *and* Mythprint] | [*at left:*] 6-97105 [*at right, in black, against a
white panel:*] ISBN 0-395-56008-X | [*bar codes*]'. Printed on front flap: '$21.95 |
[*blurb, in black except initial "W" in dark blue*] | [*in black:*] 1190'. Printed on back
flap: '[*blurb, continued*] | [*note on Christopher Tolkien*] | *Jacket illustration:* © Alan
Lee | HOUGHTON MIFFLIN COMPANY | 2 *Park Street, Boston, Massachusetts
02108*'.

Published 14 November 1990 at $21.95; 18,500 copies printed.

Typeset as for A28a, except pp. [iii–iv].

c. First paperback edition (1992):

To be published by HarperCollins, London.

A29   SAURON DEFEATED   1992

a. First edition:

[*2 lines in tengwar, between double rules*] | J. R. R. TOLKIEN | SAURON
DEFEATED | THE END OF THE THIRD AGE | (The History of The Lord of the
Rings | Part Four) | [*rule*] | THE NOTION CLUB PAPERS | and | THE
DROWNING OF ANADÛNÊ | Edited by Christopher Tolkien | [*publisher's 'fire
and water' device*] | HarperCollins*Publishers* | [*3 lines in tengwar, between double
rules*]

xii, 484 pp. + 2 plates. Collation: [1–14¹⁶15⁸16¹⁶]. 22.1 × 14.2 cm.

[i] 'SAURON DEFEATED'; [ii] '[*2 lines in tengwar, between double rules*] | THE
HISTORY OF MIDDLE-EARTH | I | THE BOOK OF LOST TALES, PART ONE |
II | THE BOOK OF LOST TALES, PART TWO | III | THE LAYS OF BELERIAND |
IV | THE SHAPING OF MIDDLE-EARTH | V | THE LOST ROAD | VI | THE
RETURN OF THE SHADOW | VII | THE TREASON OF ISENGARD | VIII | THE
WAR OF THE RING | IX | SAURON DEFEATED | [*3 lines in tengwar, between
double rules*]'; [iii] title; [iv] 'HarperCollins*Publishers* | 77–85 Fulham Palace Road,
| Hammersmith, London W6 8JB | Published by HarperCollins*Publishers* 1992 |
Copyright © HarperCollins*Publishers*, 1992 | [*at left, "JRRT" device with circled
trademark symbol; at right:*] © 1990 Frank Richard Williamson | and Christopher
Reuel Tolkien, | executors of the Estate of the late | John Ronald Reuel Tolkien |
[*below the prededing:*] A catalogue record for this book | is available from the
British Library | ISBN 0-261-10240-0 | Set in 11 on 12 point Sabon by | Nene
Phototypesetters Ltd, Northampton | and printed in Great Britain by | HarperCollins
Manufacturing, Glasgow | [*notice of restrictions*]'; [v]–vi table of contents; [vii] list
of illustrations; viii 'To | *TAUM SANTOSKI*'; [ix]–xi foreword; [xii] blank; [1]
'PART ONE | [*swelled rule*] | THE END OF THE | THIRD AGE'; [2] blank; [3]–
141 text and illustrations; [142] blank; [143] 'PART TWO | [*swelled rule*] | THE
NOTION CLUB | PAPERS'; [144] blank; [145]–327 text and illustrations; [328]
blank; [329] 'PART THREE | [*swelled rule*] | THE DROWNING | OF ANADÛNÊ |
With the Third Version of | THE FALL OF NÚMENOR | And Lowdham's Report

on | THE ADUNAIC LANGUAGE'; [330] blank; [331]–440 text; [441]–82 indexes; [483–4] blank.

Illustrations, by Tolkien: 'Arundel Lowdham's "Fragments"' from *The Notion Club Papers*, on 2 colour plates inserted before p. [i]; p. 19, manuscript page with sketch of the Tower of Kirith Ungol; sketch of Mount Doom, entitled on the work *Orodruin, Mt Doom*, and *Sam's Path*, p. 42 (cf. Ei2, no. 30); 'First copy of the King's letter', p. 130; 'Third copy of the King's letter', p. 131; *Orthanc I, II*, and *III*, pp. 138–9; *Dunharrow I* and *II*, pp. 140–1; p. 154, manuscript title page of *The Notion Club Papers*; lettered titling, 'NOTION CLUB PAPERS', p. [155]; pp. 319–21, three 'surviving page[s] of Edwin Lowdham's manuscript' from *The Notion Club Papers*. Also contains, pp. 322–7, comments on 'Lowdham's' texts written out by Christopher Tolkien.

Wove paper. Bound in red textured paper over boards. Stamped on spine in gilt: '[*double rule*] | 9 | [*double rule*] | [*running down:*] SAURON [*parallel to the preceding word:*] DEFEATED [*followed by:*] J. R. R. TOLKIEN | [*horizontal:*] [*publisher's "fire and water" device*] | Harper | Collins'. Wove endpapers. No headbands. All edges trimmed and unstained.

Dust-jacket, wove paper. Covers and spine printed against a dark red background. Printed on upper cover within a gold double rule frame interrupted at top by 'THE HISTORY OF MIDDLE-EARTH' in white: '[*in white:*] CHRISTOPHER TOLKIEN | [*"JRRT" monogram, in gold*] | [*in white:*] SAURON | DEFEATED | [*in gold:*] [*rule*] 9 [*rule*] | [*in white and gold:*] J. R. R. TOLKIEN'. Printed on spine: '[*in gold:*] [*double rule*] | 9 | [*double rule*] | [*running down, in white:*] SAURON [*parallel to the preceding word:*] DEFEATED [*followed by:*] J. R. R. TOLKIEN | [*horizontal, in gold:*] [*publisher's "fire and water" device*] | Harper | Collins'. Printed on lower cover: '[*"JRRT" monogram, within a double rule frame, in gold*] | [*in black, against a white panel obscuring the lower right corner of the frame:*] ISBN 0-261-10240-0 | [*bar code*]'. Printed on front flap in dark red: '[*blurb*] | £20.00 net'. Printed on back flap in dark red: 'ILLUSTRATED | HarperCollins*Publishers*'.

Published 6 January 1992 at £20.00; 3,000 copies printed.

The ninth volume of 'The History of Middle-earth'. Contains portions of the manuscripts of *The Lord of the Rings*, bk. 6 and epilogue; *The Notion Club Papers*, with texts of 'Imram' (cf. C37); and 'The Drowning of Anadûnê', including the third version of 'The Fall of Númenor'. Also contains, p. 12, excerpts from two unpublished letters from Tolkien to Stanley Unwin, 5 and 28 May 1947.

   The title page inscription (also printed on p. [ii]) reads: 'In this book is traced first the story of the destruction of the One Ring and the downfall of Sauron at the end of the Third Age. Then follows an account of the intrusion of the Cataclysm of the West into the deliberations of certain scholars of Oxford and the fall of Sauron named Zigûr in the drowning of Anadûnê.'

   An additional 2,000 copies of the first impression were printed for sale to book club members, identical to A29a except with no price printed on the dust-jacket.

b. First American edition (1992):

To be published by Houghton Mifflin, Boston, in October 1992.

B

Books Edited, Translated, or with Contributions by J. R. R. Tolkien

In order to keep section B to a manageable size I have omitted full descriptions of books to which Tolkien contributed only as part of an editorial staff or as an adviser or helper 'behind the scenes'; however, some of these books are mentioned in notes. The number of authors who have acknowledged Tolkien's assistance cannot easily be counted, nor, usually, can the extent of his labour be determined. He was generous with his time and scholarship in the aid of others, often at the expense of the writings which appeared (or failed to appear) under his own name. It has been said that he took endless pains with his students, giving them so much help that work they published was really his own, yet he took only pleasure in their accomplishments, without credit for himself. He helped his academic colleagues no less.

Three books which thus fall outside the scope of section B nevertheless deserve special mention:

The *Oxford English Dictionary* (or *New English Dictionary*, Oxford University Press). Tolkien was on the staff of the *OED* from late 1918 until the spring of 1920, and worked on words beginning with W. At least *wag, walrus, wampum, warm, wasp, water, wick (lamp)*, and *winter* were researched by him. Tolkien himself reviewed the half-volume *Whisking–Wilfulness* in *The Year's Work in English Studies*, vol. 5 (B8), noting its deficiencies as well as reasons for praise. He spoke on the *OED* at least once, to a joint meeting of the Yorkshire Dialect Society and the English Association during the week of 21–7 January 1922, a lecture still unpublished (if, indeed, its text survives).

Þe *Liflade ant te Passiun of Seinte Iuliene*, edited by S. R. T. O. d'Ardenne (Liège: Bibliothèque de la faculté de philosophie et lettres de l'Université de Liège, and Paris: E. Droz, 1936; reissued with corrigenda, Oxford: Published for the Early English Text Society by the Oxford University Press, 1961). Simonne d'Ardenne was a Belgian who studied Middle English with Tolkien at Oxford during the early nineteen-thirties and became Professor of English at the University of Liège. Like Tolkien, she was interested in the English dialect revealed in the *Ancrene Wisse* and other thirteenth-century manuscripts. She collaborated with him on two short articles (C34, C35), and together they began an edition of *Seinte Katerine* (eventually completed without Tolkien's assistance but with an acknowledgement to his inspiration). Humphrey Carpenter, *Biography*, notes that Tolkien 'contributed much' to d'Ardenne's edition of *The Life and Passion of St Juliene*; indeed, he says, it 'paradoxically contains more of his views on early Middle English than anything he ever published under his own name.' D'Ardenne admitted privately that the book should have been published as a joint work; but published under her name, as her academic thesis, it entitled her to be elected as a university professor. In her prefatory note to the book, d'Ardenne thanks Tolkien 'for assistance from the beginning of my work on this text, and especially during the revision of the glossary and grammar.'

The Jerusalem Bible (London: Darton, Longman & Todd; Garden City, N.Y.: Doubleday, 1966). Tolkien served as an editor of this version in a capacity nowhere definitively described. According to Tolkien himself, in a letter to Charlotte and

Denis Plimmer of 8 February 1967, he was originally to have translated a large amount of text, but under pressure from other work completed only Jonah ('one of the shortest books'), and otherwise 'was consulted on one or two points of style, and criticized some contributions of others'. According to Anthony Kenny, *A Path from Rome: An Autobiography* (London: Sidgwick & Jackson, 1985), Tolkien was asked to translate Judges and Jonah, but in the end contributed only a revision of the latter. According to Carpenter, *Biography*, Tolkien's only contribution was the original draft of a translation of Jonah, which was extensively revised by others before publication. But it was reported in the Tolkien Society bulletin, *Amon Hen*, no. 26 (May 1977), that according to Darton, Longman & Todd Tolkien also worked on the Book of Job, providing its initial draft and playing an important part in establishing its final text.

B1   OXFORD POETRY 1915   1915

a. Hardcover copies:

OXFORD POETRY | 1915 | EDITED BY | G. D. H. C. AND T. W. E. | OXFORD | B. H. BLACKWELL, BROAD STREET | 1915

viii, 72 pp. Collation: $\pi^4 1–4^8 5^4$. 19.1–19.4 × 12.6–13.0 cm. (height and width vary).

[i] 'OXFORD POETRY | 1915'; [ii] 'LONDON AGENTS | SIMPKIN, MARSHALL AND CO., LTD. | NEW YORK | LONGMANS, GREEN AND CO., FOURTH AVENUE, | AND THIRTIETH STREET'; [iii] title; [iv] blank; v–vii table of contents; viii editors' note; 1–[72] text; at foot of p. [72]: '[*rule*] | BILLING AND SONS, LTD., PRINTERS, GUILDFORD, ENGLAND'.

Includes poem, 'Goblin Feet', by J. R. R. Tolkien, pp. 64–5.

Laid paper, watermarked 'ANTIQUE DE LUXE'. Bound in dark blue paper over boards, white parchment spine. Label affixed to upper cover, printed in dark blue, within a dark blue single rule frame: 'Oxford | Poetry | 1915 | [*black letter:*] Oxford | [*roman:*] B. H. Blackwell'. Label affixed to spine, printed running up, in dark blue, within a dark blue single rule frame: 'Oxford Poetry 1915'. Laid endpapers, watermarked 'ANTIQUE DE LUXE'. No headbands. All edges untrimmed and unstained.

Issued without dust-jacket.

Published 1 December 1915 at 2s. 6d.; 150 copies printed, simultaneous with B1b.

'Goblin Feet' was written on 27–8 April 1915 to please Edith Bratt (later Mrs. J. R. R. Tolkien), who liked 'spring and flowers and trees, and little elfin people'. Later Tolkien wished that his poem, 'the unhappy little thing, representing all that I came (so soon after) to fervently dislike, could be buried for ever' (quoted in *BLT1* [A21], p. 32). Yet it was an early success and has been reprinted both for its charm and as Tolkien 'juvenilia', notably in *Oxford Poetry 1914–1916* (Oxford: Blackwell, 1917), pp. 120–2; *The Book of Fairy Poetry*, ed. Dora Owen (London: Longmans, Green, 1920), pp. 177–8, with an illustration by Warwick Goble; and *The Annotated Hobbit* (A3dd–ee), p. 77, with the Goble illustration on p. 76.

Part of a manuscript version of the poem is printed in *Biography* (pt. 2, ch. 7) but is not so identified. In the 1987 revision of *Biography* (B32e), the manuscript version is commingled in the second stanza with a misreading of the published version.

Oxford Poetry 1915 was edited by G. D. H. Cole and T. W. Earp, the latter a fellow contributor with Tolkien from Exeter College.

b. Paperback copies:

Sheets as for B1a. Bound in dark blue wove wrappers, cover label as for B1a, spine label printed running up, in dark blue: '[*vertical rule*] Oxford Poetry 1915 [*vertical rule*]'. All edges untrimmed and unstained.

Published 1 December 1915 at 1s.; 850 copies printed, simultaneous with B1a.

B2   **A SPRING HARVEST**   **1918**

A SPRING HARVEST | BY | GEOFFREY BACHE SMITH | LATE LIEUTENANT IN THE LANCASHIRE FUSILIERS | ERSKINE MACDONALD, LTD. | LONDON, W.C.1

80 pp. Collation: [1]⁴2–10⁴. 18.4–18.7 × 12.4–12.8 cm. (height and width vary).

[1–2] blank, pasted down to front board; [3] 'A SPRING HARVEST'; [4] 'To HIS MOTHER | GEOFFREY BACHE SMITH | Born ... *October* 18*th*, 1894 | Entered Corpus Christi College, | Oxford, as Exhibitioner . *October* 1913 | Received Commission ... *January* 1915 | Died of wounds at Warlencourt, | France ... *December 3rd*, 1916'; [5] title; [6] '*All Rights Reserved* | *First published June* 1918'; [7] note, signed 'J. R. R. T.'; [8] blank; 9–10 table of contents; 11 poem, 'If there be one among the Muses nine'; [12] blank; 13–[78] text; at foot of p. [78]: '[*rule*] | *Printed by Hazell, Watson & Viney, Ld., London and Aylesbury.*'; [79–80] blank, pasted down to back board.

Includes three-paragraph prefatory note by J. R. R. Tolkien, p. [7], signed 'J. R. R. T.'

Laid paper, watermarked 'Abbey Mills'. Bound in light green paper over boards. Stamped on upper cover in dark blue: 'A SPRING HARVEST | [*ornaments*] | GEOFFREY BACHE SMITH'. Stamped on spine in dark blue: '[*running up:*] A SPRING HARVEST — G. B. SMITH | [*horizontal:*] E.MD.' No headbands. Top edge trimmed, fore- and bottom edges untrimmed. All edges unstained.

Dust-jacket, light green wove paper. Printed in green. Of the copies of B2 examined, only the Bodleian Library copy retains its jacket, and that only in part, trimmed and tipped into the book. The following description is therefore only fragmentary, as noted. Printed on upper cover, between two vertical rules (or possibly within a single rule frame): 'A SPRING HARVEST | BY | GEOFFREY BACHE SMITH | Late Lieutenant in the Lancashire Fusiliers | ERSKINE MACDONALD, LTD. | LONDON, W.C.1'. Printed on spine (possibly, but not probably, with additional printing at top): 'A Spring | Harvest | G. B. | SMITH | 3/6 | NET | ERSKINE | MACDONALD | LTD.' Advertisement printed on lower cover, within a single rule frame, possibly with a heading at top: '[*18 titles, beginning with* Three Plays by Mabel Dearmer, *ending with* Soldier Poets: Songs of the Fighting Man] | [*rule*] | ERSKINE MACDONALD, LTD., LONDON, W.C.1'. Printed on front flap, within a single rule frame: '[*advertisement for Nettleingham,* Tommy's Tunes] | [*rule*] | ERSKINE MACDONALD, LTD. | London, W.C.1'. Back flap not seen.

Published June 1918 according to p. [6], but July 1918 according to the *English Catalogue*, at 3s. 6d.; number of copies not known.

Geoffrey Bache Smith was a promising poet and an early critic of Tolkien's verse-writing. This memorial collection of his work was edited, according to Carpenter, *Biography*, by J. R. R. Tolkien and Christopher Wiseman, who were close friends of Smith at King Edward's School, Birmingham. However, Wiseman revealed to John D. Rateliff that Tolkien was the sole editor of the book. Tolkien wanted Wiseman to have credit as co-editor because the two were the only members of their private society, the 'T.C.B.S.', to have survived the World War, G. B. Smith and Rob Gilson having been killed in action. Tolkien had written to Smith on 12 August 1916: 'Of course the TCBS may have been all we dreamt—and its work in the end be done by three or two or one survivor and the part of the others be trusted by God to that of the inspiration which we do know we all got and get from one another. To this I now pin my hopes, and pray God that the people chosen to carry on the TCBS may be no fewer than we three. . . .' In the event, neither Wiseman nor Tolkien were credited in the book as editors.

B3   FOURTEENTH CENTURY VERSE & PROSE   1922

a. First edition with glossary:

[*within 2 concentric single rule frames:*] Fourteenth Century | VERSE *&* PROSE | edited by | KENNETH SISAM | [*publisher's device, an open book and 3 crowns on a shield, with 'AC. OX.'*] | [*rule*] | OXFORD | AT THE CLARENDON PRESS | M D CCCC XXI

xlviii, 292, 168 pp. Collation: [a]⁸b–c⁸B–T⁸U², π²1–9⁸10¹⁰ (10₃ signed '10**'; second leaves signed '[no.]*'). 18.3 × 12.6 cm.

first section: [i] 'Fourteenth Century | VERSE & PROSE'; [ii] blank; [iii] title; [iv] 'Oxford University Press | [*12 addresses, London to Shanghai*] | Humphrey Milford Publisher to the UNIVERSITY'; [v]–vii table of contents; [viii] map; [ix]–xliii introduction; [xliv] blank; [xlv] note on the texts; [xlvi]–xlvii bibliography; [xlviii] blank; [1]–203 text; [204]–64 notes; [265]–92 appendix, 'The English Language in the Fourteenth Century'; at foot of p. 292: 'PRINTED IN ENGLAND | AT THE OXFORD UNIVERSITY PRESS'; *second section, new pagination:* [1] '[*within a single rule frame, within a frame of 184 ornaments (56 at left and right, 36 at top and bottom):*] A | MIDDLE ENGLISH | VOCABULARY | BY | *J. R. R. TOLKIEN* | [*rule*] | *Designed for use with* | SISAM'S Fourteenth Century Verse & Prose | [*rule*] | [*ornaments*] | [*rule*] | OXFORD | AT THE CLARENDON PRESS | M D CCCC XXII'; [2] list of abbreviations; [3] note; [4] list of principal variations of form or spelling; [5–162] text; [163–8] index of names, followed on p. [168] by corrigenda to *Fourteenth Century Verse & Prose*; at foot of p. [168]: 'Printed in England at the Oxford University Press'.

Includes *A Middle English Vocabulary* by J. R. R. Tolkien, second section; cf. A1.

Laid paper. Bound in dark wine red cloth over boards. Stamped on spine in gilt: '[*strip of ornaments*] | FOURTEENTH | CENTURY | VERSE AND | PROSE | SISAM | WITH | GLOSSARY | [*publisher's device, an open book and 3 crowns within a cartouche*] | OXFORD | [*strip of ornaments*]'. Wove front endpapers. 3 pp. of advertisements on 2 leaves (second leaf pasted down), inserted following 10₁₀, as for the earliest variant of A1, headed on p. [1]: 'EARLY AND MIDDLE ENGLISH | Editions of Chaucer by Professor Skeat | October 1921'. No headbands. All edges trimmed and unstained.

Dust-jacket not seen. Later impressions in buff jacket printed in dark blue.

Published 8 June 1922 at 10s. 6d.; number of copies not known (cf. A1).

Fourteenth Century Verse & Prose was first published in October 1921 without *A Middle English Vocabulary*. The original edition, without glossary, continued to be sold, at 7s. 6d. A copy of B3a with apparently a first impression of the glossary has been seen with the title page dated 1923 and plain wove front and back endpapers.

Kenneth Sisam, one of the most important twentieth-century scholars of Old and Middle English studies, was Tolkien's tutor in the Oxford English School and his unsuccessful rival in 1925 for the Rawlinson and Bosworth Professorship of Anglo-Saxon at Oxford. Sisam also had a distinguished career with the Oxford University Press.

b. First paperback impression (1975):

[*within 2 concentric single rule frames:*] Fourteenth Century | VERSE & PROSE | edited by | KENNETH SISAM | [*publisher's device, an open book and 3 crowns on a shield, with 'AC. OX.'*] | [*rule*] | OXFORD | AT THE CLARENDON PRESS

xlviii, 464 pp. Collation: [A]¹⁶B–P¹⁶[Q]¹⁶. 18.6 × 12.2 cm.

[i] 'Fourteenth Century | VERSE & PROSE'; [ii] blank; [iii] title; [iv] '*Oxford University Press, Ely House, London W. 1* | [*list of 22 cities (publisher's branches), Glasgow to Tokyo*] | *Casebound*: ISBN 0 19 811391 9 | *Paperback*: ISBN 0 19 871093 3 | *First published 1921* | *Reprinted 1923, 1924, 1927, 1933* | *1937 (with corrections), 1944, 1946, 1949, 1950* | *1955 (with corrections), 1959, 1962, 1964, 1967* | *1970 (with corrections), 1975* | *Printed in Great Britain* | *at the University Press, Oxford* | *by Vivian Ridler* | *Printer to the University*'; [v]–vii table of contents; [viii] map; [ix]–xliii introduction; [xliv] blank; [xlv] note on the texts; [xlvi]–xlvii select bibliography; [xlviii] blank; [1]–203 text; [204]–64 notes; [265]–92 appendix, 'The English Language in the Fourteenth Century'; [293] 'A | MIDDLE ENGLISH | VOCABULARY | BY | *J. R. R. TOLKIEN*'; [294] list of abbreviations; [295] note; [296] list of principal variations of form or spelling; [297]–454 text; [455–60] index of names; [461–4] blank.

Wove paper. Bound in heavy wove wrappers. Covers and spine printed against a light yellow-brown background. Printed on upper cover: '[*illustration, in brown*] | [*in yellow:*] Fourteenth Century | Verse & Prose | [*in white:*] Edited by Kenneth Sisam | [*illustration, in brown, wraps around spine*]'. Printed on spine: '[*in white:*] SISAM | [*running down, in yellow:*] Fourteenth Century [*parallel with the preceding two words:*] Verse & Prose | [*horizontal:*] [*illustration, in brown*] | [*publisher's device, an open book and 3 crowns within a cartouche, in yellow*] | [*in white:*] OXFORD'. Printed on lower cover: '[*in white:*] From the reviews | [*2 quotations, from the* Times Literary Supplement *and the* Guardian] | *The cover illustrations, depicting agricultural scenes in medieval* | *England, are taken from the Luttrell Psalter* (c. 1340). | OXFORD UNIVERSITY PRESS | £2.75 net in UK | ISBN 0 19 871093 3 | [*illustration, in brown*]'. All edges trimmed and unstained.

Published 13 November 1975 at £2.75; 8,000 copies printed.

Typeset as for B3a, except pp. [iii–iv], 292–[3].

B4   **A NORTHERN VENTURE**   1923

A NORTHERN [*2 leaf ornaments*] | VENTURE : VERSES BY | MEMBERS OF THE LEEDS | UNIVERSITY ENGLISH [*leaf ornament*] | SCHOOL ASSOCIATION. [*leaf ornament*] | LEEDS: AT THE SWAN PRESS | 52, BELLE VUE ROAD. MCMXXIII vi, 26 pp. Collation: [1¹⁶]. 15.8 × 9.8 cm.

[i–ii] blank; [iii] title; [iv] blank; [v] table of contents; [vi] blank; 1–25 text; [26] publisher's device (signboard, 'At the Sign of the Swan').

Includes three poems by J. R. R. Tolkien: 'Tha Eadigan Saelidan: The Happy Mariners,' pp. 15–16; 'Why the Man in the Moon Came Down Too Soon,' pp. 17–19; and 'Enigmata Saxonica Nuper Inventa Duo,' p. 20.

Bound in green wove wrappers, stapled through fold. Printed on upper cover: 'A NORTHERN | VENTURE [2 *leaf ornaments*] | [*illustration by Albert Wainwright, a sailing ship with a dragon prow*]'. All edges trimmed and unstained.

Published June 1923 at 1s. 6d.; 170 copies printed. One copy seen was inscribed by a contributor 22 June 1923. A 'second edition' (i.e. second impression?), not seen, was published in July 1923 at 1s., in an edition of 200 copies.

'Tha Eadigan Saelidan: The Happy Mariners' is a slightly revised version of 'The Happy Mariners' (C10). It was reprinted in *The Book of Lost Tales, Part Two* (A22), pp. 273–4, with a later revision, pp. 275–6. In *BLT2* Christopher Tolkien notes (but does not correct) 'Twilight' in l. 5 as almost certainly an error for *Twilit*, the reading of all the original texts; omits 'the' before 'twilit tinkle' in l. 19; and corrects 'murmer' to 'murmur' in l. 37. 'Why the Man in the Moon Came Down Too Soon' was originally subtitled 'An East Anglian Phantasy,' and before publication was also entitled 'A Faërie: Why the Man in the Moon Came Down Too Soon' and 'Se Móncyning'. The poem was later much revised as 'The Man in the Moon Came Down Too Soon' and published in *The Adventures of Tom Bombadil* (A6). An intermediate revision was published in *The Book of Lost Tales, Part One* (A21), pp. 204–6. 'Enigmata Saxonica Nuper Inventa Duo', in Old English, has not been reprinted.

B5   LEEDS UNIVERSITY VERSE 1914–24   1924

LEEDS UNIVERSITY | VERSE [*leaf ornament*] 1914–24 | COMPILED AND EDITED BY THE [2 *leaf ornaments*] | ENGLISH SCHOOL ASSOCIATION | LEEDS: AT THE SWAN PRESS, 52, BELLE | VUE ROAD [3 *leaf ornaments*] MCMXXIV

64 pp. Collation: [1–4⁸]. 17.0 × 14.0 cm.

[1] title; [2–3] table of contents; 4 advertisement, i.e. foreword; 5–64 text.

Includes three poems by J. R. R. Tolkien: 'An Evening in Tavrobel', p. 56; 'The Lonely Isle', p. 57; and 'The Princess Ní', p. 58.

Wove paper. Bound in wove green wrappers with yapp edges. Printed on upper cover: 'LEEDS UNIVERSITY | VERSE [*leaf ornament*] 1914–24 | [*illustration by A. H. Smith, of a sailing ship*]'. Illustration, an angel with a harp, printed on lower cover. Wove endpapers. Publisher's device (signboard, 'At the Sign of the Swan') printed on verso, back free endpaper. All text leaves trimmed and unstained.

Published May 1924 at 2s.; 500 copies printed.

A volume of verse 'written by members of the University during the past ten years'.
  'An Evening in Tavrobel' dates, perhaps, from the period of Tolkien's convalescence (from 'trench fever') in 1917 at Great Haywood in Staffordshire. *Tavrobel*, a place in Tol Eressëa in Tolkien's mythology of *The Book of Lost Tales*, was the

'ancient name' of Great Haywood. 'The Lonely Isle' was written on the occasion of Tolkien's Channel crossing with his battalion in the First World War. The poem is dated in the manuscript 'Étaples, Pas de Calais, June 1916' and is subtitled 'For England'. The manuscript also bears the Old English title 'Seo Unwemmede Íeg'. 'The Princess Ní' is a precursor of 'Princess Mee' in *The Adventures of Tom Bombadil* (A6). None of these poems has been reprinted.

B6   THE YEAR'S WORK IN ENGLISH STUDIES 1923   1924

THE YEAR'S WORK IN | ENGLISH STUDIES | VOLUME IV | 1923 | Edited for | [*black letter:*] The English Association | [*roman:*] BY | SIR SIDNEY LEE | and | F. S. BOAS | OXFORD UNIVERSITY PRESS | LONDON : HUMPHREY MILFORD | 1924

276 pp. Collation: A–Q^{8}R^{10}. 21.9–22.0 × 14.0–14.1 cm. (height and width vary).

[1] title; [2] 'PRINTED IN ENGLAND | AT THE OXFORD UNIVERSITY PRESS'; [3] preface; [4] list of abbreviations; [5]–6 table of contents; [7]–259 text; [260]–9 index; [270–2] tables of contents of *The Year's Work in English Studies*, Vols. I–III; [273] '[*within a thin-thick-thin rule frame:*] The CAMBRIDGE *University Press* | [*thin-thick-thin rule*] | [*advertisement of 11 titles, beginning with* The Sonnets of Shakespeare, *ending with* Cambridge Plain Texts: English (*i.e. 9 separate Cambridge Plain Texts*)] | FETTER LANE, LONDON, E.C. 4'; [274] '[*within a frame of ornaments:*] OXFORD BOOKS | [*advertisement of 6 titles, beginning with* Smith, The Principles of English Metre, *ending with* The Oxford Miscellany] | OXFORD UNIVERSITY PRESS'; [275] '[*within a frame of ornaments:*] OXFORD BOOKS | [*advertisement of 7 titles, beginning with* Oxford Lectures on Literature (*i.e. 5 separate lectures*), *ending with* White, The Groombridge Diary] | OXFORD UNIVERSITY PRESS'; [276] '[*within a single rule frame:*] From SIDGWICK & JACKSON'S LIST | [*rule*] | [*advertisement of 10 titles, beginning with* Poems of To-day, *ending with* Creizenach, The English Drama in the Age of Shakespeare] | [*rule*] | SIDGWICK & JACKSON LTD., 3 ADAM STREET, LONDON, W.C. 2'.

Includes review essay, 'Philology: General Works', by J. R. R. Tolkien, pp. [20]–37.

Wove paper. Bound in grey-brown paper over boards. Stamped on upper cover in black, within a frame of black diamonds: 'THE YEAR'S WORK IN | ENGLISH STUDIES | VOLUME IV | 1923 | Edited for | [*black letter:*] The English Association | [*roman:*] BY | SIR SIDNEY LEE | and | F. S. BOAS | [*leaf ornament*] | OXFORD UNIVERSITY PRESS | LONDON: HUMPHREY MILFORD'. Stamped on spine, running up, in black: 'THE YEAR'S WORK IN ENGLISH STUDIES, 1923'. Wove endpapers. No headbands. Bottom edge trimmed, top and fore-edges untrimmed. All edges unstained.

No dust-jacket seen.

Published 8 January 1925 at 7s. 6d. (3s. 6d. to members of the English Association); 1,250 copies printed.

Tolkien was to review 'Philology: General Works' in the previous number of *The Year's Work in English Studies*, 1922 (published 1923), but was prevented by illness. The essay for that year was turned over to Tolkien's young colleague at Leeds, E. V. Gordon, who also contributed to later volumes.

B7   SIR GAWAIN AND THE GREEN KNIGHT   1925

a. First edition:

SIR GAWAIN | & | The Green Knight | Edited by | J. R. R. TOLKIEN | & | E. V. GORDON | [*ornaments arranged in a cross*] | OXFORD | At the Clarendon Press | 1925

xxviii, 212 pp. + 2 plates. Collation: [a]⁸b⁶B–N⁸O¹⁰. 19.1–19.3 × 12.6–12.8 cm. (height and width vary).

[i-ii] blank; [iii] title; [iv] 'Oxford University Press | [*list of 12 cities (publisher's branches), London to Shanghai*] | Humphrey Milford Publisher to the UNIVERSITY | Printed in England'; [v]–vi preface; [vii]–xxiv introduction; [xxv]–xxvii bibliography; [xxviii] note on the text; [1]–78 text; 79–117 notes; 118–21 notes on metre; 122–32 notes on language; 133 note on glossary; 134 list of abbreviations; 135–210 glossary; 210–11 index of names; [212] 'PRINTED IN ENGLAND | AT THE OXFORD UNIVERSITY PRESS'. Illustrations, on 2 plates: 'The Lady of the Castle Visits Sir Gawain', facing p. [iii]; 'The Beginning of the Text', facing p. viii.

Laid paper, watermarked 'Abbey Mills'. Bound in green cloth over boards. Axe device stamped on upper cover in gilt, within a gilt single rule frame. Stamped on spine in gilt: '[*rule*] | SIR | GAWAIN | and the | Green Knight | Tolkien | & | Gordon | [*publisher's device, an open book and 3 crowns within a cartouche*] | OXFORD | [*rule*]'. Single rule frame stamped on lower cover in blind. Wove endpapers. No headbands. All edges untrimmed and unstained. Errata slip inserted facing p. vi. Copies have been seen with or without tissue guards over the plates. Copies have been seen with 4 pp. of advertisements, dated August 1925, inserted following the text, or without advertisements; no priority determined, but the British Library copy, without ads, was acquired on 30 April 1925.

Dust-jacket, grey wove paper. Printed on upper cover in dark blue: 'SIR GAWAIN | & | The Green Knight | Edited by | J. R. R. TOLKIEN | & | E. V. GORDON | [*ornaments arranged in a cross*] | OXFORD | AT THE CLARENDON PRESS | [*list of 12 cities (publisher's branches), London to Shanghai*] | OXFORD UNIVERSITY PRESS | Humphrey Milford'. Printed on spine in dark blue: 'SIR | GAWAIN | and the | Green Knight | Tolkien | & | Gordon | [*publisher's device, an open book and 3 crowns within a cartouche*] | OXFORD'. Printed on lower cover in dark blue: '[*within a frame of ornaments:*] Oxford Books | [*advertisement of 5 titles, beginning with Sisam*, Fourteenth Century Verse and Prose, *ending with Pollard*, English Miracle Plays] | *OXFORD UNIVERSITY PRESS* | [*below the frame:*] April 1925'.

Published 23 April 1925 at 7s. 6d.; 2,500 copies printed.

Tolkien was responsible for the text and glossary, and E. V. Gordon for the greater part of the notes, of this edition of the Middle English poem. Their work began sometime early in 1922, after Gordon joined Tolkien in the English Department of Leeds University. Tolkien later made a Modern English translation of *Sir Gawain* (see B30) and in 1953 delivered a lecture on the poem (see A19).

Corrected in later impressions from 1930, until the revised edition of 1967 (B7b–c).

Pertinent manuscript materials and correspondence are in the Bodleian Library, Oxford.

b. Second edition, hardcover copies (1967):

Sir Gawain and the | Green Knight | EDITED BY | J. R. R. TOLKIEN AND E. V. GORDON | *SECOND EDITION* | REVISED BY | NORMAN DAVIS | [*rule*] | [*publisher's device, an open book and 3 crowns on a shield, with 'AC: OX:'*] | [*rule*] | OXFORD | AT THE CLARENDON PRESS | 1967

xxviii, 232 pp. + 2 plates. Collation: [a]⁸b⁶B–P⁸Q⁴. 21.6 × 14.0 cm.

[i] 'SIR GAWAIN AND THE | GREEN KNIGHT'; [ii] blank; [iii] title; [iv] '*Oxford University Press, Ely House, London W. 1* | [*list of 20 cities (publisher's branches), Glasgow to Tokyo*] | © *Oxford University Press 1967* | FIRST EDITION 1925 | REPRINTED 1930 (WITH CORRECTIONS) | 1936, 1946, 1949, 1952, 1955, 1960, 1963, 1966 | SECOND EDITION 1967 | PRINTED IN GREAT BRITAIN | AT THE UNIVERSITY PRESS, OXFORD | BY VIVIAN RIDLER | PRINTER TO THE UNIVERSITY'; [v]–vi preface to the second edition; [vii]–viii preface to the first edition; [ix] table of contents; [x] blank; [xi]–xxvii introduction; [xxviii] note on the text; [1]–69 text; [70]–131 notes; [132]–52 appendix; [153]–6 bibliography; [157] list of abbreviations; [158] blank; [159] note on the glossary; [160] list of abbreviations used in the glossary; [161]–230 glossary; [231]–2 index of names. Illustrations, on 2 plates: 'The Lady of the Castle Visits Sir Gawain', facing p. [iii]; 'The Beginning of the Text', facing p. [1].

Laid paper. Bound in green cloth over boards. Stamped on spine in gilt: 'SIR | GAWAIN | and the | Green Knight | [*rule*] | SECOND | EDITION | [*rule*] | TOLKIEN | GORDON | DAVIS | [*publisher's device, an open book and 3 crowns within a cartouche*] | OXFORD'. Wove endpapers. No headbands. All edges trimmed and unstained.

Dust-jacket, wove paper. Covers and spine printed against a yellow-green background. Printed on upper cover: '[*in white:*] Sir Gawain and | the Green Knight | [*in black:*] Edited by J. R. R. Tolkien and E. V. Gordon | [*within a white single rule frame:*] [*in black:*] Second Edition [*ornament, in white*] [*in black:*] Edited by | [*in white:*] Norman Davis | [*illustration, "The Lady of the Castle Visits Sir Gawain", in black, within a black single rule frame, against a white panel, within a thick black single rule frame*]'. Printed on spine, running down, within a white single rule frame: '[*in white:*] Sir Gawain and the Green Knight [*in black:*] 2nd. ed. [*in white:*] [*ornament*] Oxford'. Printed on lower cover: 'OXFORD BOOKS | [*advertisement of 5 titles, beginning with* The Works of Sir Thomas Malory, *ending with* Loomis, Introduction to Medieval Literature Chiefly in England] | Oxford University Press | [*square brackets in original:*] [811479/7/67]'. Printed on front flap: '[*blurb*] | 35s. net | IN U.K. ONLY'. Printed on back flap: 'OXFORD | UNIVERSITY PRESS | [*20 addresses, London to Addis Ababa*]'.

Published October 1967 at 35s.; number of copies not known.

Reset, a revision of B7a with reference to the Early English Text Society edition of 1940 by Gollancz and collated anew against the original manuscript. Davis notes, p. [v], that Tolkien, 'long ago my teacher and now my much honoured friend, has allowed me a free hand in revising his work and has generously given me the use of his later notes. Many of these I have incorporated, but other changes are my own. . . .' E. V. Gordon had died in 1938. Davis, Tolkien's successor at Oxford as Merton Professor of English Language and Literature, largely rewrote the introduction, notes, and appendix on language.

c. Second edition, paperback copies (1968):

Sir Gawain and the | Green Knight | EDITED BY | J. R. R. TOLKIEN AND E. V. GORDON | *SECOND EDITION* | REVISED BY | NORMAN DAVIS | [*rule*] | [*publisher's device, an open book and 3 crowns on a shield, with 'AC: OX:'*] | [*rule*] | OXFORD | AT THE CLARENDON PRESS | 1968

ii, [2], iii–xxviii, [2], 240 pp. Collation: [A]^{16}B–H^{16}I^8. 20.3 × 13.5 cm.

[i] 'SIR GAWAIN AND THE | GREEN KNIGHT'; [ii] blank; [ii+1] blank; [ii+2] illustration, 'The Lady of the Castle Visits Sir Gawain'; [iii] title; [iv] '*Oxford University Press, Ely House, London W. 1* | [*list of 20 cities (publisher's branches), Glasgow to Tokyo*] | © *Oxford University Press 1967* | FIRST EDITION 1925 | REPRINTED 1930 (WITH CORRECTIONS) | 1936, 1946, 1949, 1952, 1955, 1960, 1963, 1966 | SECOND EDITION 1967 | FIRST ISSUED AS A PAPERBACK 1968 | PRINTED LITHOGRAPHICALLY IN GREAT BRITAIN | AT THE UNIVERSITY PRESS, OXFORD | BY VIVIAN RIDLER | PRINTER TO THE UNIVERSITY'; [v]–vi preface to the second edition; [vii]–viii preface to the first edition; [ix] table of contents; [x] blank; [xi]–xxvii introduction; [xxviii] note on the text; [xxviii+1] blank; [xxviii+2] illustration, 'The Beginning of the Text'; [1]–69 text; [70]–131 notes; [132]–52 appendix; [153]–6 bibliography; [157] list of abbreviations; [158] blank; [159] note on the glossary; [160] list of abbreviations used in the glossary; [161]–230 glossary; [231]–2 index of names; [233–40] blank.

Wove paper. Bound in heavy wove wrappers. Cover and spine as for B7b dust-jacket cover and spine. Printed on lower cover against a yellow-green background: '[*blurb*] | OXFORD UNIVERSITY PRESS | [*square brackets in original:*] [811486/6/67] | 15*s net* | IN U.K. ONLY | *Also available in cloth covers*'. All edges trimmed and unstained.

Published in 1968 at 15s.; date of publication and number of copies not known.

Typeset as for B7b, except pp. [iii–iv]. The illustrations are printed on integral leaves not included in the pagination.

B8   THE YEAR'S WORK IN ENGLISH STUDIES 1924   1926

THE YEAR'S WORK IN | ENGLISH STUDIES | VOLUME V | 1924 | Edited for | [*black letter:*] The English Association | [*roman:*] BY | F. S. BOAS | and | C. H. HERFORD | OXFORD UNIVERSITY PRESS | LONDON : HUMPHREY MILFORD | 1926

328 pp. Collation: A–U^{8}X^4. 21.4–22.0 × 14.0–14.4 cm. (height and width vary).

[1] title; [2] '*Printed in England* | *At the* OXFORD UNIVERSITY PRESS | *By John Johnson* | *Printer to the University*'; [3] preface; [4] list of abbreviations; [5]–6 table of contents; [7]–305 text; [306] blank; [307]–18 index; [319–22] tables of contents of *The Year's Work in English Studies*, Vols. I–IV; [323] '[*within a thin-thick-thin rule frame:*] CAMBRIDGE UNIVERSITY | Fetter Lane PRESS London, E.C. 4 | [*thin-thick-thin rule*] | [*advertisement of 12 titles, beginning with Spurgeon*, Five Hundred Years of Chaucer Criticism and Allusion, 1357–1900, *ending with Mawer and Stenton*, The Place-Names of Buckinghamshire]'; [324] '[*within a frame of ornaments:*] OXFORD BOOKS | [*advertisement of 9 titles, beginning with Murry*, Keats and Shakespeare, *ending with de Maar*, A History of Modern English Romanticism] | OXFORD UNIVERSITY PRESS'; [325] '[*within a single rule frame:*] From SIDGWICK & JACKSON's List | [*rule*] | [*advertisement of 8 titles,*

beginning with Poems of To-day, *ending with* The Review of English Studies] | [*rule*] | SIDGWICK & JACKSON LTD., 44 MUSEUM STREET, W.C. 1'; [326] '[*within a thin-thick-thin rule frame:*] The 'Teaching of English' Series | GENERAL EDITOR: SIR HENRY NEWBOLT | *A new series of School Books designed to help in carrying out the principles* | *enunciated in 'The Teaching of English in England'.* | SELECTED VOLUMES | [*advertisement of 6 titles, beginning with* Grattan and Gurrey, Our Living Language, *ending with* A Shorter Boswell] | THOMAS NELSON & SONS LTD. | 35 & 36 PATERNOSTER ROW, E.C. 4'; [327–8] blank.

Includes review essay, 'Philology: General Works', by J. R. R. Tolkien, pp. [26]–65.

Wove paper. Bound in grey-brown paper over boards. Stamped on upper cover in black, within a frame of black diamonds: 'THE YEAR'S WORK IN | ENGLISH STUDIES | VOLUME V | 1924 | Edited for | [*black letter:*] The English Association | [*roman:*] BY | F. S. BOAS | and | C. H. HERFORD | [*leaf ornament*] | OXFORD UNIVERSITY PRESS | LONDON : HUMPHREY MILFORD'. Stamped on spine, running up, in black: 'THE YEAR'S WORK IN ENGLISH STUDIES, 1924'. Wove endpapers. No headbands. Top edge trimmed, fore- and bottom edges untrimmed. All edges unstained.

No dust-jacket seen.

Published 4 March 1926 at 7s. 6d. (3s. 6d. to members of the English Association); 1,200 copies printed.

B9   REALITIES   1927

REALITIES | An Anthology of Verse | Edited by. . . . | G. S. TANCRED | Leeds: At the Swan | Press., London: Gay | and Hancock Limited, | W.C.2. MCMXXVII

32 pp. Collation: [a]⁸b⁸. 16.7 × 10.3 cm.

[1] 'REALITIES'; [2] illustration; [3] title; 4–5 table of contents, followed on p. 5 by note; [6] '*To* | MY NEPHEWS AND NIECES'; 7–'15' [i.e. 31] text; [32] publisher's circular 'swan' device.

Includes poem, 'The Nameless Land', by J. R. R. Tolkien, pp. 24–5.

Laid paper. Bound in orange-tan paper over boards. Stamped on upper cover in brown: 'REALITIES | *An Anthology of Verse* | Edited by | G. S. TANCRED'. Laid endpapers. No headbands. All edges trimmed and unstained.

Dust-jacket not seen.

Published in 1927; date of publication, price, and number of copies not known.

Tolkien wrote 'The Nameless Land' in May 1924 at Darnley Road, Leeds, in the metrical form of the medieval poem *Pearl*. It was included in *Realities* by Gwendoline S. Tancred, who edited the anthology for the benefit of the Queen's Hospital for Children, Hackney, E. The poem was reprinted in *The Lost Road and Other Writings* (A25), pp. 98–100, with two revised versions entitled 'The Song of Ælfwine', pp. 100–3.

B10   THE YEAR'S WORK IN ENGLISH STUDIES 1925   1927

THE YEAR'S WORK IN | ENGLISH STUDIES | VOLUME VI | 1925 | Edited for | [*black letter:*] The English Association | [*roman:*] BY | F. S. BOAS | and | C. H.

HERFORD | OXFORD UNIVERSITY PRESS | LONDON : HUMPHREY MILFORD | 1927

356 pp. Collation: [A]–X⁸Y¹⁰. 20.9–22.1 × 14.0–14.3 cm. (height and width vary).

[1] title; [2] 'OXFORD UNIVERSITY PRESS | [*list of 12 cities (publisher's branches), London to Shanghai*] | HUMPHREY MILFORD | *Publisher to the University* | *Printed in England at the* UNIVERSITY PRESS, OXFORD | *By John Johnson Printer to the University*'; [3] preface; [4] list of abbreviations; [5]–6 table of contents; [7]–330 text; [331]–45 index; [346] '*Printed in England at the* UNIVERSITY PRESS, OXFORD | *By John Johnson Printer to the University*'; [347–51] tables of contents of *The Year's Work in English Studies*, Vols. I-V; [352] blank; [353] '[*within a thin-thick-thin rule frame:*] PUBLISHED BY THE | CAMBRIDGE UNIVERSITY PRESS | [*thin-thick-thin rule*] | [*advertisement of 9 titles, beginning with* Wyatt, The Threshold of Anglo-Saxon, *ending with* Mawer *and* Stenton, The Place-names of Bedfordshire and Huntingdonshire] | [*thin-thick-thin rule*] | LONDON FETTER LANE, E.C. 4'; [354] '[*within a single rule frame:*] OXFORD BOOKS | *A FEW OF THE MOST IMPORTANT* 'OXFORD' | *PUBLICATIONS OF* 1926 | [*advertisement of 6 titles, beginning with* Fowler, A Dictionary of Modern English Usage, *ending with* Beresford, ed., The Diary of a Country Parson] | OXFORD UNIVERSITY PRESS'; [355] '[*within a single rule frame:*] OXFORD BOOKS | [*advertisement of 7 titles, beginning with* Wordsworth's 'Prelude', *ending with* Brinton, The Political Ideas of the English Romanticists] | OXFORD UNIVERSITY PRESS'; [356] '[*within a single rule frame:*] From SIDGWICK & JACKSON's List | [*rule*] | [*advertisement of 8 titles, beginning with* Poems of To-day, *ending with* The Review of English Studies] | [*rule*] | SIDGWICK & JACKSON LTD., 44 MUSEUM STREET, W.C. 1 | [*below the frame:*] *Printed in England by John Johnson at the* OXFORD UNIVERSITY PRESS'.

Includes review essay, 'Philology: General Works', by J. R. R. Tolkien, pp. [32]–66.

Wove paper. Bound in grey-brown paper over boards. Stamped on upper cover in black, within a frame of black diamonds: 'THE YEAR'S WORK IN | ENGLISH STUDIES | VOLUME VI | 1925 | Edited for | [*black letter:*] The English Association | [*roman:*] BY | F. S. BOAS | and | C. H. HERFORD | [*leaf ornament*] | OXFORD UNIVERSITY PRESS | LONDON : HUMPHREY MILFORD'. Stamped on spine, running up, in black: 'THE YEAR'S WORK IN ENGLISH STUDIES, 1925'. Wove endpapers. No headbands. Top edge trimmed, fore- and bottom edges untrimmed. All edges unstained.

No dust-jacket seen.

Published 24 February 1927 at 7s. 6d. (3s. 6d. to members of the English Association); 1,250 copies printed.

B11   **A NEW GLOSSARY OF THE DIALECT**   **1928**
           OF THE HUDDERSFIELD DISTRICT

A New Glossary of | THE DIALECT OF THE | HUDDERSFIELD DISTRICT | BY | WALTER E. HAIGH | F.R.HIST.S. | *Author of* '*An Analytical History of England*' | *Twenty-eight years Head of the English & History* | *Department of the Huddersfield Technical College* | *now Emeritus Lecturer in English* | OXFORD UNIVERSITY PRESS | LONDON: HUMPHREY MILFORD | 1928

[2], xxx, 168 pp. Collation: [a]⁴b–d⁴B–Y⁴. 22.2 × 14.0 cm.

[preliminary 1–2] blank; [i] '*A New Glossary of* | THE DIALECT OF THE | HUDDERSFIELD DISTRICT'; [ii] 'OXFORD | UNIVERSITY PRESS | LONDON: AMEN HOUSE, E.C. 4 | [*list of 12 cities (publisher's branches), Edinburgh to Shanghai*] | HUMPHREY MILFORD | PUBLISHER TO THE | UNIVERSITY'; [iii] title; [iv] blank; [v] 'TO THE | *YOUNG PEOPLE* OF THE HUDDERSFIELD DISTRICT | AND THEIR *TEACHERS* | IN WHOSE HANDS JOINTLY RESTS | THE FUTURE OF OUR DIALECT | THIS GLOSSARY | IS RESPECTFULLY DEDICATED | BY THE AUTHOR—| HIMSELF AN OLD TEACHER'; [vi] blank; [vii]–x preface; [xi] table of contents; [xii] blank; [xiii]–xviii foreword; [xix]–xxix introductory chapter; [xxx] blank; 1 list of abbreviations and references; 2 aids to the general reader; 3–156 text; 157–62 appendix; 163–[6] list of subscribers; [167] 'PRINTED IN ENGLAND AT THE | UNIVERSITY PRESS, OXFORD | BY JOHN JOHNSON | PRINTER TO THE UNIVERSITY'; [168] blank. A copy has been seen with 'PRINTED IN ENGLAND.' rubber-stamped on p. [iv].

Includes foreword by J. R. R. Tolkien, pp. [xiii]–xviii.

Wove paper. Bound in wine red cloth over boards. Upper cover (1) with arms stamped on upper cover in gilt, within a single rule frame stamped in blind, or (2) with only a single rule frame in blind on the upper cover, no arms; no priority determined. Stamped on spine in gilt: '[*rule*] | DIALECT | OF THE | HUDDERS-FIELD | DISTRICT | HAIGH | [*publisher's device, an open book and 3 crowns within a cartouche*] | OXFORD | [*rule*]'. Single rule frame stamped on lower cover in blind. Wove endpapers. No headbands. Top and fore-edge trimmed, bottom edge untrimmed. All edges unstained.

Dust-jacket, grey wove paper. Upper cover printed in dark blue, identical to title page except without date. Printed on spine in dark blue: 'DIALECT | OF THE | HUDDERSFIELD | DISTRICT | HAIGH | [*publisher's device, an open book and 3 crowns within a cartouche*] | OXFORD'. Printed on lower cover: '[*within a single rule frame:*] Oxford Books | [*advertisement of 5 titles, beginning with Onions, The Oxford Shakespeare Glossary, ending with Ekwall,* English River-names] | *OXFORD UNIVERSITY PRESS* | [*below the frame:*] Jan. 1928'. Printed on front flap: 'OXFORD | UNIVERSITY PRESS | [*14 addresses, London to Shanghai*] | HUMPHREY MILFORD | AMEN HOUSE | E.C. 4 | [*price? clipped on only copy seen*]'.

Published 12 January 1928 at 12s. 6d.; number of copies not known.

In his foreword Tolkien praises Haigh's work and promotes dialect studies in general. He 'first became acquainted with the manuscript in 1923, when Mr. Haigh had already lavished endless time and care upon it; almost my only contribution since has been to urge him to go on, and to assure him of the value of his work. . . .' Haigh thanks Tolkien, p. x, for his 'ever-ready advice and encouragement'.

B12   ESSAYS AND STUDIES   1929

ESSAYS AND STUDIES | BY MEMBERS OF | THE ENGLISH ASSOCIATION | VOL. XIV | COLLECTED BY | H. W. GARROD | OXFORD | AT THE CLARENDON PRESS | 1929

136 pp. Collation: [A]⁸B–H⁸I⁴. 21.4 × 13.8 cm.

[1] 'ESSAYS AND STUDIES'; [2] 'OXFORD UNIVERSITY PRESS | AMEN HOUSE, E.C. 4 | [*list of 12 cities (publisher's branches), London to Shanghai*] |

HUMPHREY MILFORD | PUBLISHER TO THE | UNIVERSITY'; [3] title; [4] 'THE ENGLISH ASSOCIATION | [*list of officers for 1928*] | Printed in Great Britain'; [5] table of contents; [6] blank; [7]–126 text; [127–33] lists of contents of vols. I–XIII in the series; [134] 'PRINTED IN ENGLAND AT THE | UNIVERSITY PRESS, OXFORD | BY JOHN JOHNSON | PRINTER TO THE UNIVERSITY'; [135–6] blank.

Includes essay, '*Ancrene Wisse* and *Hali Meiðhad*', by J. R. R. Tolkien, pp. [104]-26.

Wove paper. Bound in green cloth over boards. Four concentric single rule frames stamped on both upper and lower covers in blind. Stamped on spine in gilt: '[*2 rules*] | ESSAYS | AND | STUDIES | VOL. XIV | [*publisher's device, an open book and 3 crowns on a shield*] | OXFORD | [*2 rules*]'. Wove endpapers. No headbands. All edges trimmed and unstained.

Dust-jacket, blue-grey wove paper. Printed on upper cover in dark blue: 'ESSAYS AND STUDIES | BY MEMBERS OF | THE ENGLISH ASSOCIATION | VOL. XIV | COLLECTED BY | H. W. GARROD | [*rule*] | [*list of contents*] | [*rule*] | OXFORD | AT THE CLARENDON PRESS'. Printed on spine in dark blue: 'ESSAYS | AND | STUDIES | VOL. XIV | [*publisher's device, an open book and 3 crowns on a shield*] | OXFORD'. Printed on lower cover in dark blue, within a dark blue frame of ornaments: 'The Year's Work | in English Studies | EDITED FOR | The English Association | BY | SIR SIDNEY LEE, F. S. BOAS | AND C. H. HERFORD | [*line of ornaments*] | Now ready | [*list of 8 vols. in the series, 1919–20 through 1927*] | [*line of ornaments*] | OXFORD UNIVERSITY PRESS'. Printed on front flap in dark blue: 'OXFORD | UNIVERSITY PRESS | [*13 addresses, London to Shanghai*] | HUMPHREY MILFORD | AMEN HOUSE | E.C. 4 | [*diagonal dotted rule*] | Price 7s. 6d. net'.

Published 17 January 1929 at 7s. 6d.; number of copies not known.

The *Ancrene Wisse* (or *Ancrene Riwle*, MS Corpus Christi College Cambridge 402), an early Middle English guide for anchoresses, and the thirteenth-century homily *Hali Meiðhad* (a part, with *Sawles Warde* and others, of the 'Katherine Group', MS Bodley 34) attracted Tolkien's study throughout his career. Cf. B23, B25, C14, C34, C35, Dii52. T. A. Shippey has called '*Ancrene Wisse* and *Hali Meiðhad*' the 'most perfect' of Tolkien's academic writings: see further, *The Road to Middle-earth* (Dii54), pp. 31–3. Tolkien's June 1925 application for the Rawlinson and Bosworth Professorship of Anglo-Saxon at Oxford (Dii1) lists his essay forthcoming in *Essays and Studies* as 'The Second Weak Conjugation in the Ancren Riwle and the Katherine-Group'.

    B12 was reprinted by Wm. Dawson & Sons, London, in 1966.

B13   **REPORT ON THE EXCAVATION OF THE**   **1932**
             PREHISTORIC, ROMAN, AND POST-ROMAN
             SITE IN LYDNEY PARK, GLOUCESTERSHIRE

Reports of the Research Committee | of the | Society of Antiquaries of London | [*rule*] | No. IX | [*rule*] | Report on the | Excavation of the Prehistoric, | Roman, and Post-Roman Site in | Lydney Park, Gloucestershire | By R. E. M. Wheeler, D.Lit., F.S.A., | and T. V. Wheeler, F.S.A. | [*seal of the Society*] | Oxford | Printed at the University Press by John Johnson for | The Society of Antiquaries | Burlington House, London | 1932 viii, 140 pp. + 42 plates. Collation: [A]⁴B–I⁸K⁶. 25.6–26.1 × 17.1–17.5 cm. (height and width vary).

[i-ii] blank; [iii] title; [iv] 'PRINTED IN GREAT BRITAIN'; [v] roster of Research Committee, Society of Antiquaries; [vi] blank; [vii]–viii table of contents; [1]–131 text; 132–7 appendices; [138] blank; [139] 'PLATES'; [140] blank. Colour illustration on plate inserted facing p. [iii]. Black and white illustrations on 13 plates inserted between pp. 22–3, 26–7, 48–9, 68–9, 74–5, 76–7, 78–9, 82–3, 84–5, 86–7, 92–3, 94–5, and 100–1, and on 28 plates (4 folded) following p. [140].

Includes essay, 'Appendix I: The Name "Nodens"', by J. R. R. Tolkien, pp. 132–7.

Wove paper. Bound in blue-grey wove wrappers with yapp edges. Title page text printed on upper cover, followed by: 'Price Seven Shillings and Sixpence'. Printed on spine, running up: 'REPORT ON EXCAVATIONS IN LYDNEY PARK, GLOUCESTERSHIRE'. All edges untrimmed and unstained.

Published July 1932 at 7s. 6d.; 1,150 copies printed.

The name *Nodens* was found in three inscriptions at the Lydney Park site.

B14   TRANSACTIONS OF THE PHILOLOGICAL SOCIETY   1934

TRANSACTIONS | OF THE | PHILOLOGICAL SOCIETY. | 1934. | PUBLISHED FOR THE SOCIETY BY | DAVID NUTT (A. G. BERRY), LONDON. | 1934.

iv, 108, viii pp. Collation: [A]²B–G⁸H⁶[I]⁴. 21.4 × 13.9 cm.

[i] title; [ii] 'HERTFORD: | PRINTED BY | STEPHEN AUSTIN AND SONS, LTD.'; [iii] table of contents; [iv] blank; [1]–103 text; [104–5] Philological Society balance sheets for 1933; [106–8] blank; [i]–viii list of members of the Philological Society, corrected to June 1934.

Includes essay, 'Chaucer as a Philologist: *The Reeve's Tale*', by J. R. R. Tolkien, pp. [1]–70.

Wove paper. Bound in light green wove double wrappers (viii pp.): [i] 'TRANS-ACTIONS | OF THE | PHILOLOGICAL SOCIETY. | 1934. | PUBLISHED FOR THE SOCIETY BY | DAVID NUTT (A. G. BERRY), LONDON. | 1934.'; [ii] notice to members of the Society regarding publications; [iii] 'PHILOLOGICAL SOCIETY. | [*rule*] | COUNCIL, 1934–35. | [*list of officers, members, bankers*] | [*notes on members' fees*] | [*notes on the* Transactions *and other Society publications*]'; iv 'PHILOLOGICAL SOCIETY. | [*rule*] | [*notes on the Society*] | [*rule*] | [*note on applications for admission to the Society*] | [*rule*] | LONDON: DAVID NUTT (A. G. BERRY).'; [v] 'PROCEEDINGS AND PUBLICATIONS | OF THE | PHILO-LOGICAL SOCIETY. | [*rule*] | [*list of publications*] | [*rule*] | LONDON: DAVID NUTT (A. G. BERRY).'; vi '[*list of publications continued*] | LONDON: DAVID NUTT (A. G. BERRY).'; vii '[*list of publications continued*] | LONDON: DAVID NUTT (A. G. BERRY).'; [viii] blank. Printed on spine, running up: 'THE PHILO-LOGICAL SOCIETY'S TRANSACTIONS, 1934.' All edges trimmed and unstained.

Published in the second half of 1934; date of publication, price, and number of copies not known.

Tolkien read his paper, originally entitled 'Chaucer's Use of Dialects', on 16 May 1931 at a meeting of the Philological Society in Oxford. He remarked in a note to the version printed three years later that the delay in publication was 'principally due to hesitation in putting forward a study, for which closer investigation of words, and more still a much fuller array of readings from MSS. of the *Reeve's Tale*, were so plainly needed. But for neither have I had opportunity, and dust has merely accumulated on the pages. The paper is therefore presented . . . practically as it was read, though with the addition of a "critical text", and accompanying textual notes, as well as of various footnotes, appendices, and comments naturally omitted in reading'.

Tolkien made briefer comments on Chaucer's use of dialect in the preface to his reduction of 'The Reeve's Tale' (B16).

Manuscript materials and correspondence by Tolkien on Chaucer studies are in the Bodleian Library, Oxford.

An offprint of Tolkien's essay was issued by the Philological Society.

B15   SONGS FOR THE PHILOLOGISTS   1936

SONGS FOR THE | PHILOLOGISTS | By J. R. R. TOLKIEN, E. V. GORDON & others | Mál-Rúnar skaltu kunna. | PRIVATELY PRINTED IN THE DEPART- MENT OF | ENGLISH AT UNIVERSITY COLLEGE, LONDON | MCMXXXVI

iv, 32 pp. Collation: [1^{18}]. 21.0 × 16.3 cm.

[i] title; [ii] blank; iii–iv table of contents; at foot of p. iv: '[*double rule*] | Printed by G. TILLOTSON, A. H. SMITH, B. PATTISON and other | members of the English Department, University College, London | [*double rule*]'; 1–30 text; [31] blank; [32] device of the Department of English, University College, London.

Includes thirteen poems by J. R. R. Tolkien, as described below.

Laid paper. Bound in grey-blue wrappers, stapled through the fold. Printed on upper cover: 'SONGS FOR THE | PHILOLOGISTS | By J. R. R. TOLKIEN, E. V. GORDON & others | Mál-Rúnar skaltu kunna. | PRIVATELY PRINTED IN THE DEPARTMENT OF | ENGLISH AT UNIVERSITY COLLEGE, LONDON | MCMXXXVI'. Device of the Department of English, University College, London, printed on lower cover. Bottom edge trimmed, top and fore-edges untrimmed. All edges unstained.

Songs for the Philologists began as duplicated typescripts prepared by E. V. Gordon in 1921–6 for the amusement of English Department students at Leeds University. Gordon included verses written by himself and by J. R. R. Tolkien, as well as modern and traditional songs, chiefly in Old and Modern English, Gothic, Icelandic, and Latin. In 1935 or 1936 Dr. A. H. Smith of University College, London, formerly a student at Leeds, gave an uncorrected copy of one of the typescripts to a group of students to print at their private press as an exercise. According to H. Winifred Husbands of University College, in a letter to Tolkien of November 1940, Dr. Smith realized that he had not asked permission of Gordon or Tolkien to print their verses, and therefore did not distribute the completed booklets but retained them at the press in its rooms on Gower Street. Most of the copies were burned in a fire that destroyed part of the building in which the press was housed. However, some copies evidently had been distributed, presumably at least to the students who printed them. Husbands knew of more than thirteen surviving copies; the total number of copies printed is not known, but undoubtedly was very small. Two copies came into Tolkien's possession in 1940–1, which he annotated with corrections and changes, *circa* 19 August 1966 (according to a letter of that date from Tolkien to A. E. Skinner of the University of Texas).

The collection consists of thirty songs ('Salve', p. 23, was omitted from the table of contents). Not all of the 'Leeds Songs' were set (omitting, *inter alia*, Tolkien's 'Smakkabagms'), one new song was added, and some of the Leeds material was altered. Tolkien's 'contributions' are identified in his papers:

p. 6, 'From One to Five', revised from the Leeds version to suit University College, London, conditions, sung to the tune 'Three Wise Men of Gotham'

p. 7, 'Syx Mynet', an Old English rendering, and sung to the tune of, 'I Love Sixpence'

pp. 8–9, 'Ruddoc Hana', sung to 'Who Killed Cock Robin?'

pp. 10–11, 'Ides Ælfscýne', sung to 'Daddy Neptune'

p. 12, 'Bagmē Blomā', sung to 'O Lazy Sheep!'

p. 13, 'Éadig Béo þu!' sung to 'Twinkle, Twinkle, Little Star'

pp. 14–15, 'Ofer Wídne Gársecg', sung to 'The Mermaid'

p. 16, 'La Húru', sung to 'O'Reilly'

p. 17, 'I Sat upon a Bench', sung to 'The Carrion Crow'

p. 18, 'Natura Apis: Morali Ricardi Eremite', the concluding verse omitted, also sung to 'O'Reilly'

pp. 20–1, 'The Root of the Boot', an early version of 'The Stone Troll', sung to 'The Fox Went Out'

pp. 24–5, 'Frenchmen Froth', sung to 'The Vicar of Bray'

p. 27, 'Lit' and Lang'', listed in the table of contents as 'Two Little Schemes', also revised to omit Leeds allusions (in such a way, Tolkien noted, as to break the rhyme), sung to 'Polly Put the Kettle On'

'The Root of the Boot', commonly known as 'The Troll Song', was originally entitled 'Pero & Podex' ('Boot and Bottom'). Verse 6 of the original manuscript was published in *The Return of the Shadow* (A26), p. 144. Also printed in that work, p. 143, is a version of the song, incorporating or noting corrections by Tolkien, which differs from that published in *Songs* in a few respects:

l. 10: [*Songs*] of > [*Shadow*] o'
l. 11: lying in the churchyard > a-lyin' in churchyard
l. 23: that is > is that
l. 24: With > wi'

Noted but not incorporated in the *Shadow* version is a change suggested by Tolkien, l. 15: [*Songs*] 'In heaven on high hath an aureole' > [*Shadow*] 'Hath a halo in heaven upon its poll'. The work was revised for *The Lord of the Rings* (A5), first as Bingo's (i.e. Frodo's) song in The Prancing Pony (bk. 1, ch. 9), later as Sam's song (bk. 1, ch. 12), and in that form was still later published as 'The Stone Troll' in *The Adventures of Tom Bombadil* (A6). Three versions of the song under revision for *LR* are discussed, and the first printed, in *The Treason of Isengard* (A27), pp. 59–61, 66. The second of these versions was recorded by Tolkien in 1952 and later included in *J. R. R. Tolkien Reads and Sings His* The Hobbit *and* The Fellowship of the Ring (see section Fi). The *Songs* version was reprinted on pp. 68–9 of George Burke Johnston, 'The Poetry of J. R. R. Tolkien', in *The Tolkien Papers* (*Mankato Studies in English*, no. 2 [vol. 2, no. 1], Mankato, Minn.: Mankato State College, 1967), with comments on the revision for *LR*; and in *The Annotated Hobbit* (A3dd–ee), p. 45.

Corrected and revised versions of 'Bagmē Blomā' ('Flower of the Trees'), 'Éadig Béo þu' ('Good Luck to You'), 'Ides Ælfscýne' ('Elf-fair Lady'), and 'Ofer Wídne Gársecg' ('Across the Broad Ocean') were published, with Modern English translations, by T. A. Shippey in his *Road to Middle-earth* (Dii54), pp. [227]–33.

[*black letter:*] The Reeve's Tale | version prepared for recitation | at the 'summer diversions' | Oxford : 1939 | J. R. R. T.

16 pp. Collation: [1⁸]. 22.4 × 14.2–14.3 cm. (width varies).

[1] title; [2] blank; [3–4] introduction, signed on p. [4] 'J. R. R. T.'; 5–14 text; [15–16] blank.

Laid paper, watermarked 'Abbey Mills'. Bound in self wrappers, stapled through fold. All edges untrimmed and unstained.

Published in summer? 1939; price (if any) and number of copies not known.

In 1938 and 1939 Tolkien played the role of Geoffrey Chaucer in the 'Summer Diversions' arranged in Oxford by Nevill Coghill and John Masefield. On the first occasion, he recited 'The Nun's Priest's Tale', and on the second, 'The Reeve's Tale'. His version of the latter was devised in Oxford from *circa* 14 July 1939, when he described his intentions in a letter to Masefield, to *circa* 27–9 July (see *The Return of the Shadow*, A26, pp. 382–3). The text is slightly abbreviated and departs materially from Skeat's edition 'only in the words of the clerks', which are presented 'in a more marked and consistently northern form—in nearly every case with some manuscript authority' (p. [4]).

    The Bodleian Library copy is numbered by Tolkien in pencil to line 180, and with extensive manuscript notes by him in pen. Two copies in private hands have lines 126–69 numbered in pencil, possibly by Tolkien.

a. 'New edition':

BEOWULF | AND | THE FINNESBURG FRAGMENT | *A Translation into Modern* | *English Prose* | *By* | JOHN R. CLARK HALL, M.A., PH.D. | NEW EDITION | completely revised, with notes and | an Introduction by | C. L. WRENN, M.A. | *Professor of English Language and Literature in the* | University of London | with Prefatory Remarks by | J. R. R. TOLKIEN | *Rawlinson and Bosworth Professor of* | *Old English* | *at the University of Oxford* | London | GEORGE ALLEN & UNWIN LTD

xlii, 11–192 pp. Collation: [A]⁸B–O⁸. 18.5 × 12.4 cm.

[i] 'BEOWULF | AND | THE FINNESBURG FRAGMENT'; [ii] blank; [iii] title; [iv] 'FIRST PUBLISHED IN 1911 | COMPLETELY REVISED 1940 | *All rights reserved* | PRINTED IN GREAT BRITAIN | *in 12-Point Old Face Type* | BY UNWIN BROTHERS LIMITED | WOKING'; [v] table of contents; [vi] blank; [vii]–xli prefatory remarks; [xlii] blank; [11]–17 introduction; [18] blank; [19]–180 text; [181]–7 notes; [188] '[*publisher's square "St. George" device with lettered border*] | GEORGE ALLEN & UNWIN LTD | [*6 addresses, London to Sydney*]'; [189–92] blank ([191–2] pasted down).

Includes 'Prefatory Remarks on Prose Translation of "Beowulf"' by J. R. R. Tolkien, pp. [viii]–xli, in two parts: 'I: On Translation and Words' and 'II: On Metre'.

Wove paper. Bound in orange cloth over boards. Stamped on spine in black: 'BEOWULF | AND THE | FINNSBURG | FRAGMENT | [*swelled rule*] |

A Translation into | *Modern English* | *Prose* | *by* | JOHN R. CLARK | HALL | GEORGE ALLEN | & UNWIN LTD'. Wove front endpapers. No headbands. All edges trimmed. Top edge stained orange or unstained (no priority determined), fore- and bottom edges unstained.

Dust-jacket, orange wove paper. Printed on upper cover: '[*swelled rule*] | BEOWULF | AND THE FINNSBURG FRAGMENT | [*swelled rule*] | *New Edition* | *Completely Revised with* | *Notes and an* | *Introduction* | *by* | C. L. Wrenn | *and* | *a Preface by* | *J. R. R. Tolkien* | [*swelled rule*] | A TRANSLATION INTO MODERN | ENGLISH PROSE BY | JOHN R. CLARK HALL | M.A., PH.D.' Printed on spine: '[*swelled rule*] | BEOWULF | AND THE | FINNSBURG | FRAGMENT | [*swelled rule*] | *A Translation* | *into* | *Modern* | *English* | *Prose* | *by* | JOHN R. CLARK | HALL | [*publisher's square "St. George" device*] | GEORGE ALLEN | AND UNWIN | [*swelled rule*]'. Advertisement of Ford, *The March of Literature*, and Trilling, *Matthew Arnold*, printed on lower cover. Front flap unprinted or with price at foot; only copy seen was clipped. Printed on back flap: '*Printed in Great Britain.*'

Published 16 July 1940 at 7s. 6d.; 1,250 copies printed, approximately 1,000 bound between 1940 and 1950. 162 copies were destroyed in the binder's warehouse during the bombing of London on 7 November 1940.

Tolkien was invited, probably in early or mid-1936, to revise John R. Clark Hall's Modern English translation of *Beowulf* and the medieval 'Finnesburg Fragment', previously published in 1911. Foreseeing that he would not have time to make the revision, he declined, though he agreed to write a brief introductory note for the book. The job of revision was given instead to Elaine Griffiths, a young Oxford graduate who had been Tolkien's pupil (cf. A3a note). On 13 August 1937 Tolkien wrote from Devon, where he was on holiday, to Stanley Unwin: 'I only had time to glance at Miss Griffiths' *Beowulf* before coming away. It seemed good. But I will correct or help in correcting it, and write my small bit as soon as I get back on Saturday night week.' On 17 September 1937 he wrote to C. A. Furth at Allen & Unwin: 'I have gone through a good deal of it [*Beowulf*]. I cannot pass it, of course, without seeing Miss Griffiths. I must confess to not having written my own pages yet.' In addition to his Oxford duties, Tolkien was involved with *The Hobbit* and the beginning of *The Lord of the Rings*; and there were other difficulties, as he remarked in a letter to Stanley Unwin on 4 June 1938: 'I would quickly write my brief intro- ductory note, if I saw the book complete. It would be brief for I do not wish to anticipate the things I should say in a preface to a new [Modern English] translation [by himself, which Allen & Unwin wanted to publish].' Griffiths had not been able to complete work on the book, and by the end of June 1938 asked to be released from her contract. Though she had, Tolkien believed, the talent and scholarship for the job, she did not have the time to carry it through.

By now Tolkien felt even less desire to edit ('a dull and troublesome job') Clark Hall's translation, of which he now wrote disparagingly to Stanley Unwin; but he felt an obligation to the publisher. On 24 July 1938, in a letter to C. A. Furth, he suggested that he himself 'put the thing into such order as is now possible, for such remuneration as seems good to you, with a title to be devised. I should prefer on the whole not to be mentioned, or to put too much new stuff into it, to the prejudice of my own "translation". My concern would be primarily to put *the text* into reasonable working order, as far as can be contrived without too great or too costly cutting up of the version now in type.' His offer was accepted on 4 August; but on 13 October he wrote to Stanley Unwin: 'I now find myself rapidly getting into the same predicament as Miss Griffiths. . . . For various reasons—other commitments, my own health, and the emergency work that has fallen on me in straightening out the affairs and academic obligations of my friend and colleague Eric [E. V.] Gordon of Manchester (who died in July)—I have not been able to touch *Beowulf*.' He recommended that he relinquish the revision to C. L. Wrenn, then Oxford University Lecturer in English philology, 'a first-class Anglo-Saxon scholar' who moreover was ready to adhere to a latest date of completion. Unwin at once agreed to this course and asked Tolkien to hand on to Wrenn the two sets of corrected proofs in his possession.

The revision was complete for press by October 1939, lacking only Tolkien's note. In a letter of 19 December 1939 to Stanley Unwin, having received several inquiries from Allen & Unwin, Tolkien apologized: 'I will try and collect my weary wits and pen a sufficient foreword to the "Beowulf" translation, *at once*.' But anxiety over his own and his wife's ill health, the war, and academic duties made writing very difficult. In early 1940 he was again pressed for a note: 'a word or two' would be enough, he was told. He responded on 30 March 1940 to Stanley Unwin: 'I knew that a "word or two" would suffice (though could not feel that any words under my name would have any particular value unless they said something worth saying—which takes space). But I believed that more was hoped for.' At this stage, the preliminary matter of the book consisted of only ten lines concerning the manuscript of *Beowulf*, and an argument or summary of its story—considerably less than Clark Hall had included in the previous edition. That being so, wrote Tolkien, 'I laboured long and hard to compress (and yet enliven) such remarks on *translation* as might both be useful to students and of interest to those using the book without reference to the original text. But the result ran to 17 of my mss. pages (of some 300 words each)—not counting the metrical appendix, the most original part, which is as long again!'

At last Tolkien realized that he had written more than was expected of him. But he had delayed so long already that he sent all that he had done to Stanley Unwin, suggesting that he 'might care to consider it (submitting it to Wrenn) for inclusion later, e.g. if a further edition is required. (Retouched it might make a suitable small booklet for students. . . .)' Or, he suggested 'with grief, reluctance, and penitence', either some 1,400 words of the manuscript marked in red or 750–800 marked in blue might serve. Stanley Unwin replied with sympathy on 2 April, and decided to use Tolkien's manuscript in full though it would increase the length of the book (and evidently upset the pagination scheme prior to p. [11]).

Proofs of the foreword were sent to Tolkien on 19 April 1940. He returned them corrected on 24 April, noting in a letter to Stanley Unwin 'a fair number of errors, especially with Anglo-Saxon words.' In a postscript to his letter of 30 March he had already remarked on errors in proofs of the main body of the book. 'I hope,' he wrote on 24 April, 'that all the difficulties into which first Miss Griffiths and then I myself have led this book will now be solved, and that it will go reasonably well—as well as anything reasonable can go in this lunatic era.'

At Tolkien's suggestion, the spelling of 'Finnsburg', used in earlier editions of the book, was changed to 'Finnesburg'.

Tolkien's prefatory remarks were reprinted as 'On Translating Beowulf' in *The Monsters and the Critics and Other Essays* (A19). The essay includes extracts from his Modern English verse translation of *Beowulf*, still unpublished in its entirety.

Drafts of lectures by Tolkien on translating *Beowulf*, and manuscript and typescript drafts of his unpublished alliterative and prose translations of *Beowulf*, are in the Bodleian Library, Oxford.

b. 'New edition', revised (1950):

BEOWULF | AND THE FINNESBURG | FRAGMENT | A TRANSLATION INTO | MODERN ENGLISH PROSE | BY | JOHN R. CLARK HALL | M.A., PH.D. |

NEW EDITION | COMPLETELY REVISED WITH NOTES | AND AN INTRO-
DUCTION BY | C. L. WRENN | M.A. | *Rawlinson and Bosworth Professor of
Anglo-Saxon* | *at the University of Oxford* | WITH PREFATORY REMARKS BY |
J. R. R. TOLKIEN | *Merton Professor of English Language and* | *Literature, Oxford*
| [*publisher's open 'St. George' device*] | GEORGE ALLEN & UNWIN LTD |
RUSKIN HOUSE MUSEUM STREET LONDON

xliv, 196 pp. Collation: [A]^{8}B–P^8. 18.3 × 12.0 cm.

[i] 'BEOWULF | AND THE FINNESBURG FRAGMENT'; [ii] blank; [iii] title; [iv]
'FIRST PUBLISHED IN 1911 | COMPLETELY REVISED 1940 | AND IN 1950 |
This book is copyright under the Berne | *Convention. No portion may be
reproduced* | *by any process without written permission.* | *Inquiries should be
addressed to the publishers* | PRINTED IN GREAT BRITAIN | BY BRADFORD &
DICKENS | LONDON, W.C. 1'; v–vi foreword; [vii] table of contents; [viii] blank;
ix–xliii prefatory remarks; [xliv] blank; 1–19 introduction; 20–181 text; 182–94
notes; [195] blank; [196] '[*publisher's open "St. George" device*] | GEORGE
ALLEN & UNWIN LTD | [*6 addresses, London to Sydney*]'.

Includes 'Prefatory Remarks on Prose Translation of "Beowulf"', by J. R. R.
Tolkien, pp. ix–xliii.

Wove paper. Bound in light orange cloth over boards. Stamped on upper cover in
black: 'BEOWULF'. Stamped on spine in black: 'BEOWULF | AND THE |
FINNESBURG | FRAGMENT | [*rule*] | JOHN R. | CLARK | HALL | [*rule*] | ALLEN
| AND | UNWIN'. Wove endpapers. No headbands. All edges trimmed and
unstained.

Dust-jacket, grey wove paper. Printed on upper cover: '[*band of dotted square
ornaments in red-brown and grey, wraps around spine*] | [*in red-brown:*] BEOWULF
| *AND THE FINNESBURG* | *FRAGMENT* | Translated into Modern English Prose
by | JOHN R. CLARK HALL | [*2 bands of dotted square ornaments in red-brown
and grey, wrap around spine*] | [*in red-brown:*] A New Edition Completely Revised
with | Notes and an Introduction by | C. L. WRENN | With Prefatory Remarks by |
J. R. R. TOLKIEN | [*band of dotted square ornaments in red-brown and grey,
wraps around spine*]'. Printed on spine: '[*band of dotted square ornaments in red-
brown and grey*] | [*in red-brown:*] BEOWULF | AND THE | FINNESBURG |
FRAGMENT | *Translation* | *into* | *Modern* | *English* | *Prose* | *by* | JOHN R. |
CLARK | HALL | [*2 bands of dotted square ornaments in red-brown and grey*] | [*in
red-brown:*] [*publisher's open "St. George" device*] | ALLEN AND | UNWIN'.
Printed on lower cover in red-brown: '[*advertisement of* The Birds of Aristophanes
and Thomson, The Classical Background of English Literature] | *books that matter* |
[Unwin Brothers "UB" device]'. Printed on front flap in red-brown: '[*blurb*] | 10s.
6d. net'. Printed on back flap in red-brown: 'THE NATIONAL | BOOK LEAGUE |
President: | *John Masefield, O.M.* | [*notice about the League*] | [*League "NBL"
device*] | *Printed in Great Britain*'.

Published 2 March 1950 at 10s. 6d. (increased to 12s. 6d. on 4 October 1951,
during the life of the first impression); 2,500 copies printed. About 1,000 copies
bound before publication, the remaining copies in April 1950 and August–
September 1951.

Reset. 'The scholarship has been again revised in the light of recent scholarship, and
the opportunity has been taken to correct misprints. An entirely new Introduction
has been provided.... The Notes have been greatly enlarged.... Professor Tolkien's
Prefatory Remarks ... are here reproduced unchanged save for the correction of an

occasional misprint: for they must remain as the most permanently valuable part of the book' (pp. v–vi).

According to library catalogues, B17b was distributed in the United States by Barnes & Noble, New York, probably beginning in 1950 or 1951. A copy of the fifth impression has been seen with the Barnes & Noble imprint on a label affixed to the title page over the Allen & Unwin imprint. *Cumulative Book Index* notes, probably in error, that this work was published in the United States by Macmillan, 1950, at $2.00. No copy of the book with a Macmillan imprint has been seen.

c. Revised edition, ninth (first paperback?) impression (1980):

BEOWULF | AND THE FINNESBURG | FRAGMENT | A TRANSLATION INTO | MODERN ENGLISH PROSE | BY | JOHN R. CLARK HALL | M.A., PH.D. | *NEW EDITION* | COMPLETELY REVISED WITH NOTES | AND AN INTRO-DUCTION BY | C. L. WRENN | M.A. | *Rawlinson and Bosworth Professor of Anglo-Saxon* | *at the University of Oxford* | WITH PREFATORY REMARKS BY | J. R. R. TOLKIEN | *Merton Professor of English Language and* | *Literature, Oxford* | London | GEORGE ALLEN & UNWIN | Boston Sydney

xliv, 196 pp. Collation: 120 leaves. 18.5 × 12.0 cm.

Contents as for B17b, except pp. [iii] title, as above; [iv] 'First Published in 1911 | Revised Edition 1940 | Revised Edition 1950 | Ninth impression 1980 | [*notice of restrictions under copyright*] | GEORGE ALLEN & UNWIN LTD | 40 Museum Street, London WC1A 1LU | ISBN 0 04 829002 5 | Printed in Great Britain by | Lowe & Brydone Printers Ltd, | Thetford, Norfolk'; and [196] blank.

Wove paper. Bound in heavy wove wrappers. Covers and spine printed against a red-brown background. Printed on upper cover: '[*in pale red-brown:*] BEOWULF | AND | THE FINNESBURG FRAGMENT | With prefatory remarks by | [*in white:*] J. R. R. Tolkien | [*in pale red-brown:*] Translated into modern English prose by | [*in white:*] John R. Clark Hall | [*in pale red-brown:*] A new edition completely revised with notes and | an introduction by | [*in white:*] C. L. Wrenn'. Printed on spine, running down: '[*in pale red-brown:*] BEOWULF [*parallel to the preceding word:*] AND THE FINNESBURG FRAGMENT [*followed by, in white:*] Translated into modern English prose by [*parallel to the preceding phrase:*] John R. Clark Hall [*followed by:*] GEORGE ALLEN [*parallel to the preceding two words:*] & UNWIN'. Printed on lower cover in white: '[*blurb*] | ISBN 0 04 829002 5'. All edges trimmed and unstained.

Published 1980; date of publication, price, and number of copies not known.

Typeset as for B17b, except pp. [iii–iv].

| B18 | SIR ORFEO | 1944 |

SIR ORFEO | [*typed underline*]

ii, 18 pp. Collation: [1^{10}]. 21.1 × 13.4 cm.

[i] title; [ii] title; [1]-18 text; at foot of p. 18: '[*typed underline*] | The Academic Copying Office, Oxford; 1944.'

Wove paper, watermarked 'Croxley Hard Sized Duplicator'. Bound in tan wrappers, stapled through fold. Printed on upper cover: 'SIR ORFEO | [*typed underline*]'. All edges untrimmed and unstained.

Published in 1944; date of publication, price (if any), and number of copies not known. Five copies have been located.

In Middle English. Reproduced from typescript.

A note inside the Bodleian Library copy indicates that the booklet was reproduced by the University (by mimeograph) before the text, set for English Schools, was formally printed from type. However, the booklet seems to have been the only printing of this text. Another copy, in the English Faculty library at Oxford, contains a note, reported to be in Tolkien's hand, which states that this edition of 'Sir Orfeo' was prepared for the naval cadets' course in English, which Tolkien organized in January 1943 and directed until the end of March 1944.

The Bodleian Library copy is numbered by Tolkien in pencil, by tens, to line 340. Two copies in private hands are each numbered in pencil, probably by Tolkien, by tens to line 600, and contain two manuscript emendations: 'and wolde vp and [wende] owy' (word added), p. 3, l. 96, and 'nemoned' > 'nempned', p. 16, l. 600.

A translation of the poem into Modern English by Tolkien was published in 1975; see B30.

B19   ESSAYS PRESENTED TO CHARLES WILLIAMS   1947

a. First edition:

Essays presented to | CHARLES | WILLIAMS | [*decorative rule*] | *Contributors* | DOROTHY SAYERS | J. R. R. TOLKIEN | C. S. LEWIS | A. O. BARFIELD | GERVASE MATHEW | W. H. LEWIS | [*decorative rule*] | GEOFFREY CUMBERLEGE | OXFORD UNIVERSITY PRESS | *London New York Toronto* | 1947

xvi, 148 p. + 1 plate. Collation: [A]⁸B–I⁸K¹⁰, K2 signed. 21.5 × 13.9 cm.

[i] '*Essays presented to* | CHARLES WILLIAMS'; [ii] blank; [iii] title; [iv] '*Oxford University Press, Amen House, London, E.C. 4* | [*list of 10 cities (publisher's branches), Edinburgh to Cape Town*] | *Geoffrey Cumberlege, Publisher to the University* | PRINTED IN GREAT BRITAIN'; [v]–xiv preface; [xv] table of contents; [xvi] blank; [1]–145 text; [146] 'PRINTED IN | GREAT BRITAIN | AT THE | UNIVERSITY PRESS | OXFORD | BY | CHARLES BATEY | PRINTER | TO THE | UNIVERSITY'; [147–8] blank. Photograph of Charles Williams by Elliot & Fry, on plate facing p. [iii].

Includes essay, 'On Fairy-Stories', by J. R. R. Tolkien, pp. [38]–89.

Wove paper. Bound in dark blue cloth over boards. Stamped on spine in gilt: '[*ornaments*] | [*rule*] | ESSAYS | *presented* | *to* | Charles | Williams | [*rule*] | [*ornaments*] | OXFORD'. Wove endpapers. No headbands. All edges trimmed and unstained.

Dust-jacket, wove brownish-white paper. Printed on upper cover within a blue single rule frame, within a blue frame of ornaments: '*Essays presented to* | CHARLES | WILLIAMS | [*rule, in blue*] | [*in black:*] *With a Memoir by* C. S. Lewis | [*rule, in blue*] | [*in black:*] [*note on Charles Williams*] | *Oxford University Press*'. Printed on spine: '[*in blue:*] [*ornaments*] | [*rule*] | [*in black:*] ESSAYS | *presented* | *to* | Charles | Williams | [*in blue:*] [*rule*] | [*ornaments*] | [*in black:*] OXFORD'. Printed on lower cover: '[*in blue:*] *Some Oxford Books* | [*rule*] | [*in black:*] [*advertisement of 4 titles, beginning with* Williams, Seed of Adam and Other Plays, *ending with* Essays on the Eighteenth Century] | (ALL PRICES ARE SUBJECT TO ALTERATION

WITHOUT NOTICE) | [*rule, in blue*] | [*in black:*] OXFORD UNIVERSITY PRESS'. Printed on front flap: '[*blurb*] | *Price* | 12s. 6d. net'.

Published December 1947 at 12s. 6d.; number of copies not known. W. H. Lewis's diary entry for 11 November 1947 (*Brothers and Friends: The Diaries of Major Warren Hamilton Lewis*, ed. Clyde S. Kilby and Marjorie Lamp Mead [San Francisco: Harper & Row, 1982], p. 214) notes that the 'Charles Williams essays' are 'out at last'; however, Lewis may have been referring to an advance copy.

In 1938 Tolkien promised a lecture on fairy-stories to an undergraduate society at Worcester College, Oxford; but he did not prepare his lecture in time, and read his story 'Farmer Giles of Ham' instead. He returned to the subject of fairy-stories in his Andrew Lang Lecture at the University of St. Andrews on 8 March 1939 (not 1940 as stated in B19, p. [38], or 1938 as stated in *Tree and Leaf* [A7]). He expanded his lecture for publication in *Essays Presented to Charles Williams*, a volume originally intended as a *Festschrift* but which became a memorial after Williams' death in 1945. 'On Fairy-Stories' was finished, or nearly finished, by 21 July 1946, when Tolkien referred to it in a letter to Stanley Unwin. He corrected proofs *circa* 11 December 1946; most of his alterations were in the section 'Fantasy'. The essay was further revised for publication in *Tree and Leaf*.

Two sentences deleted by Tolkien from the manuscript of *OFS* were published by Christina Scull on p. 9 of a review (pp. 9–12) in *Amon Hen* (bulletin of The Tolkien Society), no. 113 (January 1992).

Pertinent manuscript and typescript materials, and corrected proofs, are in the Bodleian Library, Oxford; see further, A7a.

b. First American edition (1966):

Essays presented to | CHARLES | WILLIAMS | [*decorative rule*] | *Contributors* | DOROTHY SAYERS | J. R. R. TOLKIEN | C. S. LEWIS | A. O. BARFIELD | GERVASE MATHEW | W. H. LEWIS | [*decorative rule*] | WILLIAM B. EERDMANS PUBLISHING COMPANY | *Grand Rapids, Michigan*

xvi, 148 pp. Collation: [1–3^{16}4^{18}5^{16}]. 21.4 × 13.8 cm.

Contents as for B19a, except pp. [iii] title, as above; [iv] 'This book was first published by Oxford University | Press in 1947, and is here published in its first paperback | edition by special arrangement with Florence Sarah Williams through | Armitage Watkins, Inc., New York. | This edition, April 1966. All rights reserved. | PHOTOLITHOPRINTED BY GRAND RAPIDS BOOK MANUFACTURERS, INC. | GRAND RAPIDS, MICHIGAN | 1966'; and [146] blank.

Wove paper, watermarked 'Warren's Olde Style'. Bound in heavy wove wrappers. Printed on upper cover in white, against a black and orange photograph of Charles Williams: 'Essays Presented to | Charles Williams | Edited by C. S. Lewis | Sayers · Tolkien · Lewis · Barfield · Mathew · Lewis'. Printed on spine, running down: Lewis Essays Presented to Charles Williams | EERDMANS'. Printed on lower cover: 'Essays Presented to | Charles Williams | *Edited by C. S. Lewis* | [*quotation from the preface*] | $2.45 | [*at left, publisher's "books" device; at near right:*] WM. B. EERDMANS PUBLISHING CO. | 255 Jefferson Avenue, S.E. | Grand Rapids, Michigan 49502 [*at far right, running up:*] Cover Design: Friederichsen'. All edges trimmed and unstained.

Published 30 March 1966 at $2.45; 3,000 copies printed.

Typeset as for B19a, except pp. [iii–iv], [146]. Omits the frontispiece.

Reprinted by Books for Libraries, Freeport, New York, 1972, from the same typesetting.

B20   ESSAIS DE PHILOLOGIE MODERNE   1953

Bibliothèque de la Faculté de Philosophie et Lettres | de l'Université de Liège—
Fascicule CXXIX | [*rule*] | ESSAIS DE | PHILOLOGIE MODERNE | (1951) |
[*within a single rule frame:*] Communications présentées au Congrès International
de Philologie | Moderne, réuni à Liège du 10 au 13 septembre 1951, à l'occasion du
LXe Anniversaire des Sections de Philologie germanique et | de Philologie romane de
la Faculté de Philosophie et Lettres de | l'Université de Liège. | [*below the frame:*]
[*seal of the University*] | 1953 | Société d'édition «LES BELLES LETTRES» | 95,
boulevard Raspail | PARIS (VI^c)

ii, 252, 18 pp. Collation: [1]^62–17^8. 24.7 × 16.4 cm.

first section: [i–ii] blank; [1] 'ESSAIS DE PHILOLOGIE MODERNE | (1951)'; [2]
blank; [3] title; [4] blank; [5]–7 foreword; [8] blank; [9]–12 note sur les travaux du
Congrès; [13]–19 liste des participants; [20] blank; [21]–249 text; [250] blank;
[251] table des matières; [252] blank; *second section:* [1]–16 catalogue of publications of La Faculté de Philologie et Lettres de l'Université de Liège, headed on p.
[1]: 'BIBLIOTHÈQUE | DE LA FACULTÉ DE PHILOSOPHIE ET LETTRES | DE
L'UNIVERSITÉ DE LIÈGE | [*rule*] | *Administrateur*: M. DELBOUILLE—Secrétaire:
M. DE CORTE | [*rule*] | *Les prix s'entendent en francs français.* | CATALOGUE
CHRONOLOGIQUE | DES DIFFERENTES SÉRIES'; [17] 'IMPRIMERIE
GEORGE MICHIELS, S. A., 6 RUE DE LA PAIX, LIÈGE'; [18] blank.

Includes essay, 'Middle English "Losenger": Sketch of an Etymological and
Semantic Enquiry', by J. R. R. Tolkien, first section, pp. [63]–76.

Wove paper. Bound in heavy grey wove wrappers. The upper cover reprints the title
page. Printed on spine: '[*rule*] | Fascicule | CXXIX | [*rule*] | Essais de | Philologie |
Moderne | (1951) | [*rule*] | 1953 | [*rule*] | Prix: | 500 fr.fr.' Bottom edge trimmed, top
and fore-edges untrimmed. All edges unstained.

Published before 13 October 1953 at 500 fr.; number of copies not known.
Terminus ad quem determined by the date of a letter in a private collection noting an
offprint of Tolkien's essay.

For his lecture before the Congrès International de Philologie Moderne in September
1951 Tolkien examined the Middle English word *losenger* because 'a fresh scrutiny
of its etymology may afford a glimpse (if no more) into the complexities of the
contacts of Germanic and Latin in Northern Gaul' (p. [63]). He is listed as a
participant in the Congrès, first section p. 19, as 'professeur à l'Université d'Oxford
(Merton College), et représentant officiel de cette Université, Oxford (Grande-
Bretagne)'.
  The essay was also issued as an offprint, bound in buff wrappers.
  Pertinent manuscript materials and correspondence (dated 1946–51) are in the
Bodleian Library, Oxford.

B21   ESSAYS AND STUDIES   1953

ESSAYS AND STUDIES | 1953 | BEING VOLUME SIX OF THE NEW SERIES |
OF ESSAYS AND STUDIES COLLECTED FOR | THE ENGLISH ASSOCIATION
| BY GEOFFREY BULLOUGH | LONDON | JOHN MURRAY, ALBEMARLE
STREET, W.

vi, 114 pp. Collation: [A]^8B–F^8G^4H^8. 21.5 × 13.8 cm.

[i] 'ESSAYS AND STUDIES 1953'; [ii] blank; [iii] title; [iv] *'First Edition . . 1953* | *Printed in Great Britain by* | *Wyman & Sons, Ltd., London, Fakenham and Reading* | *and published by John Murray (Publishers) Ltd.*'; [v] table of contents; [vi] notes on contributors; [1]–114 text.

Includes 'The Homecoming of Beorhtnoth Beorhthelm's Son' by J. R. R. Tolkien, pp. [1]-18.

Wove paper. Bound in light yellow cloth over boards. Stamped on upper cover in red: 'ESSAYS | AND | STUDIES | 1953'. Stamped on spine in red: '[*running down:*] ESSAYS AND STUDIES 1953 | [*horizontal:*] J. M.' Wove endpapers. No headbands. All edges trimmed and unstained.

Dust-jacket, grey wove paper. Printed on upper cover in red: 'ESSAYS | AND | STUDIES | 1953 | [*flourish*] | Being Volume Six of the New Series of | ESSAYS AND STUDIES | Collected for the English Association by | GEOFFREY BULLOUGH'. Printed on spine in red: '[*running down:*] ESSAYS AND STUDIES 1953 | [*horizontal:*] J. M.' Printed on lower cover in red: 'This Volume Contains | [*list of contents*]'. Printed on front flap in red: '[*diagonal dashed rule*] | 10s. 6d. | NET'. Printed on back flap in red: '*Also Available* | [*advertisement of* English Studies 1949 *and* Essays and Studies *for 1950, 1951, and 1952*]'.

Published October 1953 at 10s. 6d.; number of copies not known.

Carpenter, *Biography*, states that 'Beorhtnoth'—probably he means the drama proper—was in existence by 1945. A dramatic dialogue in rhyming verse, clearly a precursor of 'Beorhtnoth', was written *circa* 1930–3 and published in *The Treason of Isengard* (A27), pp. 106–7, with reference to a still earlier text in the Bodleian Library, Oxford. Tolkien remarked in a letter of 24 October 1952 that he was 'producing a contribution to "Essays and Studies" by December 2nd'.

The whole of 'The Homecoming of Beorhtnoth Beorhthelm's Son' is in three parts. Part I, 'Beorhtnoth's Death', is an account of the slaying of Beorhtnoth of Essex, commander of the English in the Battle of Maldon, and is an introduction to part II, the 'Homecoming' itself. Part III, 'Ofermod', is a 'criticism of the matter and manner' of the Old English poem 'The Battle of Maldon' in which Tolkien comments on the heroic excess that was Beorhtnoth's downfall. Tolkien referred to 'The Homecoming of Beorhtnoth Beorhthelm's Son' as 'a dramatic dialogue on the nature of the "heroic" and the "chivalrous"'. He began a long poem, 'The Fall of Arthur', in the same measure, i.e. the Modern English equivalent of Anglo-Saxon alliterative verse, but abandoned it in the mid-nineteen-thirties; see B32a note.

The work was also published in *The Tolkien Reader* (A8), *Tree and Leaf, Smith of Wootton Major [and] The Homecoming of Beorhtnoth Beorhthelm's Son* (A13), and *Poems and Stories* (A16). A separate edition was published in August 1991 by Anglo-Saxon Books, Pinner, Middlesex, in a limited edition of 300 copies (with, however, numerous deviations from the *Essays and Studies* text, especially in punctuation).

B21 was reprinted for Wm. Dawson & Sons, London, in 1967.

A radio production of 'Beorhtnoth' by Rayner Heppenstall was performed on the BBC Third Programme on 3 December 1954 and was later rebroadcast; see *Letters* no. 152. 'Beorhtnoth' was performed in 1975 by the London University Dramatic Society, and on 10 and 11 August 1991 as part of the celebration of the Battle of Maldon millennium. A recording of 'Beorhtnoth' is to be issued in 1992, with readings by J. R. R. and Christopher Tolkien.

Manuscript and typescript materials by Tolkien pertinent to 'Beorhtnoth' and to his study of *The Battle of Maldon* are in the Bodleian Library.

B22   PEARL   1953

a. First edition:

PEARL | Edited by | E. V. GORDON | OXFORD | AT THE CLARENDON PRESS | 1953

lx, 168 pp. + 1 plate. Collation: [a]^{8}b–c^{8}d^{6}B–L^{8}M^4. 18.2 × 12.2 cm.

[i] title; [ii] '*Oxford University Press, Amen House, London E.C.4* | [*list of 11 cities (publisher's branches), Glasgow to Ibadan*] | *Geoffrey Cumberlege, Publisher to the University* | PRINTED IN GREAT BRITAIN'; [iii]–iv preface; [v] table of contents; [vi] blank; [vii]–viii list of abbreviations; [ix]–lii introduction; [liii]–lvii bibliography; [lviii] blank; [lix]–lx note on the edited text; [1]–44 text; [45]–86 notes; [87]–116 appendices; [117]–163 glossary; [164] index of names; [165]–7 list of biblical quotations and allusions; [168] 'PRINTED IN | GREAT BRITAIN | AT THE UNIVERSITY PRESS | OXFORD | BY | CHARLES BATEY | PRINTER | TO THE | UNIVERSITY'. Illustration, 'The Dreamer Lying Asleep on the Flowery Mound', on plate inserted facing p. [i].

Laid paper. Bound in dark blue cloth over boards. Stamped on spine in gilt: '[*rule*] | PEARL | GORDON | [*publisher's device, an open book and 3 crowns within a cartouche*] | OXFORD | [*rule*]'. Wove endpapers. No headbands. All edges trimmed and unstained.

Dust-jacket, grey wove paper. Printed on upper cover in dark blue: 'PEARL | [*grotesque ornament*] | *Edited by* | E. V. GORDON'. Printed on spine in dark blue: 'PEARL | GORDON | [*publisher's device, an open book and 3 crowns within a cartouche*] | OXFORD'. Printed on lower cover in dark blue: 'OXFORD BOOKS | [*advertisement of 7 titles, beginning with* Whitlock, The Audience of Beowulf, *ending with* Secular Lyrics of the XIVth and XVth Centuries] | (*These prices are operative in the United Kingdom only* | *and are subject to alteration without notice*) | OXFORD UNIVERSITY PRESS | [*square brackets in original:*] [5/53]'. Printed on front flap in dark blue: '[*blurb*] | [*diagonal dotted rule*] | *Price in U.K. only* | 12s. 6d. *net*'. Printed on back flap in dark blue: '[*advertisement of Gordon,* An Introduction to Old Norse, *and Tolkien and Gordon, eds.,* Sir Gawain and the Green Knight] | OXFORD | UNIVERSITY PRESS'.

Published 11 June 1953 at 12s. 6d.; 3,000 copies printed.

Ida L. (Mrs. E. V.) Gordon states in her preface to B22: 'After the publication of their edition of *Sir Gawain and the Green Knight* in 1925 [see B7] Professor J. R. R. Tolkien and my husband, Professor E. V. Gordon, started work on a similar edition of *Pearl*. Later, when he found himself unable to give sufficient time to it, Professor Tolkien suggested that my husband should continue the work alone. This he did. . . . My warmest thanks must go to Professor Tolkien, who had the original typescript for some time and added valuable notes and corrections; he has also responded generously to queries.' According to Christopher Tolkien in his preface to *Sir Gawain and the Green Knight, Pearl, and Sir Orfeo* (B30), *Pearl* was almost entirely the work of E. V. Gordon alone, but J. R. R. Tolkien contributed to it, besides notes and corrections, a small part of the introduction: 'Form and Purpose', pp. xi–xix. Gordon died in 1938, before finishing his work on *Pearl*, and at some time between that year and 1945 Tolkien undertook to put the manuscript in order as a duty to his friend and former pupil. In the event, he did not do so, and it was Mrs. Gordon, herself a professional philologist, who made the final revision, rewriting considerably in the process. Tolkien's contribution was reprinted in *SGPO*.

Tolkien collaborated with E. V. Gordon on two other projects which deserve notice. Gordon acknowledges in his edition of *The Battle of Maldon* (London: Methuen, 1937) that Tolkien read proof and 'made many corrections and contributions. . . . Professor Tolkien, with characteristic generosity, gave me the solution to many . . . textual and philological problems. . . .' Mrs. Gordon notes in the preface to *The Seafarer* (London: Methuen, 1960): 'When my husband . . . died in 1938 he left an uncompleted draft of an edition of *The Wanderer* and *The Seafarer*, on which he had been working in collaboration with Professor J. R. R. Tolkien. And my first intention, with Professor Tolkien's approval, was to bring into final form that edition.' Subsequent scholarship required, however, an approach different from that of the draft. 'Nevertheless the edition incorporates much of the original material, especially in the Notes.'

b. First paperback impression (1980):

PEARL | Edited by | E. V. GORDON | OXFORD | AT THE CLARENDON PRESS

[4], lx, 168 pp. Collation: 116 leaves. 18.5 × 11.9 cm.

[preliminary 1–3] blank; [preliminary 4] '[*illustration as titled*] | *The Dreamer lying asleep on the flowery mound* | (See p. x)'; [i] title; [ii] '*Oxford University Press, Walton Street, Oxford* OX2 6DP | [*list of 19 cities (publisher's branches), Oxford to Cape Town*] | ISBN 0 19 812675 1 | *First published 1953* | *Reprinted from sheets of the first edition* | *1958, 1963, 1966, 1970, 1974* | *Reprinted as paperback 1980* | [*notice of restrictions*] | *Printed in Great Britain* | *at the University Press, Oxford* | *by Eric Buckley* | *Printer to the University*'; [iii]–iv preface by Ida L. Gordon; [v] table of contents; [vi] blank; [vii]–viii list of abbreviations; ix–lii introduction; [liii]–lvii bibliography; [lviii] blank; [lix]–lx note on the edited text; [1]–44 text; [45]–86 notes; [87]–116 appendixes; [117]–63 glossary; [164] index of names; [165]-7 list of biblical quotations and allusions; [168] blank.

Wove paper. Bound in heavy wove wrappers. Covers and spine printed against a brown background. Printed on upper cover in white: 'Pearl | Edited by | E. V. GORDON | CLARENDON PRESS'. Printed on spine, running down, in white: 'Pearl Edited by E. V. GORDON OXFORD'. Printed on lower cover in white: '[*blurb*] | [*2 quotations, from the* Journal of English and German Philology *and* Review of English Studies] | *Also published by Oxford University Press* | [*advertisement of Tolkien and Gordon, eds.,* Sir Gawain and the Green Knight] | [*at left:*] OXFORD UNIVERSITY PRESS | £3.50 net in UK [*at right:*] ISBN 0 19 812675 1'. All edges trimmed and unstained.

Published 3 April 1980 at £3.50; 3,000 copies printed.

Typeset as for B22a, except pp. [ii], [168]. The illustration is on an integral leaf.

B23   **THE ANCRENE RIWLE**   **1955**

a. First edition:

[*within a decorative frame:*] THE ANCRENE | RIWLE | (The Corpus MS. : *Ancrene Wisse*) | Translated into Modern English by | M. B. SALU | with an Introduction by | DOM GERARD SITWELL | O.S.B. | and a Preface by | J. R. R. TOLKIEN | *Merton Professor of English Language and* | *Literature in the University of Oxford* | [*star*] | LONDON · BURNS & OATES xxviii, 196 pp. Collation: [A]⁸B–O⁸. 19.7 × 12.9 cm.

[i] 'THE ANCRENE RIWLE'; [ii] 'THE ORCHARD BOOKS | *Uniform with this volume* | [9 *titles, beginning with* The Rule of Saint Benedict, *ending with* Grou, Manual for Interior Souls]'; [iii] title; [iv] 'NIHIL OBSTAT: JOANNES M. T. BARTON, S.T.D., L.S.S. | CENSOR DEPVTATVS | IMPRIMATVR : E. MORROGH BERNARD | VICARIVS GENERALIS | WESTMONASTERII : DIE XV FEBRVARII MCMLV | *First published* 1955 | MADE AND PRINTED IN GREAT BRITAIN BY | THE BROADWATER PRESS LIMITED, WELWYN GARDEN CITY, HERTFORDSHIRE, FOR | BURNS OATES AND WASH- BOURNE LIMITED | 28 ASHLEY PLACE, LONDON, S.W.1'; v preface; [vi] blank; vii–xxii introduction; xxiii–xxvi translator's note; xxvii table of contents; [xxviii] blank; 1–192 text; 193–6 appendix.

Includes two-paragraph preface by J. R. R. Tolkien, p. v.

Wove paper. Bound in green cloth over boards. Quartered shield, bird with young on each of two quarters, group of three flowers on each of other two quarters, stamped on upper cover in gilt, within a single rule frame stamped in blind. Stamped on spine in gilt: '[*decorative rule*] | THE | ANCRENE | RIWLE | [*decorative rule*] | BURNS | OATES'. Single rule frame stamped on lower cover in blind. Wove endpapers. No headbands. All edges trimmed. Top edge stained green, fore- and bottom edges unstained.

Dust-jacket, light green wove paper. Printed on upper cover in dark blue, within a dark blue decorative frame: 'THE ORCHARD BOOKS | THE | ANCRENE | RIWLE | *Rendered into Modern English* | *and edited by* | M. B. SALU | *With a Preface by* | Prof. J. R. R. TOLKIEN | *and* | *an Introduction and Appendix by* | DOM GERARD SITWELL | BURNS & OATES'. Printed on spine in dark blue: '[*leafy ornament*] | THE | ORCHARD | BOOKS | THE | ANCRENE | RIWLE | [*flower*] | *Rendered* | *into* | *Modern English* | *and edited by* | M. B. SALU | [*flower*] | BURNS | OATES | [*leafy ornament*]'. Printed on lower cover in dark blue within a dark blue decorative frame: 'THE ORCHARD BOOKS | [*advertisement of 9 titles, beginning with* The Rule of St Benedict, *ending with* St Francis de Sales, Introduction to the Devout Life] | BURNS & OATES | 28 ASHLEY PLACE, LONDON, S.W.1'. Printed on front flap in dark blue: '[*blurb*] | 15s.'

Published November 1955 at 15s.; number of copies not known.

The preface is dated Merton College, Oxford, 29 June 1955.

   M. B. (Mary) Salu was tutored by Tolkien at Oxford University, *circa* 1944, and remained his friend. After Tolkien's death she co-edited a volume of essays in his memory (B34).
   Cf. B25.

b. First American edition (1956):

[*within a decorative frame:*] THE ANCRENE | RIWLE | (The Corpus MS. : *Ancrene Wisse*) | Translated into Modern English by | M. B. SALU | with an Introduction by | DOM GERARD SITWELL | O.S.B. | and a Preface by | J. R. R. TOLKIEN | *Merton Professor of English Language and* | *Literature in the University of Oxford* | [*star*] | UNIVERSITY OF NOTRE DAME PRESS | NOTRE DAME, INDIANA

xxviii, 196 pp. Collation: [A]⁸B–O⁸. 19.6 × 12.7 cm.

Contents as for B23a, except pp. [iii] title, as above; and [iv]: 'NIHIL OBSTAT: JOANNES M.T. BARTON, S.T.D., L.S.S. | CENSOR DEPVTATVS |

IMPRIMATVR: E. MORROGH BERNARD | VICARIVS GENERALIS | WESTMONASTERII: DIE XV FEBRVARII MCMLV | *First published* 1955 | *First American Edition* 1956 | MADE AND PRINTED IN GREAT BRITAIN'.

Wove paper. Bound in light blue cloth over boards. Stamped on spine in black uncials: '[*running down:*] THE ANCRENE RIWLE | [*horizontal:*] SALU | NOTRE | DAME | [*publisher's device, a star, cross, and open book within a shield*]'. Wove endpapers. Blue/white headbands. All edges trimmed and unstained.

Dust-jacket not seen.

Date of publication not known; p. [iv] states 1956, *Cumulative Book Index* gives 1957. Published at $2.75. Number of copies not known.

c. First paperback impression (1963):

Not seen. The first paperback impression is probably identical to the second (as in the following description), except without the note '*Reprinted* 1967' on p. [iv].

[*within a decorative frame:*] THE ANCRENE | RIWLE | (The Corpus MS. : *Ancrene Wisse*) | Translated into Modern English by | M. B. SALU | with an Introduction by | DOM GERARD SITWELL | O.S.B. | and a Preface by | J. R. R. TOLKIEN | *Merton Professor of English Language and* | *Literature in the University of Oxford* | LONDON | BURNS & OATES

xxviii, 196 pp. Collation: [A]⁸B–O⁸. 19.8 × 12.9 cm.

Contents as for B23a, except pp. [ii] blank; [iii] title, as above; and [iv] 'BURNS & OATES LIMITED | 25 Ashley Place, London, S.W.1 | *First published* 1955 | *This edition* 1963 | *Reprinted* 1967 | Nihil Obstat: Joannes M. T. Barton, S.T.D., L.S.S. | Censor Depvtatvs | Imprimatvr: E. Morrogh Bernard | Vicarivs Generalis | Westmonasterii: Die XV Febrvarii MCMLV | Introduction © Gerard Sitwell, 1955 | This translation © Burns & Oates Ltd, 1955 | Catalogue No.: 5/4017 | MADE AND PRINTED IN GREAT BRITAIN BY | THE BROADWATER PRESS LIMITED, WELWYN GARDEN CITY, HERTFORDSHIRE'.

Wove paper. Bound in heavy wove wrappers. Printed on upper cover: '*The* | [*in blue-green:*] ANCRENE | RIWLE [*to left of title, illustration, a peacock on a book, in black and light blue-green*] | [*in black:*] *Translated by* M. B. SALU | [*in blue-green:*] *Introduction by* | GERARD SITWELL, O.S.B. | [*in black:*] *Preface by* Prof. J. R. R. TOLKIEN'. Printed on spine: 'SALU | [*running down, in light blue-green:*] THE ANCRENE RIWLE | [*horizontal, in black:*] BURNS | OATES'. Printed on lower cover: '[*blurb*] | 7s 6d | [*in blue-green:*] BURNS & OATES | [*in black:*] 25 Ashley Place, London, S.W.1. | Catalogue No.: 5/4017'. Wove endpapers. All edges trimmed and unstained.

Date of publication and number of copies not known. Published at 7s. 6d.

Typeset as for B23a, except pp. [ii–iv].

B23c was reprinted from the same typesetting, but with altered preliminaries, in 1990 by University of Exeter Press, in the series *Exeter Medieval English Texts and Studies*.

B24   THE OLD ENGLISH APOLLONIUS OF TYRE   1958

THE OLD ENGLISH | *APOLLONIUS* | *OF TYRE* | EDITED BY | PETER GOOLDEN | OXFORD UNIVERSITY PRESS | 1958

[2], xxxviii, 76 pp. Collation: [a]^{8}b^{8}c^4[d]^{8}C–E^{8}F^6 (F2 signed 'F2'). 21.9 × 13.9 cm.

[preliminary 1] 'OXFORD ENGLISH MONOGRAPHS | *General Editors* | J. R. R. TOLKIEN F. P. WILSON | HELEN GARDNER'; [preliminary 2] 'OXFORD ENGLISH MONOGRAPHS | [*5 titles, beginning with* Víga-Glúms Saga, *ending with* The Peterborough Chronicle]'; [i] title; [ii] '*Oxford University Press, Amen House, London E.C.4* | [*list of 14 cities (publisher's branches), Glasgow to Accra*] | © *Oxford University Press 1958* | PRINTED IN GREAT BRITAIN'; [iii] prefatory note; [iv] blank; [v]–vi preface; [vii] table of contents; [viii] blank; [ix]–xxxiv introduction; [xxxv]–xxxvi bibliography; [xxxvii] list of abbreviations; [xxxviii] textual note; [1] 'APOLLONIUS'; [2]–43 Old English and Latin texts on facing pages; [44]–62 commentary; [63]–74 glossary; [75] glossary of proper names; [76] 'PRINTED IN | GREAT BRITAIN | AT THE | UNIVERSITY PRESS | OXFORD | BY | CHARLES BATEY | PRINTER | TO THE | UNIVERSITY'.

Includes one-paragraph prefatory note by J. R. R. Tolkien, p. [iii].

Laid paper. Bound in green cloth over boards. Stamped on spine in gilt: '[*rule*] | THE OLD | ENGLISH | Apollonius | of Tyre | GOOLDEN | [*publisher's device, an open book and 3 crowns within a cartouche*] | OXFORD | [*rule*]'. Wove endpapers. No headbands. Top edge and fore-edge trimmed, bottom edge untrimmed. All edges unstained.

Dust-jacket, grey wove paper. Printed on upper cover in dark blue: 'OXFORD ENGLISH MONOGRAPHS | *General Editors* | J. R. R. TOLKIEN F. P. WILSON HELEN GARDNER | [*rule*] | [*line of ornaments*] | THE | OLD ENGLISH | *APOLLONIUS* | *OF TYRE* | [*ornaments*] | Edited by | PETER GOOLDEN | [*line of ornaments*] | [*rule*] | OXFORD UNIVERSITY PRESS'. Printed on spine in dark blue: 'The Old | English | *Apollonius* | *of Tyre* | GOOLDEN | [*publisher's device, an open book and 3 crowns within a cartouche*] | OXFORD'. Printed on lower cover in dark blue: '*Oxford English Monographs* | [*advertisement of 5 titles, beginning with* Víga-Glúms Saga, *ending with* The Peterborough Chronicle] | (*These prices are operative in the United Kingdom only* | *and are subject to alteration without notice*) | OXFORD UNIVERSITY PRESS | [*square brackets in original:*] [7/58]'. Printed on front flap in dark blue: 'THIS is the sixth volume to appear in | the *Oxford English Monographs.* (See | back of jacket for previous volumes.) | [*swelled rule*] | [*blurb*] | *Price (in U.K. only)* | 25s. *net*'. Printed on back flap in dark blue: 'OXFORD | UNIVERSITY PRESS | [*15 addresses, London to Nairobi*]'.

Published November 1958 at 25s.; number of copies not known.

Tolkien was a general editor of the Oxford English Monographs from 1940 to 1958. His assistance is acknowledged in two other volumes in the series: B. L. Joseph, *Elizabethan Acting* (London: Oxford University Press, 1951), and Þorgils Saga ok Hafliþa, ed. Ursula Brown (London: Oxford University Press, 1952).

B25   **ANCRENE WISSE**   **1962**

THE ENGLISH TEXT OF THE | ANCRENE RIWLE | [*black letter:*] Ancrene Wisse | [*roman:*] EDITED FROM | MS. CORPUS CHRISTI COLLEGE | CAMBRIDGE 402 | BY | J. R. R. TOLKIEN | WITH AN INTRODUCTION BY | N. R. KER | *Published for* | THE EARLY ENGLISH TEXT SOCIETY | *by the* | OXFORD UNIVERSITY PRESS | LONDON NEW YORK TORONTO | 1962

[2], xviii, 224 pp. + 1 plate. Collation: [A]^{10}[B]^{8}C–P^8. 21.4 × 13.8 cm.

[preliminary 1–2] blank; [i] '[*black letter:*] Ancrene Wisse | [*rule*] | [*roman:*] EARLY ENGLISH TEXT SOCIETY | No. 249 | 1962 (for 1960) | PRICE 30s.'; [ii] blank; [iii] title; [iv] '© *Early English Text Society 1962* | PRINTED IN GREAT BRITAIN'; [v] table of contents; [vi]–viii prefatory note; [ix]–xviii introduction; [1] 'MS. Corpus Christi College Cambridge 402 | *A Rule for Nunnes or Recluses* | ANCRENE WISSE'; 2–222 text; [223] 'PRINTED IN GREAT BRITAIN | AT THE UNIVERSITY PRESS, OXFORD | BY VIVIAN RIDLER | PRINTER TO THE UNIVERSITY'; [224] blank. Illustrations, two pages from the *Ancrene Wisse* manuscript, on plate between pp. [ii–iii].

Wove paper. Bound in brown cloth over boards. Stamped on upper cover in gilt, within a single rule frame stamped in blind: '[*black letter:*] Ancrene Wisse | MS. Corpus Christi College Cambridge 402 | [*device of Early English Text Society*]'. Stamped on spine in gilt: '[*rule*] | ANCRENE | WISSE | MS. | CORPUS | CHRISTI | COLLEGE | CAMBRIDGE | 402 | TOLKIEN | EARLY | ENGLISH | TEXT | SOCIETY | 1962 | [*rule*] | 249'. Single rule frame stamped on lower cover in blind. Wove endpapers. No headbands. All edges trimmed and unstained. Description of the Early English Text Society and list of publications, separate gathering of 8 pp., inserted following p. [224]. The inserted gathering is dated January 1962 at the foot of p. [8], and *Ancrene Wisse* is the last volume (no. 249) in the list of publications, 'at press'.

Dust-jacket, unprinted glassine.

Published 7 December 1962 at 30s.; 3,000 copies printed.

The Bodleian Library holds correspondence by Tolkien regarding this edition of *Ancrene Wisse* from as early as 1936. In a letter to Stanley Unwin of 18? March 1945 Tolkien wrote that his book on the *Ancrene Riwle* is 'all typed out'—by which he meant, perhaps, only the text proper. In two letters to Rayner Unwin of late 1952 Tolkien referred to the book as overdue professional work, which he was attempting to finish in the midst of other writing and with *The Lord of the Rings*, soon to be published, distracting his attention. In a letter to Rayner Unwin of 31 July 1960 he remarked that 'my edition of the prime MS. [of the *Ancrene Wisse*] should have been completed *many years* ago! I did at least try to clear it out of the way before retirement, and by a vast effort sent in the text in Sept. *1958*'. Robert Burchfield, then the editorial secretary of the Early English Text Society, with Professor Norman Davis, the director of the EETS, 'gently bullied' Tolkien until the typescript was submitted—which, in the event, was not merely a typescript, but included initial letters elegantly drawn by Tolkien. See further, 'Robert Burchfield on J R R Tolkien', *The Independent Magazine*, London, 4 March 1989, p. 50.

A printers' strike prevented proofs from being sent to Tolkien until June 1960, when he was 'in full tide of composition for the *Silmarillion*, and had lost the threads of the M[iddle] E[nglish] work' (letter to Rayner Unwin, 31 July 1960). He subsequently worked ten hours per day 'trying to induce order into a set of confused and desperately sticky proofs, and notes. And then I have to write an introduction.' By 'introduction' Tolkien probably meant the prefatory note; N. P. Ker wrote the introduction proper. But the book was further delayed. Tolkien corrected probably the final proofs in January 1962. On 19 December 1962, in a letter to his son Michael, he reported that 'my *Ancrene Wisse* . . . got between covers this week at last'.

Pertinent manuscript and typescript materials, correspondence, and revised proofs, and other materials on *Ancrene Wisse* studies by Tolkien (with M. B. Salu and S. R. T. O. d'Ardenne) are in the Bodleian Library, Oxford.

B26   ANGLES AND BRITONS   1963

ANGLES AND | BRITONS | [*swelled rule*] | *O'Donnell Lectures* | [*seal of the University of Wales*] | CARDIFF | UNIVERSITY OF WALES PRESS | 1963

viii, 168 pp. + 1 plate (map). Collation: [A]⁴B–H⁸[I]⁸K–L⁸M⁴. 21.6 × 13.8 cm.

[i] 'ANGLES AND BRITONS | *O'Donnell Lectures*'; [ii] blank; [iii] title; [iv] 'PRINTED IN GREAT BRITAIN | AT THE UNIVERSITY PRESS, OXFORD | BY VIVIAN RIDLER | PRINTER TO THE UNIVERSITY'; [v] note; [vi] blank; [vii] table of contents; [viii] blank; [1]–168 text. Folded map inserted following p. 92.

Includes essay, 'English and Welsh', by J. R. R. Tolkien, pp. [1]–41.

Wove paper. Bound in dark blue cloth over boards. Stamped on spine in gilt: '[*running down:*] ANGLES AND BRITONS [*diamond*] O'Donnell Lectures | [*horizontal:*] University | of Wales | Press'. Wove endpapers. No headbands. All edges trimmed and unstained.

Dust-jacket, grey laid paper watermarked 'Abbey Mills'. Printed on upper cover in dark blue: 'O'Donnell Lectures | [*decorative rule*] | ANGLES AND | BRITONS | [*decorative rule*] | J. R. R. Tolkien | T. H. Parry-Williams | Kenneth Jackson | B. G. Charles | N. K. Chadwick | William Rees | [*decorative rule*] | UNIVERSITY OF WALES PRESS'. Printed on spine in dark blue: '[*running down:*] ANGLES AND BRITONS [*diamond*] O'Donnell Lectures | [*horizontal:*] University | of Wales | Press'. Printed on lower cover in dark blue: 'SELECTED PUBLICATIONS | [*advertisement of 7 titles, beginning with* Trioedd Ynys Prydein, *ending with* Loomis, The Grail: From Celtic Myth to Christian Symbol] | UNIVERSITY OF WALES PRESS | University Registry, Cathays Park, Cardiff'. Printed on front flap in dark blue: '[*blurb*] | 21s.'

Published 8 July 1963 at 21s.; number of copies not known.

Distributed in the United States by Lawrence Verry, Inc. of Mystic, Connecticut, who affixed their label over the University of Wales Press imprint on the spine of the dust-jacket.

Though suffering from laryngitis, Tolkien delivered 'English and Welsh', the first of a series of O'Donnell Lectures at Oxford University, on 21 October 1955. Overdue, the lecture had been written, as Tolkien remarked in a letter of 8 December 1955 to Naomi Mitchison, 'with "all the woe in the world", as the Gawain-poet says of the wretched fox with the hounds on his tail'. It was included in *Angles and Britons* with other previously unpublished O'Donnell Lectures, which in general are concerned with the 'British or Celtic element in the English Language and the dialects of English Counties and the special terms and words used in agriculture and handicrafts and the British or Celtic element in the existing population of England' (p. [v]). See further, Tolkien's letter to Jane Neave, 8–9 September 1962, *Letters* no. 241.

'English and Welsh' was reprinted in *The Monsters and the Critics and Other Essays* (A19).

Pertinent manuscript and typescript materials, correspondence, and revised proofs are in the Bodleian Library, Oxford.

B27   WINTER'S TALES FOR CHILDREN   1965

a. First (British) edition:

WINTER'S TALES | FOR CHILDREN 1 | EDITED BY | CAROLINE HILLIER |

[*illustration*] | *Illustrated by* | HUGH MARSHALL | MACMILLAN | London ·
Melbourne · Toronto | [*swelled rule*] | ST MARTIN'S PRESS | New York | 1965

viii, 200 pp. Collation: [A]⁸B–N⁸. 23.5 × 17.4 cm.

[i] 'WINTER'S TALES FOR CHILDREN 1'; [ii] blank; [iii] title; [iv] 'Copyright ©
Macmillan & Co. Ltd 1965 | MACMILLAN AND COMPANY LIMITED | *Little
Essex Street London WC 2* | *also Bombay Calcutta Madras Melbourne* | THE
MACMILLAN COMPANY OF CANADA LIMITED | *70 Bond Street Toronto 2* | ST
MARTIN'S PRESS INC | *175 Fifth Avenue New York 10010 NY* | Library of
Congress Catalogue Card No. 65-25196 | PRINTED IN GREAT BRITAIN BY
RICHARD CLAY (THE CHAUCER PRESS), LTD., | BUNGAY, SUFFOLK.'; v table
of contents; [vi] blank; vii editor's note; [viii] blank; 1–200 text and illustrations.

Includes two poems, 'Once upon a Time', pp. [44]–5, and 'The Dragon's Visit', pp.
[84], 86–7 (p. [85] is an illustration), by J. R. R. Tolkien.

Wove paper. Bound in dark green textured paper over boards. Illustration by Hugh
Marshall, of a dragon, stamped on upper cover in gilt. Stamped on spine in gilt:
'WINTER'S | TALES | FOR | CHILDREN | [*star*] | *Edited by* | CAROLINE | HILLIER
| MACMILLAN'. Wove endpapers. No headbands. All edges trimmed and unstained.

Dust-jacket, wove paper. Illustration by Marshall, of a dragon, printed on upper cover
in black, orange, and light green, extended with decorations and lettering around
spine and part of lower cover. Lettered on upper cover within the illustration:
'*WINTER'S* | *TALES FOR* | *CHILDREN* | *1* | *EDITED BY* | *CAROLINE
HILLIER*'. Lettered on spine within the illustration: '[*running down:*] *Edited by*
[*parallel to the preceding words:*] *Caroline Hillier* [*followed by:*] *WINTER'S TALES*
[*parallel to the preceding two words:*] *FOR CHILDREN 1* | [*horizontal:*]
MACMILLAN'. Printed on lower cover: '[*in orange:*] The Contributors | [*in black:*]
[*14 names, beginning with* Kevin Crossley-Holland, *ending with* J. R. R. Tolkien] |
[*illustration by Marshall, of a dragon*]'. Printed on front flap: '[*illustration by
Marshall, of a dragon*] | [*blurb*] | 25/-'. Printed on back flap: '[*in orange:*] CAROLINE
HILLIER | [*in black:*] [*note on the editor*] | Jacket design by Hugh Marshall |
Macmillan | *Printed in Great Britain*'.

Published October 1965 at 25s.; number of copies not known.

'The Dragon's Visit' is a revised version of the poem of the same title in the *Oxford
Magazine*, 4 February 1937 (C29). It was reprinted in *The Annotated Hobbit* (A3dd–
ee), pp. 262–3. Both poems were reprinted, with minor differences of capitalization
and punctuation, in *The Young Magicians*, ed. Lin Carter (New York: Ballantine
Books, 1969), pp. 255–6 ('Once upon a Time') and 259–62 ('The Dragon's Visit').

b. First (American) edition (1965):

WINTER'S TALES | FOR CHILDREN 1 | EDITED BY | CAROLINE HILLIER |
[*illustration*] | *Illustrated by* | HUGH MARSHALL | MACMILLAN | London ·
Melbourne · Toronto | [*swelled rule*] | ST MARTIN'S PRESS | New York | 1965

viii, 200 pp. Collation: [A]⁸B–N⁸. 23.5 × 17.3 cm.

Sheets as for B27a.

Wove paper. Bound as for B27a, except that the spine imprint is 'ST MARTIN'S PRESS'.

Dust-jacket, wove paper, as for B27a, except that the spine imprint is '*ST MARTIN'S
PRESS*' and the price on the front flap is '$4.95'.

Published 1965 at $4.95; date of publication and number of copies not known.

B28   THE ROAD GOES EVER ON   1967

a. First edition:

THE ROAD | GOES | EVER ON | [*in red:*] *A SONG CYCLE* | [*in black:*] POEMS BY
J. R. R. TOLKIEN | MUSIC BY DONALD SWANN | *with decorations by J. R. R.
Tolkien | and Samuel Hanks Bryant* | 1967 | HOUGHTON MIFFLIN COMPANY
BOSTON

xii, 68 pp. Collation: [1–5⁸]. 27.9 × 21.2 cm.

[i] 'THE ROAD GOES | EVER ON'; [ii] 'BOOKS BY | *J. R. R. Tolkien* | [*9 titles,
beginning with* H, *ending with* RGEO]'; [iii] title; [iv] 'FIRST PRINTING W | TEXT
COPYRIGHT © 1962 BY GEORGE ALLEN & | UNWIN LTD.; COPYRIGHT ©
1967 BY J. R. R. TOLKIEN | MUSIC COPYRIGHT © 1967 BY DONALD SWANN
| ALL RIGHTS RESERVED INCLUDING THE RIGHT TO | REPRODUCE THIS
BOOK OR PARTS THEREOF IN ANY FORM | LIBRARY OF CONGRESS
CATALOG CARD NUMBER: 67–20501 | PRINTED IN THE UNITED STATES OF
AMERICA'; v–viii foreword, by Donald Swann; ix table of contents; [x] blank; [xi]
'THE ROAD GOES | EVER ON'; 1–53 music and lyrics; [54] blank; [55] 'NOTES
AND TRANSLATIONS | HERE FOLLOW Professor Tolkien's scripts, translations
and | comments on the Elvish texts for "Namárië" (song Number 5) | and "A Elbereth
Gilthoniel" (in song Number 6).'; [56] blank; [57]–[68] text and reproductions.
Manuscripts formally written out by Tolkien in tengwar, 'Namárië' and 'A Elbereth
Gilthoniel', reproduced in black and red on pp. [57] and 62 respectively, and in grey
and red, line by line, as decorations along the head and foot of most pages throughout
the book. Holograph manuscript of 'Namárië' by Tolkien, with notes, reproduced in
black and red on p. [68] (transcription printed in type on p. 58). Pen-drawn
decorations by Samuel Hanks Bryant (two designs, repeated) printed in grey following
the music on pp. 3, 17, 24, and 31, and on pp. 53 and 67. Headings for the foreword
and table of contents, and song title headings, printed in red.

Order of songs: 'The Road Goes Ever On' (from *The Lord of the Rings* [A5], bk. 1, ch.
1); 'Upon the Hearth the Fire is Red' (*LR*, bk. 1, ch. 3); 'In the Willow-meads of
Tasarinan' (*LR*, bk. 3, ch. 4); 'In Western Lands' (*LR*, bk. 6, ch. 1); 'Namárië
(Farewell)' (*LR*, bk. 2, ch. 8); 'I Sit beside the Fire' (*LR*, bk. 2, ch. 3, with Elvish refrain
'A Elbereth Gilthoniel' from *LR*, bk. 2, ch. 1); 'Errantry' (from *The Adventures of
Tom Bombadil* [A6]).

Tan wove paper. Bound in red-orange cloth over boards. Stamped on upper cover in
gilt: '[*at left, decorative border stamped along the length of the spine; at right:*] THE
ROAD GOES | EVER ON'. Stamped on spine, running down: '[*in gilt:*] J. R. R.
TOLKIEN – [*in black:*] THE ROAD GOES EVER ON [*in gilt:*] – DONALD SWANN
– HMCO'. Tan wove endpapers. No headbands. All edges trimmed and unstained.

Dust-jacket, tan wove paper. Printed on upper cover: '[*to right of red vertical rule:*]
[*uncials:*] [*in red:*] THE ROAD GOES EVER ON | [*rule*] | [*in black:*] A SONG
CYCLE [*3 dots, in red*] [*in black:*] MUSIC BY | [*rule, in red*] | [*in black:*] DONALD
SWANN [*3 dots, in red*] [*in black:*] POEMS | [*rule, in red*] | [*in black:*] BY J. R. R.
TOLKIEN [*tengwar:*] [*in red:*] Namárië | [*rule*] | Attariello nainië Lóriendesse | [*to left
of vertical rule:*] Ai [*to right of rule, in grey, the remainder of Tolkien's poem
"Namárië"*]'. Printed on spine, running down, in uncials: 'TOLKIEN [*in red:*] : THE
ROAD GOES EVER ON : [*in black:*] SWANN HMCO'. Printed on lower cover:
'[*tengwar:*] [*in red:*] A Elbereth Gilthoniel | [*in grey:*] aerlinn in edhil o Imladris | [text
of Tolkien's poem "A Elbereth Gilthoniel"] | [*roman, in black:*] The front jacket

shows the Tengwar text of Song No. 5, *Namárië*. | Above is the Elvish refrain from Song No. 6, *I Sit Beside the Fire (Elbereth)*. | Both were drawn by J. R. R. Tolkien.' Printed on front flap: '$3.95 | [*to right of red vertical rule, in uncials:*] [*in red:*] THE ROAD GOES EVER ON | [*rule*] | [*in black:*] A SONG CYCLE [*3 dots, in red*] [*in black:*] MUSIC BY | [*rule, in red*] | [*in black:*] DONALD SWANN [*3 dots, in red*] [*in black:*] POEMS | [*rule, in red*] [*in black:*] BY J. R. R. TOLKIEN | [*rule, in red*] | [*in black:*] [*blurb*] | [*below blurb and vertical rule:*] [*at left, running up:*] 1067 [*at right, horizontal:*] [*in red:*] The songs from [*in black:*] The Road Goes Ever On [*in red:*] are | sung by William Elvin, the composer at the | piano, in a record album entitled [*in black:*] Poems and | Songs of Middle Earth | [*in red:*] (with Professor Tol- | kien reading the poems) produced by Caedmon, | #TC1231, and available at your record or book store for $5.95.' Printed on back flap: '[*photograph of Tolkien*] | PHOTO BY ROGER HILL | [*note on Tolkien*] | [*photograph of Swann*] | PHOTO BY BRIAN SHUEL | [*note on Swann*] | [*in red:*] HOUGHTON MIFFLIN COMPANY | 2 Park Street | Boston, Massachusetts | 02107'.

Published 31 October 1967 at $3.95; 20,000 copies printed.

Errors: foot of pp. viii, 8, 17, 26, 35, 44, 53, 65, *ilye* in the tengwar inscription lacks the diacritical mark (two superior dots) indicating *y*; foot of p. ix, most of the doubled tengwar character *númen* is lost; p. 32, the third staff is incorrectly marked with a bass clef rather than a treble clef; p. 62, the red diacritical and punctuation marks within the tengwar chant 'A Elbereth Gilthoniel' are not in register; p. 63, l. 7 of 'A Elbereth Gilthoniel', 'aeron' is misprinted for 'aearon'.

Early in 1965 the composer and pianist Donald Swann set to music several of the poems in *The Lord of the Rings*. In his autobiography, *Swann's Way: A Life in Song* (London: William Heinemann, 1991), he recalled that seven songs were written in Ramallah, outside Jerusalem; but in his foreword to *The Road Goes Ever On*, and in his first letter to Allen & Unwin concerning his work (8 March 1965), he wrote of six songs, which seems to be the correct number. Of these, he soon rejected a setting of 'O Orofarnë, Lassemista, Carnimírië!' (the ent Quickbeam's lament for the dead rowan, *LR*, bk. 3, ch. 4), which he thought too similar to Purcell's *Dido and Aeneas*. He met Tolkien on 30 May 1965 at Priscilla Tolkien's home (where there was a piano) and played for him 'The Road Goes Ever On', 'Upon the Hearth the Fire is Red', 'In the Willow-meads of Tasarinan', 'In Western Lands', and 'I Sit beside the Fire', as well as a new sixth song, a setting of 'Namárië'. Tolkien approved all except the last, which he conceived as plainchant; to Tolkien's theme Swann later added an introduction, interlude, and coda.

  Swann asked for permission to perform and publish his settings of Tolkien's poetry, and received it with enthusiasm. He became close to Tolkien, who thought him 'a most delightful person', and to Joy Hill, then responsible for rights and permissions at Allen & Unwin. Hill promoted Swann at every opportunity. She introduced him to a music student friend, baritone William Elvin, whose voice was found ideal for the songs (and whose surname Tolkien thought 'a good omen'), and she supported Swann's desire to make a phonograph record of the cycle. When, in January 1966, a representative of the music and record publisher Chappells thought that the songs would make too short a record to sell in the important American market, Hill suggested that a long-playing record could be made by combining the songs with readings from Tolkien's works by Michael Flanders, Swann's long-time partner.

  In late April 1966 Swann made an experimental tape of the songs to play to record companies. He was not yet committed to a publisher. In the first week of May he performed part of the song cycle on BBC radio, to encouraging public response. The songs were also performed by Swann and Elvin on 7 and 8 May 1966, at the Lakeland

Theatre at Rosehill, Cumberland, in a programme of poetry set to music and collectively titled *The Lyric Songs of Donald Swann*. Later in 1966 Swann and Flanders took their two-man musical show *At the Drop of Another Hat* to American theatres and included among its songs 'I Sit beside the Fire'. In the audience at their opening in Boston was Austin Olney of the publisher Houghton Mifflin, with whom Swann thereafter dealt closely. Olney suggested Caedmon of New York as a publisher for the record: not only was Caedmon a respected label, it was represented in schools and selected shops by Houghton Mifflin. The project was discussed at length, until in late December 1966 Olney, Swann, and Allen & Unwin agreed that the best recording would consist of the songs performed by Swann and Elvin, and poems read not by Flanders but by Tolkien himself. Tolkien added his agreement in April 1967, and on the afternoon of 15 June 1967 recorded five poems from *The Adventures of Tom Bombadil* and the Elvish 'A Elbereth Gilthoniel'. The recording, *Poems and Songs of Middle Earth*, was issued in the United States in autumn 1967 and in Britain in spring 1968; see section Fi.

By now Swann had also set Tolkien's 'Errantry' to music, so that the song cycle would not end 'on a sort of question mark' with 'I Sit beside the Fire' (B28a–d, foreword). Tolkien wondered, in a letter to Swann of 14 October 1966, if 'Errantry' was not too long for the arrangement Swann had in mind, and felt that abbreviation of the poem would be difficult. Swann first tried to make 'Errantry' into a duet, with the second voice (Michael Flanders) giving a slower counterpoint to the lively verses, using repeated lines of words and music; later he decided that a single voice worked best.

On 3 October 1966 Swann informed Tolkien that Austin Olney was considering the publication of *The Road Goes Ever On* as a 'booklet'. Rayner Unwin thought that the song cycle, at only some forty pages, might be too slim to be a paying proposition; so it was fleshed out with calligraphic inscriptions in Elvish, decorations, and supplementary material, including 'Namárië' which Tolkien had written out in a letter to Swann. Tolkien was to make the decorations himself, and it was suggested that he write a note on the origins of his verse and about the peregrinations of 'Errantry' (see *The Treason of Isengard* [A27], ch. 5). Instead he wrote short linguistic analyses of the two Elvish texts Swann had set to music. By March 1967 Tolkien supplied the needed lettering in tengwar but was too occupied with other work to make much progress on decorations. These were made instead by Samuel Hanks Bryant, a prolific American illustrator, to fill blank spaces at the end of songs. Titling was originally in 'quasi-Elvish' letters, changed to roman type following objections by Tolkien, Swann, and Unwin. A calligraphic figure of Tolkien's and Swann's initials, made by Tolkien for the book, arrived too late to be used.

Pertinent manuscript and typescript material by Tolkien is in the Bodleian Library, Oxford. Pertinent correspondence is in the Bodleian Library and in the library of the University of Reading.

b. First British edition (1968):

THE ROAD | GOES | EVER ON | [*in red:*] *A SONG CYCLE* | [*in black:*] POEMS BY J. R. R. TOLKIEN | MUSIC BY DONALD SWANN | *with decorations by J. R. R. Tolkien* | *London* | GEORGE ALLEN AND UNWIN LTD

xii, 68 pp. Collation: [1–5^8]. 28.0 × 21.5 cm.

Contents as for B28a, except pp. [iii] title, as above; and [iv] 'FIRST PUBLISHED IN GREAT BRITAIN | IN 1968 | [*notice of restrictions under copyright*] | Text © George Allen & Unwin Ltd, 1962 | © J. R. R. Tolkien 1967 | Music © Donald Swann 1967 |

PRINTED IN GREAT BRITAIN | BY JOHN DICKENS AND CO LTD | NORTHAMPTON'. Headings printed in red as for B28a. The decorations by Samuel Hanks Bryant are present but uncredited.

Buff laid paper. Bound in cream paper over boards. Printed on upper cover in red-orange: 'THE ROAD GOES | EVER ON'. Printed on spine in red-orange: '[*running down:*] TOLKIEN THE ROAD GOES EVER ON SWANN | [*horizontal:*] A | & | U'. Buff laid endpapers. No headbands. All edges trimmed and unstained.

Dust-jacket, cream laid paper. Printed on upper cover: '[*to right of red-orange vertical rule:*] [*uncials:*] [*in red-orange:*] THE ROAD GOES EVER ON | [*rule*] | [*in black:*] A SONG CYCLE [*3 dots, in red-orange*] [*in black:*] MUSIC BY | [*rule, in red-orange*] | [*in black:*] DONALD SWANN [*3 dots, in red-orange*] [*in black:*] POEMS | [*rule, in red-orange*] | [*in black:*] BY J. R. R. TOLKIEN [*tengwar:*] [*in red-orange:*] Namárië | [*rule*] | Attariello nainië Lóriendesse | [*to left of vertical rule:*] Ai [*to right of rule, in dark grey, the remainder of Tolkien's poem "Namárië"*]'. Printed on spine: '[*uncials:*] TOLKIEN [*in red-orange:*] : THE ROAD GOES EVER ON : [*in black:*] SWANN [*roman, horizontal:*] A | & | U'. Printed on lower cover: '[*tengwar:*] [*in red-orange:*] A Elbereth Gilthoniel | [*in dark grey:*] aerlinn in edhil o Imladris | [*text of Tolkien's poem "A Elbereth Gilthoniel"*] | [*roman, in black:*] The front jacket shows the Tengwar text of Song No: 5, Namárië. | Above is the Elvish refrain from Song No. 6, I Sit Beside the Fire (Elbereth). | Both were drawn by J. R. R. Tolkien.' Printed on front flap: '[*to right of red-orange vertical rule, in uncials:*] [*in red-orange:*] THE ROAD GOES EVER ON | [*rule*] | [*in black:*] A SONG CYCLE [*3 dots, in red-orange*] [*in black:*] MUSIC BY | [*rule, in red-orange*] | [*in black:*] DONALD SWANN [*3 dots, in red-orange*] [*in black:*] POEMS | [*rule, in red-orange*] [*in black:*] BY J. R. R. TOLKIEN | [*rule, in red-orange*] | [*in black:*] [*roman:*] [*blurb*] | [*in red-orange:*] The songs from [*in black:*] "The Road Goes Ever On" [*in red-orange:*] are | sung by William Elvin, with the composer at the | piano, in a record album entitled [*in black:*] "Poems and | Songs of Middle Earth" [*in red-orange:*] (with Professor Tolkien | reading the poems) produced by Caedmon, | #TC1231, and available at your record shop. | [*below the blurb and vertical rule, in black:*] The Road Goes Ever On | Tolkien/Swann | George Allen & Unwin Ltd. | Price in U.K.: 30s. net'. Printed on back flap: '[*photograph of Tolkien*] | [*note on Tolkien*] | [*photograph of Swann*] | [*note on Swann*] | Printed in Great Britain'.

Published 28 March 1968 at 30s.; number of copies not known.

Type, music, reproductions as for B28a, except pp. [iii–iv], the *númen* fully present on p. ix, the third staff on p. 32 correctly marked with a treble clef, and the red marks in register on p. 62.

c. Ballantine Books edition, first impression (1969):

THE ROAD | GOES | EVER ON | [*in red:*] A SONG CYCLE | [*in black:*] POEMS BY J. R. R. TOLKIEN | MUSIC BY DONALD SWANN | *with decorations by J. R. R. Tolkien | and Samuel Hanks Bryant* | BALLANTINE BOOKS • NEW YORK

xii, 68 pp. Collation: [1–5⁸]. 27.8 × 21.1 cm.

[i] '[*at left:*] 74550 [*at right:*] $2.95 | [*uncials:*] THE ROAD GOES EVER ON | [*rule*] | A SONG CYCLE [*3 dots*] MUSIC BY | [*rule*] | DONALD SWANN [*3 dots*] POEMS | [*rule*] | BY J. R. R. TOLKIEN | [*roman:*] [*blurb*] | The songs from *The Road Goes Ever On* are | sung by William Elvin, the composer at the | piano, in a record album entitled *Poems and | Songs of Middle Earth* | (with Professor Tolkien | reading the poems) produced by Caedmon, | #TC1231, and available at your record or book | store.';

[ii] 'the books of | J. R. R. Tolkien | [*10 titles, beginning with* H, *ending with* RGEO] | The works of J. R. R. Tolkien are published | in hardcover by Houghton Mifflin Company | and in the Authorized Edition in paperback | by Ballantine Books'; [iii] title; [iv] 'TEXT COPYRIGHT © 1962 BY GEORGE ALLEN & | UNWIN LTD.; COPYRIGHT © 1967 BY J. R. R. TOLKIEN | MUSIC COPYRIGHT © 1967 BY DONALD SWANN | ALL RIGHTS RESERVED INCLUDING THE RIGHT TO | REPRODUCE THIS BOOK OR PARTS THEREOF IN ANY FORM | LIBRARY OF CONGRESS CATALOG CARD NUMBER: 67-20501 | PRINTED IN THE UNITED STATES OF AMERICA | THIS EDITION PUBLISHED BY ARRANGE-MENT WITH | HOUGHTON MIFFLIN COMPANY | BALLANTINE BOOKS, INC. | 101 FIFTH AVENUE, NEW YORK, N.Y. 10003'; v–viii foreword, by Donald Swann; ix table of contents; [x] blank; [xi] 'THE ROAD GOES | EVER ON'; [xii] blank; 1–53 music and lyrics; [54] blank; [55] 'NOTES AND TRANSLATIONS | HERE FOLLOW Professor Tolkien's scripts, translations and | comments on the Elvish texts for "Namárië" (song Number 5) | and "A Elbereth Gilthoniel" (in song Number 6).'; [56] blank; [57]–[68] text and reproductions. Headings printed in red as for B28a.

Wove paper. Bound in light blue paper over boards. Stamped on upper cover in gilt: '[*to right of vertical rule:*] [*uncials:*] THE ROAD GOES EVER ON | [*rule*] | A SONG CYCLE [*3 dots*] MUSIC BY | [*rule*] | DONALD SWANN [*3 dots*] POEMS | [*rule*] | BY J. R. R. TOLKIEN [*tengwar:*] Namárië' | [*rule*]'. Colour illustration by Barbara Remington, the *Lord of the Rings* mural (see A5d), pasted onto lower part of upper cover below type and rules, in a recessed panel, within a single rule frame stamped in blind. Stamped on spine in gilt: '[*publisher's "BB" device*] | [*running down:*] [*uncials:*] SWANN · THE ROAD GOES EVER ON · TOLKIEN [*roman:*] 74550 295'. Wove endpapers. No headbands. All edges trimmed and unstained.

Published October 1969 at $2.95; number of copies not known.

Type, music, reproductions as for B28a, except pp. [i–iv], the *númen* fully present on p. ix, the third staff on p. 32 correctly marked with a treble clef, and 'aeron' corrected to 'aearon' on p. 63. The red diacritical and punctuation marks on p. 62 are out of register.

d. Ballantine Books edition, second (first paperback) impression (1975):

THE ROAD | GOES | EVER ON | [*in red:*] A SONG CYCLE | [*in black:*] POEMS BY J. R. R. TOLKIEN | MUSIC BY DONALD SWANN | *with decorations by J. R. R. Tolkien* | *and Samuel Hanks Bryant* | BALLANTINE BOOKS • NEW YORK

xii, 68 pp. Collation: 40 leaves. 28.0 × 20.9 cm.

Contents as for B28c, except pp. [ii] 'also available from | Ballantine Books | The great masterpieces of fantasy by | J. R. R. Tolkien | [*advertisement of works by and about Tolkien*]'; and [iv] 'TEXT COPYRIGHT © 1962 BY GEORGE ALLEN & | UNWIN LTD.; COPYRIGHT © 1967 BY J. R. R. TOLKIEN | MUSIC COPYRIGHT © 1967 BY DONALD SWANN | ALL RIGHTS RESERVED INCLUDING THE RIGHT TO | REPRODUCE THIS BOOK OR PARTS THEREOF IN ANY FORM | LIBRARY OF CONGRESS CATALOG CARD NUMBER: 67-20501 | SBN 345-24733-7-495 | FIRST PRINTING: OCTOBER, 1969 | SECOND PRINTING: AUGUST, 1975 | PRINTED IN THE UNITED STATES OF AMERICA | BALLANTINE BOOKS | A DIVISION OF RANDOM HOUSE, INC. | 201 EAST 50TH STREET, NEW YORK, N.Y. 10022 | SIMULTANEOUSLY PUBLISHED BY | BALLANTINE BOOKS, LTD., TORONTO, CANADA'.

Wove paper. Bound in heavy wove wrappers. Covers and spine printed against a light red-purple background. Printed on upper cover: '[*publisher's "BB" device, in black and white*] [*in white:*] Ballantine/24733/$4.95 | Poems & songs of Middle Earth ... | for the millions who have read and loved | THE LORD OF THE RINGS | [*in black, against a yellow oval panel, against a black panel, within a white, black, and yellow decorative frame:*] THE ROAD | GOES EVER | ON: | A SONG CYCLE | music by | Donald Swann | [*below the frame, in yellow:*] poetry by | [*in white:*] J. R. R. TOLKIEN | [*colour photograph of Tolkien, outlined in white*] | [*in white:*] Complete with easy-to-play chords for guitar and piano!'. Printed on spine: '[*publisher's "BB" device, in black and white*] | [*running down:*] THE ROAD GOES EVER ON: A SONG CYCLE music by Donald Swann poetry by J. R. R. TOLKIEN 345-24733-7-495'. Printed on lower cover: '[*blurb, in black, against a yellow oval panel outlined in black, within a white and yellow decorative frame*] | [*below the frame, in white:*] Printed in USA'. All edges trimmed and unstained.

Published August 1975 at $4.95; number of copies not known.

Type, music, reproductions as for B28c, except pp. [ii], [iv].

e. Second Allen & Unwin edition (1978):

THE ROAD | GOES | EVER ON | [*in dark green:*] A SONG CYCLE | [*in black:*] POEMS BY J. R. R. TOLKIEN | MUSIC BY DONALD SWANN | *with decorations by J. R. R. Tolkien* | London | GEORGE ALLEN & UNWIN | Boston Sydney

xiv, 82 pp. Collation: [1–6⁸]. 27.6 × 21.8 cm.

[i] 'THE ROAD GOES | EVER ON'; [ii] 'BOOKS BY | *J. R. R. Tolkien* | [*12 titles, beginning with* H, *ending with* Silm]'; [iii] title; [iv] 'First published in Great Britain in 1968 | Fourth impression 1974 | Second edition 1978 | [*notice of restrictions under copyright*] | GEORGE ALLEN & UNWIN LTD | 40 Museum Street, London WC1A 1LU | Text © George Allen & Unwin Ltd, 1962 | © J. R. R. Tolkien 1967 | Music © Donald Swann 1967 | Bilbo's Last Song Text © Joy Hill 1978 | [*British Library Cataloguing in Publication Data, within a single rule frame*] | Printed in Great Britain by | William Clowes & Sons Limited | London, Beccles and Colchester'; v–ix foreword, by Donald Swann; [x] blank; [xi] table of contents; [xii] blank; [xiii] 'THE ROAD GOES | EVER ON'; [xiv] notes for performers; 1–62 music and lyrics; [63] 'NOTES AND TRANSLATIONS | HERE FOLLOW Professor Tolkien's scripts, translations and | comments on the Elvish texts for "Namárië" (song Number 5) | and "A Elbereth Gilthoniel" (in song Number 6).'; [64] blank; [65]–76 text and reproductions; [77–82] blank. Manuscripts formally written out by Tolkien in tengwar, 'Namárië' and 'A Elbereth Gilthoniel', reproduced in black and dark green on pp. [65] and 70 respectively, and in grey and dark green, line by line, as decorations along the head and foot of most pages throughout the book. Holograph manuscript of 'Namárië' by Tolkien, with notes, reproduced in black and red on p. [76] (transcription printed in type on p. 66). Decorations by Samuel Hanks Bryant as for B28a, but uncredited. Headings for the foreword and table of contents, and song title headings, printed in dark green.

Order of songs as for B28a, with 'Bilbo's Last Song (at the Grey Havens)' added at end.

Cream wove paper. Bound in cream paper over boards. Printed on upper cover in dark green: 'THE ROAD GOES | EVER ON'. Printed on spine in dark green: '[*running down:*] TOLKIEN THE ROAD GOES EVER ON SWANN | [*horizontal:*] A | & | U'. Cream wove endpapers. No headbands. All edges trimmed and unstained.

Dust-jacket, cream wove paper. Printed on upper cover: '[*to right of dark green vertical rule:*] [*uncials:*] [*in dark green:*] THE ROAD GOES EVER ON | [*rule*] | [*in black:*] A SONG CYCLE [*3 dots, in dark green*] [*in black:*] MUSIC BY | [*rule, in dark green*] | [*in black:*] DONALD SWANN [*3 dots, in dark green*] [*in black:*] POEMS | [*rule, in dark green*] | [*in black:*] BY J. R. R. TOLKIEN [*in dark green:*] [*vertical rule*] SECOND [*parallel to the preceding word:*] EDITION | [*rule*] | [*tengwar:*] Attariello nainië Lóriendesse | [*to left of long vertical rule:*] Ai [*to right of rule, in dark grey, the remainder of Tolkien's poem "Namárië"*]'. Printed on spine, running down: '[*uncials:*] TOLKIEN [*in dark green:*] : THE ROAD GOES EVER ON : [*in black:*] SWANN [*roman:*] George Allen & Unwin'. Printed on lower cover: '[*tengwar:*] [*in dark green:*] A Elbereth Gilthoniel | [*in dark grey:*] aerlinn in edhil o Imladris | [*text of Tolkien's poem "A Elbereth Gilthoniel"*] | [*roman, in black:*] The front jacket shows the Tengwar text of Song No: 5, *Namárië*. | Above is the Elvish refrain from Song No. 6, *I Sit Beside the Fire (Elbereth)*. | Both were drawn by J. R. R. Tolkien.' Printed on front flap: '[*to right of dark green vertical rule:*] [*uncials:*] [*in dark green:*] THE ROAD GOES EVER ON | [*rule*] | [*in black:*] A SONG CYCLE [*3 dots, in dark green*] [*roman:*] [*in black:*] MUSIC BY | [*rule, in dark green*] | [*in black:*] DONALD SWANN [*3 dots, in dark green*] [*in black:*] POEMS | [*rule, in dark green*] | [*in black:*] BY J. R. R. TOLKIEN | [*rule, in dark green*] | [*in black:*] [*blurb*] | [*in dark green:*] The songs from [*in black:*] "The Road Goes Ever On" [*in dark green:*] are | sung by William Elvin, with the composer at the | piano, in a record album entitled [*in black:*] "Poems and | Songs of Middle Earth" [*in dark green:*] (with Professor Tolkien | reading the poems) produced by Caedmon, | #TC1231, and available at your record shop. | [*in black:*] SECOND EDITION | [*below blurb and vertical rule:*] PRICE NET | £4.75 | IN UK ONLY'. Printed on back flap: '[*photograph of Tolkien*] | [*note on Tolkien*] | [*photograph of Swann*] | [*note on Swann*] | ISBN 0 04 784011 0 | *Printed in Great Britain*'.

Published October 1978 at £4.75; number of copies not known.

For the new edition Swann rewrote his foreword and added performance directions, including indications of tempo and suggestions for the division of voices. A new, eighth setting, 'Bilbo's Last Song' (cf. A11), now ends the cycle. The final line of the lyrics to 'Bilbo's Last Song', pp. 60, 61, was corrected after the initial typesetting to agree with A11b ('above your mast'). The remainder of the music, and Tolkien's notes, are in B28e as for B28a. The preliminary matter was newly typeset except for the half-title, part of the title page, and part of the table of contents.

The diacritical and punctuation marks in the chant 'A Elbereth Gilthoniel', p. 70, are not present.

f. Second Houghton Mifflin edition (1978):

THE ROAD | GOES | EVER ON | [*in green:*] *A SONG CYCLE* | [*in black:*] POEMS BY J. R. R. TOLKIEN | MUSIC BY DONALD SWANN | *with decorations by J. R. R. Tolkien* | SECOND EDITION, REVISED | HOUGHTON MIFFLIN COMPANY BOSTON | 1978

xiv, 82 pp. Collation: [1–6⁸]. 27.8 × 21.4 cm.

Contents as for B28e, except pp. [iii] title, as above; and [iv] 'Text copyright © 1962, 1978 by George Allen & Unwin Ltd; | copyright © 1967 by J. R. R. Tolkien | Music copyright © 1967, 1978 by Donald Swann | [*notice of restrictions*] | Library of Congress Catalog Card Number 67-20501 | ISBN: 0-395-24758-6 | Printed in the United States of America | [*printing code, beginning "H", ending "1"*]'. Decorations by Samuel Hanks Bryant as for B28a, but uncredited. Headings as for B28e, printed in green.

Wove paper. Bound in dark green cloth over boards. Stamped on upper cover in gilt, to right of decorative border stamped in gilt: 'THE ROAD GOES | EVER ON'. Stamped on spine, running down in gilt: 'J. R. R. TOLKIEN – THE ROAD GOES EVER ON – DONALD SWANN – HMCO'. Tan wove endpapers. No headbands. All edges trimmed and unstained.

Dust-jacket, cream wove paper. Printed on upper cover: '[*to right of green vertical rule:*] [*uncials:*] [*in green:*] THE ROAD GOES EVER ON | [*rule*] | [*in black:*] A SONG CYCLE [*3 dots, in green*] [*in black:*] MUSIC BY | [*rule, in green*] | [*in black:*] DONALD SWANN [*3 dots, in green*] [*in black:*] POEMS | [*rule, in green*] | [*in black:*] BY J. R. R. TOLKIEN [*vertical rule, in green*] [*roman, in black:*] SECOND EDITION [*parallel to the two preceding words:*] REVISED [*in green:*] [*vertical rule*] | [*rule*] | [*tengwar:*] Attariello nainië Lóriendesse | [*to left of long vertical rule:*] Ai [*to right of rule, in grey, the remainder of Tolkien's poem "Namárië"*]'. Printed on spine, running down, in uncials: 'TOLKIEN [*in green:*] : THE ROAD GOES EVER ON : [*in black:*] SWANN HMCO'. Printed on lower cover: '[*tengwar:*] [*in green:*] A Elbereth Gilthoniel | [*in grey:*] aerlinn in edhil o Imladris | [*text of Tolkien's poem "A Elbereth Gilthoniel"*] | [*roman, in black:*] The front jacket shows the Tengwar text of Song No. 5, *Namárië*. | Above is the Elvish refrain from Song No. 6, *I Sit Beside the Fire (Elbereth)*. | Both were drawn by J. R. R. Tolkien. | ISBN 0-395-24758-6 | [*rule*] | 6-97067'. Printed on front flap: '$10.00 | [*to right of green vertical rule:*] [*uncials:*] [*in green:*] THE ROAD GOES EVER ON | [*rule*] | [*in black:*] A SONG CYCLE [*3 dots, in green*] [*roman:*] [*in black:*] MUSIC BY | [*rule, in green*] | [*in black:*] DONALD SWANN [*3 dots, in green*] [*in black:*] POEMS | [*rule, in green*] | [*in black:*] BY J. R. R. TOLKIEN | [*rule, in green*] | [*in black:*] [*blurb*] | [*in green:*] SECOND EDITION | REVISED | [*in black:*] HOUGHTON MIFFLIN COMPANY © 1978 [*to left of vertical rule, running down:*] 0478'. Printed on back flap: '[*photograph of Tolkien*] | PHOTO BY ROGER HILL | [*note on Tolkien*] | [*photograph of Swann*] PHOTO BY BRIAN SHUEL | [*note on Swann*] | [*in green:*] HOUGHTON MIFFLIN COMPANY | 2 Park Street | Boston, Massachusetts | 02107'.

Published 25 May 1978 at $10.00; 10,000 copies printed.

Type, music, reproductions as for B28e, except pp. [iii–iv], and with diacritical and punctuation marks present, in green, on p. 70.

B29   ATTACKS OF TASTE   1971

[*within a red-brown decorative frame, within a black single rule frame:*] [*in red-brown:*] ATTACKS | OF TASTE | [*in black:*] [*decorative dash*] | *Compiled and Edited* | *by* | EVELYN B. BYRNE | & | OTTO M. PENZLER | ON TEENAGE READING: | *"You must remember that youngsters (as | youngsters for some reason never remem-* | *ber) have attacks of taste like attacks of* | *measles."*—ARCHIBALD MACLEISH | [*below the frames:*] New York GOTHAM BOOK MART 1971

[4], xii, 66 pp. Collation: [1–5⁸χ1]. 23.4 × 15.5 cm.

[preliminary 1] 'ATTACKS OF TASTE'; [preliminary 2–4] blank; [i] 'DEDICATED | To those we love'; [ii] blank; [iii] title; [iv] 'Copyright © 1971 by | EVELYN B. BYRNE and OTTO M. PENZLER | All rights reserved. No portion of this book may be | reprinted without the permission of the Gotham Book Mart | and Gallery and the Editors. | PUBLISHED AND DISTRIBUTED BY | The Gotham Book Mart and Gallery, Inc. | 41 West 47th Street | New York, N.Y. 10036'; [v, misnumbered 'vii'] preface; [vi] blank; [vii] table of contents; [viii] blank; [ix] '*Attacks of Taste*'; [x] blank; xi–xii introduction; 1–49 text; [50] blank; [51] '*Index*'; [52] blank; 53–63 index; [64] blank; [65] 'Printed in Trump Mediaeval and Caslon types at the Noel Young | Press, Santa Barbara, Calif. by Noel Young & Graham Mackintosh. | This first edition is limited to 500 copies numbered and signed by | the editors, of which 100 copies are for presentation & not for sale. | [*number of copy added in pen*] | [*signatures of Byrne and Penzler*] | Printed in the United States of America'; [66] blank.

Includes one-paragraph statement by J. R. R. Tolkien, p. 43.

Wove paper. Bound in tan cloth over boards. Label affixed to upper cover, printed: '[*within a red-brown decorative frame, within a black single rule frame:*] [*decorative dash*] | [*in red-brown:*] ATTACKS OF TASTE | [*in black:*] [*decorative dash*] | *Compiled and Edited* | *by* | EVELYN B. BYRNE | *&* | OTTO M. PENZLER'. Label affixed to spine, printed: '[*ornament, in red-brown*] [*in black:*] ATTACKS OF TASTE [*ornament, in red-brown*] [*in black:*] Evelyn B. Byrne *&* Otto M. Penzler [*ornament, in red-brown*]'. Red-brown laid endpapers. No headbands. All edges trimmed and unstained.

Dust-jacket, unprinted wove paper.

Published 25 December 1971 at $15.00; 500 copies printed.

A collection of statements by authors on the books they loved while teenagers. Tolkien was interested not in literature but in books on botany and astronomy. His statement was reprinted in *Beyond Bree* (newsletter of the American Mensa Tolkien Special Interest Group), Sherman Oaks, Calif., December 1986, p. 6.

B30   **SIR GAWAIN AND THE GREEN KNIGHT,**   1975
                       PEARL, AND SIR ORFEO

a. First edition:

SIR GAWAIN | AND THE GREEN KNIGHT | PEARL | *and* | SIR ORFEO | *Translated by* | J. R. R. TOLKIEN | *London* | GEORGE ALLEN & UNWIN LTD | RUSKIN HOUSE MUSEUM STREET

152 pp. Collation: [1–8^{8}9^{4}10^8]. 23.4 × 15.5 cm.

[1–2] blank; [3] 'SIR GAWAIN | AND THE GREEN KNIGHT | PEARL | *and* | SIR ORFEO'; [4] 'J. R. R. TOLKIEN | [*9 titles, beginning with* LR, *ending with* TL] | With Donald Swann | *The Road Goes Ever On*'; [5] title; [6] 'First published in 1975 | [*notice of restrictions under copyright*] | © George Allen & Unwin Ltd. 1975 | ISBN 0 04 821035 8 | Printed in Great Britain | in 11 point Garamond type | by W & J Mackay Limited, Chatham'; 7–9 preface; [10] blank; [11] table of contents; [12] blank; 13–24 introduction; 25–137 text; 138–41 glossary; 142–8 appendix; [149] poem, 'Gawain's Leave-taking'; [150–2] blank.

Wove paper. Bound in dark green cloth over boards. Stamped on spine in gilt: '[*running down:*] J. R. R. TOLKIEN *Sir Gawain and the Green Knight* [*flower*] *Pearl* [*flower*] *Sir Orfeo* | [*horizontal:*] George | Allen | & | Unwin'. Wove endpapers. Green/white headband. All edges trimmed. Top edge stained green, fore- and bottom edges unstained.

Dust-jacket, wove paper. Printed on upper cover against a dark green background: '[*in white:*] J. R. R. TOLKIEN | [*in orange:*] Sir Gawain | and the | Green Knight | [*decorative rule, in white*] | [*in orange:*] Pearl | [*decorative rule, in white*] | [*in orange:*] Sir Orfeo'. Printed on spine, running down, against a dark green background: '[*in white:*] J. R. R. TOLKIEN [*in orange:*] Sir Gawain and the Green Knight [*flower, in white*] [*in orange:*] Pearl [*flower, in white*] [*in orange:*] Sir Orfeo [*in white:*] GEORGE ALLEN [*parallel to the preceding two words:*] & UNWIN'. Lower cover printed solid dark green. Printed on front flap in dark green: '[*blurb*] | PRICE NET | £3·95 | IN U.K. ONLY'. Printed on back flap in dark green: 'ISBN 0 04 821035 8 | *Printed in Great Britain*'.

Published September 1975 at £3.95; number of copies not known. *The Bookseller*, 20 September 1975, says 'published this week'.

Edited with a preface and notes by Christopher Tolkien.

J. R. R. Tolkien began, carried almost to the end, but never completed (to his satisfaction) Modern English translations of the medieval poems *Sir Gawain and the Green Knight*, *Pearl*, and *Sir Orfeo*. His Modern English *Sir Gawain* was begun in the nineteen-thirties or forties, following the Middle English edition of the poem he edited with E. V. Gordon (B7). By late 1950 he had prepared, or was preparing, a radio broadcast version of *Sir Gawain*: in a letter of 6 November 1950 Stanley Unwin asked if Tolkien had ever made any arrangement for its publication in book form. Unwin inquired also about Tolkien's translation of *Pearl*, 'which I believe Blackwells put into type and of which Rayner [Unwin] saw galley proofs in about 1944'. On 21 November Stanley Unwin wrote again to express interest in 'a volume of non-Chaucerian Middle English translations' with an introductory essay by Tolkien. Tolkien's Modern English *Sir Gawain* was not broadcast until December 1953, read by professional actors, on the BBC Third Programme (repeated September 1954), with an introduction and afterword recorded by Tolkien himself. Tolkien also presented on the BBC Third Programme, in January 1954, a talk on the meaning and place of *Sir Gawain and the Green Knight* in the literature of the Chaucerian period.

On 7 August 1954 Tolkien wrote to Katherine Farrer that 'they are clamouring for Gawain'—'they' being, evidently, the academic community. Tolkien's correspondence with Allen & Unwin now concerned not *Sir Gawain* but the correction of proofs of *The Lord of the Rings*. However, Allen & Unwin continued to be interested in *Sir Gawain*; and so too was the London publisher William Heinemann. The BBC copy of the translation seems to have been lent by P. H. Newby, who managed the broadcast, to James Reeves, editor of Heinemann's 'Poetry Bookshelf', who wished to include *Sir Gawain* in that series. 'Owing to distractions and incompetence' Tolkien entered into negotiations with Reeves, forgetting Allen & Unwin's long-standing interest, and was on the point of signing a contract with Heinemann when he realized that his latest contract with Allen & Unwin gave that publisher the right of first refusal of his next work after *The Lord of the Rings*. He politely broke off with Heinemann and on 4 August 1959 apologized to Rayner Unwin for his lapse. 'I think it is high time that *Sir Gawain* was published,' he wrote, 'before some competitor (whether better or worse) spoils the field. Would you welcome it soon, or not?' Unwin quickly agreed, noting that Tolkien had delayed so far in order to assemble other translations to publish together with *Sir Gawain*; but Allen & Unwin would publish *Sir Gawain* on its own. On 20 August 1959 Tolkien wrote to Unwin that he wanted to publish his translation of *Pearl* with *Sir Gawain*, but that he had promised the former work to Blackwell's. Five days later, Tolkien met with Basil Blackwell, who released *Pearl* unconditionally (see further, below).

On 27 August 1959 Tolkien wrote to Rayner Unwin that 'the best form of amends would be to get *Gawain* and *Pearl* into your hands as soon as possible. The spirit is indeed willing; but the flesh weak and rebellious' (he had contracted lumbago). On 9 December 1959 he reported to Unwin that he was 'charging well ahead with the reconstruction of the *Silmarillion* etc.' which was also wanted; but he felt 'quite clearly I must take up Gawain immediately. I shall not manage it before Christmas; but I recently ordered and inspected the material and I do not think that the actual text of the translation of *Gawain* and of *Pearl* now need very much work. . . . I am still a little uncertain about what other matter to add to them by way of introduction or notes'. Three years later, however, he was still putting the work in order. On 2 November 1962 he wrote to Unwin that the translations of *Pearl* and *Sir Gawain* were completed, 'but they need a final revision before I can send them in. *Pearl* in particular has been subjected to a good deal of criticism, much of which is justified, by an expert in this field. These translations are of course on my list as the most urgent task before me, but the return to lecturing this term has proved a much greater burden than I expected. It has taken much more work than I guessed to shake the dust of seventeen years off matter which I once thought I knew.' Even so, he hoped on 19 December 1962, in a letter to his son Michael, that the translations would be published early in the new year.

In letters to Tolkien in early 1963 Rayner Unwin hoped in vain to begin production of the book that spring for a Christmas 1963 publication. On 6 January 1965 Tolkien apologized to his grandson, Michael George Tolkien, that *Sir Gawain* and *Pearl* had not yet appeared 'largely owing, in addition to the natural difficulty of rendering verse into verse, to my discovering many minor points about words, in the course of my work, which lead me off'. Allen & Unwin finally prepared specimen pages, which Tolkien approved on 25 May 1965. But now the *Lord of the Rings* copyright problem (see A5c note) also demanded his attention. After so much labour and delay, it was surely with ironic humor that Tolkien remarked to Rayner Unwin in a letter of 8 November 1965:

> I expect you are getting anxious about [*Sir Gawain* and *Pearl*]. . . . It was rather disastrous that I had to put them aside, while I had them fully in mind. The work on the 'revision' of *The Lord of the Rings* took me clean away, and I now find work on anything else tiresome. I am finding the selection of notes [for the translations], and compressing them, and the introduction difficult. Too much to say, and not sure of my target. The main target is, of course, the general reader of literary bent with no knowledge of Middle English; but it cannot be doubted that the book will be read by students, and by academic folk of 'English Departments'. Some of the latter have their pistols loose in the holsters.

'Tiresome' work or not, Tolkien had set *Sir Gawain* aside also to write 'Smith of Wootton Major', and to attend to Donald Swann's songs (see B28), and especially *The Silmarillion* still called to him; and so it went, so many demands upon his time, until his death. A letter of 14 May 1968 still found him in 'the last throes of *Gawain* and *Pearl*'.

Tolkien's translation of *Pearl* has an even longer history than *Sir Gawain*. It was begun at Leeds in the nineteen-twenties and was in a finished form by 1926. It was offered unsuccessfully to the publisher J. M. Dent; but Guy Pocock of Dent's arranged for part of it, at least, to be broadcast on radio on 7 August 1936. It was referred to in a letter to Tolkien of 5 October 1936 by Stanley Unwin, who expressed an interest; but Tolkien's attention was with *The Hobbit* and with Clark Hall's *Beowulf and the Finnesburg Fragment* (B17). By 1942 Basil Blackwell offered to publish *Pearl*, translator's payment to be credited to Tolkien's overdue account at Blackwell's

Oxford bookshop. Tolkien wrote to his son Christopher on 23–5 September 1944 that he 'must try and get on with the Pearl and stop the eager maw of Basil Blackwell'. The work was set in type, and by *circa* 18 March 1945 the proofs needed correction and an introduction had still to be written. But the latter came to no more than rough notes, and in 1959, at Tolkien's request, Blackwell abandoned the project with grace, even refusing payment for Tolkien's default and the cost of the abortive typesetting. In fact, as Tolkien wrote to Rayner Unwin on 25 August 1959, the typesetting had 'about a thousand fatuous mistakes (from reasonable copy)' and would have been costly to correct.

It may be assumed that Tolkien translated *Sir Orfeo* into Modern English, like the other two poems, *circa* 1920–40—or perhaps *circa* 1944, when he prepared a version of the poem in Middle English for the Oxford wartime naval cadets' course (see B18). He remarked, in a letter of 28 April 1967 to a Canadian university professor compiling an anthology of early English poetry, that he had made a 'reasonably successful' translation of *Sir Orfeo* 'some years ago'. Christopher Tolkien, in his preface to B30, noted that he could find no writing by his father on *Sir Orfeo*.

The first three (of six) parts of the introduction to B30 are by J. R. R. Tolkien. Part I, on the author of *Sir Gawain* and *Pearl*, was derived by Christopher Tolkien from his father's notes. Part II, on *Sir Gawain*, is a 'slightly reduced' version of the radio talk J. R. R. Tolkien gave following the 1953–4 BBC broadcast; cf. C36. Part III, on *Pearl*, is a reprint of Tolkien's contribution to the introduction to E. V. Gordon's edition of *Pearl* (see B22). To these are added notes by Christopher Tolkien on *Sir Orfeo*, on editions of the three poems, and on the text of the translations. The glossary is also by Christopher Tolkien.

'Gawain's Leave-taking' is a translation by J. R. R. Tolkien of yet another medieval English poem, from the Vernon manuscript in the Bodleian Library, Oxford.

BBC Radio 3 broadcast a three-part version of Tolkien's *Pearl*, adapted by Kevin Crossley-Holland and read by Hugh Dickson, in May–June 1978.

Manuscript and typescript materials by Tolkien relating to his study and translations of *Sir Gawain*, *Pearl*, and *Sir Orfeo*, and proofs, correspondence, and other material relating to the aborted Blackwell edition of *Pearl*, are in the Bodleian Library.

b. First American edition (1975):

SIR GAWAIN | AND THE GREEN KNIGHT | PEARL | *and* | SIR ORFEO | *Translated by* | J. R. R. TOLKIEN | *Boston* | HOUGHTON MIFFLIN COMPANY | *1975*

160 pp. Collation: [1–5^{16}]. 23.4 × 15.4 cm.

Contents as for B30a, except pp. [5] title, as above; and [6] 'First American Edition | Copyright © 1975 by George Allen & Unwin Ltd. | [*notice of restrictions*] | Printed in the United States of America | [*Library of Congress Cataloging in Publication Data*] | [*printing code, beginning "V", ending "1"*]'.

Wove paper. Bound in blue cloth over boards. Stamped on upper cover in gilt: '[*axe ornament*] | SIR GAWAIN | AND THE GREEN KNIGHT | PEARL | SIR ORFEO | [*leafy ornament*]'. Stamped on spine, running down, in gilt: '*Tolkien* SIR GAWAIN AND THE GREEN KNIGHT · PEARL · SIR ORFEO *hmco*'. Red wove endpapers. Yellow/blue headbands. All edges trimmed. Top edge stained orange, fore- and bottom edges unstained.

Dust-jacket, wove paper. Printed on upper cover: '[*in red:*] J. R. R. | TOLKIEN | [*against a red panel:*] [*in orange outlined in red, against a blue panel, within a broken orange single rule frame:*] Sir Gawain | and the | Green Knight | [*below the frame, in orange outlined in red, against a blue panel between orange single rules at left and right:*] | Pearl | [*below the panel, in orange outlined in red, against another blue panel within a broken orange single rule frame:*] Sir Orfeo'. Printed on spine, running down, against a blue background: '[*in red:*] J. R. R. TOLKIEN [*in orange outlined in red:*] Sir Gawain and the Green Knight [*parallel to the preceding title:*] Pearl Sir Orfeo [*in red:*] HOUGHTON MIFFLIN COMPANY'. Printed on lower cover against a blue background: '[*in white:*] Photograph by B. Potter | [*black and white photograph of J. R. R. Tolkien*] | [*in white:*] 6-97068'. Printed on front flap: '[*in blue:*] $8.95 | [*upper cover design against the red panel, reduced*] | [*in red:*] Translated by | J. R. R. TOLKIEN | [*in blue:*] [*blurb; to left of blurb, running down:*] 0975'. Printed on back flap: '[*blurb, continued, in blue*] | [*in red:*] The Translator | [*note on J. R. R. Tolkien, in blue*] | [*in red:*] HOUGHTON MIFFLIN COMPANY | 2 Park Street | Boston, Massachusetts 02107'.

Published 15 October 1975 at $8.95; 10,000 copies printed.

Typeset as for B30a, except pp. [5–6].

c. First paperback edition (1978):

SIR GAWAIN | AND THE GREEN KNIGHT | PEARL | *and* | SIR ORFEO | *Translated by* | J. R. R. TOLKIEN | *Boston* | HOUGHTON MIFFLIN COMPANY | 1978

160 pp. Collation: 80 leaves. 23.4 × 15.2 cm.

Contents as for B30a, except pp. [4] 'J. R. R. TOLKIEN | [*10 titles, beginning with* LR, *ending with* Silm] | WITH DONALD SWANN | The Road Goes Ever On'; [5] title, as above; and [6] 'Copyright © 1975 by George Allen & Unwin Ltd. | [*notice of restrictions under copyright*] | Printed in the United States of America | [*Library of Congress Cataloging in Publication Data*] | [*printing code, beginning* "V", *ending* "1"]'.

Wove paper. Bound in heavy wove wrappers. Printed on upper cover: 'Three tales from the Middle Ages | translated by | [*in red-brown:*] J. R. R. TOLKIEN | [*in black:*] [*rule*] | SIR GAWAIN | and the | GREEN KNIGHT | • | PEARL • SIR ORFEO | [*colour illustration by Pauline Baynes, of the Green Knight and Sir Gawain*]'. Printed on spine, running down: '[*in red-brown:*] TOLKIEN [*in black:*] SIR GAWAIN and the GREEN KNIGHT • PEARL • SIR ORFEO [*parallel to the preceding titles:*] HOUGHTON MIFFLIN COMPANY'. Printed on lower cover: '[*in red-brown:*] J. R. R. TOLKIEN | [*in black:*] [*rule*] | SIR GAWAIN | and the | GREEN KNIGHT | • | PEARL • SIR ORFEO | [*blurb*] | [*3 quotations, from Robert Fitzgerald*, Library Journal, *and the* Pittsburgh Press, *in black and pink*] | [*in pink:*] Jacket painting by Pauline Baynes | [*in black:*] [*at left:*] $3.95 [*at right:*] ISBN 0-395-26469-3 | [*rule*] | 6-97064 | HOUGHTON MIFFLIN COMPANY © 1978'. All edges trimmed and unstained.

Published 4 May 1978 at $3.95; 15,000 copies printed.

Typeset as for B30b, except pp. [4–6].

d. Unwin Paperbacks edition (1979):

Sir Gawain and the | Green Knight | Pearl | and | Sir Orfeo | Translated by J. R. R. TOLKIEN | Edited by Christopher Tolkien | London | UNWIN PAPERBACKS | Boston Sydney

x, 150 pp. Collation: 80 leaves. 19.5 × 12.8 cm.

[i] blurb; [ii] 'Also by J. R. R. Tolkien | [*11 titles, beginning with* H, *ending with* TL] | *With Donald Swann* | THE ROAD GOES EVER ON'; [iii] title; [iv] 'First published in Great Britain by | George Allen & Unwin 1975 | First published in Unwin Paperbacks 1979 | [*notice of restrictions under copyright*] | UNWIN® PAPERBACKS | 40 Museum Street, London WC1A 1LU | © George Allen & Unwin (Publishers) Ltd 1975, 1979 | [*British Library Cataloguing in Publication Data, within a single rule frame*] | Typeset in 10 on 11 point Plantin by Trade Linotype | and printed in Great Britain by Cox & Wyman Ltd, | London, Reading and Fakenham'; v–vii preface; [viii] blank; [ix] table of contents; [x] blank; [1]–13 introduction; [14]–130 text; [131]–4 glossary; [135]–42 appendix; [143] poem, 'Gawain's Leave-taking'; [144] blank; [145] advertisement of *LR*; [146] '*Other books by J. R. R. Tolkien in Unwin Paperbacks* | [*advertisement of* H, Silm, Farmer Giles of Ham [and] The Adventures of Tom Bombadil, *and* Tree and Leaf, Smith of Wootton Major, [and] The Homecoming of Beorhtnoth Beorhthelm's Son]'; [147] '*Also in Unwin Paperbacks* | [*advertisement of Foster*, The Complete Guide to Middle-earth, *and Carpenter*, J. R. R. Tolkien: A Biography]'; [148] blank; [149] '*Also by J. R. R. Tolkien* | [*advertisement of* RGEO]'; [150] blank.

Wove paper. Bound in heavy wove wrappers. Covers and spine printed against a blue background. Printed on upper cover: '[*in orange:*] TOLKIEN | [*in white:*] Sir Gawain & the Green Knight | Pearl Sir Orfeo | [*colour illustration*, The Labours of Hercules] | [*publisher's "unwin/UNWIN PAPERBACKS" device, in orange, white, and black*]'. Printed on spine, running down: '[*in orange:*] TOLKIEN [*in white:*] Sir Gawain & the Green Knight Pearl Sir Orfeo [*publisher's "unwin/UNWIN PAPERBACKS" device, in orange, white, and black*]'. Printed on lower cover against a white panel outlined in red-orange: '[*blurb*] | [*2 quotations, from the* Birmingham Post *and the* Times Higher Education Supplement] | Cover photograph: The Bodleian Library | From *Le Mireur du Monde*, | The Labours of Hercules | [*at left:*] UNITED KINGDOM £1.50 | AUSTRALIA $3.95 (Recommended) | NEW ZEALAND $3.95 [*at right:*] TOLKIEN/ LITERATURE | ISBN 0 04 821039 0'. All edges trimmed and unstained.

Published July 1979 at £1.50; 20,000 copies planned.

Reset.

In 1990 the cover was changed to feature a wraparound illustration by Nicki Palin.

e. Ballantine Books edition (1980):

SIR GAWAIN | AND THE GREEN KNIGHT | PEARL | and | SIR ORFEO | *Translated by* | J. R. R. TOLKIEN | BALLANTINE BOOKS · NEW YORK

x, 166 pp. Collation: 88 leaves. 17.8 × 10.7 cm.

[i] note on Tolkien; [ii] 'The Fiction of J. R. R. Tolkien | *published by Ballantine Books:* | [*7 titles, beginning with* H, *ending with* Silm]'; [iii] title; [iv] 'Copyright © 1975 by George Allen & Unwin Ltd. | [*notice of restrictions*] | Library of Congress Catalog Card Number: 75-20352 | ISBN 0-345-27760-0 | This edition published by arrangement with | Allen & Unwin Ltd. | Manufactured in the United States of America | First Ballantine Books Edition: January 1980'; [v] table of contents; [vi] blank; vii–x preface; 1–17 introduction; [18] blank; 19–148 text; 149–53 glossary; [154] blank; 155–64 appendix on verse-forms; [165] poem, 'Gawain's Leave-taking'; [166] '[*3 lines and blurb between thick-thin rules at left and right:*] J. R. R. TOLKIEN'S | Epic Fantasy Classic | The Lord of the Rings | [*blurb*] | [*publisher's order form for* H, LR]'.

Wove paper. Bound in heavy wove wrappers. Covers and spine printed against a dark wine red background. Printed on upper cover within a gold single rule frame, within a white single rule frame: '[*in white:*] Three Magnificent Translations | by the renowned author of | The Hobbit and The Lord of the Rings | [*with decorative capitals:*] J. R. R. Tolkien | [*rule with flourishes at centre*] | [*in orange, with decorative capitals:*] Sir | Gawain | and the | Green Knight | [*flourish, in white*] | [*in light blue, with decorative capital:*] Pearl | [*flourish, in white*] | [*in yellow, with decorative capitals:*] Sir Orfeo | [*in gold:*] Ballantine [*publisher's "BB" device, in dark wine red and gold*] [*in gold:*] 27760/$2.95'. Printed on spine: '[*publisher's "BB" device, in dark wine red and gold*] | [*running down:*] [*in white:*] Sir Gawain and the Green Knight [*flourish, in gold*] [*in white:*] Pearl [*flourish, in gold*] [*in white:*] Sir Orfeo [*flourish, in gold*] [*in white:*] J. R. R. Tolkien [*in gold:*] 345-27760-0-295'. Printed on lower cover: '[*within a gold single rule frame, within a white single rule frame:*] '[*in orange, with decorative capitals:*] Sir | Gawain | and the | Green Knight | [*in white, blurb, punctuated by rules, each rule with flourishes at centre*] | [*outside the frames, at lower right, running down:*] Cover printed in USA'. All edges trimmed and stained yellow.

Published January 1980 at $2.95; number of copies not known.

Reset.

B31   A TOLKIEN COMPASS   1975

a. First edition, hardcover copies:

A Tolkien Compass | Edited by Jared Lobdell | Including J. R. R. Tolkien's | *Guide to the Names in The Lord of the Rings* | Open Court La Salle, Illinois

vi, 202 pp. Collation: signatures not distinct. 20.3 × 13.3 cm.

[i] 'A Tolkien Compass'; [ii] blank; [iii] title; [iv] 'Copyright © 1975 by The Open Court Publishing Company | "Nomenclature of *The Lord of the Rings*" | Copyright © 1975 by the executors of Professor J. R. R. Tolkien. | [*notice of restrictions under copyright*] | Printed in the United States of America | ISBN 0-87548-303-8 | [*Library of Congress Cataloging in Publication Data*]'; [v] table of contents; [vi] blank; [1]–7 introduction; [8] blank; [9]–201 text; [202] blank.

Includes 'Guide to the Names in *The Lord of the Rings*' by J. R. R. Tolkien, pp. [153]–201.

Wove paper. Bound in brown-speckled beige cloth over boards. Stamped on spine in gilt: '[*running down:*] Lobdell Tolkien Compass | [*horizontal:*] Open | Court | [*publisher's "O and C's" device*]'. Wove endpapers. White headbands. All edges trimmed and unstained.

Dust-jacket, wove paper. Printed on upper cover: '[*within a decorative frame:*] A Tolkien Compass | [*colour illustration by Lester Abrams, the dragon Smaug from* The Hobbit] | Edited by Jared Lobdell'. Printed on spine: '[*running down:*] Lobdell/A Tolkien Compass | [*horizontal:*] [*publisher's "O and C's" device*] | Open | Court'. Printed on lower cover: 'A TOLKIEN COMPASS | *Jared Lobdell, Editor* | [*blurb*] | [*list of contents*] | Open Court • La Salle, Illinois • 61301'. Printed on front flap: '$7.95 | A Tolkien Compass | Jared Lobdell, editor | Including J. R. R. Tolkien's "Guide | to the Names in *The Lord of the Rings*" | [*blurb*]'. Printed on back flap: '[*blurb, continued from front flap*] | ISBN 0-87548-316-X | Cover design by Lester Abrams'.

Published 1975 at $7.95; date of publication and number of copies not known. Simultaneously issued in wrappers (see B31b).

Tolkien wrote his 'Guide to the Names in *The Lord of the Rings*' (originally entitled 'Nomenclature of *The Lord of the Rings*') after Swedish and Dutch translators made (he felt) unwarranted changes in the personal and place names of *H* and *LR*; see *Letters* nos. 190 and 204. The guide was often photocopied for translators' use. It was revised for publication in *A Tolkien Compass* by Christopher Tolkien.

b. First edition, paperback copies:

A Tolkien Compass | Edited by Jared Lobdell | Including J. R. R. Tolkien's | *Guide to the Names in The Lord of the Rings* | Open Court La Salle, Illinois

vi, 202 pp. Collation: 104 leaves. 20.3 × 13.3 cm.

Sheets as for B31a.

Wove paper. Bound in heavy wove wrappers. Printed on upper cover: '[*within a decorative frame:*] A Tolkien Compass | [*colour illustration, by Lester Abrams, of the dragon Smaug from* The Hobbit] | Edited by Jared Lobdell'. Printed on spine: '[*running down:*] Lobdell/A Tolkien Compass | [*horizontal:*] [*publisher's "O and C's" device*] | Open | Court'. Printed on lower cover: '[*at top left:*] Literature [*at top right:*] Open Court Paperback | $2.95 [*publisher's "O and C's" device*] | A Tolkien Compass | Jared Lobdell, Editor | Including Tolkien's own unpublished Guide to the | Names in The Lord of the Rings | [*blurb*] | Open Court • La Salle, Illinois • 61301 | ISBN: 0-87548-303-8 | Cover design by Lester Abrams'. All edges trimmed and unstained.

Published 1975 at $2.95; date of publication and number of copies not known. Simultaneously issued in boards (see B31a).

c. Ballantine Books edition (1980):

A TOLKIEN | COMPASS | Edited by Jared Lobdell | Including J. R. R. Tolkien's | *Guide to the Names in The Lord of the Rings* | [*publisher's 'DEL REY' device*] | A Del Rey Book | BALLANTINE BOOKS • NEW YORK

vi, 218 pp. Collation: 112 leaves. 17.8 × 10.6 cm.

[i] 'A TOLKIEN COMPASS' | [*quotation from the* A.R.E. *Journal*] | [*blurb*]'; [ii] 'The Fiction of J. R. R. Tolkien | *published by Ballantine Books:* | [*7 titles, beginning with* H, *ending with* Silm]'; [iii] title; [iv] 'A Del Rey Book | Published by Ballantine Books | Copyright © 1975 by The Open Court Publishing Company | "Nomenclature of *The Lord of the Rings*" | Copyright © 1975 by the executors of | Professor J. R. R. Tolkien | [*notice of restrictions under copyright*] | Library of Congress Catalog Card Number: 74-20681 | ISBN 0-345-28855-6 | This edition published by arrangement with | The Open Court Publishing Co. | Manufactured in the United States of America | First Ballantine Books Edition: June 1980 | Cover art by Darrell K. Sweet, from | THE 1980 J. R. R. TOLKIEN CALENDAR, | Copyright © 1979 by Random House, Inc.'; [v–vi] table of contents; 1–8 introduction; 9–216 text; [217] '[*within a thick-thin rule frame:*] J. R. R. TOLKIEN: | MAN | AND MYTH | [*below the frame:*] [*advertisement of 5 titles, beginning with Carpenter,* Tolkien: A Biography, *ending with* J. R. R. Tolkien: Man and Myth *boxed set*] | [*at left, publisher's "BB" device; at right:*] Ballantine Books LG-7'; [218] '[*3 lines and blurb between thick-thin rules at left and right:*] J. R. R. TOLKIEN'S | Epic Fantasy Classic | The Lord of the Rings | [*blurb*] | [*publisher's order form for* H, LR]'.

Includes 'Guide to the Names in *The Lord of the Rings*' by J. R. R. Tolkien, pp. 168–216.

Wove paper. Bound in heavy wove wrappers. Covers and spine printed against a light orange background. Printed on upper cover: '[*at upper left, publisher's "DEL REY" device in white and red*] | [*in black:*] Fantasy | Nonfiction | 28855 | $2.50 [*at centre:*] [*in light blue and white:*] A | [*in blue and white, lower serif of "T" extends partly around the illustration:*] TOLKIEN | [*in light blue and white:*] COMPASS | [*colour illustration by Darrell K. Sweet, of Gollum and Bilbo from* The Hobbit] | [*in light blue:*] FASCINATING | STUDIES AND INTERPRETATIONS | OF J. R. R. TOLKIEN'S MOST POPULAR | EPIC FANTASIES | [*rule, in black*] | [*in red:*] EDITED BY JARED LOBDELL'. Printed on spine: '[*publisher's "DEL REY" device in white and red*] | [*in black:*] Fantasy | Nonfiction | [*running down:*] [*in light blue and white:*] A [*in dark blue and white:*] TOLKIEN [*in light blue and white:*] COMPASS [*in red:*] EDITED BY [*parallel to the preceding two words:*] JARED LOBDELL [*followed by, in black:*] 345-28855-6-250'. Printed on lower cover: '[*quotation from the* A.R.E. Journal] | [*blurb, in red, blue, and black*] | [*within a black single rule oval:*] [*in red:*] SPECIAL FEATURE | [*in blue:*] GUIDE TO THE NAMES IN THE | LORD OF THE RINGS by J. R. R. Tolkien | [*in black:*] [*blurb*] | [*below the frame:*] [*in black:*] Cover printed in USA'.

Published June 1980 at $2.50; number of copies not known.

Reset.

B32   J. R. R. TOLKIEN: A BIOGRAPHY   1977

a. First edition:

J. R. R. TOLKIEN | *A biography* | *by* | Humphrey Carpenter | London | GEORGE ALLEN & UNWIN LTD | Ruskin House Museum Street

xiv, 290 pp. + 8 plates. Collation: [1–9^{16}10^8]. 23.3 × 15.4 cm.

[i–ii] blank; [iii] 'J. R. R. TOLKIEN | *A biography*'; [iv] 'Also by Humphrey Carpenter | *A Thames Companion* | (with Mari Prichard)'; [v] title; [vi] 'First published in 1977 | [*notice of restrictions under copyright*] | © George Allen & Unwin (Publishers) Ltd, 1977 | ISBN 0 04 928037 6 | Printed in Great Britain by Westerham Press'; [vii] 'Dedicated to the memory of | The T.C.B.S.'; [viii] blank; [ix–x] table of contents; [xi–xii] list of illustrations; [xiii] author's note; [xiv] blank; [1] 'I | *A visit*'; [2] blank; 3–6 text; [7] 'II | *1892–1916: Early years*'; [8] blank; 9–86 text; [87] 'III | *1917–1925: The making of a | mythology*'; [88] blank; 89–108 text; [109] 'IV | *1925–1949(i): 'In a hole in | the ground there lived a hobbit'*'; [110] blank; 111–72 text; [173] 'V | *1925–1949(ii): The Third Age*'; [174] blank; 175–204 text; [205] 'VI | *1949–1966: Success*'; [206] blank; 207–32 text; [233] 'VII | *1959–1973: Last years*'; [234] blank; 235–56 text; [257] 'VIII | *The Tree*'; [258] blank; 259–[60] text; [261] '*Appendices*'; [262] blank; [263]–79 appendices; [280] blank; 281–7 index; [288–90] blank. 29 illustrations on 8 plates, inserted between pp. 18–19, 50–1, 82–3, 114–15, 146–7, 178–9, 242–3, 274–5.

Includes excerpts from previously unpublished letters, poetry, and prose by Tolkien:

p. 16, letter to his father, 14 February 1896, written at age four, never sent
p. 36, limerick in 'Nevbosh' or 'New Nonsense', a language invented by Tolkien and his cousin Mary Incledon

p. 47, six lines of a poem, 'Wood-sunshine' ('Come sing ye light fairy things tripping so gay'), written in July 1910

p. 71, the first eight lines of a poem, 'The Voyage of Earendel the Evening Star' (later 'The Last Voyage of Eärendel'), composed at Phoenix Farm, Gedling, Nottinghamshire, in September 1914. This was the first poem written by Tolkien on the subject of Eärendel. A version was read to the Essay Club of Exeter College, Oxford in November 1914, where it was 'well criticised' (Tolkien to Edith Bratt, 27 November 1914). Cf. *The Book of Lost Tales, Part Two* (A22), p. 268, with these lines appended to the last of five versions of the poem, pp. 267–9.

pp. 73–4, six lines of a poem, 'Sea Chant of an Elder Day' ('In a dim and perilous region'), written (according to Carpenter) on 4 December 1914, based on Tolkien's memories of a holiday in Cornwall earlier in the year. The lines quoted, however, are from a version of 1915, and the history of the poem begins in 1912 with revisions in December 1914 and March 1915; see *The Shaping of Middle-earth* (A24), pp. 213–17. The 'Sea Chant' was also entitled 'The Tides' and 'On the Cornish Coast', and was incorporated, ll. 13 ff., into 'The Horns of Ulmo [> Ylmir]' (see *Shaping*, p. 216).

p. 74, poem, or nine lines of a poem, 'Lo! young we are and yet have stood'

pp. 74–5, the first sixteen lines of a manuscript version (not so identified) of 'Goblin Feet' (cf. B1a)

p. 76, four lines of an untitled poem in Elvish, beginning 'Ai lintulinda Lasselanta', dated November 1915 and March 1916. The complete poem was published, p. 48, with a commentary, in Paul Nolan Hyde, 'Narqelion: A Single, Falling Leaf at Sunfading', *Mythlore*, 15, no. 2, whole no. 56 (Winter 1988), pp. 47–52 and (the poem in tengwar) lower cover; poem and part of commentary reprinted in *Vinyar Tengwar* (newsletter of the Elvish Linguistic Fellowship), no. 6 (July 1989), pp. 12–13.

pp. 76–7, poem, 'The Shores of Faery', in its earliest form. It was written in Moseley, Edgbaston, and Birmingham, on 8–9 July 1915 and later revised, especially in 1924. The latest version, with earliest version readings in footnotes, was published in *The Book of Lost Tales, Part Two* (A22), pp. 271–2.

p. 167, eleven lines from 'The Gest of Beren and Lúthien' ('Much love be [i.e. he] learned, and loved wisdom'), lines 344–54 of 'The Lay of the Children of Húrin' (cf. *The Lays of Beleriand* [A23], p. 14).

p. 168, six lines from a poem, 'The Fall of Arthur'

illustration facing p. 179, reproduction of an autograph page from the manuscript of *The Lord of the Rings* (A5), including the earliest drawing of the inscription and signs on the West Gate of Moria (bk. 2, ch. 4). Later published in *The Treason of Isengard* (A27), p. 182.

pp. 184–5, excerpt from a letter to Stanley Unwin, 16 December 1937, on *The Silmarillion* and a successor to *The Hobbit* (cf. *Letters* no. 19)

pp. 190–1, part of a poem, 'Mythopoeia', the quotation beginning 'The heart of man is not compound of lies'. Cf. the final version of the poem, published in *Tree and Leaf* (A7e–g).

pp. 197–9, excerpts from letters to Christopher Tolkien, 1944, elisions not indicated by Carpenter: 5 April (cf. *Letters* no. 59); 8 April; 13 April (cf. *Letters* no. 60); 14 April; 18 April (cf. *Letters* no. 61); 23 April (cf. *Letters* no. 62); 25 [?] April (cf. *Letters* no. 63, dated 26 April); 4 [?] May (cf. *Letters* no. 66, dated 6 May); 14 May (cf. *Letters* no. 69); 21 May (cf. *Letters* no. 70); 31 May (cf. *Letters* no. 72).

p. 210, excerpt from a draft of a letter to Stanley Unwin, 14 April 1950 (cf. the letter as sent, *Letters* no. 127)

p. 223, verse, untitled, beginning '*The Lord of the Rings*/is one of those things'

p. 242, part of an unfinished preface to *The Golden Key* by George MacDonald, written *circa* January 1965, discussing the meaning of *Fairy* (i.e. *Faerie*; cf. *SWM*, A9a)

p. 266, letter to Glyn Daniel, 25 August 1973, a note of thanks for a dinner

passim, miscellaneous quotations and reminiscences by Tolkien from letters, diaries, and other sources not specifically identified or dated

Wove paper. Bound in brown cloth over boards. Stamped on spine, running down, in gilt: 'J. R. R. TOLKIEN: A Biography [*parallel to title:*] Humphrey Carpenter *George Allen & Unwin*'. Cream laid endpapers, watermarked 'Glastonbury'. Brown/white headband. All edges trimmed. Top edge stained dark brown, fore- and bottom edges unstained.

Dust-jacket, wove paper. Covers and spine printed against a black background. Printed on upper cover: '[*in white outlined in green:*] J. R. R. | TOLKIEN | [*in green:*] a biography | [*colour photograph of Tolkien, outlined in white*] | [*in red:*] Humphrey Carpenter'. Printed on spine: '[*in white outlined in green:*] J. R. R. TOLKIEN [*in green:*] a biography [*parallel to title, in red:*] Humphrey Carpenter | [*horizontal, in white:*] GEORGE ALLEN | & UNWIN'. Printed on lower cover in white: '*The authorised biography* | *of the creator of* | The Lord of the Rings, | The Hobbit and The Silmarillion*'. Printed on front flap: '[*blurb*] | Jacket photograph: J. R. R. Tolkien in 1968 | (*BBC copyright*)'. Some copies seen have a label affixed below the text on the front flap, printed: '£4.95 | *net* | George Allen | and Unwin'. Other copies have had the lower corner of the front flap clipped; one clipped flap seen has the partial text 'PRI' in the lower corner. Printed in the lower corner of the front flap of a proof dust-jacket: 'PRICE NET | £4.95 | IN U.K. ONLY'. Printed on back flap: '[*note on Humphrey Carpenter*] | ISBN 0 04 928037 6 | *Printed in Great Britain*'.

Published 5 May 1977 at £4.95; number of copies not known.

b. First American edition (1977):

TOLKIEN | *A biography* | BY HUMPHREY CARPENTER | *Illustrated with photographs* | [*publisher's 'dolphin' device*] | Houghton Mifflin Company Boston 1977

xii, 292 pp. + 8 plates. Collation: [1–19⁸]. 23.3 × 15.4 cm.

[i] 'TOLKIEN | *A biography*'; [ii] 'Also by Humphrey Carpenter | *A Thames Companion* | (with Mari Prichard)'; [iii] title; [iv] 'Copyright © 1977 by George Allen & Unwin (Publishers) Ltd. | [*notice of restrictions under copyright*] | ISBN: 0-395-25360-8 | Printed in the United States of America | [*printing code, beginning "P", ending "1"*]'; [v] 'Dedicated to the memory of | 'The T.C.B.S.''; [vi] blank; [vii–viii] table of contents; [ix–x] list of illustrations; [xi] author's note; [xii] blank; [1] 'I | *A visit*'; [2] blank; 3–6 text; [7] 'II | *1892–1916: Early years*'; [8] blank; 9–86 text; [87] 'III | *1917–1925: The making of a | mythology*'; [88] blank; 89–108 text; [109] 'IV | *1925–1949(i): 'In a hole in | the ground there lived a hobbit'*"; [110] blank; 111–72 text; [173] 'V | *1925–1949(ii): The Third Age*'; [174] blank; 175–204 text; [205] 'VI | *1949–1966: Success*'; [206] blank; 207–32 text; [233] 'VII | *1959–1973: Last years*'; [234] blank; 235–56 text; [257] 'VIII | *The Tree*'; [258] blank; 259–[60] text; [261] '*Appendices*'; [262] blank; [263]–79 appendices; [280] blank; 281–[7] index; [288–92] blank. 29 illustrations on 8 plates, inserted between pp. 148–9.

Wove paper. Bound in brown cloth over boards. Stamped on upper cover: '[*flourishes, in green*] | [*in gilt:*] TOLKIEN | [*flourishes, in green*]'. Stamped on spine: '[*in gilt:*] Humphrey | Carpenter | [*flourishes, in green*] | [*running down, in gilt:*] TOLKIEN | [*horizontal:*] [*flourishes, in green*] | [*in gilt:*] Houghton | Mifflin |

Company'. Green wove endpapers. Brown/white headbands. All edges trimmed and unstained.

Dust-jacket, wove paper. Printed on upper cover: '[*in green:*] THE AUTHORIZED BIOGRAPHY | [*in black:*] TOLKIEN | [*colour photograph of Tolkien, within a black single rule circle*] | [*in black:*] HUMPHREY CARPENTER'. Printed on spine: '[*running down:*] [*in green:*] HUMPHREY [*parallel to the preceding name:*] CARPENTER [*followed by, in black:*] TOLKIEN | [*horizontal:*] HOUGHTON | MIFFLIN | COMPANY'. Printed on lower cover: 'The authorized biography | of the creator of | [*in green:*] The Lord of the Rings, | The Hobbit [*in black:*] and [*in green:*] The Silmarillion | [*in black:*] ISBN 0-395-25360-8 | [*rule*] | 6-83270'. Printed on front flap: '\$10.00 | [*blurb; to left of blurb, running up:*] 0677'. Printed on back flap: '[*blurb, continued from front flap*] | [*note on Humphrey Carpenter*] | Jacket photograph: J. R. R. Tolkien in 1968 ©BBC | HOUGHTON MIFFLIN COMPANY | 2 Park Street | Boston, Massachusetts 02107'.

Published 29 June 1977 at \$10.00; 35,000 copies printed.

Typeset as for B32a, except pp. [i–iv], [ix–x], running titles; page number removed, p. [287].

  Also published by the Book-of-the-Month Club.

c. First paperback edition (1978):

J. R. R. TOLKIEN | *A biography* | HUMPHREY CARPENTER | London | UNWIN PAPERBACKS | Boston Sydney

288 pp. + 4 plates. Collation: 144 leaves. Copies vary in size, 19.6 × 12.8 – 19.2 × 12.6 cm.

[1] blurb; [2] 'Also by Humphrey Carpenter | *A Thames Companion* | (with Mari Prichard) | *The Joshers* | *The Inklings*'; [3] title; [4] 'First published in Great Britain by George Allen & Unwin 1977 | First published in Unwin Paperbacks 1978 | [*notice of restrictions under copyright*] | UNWIN® PAPERBACKS | 40 Museum Street, London WC1A 1LU | © George Allen & Unwin (Publishers) Ltd, 1977 1978 | ISBN 0 04 928039 2 | Typeset in 10 on 11 point Times | and printed in Great Britain | by Cox & Wyman Ltd, London, Reading and Fakenham'; [5] '*Dedicated to the memory of* | 'The T.C.B.S.''; [6] blank; [7] table of contents; [8] list of illustrations; [9] author's note; [10] blank; [11]–14 text; [15] 'Part Two | *1892–1916: Early years*'; [16] blank; [17]–94 text; [95] 'Part Three | *1917–1925: The making of* | *a mythology*'; [96] blank; [97]–115 text; [116] blank; [117] 'Part Four | *1925–1949(i): 'In a hole in* | *the ground there lived a* | *hobbit*''; [118]–75 text; [176] blank; [177] 'Part Five | *1925–1949(ii):* | *The Third Age*'; [178] blank; [179]–208 text; [209] 'Part Six | *1949–1966: Success*'; [210] blank; [211]–34 text; [235] 'Part Seven | *1959–1973: Last years*'; [236] blank; [237]–57 text; [258] blank; [259]–60 text; [261] '*Appendices*'; [262] blank; [263]–78 appendices; [279]–87 index; [288] blank. 13 illustrations on 4 plates, inserted between pp. 144–5.

Wove paper. Bound in heavy wove wrappers. Covers and spine printed against a light tan background. Printed on upper cover: '[*in orange:*] J. R. R. TOLKIEN | [*in white:*] A BIOGRAPHY | [*in black:*] Humphrey Carpenter | *'one of the most interesting and readable biographies* | *of a literary figure for some time'* | The Times | [*colour photograph of Tolkien, outlined in black-white-black*] | [*publisher's "unwin/ UNWIN PAPERBACKS" device, in orange, white, and black*]'. Printed on spine, running down: 'J. R. R. TOLKIEN A BIOGRAPHY Humphrey Carpenter [*publisher's "unwin/UNWIN PAPERBACKS" device, in orange, white, and black*]'.

Printed on lower cover within a thin-thick rule frame: 'Several million readers throughout the world have enjoyed | *The Hobbit, The Lord of the Rings* and *the Silmarillion*. This | is the authorised biography of their creator, J. R. R. Tolkien. | [*6 quotations, from the* Sunday Times, Guardian, Daily Mail, Evening Standard, Listener, *and* Times Literary Supplement] | Cover Photograph © Copyright: Billett Potter | [*at left:*] United Kingdom £1.25 [*at right:*] BIOGRAPHY | ISBN 0 04 928039 2'. All edges trimmed and unstained.

In 1981, first impression sheets were bound in new wrappers as follows. Printed on upper cover: '[*publisher's "unwin" device, in orange, white, and black*] | [*in brown:*] Humphrey Carpenter | [*within a dark blue single rule frame:*] [*in dark blue:*] J R R | Tolkien | The Authorised Biography | [*coloured collage of photographs of Tolkien and his family, against a coloured photograph of Magdalen College, Oxford, extending beyond the frame at left and right*] | [*below the frame, in black:*] THE LIFE OF THE CREATOR OF *THE HOBBIT,* | *THE LORD OF THE RINGS* AND *THE SILMARILLION*'. Printed on spine, running down: '[*in dark blue:*] J. R. R. Tolkien: A Biography [*in brown:*] Humphrey Carpenter [*publisher's "unwin" device, in orange, white, and black*]'. Printed on lower cover: '[*2 quotations, from the* Sunday Times *and* Daily Mail, *in orange and dark blue*] | [*blurb, in black*] | [*3 quotations, from the* Listener, Times Literary Supplement, *and* Evening Standard, *in orange and dark blue*] | [*in black:*] [*at left, within a single rule frame:*] £1.95 [*at right:*] UNWIN PAPERBACKS | BIOGRAPHY | 0 04 928039 2'. All edges trimmed and unstained. Copies seen with this binding vary widely in size, 19.9 × 12.5 – 18.9 × 12.5 cm.

Published 24 July 1978 at £1.25, increased to £1.95 with new binding; number of copies not known.

Reset, with minor corrections, except Appendix A and the genealogical table reprinted from B32a. The chronology and bibliography now noted the publication of *The Silmarillion* (1977). Omits 16 illustrations.

d. First American paperback edition (1978):

TOLKIEN | *A Biography* | Humphrey Carpenter | BALLANTINE BOOKS • NEW YORK

viii, 328 pp. + 8 plates. Collation: 168 leaves. 17.9 × 10.5 cm.

[i] 'HIGHEST PRAISE FOR HUMPHREY | CARPENTER'S | TOLKIEN | [*5 quotations, from the* Chicago Daily News, Saturday Review, New York Times Book Review, Publishers Weekly, *and* Kirkus Reviews, *divided by rules*]'; [ii] 'The Authorized Editions | *of the works of J. R. R. Tolkien* | Published by Ballantine Books: | THE HOBBIT | *The Lord of the Rings Trilogy* | THE FELLOWSHIP OF THE RING | THE TWO TOWERS | THE RETURN OF THE KING | SMITH OF WOOTTON MAJOR | FARMER GILES OF HAM | THE TOLKIEN READER | *With Donald Swann:* | THE ROAD GOES EVER ON'; [iii] title; [iv] 'Dedicated to the memory of | 'The T.C.B.S.' | Copyright © 1977 by George Allen & Unwin (Publishers) Ltd. | [*notice of restrictions under copyright*] | ISBN: 0-345-27256-0 | This edition published by arrangement with Houghton Mifflin | Company | Manufactured in the United States of America | First Ballantine Books Edition: September 1978'; v–vi table of contents; vii author's note; [viii] blank; [1] 'I | [*swelled rule*] | *A visit*'; 2–6 text; [7] 'II | [*swelled rule*] | *1892–1916: Early years*'; 8–97 text; [98] blank; [99] 'III | [*swelled rule*] | *1917–1925: The making of a* | *mythology*'; 100–22 text; [123] 'IV | [*swelled rule*] | *1923–1949(i):* | '*In a hole in the*

ground | *there lived a hobbit*'; 124–93 text; [194] blank; [195] 'V | [*swelled rule*] | *1925–1949(ii):* | *The Third Age*'; 196–231 text; [232] blank; [233] 'VI | [*swelled rule*] | *1949–1966: Success*'; 234–63 text; [264] blank; [265] 'VII | [*swelled rule*] | *1959–1973: Last years*'; 266–90 text; [291] 'VIII | [*swelled rule*] | *The Tree*'; 292–4 text; [295] '*Appendices*'; 296–316 appendices; 317–27 index; [328] '[*within a thick-thin rule frame:*] BESTSELLERS | By J. R. R. TOLKIEN | Today's best-loved author of fantasy. | [*below the frame:*] Available at your bookstore or use this coupon. | [*publisher's order form for* H, LR, Smith of Wootton Major & Farmer Giles of Ham, TR, *and* The Hobbit: An Illustrated Edition]'. 29 illustrations on 8 plates, inserted between pp. 144–5.

Wove paper. Bound in heavy wove wrappers. Covers and spine printed against a tan background. Printed on upper cover: '[*in black:*] Ballantine/Nonfiction/27256 /\$2.50 [*publisher's "BB" device, in white and black*] | [*in brown:*] THE AUTHORIZED BIOGRAPHY | [*rule, in black*] | [*in brown:*] OF THE CREATOR OF | THE HOBBIT, THE LORD OF THE RINGS | AND THE SILMARILLION | [*rule, in black*] | [*in brown and light orange:*] TOLKIEN | [*rule, in black*] | [*in brown:*] HUMPHREY CARPENTER | [*rule, in black*] | [*colour photograph of Tolkien; to left of photograph, running up, in black:*] Photographed by Billett Potter © 1973 by George Allen & Unwin Ltd.' Printed on spine: '[*publisher's "BB" device, in white and black*] | [*in black:*] Nonfiction | [*running down:*] [*in brown and light orange:*] TOLKIEN: [*in brown:*] A BIOGRAPHY HUMPHREY [*parallel to the preceding word:*] CARPENTER [*followed by, in black:*] 345-27256-0-250'. Printed on lower cover: '[*rule, in black*] | [*quotation from the* Chicago Tribune Book World, *in red*] | [*rule, in black*] | [*quotation from* Newsweek, *in brown*] | [*rule, in black*] | [*blurb, in brown*] | [*rule, in black*] | [*3 quotations, from the* Saturday Review, Washington Post, *and* National Observer, *in brown, separated by rules in black*] | [*2 rules, in black*] | [*in brown:*] A BOOK-OF-THE-MONTH | CLUB ALTERNATE SELECTION | [*rule, in black*]'. All edges trimmed and stained yellow.

Published September 1978 at \$2.50; number of copies not known.

Reset, except the genealogical table reprinted from B32a. Appendix C was updated to 1977. The chronology was not updated. Includes all of the illustrations in B32a.

e. Revised edition (1987):

J. R. R. | TOLKIEN | [*rule*] *A BIOGRAPHY* [*rule*] | Humphrey Carpenter | UNWIN PAPERBACKS | London Sydney

288 pp. + 4 plates. Collation: 144 leaves. 19.6 × 12.8 cm.

[1] blurb, and note on Humphrey Carpenter; [2] 'Also by Humphrey Carpenter | *W.H. Auden: A Biography* | *The Inklings*'; [3] title; [4] 'First published in Great Britain by George Allen & Unwin 1977 | First published in Unwin Paperbacks 1978 | Reissued by Unwin® Paperbacks, an imprint of Unwin Hyman | Ltd, in 1987. | Copyright © George Allen & Unwin (Publishers) Ltd 1977, | 1978, 1987 | [*notice of restrictions*] | [*4 publisher's addresses, London (Denmark House) to Wellington*] | [*rule*] | [*British Library Cataloguing in Publication Data*] | [*rule*] | Printed in Great Britain by Cox & Wyman Ltd, Reading'; [5] '*Dedicated to the memory of* | 'The T.C.B.S.*'*; [6] blank; [7] table of contents; [8] list of illustrations; [9] author's note; [10] blank; [11]–14 text; [15] 'Part Two | *1892–1916: Early years*'; [16] blank; [17]–94 text; [95] 'Part Three | *1917–1925: The making of* | *a mythology*'; [96] blank; [97]–115 text; [116] blank; [117] 'Part Four | *1925–1949(i): 'In a hole in the ground there lived a* | *hobbit*''; [118]–75 text; [176] blank; [177] 'Part Five | *1925–*

1949(ii): | *The Third Age*'; [178] blank; [179]–208 text; [209] 'Part Six | *1949–1966: Success*'; [210] blank; [211]–34 text; [235] 'Part Seven | *1959–1973: Last years*'; [236] blank; [237]–57 text; [258] blank; [259]–60 text; [261] '*Appendices*'; [262]–79 appendices; [280]–8 index. 13 illustrations on 4 plates, inserted between pp. 160–1.

Wove paper. Bound in heavy wove wrappers. Covers and spine printed against a light yellow background. Printed on upper cover: '[*in dark red:*] J. R. R. | TOLKIEN | [*in red:*] [*rule*] A BIOGRAPHY [*rule*] | [*in black:*] Humphrey Carpenter | [*colour photograph of Tolkien, against a white panel outlined in red*] | [*in black:*] 'Rich and beautifully told' | *Sunday Times*'. Printed on spine, running down: '[*in dark red:*] J. R. R. TOLKIEN [*in black:*] Humphrey Carpenter [*publisher's "unwin" device, in yellow and black*]'. Printed on lower cover: '[*thick-thin rule, in red*] | [*in black:*] [*blurb*] | [*5 quotations, from the* Sunday Times, Daily Mail, Listener, Times, *and* Evening Standard] | [*thin-thick rule, in red*] | [*in black:*] Cover photograph by Billett Potter | Cover design by Behram Kapadia | [*at left:*] UNWIN PAPERBACKS/ | BIOGRAPHY | £4.95 [*at right:*] ISBN 0-04-928070-8 [*3 parallel lines*] | [*bar codes*]'. All edges trimmed and unstained.

Published 12 March 1987 at £4.95; 5,000 copies printed.

Partly reset, based on B32c. Pp. [1–4] and [7] were reset; appendices and index reimposed; 'Madelener' corrected to 'Madlener', p. 59, l. 10, and in index, new p. 283; Appendix C (checklist of Tolkien's writings) reset, corrected, and expanded through 1986 (*The Lost Road and Other Writings* is noted as 'in preparation') chiefly by Charles E. Noad, Bibliographer of The Tolkien Society; acknowledgements enlarged, new p. 278, ll. 2–4. On pp. 82–3 a manuscript version of 'Goblin Feet' is mistakenly commingled in the second stanza with a misreading of the published version (cf. B1a).

f. Trade paperback edition (1988):

TOLKIEN | *A biography* | BY HUMPHREY CARPENTER | *Illustrated with photographs* | [*publisher's 'dolphin' device*] | Houghton Mifflin Company Boston

xii, 292 pp. + 8 plates. Collation: 152 leaves. 20.8 × 13.9 cm.

Contents as for B32b, except pp. [iii] title, as above; and [iv] 'Copyright © 1977 by George Allen & Unwin (Publishers) Ltd. | This book is copyright under the Berne Convention. | All rights reserved. | For information about permission to reproduce selections from this book, write to | Permissions, Houghton Mifflin Company, 2 Park Street, Boston, Massachusetts | 02108. | [*Library of Congress Cataloging in Publication Data*] | Printed in the United States of America | [*printing code, beginning "P", ending "1"*]'.

Wove paper. Bound in heavy wove wrappers. Covers and spine printed against a mottled grey background. Printed on upper cover: '[*within a three-sided outline:*] [*against a pale pink panel:*] HUMPHREY | CARPENTER | [*against a grey panel:*] [*thick rule*] | [*thin rule*] | THE AUTHORIZED BIOGRAPHY | [*thin rule*] | [*thick rule*] | [*against a pale blue panel:*] J. R. R. | TOLKIEN | [*photograph of Tolkien, below and overlapping the preceding word, panel, and lower part of the frame*]'. Printed on spine: '[*running down:*] J. R. R. TOLKIEN HUMPHREY [*parallel to the preceding word:*] CARPENTER | [*publisher's "dolphin" device, horizontal*] | [*running down:*] HOUGHTON MIFFLIN'. Printed on lower cover: 'BIOGRAPHY FPT>>$8.95 | [*blurb*] | [*3 quotations, from the* Christian Science Monitor, Newsweek, *and* Washington Post] | Cover design: Sara Eisenman | Cover photo:

Professor Meredith Thompson | [*at left:*] 10087088 | [*rule*] | 6-82907 [*at right, against a white panel:*] ISBN 0-395-48676-9'. All edges trimmed and unstained.

Published 28 October 1988 at $8.95; 7,500 copies printed.

Typeset as for B32b, except pp. [i–iv]. Reprint of the 1977 American edition, without correction or updating.

B33   **THE INKLINGS**   **1978**

a. First edition:

THE INKLINGS | *C. S. Lewis, J. R. R. Tolkien,* | *Charles Williams,* | *and their friends* | *by* | Humphrey Carpenter | London | GEORGE ALLEN & UNWIN | Boston Sydney

xvi, 288 pp. + 8 plates. Collation: [1–8¹⁶9⁸10¹⁶]. 23.4 × 15.5 cm.

[i–ii] blank; [iii] 'THE INKLINGS'; [iv] 'Also by Humphrey Carpenter | *J. R. R. Tolkien: a biography* | *A Thames Companion* (with Mari Prichard) | For younger readers: *The Joshers*'; [v] title; [vi] 'First published in 1978. | [*notice of restrictions under copyright*] | GEORGE ALLEN & UNWIN LTD | 40 Museum Street, London WC1A 1LU | © George Allen & Unwin (Publishers) Ltd, 1978 | [*British Library Cataloguing in Publication Data, within a single rule frame*] | Typeset in 11 on 12 point Garamond by Bedford Typesetters Ltd | and printed in Great Britain | by W. & J. Mackay Ltd, Chatham'; [vii] 'Dedicated to the memory of | the late Major W. H. Lewis | ('Warnie')'; [viii] blank; ix table of contents; [x] blank; xi–xii list of illustrations; xiii–xiv preface; [xv] *"O my heart, it is all a very odd life.'* | Charles Williams in a letter to his wife, 12 March 1940'; [xvi] blank; [1] 'PART ONE'; [2] blank; 3–69 text; [70] blank; [71] 'PART TWO'; [72] blank; 73–110 text; [111] 'PART THREE'; [112] blank; 113–200 text; [201] 'PART FOUR'; [202] blank; 203–52 text; [253] 'APPENDICES'; [254] blank; 255–81 appendices; 282–7 index; [288] blank. 27 illustrations on 8 plates, inserted between pp. 16–17, 48–9, 80–1, [112]–13, 144–5, 176–7, 208–9, 240–1.

Includes excerpts from previously unpublished letters, diaries, and manuscripts by J. R. R. Tolkien (see 'Sources of Quotations', *Inklings* pp. 266–79):

pp. 30, 31, fifteen lines (in all) from a poem, 'The Gest of Beren and Lúthien' ('There once, and long and long ago', 'Hateful, thou art . . .', 'The peerless Silmarils . . .'), also known as 'The Lay of Leithian', here from the 1929 typescript as shown to C. S. Lewis. Cf. emended version in *The Lays of Beleriand* (A23), pp. 171–2, ll. 401–11; p. 185, ll. 848–9; p. 192, ll. 1135–6.

pp. 32, 121, 160, 198, from a letter to Dick Plotz, 12 September 1965; cf. *Letters* no. 276

pp. 32, 52, from a diary entry for 1 October 1933, on C. S. Lewis

p. 48, a manuscript note on C. S. Lewis

pp. 50, 51–2, 216, 232, notes on C. S. Lewis, from 'The Ulsterior Motive', an essay written in 1964 originally as a critique of Lewis's *Letters to Malcolm*; cf. Wilson, C. S. *Lewis: A Biography* (section Fiii), p. 135

p. 55, from a manuscript, quoting a poetic jibe by C. S. Lewis, and with a comment by Tolkien on Lewis

p. 65, from a letter to Allen & Unwin, 18 February 1938, i.e. to Stanley Unwin, 4 March; cf. *Letters* no. 26

pp. 65–6, from a letter to Charlotte and Denis Plimmer, [8] February 1967; cf. *Letters* no. 294

p. 66, from letters to Stanley Unwin, 4 March 1938 and 18 February 1938; cf. *Letters* nos. 24, 26

p. 67, from a letter to Stanley Unwin, 4 June 1938; cf. *Letters* no. 28

pp. 120, 194, from a letter to Anne Barrett, 7 August 1964; cf. *Letters* no. 259

pp. 120, 121, manuscript comments on Charles Williams, from Tolkien's copy of *Essays Presented to Charles Williams* (B19)

p. 121, from a letter to Christopher Tolkien, 29 November 1944; cf. *Letters* no. 91, this portion not printed

p. 122, from letters to Christopher Tolkien, November 1943 and 23 September 1944; the latter, cf. *Letters* no. 81

p. 123, from a letter to Christopher Tolkien, 13 December 1944

pp. 123–6, a poem, 'Our dear Charles Williams many guises shows', written at some time during World War Two

illustration facing p. 144 (and on lower cover of dust-jacket), a reproduction of a manuscript note to Warfield M. Firor, 1948, by some of the Inklings, including Tolkien

p. 168, from a letter to Michael Tolkien, 12 March 1941

p. 169, from a letter to Michael Tolkien, 6 March 1941; cf. *Letters* no. 43

p. 171, from a letter to Christopher Tolkien, 23 April 1944 (? 30 April, cf. *Letters* no. 64)

pp. 176–7, an unfinished poem in Old English, 'Hwæt! we Inclinga', with a Modern English translation by Carpenter

pp. 177, 186, 187, four clerihews

pp. 177, 185, from a letter to Christopher Tolkien, 1 March 1944; cf. *Letters* no. 56

pp. 177–8, from a letter to Christopher Tolkien, 18 November 1944 (? 24 November, cf. *Letters* no. 90)

p. 182, from a letter to Christopher Tolkien, 29 January 1945 (? 30 January, cf. *Letters* no. 96)

p. 189, from a letter to Christopher Tolkien, 25 May 1944; cf. *Letters* no. 71

p. 190, from remarks to Daphne Cloke

p. 191, from a letter to Christopher Tolkien, 10 June 1944; cf. *Letters* no. 73

pp. 191, 192, from a letter to Christopher Tolkien, 6 October 1944; cf. *Letters* no. 83

p. 192, from a letter to an unknown recipient, 1956

p. 194, from letters to Christopher Tolkien, 10 November 1943, and 10 April 1944 (? 13 April; cf. *Letters* no. 60)

p. 195, from letters to Christopher Tolkien, 30 March 1944, 3 April 1944, 14 May 1944, and 31 May 1944; cf. *Letters* nos. 57, 58, 69, 72

p. 197, from a letter to Christopher Tolkien, 7 November 1944; cf. *Letters* no. 89

p. 198, from undated draft of letter, '1964' (? cf. *Letters* no. 252, draft of a letter to Michael Tolkien, November or December 1963)

p. 199, from a letter to Christopher Tolkien, 23 September 1944; cf. *Letters* no. 81

p. 204, from a letter to Michal Williams, 15 May 1945; cf. *Letters* no. 99

p. 205, from letters to Christopher Tolkien, 30 September 1944, cf. *Letters* no. 82; and 9 October 1945

p. 210, from a letter to Christopher Tolkien, August 1947

p. 228, from a letter to Fr. David Kolb, 11 November 1964, cf. *Letters* no. 265; from a letter to Christopher Tolkien, 30 January 1945, cf. *Letters* no. 196; and from a letter to Stanley Unwin, 21 July 1945

pp. 232, 242, from a letter to Christopher Bretherton, 16 July 1964; cf. *Letters* no. 257

p. 252, from a draft of a letter to an unknown recipient, i.e. Michael Tolkien, November or December 1963; cf. *Letters* no. 252

Also quotes, p. 58, Tolkien's statement about C. S. Lewis and his verse 'We were talking of dragons', from Lewis's *Selected Literary Essays* (see Dii16); p. 63, ten lines from Tolkien's poem 'Mythopoeia' (cf. A7e–g); p. 67, from a letter to William Luther White, 11 September 1967 (see Dii17); and pt. 3, ch. 3, other letters, adapted.

Wove paper. Bound in black cloth over boards. Stamped on spine in silver: '[*running down:*] THE INKLINGS Humphrey Carpenter | [*horizontal:*] GEORGE | ALLEN | & | UNWIN'. Wove endpapers. No headbands. All edges trimmed. Top edge stained black, fore- and bottom edges unstained.

Dust-jacket, wove paper. Covers and spine printed against a dark blue-green background. Printed on upper cover: '[*in cream:*] Humphrey Carpenter | [*within a thick single rule frame:*] The | Inklings | [*in orange:*] C. S. Lewis | J. R. R. Tolkien | Charles Williams | and their friends'. Printed on spine: '[*running down:*] [*in cream:*] The Inklings [*in orange:*] Humphrey Carpenter | [*horizontal, in white:*] GEORGE ALLEN | & UNWIN'. Printed on lower cover: '[*in orange:*] The | Inklings | [*illustration, inscriptions by eight of the Inklings, in dark blue, against a cream panel outlined with a thick orange rule*]'. Printed on front flap in dark blue, against a cream background: '[*blurb*] | PRICE NET | £6.50 | IN U K ONLY'. Printed on back flap in dark blue, against a cream background: '[*photograph of Humphrey Carpenter*] | Photograph courtesy Billet [*sic*] Potter | [*note on Carpenter*] | Illustrated on the back of the jacket are signatures of | some of the Inklings, sent to Dr Warfield M. Firor | after he had given them a ham. | Jacket design Nicholas Rous | ISBN 0 04 809011 5 | *Printed in Great Britain*'.

Published October 1978 at £6.50; number of copies not known.

b. First American edition (1979):

THE INKLINGS | C. S. Lewis, J. R. R. Tolkien, | Charles Williams, | and their friends | by | Humphrey Carpenter | Boston | HOUGHTON MIFFLIN COMPANY 1979

xvi, 288 pp. + 8 plates. Collation: $[1–8^{16}9^810^{16}]$. 23.3 × 15.4 cm.

Contents as for B33a, except pp. [iv] 'Also by Humphrey Carpenter | *A Thames Companion* | (WITH MARI PRICHARD) | *Tolkien: A Biography*'; [v] title, as above; and [vi] 'First American Edition 1979 | Copyright © 1978 by George Allen & Unwin (Publishers) Ltd. | [*notice of restrictions under copyright*] | [*Library of Congress Cataloging in Publication Data*] | Printed in the United States of America | [*printing code, beginning "V", ending "1"*]'.

Wove paper. Bound in black cloth over boards. Stamped on upper cover in blind: 'THE | INKLINGS | [*"star" (4 interlinked loops)*]'. Stamped on spine in gilt: 'Humphrey | Carpenter | [*2 "stars"*] | [*running down:*] THE INKLINGS | [*horizontal:*] [*2 "stars"*] | HOUGHTON | MIFFLIN | COMPANY'. Tan wove endpapers. Tan headbands. All edges trimmed and unstained.

Dust-jacket, wove paper. Printed on upper cover against a dark red background: '[*in white:*] A GROUP OF | WRITERS WHOSE LITERARY | FANTASIES STILL FIRE THE | IMAGINATION OF ALL | THOSE WHO SEEK | A TRUTH BEYOND | REALITY | [*in orange:*] The | Inklings | [*in white:*] C. S. Lewis | J. R. R. Tolkien | Charles Williams | and their friends | [*thick-thin rule, in orange*] | [*in white:*] Humphrey Carpenter'. Printed on spine against a dark red background: '[*thin-thick rule, in white*] | [*running down, in orange:*] The Inklings Carpenter | [*horizontal, in white:*] [*thick-thin rule*] | HOUGHTON | MIFFLIN | COMPANY'. Printed on lower cover: '[*in dark red:*] FROM THE BRITISH REVIEW | [*4 quotations, from the*

Sunday Telegraph, Observer, New Statesman, *and* Times Educational Supplement, *in black and dark red*] | [*in black:*] ISBN: 0-395-27628-4 | [*rule*] | 6-83271 | HOUGHTON MIFFLIN COMPANY © 1979'. Printed on front flap: '$10.95 | [*blurb; to left of blurb, running down:*] 0379'. Printed on back flap: '[*blurb, continued from front flap*] | [*note on Carpenter*] | HOUGHTON MIFFLIN COMPANY | 2 Park Street, Boston, Massachusetts 02107'.

Published 27 February 1979 at $10.95; 25,000 copies printed.

Typeset as for B33a, except pp. [iv–vi].

c. First paperback edition (1981):

The Inklings | *C. S. Lewis, J. R. R. Tolkien,* | *Charles Williams,* | *and their friends* | HUMPHREY CARPENTER | London | UNWIN PAPERBACKS | Boston Sydney

xiv, 290 pp. + 4 plates. Collation: 152 leaves. 19.7 × 12.9 cm.

[i] blurb; [ii] '*Also published in Unwin Paperbacks* | J. R. R. Tolkien: A Biography | *Also by Humphrey Carpenter* | W. H. Auden (Allen & Unwin) | A Thames Companion (with Mari Prichard) (Oxford | University Press) | Jesus (Past Masters Series) (Oxford University Press) | *For Children* | The Joshers (Allen & Unwin) | The Captain Hook Affair (Allen & Unwin)'; [iii] title; [iv] 'First published in Great Britain by | George Allen & Unwin 1978 | First published in Unwin Paperbacks 1981 | [*notice of restrictions under copyright*] | UNWIN® PAPERBACKS | 40 Museum Street, London WC1A 1LU | © George Allen & Unwin (Publishers) Ltd, 1978, 1981 | [*notice of conditions of sale*] | [*British Library Cataloguing in Publication Data, within a single rule frame*] | Reproduced, printed and bound in Great Britain by | Hazell Watson & Viney Ltd, Aylesbury, Bucks'; [v] 'Dedicated to the memory of | the late Major W. H. Lewis | ('Warnie')'; [vi] blank; vii table of contents; [viii] blank; ix list of illustrations; [x] blank; xi–xii preface; [xiii] "*O my heart, it is all a very odd life.'* | Charles Williams in a letter to his wife, 12 March 1940'; [xiv] blank; [1] 'PART ONE'; [2] blank; 3–69 text; [70] blank; [71] 'PART TWO'; [72] blank; 73–110 text; [111] 'PART THREE'; [112] blank; 113–200 text; [201] 'PART FOUR'; [202] blank; 203–52 text; [253] 'APPENDICES'; [254] blank; 255–81 appendices; 282–7 index; [288] blank; [289] '*Also by Humphrey Carpenter* | [*advertisement of* J. R. R. Tolkien: A Biography]'; [290] '*Also published in Unwin Paperbacks* | [*advertisement of* Foster, The Complete Guide to Middle-earth]'. 17 illustrations on 4 plates, inserted between pp. 146–7.

Wove paper. Bound in heavy wove wrappers. Printed on upper cover: '[*publisher's "unwin" device, in red, white, and black*] | [*in green:*] Humphrey Carpenter | [*within a brown single rule frame:*] [*in brown:*] The | Inklings | [*in green:*] C. S. Lewis, J. R. R. Tolkien, Charles Williams | and their friends | [*collage of three coloured illustrations, of Williams, Tolkien, Colin Hardie, Humphrey Havard, and Lewis, overlapping the frame at left and right*] | [*below the frame, in black:*] WINNER OF THE SOMERSET MAUGHAM AWARD'. Printed on spine: '[*running down:*] [*in brown:*] The Inklings [*in green:*] Humphrey Carpenter [*publisher's "unwin" device, in red, white, and black*]'. Printed on lower cover: 'WINNER OF THE SOMERSET MAUGHAM AWARD | [*2 quotations, from the* Sunday Times *and* Observer, *in orange and brown*] | [*blurb, in black*] | [*2 quotations, from the* New Statesman *and* Sunday Telegraph, *in orange and brown*] | [*in black:*] [*at left, within a single rule frame:*] £2.95 [*at right:*] UNWIN PAPERBACKS | BIOGRAPHY | 0 04 809013 1'. All edges trimmed and unstained.

Published March 1981 at £2.95; 7,500 copies planned.

Typeset as for B33a, except pp. [i–iv]. Omits 10 illustrations.

d. First American paperback edition (1981):

THE INKLINGS | *C. S. Lewis, J. R. R. Tolkien,* | *Charles Williams, and their friends* | [*leaf ornament*] | Humphrey Carpenter | BALLANTINE BOOKS • NEW YORK

xii, 324 pp. + 8 plates. Collation: 168 leaves. 17.8 × 10.5 cm.

[i] 'INTERNATIONAL ACCLAIM FOR | THE INKLINGS | by the bestselling author of | TOLKIEN: A BIOGRAPHY | [*4 quotations, from the* Sunday Telegraph, Washington Post, Observer, *and* National Review]'; [ii] 'Also by Humphrey Carpenter | *Published by Ballantine Books:* | TOLKIEN: A BIOGRAPHY'; [iii] title; [iv] *'Dedicated to the memory of* | *the late Major W. H. Lewis* | *('Warnie')* | Copyright © 1978 by George Allen & Unwin (Publishers) Ltd. | [*notice of restrictions*] | Library of Congress Catalog Card Number: 78-26042 | ISBN 0-345-29552-8 | This edition published by arrangement with | Houghton Mifflin Company | Manufactured in the United States of America | First Ballantine Books Edition: December 1981'; [v] table of contents; [vi] blank; vii–viii list of illustrations; ix–x preface; [xi] ''O *my heart, it is all a very odd life.*' | Charles Williams in a letter to his wife, 12 March 1940'; [xii] blank; 1–279 text; 280–316 appendices; 317–24 index. 27 illustrations on 8 plates, inserted between pp. 172–3.

Wove paper. Bound in heavy wove wrappers. Printed on upper cover, within a black outline: '[*colour illustration, silhouettes of Charles Williams, J. R. R. Tolkien, and C. S. Lewis, within and, at top, extending beyond a black single rule frame, extending also beyond the larger outline*] | [*rule, in black*] | [*against a light grey-blue panel:*] [*in white:*] J. R. R. Tolkien | C. S. Lewis | Charles Williams | and their friends | [*in black, against a white panel outlined in black:*] The | [*at left and right extending beyond the frame:*] Inklings | [*within the frame:*] IN A WONDERFUL TIME, IN A | WONDERFUL PLACE, THREE | EXTRAORDINARY WRITERS | CAME TOGETHER TO GIVE | THE WORLD ITS BEST-LOVED | WORKS OF FANTASY | [*thin-thick rule*] | Humphrey Carpenter | [*below the frame:*] [*publisher's "BB" device, in black and white*] | [*in white:*] Ballantine/Biography/29552/$3.50'. Printed on spine: '[*publisher's "BB" device, in white and black*] | [*in black:*] Biography | [*running down:*] The Inklings Humphrey Carpenter 345-29552-8-350'. Printed on lower cover within a black outline: '[*colour illustration as on upper cover, within and, at top, extending beyond a black single rule frame, extending also beyond the larger outline*] | [*rule, in black*] | [*against a light grey-blue panel:*] [*in white:*] THE LORD OF THE RINGS | THE CHRONICLES OF NARNIA | [*in black:*] Timeless Works of Fantasy | [*rule*] | [*blurb*] | [*rule*] | [*quotation by Kingsley Amis*] | [*rule*] | [*quotation from the* Boston Globe] | [*against a white panel:*] [*bar codes*] | ISBN 0-345-29552-8 [*to right of white panel, running down:*] Cover printed in USA'. All edges trimmed and stained yellow.

Published December 1981 at $3.50; number of copies not known.

Reset.

B34   J. R. R. TOLKIEN, SCHOLAR AND STORYTELLER   1979

J. R. R. TOLKIEN, | *Scholar and Storyteller* | [*swelled rule*] | ESSAYS *IN MEMORIAM* | EDITED BY | *Mary Salu* | *and Robert T. Farrell* | [*publisher's 'CUP' device, in grey*] | [*in black:*] *Cornell University Press* | ITHACA AND LONDON

328 pp. Collation: [1–8^{16}9^{4}10–11^{16}]. 22.9 × 14.9 cm.

[1] 'J. R. R. TOLKIEN, | *Scholar and Storyteller* | [*rule*] | ESSAYS *IN MEMORIAM*';
[2] '[*photograph of Tolkien*] | *Professor Tolkien in the gardens of Merton College.* |
Copyright © *Billet* [*sic*] *Potter*.'; [3] title; [4] 'This book has been published with the
aid | of a grant from the Hull Memorial | Publication Fund of Cornell University. |
Copyright © 1979 by Cornell University | [*notice of restrictions*] | First published
1979 by Cornell University Press. | Published in the United Kingdom by Cornell
University Press Ltd., | 2–4 Brook Street, London W1Y 1AA. | International Standard
Book Number 0-8014-1038-X | Library of Congress Catalog Card Number 78-
58032 | Printed in the United States of America. | *Librarians: Library of Congress
cataloging information* | *appears on the last page of the book*.'; 5–6 table of contents;
7–8 preface; [9] 'PART ONE | [*swelled rule*] | [*decoration, in grey*]'; [10] blank; 11–
37 text; [38] blank; [39] 'PART TWO | [*swelled rule*] | [*decoration, in grey*]'; [40]
blank; 41–245 text; [246] blank; [247] 'PART THREE | [*swelled rule*] | [*decoration,
in grey*]'; [248] blank; 249–316 text; 317–22 handlist of the writings of J. R. R.
Tolkien, by Humphrey Carpenter; 323–5 index; [326] blank; [327] '*J. R. R. Tolkien,
Scholar and Storyteller* | [*production credits*]'; [328] Library of Congress Cataloging
in Publication Data.

Includes 'Valedictory Address to the University of Oxford, 5 June 1959' by J. R. R.
Tolkien, pp. 16–32.

Wove paper, watermarked 'Warren's Olde Style'. Bound in brown cloth over boards.
Stamped on upper cover in blind: 'J. R. R. TOLKIEN | [*rule*] | [*decoration, oak
leaves*]'. Stamped on spine: '[*in gilt:*] [*very thick rule*] | [*thick rule*] | J. R. R. | Tolkien, |
Scholar | AND | Storyteller | [*in copper:*] | [*rule*] | Essays | in Memoriam | [*rule*] |
[*decoration, oak leaves*] | [*in gilt:*] SALU & | FARRELL | Editors | [*in copper:*] |
CORNELL | UNIVERSITY | PRESS | [*in gilt:*] [*thick rule*] | [*very thick rule*]'. Red-
orange wove endpapers. Yellow/brown headbands. All edges trimmed and
unstained.

Dust-jacket, wove paper. Covers and spine printed against a red background. Printed
on upper cover: '[*in white:*] J. R. R. | Tolkien | [*at left:*] Scholar | and | Story- | teller | [*in
black:*] Essays in | Memoriam [*at right, photograph of Tolkien, outlined by a thick
rule, within a white single rule frame*] | Edited by | Mary Salu and Robert T. Farrell'.
Printed on spine: 'Salu | and | Farrell | Editors | [*running down, in white:*] J. R. R.
Tolkien Scholar [*parallel to the preceding word:*] and [*parallel to the preceding word:*]
Story- [*parallel to the preceding word:*] teller | [*horizontal, in black:*] Cornell |
University | Press'. Printed on lower cover: '[*in white:*] J. R. R. | Tolkien Scholar and
Storyteller | [*in black:*] Essays in Memoriam | Edited by Mary Salu and Robert T.
Farrell | [*list of contents, in black and white*] | [*in white:*] Cornell University Press •
Ithaca and London'. Printed on front flap: '[*in white:*] J. R. R. | Tolkien | Scholar | and
| Story- | teller | [*in black:*] Essays in Memoriam | Edited by Mary Salu | and Robert T.
Farrell | [*blurb*] | ISBN 0-8014-1038-X'. Printed on back flap: '[*note on Tolkien*] |
[*note on Salu*] | [*note on Farrell*] | Jacket photograph by Billett Potter | Jacket design by
Gregory Chambers'.

Published 31 March 1979 at $25.00; 1,560 copies printed.

Tolkien delivered his 'Valedictory Address' at Merton College Hall on 5 June 1959, at
the end of his final summer term at Oxford. An alternate version of the address was
published in *The Monsters and the Critics and Other Essays* (A19).

Pertinent manuscript materials are in the Bodleian Library, Oxford.

THE | OLD ENGLISH | *EXODUS* | TEXT, TRANSLATION, AND | COMMENTARY | BY | J. R. R. TOLKIEN | [*thick-thin rule*] | EDITED BY | JOAN TURVILLE-PETRE | OXFORD | AT THE CLARENDON PRESS | 1981

x, 86 pp. Collation: [1–6^8]. 21.6 × 13.6 cm.

[i] 'THE | OLD ENGLISH | *EXODUS*'; [ii] blank; [iii] title; [iv] '*Oxford University Press, Walton Street, Oxford OX2 6DP* | [*list of 18 cities (publisher's branches), London to Auckland*] | *and associate companies in* | *Beirut Berlin Ibadan Mexico City* | *Published in the United States by* | *Oxford University Press, New York* | © *Editorial Apparatus: Joan Turville-Petre 1981* | © *All other matter: The Executors of the* | *J. R. R. Tolkien Estate 1981* | [*notice of restrictions*] | [*British Library Cataloguing in Publication Data*] | *Printed in Great Britain* | *at the University Press, Oxford* | *by Eric Buckley* | *Printer to the University*'; [v]–vi editor's preface; [vii] table of contents; [viii] blank; [ix]–x bibliography; [1]–18 Anglo-Saxon text; [19] note to translation; [20]–32 Modern English translation; [33]–79 commentary; [80] blank; [81]–5 index; [86] blank.

Wove paper. Bound in dark blue cloth over boards. Stamped on spine in gilt: '[*running down:*] THE OLD ENGLISH *EXODUS* [*diamond*] J. R. R. TOLKIEN | [*horizontal:*] [*publisher's device (open book and 3 crowns within a cartouche)*] | OXFORD'. Stamped on lower cover in blind: '202'. Light blue laid endpapers, watermarked 'Glastonbury'. No headbands. All edges trimmed and unstained.

Dust-jacket, wove paper. Covers and spine printed against a dark blue-green background. Printed on upper cover: '[*in pale orange:*] The | Old English | *Exodus* | [*in white:*] Text, Translation, and Commentary | by | [*in pale orange:*] J. R. R. TOLKIEN | [*in white:*] Edited by | JOAN TURVILLE-PETRE'. Printed on spine, running down: '[*in white:*] TOLKIEN [*in pale orange:*] *EXODUS* [*in white:*] OXFORD'. Printed on lower cover in white: 'ISBN 0 19 811177 0'. Printed on front flap in dark blue-green: '[*blurb*] | Joan Turville-Petre is an Honorary | Research Fellow at Somerville College, | Oxford. | £7.95 net | in UK'. Printed on back flap in dark blue-green: 'RELATED OXFORD BOOKS | [*10 titles, beginning with* The Oxford Book of Medieval English Verse, *ending with* J. and E. M. Wright, Old English Grammar] | OXFORD UNIVERSITY PRESS'.

Published 28 January 1982 at £7.95 in Great Britain and $19.95 in the United States; 3,000 copies printed.

The Old English Exodus is based on Tolkien's notes for a series of informal lectures delivered in the nineteen-thirties and forties, 'retouched' in the nineteen-fifties. Joan Turville-Petre attended Tolkien's lectures while a student at Oxford. Here she abbreviated his commentary on *Exodus* (MS Junius 11, Bodleian Library, Oxford) 'systematically'. She reduced 'diffuse comments and some basic instruction', omitted 'palaeographical description that is by now irrelevant or mistaken' (p. [v]), and added her own observations and brief notes where necessary.

Tolkien's notes were also used by Peter J. Lucas in his edition of Exodus (London: Methuen, 1977). Lucas credits Tolkien with the emendations adopted on pp. 280 and 519 of his text, and incorporates his comments or suggestions in notes 33b, 38, 62, 142, 166, 275, 308–9, 344a, and 475 (not 575 as stated by Lucas, p. x).

Pertinent manuscript materials are in the Bodleian Library.

a. First edition:

J. R. R. TOLKIEN | Finn and Hengest: | The Fragment | and the Episode | Edited by
ALAN BLISS | London | GEORGE ALLEN & UNWIN | Boston Sydney

xii, 180 pp. Collation: [1–6^{16}]. 20.7 × 13.9 cm.

[i] 'Finn and Hengest'; [ii] blank; [iii] title; [iv] '© 1982 Executors of the late J. R. R.
Tolkien and Professor Alan Bliss | This book is copyright under the Berne Convention.
No reproduction | without permission. All rights reserved. | [*3 publisher's addresses,
London to North Sydney*] | First published in 1982 | [*rule*] | [*British Library
Cataloguing in Publication Data*] | [*rule*] | Set in 10 on 12 point Times by Bedford
Typesetters Ltd | and printed in | United States of America'; v–ix preface; × table of
contents; xi list of abbreviated titles; xii list of abbreviations; 1–6 editor's introduction; [7] 'Introduction'; [8] blank; 9–16 introduction; [17] 'Texts'; [18] blank;
19–23 texts; [24] blank; [25] 'Glossary of Names'; [26] blank; 27–79 glossary of
names; [80] blank; [81] 'Textual Commentary'; [82] blank; 83–143 textual commentary; [144] blank; [145] 'The Translations'; 146–55 translations; [156] blank; [157]
'Reconstruction'; [158] blank; 159–62 reconstruction; 163–80 appendices.

Wove paper. Bound in dark brown textured paper over boards. Stamped on spine,
running down, in gilt: '*J. R. R. TOLKIEN* Finn and Hengest Edited by [*parallel to the
preceding two words:*] ALAN BLISS [*followed by:*] GEORGE ALLEN [*parallel to the
preceding two words:*] & UNWIN'. Wove endpapers. No headbands. All edges
trimmed and unstained.

Dust-jacket, wove paper. Printed on upper cover against a dark brown background:
'[*in white:*] *J. R. R. TOLKIEN* | [*in orange:*] Finn and | Hengest | The Fragment | and
the Episode | [*in white:*] Edited by | ALAN BLISS'. Printed on spine, running down,
against a dark brown background: '[*in white:*] J. R. R. TOLKIEN [*in orange:*] Finn
and Hengest [*parallel to the title:*] The Fragment and the Episode [*followed by, in
white:*] Edited by [*parallel to the preceding two words:*] ALAN BLISS [*followed by:*]
GEORGE ALLEN [*parallel to the preceding two words:*] & UNWIN'. Lower cover
printed solid dark brown. Blurb printed on front flap in dark brown. Label affixed to
front flap, printed: 'A&U | £9.95'. Printed on back flap in dark brown: 'ISBN 0 04
829003 3 | *Printed in Great Britain*'.

Published 20 January 1983 at £9.95; number of copies not known.

Tolkien lectured on the medieval story of Finn and Hengest at Oxford in the late
nineteen-twenties, through the thirties and into the forties (separately or in conjunction with lectures on *Beowulf*), and again in 1963. In 1966 he offered to lend his
lecture notes to Alan Bliss, who was writing on Finn and Hengest. The notes were in
disarray when Tolkien died in 1973, and in 1979 came to Bliss with the suggestion
that he edit them for publication. Tolkien himself may have looked ahead to
publication of his lectures: the long version of the glossary of names printed in B36
was 'more carefully penned [than the other notes] in a more formal style, and is
liberally supplied with footnotes' (p. vi). The text of the book is by Tolkien except for
the editor's introduction and other preliminary matter, the translation of the
Fragment, Appendix C, and occasional comments, silent expansion of references, and
some footnotes.

'Fragment' refers to the surviving scrap of the poem 'The Fight at Finnesburg',
'Episode' to the allusion to the events of the poem in *Beowulf*.

Pertinent manuscript materials are in the Bodleian Library, Oxford.

b. First American edition (1983):

Finn and Hengest: | The Fragment | and the Episode | J. R. R. TOLKIEN | Edited by ALAN BLISS | Houghton Mifflin Company Boston 1983

xii, 180 pp. Collation: [1–6¹⁶]. 20.7 × 13.9 cm.

Contents as for B36a, except pp. [iii] title, as above; and [iv] 'First American edition 1983 | Copyright © 1982 by the Executors of the late J. R. R. Tolkien and | Professor Alan Bliss | [*notice of restrictions under copyright*] | [*rule*] | [*Library of Congress Cataloging in Publication Data*] | [*rule*] | Printed in United States of America | [*printing code, beginning "V", ending "1"*]'.

Wove paper. Bound in dark brown textured paper over boards. Stamped on spine, running down, in gilt: '*J. R. R. TOLKIEN* Finn and Hengest Edited by [*parallel to the preceding two words:*] ALAN BLISS [*followed by:*] HMCo'. Wove endpapers. No headbands. All edges trimmed and unstained.

Dust-jacket, wove paper. Covers and spine printed against a dark brown background. Printed on upper cover: '[*in white:*] *J. R. R. TOLKIEN* | [*in orange:*] Finn and | Hengest | The Fragment | and the Episode | [*in white:*] Edited by | ALAN BLISS'. Printed on spine, running down: '[*in white:*] J. R. R. TOLKIEN [*in orange:*] Finn and Hengest [*parallel to the title:*] The Fragment and the Episode [*followed by, in white:*] Edited by [*parallel to the preceding two words:*] ALAN BLISS [*followed by, in orange:*] HOUGHTON [*parallel to the preceding word:*] MIFFLIN [*parallel to the preceding word:*] COMPANY'. Printed on lower cover: '[*at left, against a white panel:*] 6-7086 [*at right, against a white panel:*] ISBN 0-395-33193-5'. Printed on front flap: 'FPT ISBN 0-395-33193-5 >$15.95 | [*blurb, in dark brown*] | [*in black:*] 05154583'. Printed on back flap in dark brown: 'HOUGHTON MIFFLIN COMPANY | 2 Park Street, Boston, Massachusetts 02108'.

Planned for publication 20 May 1983, but delayed, actually published no later than 6 October 1983, at $15.95; 4,000 copies printed.

Typeset as for B36a, except pp. [iii–iv].

C

Contributions to Periodicals

Listed here are works by J. R. R. Tolkien known to have appeared first in periodicals, exclusive of letters (see section Dii) and miscellaneous quotations (see section F). Contributions to annuals are described in section B. Entries are arranged chronologically in order of publication, where order can be determined, otherwise alphabetically by periodical title. The place of publication is given after the title when a periodical appears in this list for the first time. Each work is signed 'J. R. R. Tolkien' unless otherwise stated.

Cuttings preserved in Tolkien's papers indicate two periodicals to which he contributed but for which complete citations cannot be provided. The first of these periodicals, published in the late nineteen-twenties in Oxford by a Catholic organization at the University, includes two poems by Tolkien, 'Tinfang Warble' and 'The Grey Bridge of Tavrobel', possibly in two different numbers. Later manuscript notes by Tolkien suggest that the title of the periodical was *I. U. Magazine*; one of the preserved cuttings mentions *I. U. M.*, though this may refer only to the International University Movement. 'Tinfang Warble' was written at Oxford in 1914, rewritten at Leeds in 1920–3, and further revised for publication; it was reprinted in *The Book of Lost Tales, Part One* (A21), p. 108, where it was assigned the date of publication 1927. 'The Grey Bridge of Tavrobel' has not been reprinted. The second periodical that has not been located is possibly titled *Abingdon Chronicle* and includes, at least, an early version of 'Shadow-Bride' (cf. *The Adventures of Tom Bombadil* [A6]).

Tolkien's authorship of C4 and C5 is revealed in his papers. C1–3 and 6–8 may be assigned with sufficient (if not absolute) certainty, on the strength of style and content, and because Tolkien was Secretary of the Debating Society at King Edward's School, Birmingham, in 1910–13, and editor of the *King Edward's School Chronicle* for the June and July 1911 numbers.

C1 'Debating Society [Report]'. *King Edward's School Chronicle*, Birmingham, n.s. 25, no. 183 (November 1910), pp. 68–71.
Unsigned.

C2 'Debating Society [Report]'. *King Edward's School Chronicle*, n.s. 25, no. 184 (December 1910), pp. 94–5.
Unsigned. Summarizes Tolkien's part in a debate, 4 November 1910, deploring the effects of the Norman Conquest on the English language.

C3 'Debating Society [Report]'. *King Edward's School Chronicle*, n.s. 26, no. 185 (February 1911), pp. 5–9.
Unsigned. Notes that Tolkien spoke in a debate, 18 November 1910, against a system of arbitration preferred to war, summarizes Tolkien's affirmative argument on the theme 'We are Degenerating' in a debate of 2 December 1910, and records an objection by Tolkien in another debate, 27 January 1911, which reveals his habit of 'wearing a yellow pencil in his mouth'.

C4 'The Battle of the Eastern Field'. *King Edward's School Chronicle*, n.s. 26, no. 186 (March 1911), pp. 22–6.

Poem. Unsigned, with mock comments signed 'G. A. B.' Reprinted in *Mallorn* (journal of The Tolkien Society), no. 12 (1978), pp. 24–8, with a foreword by K. J. Young and illustrations by Lucy P. Matthews. Jessica Yates has shown (*Mallorn*, no. 13 [1979], pp. 3–5) that the poem is a parody of Macaulay's 'Battle of Lake Regillus'.

C5 'Acta Senatus'. *King Edward's School Chronicle*, n.s. 26, no. 186 (March 1911), pp. 26–7.
Report. Unsigned. In Latin.

C6 'Editorial'. *King Edward's School Chronicle*, n.s. 26, no. 187 (June 1911), pp. [33]–4.
Unsigned. Comments on writing editorials and on school sports.

C7 'Debating Society [Report]'. *King Edward's School Chronicle*, n.s. 26, no. 187 (June 1911), pp. 42–5.
Unsigned. Summarizes Tolkien's support in a debate, 4 April 1911, of the motion that the works attributed to Shakespeare were written by Francis Bacon.

C8 'Editorial'. *King Edward's School Chronicle*, n.s. 26, no. 188 (July 1911), pp. [53]–4.
Unsigned. A review of the school term past, and *envoi*.

C9 ['From the many-willow'd margin of the immemorial Thames']. *Stapeldon Magazine*, Exeter College, Oxford, 4, no. 20 (December 1913), p. 11.
The first stanza of a two-stanza poem, 'From Iffley', here untitled. Signed 'J'. Written in October 1911. The editor of the *Stapeldon Magazine* lost the second stanza.

C10 'The Happy Mariners'. *Stapeldon Magazine*, 5, no. 26 (June 1920), pp. 69–70.
Poem. Signed 'J. R. R. T.' Composed in Barnt Green, outside Birmingham, on 24 July 1915, and rewritten at Bedford on 9 September 1915. Slightly revised as 'Tha Eadigan Saelidan: The Happy Mariners' in *A Northern Venture* (B4).

C11 'The Clerke's Compleinte'. *Gryphon*, Leeds University, n.s. 4, no. 3 (December 1922), p. 95.
Poem. Signed 'N. N.' In Middle English. Reprinted in *Arda 1984* (publication of Arda-sällskapet, with support from Tolkiensällskapet Forodrim), Uppsala (1988), pp. 1–2, with commentary (pp. 3–7) by T. A. Shippey, a translation into Modern English (pp. 7–8) by *Arda* editor Anders Stenström and Nils-Lennart Johannesson, and a translation into Swedish (pp. 9–10) by Stenström with the assistance of Johannesson. A later, revised manuscript of the poem was printed in facsimile, with commentary, in 'The Clerkes Compleinte Revisited', *Arda 1986* (1990), pp. 1–13.

C12 'Iúmonna Gold Galdre Bewunden'. *Gryphon*, n.s. 4, no. 4 (January 1923), p. 130.
Poem. Based on line 3052 of *Beowulf*, 'the gold of men of long ago, enmeshed in enchantment'. Reprinted in *The Annotated Hobbit* (A3dd–ee), pp. 288–9. Cf. revision, C31.

C13 'The City of the Gods'. *Microcosm*, Leeds, 8, no. 1 (Spring 1923), p. 8.
Poem. Written 30 April 1915, originally entitled 'Kôr: In a City Lost and Dead'. Reprinted in *The Book of Lost Tales, Part One* (A21), p. 136.

C14 'Holy Maidenhood'. *Times Literary Supplement*, London, 26 April 1923, p. 281.
Review of *Hali Meidenhad: An Alliterative Prose Homily of the Thirteenth Century*, ed. F. J. Furnivall (Early English Text Society, 1923). Unsigned, but Tolkien's authorship is revealed in his diary.

C15 'Henry Bradley, 3 Dec., 1845–23 May, 1923'. *Bulletin of the Modern Humanities Research Association*, London, October 1923, pp. 4–5.
Obituary. Signed 'J. R. R. T.' Dr. Henry Bradley supervised Tolkien's work on the *Oxford English Dictionary* in 1918–20.

C16 'The Cat and the Fiddle: A Nursery-Rhyme Undone and Its Scandalous Secret Unlocked'. *Yorkshire Poetry*, Leeds, 2, no. 19 (October–November 1923), pp. [1–3].
Poem. The original manuscript version was published in *The Return of the Shadow* (A27), pp. 145–6. A revised version was published in *The Lord of the Rings* (A5), bk. 1, ch. 9, without title, and in *The Adventures of Tom Bombadil* (A6) as 'The Man in the Moon Stayed Up Too Late'.

C17 'Some Contributions to Middle-English Lexicography'. *Review of English Studies*, London, 1, no. 2 (April 1925), pp. 210–15.
Essay. 'Scraps of lexicographical and etymological information and suggestion', half of them notes on the glossary to the Early English Text Society edition of *Hali Meidenhad* (cf. C14). A publisher's reprint was issued bound in tan wrappers.

C18 'Light as Leaf on Lindentree'. *Gryphon*, n.s. 6, no. 6 (June 1925), p. 217.
Poem. Begun in Oxford 1919–20, revised in Leeds 1933–4. The word 'brokenhearted' in introductory line 1 is a printer's error for 'boldhearted'. The poem, revised, was incorporated into 'The Lay of the Children of Húrin' and in that form was published in *The Lays of Beleriand* (A23), pp. 108–10, with parts of the poem as it stood in typescript, pp. 120–3.

C19 'The Devil's Coach-Horses'. *Review of English Studies*, 1, no. 3 (July 1925), pp. 331–6.
Essay. On Old English *eafor*, Middle English *aver*. A publisher's reprint was issued bound in tan wrappers. A probably unauthorized reprint, 6 pp., was published under the imprint 'Jersey: Edward Brothers, 1925' but is reset in Monotype Bembo, a typeface cut in 1929.

C20 'Adventures in Unnatural History and Medieval Metres, being the Freaks of Fisiologus: (i) Fastitocalon, (ii) Iumbo, or ye Kinde of ye Oliphaunt'. *Stapeldon Magazine*, 7, no. 40 (June 1927), pp. 123–7.
Two poems. Signed 'Fisiologus'. Written in the manner of old bestiaries, precursors of 'Fastitocalon' (*The Adventures of Tom Bombadil* [A6]) and 'Oliphaunt' (*The Lord of the Rings* [A5], bk. 4, ch. 3, and *ATB*). Two of a series of four poems; 'Reginhardus, the Fox' and 'Monoceros, the Unicorn' have not been published.

C21 'The Oxford English School'. *Oxford Magazine*, 48, no. 21 (29 May 1930), pp. 778–80, 782.
Essay. Suggests reforms of the divergent 'language' and 'literature' curricula of the English School.

C22 'Progress in Bimble Town'. *Oxford Magazine*, 50, no. 1 (15 October 1931), p. 22.
Poem. Signed 'K. Bagpuize' (for Kingston Bagpuize, a village west of Oxford). Reprinted in *Tolkien and the Spirit of the Age: Papers (& Discussion) as*

Presented at the First Lustrum Celebration of the Dutch Tolkien Society 'Unquendor', 23–25 May 1986 (Leiden: Tolkien Genootschap 'Unquendor', 1987), p. 22, and in *The Annotated Hobbit* (A3dd–ee), p. 212. One of six poems collectively known as 'Tales and Songs of Bimble Bay'. See also C29. Four poems in the series, including 'Glip' (noted in *Biography*), have not been published, though one, 'The Bumpus', was revised as 'Perry-the-Winkle' in *The Adventures of Tom Bombadil* (A6).

C23 'Sigelwara Land [Part 1]'. *Medium Aevum*, Oxford, 1, no. 3 (December 1932), pp. [183]–96.
Essay. On Old English *Sigelhearwa*. See also C28. An offprint was issued. Pertinent manuscript materials and proofs are in the Bodleian Library, Oxford.

C24 'Errantry'. *Oxford Magazine*, 52, no. 5 (9 November 1933), p. 180.
Poem. In its earliest complete form it was read to The Inklings (the short-lived Oxford literary club organized by Edward Tangye-Lean) *circa* 1932–3. Both the earliest surviving version and the version that appeared in the *Oxford Magazine* were published in *The Treason of Isengard* (A27), pp. 85–9. A revised version was published in *The Adventures of Tom Bombadil* (A6). For an account of the development of the poem both as 'Errantry' and as Bilbo's song at Rivendell ('Eärendil was a mariner', *The Lord of the Rings*, bk. 2, ch. 2), see *Treason*, ch. 5.

C25 'Firiel'. *Chronicle*, Convent of the Sacred Heart, Roehampton, 4 (1934), pp. 30–2.
Poem. Illustrations by an unidentified artist. Revised as 'The Last Ship' in *The Adventures of Tom Bombadil* (A6).

C26 'Looney'. *Oxford Magazine*, 52, no. 9 (18 January 1934), p. 340.
Poem. Revised as 'The Sea-Bell' in *The Adventures of Tom Bombadil* (A6).

C27 'The Adventures of Tom Bombadil'. *Oxford Magazine*, 52, no. 13 (15 February 1934), pp. 464–5.
Poem. Its manuscript 'germ' was published in *The Return of the Shadow* (A26), pp. 115–16. A revised version was published in *The Adventures of Tom Bombadil* (A6). Tom Bombadil was based on a Dutch doll that belonged to Tolkien's son Michael. The character came to signify, for Tolkien, 'the spirit of the (vanishing) Oxford and Berkshire countryside' (letter to Stanley Unwin, 16 December 1937).

C28 'Sigelwara Land [Part 2]'. *Medium Aevum*, 3, no. 2 (June 1934), pp. [95]–111.
Essay. See C23. An offprint was issued. *Medium Aevum* vol. 3 was reprinted for Wm. Dawson & Sons, London, in 1966.

C29 'The Dragon's Visit'. *Oxford Magazine*, 55, no. 11 (4 February 1937), p. 342.
Poem. One of six poems collectively known as 'Tales and Songs of Bimble Bay'; see also C22. Reprinted in *The Annotated Hobbit* (A3dd–ee), pp. 262–3. A revised version was published in *Winter's Tales for Children 1* (B27).

C30 'Knocking at the Door: Lines Induced by Sensations when Waiting for an Answer at the Door of an Exalted Academic Person'. *Oxford Magazine*, 55, no. 13 (18 February 1937), p. 403.
Poem. Signed 'Oxymore'. Revised as 'The Mewlips' in *The Adventures of Tom Bombadil* (A6).

C31 'Iumonna Gold Galdre Bewunden'. *Oxford Magazine*, 55, no. 15 (4 March 1937), p. 473.
Poem. Revision of C12. Further revised as 'The Hoard' in *The Adventures of Tom Bombadil* (A6).

C32 'Leaf by Niggle'. *Dublin Review*, London, January 1945, pp. 46–61.
Story. Signed 'J. R. R. T.' In a letter to his aunt Jane Neave, 8–9 September 1962, Tolkien recalled having written 'Leaf by Niggle' just before World War Two began, and having first read it aloud to friends early in 1940. He woke up one morning with the work, originally entitled 'The Tree', virtually complete in his head. 'It took only a few hours to get down, and then copy out', he told Stanley Unwin in a letter of 18? March 1945; but the story did not go unrevised, as its manuscript and typescripts in the Bodleian Library, Oxford, reveal. On 6 September 1944 T. S. Gregory, editor of the *Dublin Review*, wrote to Tolkien among other Roman Catholic authors, asking for contributions in order that the magazine be 'an effective expression of Catholic humanity'. Tolkien sent him 'Leaf by Niggle' on 12 October 1944. The tale was first reprinted, with minor revisions, in *Tree and Leaf* (A7).

C33 'The Lay of Aotrou and Itroun'. *Welsh Review*, Cardiff, 4, no. 4 (December 1945), pp. [254]–66.
Poem. Based on Breton ballads; see Jessica Yates, 'The Source of "The Lay of Aotrou and Itroun"', *Leaves from the Tree: J. R. R. Tolkien's Shorter Fiction* (London: The Tolkien Society, 1991), pp. 63–71. The poem was completed in its original form in 1930, and later heavily revised for publication; see *The Treason of Isengard* (A27), p. 345, n. 1.

C34 '"Iþþlen" in Sawles Warde'. *English Studies*, Amsterdam, 28, no. 6 (December 1947), pp. 168–70.
Essay, in the section 'Notes and News'. Written in collaboration with S. R. T. O. d'Ardenne. A publisher's reprint was issued bound in white wrappers. The complete issue of *English Studies* was reprinted by Swets & Zeitlinger, Amsterdam, in 1978. Manuscript notes by Tolkien regarding *Sawles Warde* are in the Bodleian Library, Oxford.

C35 'MS. Bodley 34: A Re-Collation of a Collation'. *Studia Neophilologica*, Uppsala, 20, nos. 1–2 (1947–8), pp. [65]–72.
Essay. Written in collaboration with S. R. T. O. d'Ardenne. A response to R. Furuskog, 'A Collation of the *Katherine Group* (MS. Bodley 34)', in an earlier issue of *Studia Neophilologica*. *Studia Neophilologica*, 20, nos. 1–2 was reprinted by Swets & Zeitlinger, Amsterdam, in 1972.

C36 'A Fourteenth-Century Romance'. *Radio Times*, London, 4 December 1953, p. 9.
Foreword to a new translation of *Sir Gawain and the Green Knight* broadcast in the BBC Third Programme. See B30.

C37 'Imram'. *Time and Tide*, London, 3 December 1955, p. 1561.
Poem. Illustrations by Robert Gibbings (for the story of St. Brendan in *Beasts and Saints* by Helen Waddell). Entitled in earlier forms 'The Ballad of St. Brendan's Death' and 'The Death of St. Brendan'. For its history and one earlier version, contained in Tolkien's 1945 manuscript, *The Notion Club Papers*, see *Sauron Defeated* (A29), pp. 261–4, 295–6. Reprinted in *Angerthas* (publication of the Arthedain-Norges Tolkienforening), Oslo, 25 (29 June 1989), pp. 13–14, with a translation into Norwegian, pp. 14–15, and commentary by Nils-Ivar Agøy; and in *Sauron Defeated*, pp. 296–9.

C38 'Tolkien on Tolkien'. *Diplomat*, New York, October 1966, p. 39.
Article, incorporating part of an autobiographical statement prepared by Tolkien for the Houghton Mifflin Co., plus three additional paragraphs. Cf. *Letters* no. 165.

C39 'For W. H. A.' *Shenandoah: The Washington and Lee University Review*, Lexington, Va., 18, no. 2 (Winter 1967), pp. [96–7].
Poem. In Old English with facing Modern English version. A tribute to W. H. Auden on his sixtieth birthday. Reprinted in *Shenandoah*, 35, nos. 2–3 (1984), pp. 31–2. Auden admired Tolkien's public lectures at Oxford on Old English poetry, and his enthusiastic reviews of *The Lord of the Rings* boosted Tolkien's popularity in the United States.

D

Published Letters

i. Published Letters in Collections

Di1   LETTERS OF J. R. R. TOLKIEN   **1981**

a. First edition:

LETTERS OF | J. R. R. TOLKIEN | *A selection edited by* | Humphrey Carpenter | *with the assistance of* | Christopher Tolkien | London | GEORGE ALLEN & UNWIN | Boston Sydney

viii, 464 pp. + 1 plate. Collation: as described below. 22.1 × 14.2 cm.

[i–ii] blank; [iii] 'LETTERS OF J. R. R. TOLKIEN'; [iv] blank; [v] title; [vi] 'First published in 1981 | [*notice of restrictions under copyright*] | GEORGE ALLEN & UNWIN LTD | 40 Museum Street, London WC1A 1LU | © George Allen & Unwin (Publishers) Ltd. 1981 | [*within a single rule frame:*] [*British Library Cataloguing in Publication Data*] | ISBN 0-04-826005-3 | [*below the frame:*] Set in 10 on 12 point Garamond by | Bedford Typesetters Limited | and printed in Great Britain | by Mackays of Chatham'; [vii] table of contents; [viii] blank; 1–3 introduction; [4] blank; [5] 'LETTERS'; [6] blank; 7–432 text; [433] blank; 434–53 notes; 454–63 indexes; [464] 'NOTES'. Autograph letter signed from Tolkien to C. A. Furth, 4 February 1938 (cf. *Letters* no. 22), reproduced on plate facing p. [v].

Wove paper. Bound in brown cloth over boards. Stamped on spine in gilt: '[*running down:*] The Letters of J. R. R. TOLKIEN | [*horizontal:*] GEORGE ALLEN | & UNWIN'. Wove endpapers. No headbands. All edges trimmed. Top edge stained brown, fore- and bottom edges unstained.

Dust-jacket, wove paper. Stamped or printed on upper cover against a dark brown background: '[*"JRRT" monogram, stamped in gilt*] | [*printed in white:*] The Letters of | J. R. R. | TOLKIEN | [*rule, stamped in gilt*] | [*printed in white:*] Edited by Humphrey Carpenter | with the assistance of Christopher Tolkien'. Printed on spine in white, against a dark brown background: '[*running down:*] The Letters of J. R. R. TOLKIEN | [*horizontal:*] GEORGE ALLEN | & UNWIN'. Lower cover printed solid dark brown. Blurb printed on front flap in dark brown. Printed on back flap in dark brown: '[*note on Humphrey Carpenter*] | [*note on Christopher Tolkien*] | [*advertisement for Book Tokens*] | ISBN 0 04 826005 3 | *Printed in Great Britain*'.

Published 20 August 1981 at £9.95; 7,500–10,000 copies planned.

Three states, priority as follows:

(1) Pages 406–7 and 428–9 imposed in reverse order. Collation: $[1–13^{16}14^{12}15^{16}]$. On 3 August 1981 Allen & Unwin issued a letter to reviewers apologizing for the error in imposition and noting that 'the rest of the print run have been returned for correction'.

(2) Original pp. 405–8 replaced with a fold, new pp. 405–8, attached to the stub of original pp. 405–6; and original pp. 427–30 replaced with two disjunct leaves attached to the stubs of original pp. 427–8 and 429–30. Collation: $[1–13^{16}(-13_{15,16}+13_{15,16})14^{12}(\pm14_{10,11})15^{16}]$.

(3) Original pp. 405–8 replaced with a fold, new pp. 405–8, attached to the stub of original pp. 405–6; and gathering [14] replaced in its entirety, correcting previously misimposed pp. 428–9. Collation: $[1-13^{16}(-13_{15,16}+13_{15,16})14^{12}(\pm14^{12})15^{16}]$. Two variants of this state have been noted, no priority determined: (a) with cancellans gathering [14] printed on the same paper stock as the original gatherings, and (b) with the gathering printed on paper smoother and of lighter weight than the stock used for the rest of the book.

Includes 354 letters, excerpts from letters, and drafts, with endnotes. Priority of selection was 'given to those letters where Tolkien discusses his own books; but the selection has also been made with an eye to demonstrating the huge range of Tolkien's mind and interests, and his idiosyncratic but always clear view of the world' (p. 1). Omitted from this selection, for the most part, is a 'very large body of letters . . . highly personal in character', dated 1913–18, between Tolkien and his future wife, Edith Bratt.

Correspondence by Tolkien is held in numerous collections, including the BBC Written Archives Centre, Reading; the Bodleian Library, Oxford; the British Library, London; the Brotherton Library, Leeds; the John Rylands University Library, Manchester; the Lambeth Palace library, London; the library of Pembroke College, Oxford; the Pierpont Morgan Library, New York; the Royal Society of Literature, London; the library of University College, Dublin; the library of University College, London; the library of the University of St. Andrews; the Humanities Research Center, University of Texas at Austin; and the Marion E. Wade Center, Wheaton College, Wheaton, Illinois. Many of the letters printed in *Letters* are contained in the Tolkien-George Allen & Unwin archive now held by HarperCollins, and in private collections.

b. First American edition (1981):

THE LETTERS OF | J. R. R. TOLKIEN | [*swelled rule*] | SELECTED AND EDITED BY | *Humphrey Carpenter* | WITH THE ASSISTANCE OF | *Christopher Tolkien* | Houghton Mifflin Company Boston | 1981

x, 470 pp. Collation: gatherings not distinct. 22.8 × 15.2 cm.

[i–ii] blank; [iii] 'THE LETTERS OF | J. R. R. TOLKIEN'; [iv] blank; [v] title; [vi] 'Copyright © 1981 by George Allen & Unwin (Publishers) Ltd. | [*notice of restrictions under copyright*] | [*Library of Congress Cataloging in Publication Data*] | Printed in the United States of America | [*printing code, beginning "D", ending "1"*]'; [vii] table of contents; [viii] blank; [ix] 'THE LETTERS OF | J. R. R. TOLKIEN'; [x] blank; 1–3 introduction; [4] blank; [5] 'The Letters'; [6] blank; 7–432 text; [433] 'Notes'; 434–53 notes; 454–63 indexes; [464–70] blank.

Wove paper. Bound in black cloth over boards. 'JRRT' monogram stamped on upper cover in gilt. Stamped on spine in gilt, within a gilt decorative rule frame: '[*running down:*] THE LETTERS OF [*parallel to the preceding words:*] J. R. R. TOLKIEN [*followed by:*] [*4-dot ornament*] EDITED BY [*parallel to the two preceding words:*] *Humphrey Carpenter* [*followed by:*] [*4-dot ornament*] | [*horizontal:*] H M Co'. Wove endpapers. Yellow/brown headbands. All edges trimmed and unstained.

Dust-jacket, wove paper. Covers, spine, and flaps printed against a cream-yellow background. Printed on upper cover: '[*in purple:*] The Letters of | [*in black:*] J [*compass rose, in red, purple, and black*] [*in black:*] R [*crown and 3 stars, in red, purple, and black*] R | [*rule, in red*] | [*in black:*] TOLKIEN | [*in purple:*] SELECTED AND EDITED BY | [*in red:*] HUMPHREY CARPENTER | [*in black:*]

With the assistance of | [*in purple:*] CHRISTOPHER TOLKIEN | [*rule, "pierced" at centre, in red*] | [*diamond, in black with purple center*]'. Printed on spine: '[*running down:*] [*in purple:*] The Letters of [*in black:*] J [*diamond, in purple*] [*in black:*] R [*diamond, in purple*] [*in black:*] R TOLKIEN | [*parallel to preceding words, in red:*] SELECTED AND EDITED BY HUMPHREY CARPENTER [*3 flourishes*] | [*in purple:*] [*rule, parallel to the preceding words*] | [*horizontal, at foot of spine:*] HOUGHTON | MIFFLIN | COMPANY'. Printed on lower cover: '[*reproduction of autograph letter signed from Tolkien to C. A. Furth, 4 February 1938*] | [*at left, against a white panel:*] ISBN 0-395-31555-7 [*at right:*] 6-83269'. Printed on front flap: '$16.95 | [*blurb*] [*to left of blurb, running down:*] 1081'. Printed on back flap: '[*blurb, continued*] | [*note on Humphrey Carpenter*] | [*in red:*] JACKET DESIGN: G. G. LAURENS © 1981 | [*in purple:*] HOUGHTON MIFFLIN COMPANY | 2 Park Street, Boston, Massachusetts 02107'.

Published 15 October 1981 at $16.95; 100,000 copies printed.

Typeset as for Di1a, except pp. [iii], [v–vi], [ix], [5], [433], [464]. Omits the plate of Di1a, prints the letter to Furth on the dust-jacket.

The American edition of *Letters* sold poorly, and was largely remaindered (reportedly 92% of the impression). However, a second impression of 3,000 copies was issued in 1991 on the eve of the Tolkien centenary.

c. First paperback edition (1990):

LETTERS OF | J. R. R. TOLKIEN | *A selection edited by* | Humphrey Carpenter | *with the assistance of* | Christopher Tolkien | [*publisher's 'man drawing a circle' device*] | UNWIN | PAPERBACKS | LONDON SYDNEY WELLINGTON

vi, 470 pp. Collation: 238 leaves. 19.7 × 12.9 cm.

[i] blurb; [ii] reproduction of autograph letter signed from Tolkien to C. A. Furth, 4 February 1938; [iii] title; [iv] 'First published by George Allen & Unwin (Publishers) Ltd, 1981 | First published by Unwin Paperbacks, an imprint of Unwin Hyman | Limited, 1990 | C. [*sic, for* ©] George Allen & Unwin (Publishers) Ltd 1981 | [*notice of restrictions*] | [*3 publisher's addresses, London to Wellington*] | [*rule*] | [*British Library Cataloguing in Publication Data*] | ISBN 0-04-440664-9 | [*rule*] | Printed in Finland by Werner Söderström Oy'; [v] table of contents; [vi] blank; 1–3 introduction; [4] blank; [5] 'LETTERS'; [6] blank; 7–432 text; [433] 'NOTES'; 434–53 notes; 454–63 indexes; [464] blank; [465] advertisement of *H*; [466] advertisement of *LR*; [467] advertisement of *Silm*; [468] advertisement of *UT*; [469] advertisement of *BLT1*; [470] advertisement of *BLT2*.

Wove paper. Bound in heavy wove wrappers. Printed on upper cover in white, against a colour photograph of a desk, books, letters, and paraphernalia: 'The Letters | of | J. R. R. | TOLKIEN | edited by Humphrey Carpenter | with the assistance of | Christopher Tolkien'. Printed on spine against a beige background: 'The | Letters | of | [*in red:*] J. R. R. | TOLKIEN | [*colour photograph as on upper cover, outlined in red*] | [*in black:*] edited by | Humphrey | Carpenter | with the | assistance | of | Christopher | Tolkien | [*publisher's 'man drawing a circle' device*]'. Printed on lower cover against a beige background: '[*2 quotations from Tolkien's letters*] | [*blurb*] | [*at left:*] Cover photograph by Hanya Chlala | UNWIN PAPERBACKS | BIOGRAPHY/LETTERS | £6.99 net U.K. [*at right, against a white panel:*] ISBN 0-04-440664-9 | [*bar code*]'. All edges trimmed and unstained.

Published 20 March 1990 at £6.99; 7,500 copies printed.

Typeset as for Di1a, except pp. [i–iv], [433], [464–70].

Di2   J. R. R. TOLKIEN'S LETTERS TO RHONA BEARE   1985

J. R. R. TOLKIEN'S | LETTERS TO RHONA BEARE | The New England Tolkien Society | 1985

20 pp. Collation: [1^{10}]. 21.6 × 17.9 cm.

[1] title; [2] '[*dedication*] | [*acknowledgements*] | This is a limited edition of 95 copies. This is copy # [*numeral, added by hand in ink*].'; [3] foreword, signed 'S. G. H. [*Sumner Gary Hunnewell*], February, 1985'; [4] '[*4-sided, dot-toned ornament*] 14 October 1958 [*4-sided, dot-toned ornament, extends onto p. [17]*] | [*4-sided, thick rule ornament*] Letter #211 [*4-sided, thick rule ornament, extends onto p. (17)*]'; [5–16] reproduction of autograph letter signed from Tolkien to Beare, 14 October 1958; [17] '[*4-sided, dot-toned ornament, extends from p. [4]*] 8 June 1961 [*4-sided, dot-toned ornament*] | [*4-sided, thick rule ornament, extends from p. [4]*] Letter #230 [*4-sided, thick rule ornament*]'; [18–19] reproduction of typed letter signed, emended in holograph, from Tolkien to Beare, 8 June 1961; [20] blank.

Wove paper. Bound in grey wrappers, stapled through the fold. Wraparound geometrical decoration by Sylvia Hunnewell, incorporating a modification of Tolkien's drawing of a crown of Gondor (reproduced p. [11] of Di2), printed on covers. Printed on upper cover, above decoration: 'J. R. R. TOLKIEN'S | LETTERS TO RHONA BEARE'. Printed on lower cover, below decoration: 'The New England Tolkien Society · 5611B Ed-Lou · St. Louis, MO · USA'. All edges trimmed.

Published March 1985, distributed without charge to members of the New England Tolkien Society; 95 copies printed.

The letter of 14 October 1959 was printed in *Letters*, no. 211, with editorial changes, notably the omission of some marginal comments and the substitution of one paragraph of the letter as sent with one (on the same point) from a draft, and with a prefatory note summarizing Dr. Beare's questions to which the letter is a response. For comparisons of the original letter with the version in *Letters*, see Taum Santoski, letter to the editor, *Ravenhill* (newsletter of the New England Tolkien Society), 6, no. 1 (1985), pp. 7–8, and Donald O'Brien, 'The Transcription of J. R. R. Tolkien's Letters', *Beyond Bree* (newsletter of the American Mensa Tolkien Special Interest Group), January 1989, pp. 1–4. *Letters* no. 212 is a draft of a continuation of no. 211.

The letter of 8 June 1961 was printed in *Letters*, no. 230, without its first two paragraphs and final paragraph. The second paragraph is a translation of the Elvish hymn to Elbereth in *The Lord of the Rings* (bk. 2, ch. 1) which differs in detail (though not in substance) from the literal translation given in *The Road Goes Ever On* (B28).

ii. Separately Published Letters and Excerpts

Entries are arranged chronologically in order of publication, where order can be determined, otherwise by date of auction, etc. or alphabetically by author and title within the year of publication. The place of publication is given after the title when a periodical appears in this list for the first time. Excerpts range in length from a few words to several paragraphs. Priority is given to the first publication of a letter or excerpt. References are made to *Letters of J. R. R. Tolkien* (Di1) and to secondary printings and related excerpts. Not listed are quotations taken directly from *Letters*. See also A26, A29, B32, B33.

Dii1 *An Application for The Rawlinson and Bosworth Professorship of Anglo-Saxon in the University of Oxford by J. R. R. Tolkien, Professor of the English Language in the University of Leeds. June 25, 1925.*
A 12-page pamphlet, chiefly a letter to the Electors to the Rawlinson and Bosworth Professorship of Anglo-Saxon, dated 27 June 1925 at the end of the letter (though 25 June on the cover page). Accompanied by a list of Tolkien's publications, and testimonials by Lewis R. Farnell, Joseph Wright, Henry Bradley, M. E. Sadler, George Gordon, Allen Mawer, and Lascelles Abercrombie. The letter proper is printed in *Letters*, no. 7.

Dii2 Wright, E. M. *The Life of Joseph Wright.* Oxford: Oxford University Press, 1932.
Quotes, II, 651, from a letter to Joseph Wright, 26 January 1925, extending best wishes 'as a grateful disciple'. Tolkien was introduced to Gothic through Wright's *Primer of the Gothic Language*, and was his pupil at Oxford.

Dii3 Tolkien, J. R. R. [Letter to the editor]. *Observer*, London, 20 February 1938, p. 9.
A 'jesting reply' to a letter by 'Habit' (*Observer*, 16 January 1938), on sources for *H*. Written between 16 January and 20 February 1938, not intended for publication (see *Letters* no. 26). Printed in *Letters*, no. 25.

Dii4 Tolkien, J. R. R. 'The Name Coventry'. *Catholic Herald*, London, 23 February 1945, p. 2.
Letter to the editor, written 10 or 11 February 1945 (see *Letters* no. 97) in response to a query by 'H. D.' ('Coventry Charter Commemoration', *Catholic Herald*, 9 February 1945), on the etymology of *Coventry*, and on English place-names in general. Excerpts printed in 'Letter by J. R. R. Tolkien is Rediscovered after 30 Years', *Catholic Herald*, 18 September 1981.

Dii5 Breit, Harvey. 'In and Out of Books: Oxford Calling'. *New York Times Book Review*, 5 June 1955, p. 8.
Quotes from a letter to the *New York Times*, written before June 1955, on *LR* and *H* as 'serious' works. Printed in the prefatory notes to *Letters* no. 165.

Dii6 Everett, Caroline Whitman. *The Imaginative Fiction of J. R. R. Tolkien.* M.A. thesis, Florida State University, 1957.
Quotes, pp. 85–7, from a letter to Everett, 24 June 1957, chiefly on *LR*. Excerpts printed in *Letters*, no. 199. Partly different excerpts printed in Richard C. West, 'Progress Report on the Variorum Tolkien', *Orcrist* (bulletin of the University of Wisconsin J. R. R. Tolkien Society), no. 4 (1969–70) = *Tolkien Journal* (journal of the Tolkien Society of America), 4, no. 3, whole no. 13, p. 7. Briefer excerpt printed in Dii34. Additional excerpt printed in Dii62.

Dii7 Opie, Iona and Peter. *The Lore and Language of Schoolchildren.* Oxford: Clarendon Press, 1959; paperback, Oxford: Oxford University Press, 1976; new paperback, with addition to the preface, Oxford: Oxford University Press, 1987.
Quotes, p. 151, from a letter to the Opies, not after 1959, on *fains I* and related terms, within the context of a discussion of *fains* and *fainites* as used by English schoolchildren.

Dii8 Tolkien, J. R. R. [Letter to the editor]. *Triode*, Manchester, England, no. 18 (May 1960), p. 27.
Comments, written between January and May 1960, on an article by Arthur R. Weir ('No Monroe in Lothlorien!', *Triode*, no. 17 [January 1960], pp. 31–3).

Tolkien contemplates the 'horror' of making *LR* into a film. Partly reprinted, with Weir's article, in *I Palantir* (journal of the Fellowship of the Ring), Los Angeles, no. 3 (April 1964), pp. [17–19].

Dii9   Lupoff, Richard A. *Edgar Rice Burroughs: Master of Adventure*. New York: Canaveral Press, 1965; rev. and enl. ed., New York: Ace Books, 1968. Page references are to the first edition.

Quotes, pp. 246–7, from a letter to Lupoff, *circa* 1964, discounting Burroughs' 'John Carter of Mars' books as a source for Shelob in *LR*. Also printed in Richard C. West, *Tolkien Criticism: An Annotated Checklist*, 1st ed. (Kent, Ohio: Kent State University Press, 1970), p. 34. Excerpt printed in Bob Mesibov, 'Tolkien and Spiders', *Orcrist*, no. 4 (1969–70) = *Tolkien Journal*, 4, no. 3, whole no. 13, p. 3.

Dii10   Plotz, Dick. 'The Ace Books Controversy'. *Tolkien Journal*, 1, no. 2, whole no. 2 (Winterfilth 1965), pp. [1]–2.

Quotes from a letter to Plotz, after 12 September 1965 (cf. *Letters* no. 276), on property rights relative to Ace Books' unauthorized edition of *LR* (A5c). Also printed in Bonniejean Christensen, 'An Ace Mystery: Did Tolkien Write His Own Retraction?' *Orcrist*, no. 4 (1969–70) = *Tolkien Journal*, 4, no. 3, whole no. 13, p. 16.

Dii11   Plotz, Dick. 'Tolkien Notes from All Over'. *Tolkien Journal*, 1, no. 2, whole no. 2 (Winterfilth 1965), p. 3.

Quotes from a letter to Plotz, after 12 September 1965 (cf. *Letters* no. 276), regarding the cover painting for the first Ballantine Books edition of *H* (A3f).

Dii12   Meškys, Ed. 'Tolkien Notes from All Over'. *Tolkien Journal*, 3, no. 3, whole no. 9 (Late Summer 1968), p. 3.

Quotes from a letter to the Tolkien Society of America, 8 April 1968, expressing disapproval of *The Tolkien Relation* by William Ready (Dii13). Also printed, without the closing, in Bonniejean McGuire Christensen, 'A Ready Answer', *Tolkien Journal*, 3, no. 4, whole no. 10 (November 1969), p. 15. The complete typed letter signed is reproduced in *Tolkien in aller Welt: Eine Ausstellung der Inklings-Gesellschaft anlässlich des 100. Geburtstags von J. R. R. Tolkien und des Internationalen Tolkien-Symposions in Aachen* ([Aachen: Öffentliche Bibliothek der Stadt Aachen], 1992), p. [12].

Dii13   Ready, William. *The Tolkien Relation*. Chicago: Henry Regnery, 1968; reprinted as *Understanding Tolkien and The Lord of the Rings*, New York: Paperback Library, 1969; New York: Warner Books, 1969; London: Warner Books/New English Library, 1978. Page references are to the first edition.

Quotes from letters to Ready: pp. 55–6 (one sentence repeated on p. 144), 2 February 1967, expressing dislike for being written about, and refusing to provide biographical information; pp. 59–60, Whit Sunday (9 June) 1957, apologizing for tardy correspondence; and p. 60, August 1957, remarking on Tolkien's crowded schedule and ill health. The quotation from 2 February 1967 was also published, p. 288, in Ready, 'The Heroic Theme', *Library Review*, London, 21 (1968), pp. 283–8.

Dii14   *Wisterian* (newspaper of La Salle College High School), Philadelphia, 20 December 1968.

Reproduces, p. 3, an autograph letter signed to Billy Callahan, 29 September 1968, on Tolkien's pleasure that Callahan enjoyed *LR*. With a slightly inaccurate transcription of the letter.

Dii15 *An Afternoon in Middle-earth*. Birmingham [England]: Studio Theatre, Midlands Arts Centre, Cannon Hill, 1969.

Programme for an afternoon of readings, talks, and discussion, 30 November 1969, produced by Leslie Holloway. Reproduces, p. 1, (an excerpt from?) an autograph note signed to the event organizers, November? 1969, sending regrets that Tolkien cannot attend, and declaring himself ever 'a Birmingham man'.

Dii16 Lewis, C. S. *Selected Literary Essays*. Ed. Walter Hooper. Cambridge [England]: Cambridge University Press, 1969.

Quotes, p. 18 note, in the essay 'The Alliterative Metre', from a note to Hooper regarding Lewis's poem 'We were talking of dragons'. Also printed in *Inklings* (B33).

Dii17 White, William Luther. *The Image of Man in C. S. Lewis*. Nashville: Abingdon Press, 1969; London: Hodder & Stoughton, 1970.

Quotes, pp. 221–2, a letter to White, 11 September 1967, on the name 'Inklings' as applied by Edward Tangye-Lean and C. S. Lewis to literary discussion groups at Oxford. Printed in *Letters*, no. 298. Excerpts printed in Dii27, Dii33.

Dii18 Hill, Joy. [Excerpt from a letter to the editor]. *Carandaith* (journal of the Australian Tolkien Society), 2, no. 1 (January 1970), p. 67.

Quotes from a letter to an unknown recipient, written *circa* 1969, regarding the adaptation of *LR* for film.

Dii19 Chapman, Vera ('Belladonna Took'). 'Pro-editorial from the Pro-editor'. *Mallorn* (journal of The Tolkien Society), no. 5 (1972), p. 2.

Quotes a letter to Chapman, 6 February 1972, thanking The Tolkien Society for their gift to Tolkien on his eightieth birthday.

Dii20 Tolkien, J. R. R. 'Beautiful Place because Trees are Loved'. *Daily Telegraph*, London, 4 July 1972, p. 16.

Letter to the editor, dated 30 June 1972, in response to an editorial ('Forestry and Us', *Daily Telegraph*, 29 June 1972, p. 18), regarding trees, whose part Tolkien takes 'against all their enemies'. Printed in *Letters*, no. 339.

Dii21 Rogers, Deborah Webster. *The Fictitious Characters of C. S. Lewis and J. R. R. Tolkien in Relation to Their Medieval Sources*. Ph.D. dissertation, University of Wisconsin, 1972.

Quotes, pp. 197–9, an autobiographical letter to Rogers, 25 October 1958. Also printed in Deborah Webster Rogers and Ivor A. Rogers, *J. R. R. Tolkien* (Boston: Twayne, 1980; New York: Hippocrene Books, 1982), pp. 125–6. Substantially printed in *Letters*, no. 213. The passage beginning 'I am in fact a *hobbit*' was printed in Dii33, Dii37, and *Biography* (B32), and is frequently quoted.

Dii22 Tolkien, J. R. R. 'A Letter from Tolkien'. *Amon Dîn* (bulletin of the Tolkien Society of Treewood), Englewood, Colo., 2, no. 4, whole no. 4 (21 January 1973), p. 2.

Reproduces a typed letter signed to Randy Trimmer, 7 April 1971, a form response to a fan via George Allen & Unwin, apologizing that Tolkien cannot answer questions if he is to work on *Silm*.

Dii23 Sotheby & Co. *Catalogue of Nineteenth Century and Modern First Editions, Presentation Copies, Autograph Letters and Literary Manuscripts*. London, 16–17 July 1973.

Quotes, lot 757, from a letter to Stanley Unwin, 30 April 1954, expressing pleasure over Richard Hughes' opinion of *LR*.

Dii24 Falconer, Joan O. [Letter to the editor]. *Mythprint* (bulletin of the Mythopoeic Society), 8, no. 3 (September 1973), p. 3.
Quotes from a letter to Falconer, late 1964 or early 1965, on Sam Gamgee's character in *LR*. Excerpt printed in Dii34.

Dii25 Tolkien, Michael. 'J. R. R. Tolkien—The Wizard Father'. *Sunday Telegraph*, London, 9 September 1973.
Quotes from a letter to Michael Tolkien, late nineteen-sixties?, remarking that the addressee is one of the few who know what *LR* is really about. The article was reprinted in *Mythprint*, 11, no. 1 (January 1975), pp. 3–4.

Dii26 Murray, Robert. 'A Tribute to Tolkien'. *The Tablet*, London, 15 September 1973, pp. 879–80.
Quotes from a letter to Fr. Robert Murray, 2 December 1953, describing *LR* as a 'fundamentally religious and Catholic work'. Also printed, without one phrase, in William Dowie, 'The Gospel of Middle-Earth According to J. R. R. Tolkien', *J. R. R. Tolkien, Scholar and Storyteller* (B34), p. 284. Excerpt printed in Dii34. Printed with additional excerpts in *Letters*, no. 142. Murray also quotes, p. 879, Tolkien's (1967?) description of *SWM* (A9) as a 'counterblast to [C. S.] Lewis'.

Dii27 Green, Roger Lancelyn, and Walter Hooper. *C. S. Lewis: A Biography*. London: Collins; New York: Harcourt Brace Jovanovich, 1974; paperback, New York: Harcourt Brace Jovanovich, 1976; London: Fount, 1979.
Quotes, p. 155, from a letter to William Luther White, 11 September 1967, on C. S. Lewis and the Inklings (excerpted from Dii17); and p. 177, from a letter, presumably to Green, 1971? (cf. *Letters* no. 325, with related comments), on Lewis's use of *Numinor* in his *That Hideous Strength*, after Tolkien's *Númenor*. Also quotes, p. 241, remarks made by Tolkien to Green, *circa* 1949, deriding Lewis's *The Lion, the Witch and the Wardrobe*.

Dii28 Stratford, Jenny [ed.]. *The Arts Council Collection of Modern Literary Manuscripts 1963–1972*. London: Turret Books, 1974.
Reproduces, plate 3, an autograph letter signed to Elizabeth Jennings, 3 December 1955, congratulating her on the publication of *A Way of Looking*, and referring to Tolkien's recent contribution to *Time and Tide* (C37). The original letter is in the British Library (Add. MSS 52599, ff. 123, 124).

Dii29 Wolfe, Gene. 'The Tolkien Toll-Free Fifties Freeway to Mordor & Points Beyond Hurray!' *Vector* (journal of the British Science Fiction Association), London, no. 67/68 (Spring 1974), pp. 7–11.
Reproduces, p. 9, a typed letter signed to Wolfe, 7 November 1966, on the etymology of *orc* and *warg*.

Dii30 GoodKnight, Glen. ' "Death and the Desire for Deathlessness": The Counsel of Elrond'. *Mythlore* (journal of the Mythopoeic Society), 3, no. 2, whole no. 10 (1975), p. 19.
Quotes a letter to Dr. Herbert Schiro, 17 November 1957, arguing that *LR* is not about power and dominion, but about 'death and the desire for deathlessness'. Emended excerpt printed in *Letters*, no. 203.

Dii31 Manlove, C. N. *Modern Fantasy: Five Studies*. Cambridge [England]: Cambridge University Press, 1975.
Quotes, p. 158, from a letter to Manlove, 8 February 1967, on *LR* as an adult fairy-story.

Dii32 Power, N. S. 'Tolkien's Walk: An Unexpected Personal Link with Tolkien'. *Mallorn*, no. 9 (1975), pp. 16–17, 19.
Quotes separately, p. 19, a letter to Canon Power, 8 July 1973, regarding Tolkien's former residence at no. 26, Oliver Road, Ladywood, Birmingham. Quotations from the letter are also included in the article proper. Excerpts printed (partly incorrect) in N. S. Power, 'Ring of Doom', *Tablet*, London, 20/27 December 1975, pp. 1247–8.

Dii33 Grotta-Kurska, Daniel. *J. R. R. Tolkien: Architect of Middle Earth*. Philadelphia: Running Press, 1976; New York: Warner Books, 1977; 2nd (enl.) ed., *The Biography of J. R. R. Tolkien, Architect of Middle-earth* by Daniel Grotta, Philadelphia: Running Press, 1978; New York: Grosset & Dunlap, 1978. Page references are to the first edition.
Quotes, p. 8, from a letter to Deborah Webster Rogers, 25 October 1958 (excerpted from Dii21); pp. 37–8, from a letter to Allen Barnett, date not given, telling an off-colour story; pp. 86–7, from a letter to William Luther White, 11 September 1967 (excerpted from Dii17); and p. 140, from a letter to an unknown recipient, 2 February 1967, expressing concern over Mrs. J. R. R. Tolkien's health and Tolkien's many commitments. Also quoted, *passim*, are portions of interviews with Tolkien.

Dii34 Kilby, Clyde S. *Tolkien &* The Silmarillion. Wheaton, Ill.: Harold Shaw, 1976; Berkhamsted, Hertfordshire: Lion Publishing, 1977.
Quotes, pp. 16–18, from a letter to Kilby, 18 December 1965, accepting Kilby's offer of assistance to facilitate the completion of *Silm* (briefer excerpt printed in *Letters*, no. 282); pp. 21–2, from a letter to W. H. Auden, 23 February 1966, disapproving Auden's intention to write a book about Tolkien (printed with additional excerpts in *Letters*, no. 284); p. 31, from a letter to Joan O. Falconer (not, as Kilby states, to Vera Chapman), late 1964 or early 1965 (excerpted from Dii24); p. 39, from a letter to Kilby, October 1966, briefly regarding a cruise with Mrs. Tolkien; pp. 39–40, from a letter to Kilby, December 1967, regarding Tolkien's work, hardly proceeded due to distractions; p. 40, from a letter to Kilby, June 1968, regarding Tolkien's move from Oxford to the southwest of England, and the impertinence of William Ready (cf. Dii13); p. 40, from a letter to Kilby, February 1973, declining an invitation to visit the United States due to Tolkien's age and health; pp. 46–7, from a letter to Caroline W. Everett, 24 June 1957 (excerpted from Dii6); p. 56, from a letter to Kilby, date not given, denying that Tolkien had a conscious Christian 'schema' in mind when writing *LR*; pp. 56–7, from a letter to Fr. Robert Murray, 15 September 1973 (excerpted from Dii26); p. 57, from a letter to Kilby, 18 December 1965, quoting Cynewulf 'Eala Earendel'; pp. 71, 73, from a letter to Roger Verhulst, 9 March 1966, on Charles Williams; p. 73, from a letter to Mrs. Charles Williams, 15 May 1945, expressing condolences after Williams' death (full text printed in *Letters*, no. 99; the original autograph letter is reproduced in *C. S. Lewis: Images of His World*, ed. Clyde S. Kilby and Douglas Gilbert [Grand Rapids, Mich.: Wm. B. Eerdmans; London: Hodder & Stoughton, 1973], p. 189, and in part [obscured] in the Wheaton College *1987 Daily Events Calendar* [Wheaton, Ill.: Wheaton

Alumni Association, 1987], p. [34] opposite calendar page for June 14–20).
Also quotes, p. 71, three and one-half lines from a poem by Tolkien about Charles
Williams (full text, 'Our dear Charles Williams many guises shows', printed in
Inklings [B33]); p. 77, an inscription written by Tolkien in a copy of C. S.
Lewis's *Perelandra*; and *passim* from conversations between Tolkien and Kilby.

Dii35 Sotheby Parke Bernet. *Catalogue of Modern Literary Manuscripts and
Autograph Letters.* London, 23 July 1976.
Quotes, lot 180, from a letter to [Rayner?] Unwin, 14 August 1969, regarding
Tolkien's health.

Dii36 Sotheby Parke Bernet. *Catalogue of Nineteenth Century and Modern First
Editions, Presentation Copies, Autograph Letters and Literary Manuscripts.*
London, 28–9 July 1977.
Quotes, lot 537, from a letter to G. E. Selby, 14 December 1937, on *H* (partly
different excerpts printed, with some inaccuracies, in Glenn Horowitz,
Bookseller, *Catalogue 4: Modern First Editions*, New York, [1981], item 588;
full text printed in Dii66); lot 538, from a postcard to Selby, 19 September
1944, noting that *LR* is being typed, and on miscellaneous matters; lot 539,
from a letter to Selby, 7 July 1946, explaining that Tolkien has not yet resigned
his chair at Merton College, Oxford, and on miscellaneous matters (identical
excerpts printed in Dii41, partly different excerpts in Dii63; different excerpts
printed in Maggs Bros. (booksellers), *Autograph Letters and Historical
Documents: Catalogue 1086* [London, 1988], item 168); and lot 540, from a
letter to Selby, 1955? (cf. letter to David I. Masson, 12 December 1955, in T. A.
Shippey, *The Road to Middle-earth* [Dii54]; and *Letters* no. 191), on the
'significance' of the story of *LR* (partly different excerpts printed in Ronald
Belanske [bookseller], *[Catalogue of] Rare Books, Literary 1st Editions and
Autographs*, [New York, *circa* March 1989], on *LR* as neither a trilogy nor an
allegory, and on Charles Williams).

Dii37 Carpenter, Humphrey. 'A World of His Own'. *Telegraph Sunday Magazine*,
London, 11 September 1977, pp. 29, 31–2, 34.
Quotes, p. 32, from a letter to Deborah Webster Rogers, 25 October 1958 (see
Dii21); p. 34, from a letter to Colonel Worskett, 20 September 1963, describing
Silm ('grim and tragic . . .'; draft printed in *Letters*, no. 247); and p. 34, from a
letter to Milton Waldman, 10 March 1950, on *Silm* ('I had a mind to make a
body of more or less connected legend . . .'; draft printed in *Letters*, no. 126).

Dii38 Sotheby Parke Bernet. *Catalogue of Valuable Autograph Letters, Literary
Manuscripts and Historical Documents.* London, 12–13 December 1977.
Quotes from letters to Naomi Mitchison: lot 363, 18 December 1949,
announcing the completion (as Tolkien then considered them) of *LR* and *Silm*,
and discussing *H* and *FGH* (identical excerpts printed in Dii41; briefer
excerpts printed in Dii43, Dii63; partly different excerpts printed in *Letters*,
no. 122); lot 364, 25 April 1954, on language in *LR*, and on *Silm* (briefer
excerpts printed in Sotheby's, *[Catalogue of] Valuable Printed Books and
Manuscripts*, London, 27 September 1988, lot 151; printed with additional
excerpts in *Letters*, no. 144); lot 365, 25 September 1954, on *LR* and Tolkien's
earlier mythic writings, with a reproduction of the final page of the autograph
letter (excerpts printed in Sotheby's, *[Catalogue of] English Literature and
History*, London, 18 December 1986, lot 183, with a reproduction of the final
three lines of the letter, closing, and signature; full text printed in *Letters*, no.
154); lot 366, 29 June 1955, chiefly regarding the publication of *RK* (partly

different excerpts printed in *Letters*, no. 164); lot 367, 8 December 1955, chiefly regarding Tolkien's disappointment at the BBC radio adaptation of *LR* (see A5a; partly different excerpts printed in *Letters*, no. 176; partly different excerpts printed in Paul C. Richards Autographs, *Catalogue 236* [Templeton, Mass., 1989], item 100, also on Tolkien's receipt of an advance copy of *LR*, on his writing 'English and Welsh' [B26], and on his critics, with a reproduction of the final paragraph of the autograph letter, closing, and signature); lot 368, 15 October 1959, regarding Tolkien's retirement from Oxford (partly different excerpt printed in *Letters*, no. 220); and lot 369, 8 November 1959, chiefly regarding Tolkien's holiday in Bournemouth (partly different excerpts printed in Melissa and Mark Hime [booksellers], *Biblioasis One, or, The Quencher* [catalogue, Idyllwild, Calif., 1980], item 114).

Dii39 Lobdell, Jared C. 'A Medieval Proverb in *The Lord of the Rings*'. *American Notes and Queries Supplement*, no. 1 (1978), pp. 330–1.
Quotes from a letter to Lobdell, 31 July 1964, on the proverb 'third time proves best'.

Dii40 Sotheby Parke Bernet. *Catalogue of Autograph Letters and Historical Documents including Modern Literature*. London, 6 June 1978.
Quotes from letters to Mrs. Ogden: lot 499, 7 August 1968, inquiring about an expected stay in hospital; and lot 499A, 19 November 1968, regarding Tolkien's recuperation from a leg injury (additional excerpt printed in Dii63).

Dii41 Sotheby Parke Bernet. *Catalogue of Autograph Letters, Literary Manuscripts and Historical Documents*. London, 16 October 1978.
Quotes, lot 382, from a postcard to G. E. Selby, 7 July 1946 (see Dii36); lot 383, from a letter to Miss Jaworski, 9 December 1965, refusing to have *LR* dramatized; and lot 384, from a letter to Naomi Mitchison, 18 December 1949 (see Dii38).

Dii42 Sotheby Parke Bernet. *Catalogue of Autograph Letters, Literary Manuscripts and Historical Documents*. London, 18, 20 June 1979.
Quotes, lot 778, from a letter to Mr. Capan of the Cambridge University English Club, 16 December 1955, declining an invitation to speak. Identical excerpts printed in Doris Harris Autographs, *Catalogue 36* (Los Angeles, 1987), item 96.

Dii43 Carpenter, Humphrey. *The Lord of the Rings: Souvenir Booklet Commemorating Twenty Five Years of Its Publication*. [London]: George Allen & Unwin, 1980. Distributed both separately and with the 'Twenty-fifth Anniversary' Unwin Paperbacks *LR* (A5n note). Page references include wrappers.
Quotes, p. [3], from a letter to C. A. Furth, 19 December 1937, mentioning the beginning of 'a new story about Hobbits', *LR* (printed with additional excerpts in *Letters*, no. 20); p. [3], from a letter to Stanley Unwin, 16 December 1937, on *Silm* ('the Silmarils are in my heart . . .'; printed with additional excerpts in *Letters*, no. 19); p. [6], from a letter to Stanley Unwin, 18? March 1945, declaring Christopher Tolkien to be the 'primary audience' for Tolkien's works; and p. [6], from a letter to Naomi Mitchison, 18 December 1949 ('I hope to give you soon two books . . .'; see Dii38). Reproduces: p. [8], the first page of an autograph letter to Rayner Unwin, 24 October 1952 (cf. *Letters* no. 135, without the first two paragraphs here reproduced); and p. [9], a page from the manuscript of *LR*, part of bk. 1, ch. 2, from the Marquette University Archives. Also quotes, p. [10], from Tolkien's autobiographical statement for Houghton Mifflin Co. (full text printed in *Letters*, no. 165).

Dii44 Serendipity Books. *Catalogue 39*. Berkeley, Calif., [1980].

Quotes, item L&M 48, from a letter to Christine Jones, 9 December 1965, a brief acknowledgement of Jones's comments on *LR*; and item L&M 49, from a letter and a commentary appended to the letter, to Charlotte and Denis Plimmer, 8 February 1967 (partly different excerpts printed in *Letters*, no. 294, and in Dii46), and from a letter to the Plimmers, 16 February 1967, requesting the omission of a reference to lembas (the Elves' waybread in *LR*) as derived from the Eucharist, and commenting on the pressures of his work. The Plimmers had conducted an interview with Tolkien; see section Fii.

Dii45 Sotheby Parke Bernet. *Catalogue of Valuable Autograph Letters, Literary Manuscripts and Historical Documents*. London, 21–2 July 1980.

Quotes, lot 581, from a letter to Miss R. W. How, 12 November 1949, presenting a copy of and commenting on *FGH* (partly different excerpts printed in Melissa and Mark Hime [booksellers], *Ink and Lead, or, The Bibliolograph* [catalogue, Idyllwild, Calif., 1980], item 31); and lot 582, from a letter to Miss A. P. Northey, 19 January 1965, on the eventual fate of Shadowfax (of *LR*), and the 'applicability' of *LR* (partly different excerpt printed in *Letters*, no. 268). Reproduces Tolkien's autograph inscription to Miss How in the copy of *FGH*.

Dii46 Melissa and Mark Hime [booksellers]. *Precious Stones* [catalogue]. Idyllwild, Calif., 1980.

Quotes, item 45, from letters to Colin Smythe, 10 April 1968 and 4 June 1968, part of a series offered here, 1964–71; and item [63], from a letter and commentary to Charlotte and Denis Plimmer, 8 February 1967 (partly different excerpts printed in *Letters*, no. 294, and in Dii44). Reproduces: the poem 'Three Rings for the Elven-kings' as printed in a proof copy of the first edition of *FR* (item 29), with one holograph correction by Tolkien; an autograph inscription by Tolkien, partly in Anglo-Saxon, written in a copy of *H* (item 14); one page of a proof copy of the first edition of *RK* (item 29), heavily corrected by the author; and (item 47) a fair copy by Tolkien of the first two sentences of Galadriel's lament (from *FR*, 2nd ed., bk. 2, ch. 8) in Quenya and English, written out in tengwar and roman scripts, and dated 5 February 1966, opening with 'Alas!' for 'Ah!'

Dii47 Bradford Morrow, Bookseller. *Catalogue Nine*. Santa Barbara, Calif., [1980].

Quotes, item 542, from a letter to 'Mrs.' (i.e. Mr.) Earle, 12 April 1956, on *LR* as an 'invention'. Also printed, more accurately, in California Book Auction Galleries, *Highlights from Barry R. Levin Science Fiction & Fantasy Literature: Sale 234* (catalogue, San Francisco, 28–9 September 1986), lot 1244, with a reproduction of the first page of the autograph letter.

Dii48 Sotheby Parke Bernet, Hodgson's Rooms. *Catalogue of Nineteenth Century and Modern First Editions and Presentation Copies*. London, 18–19 December 1980.

Quotes, lot 650, from a letter to Peter Alford, written between 14 January 1956 and 2 April 1958 (the range of dates of the four letters to Alford offered here), probably early 1956, regarding the 1955–6 BBC radio dramatization of *LR* (see A5a). Reproduces Tolkien's signature and autograph inscription in tengwar in a copy of *FR* presented to Alford.

Dii49 George Allen & Unwin (Publishers). [Catalogue. July–December 1981.]

Reproduces, in an advertisement for *Letters*, two partly obscured and one complete first pages of autograph letters, respectively: to Rayner Unwin, 22

June 1952, remarking that Tolkien is again chairman of the (Oxford) English examiners (printed in *Letters*, no. 133); to Stanley Unwin, 16 December 1937, noting queries from Arthur Ransome, et al. and criticisms about *H* (excerpt printed in *Letters*, no. 19); and to C. A. Furth of Allen & Unwin, 19 December 1937, regarding a new impression of *H* (excerpts printed in *Letters*, no. 20; cf. Dii50, Dii65).

Dii50 George Allen & Unwin (Publishers). *J. R. R. Tolkien: Are You Up to Date on Tolkien Books?* [catalogue]. [Late 1981?]

Reproduces, in an advertisement for *Letters*, three partly obscured pages from autograph letters: to Rayner Unwin, 22 June 1952, regarding 'Errantry', and the progress of *LR* and *Silm* (printed in *Letters*, no. 133); to Stanley Unwin, 25 July 1938, on Rütten & Loening, prospective publishers of a German translation of *H* (printed in *Letters*, no. 29); and to C. A. Furth of Allen & Unwin, 19 December 1937, second page of two, giving corrections to *H* (excerpts printed in *Letters*, no. 20; cf. first page, Dii49, and unobscured reproduction of second page, Dii65).

Dii51 Lightowlers, Michael. 'A Letter from J. R. R. T.' *Mallorn*, no. 17 (October 1981), pp. 31–2.

Reproduces, p. 32, an autograph letter signed to Justin Arundale, 18 January 1964, remarking that *Silm* will not be published for some time. Also includes the letter by Arundale to which Tolkien is responding, with commentary by Lightowlers.

Dii52 D'Ardenne, S. R. T. O. 'Two Words in *Ancrene Wisse* and the Katherine Group'. *Notes and Queries*, 227 (1982), p. 3.

Quotes from a letter to d'Ardenne, 11 January 1939, on the etymology of *utnume*.

Dii53 Sotheby Parke Bernet. *[Catalogue of] Valuable Autograph Letters, Literary Manuscripts and Historical Documents*. London, 29–30 June 1982.

Quotes, lot 414, from a letter to Miss A. Munro-Kerr of the Society of Authors, 6 September 1955, accompanying Tolkien's membership application form, also dated 6 September. Reproduces two pages of the printed form completed in manuscript, on which Tolkien listed *H*, *OFS*, *FGH*, *FR*, *TT*, and *RK* under 'Books and Plays', *Dublin Review* and *Welsh Review* as periodicals contributed to, and three radio scripts. Printed with additional excerpts in Paul C. Richards Autographs, *Catalogue 211* (Templeton, Mass., [1986]), item 239, also with a reproduction of the completed application form. The Sotheby Parke Bernet catalogue also describes, without quoting, lot 625, a letter to an unnamed recipient, 28 October 1971.

Dii54 Shippey, T. A. *The Road to Middle-earth*. London: George Allen & Unwin, 1982; Boston: Houghton Mifflin, 1983.

Quotes, p. 110, from a letter to David I. Masson, 12 December 1955, on the application of the Lord's Prayer, 'And lead us not into temptation, but deliver us from evil', to *The Lord of the Rings* in general and to its denouement in the Sammath Naur (bk. 6, ch. 3). Also includes four poems by Tolkien, corrected and revised by Shippey, from *Songs from the Philologists* (see B15).

Dii55 Melissa and Mark Hime [booksellers]. *Catalogue 8: Holding Together, or, The Ink of the Octopus*. Idyllwild, Calif., 1983.

Quotes, item 30, from letters to Colin Smythe: 10 April 1968, casually remarking on Tolkien's poems in *Winter's Tales for Children 1* (B27); and

4 June 1968, hoping to find a poem about 'Westernesse' for publication by Smythe. Offered with these letters, but not quoted, is a letter from Tolkien to Smythe of July 1964, and an exchange of correspondence between Smythe and Joy Hill, Tolkien's secretary.

Dii56 Vink, Renée. 'Tolkien in Rotterdam'. *Lembas* (bulletin of the Tolkien Genootschap 'Unquendor'), 2, no. 10 (June 1983), pp. 20–2.
Quotes, p. 20, from letters to C. Ouboter, Voorhoeve en Dietrich, booksellers, of Rotterdam: 18 March 1958, responding to an invitation to a dinner in his honour in Rotterdam (cf. *Letters* no. 206); and 2 April 1958, expressing appreciation for Holland and the hospitality shown him at the 'Hobbit-maaltijd'. Reproduces: p. 21, part of an autograph letter, presumably to Ouboter, before 27 March 1958, regarding Tolkien's travel to Rotterdam, and his concern over what he is to say at the 'Hobbit-maaltijd'; and p. 22, the closing of an autograph letter signed to Ouboter, probably 2 April 1958, thanking Voorhoeve en Dietrich for their kindness and their promotion of *LR*. The article proper includes reminiscences of Tolkien by Ouboter.

Dii57 Sotheby Parke Bernet. *[Catalogue of] English Literature Comprising Printed Books, Autograph Letters and Manuscripts*. London, 21–2 July 1983.
Quotes from letters to Graham Tayar: lot 535, 4–5 June 1971, chiefly on linguistics in *LR*, and on the origins of the name *Tolkien* (partly different excerpts printed in *Letters*, no. 324); and lot 536, 3 May 1972, accepting an invitation to dine with the London Old Edwardians. Reproduces the autograph closing, signature, and postscript of lot 535. Also describes, without quoting, lot 534, three letters to Daphne Cloke (née Castell), written between 28 September 1954 and 6 March 1973, and quotes from comments by Tolkien on the transcript of an interview of Tolkien conducted by Miss Castell (*circa* 1966; see section Fii), on the enjoyment vs. analysis of a work of fiction; and lot 537, another letter to Tayar, 3 November 1972, declining on grounds of ill health the invitation accepted on 3 May. Also reproduces Tolkien's autograph inscription to Henry, Mary, Aileen, and Elizabeth Jennings, October 1937, in a copy of *H*, lot 531.

Dii58 Tolkien, Christopher. '"Moria Gate": Another Look'. *Amon Hen* (bulletin of The Tolkien Society), no. 70 (November 1984), p. 3.
Quotes from a letter to Rayner Unwin, 12 October 1972, regarding a picture by Tolkien not meant to be used but printed in *The J. R. R. Tolkien Calendar 1973* (Eii5; see Ei2, no. 24).

Dii59 Sotheby's. *[Catalogue of] English Literature and English History*. London, 6–7 December 1984.
Quotes from letters to Eileen Elgar: lot 273, 24 December 1971, regarding the death of Mrs. J. R. R. Tolkien and other personal matters, and on 'Bilbo' as a pet animal's name; lot 276, 5 March 1964, on Tolkien's myth of the Silmarils (different excerpts, or part of another letter of the same date to Mrs. Elgar, printed in *Letters*, no. 255); and lot 277, begun 22 September 1963, on Frodo's 'failure' as a hero in *LR* (partly different excerpts printed in Lion Heart Autographs, *Catalogue 12* [New York, (1985)], item 102, with a reproduction of Tolkien's signature, and in Paul C. Richards Autographs, *Catalogue 208* [Templeton, Mass., (1986)], item 99; cf. drafts, *Letters* no. 246). Reproduces, as part of lot 276, a holograph genealogical chart by Tolkien, 'Kinship of the Half-elven'. The catalogue entries and genealogical

chart were reprinted in 'Letters by J. R. R. Tolkien Sold at Auction', *Beyond Bree* (newsletter of the American Mensa Tolkien Special Interest Group), May 1985, pp. 4–6, with further elucidation of the chart in *Beyond Bree*, June 1985, p. 7.

Dii60   Walter R. Benjamin Autographs. *The Collector*, Hunter, N.Y., no. 910 (1985).
Quotes, item S-1130, from a letter to Peter H. Salus, 1 December 1965, on the appendices to *LR*.

Dii61   Blackwell's Rare Books. *[Catalogue of] Rare Modern Books*. Fyfield, Oxfordshire, May 1985.
Quotes, item 131, from a letter to an unnamed recipient, 24 June 1973, suggesting a luncheon engagement, and remarking on Tolkien's dietary restrictions; and item 132, from a letter to an unnamed (same?) recipient, 28 July 1973, commenting on a fine lunch, and again about Tolkien's diet. Identical excerpts printed later in Blackwell's Rare Books *Catalogue* A81, items 511 and 512.

Dii62   Rateliff, John D. '"And Something Yet Remains to be Said": Tolkien and Williams'. *Mythlore*, 12, no. 3, whole no. 45 (Spring 1986), pp. 48–54.
Quotes, p. 53, from a letter to Caroline Whitman Everett, 24 June 1957, on Charles Williams and his work (different excerpts, see Dii6); and p. 53, from a letter to Mother Mary Anthony, 12 April 1966, also regarding Williams. The original letter of 12 April is in the Marion E. Wade Center, Wheaton College, Wheaton, Illinois. The article also briefly quotes, p. 52, from marginalia in the manuscript of *LR* at Marquette University.

Dii63   Sotheby's. *[Catalogue of] Printed Books, Manuscripts and Music*. London, 27 May, 10 June 1986.
Quotes, lot 555, from a letter to Mrs. Ogden, 19 November 1968, on the kindness the writer received in hospital (additional excerpt printed in Dii41); lot 556, from a letter to G. E. Selby, 7 July 1946 (see Dii36); lot 557, from a letter to Naomi Mitchison, 18 December 1949 (see Dii38); lot 558, from a letter to J. D. Gilbert, 17 April 1967, on the quality of books read in childhood, and on Tolkien's contract to publish *Silm*. The catalogue also describes, without quoting, lot 554, another letter to Mrs. Ogden, 7 August 1968 (see Dii41).

Dii64   Unwin, Rayner. 'The Hobbit 50th Anniversary'. *The Bookseller*, London, 16 January 1987, pp. 166–7.
Quotes, p. 166, from a letter to C. A. Furth of George Allen & Unwin, 17 January 1937, looking forward to learning by what method the publisher would reproduce 'moon-letters' in *H* (see A3a; additional excerpt printed in *Letters*, no. 10); p. 166, from a letter to Allen & Unwin, 5 February 1937, leaving *H* in the hands of the publisher's production department; p. 166–7, from letters to C. A. Furth, 25 April 1937, and to Allen & Unwin, 9? July 1937, regarding production of the dust-jacket and binding for *H*; p. 167, from a letter to Allen & Unwin, 28 May 1937, on *H* as one of his 'procrastinations'; p. 167, slightly abridged, from a letter to Stanley Unwin, 15 October 1937, regarding Oxford interest in *H* (printed with additional excerpts in *Letters*, no. 17); p. 167, from a letter to C. A. Furth, 13 May 1937, remarking unfavourably on the Disney Studios' work; p. 167, from a letter to C. A. Furth, 31 August 1937, expressing hope that *H* would succeed, if moderately; and p. 167, from a letter to C. A. Furth (not, as stated, Stanley

Unwin), 19 December 1937, announcing that he had begun 'a new story about Hobbits', i.e. *LR* (printed in *Letters*, no. 20). The article, which describes the publication history of *H*, also includes excerpts from relevant letters from Allen & Unwin to Tolkien. It was reprinted in *Science Fiction Chronicle*, New York, June 1987, pp. 48, 50; and in *Books for Keeps*, London, no. 46 (September 1987), pp. 8–9.

Dii65 Alderson, Brian. *The Hobbit 50th Anniversary, 1937–1987*. [Oxford]: Blackwell Bookshops; London: Unwin Hyman, 1987. Pagination includes wrappers.
Reproduces, p. [10], the second of two pages of an autograph letter signed to C. A. Furth of George Allen & Unwin, 19 December 1937, noting corrections to *H*, and mentioning a 'new story about Hobbits' (*LR*). Printed in *Letters*, no. 20, but without most of the passage here reproduced. The reproduction was also printed in *The Hobbit Fiftieth Anniversary, 1938–1988* ([Boston]: Houghton Mifflin, 1988), p. [10]. Both pamphlets also quote, *passim*, from *Letters*. A reproduction of the first page of the letter was printed in Dii49.

Dii66 Patrick & Beatrice Haggerty Museum of Art, Marquette University. *J. R. R. Tolkien:* The Hobbit *Drawings, Watercolors, and Manuscripts, June 11– September 30, 1987*. Milwaukee: Marquette University, 1987.
Quotes, p. 4 (described, p. 41, as exhibit no. 53), a letter to G. E. Selby, 14 December 1937, regarding *H*. Cf. Dii36. The original autograph letter signed is in the Pierpont Morgan Library, New York (MS MA 4373). In the catalogue transcription of the letter, the last word of the second sentence before the closing, 'better', is a misreading for 'tottery'. This exhibition catalogue also describes and reproduces drawings and paintings for *H*; see entry following Ei3.

Dii67 Paul C. Richards Autographs. *Catalogue 223*. Templeton, Mass., [1987].
Quotes, item 35, from a letter to Jane Dixon, 9 December 1965, regarding the publication of *H* and *LR* in the United States, and the prospects of film versions of Tolkien's works.

Dii68 Paul C. Richards Autographs. *Catalogue 224*. Templeton, Mass., [1987].
Quotes, item 40, from a letter to William McCullam, 9 December 1965, on American editions of *LR*, the use by others of words and names from Tolkien's writings, and the word *grey* in Elvish. Identical excerpts printed in Richards' *Catalogue 251* [1990], item 166.

Dii69 David Schulson Autographs. *[Catalogue] 42*. [Los Angeles?], 1987.
Quotes, item 140, from a letter to Mr. Burns, 15 November 1952, on the character of a scholar who had written for advice about her work, on the current view of Anglo-Saxons, and on Anglo-Saxon verse.

Dii70 Mitchell, Bruce. *On Old English*. Oxford: Basil Blackwell, 1988.
Quotes, pp. 53–4, from a letter to Mitchell, date not given, on *Beowulf*. Also quotes, p. 340, remarks by Tolkien on the *Exodus* poet made in a lecture at Oxford and recorded in notes by then-student Mitchell.

Dii71 Paul C. Richards Autographs. *Catalogue 227*. Templeton, Mass., [1988].
Reproduces, item 43, an autograph letter signed to J. L. N. O'Loughlin, 29 January 1943, congratulating him on the birth of a son, and commenting on wartime matters. With a transcription of parts of the text. Excerpts printed in Tollett and Harman (booksellers), *Catalogue 12* (New York, [1991]), item 112, with a reproduction of the closing and signature.

Dii72 Paul C. Richards Autographs. *Catalogue 228.* Templeton, Mass., [1988].
Reproduces, item 210, an autograph postcard signed to J. L. N. O'Loughlin,
18 January 1948, thanking him for a parcel, and remarking on Tolkien's
health. With a transcription of most of the text.

Dii73 Paul C. Richards Autographs. *Catalogue 229.* Templeton, Mass., [1988].
Quotes, item 309, from a letter to J. L. N. O'Loughlin, 30 October 1965,
praising an article by O'Loughlin, and remarking on the omission of
O'Loughlin from *English and Medieval Studies Presented to J. R. R. Tolkien
on the Occasion of His Seventieth Birthday* (ed. Davis and Wrenn, 1962).

Dii74 Paul C. Richards Autographs. *Catalogue 230.* Templeton, Mass., [1988].
Quotes, item 287, from a letter to J. L. N. O'Loughlin, 7 January 1949,
acknowledging a letter from O'Loughlin.

Dii75 Sibley, Jane T. 'J. R. R. Tolkien's Runes'. *Niekas*, no. 38 (January 1989), pp.
13, 67.
Quotes, p. 13, a letter to Sibley, 30 May 1964, on runes in *H* and *LR*. A
corrected version of the article, with a more accurate transcription of
Tolkien's letter (still with minor inaccuracies), was published in *Vinyar
Tengwar* (newsletter of the Elvish Linguistic Fellowship), San Diego, no. 6
(July 1989), pp. 7–8, with a reproduction of the typed letter signed, p. [15].

Dii76 Tolkien, J. R. R. 'The Dick Plotz Letter: Declension of the Quenya Noun'.
Beyond Bree, March 1989, p. 7.
Reproduces part of an autograph letter to Dick Plotz, late 1966–early 1967,
declining in 'Book Quenya' the nouns *cirya* and *lasse*. With a commentary by
Nancy Martsch. The letter was earlier printed, with a commentary by Jim
Allan, in 'Tolkien Language Notes #2' (1974, p. 4), a working paper
privately circulated by Allan to people involved in writing *An Introduction to
Elvish* (ed. Allan, 1978). A transcription of the letter, with an additional note
by Tolkien and commentary by Jorge Quiñonez, was published in *Vinyar
Tengwar*, no. 6 (July 1989), pp. 13–[14].

Dii77 Maggs Bros. [booksellers]. *Autograph Letters & Historical Documents:
Catalogue 1096.* London, 1989.
Quotes, item 203, from a letter to Molly Waldron, 30 November 1955, on
the genesis of *LR*, and on the work's unsuitability for 'dramatization'.
Reproduces the final two sentences of the autograph letter, closing, and
signature. Partly different excerpt printed in *Letters*, no. 175.

Dii78 Paul C. Richards Autographs. *Catalogue 249.* Templeton, Mass., [1990].
Reproduces, item 62, a typed letter signed to Andrew Schiller, 22 June 1957,
on metre and prosody, and *Sir Gawain and the Green Knight*.

Dii79 George J. Houle [bookseller]. *Catalogue 54: Autographs.* Los Angeles, 1990.
Quotes, item 118, from a letter to Mr. Wood, *circa* 1970, regarding Tolkien
having moved from Oxford, and the binding decoration for the 'India Paper
edition' of *LR* (see A5h).

Dii80 Sotheby's. *[Catalogue of] English Literature and History.* London, 19 July
1990.
Quotes, lot 202, with a reproduction of an autograph page, from a letter to
Miss Clark, on *LBN* and *HBBS*, and on the design of the dust-jacket of the
first edition of *LR* (A5a).

Dii81 Sotheby's. *[Catalogue of] English Literature and History*. London, 18 July 1991.

Quotes, lot 359, from one or both of two letters to Miss Turnbull, 2 and 19 May 1955, sentiments on the completion of *RK* (briefer excerpts printed in R. A. Gekoski [bookseller], London, *Catalogue 16*, spring 1992, item 108); lot 361, from a letter to Leila and Patricia Kirke, 9 January 1945, on the help his children Christopher and Priscilla are giving him with *LR*, and (with several errors in the transcription) on the characters and plot of *LR*; and lot 362, from one or two of eight letters to Patricia Kirke, 1954–9, on holy relics, and on his calligraphic handwriting; and reproduces, lot 360, an autograph page from a letter to Miss R. Turnbull, 11 March 1949, noting the approaching publication of *FGH* and the typing of *LR*, and mentioning a friend among the Sisters of Mercy of Hull (excerpt printed in R. A. Gekoski, *Catalogue 16*, item 107). The entry for lot 360 and the facsimile autograph page were reprinted in *Beyond Bree*, September 1991, p. 3. Cf. Dii86.

Dii82 Lobdell, Jared C. 'C. S. Lewis's Ransom Stories and Their Eighteenth-Century Ancestry'. *Word and Story in C. S. Lewis*. Ed. Peter J. Schakel and Charles A. Huttar. Columbia: University of Missouri Press, 1991. Pp. 213–31.

Quotes, p. 230, from letter to Lobdell, December 1963, on C. S. Lewis's qualities as a reader.

Dii83 David J. Holmes Autographs. *Catalogue 37: Books from a Private Library (with Additions)*. Philadelphia, [December 1991].

Quotes, item 161, from two letters to H. F. B. Brett-Smith, 22 July and 8 August 1925, on Tolkien's academic duties at Leeds, and on his aspirations as a poet. Included with these letters are two by H. C. Wyld to Brett-Smith, concerning their (aborted?) plan to circulate a poem by Tolkien as a 'discovered' eighteenth-century text.

Dii84 *The Tolkien Family Album*. London: Grafton Books; Boston: Houghton Mifflin, 1992.

Reproduces, p. 22, a 'coded' autograph letter or card, [1900], a limerick; and p. 35, an autograph postcard signed to Edith Bratt, postmarked 2 February 1913, on his life at Oxford. Also reproduces, p. 32, an Exeter College 'smoker' programme cover by Tolkien (see Eii2); p. 33, the poem 'Namárië', written out in tengwar by Tolkien for *RGEO* (B28); p. 40, a trench map drawn by Tolkien in World War One; p. 57, the poster for the Bodleian Library *Hobbit* exhibition, 1987, with Tolkien's painting *Bilbo Comes to the Huts of the Raft-elves* (see Eii24); p. 58, Tolkien's drawing *Beorn's Hall* from *H* (A3); p. 59, an address panel by Tolkien written as Father Christmas (*FCL*, A14, p. [5]); p. 60, a page from a Father Christmas letter, from (*FCL*, p. [9]); p. 63, the title page from *Mr. Bliss* (A18a); and p. 70, part of the standard dust-jacket for *H*, with later lettering (see A3h).

Dii85 Rossenberg, René van. *Hobbits in Holland: Leven en werk van J R R Tolkien (1892–1973)*. The Hague: Koninklijke Bibliotheek, 1992.

Reproduces, p. 68, typed letter signed to S. E. O. Joukes, on the meaning of names in *The Lord of the Rings*. Also reproduces, p. 56, an inscription by Tolkien in tengwar on the title page of a copy of *FR*. Quotes, p. 31, from Tolkien's remarks at the 'Hobbit-maaltijd', 1958 (cf. Dii56).

Dii86 Superior Galleries. *[Catalogue of] The Superior Galleries May 9th, 1992 Auction of Autographs, Manuscripts & Select Books*. Beverly Hills, Calif., 1992.

Reproduces, lot 69, portions of three autograph letters and one typed letter to Patricia Kirke, displayed in a photograph layered one on top of another. The dates of two letters are visible (20 June 1955, 5 July 1959); another letter is undated, and the last is obscured except for the closing, but both were written between 1955 and 1959. On personal matters, and arranging to meet Kirke. Cf. Dii81.

Dii87 Sotheby's, London. [Draft of a catalogue entry]. 'Reports'. *Amon Hen*, no. 115 (May 1992), pp. 9–11.

Quotes from a letter to Rayner Unwin, 30 December 1953, regarding an upside-down illustration in a proof of *FR*. Also quotes from Tolkien's remarks written on proof pages of *LR*. The full, correct text of the entry was printed in Sotheby's, *[Catalogue of] English Literature and History, Private Press and Illustrated Books, Related Drawings and Animation Art*, London, 21–2 July 1992, lot 183.

E

Art by J. R. R. Tolkien

i. Art in Collections

Described here are books containing several paintings or drawings by Tolkien, exclusive of bound calendars and diaries (see Eii), books in sections A and B with illustrations by Tolkien, and collections with commentary not in English (see section G).

Ei1   DRAWINGS BY J. R. R. TOLKIEN   1976

First edition:

Catalogue | of an Exhibition of | *Drawings by* | *J. R. R. TOLKIEN* | *at the* | ASHMOLEAN MUSEUM | OXFORD | 14th December – 27th February | 1976– 1977 | *and at* | THE NATIONAL BOOK LEAGUE | 7 ALBEMARLE STREET | LONDON W1 | 2nd March – 7th April | 1977

36 pp.; text also printed on inside covers. Collation: $[1^{18}]$. 23.5 × 15.7 cm.

[inside upper cover] notes on cover illustrations and monogram on p. [1]; [1] 'J. R. R. TOLKIEN | ASHMOLEAN MUSEUM | OXFORD | NATIONAL BOOK LEAGUE | LONDON | [*"JRRT" monogram, misprinted as mirror image*]'; [2] photograph of Tolkien, by John Wyatt; [3] title; [4] 'Catalogue Copyright © The Ashmolean Museum, Oxford 1976 | All Rights Reserved | ISBN 0 90009042 1 | 0 85353 251 6 (NBL) | Published jointly by The Ashmolean Museum, Oxford and the | National Book League, Albemarle Street, London, in conjunction | with George Allen & Unwin (Publishers) Ltd | Introduction © Baillie Tolkien 1976 | Biographical Introduction © Humphrey Carpenter 1976 | Illustrations © George Allen & Unwin (Publishers) Ltd 1976 | Catalogue designed by George Allen & Unwin (Publishers) Ltd | set in 'Monotype' Baskerville (Series 169/312) | and printed in Great Britain by | Wood Westworth & Co Ltd, St Helens, Merseyside | First published 1976'; [5] foreword, by K. J. Garlick; [6–7] introduction, by Baillie Tolkien (Mrs. Christopher Tolkien); [8– 10] biographical note, by Humphrey Carpenter; at foot of p. [10]: 'CATALOGUE | [*note*]'; [11–35] text and illustrations; [36—inside lower cover] annotated list of 'J. R. R. Tolkien's Books', beginning with *H*, ending with *FCL*.

Includes previously unpublished art by Tolkien, reproduced in black and white except on covers:

    upper cover, *The Green Dragon*, a painting inspired by *Beowulf* (cf. Ei2, no. 40 [top]), executed in September 1927 in a sketch book entitled *The Book of Ishness*
        p. [11], a dragon, an unused drawing for the binding of *The Hobbit* (see A3a)
        p. [13], *Dwarves Marching*, a sketch for *The Hobbit*
        p. [17], *Dragon and Warrior*, a painting inspired by *Beowulf*, executed in May 1928 on a sheet tipped into the *Book of Ishness* sketch book (cf. Ei2, no. 40 [lower right])
        p. [19], *Smaug*, a sketch for *Smaug Flies Round the Mountain* (see Ei2, no. 18)

p. [22], detail from a painting of Father Christmas and his reindeer over Oxford (cf. *FCL*, A14, p. [7])

p. [26], *North Pole Post*, a painted 'stamp' (cf. *FCL*, p. [7])

p. [27], *North Pole 1924* and *2*, two painted 'stamps' (cf. *FCL*, pp. [7], [16])

p. [30], *By Elf Messenger*, a painted and written decoration (cf. *FCL*, p. [4])

p. [31], two drawn 'patterns'

lower cover, 'Ring and Eye' device, here identified as 'the design for the dust jacket of *The Fellowship of the Ring*'

Wove paper. Bound in heavy wove wrappers, stapled through fold. Printed on upper cover: '*Drawings | by |* TOLKIEN | [*colour illustration by Tolkien,* The Green Dragon]'. 'Ring and Eye' device for the dust-jackets of *The Lord of the Rings* (A5a) printed on lower cover in black, red, and orange. All edges trimmed.

Published December? 1976 at £1.35; total number of copies not known, from which the Ashmolean Museum received 960. Copies were later distributed by Allen & Unwin to friends without charge.

The art was selected and the catalogue entries written by the Countess of Caithness and Ian Lowe, assisted by Christopher Tolkien. Includes transcriptions of manuscript notes added by J. R. R. Tolkien to some illustrations.

In 1975 the Ashmolean Museum, Oxford, at the request of Tolkien's executors, assumed custody of these drawings and paintings. The works were later transferred to the Bodleian Library, Oxford.

Ei2   PICTURES BY J. R. R. TOLKIEN   1979

a. First edition:

[*colour triangular ornament by Tolkien, extracted from a larger pattern (no. 44, lower right)*] | [*line closely spaced:*] PICTURES·BY·J.R.R.TOLKIEN | [*colour triangular ornament by Tolkien, as above, but inverted*] | *Foreword and Notes by* | CHRISTOPHER TOLKIEN | London | GEORGE ALLEN & UNWIN | Boston Sydney

108 pp. Collation: [1–3^{12}4^{6}5^{12}]. 30.9 × 29.8 cm.

[1–2] blank; [3] line closely spaced: 'PICTURES·BY·J.R.R.TOLKIEN'; [4] colour photograph of Tolkien, by Billett Potter; [5] title; [6] 'First published in 1979 | [*notice of restrictions under copyright*] | GEORGE ALLEN & UNWIN LTD | 40 Museum Street, London WC1A 1LU | This book © George Allen & Unwin (Publishers) Ltd. 1979 | ISBN 0 04 741003 5 Hardback | [*two-column list of illustrations with copyright information*] | Typeset in 12 on 14 pt Goudy by Bedford Typesetters Ltd | and printed in Great Britain by Chorley & Pickersgill Ltd, Leeds'; [7–8] foreword; [9] 'JRRT' monogram; [10–105] text and illustrations, rectos in full colour; [106–8] blank.

Includes the following art by J. R. R. Tolkien, with notes by Christopher Tolkien:

1 *The Hill: Hobbiton-across-the Water.* (a) pencil sketch for *H*, preliminary to (and here misidentified as) the pen-and-ink frontispiece of the first impression of A3a; (b) painted version, first published in the second impression of A3a.

2 *The Trolls*: (a) drawing for *H*, first published in A3a; (b) the drawing as coloured by H. E. Riddett for *The Hobbit Calendar 1976* (Eii10).

3 *The Three Trolls are Turned to Stone*: (a) unused drawing for *H*, published here

for the first time in its original form; (b) the drawing as coloured by H. E. Riddett for the *J. R. R. Tolkien Calendar 1979* (Eii18).

4 *Rivendell Looking West*: unfinished colour sketch, first published in *The Lord of the Rings 1977 Calendar* (Eii13).

5 *Rivendell Looking East*: colour sketch, first published in *The Lord of the Rings 1977 Calendar* (Eii13).

6 *Rivendell*: painting for *H*, first published in the second impression of A3a.

7 *The Mountain-path*: (a) drawing for *H*, first published in A3a; (b) the drawing as coloured by H. E. Riddett for *The Hobbit Calendar 1976* (Eii10).

8 *The Misty Mountains Looking West from the Eyrie towards Goblin Gate*: (a) drawing for *H*, first published in A3a; (b) the drawing as coloured by H. E. Riddett for *The Hobbit Calendar 1976* (Eii10).

9 *Bilbo Woke with the Early Sun in His Eyes*: painting for *H*, first published in A3b as *Bilbo Woke Up with the Early Sun in His Eyes* (and sometimes reproduced under the fuller title, more accurately quoted from the text of *H*).

10 *Beorn's Hall*: (a) drawing for *H*, first published in A3a; (b) the drawing as coloured by H. E. Riddett for *The Hobbit Calendar 1976* (Eii10).

11 *The Elvenking's Gate (I)*: unfinished painting for *H*, first published in the *J. R. R. Tolkien Calendar 1979* (Eii18).

12 *The Elvenking's Gate (II)*: (a) drawing for *H*, first published in A3a; (b) the drawing as coloured by H. E. Riddett for *The Hobbit Calendar 1976* (Eii10).

13 *Bilbo Comes to the Huts of the Raft-elves (I)*: painting for *H*, titled on the work *Sketch for The Forest River*, first published in the *J. R. R. Tolkien Calendar 1979* (Eii17).

14 *Bilbo Comes to the Huts of the Raft-elves (II)*: painting for *H*, first published in the second impression of A3a.

15 *Lake Town*: (a) drawing for *H*, first published in A3a; (b) the drawing as coloured by H. E. Riddett for *The Hobbit Calendar 1976* (Eii10).

16 *The Front Gate*: (a) drawing for *H*, first published in A3a; (b) the drawing as coloured by H. E. Riddett for *The Hobbit Calendar 1976* (Eii10).

17 *Conversation with Smaug*: painting for *H*, first published in the second impression of A3a as *O Smaug, the Chiefest and Greatest of All Calamities!*.

18 *Smaug Flies Round the Mountain*: painting for *H*, first published in the *J. R. R. Tolkien Calendar 1979* (Eii18).

19 *Death of Smaug*: colour sketch for *H*, with manuscript notes, first published on the cover of A3h.

20 *The Hall at Bag-End, Residence of B. Baggins Esquire*: (a) drawing for *H*, first published in A3a; (b) the drawing as coloured by H. E. Riddett for A3o.

21 *Old Man Willow*: colour drawing for *LR*, first published in *The J. R. R. Tolkien Calendar 1973* (Eii5).

22 *Doors of Durin* and *Moria Gate*: (a) drawing, with text, of the Doors of Durin in *LR*, first published in A5a; (b) colour drawing of the West Gate of Moria, first published in *The J. R. R. Tolkien Calendar 1973* (Eii5, October).

23 'Leaves from the Book of Mazarbul': colour 'facsimile pages', as if from the Dwarves' book in *LR*, bk. 2, ch. 4–5, first published in *The Lord of the Rings 1977 Calendar* (Eii13).

24 *Moria Gate (The Steps to the East Gate)*: the discarded bottom part of the colour drawing in no. 22 above, here incorrectly identified as the eastern steps leading to Moria in *LR*, first published in *The J. R. R. Tolkien Calendar 1973* (Eii5, September). See Christopher Tolkien, '"Moria Gate": Another Look', *Amon Hen* (bulletin of The Tolkien Society), no. 70 (November 1984), p. 3.

25 *The Forest of Lothlorien in Spring*: colour drawing for *LR*, first published in the *J. R. R. Tolkien Calendar 1974* (Eii6).

26 *Helm's Deep & the Hornburg*: sketch for *LR*, first published in *The Lord of the Rings 1977 Calendar* (Eii13).

27 *Orthanc* and *Minas Tirith*: (a) sketch of Orthanc for *LR*; (b) unfinished colour drawing of Minas Tirith for *LR*, entitled on the work *Stanburg* and *Steinborg*; (a) and (b) first published in *The Lord of the Rings 1977 Calendar* (Eii13).

28 *Shelob's Lair*: manuscript page of *TT* including a colour sketch, first published in *The Lord of the Rings 1977 Calendar* (Eii13).

29 *Dunharrow*: colour drawing for *LR* (an earlier conception of the appearance of Dunharrow), first published in *The Lord of the Rings 1977 Calendar* (Eii13).

30 *Orodruin* and *Barad-dûr*: (a) sketch of Mount Doom for *LR*, entitled on the work *Orodruin, Mt Doom*, and *Sam's Path*, here in black and white, first published in colour in *The Lord of the Rings 1977 Calendar* (Eii13); (b) colour drawing of Barad-dûr for *LR*, first published in *The J. R. R. Tolkien Calendar 1973* (Eii5).

31 *Taniquetil*: painting for *Silm*, executed (probably, like all of the Silmarillion paintings) *circa* 1927–8, first published in the *J. R. R. Tolkien Calendar 1974* (Eii6).

32 *Lake Mithrim*: painting for *Silm*, dated 1927, first published in *The Silmarillion Calendar 1978* (Eii15).

33 *Nargothrond (I)*: unfinished painting for *Silm*, probably executed in 1928, first published in *The Silmarillion Calendar 1978* (Eii15).

34 *Nargothrond (II)*: (a) drawing for *Silm*, executed at Lyme Regis in Dorset, dated 1928, published here for the first time in its original form; (b) the drawing as coloured by H. E. Riddett for *The Silmarillion Calendar 1978* (Eii15).

35 *Gondolin and the Vale of Tumladen [from Cristhorn]*: (a) drawing for *Silm*, dated September 1928, published here for the first time in its original form; (b) the drawing as coloured by H. E. Riddett for *The Silmarillion Calendar 1978* (Eii15).

36 *Tol Sirion*: (a) drawing for *Silm*, executed at Lyme Regis, Dorset, in July 1928, published here for the first time in its original form; (b) the drawing as adapted (with the mountain Thangorodrim much reduced in size according to later revisions to *Silm*) and coloured by H. E. Riddett for *The Silmarillion Calendar 1978* (Eii15).

37 *Mirkwood* and *Beleg Finds Gwindor in Taur-nu-Fuin (Fangorn Forest)*: (a) *Mirkwood*, wash drawing for *H*, first published in A3a; (b) painting for *Silm*, of Beleg finding Gwindor in the forest of Taur-nu-Fuin, entitled on the work *Fangorn Forest* for its first reproduction, in *The J. R. R. Tolkien Calendar 1974* (Eii6).

38 *Glaurung Sets Forth to Seek Túrin*: painting for *Silm*, dated on the work September 1927; first published with its original title (*Glórund Sets Forth . . .*) in *The Silmarillion Desk Calendar 1979* (Eii20); also published, with its title relettered by Christopher Tolkien with the name of the dragon as in the published *Silm*, in *The Silmarillion Calendar 1978* (Eii15).

39 *Polar Bear had Fallen from Top to Bottom onto His Nose*: painting, made for Christmas 1928, first published in *FCL* (A14).

40 Three dragons, made *circa* 1927–8: (a) top, painting, *The Green Dragon*, first published in *Drawings by J. R. R. Tolkien* (Ei1); (b) lower left, painting of a dragon coiled around a tree, first published in the *J. R. R. Tolkien Calendar 1979* (Eii18) with the other two dragons; (c) painting of a dragon and warrior, first published (in black and white) in Ei1.

41 Trees: (a) *The Tree of Amalion*, drawing made December 1963–January 1964 for the cover of the paperback edition of *TL* (A7a); (b–d) three colour drawings, two versions of *The Tree of Amalion* and one of an upright tree, the drawing at upper left made *circa* 1927–8, all three first published in the *J. R. R. Tolkien Calendar 1979* (Eii18).

42 Flowering tree with friezes, five colour drawings combined, made in the late nineteen-twenties except two flowers (at left and right) from the nineteen-sixties; first published in the *J. R. R. Tolkien Calendar 1979* (Eii18).

43 Patterns (I), colour drawings made in the nineteen-sixties on newspaper pages, floral and geometric forms perhaps meant to be associated with the world of *The Silmarillion*; first published in the *J. R. R. Tolkien Calendar 1979* (Eii18).

44 Patterns (II), more coloured drawings like those in 43; first published in the *J. R. R. Tolkien Calendar 1979* (Eii18).

45 Floral designs: one drawing, *Pilinehtar*, and four paintings of plants, combined within a decorative frame, made in the nineteen-sixties; first published in the *J. R. R. Tolkien Calendar 1979* (Eii18).

46 Númenórean tile and textiles: three colour drawings; tile first published in the *J. R. R. Tolkien Calendar 1974* (Eii6); textiles first published (with the tile printed again) in *The Silmarillion Calendar 1978* (Eii15).

47 Heraldic devices, sixteen colour drawings or paintings of devices for *Silm*: Elwë, Melian, Fingolfin, Finwë, Fëanor, Lúthien (two versions), Beren, Finrod Felagund, Idril Celebrindal, Gil-galad, Bëor, Eärendil, Hador, the Silmarils, and the House of Haleth; first published in the *J. R. R. Tolkien Calendar 1974* (Eii6) and *The Silmarillion Calendar 1978* (Eii15).

48 Elvish script, three pages of calligraphy: (a, top) the beginning of 'Errantry' in black and coloured inks; (b–c, lower left and right) versions of 'The Adventures of Tom Bombadil' in black ink; first published in *The Silmarillion Calendar 1978* (Eii15).

Wove paper. Bound in dark brown cloth over boards. 'JRRT' monogram stamped on upper cover in gilt. Stamped on spine, running down, in gilt: 'PICTURES·BY·J.R.R.TOLKIEN GEORGE ALLEN [*parallel to the two preceding words:*] & UNWIN'. Wove endpapers. Copies have been seen (1) with brown/cream headband and (2) with no headbands; no priority determined. All edges trimmed and unstained.

Slipcase, paper over boards with dark brown cloth top and bottom edges, the paper printed in dark brown and cream to imitate three-quarter binding. Printed on upper cover against a cream background: '[*colour triangular ornament by Tolkien, as on the title page*] | [*closely spaced, in black:*] PICTURES·BY·J.R.R.TOLKIEN | [*colour triangular ornament, as above, but inverted*]'. Printed on spine, running down, in cream: 'PICTURES·BY·J.R.R.TOLKIEN'. Blurb printed on lower cover against a cream background. A copy has been noted in a bookseller's catalogue (but none examined) in glassine dust-wrapper, in slipcase.

Published 1 November 1979 at £15.00; number of copies not known. Copies were given away by Allen & Unwin as premiums with the purchase of some copies of the 1982 limited edition of *Silm* (A15h). More copies of the bound volume Ei2a were produced than slipcases, and were sold without slipcases when the supply was exhausted.

'The primary purpose of this book is to collect together all the pictures (paintings, drawings, designs) by J. R. R. Tolkien which were published in a series of six Calendars from 1973 to 1979, with a gap in 1975', by George Allen & Unwin and Ballantine Books (p. [7]); see Eii. Some of Christopher Tolkien's notes in the 1977–9 Allen & Unwin calendars were reprinted in, or adapted for, the present book.

b. First American edition (1979):

[*colour triangular ornament by Tolkien, extracted from a larger pattern (no. 44, lower right)*] | [*line closely spaced:*] PICTURES·BY·J.R.R.TOLKIEN | [*colour triangular ornament by Tolkien, as above, but inverted*] | *Foreword and Notes by* | CHRISTOPHER TOLKIEN | Houghton Mifflin Company Boston | 1979

108 pp. Collation: [1–3^{12}4^{6}5^{12}]. 30.9 × 29.8 cm.

Contents as for Ei2a, except pp. [5] title; and [6] 'First American Edition | Copyright © George Allen & Unwin (Publishers) Ltd. 1979 | [*notice of restrictions under copyright*] | ISBN 0 – 395 – 28523 – 2 | Printed in Great Britain | [*printing code, beginning "H", ending "1"*] | [*two-column list of illustrations with copyright information*] | Typeset in 12 on 14 pt Goudy by Bedford Typesetters Ltd | and printed in Great Britain by Chorley & Pickersgill Ltd, Leeds'.

Wove paper. Bound in dark brown cloth over boards. 'JRRT' monogram stamped on upper cover in gilt. Stamped on spine, running down, in gilt: 'PICTURES·BY·J.R.R.TOLKIEN   HMCO'. Wove endpapers. Brown/cream headbands. All edges trimmed and unstained.

Slipcase, paper over boards, printed in brown and creamy yellow to imitate three-quarter binding. Printed on both upper and lower covers: '[*colour triangular ornament by Tolkien, as on t.p.*] | [*normally spaced:*] PICTURES · BY · J. R. R. TOLKIEN | [*colour triangular ornament by Tolkien, as above, but inverted*]'.

Published 19 November 1979 at $29.95; 25,000 copies printed.

Sheets imported from Allen & Unwin, with altered pp. [5–6].

c. New edition (1992):

To be published by HarperCollins, London, with new text by Christopher Tolkien.

Ei3   CATALOGUE OF THE MANUSCRIPTS OF JRRT   1984

CATALOGUE | OF AN EXHIBIT OF | THE MANUSCRIPTS | OF JRRT | ['*JRRT*' *monogram*] | Marquette University | Memorial Library | Department of Special Collections | and University Archives | Milwaukee, Wisconsin | September 12–23, 1983 | Funded in part by | the Wisconsin Humanities Committee | serving on behalf of | The National Endowment for the Humanities

[2], vi, 32 pp. Collation: [1^{20}]. 21.7 × 13.8 cm.

[preliminary 1] title; [preliminary 2] 'Published by the Marquette University Department | of Special Collections and University Archives. | "The West-gate of Moria," (3/4/15:1a), Front | Cover, Copyright (c) [*sic*, for ©] 1983 by Christopher R. | Tolkien and F.R. Williamson, as Executors | of the Estate of J. R. R. Tolkien, deceased. | Printed with Permission. | J. R. R. T. Monogram appearing on Title Page | is from the cover of *Pictures by J. R. R. Tolkien* | (1979). Copyright (c) [*sic*, for ©] George Allen & Unwin | Publishers, Ltd., 1979. Reprinted with Per- | mission.'; i–ii preface by T. J. R. Santoski; iii acknowledgements; iv–v notes; [vi] blank; 1–31 text; [32] blank.

Includes previously unpublished art and inscriptions by Tolkien relating to *The Lord of the Rings*, reproduced in black and white:

upper cover, *The West-gate of Moria* (exhibit no. 58), the second of three versions (cf. Ei2, no. 22 [black and white]).

p. 15, *Orthanc and Isengard* (exhibit no. 56, there entitled *Isengard & Orthanc*).

p. 21, map of Anórien and Minas Tirith (exhibit no. 59, there entitled *The Lands of Anorien and Minas Tirith*).

p. 27, calligraphic inscriptions in tengwar, draft of the Ring inscription and 'The Lord of the Rings—Herumillion'

Wove paper. Bound in ivory wove wrappers, stapled through fold. Printed on upper cover: '[*thick rule*] | [*thin rule*] | THE [*square ornament*] MANUSCRIPTS [*square ornament*] OF [*rule*] | J [*diamond*] R [*diamond*] R [*diamond*] T | [*thin rule*] | [*thick rule*] | [*illustration by Tolkien,* The West-gate of Moria]'. All edges trimmed.

Published June 1984, gratis to participants in 'The Road Goes Ever On', a conference on J. R. R. Tolkien and his critics held at Marquette University 15–17 September 1983; 150 copies printed.

The exhibition and catalogue were prepared by T. J. R. (Taum) Santoski. Santoski privately noted three emendations to the catalogue: p. 20, exhibit no. 44, 'The Valaquenta' is dated *circa* 1949; p. 29, exhibit no. 62 is inscribed at upper left, not upper right; and p. 30, exhibit no. 66, 'conjugations' should read 'adjectival forms'.

(Dii66)	THE HOBBIT DRAWINGS, WATERCOLORS, AND MANUSCRIPTS	1987

Patrick & Beatrice Haggerty Museum of Art, Marquette University. *J. R. R. Tolkien: The Hobbit Drawings, Watercolors, and Manuscripts, June 11–September 30, 1987.* Milwaukee: Marquette University, 1987. Entered as Dii66, for Tolkien's letter to G. E. Selby, p. 4. This exhibition catalogue also describes and reproduces drawings and paintings for *The Hobbit*, in black and white except as noted:

cover (in colour), *Bilbo Comes to the Huts of the Raft-elves* (cf. Ei2, no. 14)

pp. 8–9, fragment of a sketch for the dust-jacket of *H* (A3a)

p. 13, *The Hill: Hobbiton,* an early drawing of the subject

p. 16, *The Hill: Hobbiton across the Water,* drawing, first published as the frontispiece of A3a, 1937

p. 17, *One Morning Early in the Quiet of the World,* sketch for *H,* ch. 1

p. 18, *The Trolls* (cf. Ei2, 2a)

p. 19, *Trolls' Hill,* drawing for *H,* ch. 2

p. 20 (colour), *Bilbo Woke Up with the Early Sun in His Eyes* (cf. Ei2, no. 9)

p. 23, *Rivendell Looking East* (cf. Ei2, no. 5)

p. 25 (colour), *Conversation with Smaug* (cf. Ei2, no. 17)

p. 28, *The Mountain-path* (cf. Ei2, no. 7a)

p. 29, *Rivendell Looking West* (cf. Ei2, no. 4); and *The Misty Mountains Looking West from the Eyrie towards Goblin Gate* (cf. Ei2, no. 8a)

p. 30, *Beorn's Hall* (cf. Ei2, no. 10a)

p. 31, map of the upper river and Mirkwood, sketch on a holograph page of the *Hobbit* manuscript in the Marquette University Archives; and *The Elvenking's Gate* (cf. Ei2, no. 12a)

p. 32, *Lake Town* (cf. Ei2, no. 15a); and *The Lonely Mountain* (cf. Eii20)

p. 33, *The Front Gate* (cf. Ei2, no. 16a)

p. 34, *The Hall at Bag-End, Residence of B. Baggins Esquire* (cf. Ei2, no. 20a)

p. 44, *Wilderland,* first published as an endpaper in A3a

ii. Posters, Puzzles, Calendars, Cards, and Miscellaneous Art

Listed here are major ephemera that reproduce art by Tolkien (except Eii4, art to which Tolkien contributed editorially). Not listed (though occasionally referenced) are the many books and articles about Tolkien, and booksellers' and auction catalogues, that reproduce his paintings and drawings. See also collections, Ei, and books in A, B, and G with illustrations by Tolkien. Entries in Eii are in chronological order, when order can be determined, otherwise are alphabetical by title of the larger work. Numeric citations in square brackets are to *Pictures by J. R. R. Tolkien*, Ei2a–b. All reproductions are in colour unless otherwise noted. Cropping and colour values vary considerably from reproduction to reproduction.

Eii1 *Nov. 19th 1912 Exeter College Smoker.* [Oxford, 1912].
Menu cover. Black and white. Signed with early 'JRRT' monogram. Tolkien is listed among the names on p. [3].

Eii2 *Exeter College 'Smoker' Nov. 19th 1913.* [Oxford, 1913].
Programme cover. Black and white. Signed with 'JRRT' monogram. Reproduced in *The Tolkien Family Album* (Dii84), p. 32.

Eii3 *Ye Chequers Clubbe Binge June 1914.* [Oxford, 1914].
Programme cover. Black and white. Signed with 'JRRT' monogram.

Eii4 *A Map of Middle-earth.* [London]: George Allen & Unwin, 1970.
'Drawn and embellished by Pauline Baynes. Based on the cartography of J. R. R. and C. J. R. Tolkien.' According to an Allen & Unwin memo, 50 copies were to be printed on Cartridge paper with a 'privately printed' label, followed by 7,500 copies on Cartridge as the normal trade edition, followed by an unspecified quantity on glossy stock. An unknown number of copies were signed by Tolkien, some, unfortunately, with a water-based ink which bled. The memo suggests that additional copies were then printed for Ballantine Books with their imprint, but no such copy has been seen.
Tolkien gave Pauline Baynes additional place names for this map: Andrast, Drúwaith Iaur (Old Púkel-land), Edhellond, Eryn Vorn, Framsburg, Lond Daer (ruins), R. Adorn, R. Swanfleet (R. Glanduin). 'Kelos' is here 'Celos', 'Kiril' is 'Ciril', and 'Enedwaith' is 'Enedhwaith'. In later impressions, 'Cara Dûm' was corrected to 'Carn Dûm', 'Dimril Dale' to 'Dimrill Dale', 'Eryn Voru' to 'Eryn Vorn', 'Esgarath' to 'Esgaroth', and 'Isenmouth' to 'Isenmouthe'. Also printed in Eii5, Eii6, Eii7, Eii8, Eii10, Eii16; in J. B. Post, *An Atlas of Fantasy*, rev. ed. (New York: Ballantine Books, 1979; London: Souvenir Press, 1979); and partly on the slipcase of A5i.

Eii5 *The J. R. R. Tolkien Calendar 1973.* New York: Ballantine Books, 1972.

January: *There and Back Again* (*Hobbit* map) by Pauline Baynes
February: *The Hill: Hobbiton-across-the Water* [1 (colour)]
March: *Rivendell* [6]
April: *Bilbo Woke Up with the Early Sun in His Eyes* [9]
May: *Bilbo Comes to the Huts of the Raft-elves* [14]
June: *Conversation with Smaug* [17]
July: *Death of Smaug* [19]
August: *Old Man Willow* [21]
September: *Moria Gate* (i.e. *The Steps to the East Gate*) [24]
October: *Moria Gate* [22 (colour)]
November: *Barad-dûr* [30 (colour)]
December: photograph of Tolkien by John Wyatt

Centre spread: *A Map of Middle-earth* by Pauline Baynes. Mailing box.

Eii6 *The J. R. R. Tolkien Calendar 1974.* London: George Allen & Unwin, 1973.

January: *Mount Everwhite* (i.e. *Taniquetil*) [31]
February: *The Hill: Hobbiton-across-the Water* [1 (colour)]

March: *Bilbo Woke with the Early Sun in His Eyes* [9]
April: *The Forest of Lothlorien in Spring* [25]
May: *Bilbo Comes to the Huts of the Raft-elves* [14]
June: *Rivendell* [6]
July: *Conversation with Smaug* [17]
August: *Old Man Willow* [21]
September: *Death of Smaug* [19]
October: *Barad-dûr* [30 (colour)]
November: *Moria Gate* [22 (colour)]
December: *Fangorn Forest* (i.e. *Beleg Finds Gwindor in Taur-nu-Fuin*)
   [37 (colour)]

Overleaf after December: *A Map of Middle-earth* by Pauline Baynes. On upper cover: photograph of Tolkien by Billett Potter. On lower cover: heraldic devices of Lúthien Tinúviel (version I), Fingolfin, Finwë, Fëanor, Eärendil, Lúthien Tinúviel (version II), Idril Celebrindal, and Elwë [all 47], and a Númenórean tile [46 (top)]. Mailing box.

Eii7 *The J. R. R. Tolkien Calendar 1974*. New York: Ballantine Books, 1973.
   Illustrations as for Eii5. For the 1974 calendar, Middle-earth dates were added and the accent colour changed from light brown to purple. Mailing box.

Eii8 *The Lonely Mountain*. [New York: Science Fiction Shop, 1974].
   Poster. Black and white. 500 copies printed. Also printed, pp. [114–15], in *The Tolkien Scrapbook*, ed. Alida Becker (Philadelphia: Running Press; New York: Grosset & Dunlap, 1978), reprinted as *A Tolkien Treasury* (Philadelphia: Courage Books, 1989); and in the fiftieth anniversary edition of *H* (A3y, A3aa–bb). Tolkien sent this drawing, made for *The Hobbit* but not used, to Paul Banham of Salt Lake City, Utah, in September 1960. Banham later presented it to Baird Searles, owner of the Science Fiction Shop in New York. The original drawing is now in the Bodleian Library.

Eii9 [Posters]. London: [variously noted as published or distributed by Poster Shops, Camden Graphics, Posters by Post, 1974?].

   Bilbo Comes to the Huts of the Raft-elves [14]
   Bilbo Woke with the Early Sun in His Eyes [9]
   Conversation with Smaug [17]
   Death of Smaug [19]
   The Forest of Lothlorien in Spring [25]
   The Hill: Hobbiton-across-the Water [1 (colour)]

   A Map of Middle-earth and *There and Back Again* by Pauline Baynes were also reproduced in this series.

Eii10 *The Hobbit Calendar 1976*. London: George Allen & Unwin, 1975.

   January: *Beorn's Hall** [10 (colour)]
   February: *The Trolls** [2 (colour)]
   March: *The Misty Mountains Looking West . . .** [8 (colour)]
   April: *The Hill: Hobbiton-across-the Water* [1 (colour)]
   May: *Rivendell* [6]
   June: *Bilbo Comes to the Huts of the Raft-elves* [14]
   July: *The Elvenking's Gate** [12 (colour)]
   August: *Lake Town* [15 (colour)]
   September: *Bilbo Woke with the Early Sun in His Eyes* [9]

October: *The Front Gate* [16 (colour)]
November: *The Mountain-path** [7 (colour)]
December: *Conversation with Smaug* [17]

* Coloured by H. E. Riddett. Cover adapted from the *Hobbit* dust-jacket (see A3a). Mailing envelope, with adaptation of the dust-jacket art.

Eii11   *The Hobbit: A Two-Sided Jigsaw Puzzle.* New York: International Polygonics, 1976.
Reproduction of *Bilbo Comes to the Huts of the Raft-elves* [14] on one side, *There and Back Again* by Pauline Baynes on the other. Box, with reproductions of the finished puzzle(s). International Polygonics also issued a two-sided puzzle with reproductions of *A Map of Middle-earth* by Pauline Baynes and the British broadside 'Bilbo's Last Song' (A11b); a one-sided puzzle with three colour photographs of Tolkien by Billett Potter; and Eii14.

Eii12   *The Lord of the Rings 1977 Calendar.* London: George Allen & Unwin, 1976.

January: *Old Man Willow* [21]
February: *Rivendell Looking East* [5]
March: *Moria Gate* [22]
April: *The Forest of Lothlorien in Spring* [25]
May: *Fangorn Forest* (i.e. *Beleg Finds Gwindor in Taur-nu-Fuin*) [37 (colour)]
June: *Helm's Deep* [26]
July: *Dunharrow* [29]
August: *Orthanc* and *Minas Tirith* [27]
September: *Shelob's Lair* (i.e. page of manuscript of *TT* with drawings) [28]
October: *Mount Doom and the Walls of Barad-dûr* (i.e. *Orodruin* and *Barad-dûr*) [30]
November: *Rivendell Looking West* [4]
December: Leaves from the Book of Mazarbul [23]

On cover: 'Ring and Eye' device (see A5a). With notes by Christopher Tolkien. Mailing envelope, with reproduction of 'Ring and Eye' device.

Eii13   *The Hobbit Desk Calendar 1978.* New York: Ballantine Books, 1977.
Includes the same illustrations, in the same order, as Eii10.

Eii14   *J. R. R. Tolkien's Father Christmas.* New York: International Polygonics, 1977.
One-sided jigsaw puzzle, reproduction of *Polar Bear had Fallen from Top to Bottom on His Nose* [39]. Box, with reproduction of the finished puzzle.

Eii15   *The Silmarillion Calendar 1978.* London: George Allen & Unwin, 1977.

January: *Gondolin and the Vale of Tumladen** [35 (colour)]
February: *Lake Mithrim* [32] and heraldic devices of Fëanor, Fingolfin, Hador [all 47], and Eärendil (cf. variant, [47])
March: *Taniquetil* [31]
April: heraldic devices of Elwë, Idril Celebrindal, Finwë, Lúthien Tinúviel (version I), Finrod Felagund, Melian, Gilgalad, the Silmarils, Bëor, House of Haleth, and Beren [all 47]
May: *Nargothrond* [33]
June: *Nargothrond** [34 (colour)]
July: Númenórean tile and textiles [46]

August: *Beleg Finds Gwindor in Taur-nu-Fuin* [37 (colour)]
September: *Tol Sirion** [36 (colour)]
October: Elvish script [48]
November: *Glaurung Sets Forth to Seek Túrin* [38]
December: *Map of Beleriand and the Lands to the North** by Christopher Tolkien

* Coloured by H. E. Riddett. With notes by Christopher Tolkien. On cover: heraldic device of Lúthien Tinúviel (version I) [47]. Mailing envelope, with reproduction of the same Lúthien device.

Eii16 *Tolkien: An Exhibition of His Drawings*. Oxford: Ashmolean Museum, 1977. Poster for an exhibition, 14 December–27 February 1977. Reproduces *The Hill: Hobbiton-across-the Water* [1 (colour)].

Eii17 *Tolkien Cards*. [London]: George Allen & Unwin, [1977].
Three sets, each issued with 8 cards as described, 8 blank envelopes, and a printed contents sheet, all within a poly bag.

The Hobbit Series One:
1 *The Hill: Hobbiton-across-the Water* [1 (colour)]
2 *The Hall at Bag-End . . .** [20 (colour)]
3 *Rivendell* [6]
4 *The Trolls** [2 (colour)]
5 *Beorn's Hall** [10 (colour)]
6 *The Misty Mountains Looking West . . .** [8 (colour)]
7 *The Elvenking's Gate** [12 (colour)]
8 *The Green Dragon* [40 (top)]

The Hobbit Series Two:
1 *Bilbo Comes to the Huts of the Raft-elves* [14]
2 *Lake Town** [15 (colour)]
3 *The Front Gate** [16 (colour)]
4 *The Mountain-path** [7 (colour)]
5 *Conversation with Smaug* [17]
6 *Death of Smaug* [19]
7 *There and Back Again* by Pauline Baynes
8 *Bilbo Woke with the Early Sun in His Eyes* [9]

The Lord of the Rings
1 *Old Man Willow* [21]
2 *Moria Gate* [22 (colour)]
3 *The Forest of Lothlorien in Spring* [25]
4 *Dunharrow* [29]
5 *Barad-dûr* [30 (colour)]
6 *A Map of Middle-earth* by Pauline Baynes
7 *Minas Tirith* [27 (colour)]
8 *Helm's Deep* [26]

* Coloured by H. E. Riddett.

Eii18 *J. R. R. Tolkien Calendar 1979*. London: George Allen & Unwin, 1978.

January: Three dragons [40]
February: *The Hall at Bag-End . . .** [20 (colour)]
March: Patterns [43]
April: *The Elvenking's Gate* (painting) [11]

May: Trees [41 (colour)]
June: *The Three Trolls are Turned to Stone** [3 (colour)]
July: Patterns [44]
August: *Bilbo Comes to the Huts of the Raft-elves* (version 1) [13]
September: Floral designs [45]
October: *Smaug Flies Round the Mountain* [18]
November: Flowering tree with friezes [42]
December: *Polar Bear had Fallen from Top to Bottom on His Nose* [39]

* Coloured by H. E. Riddett. With notes by Christopher Tolkien. On upper cover: photograph portrait of Tolkien by Billett Potter. Mailing envelope, with reproduction of *The Tree of Amalion* [41 (black and white)].

Eii19 *Map of Beleriand and the Lands to the North.* London: George Allen & Unwin, 1978.
At centre: map, drawn by Christopher Tolkien for *The Silmarillion* (A15). At top and bottom: 14 heraldic devices by J. R. R. Tolkien [47]. Map coloured by H. E. Riddett.

Eii20 *The Silmarillion Desk Calendar 1979.* New York: Ballantine Books, 1978.

January: *Nargothrond** (version 2) [34 (colour)] and heraldic device of Beor [47], and a Númenórean textile design [46 (lower left)]
February: Elvish script [48 (top)] and two heraldic devices of Eärendil [the first only, 47]
March: *Beleg Finds Gwindor in Taur-nu-Fuin* (i.e. *Fangorn Forest*) [37 (colour)], printed as mirror image, and a Númenórean tile [46 (top)]
April: *Nargothrond* [33], unidentified heraldic device (of Eärendil?) and heraldic device of Gil-galad [47]
May: *Tol Sirion** [36 (colour)] and heraldic devices of Elwë and Finwë [both 47]
June: *Lake Mithrim* [32] and unidentified heraldic device (Númenórean tile design?)
July: Elvish script [48 (lower left)] and heraldic devices of Lúthien Tinúviel (version II) and Idril Celebrindal [both 47]
August: *Gondolin and the Vale of Tumladen** [35 (colour)] and heraldic devices of Finrod Felagund and Beren [both 47]
September: *Silmarillion* map* (by Christopher Tolkien) and heraldic device of Melian [47]
October: *Glórund [i.e. Glaurung] Sets Forth to Seek Túrin* [38], heraldic device of Fëanor [47], and unidentified heraldic device (Númenórean tile design?)
November: Elvish script [48 (lower right)], Númenórean textile? [46 (lower right)], and heraldic device of Fingolfin [47]
December: *Taniquetil* [31] and heraldic device of Lúthien Tinúviel (version I) [47]

On covers: *Taniquetil.* Unidentified 'devices' may be 'patterns' without reference to characters.

Eii21 *Thror's Map [and] Wilderland.* London: George Allen & Unwin, 1979.
Poster, combining the maps from *The Hobbit*, coloured by H. E. Riddett. Also referred to by the publisher as *Wilderland* and *The Hobbit Map*. The 'moon-letters' of *Thror's Map* are printed on the verso of the poster so that they show through the sheet when held up to the light—thus achieving, more than four decades later, the 'magical' effect Tolkien argued for in 1937–8 (see A3a note).

Eii22 [Upper cover and right half of spine of the *Hobbit* (A3a) dust-jacket.] Idyllwild, Calif.: Biblioctopus, 1980.
Print, reproduction of a colour photograph by Jed Wilcox. 22 copies, numbered and signed by Wilcox. The photograph was first published as the frontispiece to Melissa and Mark Hime [booksellers], *Precious Stones* (see Dii46). Later reproduced on p. [1] of Biblioctopus broadsheet *List 27*, distributed at the Boston Book Fair, November 1991.

Eii23 *Drawings for 'The Hobbit' by J. R. R. Tolkien*. Oxford: Bodleian Library, [1987].

The Hall at Bag-End . . . [20 (black and white)]
The Mountain-path [7 (black and white)]
The Front Gate [16 (black and white)]
The Trolls [2 (black and white)]

Four postcards and printed title slip, issued in poly bag. All illustrations in black ink. Published to accompany an exhibition at the Bodleian Library, 24 February–23 May 1987.

Eii24 *Drawings for 'The Hobbit' by J R R Tolkien*. Oxford: Bodleian Library, 1987. Poster for the exhibition (cf. Eii21). Reproduces *Bilbo Comes to the Huts of the Raft-elves* [14].

Eii25 *J. R. R. Tolkien: 'Drawings, Watercolors and Manuscripts from* The Hobbit'. Milwaukee: Haggerty Museum of Art, Marquette University, 1987. Poster for an exhibition, 11 June–30 September 1987 (see Dii66). Reproduces *Bilbo Comes to the Huts of the Raft-elves* [14].

Eii26 *The Tolkien Calendar 1988*. London: Unwin Paperbacks, 1987.

January: *Rivendell* [6]
June: *Bilbo Comes to the Huts of the Raft-elves* [14]
July: *Conversation with Smaug* [17]
December: *The Hill: Hobbiton-across-the Water* [1 (colour)]

The illustrations are considerably cropped. The calendar also includes art by Roger Garland, John Howe, and Ted Nasmith. Mailing envelope.

Eii27 *The 1988 J. R. R. Tolkien Calendar*. New York: Ballantine Books, 1987. Illustrations as for Eii26, but not cropped.

Eii28 *The Hobbit Birthday Book*. London: Grafton Books, 1991.

January: *Bilbo Woke with the Early Sun in His Eyes*, here entitled *Bilbo Awoke One Morning* . . . [9]
February: *The Front Gate** [16 (colour)]
March: *Bilbo Comes to the Huts of the Raft-elves*, here labelled in type *Raftelves* [14]
April: *Conversation with Smaug* [17]
May: *The Hill: Hobbiton-across-the Water*, here entitled *The Hill: Hobbiton-Upon-The-Water* [1 (colour)]
June: *Lake Town** [15 (colour)]
July: *The Elvenking's Gate** [12 (colour)]
August: *Rivendell* [6]
September: *The Hall at Bag-End: Residence of B. Baggins Esquire** [20 (colour)]
October: *The Trolls** [2 (colour)]

November: *The Mountain-path**, here *The Mountain Path* [7 (colour)]
December: *Beorn's Hall** [10 (colour)]

* Coloured by H. E. Riddett. Upper cover: *Conversation with Smaug* (with
inset title). Front and back endpapers: *Wilderland*, in purple against a pink
panel, with runic inscriptions (for *The Lord of the Rings*).

Eii29 *The Tolkien Diary*. London: Grafton Books, 1991.

introduction: heraldic device of Finwë [47]
facing 30–31 December 1991 – 1–2 January: *The Misty Mountains Looking
    West . . .** [8 (colour)]
3–5 January: heraldic device of Beren [47]
17–19 January: flowering tree, printed as mirror image [relative to 42 (centre)]
24–26 January: heraldic device of Lúthien Tinúviel (version II) [47]
facing 3–6 February: *Taniquetil* [31]
7–9 February: 'JRRT' monogram
21–23 February: floral design [45 (upper right)]
facing 24–27 February: *The Front Gate** [16 (colour)]
6–8 March: heraldic device of Fingolfin [47]
13–15 March: spider's web, detail from *Thror's Map*, rotated ninety degrees
    clockwise (cf. A3)
27–29 March: dragon, detail from *Thror's Map* (cf. A3)
30–31 March – 1–2 April: *Bilbo Comes to the Huts of the Raft-elves*
3–5 April: heraldic device of the Silmarils [47]
17–19 April: *Pilinehtar* [45 (centre)]
24–26 April: heraldic device of Gil-galad [47]
facing 27–30 April: *Lake Town** [15 (colour)]
1–3 May: floral design [45 (lower left)]
8–10 May: heraldic device of the House of Haleth [47]
29–31 May: dragon looking left, originally from the upper binding of A3a
facing 1–4 June: *Rivendell* [6]
26–28 June: dragon, detail from *Wilderland* (cf. A3)
facing 29–30 June – 1–2 July: *The Hill: Hobbiton-across-the Water*
    [1 (colour)]
10–12 July: mountains, moon, and sun, detail from the upper binding of A3a
17–19 July: heraldic device of Fëanor [47]
24–26 July: *The Tree of Amalion* [41 (black and white)]
facing 3–5 August: *Conversation with Smaug* [17]
7–9 August: flower [42 (left centre)]
14–16 August: heraldic device of Melian [47]
21–23 August: dragon around a tree [40 (lower left)]
28–30 August: floral design, printed as mirror image [relative to 45, upper left]
facing 31 August – 1–3 September: *Glórund Sets Forth to Seek Túrin* [38]
18–20 September: dragon facing right, originally from the upper binding of
    A3a
25–27 September: pointing hand and runes, detail from *Thror's Map* (cf. A3)
facing 5–7 October: *The Trolls** [2 (colour)]
facing 2–4 November: *Smaug Flies Round the Mountain* [18]
6–8 November: *The Green Dragon* [40 (top)]
13–15 November: floral design [42 (right centre)]
facing 30 November – 1–3 December: *Fangorn Forest* (i.e. *Beleg Finds
    Gwindor in Taur-nu-Fuin*) [37 (colour)]

4–6 December: dragon and warrior, printed as mirror image [relative to 40 (lower right)]

11–13 December: *The Tree of Amalion*, printed as mirror image [relative to 41 (colour, upper left)]

18–20 December: 'JRRT' monogram

25–27 December: *My Latest Portrait – Father Christmas Packing 1931* (cf. *FCL*, A14, p. [20])

1–3 January 1993: heraldic device of Lúthien Tinúviel (version I) [47]

* Coloured by H. E. Riddett. Upper cover: *Rivendell* [6], partly obscured by book title.

Eii30 *J. R. R. Tolkien Greeting Cards*. Deddington, Oxfordshire: Duns Tew Publishing, [1992].

Sold to the trade in dozens of one design, with envelopes; sold by The Tolkien Society as complete set of 12 cards, or in packs of 6 cards of one design.

The Hill: Hobbiton-across-the Water [1 (colour)]
Rivendell [6]
Bilbo Woke with the Early Sun in His Eyes [9]
The Elvenking's Gate* [12 (colour)]
Bilbo Comes to the Huts of the Raft-elves [14]
Lake Town* [15 (colour)]
The Front Gate* [16 (colour)]
Conversation with Smaug [17]
The Hall at Bag-End . . .* [20 (colour)]
The Forest of Lothlorien in Spring [25]
Taniquetil [31]
Glaurung Sets Forth to Seek Túrin [38]

* Coloured by H. E. Riddett.

F

Miscellanea

i. Audio Recordings

Arranged chronologically. Recordings of Tolkien's works by other voices are noted with the printed works in sections A and G.

At the Tobacconist's. English Lesson 20. London: Linguaphone, [*circa* 1940]. LP no. EC.20.E.
Tolkien with Professor A. Lloyd James.

Wireless. English Lesson 30. London: Linguaphone, [*circa* 1940]. LP no. EC.30.E.
Tolkien with Professor A. Lloyd James.

Poems and Songs of Middle Earth. New York: Caedmon Records, 1967. LP no. TC 1231. Issued by Caedmon as a cassette, no. CDL 51231, in 1972. Re-issued 1977 by Caedmon in *The J. R. R. Tolkien Soundbook*, LPs SBR 101, cassettes SBC 101.
In three parts: (1) 'J. R. R. Tolkien Reads from *The Adventures of Tom Bombadil*': 'The Adventures of Tom Bombadil'; 'The Mewlips'; 'The Hoard'; 'Perry-the-Winkle'; 'The Man in the Moon Came Down Too Soon'. (2) 'A Elbereth Gilthoniel' (from *LR*, bk. 1, ch. 2, read by Tolkien). (3) *The Road Goes Ever On*, sung by William Elvin with Donald Swann, piano: 'The Road Goes Ever On'; 'Upon the Hearth the Fire is Red'; 'In the Willow-Meads of Tasarinan'; 'In Western Lands'; 'Namárië'; 'I Sit beside the Fire' and refrain, 'A Elbereth Gilthoniel'; 'Errantry'.
    Sleeve notes by W. H. Auden. Colour sleeve illustration by Pauline Baynes, earlier printed on the slipcase for the Allen & Unwin deluxe three-volume *LR* (see A5a).

J. R. R. Tolkien Reads and Sings His The Hobbit *and* The Fellowship of the Ring. New York: Caedmon Records, 1975. LP TC 1477; cassette CDL 51477. Re-issued 1977 by Caedmon in *The J. R. R. Tolkien Soundbook*, LP set SBR 101, cassettes SBC 101.
A recording of most of *H* revised ch. 5, and selections from *FR*, with one misidentified selection from *TT*. Sleeve notes by Ward Botsford and George Sayer. Botsford incorrectly identifies side B, band 16 as an unpublished poem for *LR*, bk. 2, ch. 7 ('The Mirror of Galadriel'); in fact the verse ('In Dwimordene, in Lórien . . .') was published in *LR*, bk. 3, ch. 6.
    The album is based on a tape recording made by Tolkien while a guest in the house of his friend George Sayer, in Malvern, Worcestershire, in August 1952. He read from the second edition text of *The Hobbit* and from the then unpublished manuscript of *The Lord of the Rings*, occasionally at variance with the texts as published.
    Colour sleeve illustration, *Conversation with Smaug*, by Tolkien.

J. R. R. Tolkien Reads and Sings His Lord of the Rings: The Two Towers/The Return of the King. New York: Caedmon Records, 1975. LP TC 1478, cassette CDL 51478. Re-issued 1977 by Caedmon in *The J. R. R. Tolkien Soundbook*, LP set SBR 101, cassettes SBC 101.
Selections from *TT* and *RK*, and one selection from *FR* ('Namárië'), tape recorded by Tolkien in August 1952; cf. the preceding entry. Sleeve notes by Ward Botsford

and George Sayer. Botsford incorrectly states that 'Ai! laurië lantar lassi surinen' (i.e. 'Namárië') was also recorded in a spoken version on the companion Caedmon album, *J. R. R. Tolkien Reads and Sings His* The Hobbit *and* The Fellowship of the Ring, side B, band 6. That band is the song 'Farewell we call to hearth and hall', and the same recording of 'Namárië' in plainchant is the final band on both albums.

Tolkien read from the then unpublished manuscript of *The Lord of the Rings*, occasionally at variance with the texts as published.

Colour sleeve photograph of Tolkien by Billett Potter.

Tolkien and Basil Bunting. London: BBC Cassettes, 1980. Distributed in the United States by Audio-Forum, Guilford, Connecticut.
Recording of a 1964 BBC radio interview with Denis Gueroult. Transcriptions were published in 'Council of Elrond', *News from Bree*, Beaconsfield, Buckinghamshire, 13 (November 1974), pp. 3–5, and 'An Interview with J R R T', *Minas Tirith Evening-Star* (journal of The American Tolkien Society), 12, no. 1 (1984), pp. 3–7. Portions of the interview have been rebroadcast on BBC radio.

ii. Printed Interviews

This list includes, for the most part, articles and reviews incorporating material from interviews with Tolkien, arranged alphabetically by author and title. Page references are given when known. See also Gueroult recording, above.

Brace, Keith. 'In the Footsteps of the Hobbits'. Photographs by Alan Hill. *Birmingham Post Midland Magazine*, England, 25 May 1968, p. 1.

Castell, Daphne. 'Talking to a Maker of Modern Myths'. *Glasgow Herald*, 6 August 1966. Also published as? 'Tolkien on Tolkien: Making of a Myth', *Christian Science Monitor*, 11 August 1966, p. 11. The interview was also used as the basis for Castell, 'The Realms of Tolkien', *New Worlds SF*, 50 (November 1966), pp. 143–54, also printed in *Carandaith* (journal of the Australian Tolkien Society), 1, no. 2 (1969), pp. 10–15, 27.

Cater, William. 'Lord of the Hobbits'. *Daily Express*, London, 22 November 1966, p. 10.

Cater, William. 'The Lord of the Legends'. *Sunday Times Magazine*, London, 2 January 1972, pp. 24–5, 27–8. Also published as 'More and More People are Getting the J. R. R. Tolkien Habit', *Los Angeles Times*, 9 April 1972.

Curtis, Anthony. 'Remembering Tolkien and Lewis'. *British Book News*, June 1977, pp. 429–30.

Curtis, Anthony. 'Hobbits and Heroes'. *Sunday Telegraph*, 10 November 1963.

Ezard, John. 'Writers Talking 1: The Hobbit Man'. *Oxford Mail*, England, 3 August 1966, p. 4.

Foster, William. 'A Benevolent and Furry-footed People'. *Scotsman Week-end Magazine*, Edinburgh, 25 March 1967, p. 1.

Foster, William. 'An Early History of the Hobbits'. *Scotsman*, Edinburgh, 5 February 1972.

Norman, Philip. 'The Hobbit Man'. *Sunday Times Magazine*, London, 15 January 1967, pp. 34–6. Also published as 'The Prevalence of Hobbits', *New York Times Magazine*, 15 January 1967, pp. 30–1, 97, 100, 102, with photographs not published in the *Sunday Times*.

Norman, Philip. 'Lord of the Flicks'. *Show*, Hollywood, 1, no. 1 (January 1970), p. 29.

Plimmer, Charlotte and Denis. 'The Man Who Understands Hobbits'. *Daily Telegraph Magazine*, 22 March 1968, 31–2, 35.

Plotz, Richard. 'J. R. R. Tolkien Talks about the Discovery of Middle-earth, the Origins of Elvish'. *Seventeen*, January 1967, pp. 92–3, 118.

Resnik, Henry. 'An Interview with Tolkien'. *Niekas*, Late Spring 1967, pp. 37–47. Transcription of a telephone interview, 2 March 1966, which formed the basis for Resnik, 'The Hobbit-forming World of J. R. R. Tolkien', *Saturday Evening Post*, 2 July 1966, pp. 90–2, 94.

'Tolkien Talking'. *Sunday Times*, 27 November 1966.

Wood, Anthony. 'Fireworks for the Author–and B.B.C. 2 Viewers'. *Oxford Mail*, 9 February 1968.

iii. Miscellaneous writings and manuscripts

Here are listed items not included as notes in other sections, or as entries in Dii. Arranged alphabetically by author and title of the item.

Rules of Exeter College Essay Club. Oxford, January 1914. Signed 'C. C.' (Colin Cullis) and 'J. R. R. T.' [4] pp.

A Elbereth Gilthoniel (newsletter of The Fellowship of Middle Earth, Monash University), [v. 1, no. 1, early 1978?].
Contains excerpt from the manuscript of *Doworst*, a humourous report by Tolkien on oral exams at Oxford, given to R. W. Chambers 21 December 1933.

Gilson, Christopher, and Patrick Wynne. 'The Elves at Koivienéni: A New Quenya Sentence'. *Vinyar Tengwar* (newsletter of the Elvish Linguistic Fellowship), no. 14 (November 1990), pp. 5–7, 12–20.
Contains and analyses a previously unpublished sentence in Quenya written on the manuscript of *LR*. The sentence and commentary were reprinted in *Mythlore*, 17, no. 3, whole no. 65 (Spring 1991), pp. 23–30.

Hostetter, Carl F. '*Sauron Defeated*: A Linguistic Review'. *Vinyar Tengwar*, no. 24 (July 1992), pp. 4–13.
Quotes, p. 5, previously unpublished lines, in Quenya, in a draft of 'Namárië' in *LR*.

Hyde, Paul Nolan. 'The "Gondolinic Runes": Another Picture'. *Mythlore*, 18, no. 3, whole no. 69 (Summer 1992), pp. 20–5.
Reproduces, p. 21, a manuscript page by Tolkien detailing a runic alphabet. With commentary by Hyde.

Peter Jolliffe [bookseller]. *Catalogue 27*. London, 1983. Describes, as Item 487 (not illustrated), a cartoon by Tolkien of himself sitting in a chair, drawn in response to one given him by a student. The student, Sarah Harvey, had drawn a cartoon of herself in a chair, with the caption 'But Professor, I've been *introduced* to Grendel's mother!' In his cartoon, Tolkien replied 'But which of them, Madam? He has several in Oxford.' Item 487 included both drawings, a typed letter signed by Tolkien to his student, 18 February 1960, and a letter by Sarah Harvey explaining the circumstances of the exchange.

Kotowski, Nathalie. [Letter to the editor.] *Vinyar Tengwar*, no. 23 (May 1992), p. 16.

Includes a reproduction of a tengwar inscription by Tolkien in Simonne d'Ardenne's copy of *RK*.

Plotz, Dick. 'Poetry Contest'. *Tolkien Journal*, 2, no. 1 (Afteryule 1966), p. 8.
Includes Tolkien's poem 'A Elbereth Gilthoniel' in Elvish, with 'a word-for-word [English] translation as sent by Professor Tolkien'. The translation differs from that printed later in *RGEO* (B28).

Scull, Christina. 'Dragons from Andrew Lang's Retelling of Sigurd to Tolkien's Chrysophylax'. *Leaves from the Tree: J. R. R. Tolkien's Shorter Fiction*. London: The Tolkien Society, 1991. Pp. 49–62.
Includes, pp. 59, an extract from an unpublished lecture by Tolkien on dragons, delivered to children at the University Museum, Oxford, 1 January 1938.

Sotheby Parke Bernet. *Catalogue of the Well-known Collection of Autograph Letters, Historical Documents and Signed Photographs Formed between 1930 and 1979 by the Late R. E. D. Rawlins Esq.* London, 2–4 June 1980.
Reproduces, lot 1231, an autograph statement signed by Tolkien, 'In all my works I take the part of the trees as against all their enemies' (from his 30 June 1972 letter to the *Daily Telegraph* [Dii20]).

Sotheby's Belgravia. *Fine English and Continental Furniture*. London, 1 November 1972.
Reproduces, lot 116, a statement, dated 27 July 1972, to accompany the sale of the desk upon which Tolkien wrote *The Hobbit* and parts of *The Lord of the Rings* and which he donated to the charity Help the Aged in memory of his late wife, Edith. With a photograph of the desk.

Sotheby's. *Catalogue of Modern First Editions and Presentation Copies*. London, 19 July 1982.
Reproduces, lot 315, a crossword puzzle by Tolkien in Old English (incorrectly described as in Elvish), accompanying a set of the first edition of *LR* inscribed to C. M. Kilbride.

Sotheby's. *The Library of Richard Manney*. New York, 11 October 1991.
Reproduces, lot 297, an Elvish inscription in tengwar by Tolkien to 'Sarah', dated 1954, in a copy of *FR*, with a scribbled translation 'who now shall refill the cup for me?'. The quotation is from the poem 'Namárië', *LR*, bk. 2, ch. 8. The catalogue gives the Elvish as in the published book, 'Sí! man i yulma nin enquantuva?' However, Carl F. Hostetter, in *Vinyar Tengwar*, no. 21 (January 1992), pp. 6–7, 10, notes that the inscription actually reads 'Sí man i·yulmar n(g)win enquatuva', a variant form. A further note, by Nancy Martsch, was published in *Vinyar Tengwar*, no. 22 (March 1992), pp. 7–8.

Tolkien, Christopher. 'Notes on the Differences in Editions of *The Hobbit* Cited by Mr. David Cofield'. *Beyond Bree* (newsletter of the American Mensa Tolkien Special Interest Group), July 1986, pp. 1–3.
Reproduces, p. 2, the opening two text pages of the copy of A3c owned by J. R. R. Tolkien, with his author's note revised in manuscript.

Tolkien, Christopher. 'The Tengwar Numerals'. *Quettar* (bulletin of the Linguistic Fellowship of The Tolkien Society), no. 13 (February 1982), pp. 8–9, with remarks by editor Steve Pillinger, p. 7. Notes on the expression of numerals in tengwar, written out by Christopher after J. R. R. Tolkien. Reprinted in *Beyond Bree*, December 1984, p. 1. Further notes by Christopher Tolkien were published in *Quettar*, no. 14 (May 1982), pp. 6–7.

Robin Waterfield Ltd. [booksellers]. *Catalogue 40: English Literature*. Oxford, 1981.
Quotes, item 709, Tolkien's presentation inscription in a copy of the Japanese translation of *The Hobbit*; and item 712, from Tolkien's dismissive manuscript notes in his copy of 'From Academic Darkness' by Kemp Malone (offprint from *PMLA*, March 1963). Reproduces, from the latter item, part of a note by Tolkien in code. The catalogue offers several items from Tolkien's library. The notes quoted in item 712 were quoted again in James Fergusson Books & Manuscripts, *Catalogue One*, London, 1988, item 524.

Robin Waterfield Ltd. [booksellers]. *Catalogue 45: A Fair Choice*. Oxford, 1983.
Quotes, item 136, Tolkien's presentation inscription in a copy of the Japanese translation of *The Hobbit* (as in Waterfield's *Catalogue 40*); and item 137, his manuscript note in his copy of *Adam's Opera* by Clemence Dane (1928), on the provenance of the copy. The latter quotation was printed again in David J. Holmes [bookseller], *Catalogue 12*, Philadelphia, 1985, item 262.

Wilson, A. N. *C. S. Lewis: A Biography*. London: Collins; New York: W. W. Norton, 1990. Paperback editions, London: Flamingo; New York: Fawcett Columbine, 1991.
Includes excerpts from previously unpublished remarks by Tolkien on C. S. Lewis: p. xvii, from a manuscript note in Tolkien's copy of Lewis's *Letters to Malcolm*; pp. 135–6, from a note on Lewis and Christianity, the quotation including some of the lines quoted in *Inklings*, p. 50, as from 'The Ulsterior Motive', with minor differences in punctuation and with 'take up again' for 'take up'; p. 179, from a note on Lewis's talks to men at R.A.F. stations as 'an imitation of St. Paul'; and p. 217, two words from 'The Ulsterior Motive'. Also includes miscellaneous quotations, previously published, primarily from *Letters*.

Tolkien also wrote countless printed notices, examination questions, etc. as part of his academic duties at Leeds and Oxford. Some of these may be found, their originally blank pages used as writing paper, among Tolkien's manuscripts.

G

Translations

In this section, entries are arranged alphabetically by language and, within each language group, chronologically and alphabetically according to the first appearance of a translation. Priority is given to text, not format. Revised translations, first separate publications, and mixed collections are given separate entries. Changes of publisher and the extent of volumes in an edition are noted, but hardcover and paperback formats are not distinguished. Dramatizations are omitted.

Titles originally in Cyrillic and Greek have been romanized according to the *Chicago Manual of Style*. Hebrew and Japanese titles are given in English in square brackets, with other information in English as given in Bertenstam, *En Tolkien-bibliografi 1911–1980*, its supplements, and other reference sources.

No attempt has been made to evaluate the accuracy or completeness of translations; but a bibliography of relevant criticism may be found at the end of this section. See also *Letters* for Tolkien's own criticisms, and his 'guide to nomenclature' prepared for translators, published in *A Tolkien Compass* (B31).

Afrikaans

1 *Die Smid van Groot Wootton*. Kaapstad: Human & Rousseau, 1968.
  Translation, by Chris van Lille, of *SWM*. Illustrations by Pauline Baynes.

Armenian

1 [*The Hobbit*]. Yerevan: Sovetakan Groch, 1984.
  Translation by E. Makaryan. Illustrations by Mikhail Belomlinskiy. The Soviet Union national bibliography gives only the title in Russian: *Khobbit, ili, Tuda i obratno*.

2 [*Fellowship of the Ring*]. Yerevan: Arevik, 1989.
  Translation by E. Makaryan. Illustrations by T. S. Mangasaryan. The Soviet Union national bibliography gives only the title in Russian: *Khraniteli*.

Bulgarian

1 *Bilbo Begins, ili, Dotam i obratno*. Sofia: Narodna Mladezh, 1975.
  Translation, by Krasimira Todorova (prose) and Asen Todorov (verse), of *H*. Illustrations by Petyr Chuklev. Published by Narodna Mladezh in 1979 with slightly different illustrations.

2 *Chervenokosiya Dzhayls*. Sofia: Izdatelstvo Otechestvo, 1988.
  Translation, by Teodora Davidova, of *FGH*. Illustrations by Pauline Baynes.

3 *Vlastelin't na pr'stenite*. Sofia: Narodna Kultura, 1990–1.
  Translation, by Lyubomir Nikolov, of *LR*. 3 vols. in 2: I, *Vlastelin't na pr'stenite*; II/III, *Dvete kuli, Zvr 'shtaneto na kralya*. Illustrations by Yasen Panov. Omits foreword.

Catalan

1 *El hòbbit, o, Viatge d'anada i tornada.* Barcelona: Edicions de la Magrana, 1983.
Translation, by Francesc Parcerisas, of *H.*

2 *El senyor dels anells.* Barcelona: Vicens-Vives, 1986–8.
Translation, by Francesc Parcerisas, of *LR.* 3 vols.: I, *La germandat de l'anell*; II, *Les dues torres*; III, *El retorn del rei.* Omits appendices and indexes.

3 *Gil, el pagès de Ham.* Barcelona: Edhasa, 1988.
Translation, by Carles Llorach, of *FGH.* Illustrations by Pauline Baynes.

4 *El ferrer de Wootton Major, 'La fulla' d'en Niggle.* Barcelona: Edhasa, 1988.
Translation, by Jordi Arbonès, of *SWM* and *LBN.* Illustrations by Pauline Baynes.

5 *El Silmarillion.* Barcelona: Edhasa, 1991.
Translation, by Dolors Udina, of *Silm.*

Czech

1 *Hobit, aneb, Cesta tam a zase zpátky.* Prague: Odeon, 1979.
Translation, by Lubomír Doruzka, of *H.* Illustrations by Jirí Salamoun.

2 *Laser,* no. 5 (1986).
Includes, pp. 21–53, 'Pán prstenů': 'Vpodzemní Říši Moria' (translation of *LR,* bk. 2, ch. 4–5); 'Doupě Oduly', 'Mistr Samvěd volí' (translation of *LR,* bk. 4, ch. 9–10). Translator(s) unknown.

3 *Farmàř Giles z Hamu, Nimralův List, Kovàř z Wooton [sic] Major.* Prague?: Povìdky, 1990.
Translation of *FGH, LBN, SWM.* 'Povìdky' on upper cover may be the publisher or the translator, or both.

4 *Silmarillion.* Prague: Vytiskla Početnická a Organizační Služba, 1990.
Anonymous translation of *Silm.* Prepared for 'Parconu 90', apparently a fan convention. A different anonymous translation was privately published in Prague in 1987 and distributed in typescript.

5 *Pán prstenů.* Prague: Mladá Fronta, 1990–1 [–92?].
Translation, by Stanislava Pošustová, of *LR.* 3 vols.: I, *Společenstvo prstenu*; II, *Dvě věže*; III, *Návrat krále* (forthcoming?).

Danish

1 *Ringenes herre.* Copenhagen: Gyldendal, 1968–70.
Translation, by Ida Nyrop Ludvigsen, of *LR.* 3 vols.: I, *Eventyret om ringen*; II, *De to tårne*; III, *Kongen vender tilbage.* Includes Appendices A, B, C, the latter with a few omissions; of Appendix D, only the Shire Calendar and its explanatory note; the first five paragraphs of E, pt. 2; and F, pt. 1. Published by Gyldendals Bogklub, Copenhagen, in 1973 and later. Published by Forum, Copenhagen, in 1977 in 3 vols., with illustrations by 'Ingahild Grathmer' (H.M. Queen Margrethe II of Denmark), drawn by Eric Fraser (cf. A51). Published by Gyldendal in 1990 in 3 vols., with illustrations by 'Ingahild Grathmer' and Eric Fraser.

2 *Hobbitten, eller, Ud og hjem igen.* Copenhagen: Gyldendal, 1969.
Translation, by Ida Nyrop Ludvigsen, of *H.* Drawings and colour plates by Tolkien (plates omitted in later impressions). First published by Gyldendals Bogklub, Copenhagen, in 1975.

3 *Silmarillion*. Copenhagen: Gyldendal, 1978.
   Translation, by David Gress-Wright, of *Silm*. Published by Gyldendals Bogklub, Copenhagen, in 1978.

4 *Niels Bonde fra Bol, Tom Bombadils eventyr*. Copenhagen: Gyldendal, 1979.
   Translation, by David Gress-Wright, of *FGH* and *ATB*.

5 *Hr. Fryd*. Copenhagen: Gyldendal, 1983.
   Translation, by Ida Elisabeth Hammerich, of *Mr. Bliss*, with Tolkien's illustrated manuscript in English.

6 *Smeden fra Store Wootton*. Copenhagen: Lina, 1985.
   Translation, by Erik Vestbo, of *SWM*. Illustrations by Pauline Baynes.

7 *Træer og blade*. Copenhagen: Zac, 1987.
   Translation, by Erik Vestbo, of *TL*. Illustrations by Lars Physant.

8 *Niels Bonde fra Bol*. Copenhagen: Gyldendal, 1992.
   Translation, by David Gress-Wright, of *FGH*. Illustrations by Roger Garland.

Dutch

Spectrum editions are also published in Belgium.

1 *In de ban van de ring*. Utrecht: Spectrum, 1956–7.
   Translation, by Max Schuchart, of *LR*. 3 vols.: I, *De reisgenoten*; II, *De twee torens*; III, *De terugkeer van de koning*. Omits foreword and indexes. Includes Appendices A, B, part of D (as 'C'). Published by Spectrum in 1965 in 1 vol. Published by Spectrum in 1980 in 1 vol. without appendices (cf. 14, below), with a note by the translator, Schuchart; includes Middle-earth and Shire maps, redrawn.

2 *De hobbit*. Utrecht: Prisma-boeken, 1960.
   Translation, by Max Schuchart, of *H*.

3 *De Smid van Groot-Wolding*. Utrecht: Spectrum, 1968.
   Translation, by W. Wielek-berg, of *SWM*. A Spectrum edition not for sale appeared in 1967.

4 *Sprookjes*. Utrecht: Spectrum, 1971.
   Translation, by W. Wielek-berg, of *SWM, FGH, LBN*. Illustrations by Pauline Baynes. Cf. 11, below.

5 *Tolkien Kalendar 1974*. Utrecht: Spectrum, 1973.
   Cf. Eii7.

6 *De avonturen van Tom Bombadil, en andere verzen uit het Rode boek*. The Hague: Bert Bakker, 1975.
   Translation, by Max Schuchart, of *ATB*. Illustrations by Pauline Baynes. Published by Spectrum, Utrecht, in 1980, without illustrations.

7 *Brieven van de Kerstman*. Utrecht: Spectrum, 1976.
   Translation, by Max Schuchart, of *FCL*.

8 *De hobbit*. Utrecht: Spectrum, 1976.
   Revised edition of 2, above. Drawings and colour plates by Tolkien.

9 *Boer Gilles van Ham*. Utrecht: Spectrum, 1977.
   Translation, by W. Wielek-Berg, of *FGH*. Illustrations by Walt de Rijk.

10 *De Smid van Groot-Wolding.* Utrecht: Spectrum, 1977.
Translation, by W. Wielek-Berg, of *SWM*. Illustrations by Walt de Rijk.

11 *Sprookjes van Tolkien.* Utrecht: Spectrum, 1977.
Translation of *TL* (*Boom en blad*), *SWM*, *FGH*: *LBN* ('Blad van Klein'), *SWM* ('De Smid van Groot-Wolding'), *FGH* ('Boer Gilles van Ham') translated by W. Wielek-Berg, *OFS* ('Over sprookjesverhalen') translated by Max Schuchart.

12 *Het leven van J. R. R. Tolkien.* Utrecht: Spectrum, 1978.
Translation, by Max Schuchart, of Carpenter, *Biography* (B32).

13 *De silmarillion.* Utrecht: Spectrum, 1978.
Translation, by Max Schuchart, of *Silm*.

14 *In de ban van de ring.* Utrecht: Spectrum, 1980.
Revised edition of 1, above. 3 vols. Published by Spectrum in 1989 with foreword and translator's note, without appendices and indexes. Published by Spectrum in 1991 in 1 vol., without appendices and indexes.

15 *In de ban van de ring: aanhangsels.* Utrecht: Spectrum, 1980.
Translation, by Max Schuchart, of the appendices to *LR*.

16 *Nagelaten vertellingen.* Utrecht: Spectrum, 1981.
Translation, by Max Schuchart, of *UT*.

17 *Brieven.* Utrecht: Spectrum, 1982.
Translation, by Max Schuchart, of *Letters*.

18 *Meneer Blijleven.* Utrecht: Spectrum, 1983.
Translation, by André Abeling, of *Mr. Bliss*, with Tolkien's illustrated manuscript in English.

Esperanto

1 'La Hobbito'. *Literatura suplemento.* El Cerrito, Calif.: Esperanto League for North America, 1991. Pp. 11–12.
Translation, by Don Harlow, of part of ch. 12 of *H*.

Estonian

1 *Kääbik, ehk, Sinna ja tagasi.* Tallinn: Eesti Raamat, 1977.
Translation, by Lia Rajandi (verse co-translated with Harald Rajamets), of *H*. Illustrations by Maret Kernumees. Nine of the illustrations were reprinted in *The Annotated Hobbit* (A3dd–ee), pp. 62, 74, 83, 129, 156, 259, 283, 300, 304.

Faeroese

1 *Hobbin, ella, Út og heim aftur.* Hoyvík: Stiðin, 1990.
Translation, by Axel Tógarð. Illustrations by Tolkien.

2 *Klávus bónda á Bóli.*
Translation of *FGH*, said to be forthcoming.

Finnish

1 *Lohikäärmevuori, eli, Erään hoppelin matka sinne ja takaisin.* Helsinki: Tammi, 1973.
Translation, by Risto Pitkänen, of *H*. Illustrations by Tove Jansson (identical to those published in the 1962 Swedish edition).

2 *Taru sormusten herrasta.* Porvoo: Werner Söderström, 1973–4.
Translation, by Kersti Juva and Eila Pennanen (prose) and Panu Pekkanen (verse), of *LR*. 3 vols.: I, *Sormuksen ritarit*; II, *Kaksi tornia*; III, *Kuninkaan paluu*. Omits indexes. Published by Söderström in 1985 in 1 vol. Audio recording published by Synskadades Bibliotek, Helsinki, in 1974–6, read by Soila Särkelä. Audio recording of *FR* published by Söderström in 1992, read by Heikki Määttänen.

3 *Maamies ja lohikäärme.* Porvoo: Werner Söderström, 1978.
Translation, by Panu Pekkanen, of *FGH*. Illustrations by Pauline Baynes.

4 *Silmarillion.* Porvoo: Werner Söderström, 1979.
Translation, by Kersti Juva and Panu Pekkanen, of *Silm*.

5 *Herra Bliss.* Porvoo: Werner Söderström, 1983.
Translation, by Panu Pekkanen, of *Mr. Bliss*, with Tolkien's illustrated manuscript in English.

6 *Seppä ja Satumaa.* Porvoo: Werner Söderström, 1983.
Translation, by Panu Pekkanen, of *SWM*. Illustrations by Pauline Baynes.

7 *Hobitti, eli, Sinne ja takaisin.* Porvoo: Werner Söderström, 1985.
Translation, by Kersti Juva (prose) and Panu Pekkanen (verse), of *H*. Illustrations by Tolkien. Audio recording published by Synskadades Bibliotek, Helsinki, in 1986, read by Tuomo Holopainen; reissued by Tal- och Punktskriftbiblioteket, Enskede, in 1989. Audio recording published by Söderström in 1990, read by Lauri Komulainen.

8 *Keskenräisten tarujen kirja.* Porvoo: Werner Söderström, 1986.
Translation, by Kersti Juva and Panu Pekkanen, of *UT*.

French

1 *Bilbo le hobbit, ou, Histoire d'un aller et retour.* Paris: Éditions Stock, 1969.
Translation, by Francis Ledoux, of *H*. Published by Éditions J'ai Lu, Paris, in 1974. Published by Hachette, Paris, in 1976 with illustrations by Chica (five of the illustrations were reprinted in *The Annotated Hobbit* [A3dd–ee], pp. 21, 206, 239, 270, 284). Published by Hachette in 1980 with illustrations by Tolkien. Published by Éditions Stock ('Le Livre de poche') in 1983 with illustrations by Evelyne Drouhin. Published by Éditions Stock ('Le Livre de poche') in 1989 without illustrations except maps.

2 *Le Seigneur des anneaux.* Paris: Christian Bourgois, 1972–3. Translation, by Francis Ledoux, of *LR*. 3 vols.: I, *La Communauté de l'anneau*; II, *Les Deux tours*; III, *Le Retour du roi*. Omits foreword, appendices except for the 'Tale of Aragorn and Arwen', and indexes. Published by Bourgois ('Le Livre de poche') in 1976 in 3 vols. Published by Jean-Jacques Pauvert, Paris, in 1978 in 1 vol. Published by Éditions Famot, Geneva, in 1980 in 2 vols. with illustrations by Jean-Pierre Evrard. The Famot edition was reissued in 1980? with illustrations from the Bakshi *LR* film. Published by Gallimard, Paris, in 1980 in 3 vols. Published by France Loisirs, Paris, in 1983 in 3 vols. Published by Bourgois in 1986 in 4 vols. with (as vol. 4) all appendices, translated by Tina Jolas, and an index by Alain Lefèvre. Published by Bourgois ('Presses pocket') in 1986 in 3 vols. with Appendices B, C, D, and part of A (the 'Tale of Aragorn and Arwen'). Published by Bourgois ('Collection folio junior') in 1988 in 6 vols. with illustrations by Philippe Munch and Appendices A, B, C, and F, pt. 1 (as 'D'), without indexes. Published by Bourgois in 1990 in 1 vol. with all appendices and index, without foreword.

3 *Fäerie*. Paris: Christian Bourgois, 1974.
Translation, by Francis Ledoux, of *FGH, SWM, LBN, OFS*. Published by Union Générale d'Éditions, Paris, in 1978.

4 *Les Aventures de Tom Bombadil*. Paris: Christian Bourgois, 1975.
ATB in French and English, French translation by Dashiell Hedayat. Includes reproduction of 2 manuscript pages by Tolkien: 'A Elbereth Gilthoniel' and partial and full versions (slightly different) of 'Namárië'; and two passages from *LR*, the second abruptly broken off: ' "Quite right said, Sam' (= ' "Quite right, Sam," laughed Bilbo', *LR*, bk. 2, ch. 1) and 'Not all that was spoken and debated . . .' (*LR*, bk. 2, ch. 2), in part using Anglo-Saxon characters. The pages by Tolkien are introduced, in English, by Christopher Tolkien, reproduced from his holograph; attests 'This page [i.e. leaf] was written by J. R. R. Tolkien and was given to M. Christian Bourgois by Christopher & Priscilla Tolkien, March 1974'. See further, Taum Santoski, 'A Manuscript by J. R. R. Tolkien in the French Edition of *The Adventures of Tom Bombadil*', *Beyond Bree* (newsletter of the American Mensa Tolkien Special Interest Group), October 1985, pp. 6–7. Published by Union Générale d'Éditions, Paris, in 1978.

5 *Maître Gilles de Ham*. Liège: Association des Romanistes de l'Université de Liège, 1975.
Translation, by Simonne d'Ardenne, of *FGH*, from a pre-1938 manuscript, not the published text of 1949. Tolkien mentioned d'Ardenne's translation of *FGH* in a letter to Stanley Unwin of 17 November 1937.

6 *Les Lettres du Père Noël*. Paris: Christian Bourgois, 1977.
Translation, by Gérard-Georges Lemaire, of *FCL*.

7 *Le Silmarillion: histoire des silmarils*. Paris: Christian Bourgois, 1978.
Translation, by Pierre Alien, of *Silm*. Published by Éditions J'ai Lu, Paris, in 1980 in 2 vols. Published by Bourgois ('Presses-pocket') in 1984.

8 *J. R. R. Tolkien: une biographie*. Paris: Christian Bourgois, 1980.
Translation, by Pierre Alien, of Carpenter, *Biography* (B32).

9 *Contes et légendes des inachevés*. Paris: Christian Bourgois, 1982.
Translation, by Tina Jolas, of *UT*. Published by Bourgois ('Presses-pocket') in 1988 in 3 vols.: I, *Le Premier âge*; II, *Le Second âge*; III, *Le Troisième âge*.

10 *Le Fermier Gilles de Ham*. Lyons: Chardon Bleu, 1984.
Translation, by Francis Ledoux, of *FGH*. Illustrations by Philippe Pauzin.

11 *Smith de Grand-Wootton*. Lyons: Chardon Bleu, 1986.
Translation, by Francis Ledoux, of *SWM*. Illustrations by Philippe Pauzin.

12 *Smith of Wootton Major = Ferrant de Bourg-aux-Bois*. Paris: Presses Pocket, 1990.
English-French edition for students, translation by Annie Richelet.

13 *L'Album de Bilbo le hobbit: adieu à la Terre du Milieu*. Paris: Gallimard, 1991.
Translation, by Pierre de Laubier, of *Bilbo's Last Song*. Illustrations by Pauline Baynes.

German

See also A3s note.

1 *Kleiner Hobbit und der grosse Zauberer*. Recklinghausen: Paulus Verlag, 1957.

Translation, by Walter Scherf, of *H*. Illustrations by Horus Engels. Reprinted by Paulus in 1967 as *Der kleiner Hobbit*. Three of the illustrations were reprinted in *The Annotated Hobbit* (A3dd–ee), pp. 136, 185, 193.

2 *Der Herr der Ringe*. Stuttgart: Hobbit Presse im Ernst Klett, 1969–70.
Translation, by Margaret Carroux (prose) and E. M. von Freymann (verse), of *LR*. 3 vols.: I, *Die Gefährten*; II, *Die zwei Türme*; III, *Die Rückkehr des Königs*. Includes all appendices except E, pt. 1, omits major part of indexes. Published by Hobbit Presse/Klett-Cotta in 1972 in 3 vols. without appendices except the 'Tale of Aragorn and Arwen' (cf. 9, below). Published by Europ. Bildungsgemein-schaft, Stuttgart, and other book clubs in the Federal Republic of Germany, in 1983, 1984, 1985. Published by Hobbit Presse/Klett-Cotta in 1984 in 3 vols. with appendices. Published by Hobbit Presse/Klett-Cotta in 1990 in 3 vols. with appendices, and with illustrations by Heinz Edelmann (uncredited). A selection from this translation, 'Der Kampf auf der Wetterspitze' from bk. 1, ch. 11–12, was published in *Das grosse Buch der Fantasy*, ed. Michael Gördern (Bergisch Gladbach: Bastei-Lübbe, 1982). Another selection, 'Aufbrach mit den Hobbits' (from bk. 1, ch. 6–8), was published in *Aufbrach mit den Hobbits: das Fantasy-Buch* (Munich: Deutscher Taschenbuch, 1984).

3 *Die Geschichte vom Bauern Giles und dem Drachen Chrysophylax* = *Farmer Giles of Ham*. Munich: Langewiesche-Brandt, 1970.
Translation, by Angela Uthe-Spencker, of *FGH*. Parallel texts, German and English. Illustrations by Pauline Baynes. Published by Deutscher Taschenbuch, Munich, in 1974. German text published by Esslinger im ÖBV [Österreichischer Bundesverlag Wien], Esslingen, 1991, as *Bauer Giles von Ham*, with illustra-tions by Sergei Kovalenkov.

4 *Der kleine Hobbit*. Recklinghausen: Georg Bitter, 1971.
Revised edition of 1, above. Illustrations by Klaus Ensikat. Published by Deutscher Taschenbuch, Munich, in 1974. First published by Europ. Bildungs-gemeinschaft, Stuttgart, and other book clubs in the Federal Republic of Germany, in 1981. Published by Deutscher Bücherbund, Stuttgart, in 1983. Published in braille by Deutscher Blindenstudieanst, Marburg, in 1983, in 3 vols. Published by Deutscher Taschenbuch, Munich, in 1991 without illustrations, with map by Juliane Hehn-Kynast.

5 *Fabelhafte Geschichten*. Stuttgart: Hobbit Presse im Ernst Klett, 1975?
Translation, by Angela Uthe-Spencker, of *FGH* ('Bauer Giles von Ham'); by Karl A. Klewer, of *SWM* ('Der Schmied von Grossholzingen'); and by Margaret Carroux, of *LBN* ('Blatt von Tüftler'). Illustrations by Heinz Edelmann. Cf. 3, above; cf. 10, below.

6 *Die Briefe vom Weinachtsmann*. Stuttgart: Hobbit Presse/Klett-Cotta, 1977.
Translation, by Anja Hegemann, of *FCL*. Published by Klett-Cotta im Ullstein Taschenbuch, Frankfurt am Main, in 1981.

7 *Das Silmarillion*. Stuttgart: Hobbit Presse/Klett-Cotta, 1978.
Translation, by Wolfgang Krege, of *Silm*. Illustrations by Heinz Edelmann. A translation by Hans J. Schütz and Wolfgang Krege of 'Tuor and His Arrival in Gondolin' ('Von Tuor und dem Fall von Gondolin'), with a translation of part of Christopher Tolkien's introduction to *UT* and maps by Karen Wynn Fonstad with German text, collectively *Tuor und seine Ankunft in Gondolin*, was published by Deutscher Taschenbuch, Munich, in 1985. Selections from Krege's translation of *Silm*, with maps by Karen Wynn Fonstad, were published as

Feanors Fluch (Munich: Klett-Cotta im Deutschen Taschenbuch, 1991): 'Von Fëanor und der Loskettung Melkors' ('Of Fëanor and the Unchaining of Melkor'); 'Von den Silmaril und der Unruhe der Noldor' ('Of the Silmarils and the Unrest of the Noldor'); 'Von der Verdunkelung Valinors' ('Of the Darkening of Valinor'); 'Von der Verbannung der Noldor' ('Of the Flight of the Noldor'); 'Von Sonne und Mond und der Verhüllung Valinors' ('Of the Sun and Moon and the Hiding of Valinor'); 'Von den Menschen' ('Of Men'); and 'Von der Rückkehr der Noldor' ('Of the Return of the Noldor').

8 *J. R. R. Tolkien: eine Biographie.* Stuttgart: Hobbit Presse/Klett-Cotta, 1979. Translation, by Wolfgang Krege, of Carpenter, *Biography* (B32).

9 *Der Herr der Ringe: Anhange.* Stuttgart: Hobbit Presse/Klett-Cotta, 1981. Translation, by Margaret Carroux, of the appendices to *LR*. Incidental art by Heinz Edelmann.

10 *Baum und Blatt.* Frankfurt am Main: Klett-Cotta im Ullstein Taschenbuch, 1982.
Translation of *TL*. *OFS* ('Über Märchen') translated by Wolfgang Krege, *LBN* ('Blatt von Tüftler') translated by Margaret Carroux.

11 *Herr Glück.* Stuttgart: Hobbit Presse/Klett-Cotta, 1983.
Translation, by Anja Hegemann, of *Mr. Bliss*, with Tolkien's illustrated manuscript in English.

12 *Nachrichten aus Mittelerde.* Stuttgart: Hobbit Presse/Klett-Cotta, 1983.
Translation, by Hans J. Schütz, of *UT*. Illustration by Heinz Edelmann. The Schütz translation of *Narn i Hîn Húrin* was also published as *Die Geschichte der Kinder Húrins* (Munich: Klett-Cotta im Deutschen Taschenbuch, 1988), with a translation of Christopher Tolkien's introduction.

13 *Die Abenteuer des Tom Bombadil und andere Gedichte aus dem Roten Buch.* Stuttgart: Hobbit Presse/Klett-Cotta, 1984.
Translation, by E. M. von Freymann, of *ATB*.

14 *Gute Drachen sind rar: drei Aufsätze.* Stuttgart: Klett-Cotta, 1984.
Translation, by Wolfgang Krege, of 'A Secret Vice', *OFS*, and 'Beowulf: The Monsters and the Critics'.

15 *J. R. R. Tolkien: Bilder aus Mittelerde Postkartenbuch.* Munich: Deutscher Taschenbuch, 1984.
21 illustrations by Tolkien, 7 with colour added by H. E. Riddett, on postcards, with anonymous note on Tolkien and notes on the pictures.

16 *J. R. R. Tolkien, der Mythenschöpfer.* Ed. Helmut W. Pesch. Meitingen: Corian, 1984.
Includes translations: by Helmut W. Pesch, of 'Bilbo's Last Song' ('Bilbos Abschied [an den Grauen Anfurten]'); by Wolfgang Krege, of *Letters* no. 131 ('Brief an Milton Waldman'); and by Hans J. Schütz, 'Die Hütte des vergessenen Spiels' ('The Cottage of Lost Play'), from *BLT1*, omitting commentary by Christopher Tolkien.

17 *Der Zauberwald von Fangorn: das zweite Fantasy-Buch.* Munich: Deutscher Taschenbuch, 1985.
Includes translations: by Margaret Carroux and E. M. von Freymann, 'Nach Isengart!', from *LR*, bk. 3, ch. 3–4; by Hans J. Schütz, 'Die Bäume von Númenor' ('[A Description of] the Island of Númenor'), from *UT*, omitting

commentary; by Wolfgang Krege, 'Die Zwei Baume von Valinor', from *Silm*, ch. 1, 7, 8).

18 *Das Buch des verschollenen Geschichten*. Stuttgart: Hobbit Presse/Klett-Cotta, 1986–7.
Translation, by Hans J. Schütz, of *BLT1–2*. 2 vols.

19 *Zu Gast bei den Elben: das dritte Fantasy-Buch*. Munich: Deutschen Taschenbuch, 1986.
Includes translations: by Hans J. Schütz, 'Eriol geniesst die Gastfreundschaft der Elben', from *BLT1*, ch. 1, omitting commentary; by Margaret Carroux and E. M. von Freymann, 'Galadriels Spiegel', from *LR*, bk. 2, ch. 6–7; and by E. M. von Freymann, of 'The Mewlips' from *ATB* ('Die Muhlipps').

20 *Die Ungeheuer und ihre Kritiker: gesammelte Aufsätze*. Stuttgart: Hobbit Presse/Klett-Cotta, 1987.
Translation, by Wolfgang Krege, of *The Monsters and the Critics and Other Essays*, omitting 'English and Welsh'.

21 *Das Hobbitbuch*. Munich: Deutscher Taschenbuch, 1988.
Includes translations ('Fragmente aus der Chronik Mittelerdes'), by Hans J. Schütz, of 'Ælfwine of England' from *BLT2* ('Ælfwine aus England'); and from *UT*, of 'Tuor and His Banishment from Gondolin' ('Tuor und die Verbanntenvon Gondolin'); 'A Description of the Island of Númenor' ('Die Insel Númenor'); 'The Elessar' ('Der Elessar'); 'The Disaster of the Gladden Fields' ('Das Verhängnis auf den Schwertelfeldern'); 'The Hunt for the Ring' ('Das Jagd nach dem Ring'); and 'The Drúedain' ('Die Drúedain'). Omits commentary by Christopher Tolkien.

22 *Bilbos Abschiedslied in den grauen Häfen*. Esslingen: J. F. Schreiber, 1991.
Translation, by E. M. von Freymann, of *Bilbo's Last Song*. Illustrations by Pauline Baynes.

23 *Briefe*. Stuttgart: Hobbit Presse/Klett-Cotta, 1991.
Translation, by Wolfgang Krege, of *Letters*.

24 *Der Herr der Ringe*. Stuttgart: Klett-Cotta, 1991.
Revised edition of 2, above. 1 vol. Revised by Roswith Krege-Mayer. Complete Appendix E translated by Helmut Pesch. Illustrations by Anke Doberauer.

25 *Der kleine Hobbit*. Stuttgart: Klett-Cotta, 1991.
Revised edition of 3, above. Published in large print by Deutscher Taschenbuch, Munich, 1991.

26 *Das Tolkien Lesebuch*. Ed. with an afterword by Ulrike Killer. Munich: Klett-Cotta im Deutschen Taschenbuch, 1991.
Includes translations: by Wolfgang Krege, of Carpenter, *Biography* (B32), pt. 1 ('Besuch bei J. R. R. Tolkien'); by Hans J. Schütz, of 'Ælfwine of England' from *BLT2* ('Ælfwine aus England'); by Krege, of *Letters* nos. 1–2 ('Briefe an Edith Bratt'); by Schütz, of 'Éala Éarendel Engla Beorhtast' from *BLT2* ('Die Fahrt von Earendel, dem Abendstern'); by Krege, of 'A Secret Vice' from *The Monsters and the Critics and Other Essays* ('Ein heimliches Laster'); by Schütz, of 'The Music of the Ainur' from *BLT1* ('Die Musik der Ainur'); by Schütz, of 'The Fall of Gondolin' from *BLT2* ('Der Fall Gondolins'); by Schütz, of 'The Tale of Tinúviel' from *BLT2*, ch. 1 ('Die Geschichte von Tinúviel'); by Krege, of 'Of Beleriand and Its Realms' from *Silm* ('Von Beleriand und seinen Reichen'); by

Schütz, of 'The Drúedain' from *UT* ('Die Drúedain'); by Krege, of 'The Downfall of Númenor' (i.e. 'Akallabêth') from *Silm* ('Der Untergang von Númenor'); by Krege, of *Letters* no. 27 (' "Was, Dr. Tolkien, macht Sie ticken?": Brief an Houghton Mifflin Co.'); by Krege, of *Letters* no. 90 ('Ein Abend in der Kneipe: Brief an Christopher Tolkien'); by Krege, of *Letters* no. 53 (' "Unser kleiner Cherub": Brief an Christopher Tolkien'); by Krege, of *Letters* no. 45 (' "Der edle nordische Geist": Brief an Michael Tolkien'); by Anja Hegemann, 'Ein Brief vom Weihnachtsmann 1932' from *FCL*, with Tolkien's 'cave painting' illustration; by Hegemann, 'Brief vom Polarbären' from *FCL*, with the goblin alphabet; by Walter Scherf, 'Rätsel in der Finsternis', from *H*, ch. 5 ('Riddles in the Dark'); by Krege, of *Letters* no. 19 (' "Jene verrückte, glanzäugige Schönheit": Brief an Stanley Unwin'); by Krege, of *Letters* no. 25 (' "Über den Namen und die Herkunft seines merkwürdigen Helden": Brief an den Herausgeber des "Observer" '); by Krege, of *Letters* no. 17 ('Bilbo und die Oxforder Intelligenzija: Brief an Stanley Unwin'); by M. Carroux and E. M. von Freymann, 'Der Rat von Elrond', from *LR*, bk. 2, ch. 2 ('The Council of Elrond'); by Krege, of *Letters* no. 214 ('Des Brauch des Schenkens bei den Hobbits Briefentwurf'); by Krege, of *Letters* no. 184 ('Brief an Sam Gamgee'); by Krege, of *Letters* nos. 211–12 (' "War die Flügelkrone von Gondor wie die einer Walküre oder wie die auf einer Gauloises-Packung?": Brief an eine neugierige Leserin'); by Carroux and von Freymann, of 'Three is Company', *LR*, bk. 1, ch. 3 ('Drei Mann hoch'); by Carroux and von Freymann, 'Baumbart', from *LR*, bk. 3, ch. 4 ('Treebeard'); by Schütz, of 'The Palantíri' from *UT* ('Die Palantíri'); by Carroux and von Freymann, of 'The Forbidden Pool', *LR*, bk. 4, ch. 6 ('Der verbotene Weiher'); by Krege, of *Letters* no. 163 (' "At the End of the Quest, Victory": Briefentwurf an W. H. Auden'); by Krege, of *Letters* no. 258 ('Hydrofolie Schattenfell: Brief an Rayner Unwin'); by Krege, of *Letters* no. 345 ('Göttin der Milch: Brief an eine Mrs. Meriel Thurston'); by Krege, of *Letters* no. 267 ('Tolkien trifft Ava Gardner: Brief an Michael Tolkien'); by Krege, of *Letters* no. 332 ('Das letzte Domizil: Brief an Michael Tolkien'); by Krege, of *Letters* no. 340 ('Edith Tolkien Lúthien: Brief an Christopher Tolkien'); by Carroux, of *LBN* ('Blatt von Tüftler'). Omits commentary by Christopher Tolkien to *UT*, *BLT1*, *BLT2*.

Greek

1 *Khompit.* Athens: Kedros, 1979.
Translation, by A. Gabrielide and Kh. Delegianne, of *H*. Drawings by Tolkien.

2 *O arkhontas ton dachtylidion.* Athens: Kedros, 1985–8?
Translation, by Eugenia Khatzethanase-Kollia, of *LR*. 3 vols.: I, *É syntrophiá tou dakhtylidioú*; II, *Hoi dyo pyrgoi*; III, *É epistrophi tou vasilia*.

Hebrew

1 [*Farmer Giles of Ham*]. Tel-Aviv [? printed in Jerusalem]: M. Newman, 1968.
Translation by D. Tessler.

2 [*The Hobbit, or, There and Back Again*]. Tel Aviv: Zmora, Bitan, Modan, 1976.
Translation by Moshe Hanaami. Drawings by Tolkien.

3 [*The Hobbit, or, There and Back Again*]. Tel Aviv: Zmora, Bitan, Modan, 1977.
Translation 'by the P.O.W. of the Israeli Air-Force Pilots and their comrades in Abasya Prison, Cairo, 1970–1973'.

4 [*The Lord of the Rings*]. Tel Aviv: Zmora, Bitan, Modan, 1979–80.

Translation by Ruth Livnit (prose) and Uriel Ofek (verse). 3 vols. Omits 'Note on the Shire Records' and appendices.

5 [*Smith of Wootton Major*]. Tel Aviv: Zmora, Bitan, 1983.
Translation by Yehi'am Paddam.

6 [*The Adventures of Tom Bombadil*]. Tel Aviv: Zmora, Bitan, 1984.
Translation by Uriel Ofek.

7 [*The Silmarillion*]. Tel Aviv: Zmora, Bitan, 1990.
Translation by Imanuel Lotem.

Hungarian

1 *A babó.* Budapest: Móra Könyvkiadó, 1975.
Translation, by István Tótfalusi (verse) and Tibor Szobotka (prose), of *H*.
Illustrations by Tamás Szecskó. Five of the illustrations were reprinted in *The Annotated Hobbit* (A3dd–ee), pp. 13, 29, 237, 260, 287.

2 *A gyűrűk ura.* Budapest: Gondolat, 1981.
Translation, by Ádám Réz (vol. 1, ch. 1–2, and verse) and Árpád Göncz (remainder of prose), of *LR*. 3 vols.: I, *A gyűrű szövetsége*; II, *A két torony*; III, *A király visszatér.* Includes all appendices. Published by Arkádia, Budapest, in 1990, 3 vols.

3 *Tavirózska kisasszony: angol versek és mesék gyerekeknek.* Ed. Elizabeth Szász.
Illustrations by Renyi Krisztina. Budapest: Világjáró Varázscipők, 1987.
Includes, pp. 236–[46], translation by Árpád Göncz of part of *TT*, bk. 3, ch. 4 ('Treebeard').

4 *A sonkádi egyed Gazda.* Budapest: Móra Ferenc Könyvkiado, 1988.
Translation, by Árpád Göncz, of *FGH*. Illustrations by István Keleman.

5 *A Szilmarilok.* Budapest: Árkákia, 1991.
Translation, by Judit Gálvölgyi, of *Silm*.

Icelandic

1 *Hobbit.* Reykjavik: Almenna Bókafélagið, 1978.
Translation, by Úlfur Ragnarsson and Karl Agúst Úlfsson, of *H*.

2 *Gvendur bóndi á Svínafelli.* Reykjavik: Iðunn, 1979.
Translation, by Ingibjörg Jónsdóttir, of *FGH*. Illustrations by Pauline Baynes.

Indonesian

1 *Hobbit.* Jakarta: P. T. Gramedia, 1977.
Translation, by Anton Adiwiyoto, of *H*.

2 *Petani Penakluk Naga.* Jakarta: P. T. Gramedia, 1980.
Translation, by Anton Adiwiyoto, of *FGH*.

Italian

1 *Il signore degli anelli.* Rome: Astrolabio, 1967.
Translation, by Vicky Alliata, of *FR* (*La compagnia dell'anello*). Omits foreword.

2 *Il signore degli anelli.* Milan: Rusconi, 1970.
   Translation, by Vicky Alliata di Villafranca, of *LR*. 1 vol. Introduction and notes by Elémire Zolla. Omits foreword and appendices except the 'Tale of Aragorn and Arwen'. Published by Rusconi in 1974–5 in 3 vols.: I, *La compagnia dell'anello*; II, *Le due torri*; III, *Il ritorno del re*. Revised translation? published by Rusconi in 1977 in 1 vol. without foreword but with all appendices. Published by Euroclub, Bergamo? in 1979 in 1 vol. Published by Istituto Geografico de Agostini, Novara, in 1982–3 in 3 vols., without appendices.

3 *Lo hobbit, o, La riconquista del tesoro.* Milan: Adelphi Edizioni, 1973.
   Translation, by Elena Jeronimidis Conte, of *H*. Illustrations by Tolkien. Published by Tascabili Bompiani, Milan, in 1981. Published by Euroclub, Bergamo? in 1980. Published by Arnoldo Mondadori, Milan, in 1986 with illustrations by Michael Hague.

4 *Il cacciatore di draghi, ovverossa, Giles l'agricoltore di Ham.* Torino: Einaudi, 1975.
   Translation, by Camillo Pennati, of *FGH*. Illustrations by Pauline Baynes.

5 *Albero e foglia* [*Tree and Leaf*]. Milan: Rusconi, 1976.
   Translation, by Francesco Saba Sardi, of *OFS* ('Sulle fiabe'), *LBN* ('Foglia di Niggle'), *SWM* ('Fabbro di Wootton Major'), *HBBS* ('Il ritorno di Beorhtnoth figlio di Beorhthelm'). Illustrations by Piero Crida.

6 *Le avventure di Tom Bombadil.* Milan: Rusconi, 1978.
   Translation, by Bianca Pitzorno and Maria Teresa Vignoli, of *ATB*.

7 *Il silmarillion.* Milan: Rusconi, 1978.
   Translation, by Francesco Saba Sardi, of *Silm*. Published by Club degli Editori, Milan, in 1979. Published by Euroclub, Bergamo? in 1987.

8 *Le lettere di Babbo Natale.* Milan: Rusconi, 1980.
   Translation, by Francesco Saba Sardi, of *FCL*.

9 *Racconti incompiuti di Númenor e della Terra-di-mezzo.* Milan: Rusconi, 1981.
   Translation, by Francesco Saba Sardi, of *UT*.

10 *Vita di J. R. R. Tolkien.* Milan: Rusconi, 1983.
   Translation, by Francesco Saba Sardi, of Grotta, *The Biography of J. R. R. Tolkien* (Dii33). Excerpt, Tolkien's letter to Allan Barnett ('Uno scherzo coi guanti'), published in *Tuttolibri*, Torino, no. 372, 10 Settembre 1983, p. 4.

11 *Mr. Bliss.* Milan: Rusconi, 1984.
   Translation, by Francesco Saba Sardi, of *Mr. Bliss*, with Tolkien's illustrated manuscript in English.

12 *Gli Inklings: Clive S. Lewis, John R. R. Tolkien, Charles Williams & Co.* Milan: Jaca Book, 1985.
   Translation, by Maria Elena Ruggerini, of Carpenter, *The Inklings* (B33).

13 *Racconti ritrovati.* Milan: Rusconi, 1986.
   Translation, by Cinzia Pieruccini, of *BLT1*. Published by Euroclub, Bergamo? in 1988.

14 *Racconti perduti.* Milan: Rusconi, 1987.
   Translation, by Cinzia Pieruccini, of *BLT2*.

15 *Immagini.* Milan: Rusconi, 1989.
   Translation, by Quirino Principe, of *Pictures*.

16 *La realtà in trasparenza: lettere 1914–1973*. Milan: Rusconi, 1990.
Translation, by Cristina De Grandis, of *Letters*.

17 *Lo hobbit, o, La riconquista del tesoro*. Milan: Rusconi, 1991.
Translation of *The Annotated Hobbit*. Text by Tolkien translated by Conte, as
for 2, above. Annotations by Douglas A. Anderson (omitting textual notes)
translated by Grazia Maria Griffini. Illustrations by Tolkien, et al.

Japanese

See also A4a, A9a notes.

1 [*The Hobbit, or, There and Back Again*]. Tokyo: Iwanami Shoten, 1965.
Translation by Teiji Seta. Illustrations by Ryuichi Terashima. Eight of the
illustrations were reprinted in *The Annotated Hobbit* (A3dd–ee), pp. 62, 68, 84,
137, 161, 194, 223, 254.

2 [*Farmer Giles of Ham*]. Tokyo: Hyoronsha, 1972.
Translation by Shinichi Yoshida. Illustrations after Pauline Baynes. Cf. 5, below.

3 [*The Lord of the Rings*]. Tokyo: Hyoronsha, 1972.
Translation by Teiji Seta. 6 vols. Illustrations by Ryuichi Terashima. Includes
Appendices A, B, C, D.

4 [*On Fairy-Stories*]. Tokyo: Fukuinkan-Shoten, 1973.
Translation by Yoko Inokima.

5 [*Farmer Giles of Ham, Smith of Wootton Major, Tree and Leaf, The Adventures
of Tom Bombadil*]. Tokyo: Hyoronsha, 1976.
Translation by Shinichi Yoshida, Yoko Inokuma, and Tadashi Saotome. Illustrations by Pauline Baynes.

6 [*The Father Christmas Letters*]. Tokyo: Hyoronsha, 1976.
Translation by Teiji Seta.

7 [*The Silmarillion*]. Tokyo: Hyoronsha, 1982.
Translation by Akiko Tamura [Tanaka?]. 2 vols.

8 [*The White Rider*, Tokyo?].
Issue no. 1 (May 1982) of this periodical includes translations of *LR* Appendices
D, E, and F, with the tengwar and Angerthas tables reproduced from A5a etc.;
'Guide to the Names in *The Lord of the Rings*'; and part of *UT*. No. 2
(December 1983) includes a translation of a further part of *UT*. No. 3 (August
1987) includes a translation of a further part of *UT* and part of the *LR* index. A
separate index to *H* was published in August 1986.

9 [*The Quotations from Gandalf*]. Tokyo?: *The White Rider, circa* 1987.
Translation of selected passages from *LR*?

10 [*Bilbo's Last Song*]. Tokyo: Iwanami Shoten, 1991.

Latvian

1 '*Hobits, jeb, Turp un atpakal*: fragments'. *Gramata* (1990).
Translation, by Katarina Petersone, of *H*, ch. 1.

2 *Hobits, jeb, Turp un atpakaļ*. Riga: Sprīdītis, 1991.
Translation, by Zane Rozenberga, of *H*. Illustrations and maps by Laima Eglīte.
Afterword by the translator.

3 [*Lord of the Rings*].
   Said to be forthcoming.

Lithuanian

1 *Hobitas, arba, Ten ir atgal: Apysaka-pasaka*. Vilnius: Vyturys, 1985.
   Translation, by Bronė Balčienė, of *H*. Illustrations by Mikhail Belomlinskiy.

Moldavian

1 *Hobbitul*. Kishinev: Literatura Artistike, 1987.
   Translation, by Aleksey Zurhkanu, of *H*. Illustrations by Igor Hmelnickij.

Norwegian

See also C37.

1 *Hobbiten, eller, Fram og tilbake igjen*. Oslo: Tiden Norsk Forlag, 1972.
   Translation, by Finn Aasen (pp. 7–196) and Oddrun Grønvik (pp. 197–305),
   of *H*.

2 *Krigen om ringen*. Oslo: Tiden Norsk Forlag, 1973–5.
   Translation, by Nils Werenskiold, of *LR*. 3 vols.: I, *De sorte rytterne*; II, *De to
   tårne*; III, *Kongen kommer tilbake*. Omits indexes.

3 *Eigil bonde fra Heim*. Oslo: Tiden Norsk Forlag, 1980.
   Translation, by Torstein Bugge Høverstad, of *FGH*. Illustrations by Pauline
   Baynes.

4 *Ringenes herre*. Oslo: Tiden Norsk Forlag, 1980–1.
   Translation, by Torstein Bugge Høverstad, of *LR*. 3 vols.: I, *Ringens brorskap*;
   II, *To tårn*; III, *Atter en konge*. Omits indexes. Published by Tiden in 1990 in 1
   vol. Edition with Alan Lee illustrations forthcoming.

Polish

1 *Hobbit, czyli, Tam i z powrotem*. Warsaw: Iskry, 1960.
   Translation, by Maria Skibniewska, of *H*. Illustrations by Jan Mlodozeniec.

2 *Władca pierścieni*. Warsaw: Czytelnik, 1961–3.
   Translation, by Maria Skibniewska (prose), Wlodzimierz Lewik (verse, *FR*, *TT*),
   and Andrzej Nowicki (verse, *RK*), of *LR*. 3 vols.: I, *Wyprawa*; II, *Dwie
   wieże*; III, *Powrót króla*. Omits Shire map; includes Appendices A, B, C, F
   (as 'D'). Published by Czytelnik in 1981 in 3 vols., with illustrations by Jerzy
   Czerniawski. Published jointly by Czytelnik, Warsaw, and CiA-Books/SVARO,
   Poznań, in 1990 in 3 vols., without illustrations.

3 *Rudy Dzil i jego pies*. Warsaw: Iskry, 1962.
   Translation, by Maria Skibniewska, of *FGH*. Illustrations by Pauline Baynes.

4 'Liść Drobniaka'. *Zycie i Mysl*, Warsaw? 24, no. 4 (1974).
   Translation, by Jerzy Brodzki, of *LBN*.

5 *Rudy Dzil i jego pies, Kowal z Podlesia Wiekszego*. Warsaw: Iskry, 1980.
   Translation, by Maria Skibniewska, of *FGH*, *SWM*. Illustrations by Pauline
   Baynes.

6 'Listy gwiazdkowe'. *Lad*, Warsaw? 2, no. 38 (1982).
Translation, by Hanna Truba and Piotr Paszkiewicz, of excerpts from *FCL*.
Illustration(s?) by Jerszy Kabacinski.

7 *Radar* Warsaw?, 34, no. 51/52 (1984); 36, nos. 3–13, 16–51/52 (1985); 37, nos. 1–13 (1986).
Includes translation, by Maria Skibniewska, of *Silm*. Illustration(s?) by Henryk Ziembicki. Cf. 10, below.

8 *Hobbit, czyli, Tam i z powrotem*. Warsaw: Iskry, 1985.
Revised edition of 1, above. Illustrations by Maciej Buszewicz.

9 'Liść, dzieło Niggle'a'. *Fantastyka*, Warsaw? no. 2 (1985).
Translation, by Krysztof Sokołowski, of *LBN*.

10 *Silmarillion*. Warsaw: Czytelnik, 1985.
Translation, by Maria Skibniewska, of *Silm*. Endpaper illustrations by Stasys Eidrigevićius. Cf. 7, above.

Portuguese

1 *O gnomo*. Porto: Livraria Civilização, 1962.
Translation, by Maria Isabel Braga and Mario Braga, of *H*. Illustrations by António Quadros. Three of the illustrations were reprinted in *The Annotated Hobbit* (A3dd–ee), pp. 15, 43, 236.

2 *O senhor dos anéis*. Rio de Janeiro: Editora Artenova, 1974.
Translation, by Antonio Ferreira da Rocha (vols. 1–2) and Luiz Alberto Monjardim (vols. 3–6), of *LR*. 6 vols.: I, *A terra mágica*; II, *O povo do anel*; III, *As duas torres*; IV, *A volta do anel*; V, *Cerdo de Gondor*; VI, *O retorno do rei*. Omits appendices.

3 *O hobbit*. Rio de Janeiro: Editora Artenova, 1976.
Translation, by Luiz Alberto Monjardim, of *H*.

4 *O senhor dos anéis*. Mem Martins: Publicações Europa-América, 1981.
Translation, by Fernanda Pinto Rodrigues, of *LR*. 3 vols.: I, *A irmandade do anel*; II, *As duas torres*; III, *O regresso do rei*. Omits indexes; small omissions in appendices.

5 *O silmarillion*. Mem Martins: Publicações Europa-América, 1984.
Translation, by Fernanda Pinto Rodrigues, of *Silm*.

6 *Contos inacabados de Númenor e da Terra Média*. Mem Martins: Publicaçoes Europa-América, 1985.
Translation, by Fernanda Pinto Rodrigues, of *UT*.

7 *O hobbit*. Mem Martins: Publicações Europa-América, 1985.
Translation, by Fernanda Pinto Rodrigues, of *H*. Drawings and colour plates by Tolkien.

8 *As aventuras de Tom Bombadil e outras histórias*. Mem Martins: Publicações Europa-América, 1986.
Translation, by Ersílio Cardoso, of *ATB*; and by Fernanda Pinto Rodrigues, of *SWM*, *FGH*, and *LBN*.

Romanian

1 *O poveste cu un hobbit*. Bucharest: Editura Ion Creangă, 1975.
Translation, by Catinca Ralea, of *H*. Illustrations by Livia Rusz. Four of the illustrations were reprinted in *The Annotated Hobbit* (A3dd–ee), pp. 15, 71, 180, 238.

Russian

See also A3c, A3h notes.

1 *Khobbit, ili, Tuda i obratno*. Leningrad: Detskaya Literatura, 1976.
Translation, by N. Rakhmanova (prose) and G. Usova and I. Komarova (verse), of *H*. Illustrations by Mikhail Belomlinskiy. Four of the illustrations were reprinted in *The Annotated Hobbit* (A3dd–ee), pp. 14, 173, 187, 225.

2 'List raboty Melkina'. *Khimiya i zhizn'* [*Chemistry and Life*], Moscow, no. 7 (1980), pp. 84–92.
Translation, by S. Koshelev, of *LBN*. Foreword by Yu. Shreider.

3 *Khraniteli: Letopis' pervaya iz epopei 'Vlastelin Kolets'*. Moscow: Detskaya Literatura, 1982.
Translation, by A. Kistyakovskiy (prose and verse) and V. Murav'yov (prose), of *FR*. Afterword by V. Murav'yov. Illustrations by G. Kalinovskiy.

4 'Zhanrovaya priroda "Pvelitelya kolets" Dzh. R. R. Tolkiyena' ['The Genre Nature of "The Lord of the Rings" by J. R. R. Tolkien']. *Zhanrovoye svoyeobraziye literatury Anglii i SSha XX veka* [*Genre Originality in 20th-Century Literature of England and the U.S.A.*]. Chelyabinsk: Mezhvuz, 1985. Pp. 39–58.
Essay by S. Koshelev, includes a translation of 'I Sit beside the Fire' from *LR*.

5 'Fermer Dzhails iz Khema'. *Skazki angliyskikh pisateley* [*Fairy-tales by English Writers*]. Leningrad: Lenizdat, 1986. Pp. 492–536.
Translation, by G. Usova, of *FGH*. Commentary by N. Tikhonova.

6 *Moskovskiy Khobbit* [*Moscow Hobbit*], Moscow, no. 1 (1987 or 1988?).
Includes translations: by N. Grigoryeva and V. Grushetskiy, of 'The Tale of Beren and Lúthien' ('Povest' o Berene i Luchien') from *Silm*, pp. 15–46; by unidentified translator(s), of excerpts from *OFS* ('O volshebnykh skazkakh'), pp. 47–70; by V. Zarya and A. Burtsen, of the foreword by Donald Swann to the second edition, and Tolkien's notes on the Elvish texts, of *RGEO* (*Doroga ukhodit vdal'*), pp. 71–90, with facsimiles of Tolkien's 'Namárië' manuscript, pp. 91–2; and by unidentified translator, of 'The Road Goes Ever On', p. 93. The issue was prepared by Vladimir Grushetskiy and Natalya Grigoryeva, but the 'compiler's' introduction is signed 'A. P.'

7 *Kuznets iz Bol'shogo Vuttona: skazka*. Moscow: Detskaya Literatura, 1988.
Translation, by Yuriy Nagibin and Yelena Gippius, of *SWM*. Illustrations by S. Ostrov.

8 *Khobbit, ili, Tuda i obratno*. Leningrad: Detskaya Literatura, 1989.
Revised edition of 1, above. Illustrations by Mikhail Belomlinskiy. Published by Novosibirskoe Knizhnoe Izdatel'stvo, Novosibirsk, in 1989 with illustrations by A. Shurits. Published by Pravda, Moscow, in 1990 in *Zabytiy den' rozhdeniya: skazki angliyskikh pisateley* [*The Forgotten Birthday: [Fairy] Tales by English Writers*], comp. Olga Aleksandrovna Kolesnikova, with epilogue by N. Sherevskaya and illustrations by Ilya A. Markevich.

9 *Vlastelin kolets*. Moscow: Raduga, 1989–
Translation, by V. Murav'yov (prologue and bk. 1) and A. Kistyakovskiy (bk. 2 and all verse), of *LR*. 3 vols.: I, *Khraniteli*; II, *Dve tverdyni*; *RK* forthcoming. Illustrations by E. Zaryanskiy. Foreword by V. Murav'yov.

10 *Khobbit, ili, Tuda i obratno*. Khabarovsk: Amur, 1990.
Translation, by V. A. M. [Valeriya Aleksandrovna Matorina], of *H*.

11 'List kisti Nigglya'. *Publikator*, Khabarovsk, no. 6 (1990), pp. 4–5, 14.
Translation, not attributed but by Valeriya Aleksandrovna Matorina, of *LBN*.

12 *Pesni Aloy knigi: sbornik stikhov* [*Songs of the Red Book*]. 2nd (expanded) ed. Ufa: Jabberwocky-SF, 1990.
Translation, by Tolkien fans in Ufa and Novosibirsk, of poems from *LR*, with original verses on Tolkienian themes. Ed. A. Allikas. Preface by Ye. Yekhina and V. A. Matorina.

13 *Derevo i list; O volshebnykh istoriyakh; List raboty Melkina*. Moscow: Progress; Gnosis, 1991.
Translation of *TL*: by Natalya Prokhorova, of *OFS*, and by S. Koshelev, of *LBN* (cf. 2, above). Illustrations by Denis Gordeyev.

14 *Fermer Dzhails iz Khema*. Leningrad: Petrodvorets, 1991.
Translation, by G. Abramyan, of *FGH*. Notes by M. Kapustina. Illustrations by G. Yabkevich.

15 'List Naygla: iz knigi "Derevo i list"'. *Urania*, Moscow, January 1991, pp. 52–9.
Translation, by Tat'yana Antonyan, of *LBN*.

16 *List raboty Melkina i drugie volshebnye skazki*. Moscow: RIF, 1991.
Translations: by Rakhmanova, Usova, and Komarova, of *H*, as for 1, above; by Koshelev, of *LBN*, as for 3, above; of *FGH*, a new? translation credited to G. Usova, with notes by N. Tikhonova (cf. 5, above; but the translation and notes appear identical to those by Abramyan and Kapustina, cf. 14, above); by Nagibin and Gippius, of *SWM*, as for 7, above; and by S. Koshelev, of *OFS*. Ed. with an afterword by V. L. Gopman. Compiled by Vitaliy Babenko.

17 *Povest' o kol'tse: roman v tryokh chastyakh*. Moscow: SP Interprint, 1991.
Translation (abridged), by Z. A. Bobyr', of *LR*. 1 vol.

18 *Vlastelin kolets*. Leningrad: Severo-Zapad, 1991.
Translation, by Natalya Grigoryeva and Vladimir Grushetskiy, of *LR*. 1 vol. (*Bratstvo kol'tsa, Dve kreposti, Vozvrashcheniye korolya*). Includes selected appendices in separate pamphlet laid in. Illustrations by Aleksandr Nikolayev.

19 *Vlastelin kolets: Letopis' pervaya; Sodruzhestvo kol'tsa*. Khabarovsk: Amur, 1991.
Translation, by V. A. M. [Valeriya Aleksandrovna Matorina], of *FR*.

20 [*Silmarillion*]. Moscow: 'Master' publishers, 1992?
Translation by V. A. Matorina, said to be forthcoming.

Serbo-Croat

1 *Hobit*. Belgrade: Nolit, 1975.
Translation, by Meri and Milan Milišić, of *H*.

2 *Gospodar prstenova*. Belgrade: Nolit, 1981.
   Translation, by Zoran Stanojević, of *LR*. 3 vols.: I, *Družina prstena*; II, *Dve kule*;
   III, *Povratak kraha*. Introduction by Vlada Uroševic. Illustrations by Tolkien, and
   A Map of Middle-earth by Pauline Baynes. Omits foreword. Published in 1988 by
   Stilos, Belgrade, in 3 vols. Includes foreword, prologue, appendices, and index.
   Includes Shire map in text, and separate folded Middle-earth map by Dobrosav
   BoB Živković.

3 *Kovač iz Velikog Vutona*. Gornji Milanovac: Dečje Novine, 1984.
   Translation, by Ana Selić, of *SWM*. Illustrations by Pauline Baynes.

4 *Farmer Gil od Buta*. Belgrade: Rad, 1986.
   Translation, by Radoslav Petković, of *FGH*. Illustrations by Pauline Baynes.

5 'O Barenu i Lutijeni'. *ALEF*, no. 10 (May 1988).
   Translation, by Pedja Vuković, of 'Of Beren and Lúthien' from *Silm*.

Slovak

1 *Hobbiti*. Bratislava: Mladé Letá, 1973.
   Translation, by Viktor Krupa, of *H*. Illustrations by Nada Rappensbergerová.
   Five of the illustrations were reprinted in *The Annotated Hobbit* (A3dd–ee), pp.
   20, 43, 163, 264, 294.

Slovenian

1 *Hobit, ali, Tja in spet nazaj*. Ljubljana: Mladinska Knjiga, 1986.
   Translation, by Dušan Ogrizek, of *H*. Illustrations by Mirna Pavlovec. Two of the
   illustrations were reprinted in *The Annotated Hobbit* (A3dd–ee), pp. [55], [65].

Spanish

Minotauro editions are also published in Mexico and Argentina.

1 *El hobito*. Buenos Aires: Fabril, 1964.
   Translation, by Teresa Sanchez Luevas, of *H*.

2 *El señor de los anillos*. Barcelona: Ediciones Minotauro, 1977–80.
   Translation, by Luis Domènech (*FR*) and Matilde Horne and Luis Domènech
   (*TT*, *RK*), of *LR*. 3 vols.: I, *La comunidad del anillo*; II, *Las dos torres*; III, *El
   retorno del rey*. Omits foreword, indexes, and appendices except for the 'Tale of
   Aragorn and Arwen'. Published by Printer International de Panama, Panama
   City, in 1981 in 3 vols. Published by Circulo de Lectores, Barcelona, in 1982 in 1
   vol. Published by Ediciones Nacionales, Bogotá ('Circulo de lectores'), in 1981
   in 3 vols.

3 *El homejo*. La Coruña: [unpublished photocopy?], 1979.
   Translation, by Guillermo Debén Ariznavarreta et al., of *H*.

4 *Egedio, el granjero de Hom, Hoja por Niggle, El herrero de Wootton*.
   Barcelona: Minotauro, 1981.
   Translation, by Julio César Santoyo and José Maria Santamaria, of *FGH*, *LBN*,
   SWM.

5 *El hobbit*. Buenos Aires: Ediciones Minotauro, 1981.
   Translation, by Jose Valdivieso, of *H*.

6 *El hobbit*. Barcelona: Ediciones Minotauro, 1982.

Translation, by Manuel Figueroa, of *H*. Published by Circulo de Lectores, Barcelona, in 1984.

7 *Tolkien*. Barcelona: Planeta, 1982.
Translation, by S. Silió, of Grotta, *The Biography of J. R. R. Tolkien* (Dii33).

8 *Las cartas de Papá Noel*. Barcelona: Ediciones Minotauro, 1983.
Translation, by Manuel Figueroa, of *FCL*.

9 *El señor Bliss*. Barcelona: Minotauro, 1984.
Translation, by Rubén Masera, of *Mr. Bliss*, with Tolkien's illustrated manuscript in English.

10 *El silmarillion*. Barcelona: Ediciones Minotauro, 1984.
Translation, by Rubén Masera and Luis Domènech, of *Silm*.

11 *El señor de los anillos: appendixes*. Barcelona: Ediciones Minotauro, 1987?
Translation, by Rubén Masera, of *LR* appendices.

12 *Cuentos inconclusos de Númenor y la Tierra Media*. Barcelona: Minotauro, 1988–9.
Translation, by Rubén Masera, of *UT*. 3 vols.: I, *La primera edad*; II, *La segunda edad*; III (in 2 pts.), *La tercera edad, Los Drúedain, los Istari, los palantíri*. Published by Minotauro in 1990 in 1 vol. Published by Sudamericana, Buenos Aires, in 3 vols, 1990?–1.

13 *El hobbit anotado*. Barcelona: Ediciones Minotauro, 1990.
Translation, by Manuel Figueroa, of *H* (cf. 6, above). Notes by Douglas A. Anderson, translated by Rubén Masera.

14 *J. R. R. Tolkien: una biografía*. Barcelona: Minotauro, 1990.
Translation, by Carlos Peralta, of Carpenter, *Biography* (B32).

15 *El libro de los cuentos perdidos I*. Barcelona: Minotauro, 1990.
Translation, by Rubén Masera, of *BLT1*.

16 *El libro de los cuentos perdidos II*. Barcelona: Minotauro, 1991.
Translation, by Teresa Gottlieb, of *BLT2*.

17 *Las conciones de Beleriand*. Barcelona: Minotauro.
Translation of *Lays*, forthcoming.

Swedish

See also C11.

1 *Hompen, eller, En resa dit och tillbaksigen*. Stockholm: Kooperativa Förbundets Bokförlag, 1947.
Translation, by Tore Zetterholm, of *H*. Illustrations by Torbjörn Zetterholm and Charles Sjöblom. Five of the illustrations were reprinted in *The Annotated Hobbit* (A3dd–ee), pp. 22, 43, 76, 172, 207.

2 *Sagan om ringen*. Stockholm: Gebers [later Almqvist & Wiksell], 1959–61.
Translation, by Åke Ohlmarks, of *LR*. 3 vols.: I, *Sagan om ringen*; II, *Sagan om de två tornen*; III, *Sagan om konungens aterkomst*. Omits foreword, indexes, and Shire map; omits appendices except the 'Tale of Aragorn and Arwen' and Appendix D. With a preface by the translator in each volume. Published by Gebers in 1967 without the translator's prefaces. In 1971 the appendices were omitted entirely (cf. 5, below). Published by Almqvist & Wiksell, Stockholm, in

1981 in 1 vol. as *Trilogin om Härskarringen*. Edition with Alan Lee illustrations forthcoming. Audio recording published by Tal- och punktskriftbiblioteket, Enskede in 1967–9?, read by Alf Söderkvist. Audio recording published by Tal- och punktskriftbiblioteket, Enskede in 1989, read by Inga Lüning.

The bibliography of the Swedish *LR* is very complex, with many reprintings and changes of format, revisions to the poetry, and reversions to the original text. The Swedish bibliographer Åke Bertenstam hopes one day to bring the full picture of the work into focus.

The Lord of the Rings in Swedish is also known under the titles *Härskarringen* and *Sagorna om Härskarringen*.

3   *Gillis Bonde från Ham*. Stockholm: Gebers, 1961.
Translation, by Åke Ohlmarks, of *FGH*. Illustrations by Pauline Baynes. Published by AWE/Gebers, Stockholm, in 1985 in the children's literature series 'Sagas berömda böcker'. Audio recording published by Tal- och punktskriftbiblioteket, Enskede in 1981, read by Inga Lüning.

4   *Bilbo: en hobbits äventyr*. Stockholm: Rabén & Sjögren, 1962.
Translation, by Britt G. Hallqvist, of *H*. Illustrations by Tove Jansson. Four of the illustrations were reprinted in *The Annotated Hobbit* (A3dd–ee), pp. 41, 116, 248, 296. Published by Rabén & Sjögren, Stockholm, in 1971 with drawings by Tolkien. Extracts were published as 'Ur Bilbo' in *Textbok 3: svenska: litteraturläsning*, ed. Kerstin Rimsten-Nilsson, illustrations by Mats Norryd (Stockholm: Liber Läromedel, 1975). Published by Rabén & Sjögren, Stockholm, in 1979 with drawings and colour plates by Tolkien. Audio recording published by Tal- och punktskriftbiblioteket, Enskede in 1977, read by Ulf Palme.

5   *Ringens värld*. Stockholm: Gebers, 1971.
Translation, by Åke Ohlmarks, of *LR* Appendices A–D complete; E, pt. 1; a compressed extract of E, pt. 2; F, pt. 1; and the first half, abruptly broken off, of F, pt. 2. Cf. 13, below.

6   *Sagan om Smeden och Stjärnan*. Stockholm: Rabén & Sjögren, 1972.
Translation, by Britt G. Hallqvist, of *SWM*. Illustrations by Pauline Baynes. Published by Litteraturfrämjandet, Stockholm, in 1982. Audio recording published by Tal- och Punktskriftbiblioteket, Enskede, in 1983, read by Erik Nyman.

7   *Tom Bombadils äventyr och andra verser ur Västmarks Röda bok*. Stockholm: Gebers, 1972.
Translation, by Åke Ohlmarks, of *ATB*. Audio recording published by Tal- och Punktskriftbiblioteket, Enskede, in 1987, read by Leif Liljeroth.

8   *Träd och blad*. Stockholm: Gebers, 1972.
Translation, by Åke Ohlmarks, of *TL*. Audio recording published by Tal- och Punktskriftbiblioteket, Enskede, in 1974, read by Hans-Erik Stenborg. An excerpt from *OFS* ('Barn och sagor') was also published in *Ord och bilder för barn och ungdom*, vol. 2: *Utblick över barn och ungdomslitteraturen: debatt och analys* (Stockholm: Rabén & Sjögren, 1986).

9   *Om Beowulfsagan: tre essäer*. Stockholm: AWE/Gebers, 1975.
Translation, by Åke Ohlmarks, of 'Beowulf: The Monsters and the Critics' ('Beowulf, vidundren och kritikerna'), the preface to Clark Hall's *Beowulf and the Finnesburg Fragment* ('Inledade kommentarer til prosaversionen av Beowulf'), and 'English and Welsh' ('Om engelskan och walesiskan').

10 *Breven från Jultomten.* Stockholm: AWE/Gebers, 1976.
Translation, by Åke Ohlmarks, of *FCL*. An excerpt was published, reproducing an envelope from 1933 and an illustration from 1930, as 'Juldagen: post scriptum av Ilbereth' in Pernilla Tunberger, *Böckernas mat* (Höganäs: Bra Böcker, 1981).

11 *J. R. R. Tolkien: en biografi.* Stockholm: AWE/Gebers, 1978.
Translation, by Disa Törngren and (poetry) Åke Ohlmarks, of Carpenter, *Biography* (B32). New edition published by Gebers in 1989, omitting the plates. Audio recording published by Tal- och Punktskriftbiblioteket, Enskede, in 1979, read by Svante Odqvist.

12 *Silmarillion.* Stockholm: AWE/Gebers, 1979.
Translation, by Roland Adlerberth, of *Silm*. Audio recording published by Tal- och Punktskriftbiblioteket, Enskede in 198–?, read by Inga Lüning.

13 *Ringens värld.* Stockholm: AWE/Gebers, 1980.
Translation, by Åke Ohlmarks, of most of the appendices to *LR* (not all of E, pt. 2, and F, pt. 2; cf. 5, above), and of *ATB*, *TL*, and *HBBS*. Cf. 6, 7, above.

14 *Sagor från Midgård.* Stockholm: Almqvist & Wiksell, 1982.
Translation, by Roland Adlerberth, of *UT*. Audio recording published by Tal- och Punktskriftbiblioteket, Enskede in 1982, read by Inga Lüning.

15 *Herr Salig.* Stockholm: AWE/Gebers, 1983.
Translation, by Roland Adlerberth, of *Mr. Bliss*, with Tolkien's illustrated manuscript in English. Audio recording published by Tal- och Punktskrift-biblioteket, Enskede, in 1984, read by Solveig Wikander.

16 *De förlorade sagornas bok.* Stockholm: AWE/Gebers, 1986–8.
Translation, by Roland Adlerberth, of *BLT1–2*. 2 vols. Includes English text of poems. Audio recording published by Tal- och Punktskriftbiblioteket, Enskede, in 1986–9, read by Thomas Ekelöf.

Ukrainian

1 *Hobit, abo, Mandrivka za imlysti hory.* Kiev: Veselka, 1985.
Translation, by Oleksandr Mokrovol's'kiy, of *H*. Illustrations by Mikhail Belomlinskiy.

Appendix: Commentary on Translations

Doughan, David. 'Khobbit'. *Amon Hen* (bulletin of The Tolkien Society), no. 55 (April 1982), pp. 12, 14. (1976 Russian *H*)

Doughan, David. 'Frodo Torbins in Kretlorien'. *Quettar* (bulletin of the Linguistic Fellowship of The Tolkien Society), no. 40 (June 1990), pp. 8–9. (1989 Russian *FR*)

Kotowski, Nathalie. 'The Russian *Lord of the Rings*'. *Beyond Bree* (newsletter of the American Mensa Tolkien Special Interest Group), November 1990, p. 4. (1989 Russian *FR*)

Kotowski, Nathalie, and René van Rossenberg. 'Comrade Frodo and Hobbitania: Tolkien in Russian'. *Elrond's Holy Round Table: Essays on Tolkien, Sayers and the Arthur Saga*. Ed. René van Rossenberg. Leiden: Tolkien Genootschap 'Unquendor', 1990. Pp. 71–7. (Russian *SWM*, 1989 *H*, 1989 *LR*)

Smith, Arden R., ed. 'Transitions in Translations'. *Vinyar Tengwar* (newsletter of the Elvish Linguistic Fellowship), notably in the following issues (and continuing):

No. 7 (September 1989), pp. 10–11 (Spanish *LR*)

No. 8 (November 1989), pp. 10–11 (Portuguese *H*, French *H*, 1982 and 1989 Russian *FR*)

No. 9 (January 1990), pp. 11–12 (Danish *LR*, French *LR*, German *UT*)

No. 10 (March 1990), pp. 16–20 (Portuguese *H*)

No. 11 (May 1990), pp. 16–17 (Greek *H*, 1989 Russian *H*, Russian *SWM*, 1989 Russian *LR*, French *LR*)

No. 12 (July 1990), pp. 18–20 (German *LR*, 1989 Russian *FR*, Russian *SWM*)

No. 13 (September 1990), pp. 18–20 (1974 German *H*, French *LR*)

No. 15 (January 1991), pp. 11–12 (1974 German *H*, Finnish *H*, Danish *LR*)

No. 18 (July 1991), pp. 33–6 (Danish *H* and *LR*, 1989–90 Russian *FR*, *TT*)

No. 19 (September 1991), pp. 26–8 (Finnish *H*, 1990 Russian *TT*)

No. 20 (November 1991), pp. 18–20 (Grigoryeva and Grushetskiy Russian *LR*, miscellaneous Russian translations)

No. 22 (March 1992), pp. 26–30 (Italian *H*, Finnish *H* and *LR*, Matorina Russian *FR*)

No. 23 (May 1992), pp. 24–6 (*Das Tolkien Lesebuch*)

Translations of The Hobbit *Reviewed. Quettar Special Publication* no. 2. London: The Tolkien Society, 1988. (German, Dutch, Norwegian, Portuguese, Japanese, Polish, Finnish, Hungarian, Russian, French *H*)

Selected References

Allan, Jim, ed. *An Introduction to Elvish*. Hayes, Middlesex: Bran's Head Books, 1978.

Allan, Jim. 'Tolkien in Britain and Canada'. *Minas Tirith Evening Star* (journal of the American Tolkien Society), 5, no. 4 (July 1976), pp. 14–15, 17–19.

Anderson, Douglas A. 'Note on the Text'. J. R. R. Tolkien. *The Lord of the Rings*. Boston: Houghton Mifflin, [1987]. Pp. [v]–viii.

Anderson, Douglas A. 'Textual and Revisional Notes'. J. R. R. Tolkien. *The Annotated Hobbit*. Boston: Houghton Mifflin; London: Unwin Hyman, 1988. Pp. [321]–8.

Bertenstam, Åke (Jönsson). 'The Kings' Reckoning: Did Tolkien Reckon Correct?' *Beyond Bree* (newsletter of the American Mensa Tolkien Special Interest Group), November 1985, pp. 5–6.

Bertenstam, Åke (Jönsson). *En Tolkienbibliografi 1911–1980: verk av och om J. R. R. Tolkien = A Tolkien Bibliography 1911–1980: Works by and about J. R. R. Tolkien*. Rev. ed. Uppsala: Bertenstam, 1986. Supplements published in *Arda* (publication of Arda-sällskapet, with support from Tolkiensällskapet Forodrim).

Bodleian Library. *Drawings for 'The Hobbit' by J. R. R. Tolkien*. Oxford: Bodleian Library, 1987.

Bodleian Library. *Oxford Writers 1914–1977: Catalogue of an Exhibition*. Oxford: Bodleian Library, 1977. Pp. 49–51.

Bradfield, Julian C. 'Changes in *The Lord of the Rings*, Appendices D & E between the First and Second Allen & Unwin Editions (1955, 1966)'. *Beyond Bree*, October 1984, p. 3. With a note by Nancy Martsch.

Brooks, Paul. *Two Park Street*. Boston: Houghton Mifflin, 1986.

Carpenter, Humphrey. *The Inklings: C. S. Lewis, J. R. R. Tolkien, Charles Williams, and Their Friends*. London: George Allen & Unwin, 1978; Boston: Houghton Mifflin, 1979.

Carpenter, Humphrey. *J. R. R. Tolkien: A Biography* (American title: *Tolkien: A Biography*). London: George Allen & Unwin; Boston: Houghton Mifflin, 1977. Rev. ed., London: Unwin Paperbacks, 1982. Appendix C: 'The Published Writings of J. R. R. Tolkien'. Checklist revised 1982 by Charles E. Noad, et al.

Catalogue of an Exhibition of Drawings by J. R. R. Tolkien. Oxford: Ashmolean Museum; London: National Book League, in conjunction with George Allen & Unwin, 1976. Introd. by Baillie Tolkien. Biographical introd. by Humphrey Carpenter. Catalogue entries by the Countess of Caithness and Ian Lowe, assisted by Christopher Tolkien.

Christensen, Bonniejean McGuire. 'J. R. R. Tolkien: A Bibliography'. *Bulletin of Bibliography & Magazine Notes*, 27, no. 3 (July–September 1970), pp. 61–7. Addenda by Wayne G. Hammond in 34, no. 3 (July–September 1977), pp. 119–27.

Christopher, J. R. 'Three Letters by J. R. R. Tolkien at the University of Texas'. *Mythlore* (journal of The Mythopoeic Society), 7, no. 2, whole no. 24 (Summer 1980), p. 5.

Cofield, David. 'Changes in Hobbits: Textual Differences in Editions of *The Hobbit*'. *Beyond Bree*, April 1986, pp. 3–4.

Currey, L. W., with the editorial assistance of David G. Hartwell. *Science Fiction and Fantasy Authors: A Bibliography of First Printings of Their Fiction and Selected Nonfiction*. Boston: G. K. Hall, 1979. Pp. [476]–80.

Epstein, Louis. 'Index Difference Roundup'. *Frodo Fortnightly* (newsletter of the National Tolkien League, Carmel, N.Y.), nos. 141 (19 September 1982)–154 (20 March 1983).

Foster, Robert. *The Complete Guide to Middle-Earth: From* The Hobbit *to* The Silmarillion. New York: Ballantine Books; London: George Allen & Unwin, 1978.

GoodKnight, Glen H. 'Tolkien in Translation'. *Mythlore*, 9, no. 2, whole no. 32 (Summer 1982), pp. 22–7. Rev. version, 'J. R. R. Tolkien in Translation', *Mythlore*, 18, no. 3, whole no. 69 (Summer 1992), pp. 61–9.

Patrick & Beatrice Haggerty Museum of Art, Marquette University. *J. R. R. Tolkien: The* Hobbit *Drawings, Watercolors, and Manuscripts, June 11–September 30, 1987*. Milwaukee: Marquette University, 1987.

Hieatt, Constance B. 'The Text of *The Hobbit*: Putting Tolkien's Notes in Order'. *English Studies in Canada*, Ottawa, 7, no. 2 (Summer 1981), pp. [212]–24.

Hunnewell, S. Gary. Unpublished bibliography of Tolkien fanzines. Arnold, Mo., 1988.

Johnson, Judith A. *J. R. R. Tolkien: Six Decades of Criticism*. Westport, Conn.: Greenwood Press, 1986.

Marquette University Library. *Selections from the Marquette J. R. R. Tolkien Collection*. Milwaukee: Marquette University Library, 1987. Essays by Jared C. Lobdell, Taum Santoski, and Verlyn Flieger.

Martsch, Nancy. 'A Discrepancy in the Took Family Tree'. *Beyond Bree*, April 1988, p. 7.

Melmed, Susan Barbara. *John Ronald Reuel Tolkien: A Bibliography*. Johannesburg: University of the Witwatersrand, Dept. of Bibliography, Librarianship and Typography, 1972.

O'Brien, Donald. 'More Differences between the Allen & Unwin and the Ballantine Editions of *The Lord of the Rings*'. *Beyond Bree*, October 1986, p. 9.

Rateliff, John D., and Wayne G. Hammond. ' "Fastitocalon" and "Cat": A Problem in Sequencing'. *Beyond Bree*, August 1987, pp. 1–2. Additional comment by David Bratman, *Beyond Bree*, September 1987, p. 6.

Santoski, T. J. R. *Catalogue of an Exhibit of the Manuscripts of J R R T*. Milwaukee: Marquette University, Memorial Library, Department of Special Collections and University Archives, 1983.

Scull, Christina. 'A Preliminary Study of Variations in Editions of *The Lord of the Rings*'. *Beyond Bree*, April 1985, pp. 3–6; August 1985, pp. 1–6, with a comment by Robert Acker.

Smith, Arden, with the assistance of Nancy Martsch. 'Discography: Tolkien-Inspired Recordings'. *Beyond Bree*, May 1991, pp. 1–5. Supplement in *Beyond Bree*, April 1992, pp. 1–3.

Thompson, George H. 'Early Articles, Comments, Etcetera about J. R. R. Tolkien'. *Mythlore*, 13, no. 3, whole no. 49 (Spring 1987), pp. 58–63.

Thompson, George H. 'Early Reviews of Books by J. R. R. Tolkien'. *Mythlore*, 11, no. 2, whole no. 40 (Autumn 1984), pp. 56–60; 11, no. 3, whole no. 41 (Winter–Spring 1985), pp. 59–62; 12, no. 1, whole no. 43 (Autumn 1985), pp. 58–63; 12, no. 3, whole no. 45 (Spring 1986), pp. 61–2; 12, no. 4, whole no. 46 (Summer 1986), pp. 59–62; and 13, no. 1, whole no. 47 (Autumn 1986), pp. 54–9.

Tolkien, Christopher. 'Foreword'. J. R. R. Tolkien. *The Hobbit*. Fiftieth anniversary ed. London: Unwin Hyman; Boston: Houghton Mifflin, 1987.

Tolkien, Christopher. 'Notes on the Differences in Editions of *The Hobbit* Cited by Mr. David Cofield'. *Beyond Bree*, July 1986, pp. 1–3.

Tolkien, J. R. R. *Letters of J. R. R. Tolkien*. London: George Allen & Unwin; Boston: Houghton Mifflin, 1981.

Tolkien, J. R. R. *Pictures by J. R. R. Tolkien*. Foreword and notes by Christopher Tolkien. London: George Allen & Unwin; Boston: Houghton Mifflin, 1979.

Unwin, Philip. *The Printing Unwins: A Short History of Unwin Brothers, The Gresham Press, 1826–1976*. London: Published for Unwin Brothers by George Allen & Unwin, 1976.

Unwin, Philip. *The Publishing Unwins*. London: William Heinemann, 1972.

Unwin, Rayner. 'The Hobbit 50th Anniversary'. *The Bookseller*, London, 16 January 1987, pp. 166–7. Reprinted in *Science Fiction Chronicle*, New York, June 1987, pp. 48, 50; and in *Books for Keeps*, London, no. 46 (September 1987), pp. 8–9.

Unwin, Rayner. 'Taming the Lord of the Rings'. *The Bookseller*, 19 August 1988, pp. 647–50.

Vanhecke, Johan. *J. R. R. Tolkien 1892–1992*. Antwerp: Archief en Museum voor het Vlaamse Cultuurleven, 1992. Catalogue of an exhibition, 25 January–14 March 1992.

West, Richard C. *Tolkien Criticism: An Annotated Checklist*. Kent, Ohio: Kent State University Press, 1970. Rev. ed., Kent State University Press, 1981.

Yates, Jessica (Kemball-Cook). 'The Hobbit'. *Amon Hen* (bulletin of The Tolkien Society), no. 22 (October 1976), pp. 13–14; no. 23 (December 1976), pp. 11–12; no. 25 (April 1977), pp. 12–14.

Other references are cited in the text.

Index

All entries for Tolkien's works are indexed here by author, translator, illustrator, publisher, printer, and other related persons and bodies, with few exceptions by title, and in small part by subject. Secondary literature mentioned in the notes is indexed selectively by author and journal title. Omitted are (usually generic) titles of booksellers' and auction catalogues; works listed only in the secondary bibliography preceding this index; references to individual chapters and poems in *The Hobbit* and *The Lord of the Rings* except when specially noted; and references to the parts of *The Silmarillion, Unfinished Tales*, and 'The History of Middle-earth' in translation (section G). However, the non-English titles of the parent volumes of these latter works, and of separately published parts, are indexed. The reader who wishes to find, for example, a German translation of 'Aldarion and Erendis' may refer either from the index entry for that tale to the index entry for the parent work, *Unfinished Tales*, and from there to section G, or to the title entry for the larger work, *Nachrichten aus Mittelerde*.

The alphabetical placement of each index entry has been determined by its most significant element, usually the first word, excluding initial articles. Abbreviations (e.g. 'Mr.', 'MS.') are alphabetized as if spelled out. In lists of references, primary bibliography entries are selectively indicated in boldface.

413

Lonely Mountain, schematic drawing of, A3y, aa–bb, dd–ee
Longmans, Green, A3g–h; B1
'Looney', A6a; C26
'Lord of the Flicks', Fii
'Lord of the Hobbits', Fii
'The Lord of the Legends', Fii
The Lord of the Rings, A3c, e–h, n, r–t, cc, 4a, **5**, 6a, 8a, 11b–f, 15a, 17a, 18a, 21–9 introduction, 21a, 26–9; B15, 17a, 25, 28a, c, 30a, 31, 32a; C16, 20, 24, 39; Di2; Dii5–6, 8–9, 14, 23–6, 30–1, 34, 36, 38, 41, 43–7, 50, 53–4, 56–7, 59–60, 62, 64–5, 67–8, 75, 77, 79, 80–1, 85, 87; Ei1–3; Eii12, 17, 28; Fi; Fiii; Armenian 2, Bulgarian 3, Catalan 2, Czech 2, 5, Danish 1, Finnish 2, French 2, 4, German 2, 9, 17, 19, 26, Greek 2, Hebrew 4, Hungarian 2, Italian 1–2, Japanese 2–3, 7–8, Latvian 3, Norwegian 2, 4, Polish 2, Portuguese 2, 4, Russian 3–4, 9, 12, 17–19, Serbo-Croat 2, Spanish 2, 11, Swedish 2, 5, 13
The Lord of the Rings, audio recordings, Finnish 2
The Lord of the Rings, copyright dispute, A3f, 5c–d; B30a
The Lord of the Rings, film versions, A5a; Dii18; French 2
The Lord of the Rings, radio versions, A5e; Dii38, 48
The Lord of the Rings (film), A5a; French 2
The Lord of the Rings: Souvenir Booklet, Dii43
The Lord of the Rings 1977 Calendar, Ei2; **Eii12**
The Lore and Language of Schoolchildren, Dii7
Lorraine, Walter, A5b
The Lost Road, A15a, 24a, 25
The Lost Road and Other Writings, **A25**; B9
Lotem, Imanuel, Hebrew 7
Lovelace Society, A4a; B19a
Lowe, Ian, Ei1
Lowe & Brydone, B17c
Lucas, Peter J., B36
Ludvigsen, Ida Nyrop, Danish 1–2
Luevas, Teresa Sanchez, Spanish 1
Lüning, Inga, Swedish 2–3, 12, 14
Lupoff, Richard A., Dii9
Lynch, John S., A3p–q
The Lyric Songs of Donald Swann, B28a
Maamies ja lohikäärme, Finnish 3
Määttänen, Heikki, Finnish 2
Erskine Macdonald, B2
MacDonald, George, A9a; B32a
W. & J. Mackay, A3o, u, 4c, 5l, 9c, 16; B30a, 33a
Mackays of Chatham, A3bb, gg, y, 5u, 15k, 19a, 21a, 22a, 23a, 24a, 25a, 26a, 27a; Di1a
Mackintosh, Graham, B29

Macmillan, B17b, 27
Maggs Bros., Dii36, 77
Edicions de la Magrana, Catalan 1
Maître Gilles de Ham, French 5
Makaryan, E., Armenian 1–2
Mallorn, A15a; C4; Dii19, 32, 51
Malone, Kemp, Fiii
'The Man in the Moon Came Down Too Soon', A4a, **6**, 8, 12, 16; B4; Fi; Danish 4, Dutch 6, French 4, German 13, Hebrew 6, Italian 6, Japanese 5, Portuguese 8, Swedish 7, 13
'The Man in the Moon Stayed Up Too Late', **A6**, 8, 12, 16; C16; Danish 4, Dutch 6, French 4, German 13, Hebrew 6, Italian 6, Japanese 5, Portuguese 8, Swedish 7, 13
'The Man Who Understands Hobbits', Fii
Mangasaryan, T. S., Armenian 2
Mankato Studies in English, B15
Manlove, C. N., Dii31
Manney, Richard, Fiii
'MS. Bodley 34: A Re-Collation of a Collation', C35
Map of Beleriand and the Lands to the North, A15; Eii15, 19–20
A Map of Middle-earth, A5e, i, 11b; Eii4–7, 9, 11, 17; Dutch 5, Serbo-Croat 2
'Mar Vanwa Tyaliéva', A21
Margrethe II, A5l; Danish 1
'The Mariner's Wife', A17
Markevich, Ilya A., Russian 8
Marleybone Players, A3c
Marquette Journal, A3a, 5a
Marquette University, Dii66; [Ei4]; Eii25
Marquette University Library, A3a, 4a, 5a, 18a, 21–9 introduction; Dii43, 62; Ei3, [4]
Marshall, Hugh, B27
Marshall, Rita, A5s
Martsch, Nancy, A5e; Dii76; Fiii
Masefield, John, B16
Masera, Rubén, Spanish 9–13, 15
Masson, David I., Dii36, 54
'Master', Russian 20
Masterpieces of Terror and the Supernatural, A3a
Matorina, Valeriya Aleksandrovna, Russian 10–12, 19–20
Matthews, Lucy P., C4
Mawer, Allen, Dii1
Mayes, Bernard, A5e
McCullam, William, Dii68
Medcalf, Stephen, A7e
'A Medieval Proverb in *The Lord of the Rings*', Dii39
Medium Aevum, C23, 28
Meneer Blijleven, Dutch 18
Mesibov, Bob, Dii9
Meškys, Ed, Dii12
Methuen, A3h, q, 5e, 14a, 23c; B22a, 36
'The Mewlips', **A6**, 8, 12, 16; C30; Fi; Danish 4, Dutch 6, French 4, German 13,

19, Hebrew 6, Italian 6, Japanese 5,
Portuguese 8, Swedish 7, 13
Mezhvuz, Russian 4
The Microcosm, C13
'Middle English "Losenger" ', B20
A Middle English Vocabulary, **A1**; B3
The Middle-earth Collection, A3s, 5n
Midlands Arts Centre, Dii15
Milišić, Meri, Serbo-Croat 1
Milišić, Milan, Serbo-Croat 1
The Milwaukee Sentinel, A18a
Minas Morgul gate, sketch of, A27
Minas Tirith, Ei2; Eii12, 17
Minas Tirith, map of, Ei3
Minas Tirith, sketches of, A28; Ei2; Eii12, 17
Minas Tirith Evening-Star, Fi
Mind's Eye, A3c, 5e
Mindolluin, sketch of, A28
Minotauro, Spanish 2, 4–6, 8–17
Mirkwood, A3a–b, y, aa–bb, dd–ee; Ei2
Mirkwood, map of, [Ei4]
University of Missouri Press, Dii82
Mr. Baggins, A3a
Mr. Bliss, A8a, 15a, **18**; Dii84; Danish 5,
Dutch 18, Finnish 5, German 11, Italian
11, Spanish 9, Swedish 15
'Mistr Samvěd volí', Czech 2
*The Misty Mountains Looking West from the
Eyrie towards Goblin Gate*, A3a–d, i–j, l,
n–o, r–t, x–y, aa–bb, dd–ee, gg–hh; Ei2,
[4]; Eii10, 13, 17, 29; Danish 2, Dutch 8,
Faeroese 1, Finnish 7, French 1, German
15, Greek 1, Hebrew 2, Italian 3, 17,
Portuguese 7, Swedish 4
Mitchell, Bruce, Dii70
Mitchison, Naomi, B26; Dii38, 41, 43, 63
Mladá Fronta, Czech 5
Mladé Letá, Slovak 1
Mladinska Knjiga, Slovenian 1
Mlodozeniec, Jan, Polish 1
Modern Fantasy: Five Studies, Dii31
Mokrovol's'kiy, Oleksandr, Ukrainian 1
Arnoldo Mondadori, Italian 3
Monjardim, Luiz Alberto, Portuguese 2–3
'Monoceros, the Unicorn', C20
*The Monsters and the Critics and Other
Essays*, **A19**; B17a, 26, 34; German 20, 27
Móra Könyvkiado, Hungarian 1, 4
'More and More People are Getting the
J. R. R. Tolkien Habit', Fii
Moria gate, earliest drawing, A27
Moria gate illustration (drawing for *LR*), A5,
26; B32; Ei3
Moria Gate, Ei2; Eii5–7, 12, 17; Dutch 5,
German 15
Moria Gate (The Steps to the East Gate), Ei2;
Eii5
Morley Books, A28a
Bradford Morrow, Bookseller, Dii47
Morrow, Gray, A3p–q
Moskovskiy Khobbit, Russian 6

Mount Doom, sketch of, A29
Mount Everwhite, see *Taniquetil*
The Mountain-path, A3a–d, i–j, l, n–o, r–t,
x–y, aa–bb, dd–ee, gg–hh, 15c–d, g; Ei2,
[4]; Eii10, 13, 17, 23, 28; Danish 2, Dutch
8, Faeroese 1, Finnish 7, French 1, Greek 1,
Hebrew 2, Italian 3, 17, Portuguese 7,
Swedish 4
'Die Muhlipps', German 19
Muller, Romeo, A3p
Munch, Philippe, French 2
Munro-Kerr, A., Dii53
Murav'yov, V., Russian 3, 9
Murray, John, B21
Murray, Robert, Dii26, 34
Music Drama in Schools, A3c
'The Music of the Ainur', A21
Mythlore, A3j; B32a; Dii30, 62; Fiii
'Mythopoeia', A7e–g; B32–3
Mythopoeic Society, see *Mythlore*, *Mythprint*
Mythprint, A5d, 15a; Dii24–5
Nachrichten aus Mittelerde, German 12
Nagelaten vertellingen, Dutch 16
Nagibin, Yuriy, Russian 7, 16
'Namárië', A5; B28; Dii46, 84; Fi, iii;
French 4, Russian 6
'The Name Coventry', Dii4
'The Name "Nodens" ', B13
'The Nameless Land', A25; **B9**
Nargothrond (drawing), Ei2; Eii15, 20
Nargothrond (unfinished painting), Ei2;
Eii15, 20
'Narn i Hîn Húrin', A17
Narodna Kultura, Bulgarian 3
Narodna Mladezh, Bulgarian 1
'Narqelion: A Single, Falling Leaf at Sun-
fading', B32a
Nasmith, Ted, A3s, 5n; Eii26–7
National Book League, Ei1
'Natura Apis: Morali Ricardi Eremite', B15
'Nauglafring', A22
Naval Cadets' course, Oxford, B18
Návrat krále, Czech 5
Neave, Jane, A6a; B26; C32
'The Necklace of the Dwarves', A22
Thomas Nelson & Sons, A4b
'Nevbosh', B32
New England Tolkien Society, Di2
New English Library, Dii13
*A New Glossary of the Dialect of the
Huddersfield District*, B11
New Worlds SF, Fii
The New York Times Book Review, Dii5
The New York Times Magazine, Fii
Newby, P. H., B30a
M. Newman, Hebrew 1
News from Bree, Fi
Nichida, Minoru, A3p–q
Nicholson, Lewis E., A2
Niekas, Dii75; Fii
Niels Bonde fra Bol, Danish 4, 8